T0119540

THE ULTIMATE ENCYCLOPEDIA OF
MYTHOLOGY

MOSE

THE ULTIMATE ENCYCLOPEDIA OF
MYTHOLOGY

The myths and legends of the ancient worlds, from Greece, Rome and Egypt to the Norse and Celtic lands, through Persia and India to China and the Far East

ARTHUR
COTTERELL
& RACHEL
STORM

southwater

C O N

This edition is published by Southwater
an imprint of Anness Publishing Ltd
info@anness.com
www.southwaterbooks.com
www.annesspublishing.com

Anness Publishing has a new picture agency outlet for images for publishing,
promotions or advertising. Please visit our website www.practicalpictures.com
for more information.

© Anness Publishing Ltd 2020

All rights reserved. No part of this publication may be reproduced, stored
in a retrieval system, or transmitted in any way or by any means, electronic,
mechanical, photocopying, recording or otherwise, without the prior written
permission of the copyright holder.

A CIP catalogue record for this book is available from the British Library.

Publisher: Joanna Lorenz
Editorial Director: Helen Sudell
Editor: Emma Gray
Editorial Assistant: Helen Marsh
Designer: Artmedia
Illustrators: James Alexander, Nick Beale and Glenn Steward

PUBLISHER'S NOTE
Although the advice and information in this book are believed to be accurate
at the time of going to press, neither the author nor the publisher can accept
any legal responsibility or liability for any errors or omissions that may have
been made.

The entries in this encyclopedia are all listed alphabetically. When more than one
name exists for a character the entry is listed under the name used in the original
country of origin for that particular myth. Names in italic capital letters indicate
that that name has an individual entry. Special feature spreads examine specific
mythological themes in more detail. If a character is included in a special feature
spread it is noted at the end of their individual entry.

T E N T S

PREFACE

Every culture has evolved its own mythology, defining its character and offering a way to understand the world. This collection of myths contains stories drawn from the three outstanding traditions of Europe and from the great civilizations of Asia, some of the oldest, most powerful narratives in the world. Greek, Celtic and Norse legends form the core of European mythological thought. Myths from the Middle East include those of the Sumerians and Babylonians; the ancient Iranians; the Egyptians; the Canaanites and Hebrews. The section on South and Central Asia deals with the Hindu and Buddhist deities of India, Sri Lanka, Tibet and Nepal. Daoist and Buddhist myths; the folk religion of China; the Shinto deities of Japan; and animist and shamanistic religions practised from Siberia to the South-east Asian archipelago are included in the section on East Asia.

GILGAMESH was the Assyro-Babylonian hero of a great epic poem dating from the second millennium BC. Here, flanked by centaur-like figures wearing the horned crowns of the gods, Gilgamesh supports the winged disc which represents the Assyrian creator god, Ashur. (SYRIO-HITTITE STELE, 9TH CENTURY BC.)

From Mesopotamia, the cradle of Western civilization, come legends of which we are able to glimpse only fragments, while the belief systems of other ancient societies, such as the Egyptians and

A CELTIC DEITY, possibly Dagda, dangles two warriors high above his head, and thus reveals his awesome power, while the warriors in turn lift two boars, showing their supremacy over animals. (GUNDESTRUP CAULDRON, GILDED SILVER, C. 100 BC.)

Greeks, are far more readily accessible. The stories that have survived from these ancient civilizations describe gods that have long passed into history. Other deities, such as those of Hinduism and Buddhism, remain at the centre of living faiths, worshipped by millions of present-day devotees. But whether the myths recounted in this book belong to current or long-vanished cultures, they continue to exert their influence on the civilizations of the world, as their themes are explored in literature and the visual arts, and the archetypes they present help to deepen our understanding of human psychology.

All human societies recognize powers that are greater than themselves, such as light and dark; sun, storm and frost; flood and drought; and the growth of the plants on which their lives depend.

Investing such powers with spirits that have a recognizably human nature has allowed people to make greater sense of a random and threatening universe. Propitiating the spirits with offerings and prayers allows their worshippers to feel that they have a degree of control. At the same time, by seeking the protection of a deity, devotees are able to relinquish responsibility for their own lives to a higher authority. Myths concerning gods and goddesses help to give shape to the powers that are seen to preserve or endanger humanity.

Another strand of mythology recounts the experiences of human or semi-divine heroes, and touches upon the fundamental issues of existence. These stories deal with the large themes which underlie our present-day consciousness, expressing these profound ideas in terms of individual biographies and events comprehensible in human terms. The legends of heroes endure from age to age, and hold our attention because they dare to go to the extremes of human terror and delight. Myths of every culture reveal the power of love,

SIGURD, the great Norse hero, helps his mentor, Regin, re-forge his wondrous sword. With it, Sigurd slew the dragon, Fafnir. (WOOD CARVING, 12TH CENTURY.)

with its accompanying anxiety and jealousy; the conflict between the generations, the old and the new; the violence of men, especially on the battlefield or in hand-to-hand combat; the mischief of the trouble-maker, bored by the steady pace of everyday events; the sadness of illness or injury; the mystery of death; and the possibility of another life after it. Stories about individual heroes chart the effect of enchantment upon the mind and body; the horror of madness with its disruption of human relations; the incidence of good luck and misfortune, and the whole issue of fate; the challenge of the unknown, whether a voyage into uncharted waters or a quest for a sacred object; the personal danger of a contest with a monster, even a beheading game; and the sadness of betrayal and treachery by family or friends. Myths about the wider world try to explain its mysteries, dealing with the cycle of fertility in human beings, animals, and plants; the relationship between humankind and the gods; the creation of the world and the origins of society; and, last, but not least, the nature of the universe.

Different myths tackle these great questions in distinct ways. But the heroes and heroines of every civilization find themselves facing the same basic problems. The Athenian hero Theseus successfully confronts the Minotaur on Crete, but, full of his success against the bull-man, forgets the agreement made with his father about raising a white sail on his ship if he escapes death himself. As a result of this moment of carelessness, Theseus' father commits suicide by leaping from the Athenian acropolis when a black sail is sighted. Similarly, in Ireland, the inability of Cuchulainn to stop and think for a moment leads to his killing of Conlai, his own son by the Amazon Aoifa. The Hindu hero Arjuna, on the eve of the great battle of Kurukshetra against his enemies the villainous Kauravas, has a crisis of conscience when he realizes that he can only achieve victory at the cost

NESSUS, a wild Greek centaur, tries to abduct Heracles' new bride while ferrying her across the River Evenus. (THE RAPE OF DEIANIRA BY GUIDO RENI, CANVAS, 1621.)

of killing his own relatives, and is only saved from his loss of nerve by the encouragement of his close friend, the god, Krishna.

Such stories underline both the variety and the continuity of human nature. Though the great myths concern gods, heroes and monsters, much of their fascination lies in the human values they illuminate. It is easy to identify with the grief of the widowed Isis or the bereaved Orpheus; with the disgust of Amaterasu at the awful behaviour of Susano-Wo, and her consequent sulk in her cave; with the happy family life of Shiva and Parvati; or with the hopeless love of Guinevere and Lancelot.

Very many myths reveal an interwoven pattern of circumstances outside the control of both mortals and gods. Fate and destiny in mythology are almost beyond manipulation. Attempts may be made to slow down the operation of fate's decrees, sometimes to thwart them entirely, but they never work. The great hero Gilgamesh accomplishes feats beyond the strength of any other man. He even succeeds in reaching the underworld in his search for the secret of immortality. But the knowledge he ultimately returns with is that he cannot avoid his own death. The tangled web of difficulties which besets the Greek hero Theseus can be traced to a number of actions, but one stands out clearly: the refusal of King Minos of Crete to sacrifice the white bull from the sea to the god Poseidon, its real owner. Once this sacrilege has been committed, the fate of Minos and his family, intertwined with that of Theseus, is sealed.

The gods are equally subject to the workings of fate. Odin can do nothing about his future death at Ragnarok, the doom of the gods. The Celtic sun god Lugh cannot save his son Cuchulainn on the battlefield. And even immortal Zeus, the chief god of the Greeks, has a duty to see that fate takes its proper course. He cannot control events.

One of the most striking characteristics of myths is the way they have been adopted and adapted by successive cultures. The myths of Asia were carried by missionaries from one part of the continent to another, giving rise to subtle variations in archetypal legends, and different manifestations of important mythological figures. Buddhism, for instance, which arose with the teachings of Gautama Buddha in northern India around 500 BC, was introduced to China around the time of Christ and to Japan in the sixth century AD. The buddha Amitabha, whose cult may in turn have been influenced by Iranian religion, became the leading figure of Japanese Buddhism as Amida, who was more highly venerated in Japan than Gautama himself. Gautama, meanwhile, was accommodated in Hindu myth as an avatar of Vishnu. Similarly, when the Romans absorbed

KRISHNA, the divine hero and the most beguiling incarnation of the great Hindu god, Vishnu, is accompanied by musicians as he dances in the rain, holding a lotus flower, a Hindu symbol of life and consciousness. (MINIATURE, RAJASTHAN SCHOOL, 17TH CENTURY.)

power of the gods to destroy humankind, and arising from a universal awareness of the precariousness of human existence. Thus do the myths peculiar to each culture and religion point to the essential truths common to all humanity.

The abiding interest of mythology is its frankness about basic human drives. It could almost be described as sacred literature undisturbed by theologians. The raw and ragged ends of existence are still visible in its tales of both men and gods.

BAAL, which means "Lord", was the name given to the chief god of the Canaanites to conceal his true name, which could not be uttered and was known only to initiates. As a weather god, Baal wielded thunderbolts and dispensed rain. (BRONZE AND GOLD STATUETTE FROM RAS SHAMRA, UGARITIC, 1400–1200 BC.)

Greek mythology, they adopted figures such as Aphrodite – translated into the goddess Venus – who had evolved from older Mesopotamian deities including Inana, Ishtar and Astarte.

The themes of the great myths are universal. Creation myths have evolved in every culture, often with striking similarities – such as the limitless ocean from which the universe arises. A major preoccupation is that of life after death, which is explained in terms of parallel worlds: the underworld to which the dead descend to be judged; and the heavens to which the righteous aspire. Even within Hinduism and Buddhism, in which life is seen as a succession of reincarnations leading to the final release of nirvana, complex pictures of these unearthly realms have arisen. The idea of a catastrophic flood is another powerful and recurring theme, illustrating the potential

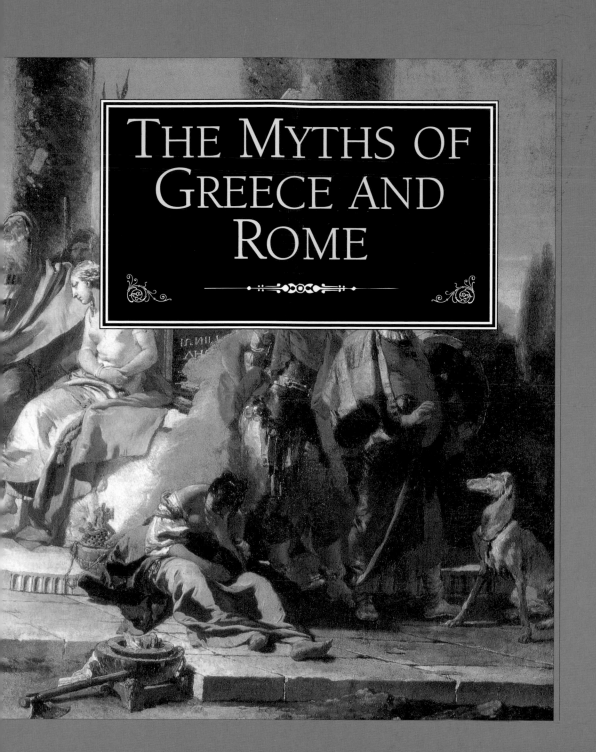

THE MYTHS OF
GREECE AND
ROME

INTRODUCTION

T HE ANCIENT GREEKS WERE THE great myth-makers of Europe. They even gave us the name by which we refer today to the amazing stories told about gods, heroes, men and animals. Around 400 BC the Athenian philosopher Plato coined the word *mythologia* in order to distinguish between imaginative accounts of divine actions and factual descriptions of events, supernatural or otherwise. Although he lived in an age that was increasingly scientific in outlook, and no longer inclined to believe every detail related about gods and goddesses, Plato recognized the power that resided in myth, and warned his followers to beware of its seductive charm.

The strength of Greek mythology, like all active traditions, lay in its collective nature. Unlike a story composed by a particular author, a myth always stood on its own, with a plot and a set of characters readily under-

MARS AND NEPTUNE, two gods of ancient Rome, ride over the Eternal City, guarding its military and maritime interests. At left, an airborne putto above Mars bears his horse's helmet, while Neptune's putto carries a seashell, symbol of the god's dominion over the waves. (MARS AND NEPTUNE BY PAOLO VERONESE, CANVAS, C.1575.)

stood by those who listened to the story-teller or dramatist making use of it. When, for instance, the Athenians watched the great cycle of plays that Aeschylus staged about the murder of Agamemnon, they were already aware of the main characters and their actions. The audience knew how the House of Atreus, Agamemnon's father, was fated to endure a terrible period of domestic strife. Not only had Atreus and his brother Thyestes been cursed by their own father, Pelops, for killing his favourite child, their half-brother Chrysippus, but a bloody quarrel of their own had also added to the family misfortune. A dispute over the succession to Pelops' throne at Mycenae led Atreus to kill three of Thyestes' sons, although they had sought sanctuary in a temple dedicated to Zeus, the supreme god. Even worse, the murderer then served the bodies of his nephews up to his brother at a banquet, after which he dared to show Thyestes their feet and hands. Atreus paid for the outrage with his life at the hands of Thyestes' surviving son, Aegisthus, who later became the lover of Agamemnon's

wife Clytemnestra during his absence at the Trojan War.

All this would have been familiar to the Athenians before Aeschylus' treatment of the myth began with Agamemnon returning home from the Trojan War. Some of the audience doubtless recalled an even older curse laid on Pelops himself by the messenger god Hermes. Pelops had provoked the god by refusing a promised gift to one of his sons. Nothing that Aeschylus included in his plays was unexpected: neither the murder of Agamemnon, nor the revenge of his son Orestes, nor Orestes' pursuit by the Furies for shedding a mother's blood. What would have fascinated the audience was the dramatist's approach to these tangled incidents, his view of motive, guilt and expiation. For that reason another dramatist was able to tackle the same story later in Athens during the fifth century BC. It needs to be remembered that such drama remained very much part of ancient religion. Today we cannot expect to appreciate the full meaning of these performances, but we are fortunate in having the raw materials from which they were made, the myths themselves.

Myths retain much of their power, even when told in summary, as they are in this encyclopedia. Because Greek myths were fashioned and refashioned over so many generations, they acquired their essential form, a shape that had been collectively recognized for longer than anyone could remember. Even now, we continue to be fascinated by the stories of Oedipus, the man who murdered his father and married his mother; of the Athenian hero Theseus, slayer of the strange bull-headed man, the Minotaur; of the great voyager Jason, who sailed across the Black Sea to distant Colchis in order to fetch the Golden Fleece; of Agamemnon, the doomed leader of the Greek expedition against Troy; of cunning Odysseus, one of the bravest of the Greeks and the inventor of the Wooden Horse, the means by which Troy was taken; of the hapless Pentheus, victim of Dionysus' ecstatic worshippers, who included his own mother; of the unbeatable champion Achilles; of the labours of Heracles, Zeus' own son and the only hero to be granted immortality; and many others. As Greeks living before and after Plato evidently understood, myths were fictitious stories that illustrated truth.

The Romans were no less impressed by the range and interest of Greek mythology. Indeed, they adopted it wholesale and identified many of their own Italian deities with those in the Greek pantheon, even adopting others for whom they possessed no real equivalent. The unruly Dionysus gave Rome considerable trouble. This god of vegetation, wine and ecstasy was by no means a comfortable deity for the Greeks, but the Romans were more deeply disturbed by his orgiastic rites. In 186 BC the Roman Senate passed severe laws against the excesses of his worshippers. It is likely that several thousand

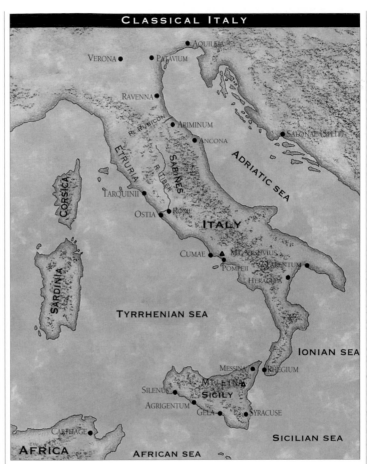

CLASSICAL ITALY

people were executed before the cult of the native wine god Bacchus discarded those aspects of Dionysus which met with official disproval. This taming of a Greek god, albeit Thracian in origin, could stand for the entire process by which Greek and Roman mythology merged in the second century BC. There were just too many myths for the Romans to resist, although they chose to impose a typical restraint on Greek extravagance.

Roman heroes could never compare with Heracles, Jason, Theseus, Perseus or Bellerophon. Something synthetic can be felt in the story of Aeneas, the leader of the refugees from Troy. His adoption as a founder-hero made him of particular concern to the first Roman emperor Augustus, but The Aeneid, the epic poem about Aeneas written by Virgil in the 20s BC, turned out to be a balanced celebration of Roman authority rather than an exciting heroic narrative. The hero heeded the call of duty and abandoned the woman he loved, as Roman heroes were expected to do in every myth.

A

ACHILLES was the son of King Peleus of Thessaly and the sea nymph *THETIS*. He was the greatest of the Greek warriors, although in comparison with *AGAMEMNON* and the other Greek kings who went on the expedition against Troy, he appears to have been something of a barbarian. His anger was as legendary as his prowess.

The uncertain nature of Achilles is apparent in the story of his birth. Both *ZEUS* and *POSEIDON* wanted to have a son by the beautiful Thetis, but *PROMETHEUS*, the fire god, had warned them that her offspring would be greater than his father. Anxious to avoid the emergence of a power superior to themselves, the gods carefully

arranged the marriage of Thetis to a mortal. Because she was so attached to Achilles, Thetis tried to make him immortal by various means. The best known was dipping the new-born baby in the Styx, the river that ran through *HADES*, the world of the dead. Since Thetis had to hold him by the heel, this one spot was left vulnerable and at Troy brought about Achilles' death from a poisoned arrow shot from the bow of *PARIS*.

Achilles learned the skills of warfare from *CHIRON*, leader of the *CENTAURS*, who also fed him on wild game to increase his ferocity. Under Chiron's care Achilles became renowned as a courageous fighter, but his immortal mother

knew that he was doomed to die at Troy if he went on the expedition. So Thetis arranged for him to be disguised as a girl and hidden among the women at the palace of King Lycomedes on the island of Scyros. The Greeks felt that without Achilles their chances of beating the Trojans were slim, but no one could identify the hidden hero. At last, cunning *ODYSSEUS* was sent to discover Achilles, which he did by means of a trick.

Having traced the young man to Scyros, Odysseus placed weapons among some jewellery in the palace. While Achilles' female companions were admiring the craftsmanship of the jewels, a call to arms was sounded and the

warrior quickly reached for the weapons, giving himself away. Unmasked, Achilles had no choice but to sail for Troy.

There he bitterly quarrelled with Agamemnon, the leader of the Greeks. It may be that he was angered by Agamemnon's use of his name to bring *IPHIGENIA* to Aulis, for she had been told she was to marry Achilles, whereas Agamemnon intended to sacrifice

ACHILLES, *relaxing beside his tent with his companion, Patroclus, welcomes his comrades, Odysseus (centre) and Ajax (right), who implore the moody hero to return to battle where he is sorely needed.* (ACHILLES RECEIVES AGAMEMNON'S MESSENGERS, BY JEAN-AUGUST INGRES, CANVAS, 1801.)

her to the goddess *ARTEMIS*, to ensure a favourable wind for the Greek fleet. For a long time Achilles stayed in his tent and refused to fight the Trojans. He even persuaded his mother to use her influence with Zeus to let the tide of war go against the Greeks. But Achilles was roused to action by the death of Patroclus, his squire and lover, at the hands of the Trojan *HECTOR*. Patroclus had borrowed Achilles' armour, which had been forged by the smith god *HEPHAISTOS*, and entered the fray, but he came up against Hector who easily defeated him.

In brand-new armour Achilles sought out Hector, who asked for respect to be shown for his body if he was defeated. Achilles refused, slew Hector with his spear and dragged the Trojan hero round the tomb of Patroclus for twelve days. Only Thetis could persuade her son to let the Trojans recover the corpse and arrange a funeral, a serious obligation for the living.

Back in the fight, Achilles struck fear into the Trojans, of whom he killed hundreds. But his own life was coming to an end, which he

ACHILLES falls beneath the Trojan walls, shot by Paris. The sun god aims his arrow straight for Achilles' heel, the only mortal part of the hero's body. In some myths, Apollo guided Paris' bow; in others, the god shot the arrow, as seen here. (APOLLO SLAYS ACHILLES BY FRANZ STASSEN, WATERCOLOUR, 1869.)

ACTAEON was a young Greek hunter who unluckily chanced upon the pool where Artemis and her nymphs were bathing. In outrage, the virgin goddess turned him into a stag and he was torn apart by his own hounds. (ILLUSTRATION FROM DICTIONARY OF CLASSICAL ANTIQUITIES, 1891.)

had been warned about by his steed *XANTHUS*, before the *FURIES* struck the divine creature dumb. An arrow from the bow of Paris, guided by the god of prophecy *APOLLO*, gave Achilles a mortal wound. Heroic yet also arrogant, Achilles was the mythical figure most admired by Alexander the Great. At the commencement of his Asian campaign against the Persians, the youthful Alexander participated in funeral games that were held at Troy in memory of Achilles. (See also *HEROES*)

ACTAEON was the son of a minor royal god and Autonoe, daughter of *CADMUS*. A Greek hunter trained by *CHIRON*, he offended the goddess *ARTEMIS* and paid with his life. There are several reasons given for his terrible end. Actaeon may have boasted of his superior skill as a hunter, or annoyed the goddess by seeing her bathing naked. To stop his boasting, Artemis turned him into a stag and he was chased and devoured by his own hounds. But these faithful animals were broken-hearted at the loss of their master, until Chiron carved a statue of Actaeon so lifelike that they were satisfied.

AEGEUS was the son of King Pandion of Athens, and father of the hero *THESEUS*. Having twice married without begetting any children, Aegeus went to consult the Delphic Oracle but received only the ambiguous answer that he should not untie his wine skin until he reached home. When he sought advice from his friend Pittheus, another ruler, the latter realized that the oracle had foretold how Aegeus would father a heroic son. To secure the services of such a man, Pittheus made Aegeus drunk and let him sleep with his daughter Aethra. When Aegeus understood what had happened, he placed a sword and a pair of sandals beneath an enormous boulder. He told the princess that if she bore a son who could move the rock, he was to bring these tokens to him in Athens on reaching manhood. Thus it was that Theseus grew up and was eventually reunited with his father.

Meantime, Aegeus had married the sorceress *MEDEA*, whose magical powers had given him another son, Medus. It was for this reason that Medea did everything she could to thwart Theseus. At her

suggestion Theseus was sent to fight the wild bull of Marathon, which he captured alive. Once Aegeus recognized his son, Medea returned in disgust to her native Colchis on the Black Sea. But bad luck continued to dog Aegeus and eventually caused his death. For it was agreed that Theseus should travel to Crete with the seven girls and seven boys sent as tribute each year to feed the *MINOTAUR*, a bull-headed man. If Theseus was successful in his dangerous mission to kill the Minotaur, the ship bringing him home was to fly a white sail; if unsuccessful, a black sail would signal his death. Returning to Athens after an incredible adventure in the Labyrinth at Knossos, Theseus forgot the agreement to change his sail from black to white, with the result that, upon seeing the vessel with its black sail, Aegeus threw himself off the Athenian acropolis to certain death.

AEGEUS, looking out to sea, sees his son's ships returning home, all with black sails hoisted. Thinking that his son had died, Aegeus hurled himself into the sea, afterwards named the Aegean. (ILLUSTRATION BY NICK BEALE, 1995.)

AENEAS was a Trojan hero and the son of Anchises and *VENUS*, the Roman goddess of love. He was the favourite of the Romans, who believed that some of their eminent families were descended from the Trojans who fled westwards with him from Asia Minor, after the Greek sack of their city. Upstart Rome was only too aware of its lack of tradition and history in comparison with Greece (there was a notable absence of a glorious past peopled with mythical heroes and gods), so the exploits of Aeneas conveniently provided a means of reasserting national pride. It was not a coincidence that the first Roman emperor, Augustus, took a personal interest in the myth.

During the Trojan War Anchises was unable to fight, having been rendered blind or lame for boasting about his relationship with Venus. But young Aeneas distinguished himself against the Greeks, who feared him second only to *HECTOR*, the Trojan champion. In gratitude *PRIAM* gave Aeneas his daughter Creusa to have as his wife, and a son was born named *ASCANIUS*. Although Venus warned him of the impending fall of Troy, Anchises refused to quit the city until two omens occurred: a small flame rose from the top of Ascanius' head and a meteor fell close by. So, carrying

Anchises on his back, Aeneas managed to escape Troy with his father and his son. Somehow Creusa became separated from the party and disappeared. Later, Aeneas saw her ghost and learned from it that he would found a new Troy in distant Italy.

After sailing through the Aegean Sea, where the small fleet Aeneas commanded stopped at a number of islands, the fleet came to Epirus

AENEAS gazes in wonder at the decorative temple in Carthage, while Dido, the queen, welcomes him to her exotic kingdom. Around them, pillars, doors and beams are made of bronze, while the fabulous walls are decorated with the famous tale of Aeneas and the Trojans.
(ILLUSTRATION BY NICK BEALE, 1995.)

on the eastern Adriatic coast. From there it made for Sicily, but before reaching the Italian mainland it was diverted to North Africa during a sudden storm sent by the goddess *JUNO*, the Roman equivalent of *HERA*, who harassed Aeneas throughout the voyage. Only the timely help of *NEPTUNE*, the Roman sea god, saved the fleet from shipwreck. At the city of Carthage, the great trading port founded by the Phoenicians (which was located in present-day Tunisia), Venus ensured that Aeneas fell in love with its beautiful queen, the widow *DIDO*. Because of her own flight to Carthage, Dido welcomed the Trojan refugees with great kindness and unlimited hospitality.

Time passed pleasantly for the lovers, as Aeneas and Dido soon

became, and it seemed as if Italy and the new state to be founded on its shores were both forgotten. But watchful *JUPITER*, the chief Roman god, dispatched *MERCURY* with a message to Aeneas, recalling him to his duty and commanding him to resume the voyage. Horrified by his intention to leave, Dido bitterly reproached Aeneas, but his deep sense of piety gave him strength enough to launch the fleet again. Then the weeping queen mounted a pyre which she had ordered to be prepared and, having run herself through with a sword, was consumed by the flames.

When the Trojans finally landed in Italy, near the city of Cumae, Aeneas went to consult the *SIBYL*, who was a renowned prophetess. She took him on a visit to the

AENEAS and his comrades battle with a flock of raging harpies who hover above them in the sky, waiting to carry off the weak and wounded. Beside Aeneas shelter his family: his blind father Anchises, his wife Creusa and their two sons. (AENEAS AND HIS COMPANIONS FIGHT THE HARPIES BY FRANÇOIS PERRIER, CANVAS, 1646–47.)

AGAMEMNON watches coolly as his daughter, Iphigenia, is offered as a "sacrificial lamb" to appease the anger of Artemis; but at the last moment, the goddess herself relented and, descending from heaven, she carried Iphigenia off to Taurus. (THE SACRIFICE OF IPHIGENIA BY GIOVANNI BATTISTA, TEMPERA, 1770.)

underworld. There Aeneas met his father's ghost, who showed him the destiny of Rome. Anchises had died of old age during the stay in Sicily, but his enthusiastic outline of the future encouraged his son. Aeneas also saw Dido's ghost, but it did not speak to him and hurriedly turned away.

Afterwards, Aeneas steered for the mouth of the River Tiber, on whose river banks the city of Rome would be built centuries later. Conflict with the Latins, the local inhabitants, was bloody and prolonged. But peace was made when Aeneas married Lavinia, the daughter of King Latinus. It had been foretold that for the sake of the kingdom Lavinia must marry a man from abroad. The Trojans, in order to appease Juno, adopted the Latins' traditions and language. (See also *VOYAGERS*)

AGAMEMNON, according to Greek mythology, was the son of *ATREUS* and the brother of *MENELAUS*, king of Sparta. He was married to *CLYTEMNESTRA*. From his citadel at Mycenae, or nearby Argos, he sent out a summons to the Greeks to join the expedition against Troy. The cause of the war was the flight of Menelaus' wife, *HELEN*, to that city with *PARIS*.

However, the Greek fleet was delayed at Aulis by contrary winds. Agamemnon then realized that he would have to make a human sacrifice in order to appease *ARTEMIS*, the goddess of the forest and wild animals. His daughter *IPHIGENIA* was therefore sent to Aulis under the pretext that she was to be married to the Greek champion and hero *ACHILLES*. According to one tradition, Iphigenia was sacrificed, but according to another, she was saved by Artemis herself and taken to Taurus to become a priestess in the goddess's temple.

Clytemnestra never forgave Agamemnon for Iphigenia's loss, and she took Aegisthus for a lover during the ten-year siege of Troy. Aegisthus was the son of Thyestes, the brother and enemy of Atreus,

Agamemnon's father. On her husband's return, Clytemnestra at first pretended how pleased she was to see him. Thanking the gods for his safe return, Agamemnon crossed the threshold of his palace, ignoring the warning of his slave *CASSANDRA*, the prophetic daughter of *PRIAM*, the defeated Trojan king. He then retired to a bathroom in order to change his clothes. Clytemnestra quickly threw a large net over Agamemnon and twisted

AJAX heads off the Trojan onslaught with typical might and courage. Beside him, his brother, Teucer the archer, aims his bow at the Trojans who, with flaming torches, hope to set the Greek ships alight. (ILLUSTRATION FROM STORIES FROM HOMER, 1885.)

it around his body, rendering him an easy target for Aegisthus' axe.

AJAX was the son of Telamon of Salamis and, like *ACHILLES*, was a powerful aid to the Greeks in their assault on Troy. After Achilles' death there was a contest for the armour of this great warrior, which had been forged by the smith god *HEPHAISTOS*. When *ODYSSEUS* was awarded the armour, Ajax became mad with jealousy. He planned a night attack on his comrades, but the goddess *ATHENA* deceived him into slaughtering a flock of sheep instead. In the light of dawn, Ajax was suddenly overwhelmed by a fear of his evil intentions, and fell on his sword and died.

ALCESTIS, according to Greek mythology, was the daughter of King Pelias of Thessaly. When she was of an age to marry, many suitors appeared and her father set a test to discover who would be the most suitable husband. Alcestis was to be the wife of the first man to yoke a lion and a boar (or, in some versions, a bear) to a chariot. With the aid of *APOLLO*, the god of prophecy, a neighbouring monarch named Admetus succeeded in this seemingly impossible task. But at the wedding he forgot to make the necessary sacrifice in gratitude to *ARTEMIS*, the goddess of the forest and wild animals, and so found his wedding bed full of snakes. Once again Apollo came to the king's assistance and, by making the *FATES* drunk, extracted from them a promise that if anyone else would die on Admetus' behalf, he might continue to live. As no one would volunteer, Alcestis gave her life for him. *PERSEPHONE*, the underworld goddess, was so impressed by this complete devotion that she restored Alcestis to Admetus, and they had two sons who later took part in the Greek expedition against the city of Troy.

ALCESTIS (below) welcomes her suitor, Admetus, who arrives in a chariot drawn by lions and bears, while Alcestis' father, Pelias, looks on in disbelief. Admetus was the only hero to yoke the beasts, so winning the hand of Alcestis. (ILLUSTRATION FROM STORIES FROM GREECE AND ROME, 1920.)

ALCMENE was the daughter of Electryon, son of *PERSEUS*, and the mother of *HERACLES*. She married Amphitryon, king of Tiryns, near Mycenae in the Peloponnese. Alcmene refused to consummate her marriage to Amphitryon until he had avenged the murder of her brothers. This the king did, but when he returned he was amazed to learn from Alcmene that she believed she had already slept with him. Amphitryon was enraged until

ALCMENE (right) was one of the sky god Zeus' many lovers, but was punished for her infidelity by her angry husband, Amphitryon, who here is portrayed setting alight a pyre beneath her. She was saved by a heavenly downpour sent by Zeus. (ILLUSTRATION BY NICK BEALE, 1995.)

the seer *TIRESIAS* explained that *ZEUS* had come to Alcmene disguised as her husband in order to father a mortal who would aid the gods in their forthcoming battle against the *GIANTS*.

So Alcmene became pregnant with twins: Heracles, the son of Zeus, and Iphicles, the son of Amphitryon. Zeus could not hide his satisfaction from his wife *HERA* who realized what had happened. She sent the goddess of childbirth,

Eileithyia, to frustrate the delivery, but a trick saved Alcmene and her two sons. Hera then put snakes into Heracles' cradle, but the infant hero strangled them.

Zeus never let Hera fatally injure Heracles, and always protected Alcmene. Once Amphitryon tried to burn her for infidelity, but was stopped by a sudden downpour. When Alcmene died naturally of old age, Zeus sent *HERMES* to bring her body to the Elysian Fields.

THE AMAZONS (opposite), fierce and independent maiden warriors, fought with passion and skill. In early images, they appear in exotic Scythian leotards, bearing half-moon shields, but in later Greek art, they wore Dorian chitons, with one shoulder bare, as seen here. (THE BATTLE OF THE AMAZONS BY PETER PAUL RUBENS, WOOD, 1600.)

AMULIUS (left) casts out his nephews, Romulus and Remus, the twin sons of Rhea Silvia and the war god Mars, ordering that they be drowned in the river Tiber. But they are eventually found by a she-wolf who suckles them until a shepherd, Faustulus, takes them home. (ILLUSTRATION FROM STORIES FROM LIVY, 1885.)

THE AMAZONS

THE AMAZONS were a tribe of female warriors, supposedly descended from *ARES*, the Greek war god, and the *NAIAD* Harmonia. Their home was situated beyond the Black Sea. It is thought that their name refers to their breastless condition, for Amazons voluntarily removed their right breasts in order that they might more easily draw a bow. The ancient Greeks believed these fierce warriors periodically mated with the men from another tribe, afterwards rearing their female children but discarding or maiming all the males.

During the Trojan War they fought against the Greeks. Although he killed the Amazon queen Penthesilea, *ACHILLES* never succeeded in shaking off the rumour that he had been in love with her. He even slew a comrade who mentioned it. Fascination with Amazon power affected other heroes besides Achilles. The adventures of both *HERACLES* and *THESEUS* involved battles with Amazons. One of Heracles' famous labours was the seizure of a girdle belonging to the Amazon queen Hippolyta, a theft that required considerable nerve.

AMULIUS, in Roman mythology, was a descendant of the Trojan hero *AENEAS*. He usurped the throne of Alba Longa from his younger brother Numitor and forced Numitor's daughter *RHEA SILVIA* to become a Vestal Virgin so as to deny her father an heir. When Rhea Silvia was raped by the war god *MARS*, Amulius imprisoned her and ordered that her twin sons, *REMUS AND ROMULUS*, be drowned in the Tiber. But the two boys escaped a watery death and grew up in the countryside. Once they realized their parentage, Romulus and Remus returned to Alba Longa and killed their uncle Amulius.

ANDROMACHE, the daughter of Eetion, a king of Mysia in Asia Minor, was the wife of *HECTOR*, the foremost Trojan warrior. Her entire family – parents, brothers, husband and son – was killed during the Trojan War. After the sack of Troy, Andromache was taken off into captivity by Neoptolemus, the son of the great Greek hero *ACHILLES*. Neoptolemus had shown the same violent and tempestuous temper as his father when he ruthlessly killed the Trojan king, *PRIAM*, at the altar of *ZEUS*' temple. Andromache bore Neoptolemus three sons, and in consequence suffered the hatred of his barren Greek wife. When Neoptolemus died, Andromache went on to marry Helenus who, like her, was a Trojan captive. Her final years were spent in Asia Minor at Pergamum, which was a new city founded by one of her sons.

ANDROMACHE, Hector's young wife, bows her head in captivity. One of the noblest but most ill-starred of heroines, she sees her husband, father and seven brothers killed by Achilles, and her son hurled from the city walls; while she falls as a prize of war to Achilles' son. (CAPTIVE ANDROMACHE BY LORD LEIGHTON, CANVAS, C. 1890.)

ANTIGONE (above) sprinkles earth on the body of her brother, Polynices, as a symbolic act of burial. For the Greeks, burial was a sacred duty, without which a soul could not rest; yet Creon, her uncle, had denied Polynices a burial, violating divine law. (ILLUSTRATION BY NICK BEALE, 1995.)

ANDROMEDA (left), chained to a rock as a sacrifice to a sea monster, can only pray, while high overhead, the hero Perseus is on his way. Swooping down on the winged horse, Pegasus, he cuts Andromeda free and slays the monster. (PERSEUS RELEASES ANDROMEDA BY JOACHIM WIEWAEL, CANVAS, 1630.)

ANDROMEDA was the daughter of Cassiope and Cepheus, king of the Ethiopians. When Cassiope boasted that Andromeda was more beautiful than the Nereids, the sea nymphs, they complained to the sea god *POSEIDON*. He avenged this insult by flooding the land and sending a sea monster to devastate Cepheus' kingdom. To avoid complete disaster it was decided to sacrifice Andromeda to the beast and she was chained to a rock at the foot of a cliff. There *PERSEUS* saw her as he flew past on winged sandals carrying the head of the Gorgon Medusa. He fell in love with Andromeda, and obtained both her and her father's consent to marriage if he defeated the monster. This Perseus did by using Medusa's head, the sight of which turned all living things to stone. After some time, Perseus and Andromeda settled in Tiryns, which Perseus ruled. The constellation of Andromeda lies close to that of Pegasus, and both Cepheus and Cassiope were also commemorated in the stars.

ANTIGONE was the daughter of *OEDIPUS*, king of Thebes, and his wife and mother Jocasta. On learning of their unwitting incest, Oedipus tore out his eyes while Jocasta hanged herself. The penitent Oedipus was then guided by Antigone in his wanderings round Greece. She was with him at the sanctuary of Colonus, near Athens, when her distraught father gained some kind of peace just before his death. She returned to Thebes, but her troubles were not over. Her brother Polynices had been killed in an uprising against the new ruler *CREON*, and his body was condemned to rot unburied outside the city. Antigone refused to accept this impiety and sprinkled earth over the corpse as a token burial. For this she was walled up in a cave, where she hanged herself like her mother Jocasta. There are a number of different versions of the myth, but they all cast Antigone as the heroic victim of a family wrecked by a terrible deed.

ANTIOPE see *LOVERS OF ZEUS*

APHRODITE was the Greek goddess of love, beauty and fertility. Unlike her Roman counterpart *VENUS*, with whom she was identified, Aphrodite was not only a goddess of sexual love but also of the affection that sustains social life. The meaning of her name is uncertain, although the ancient Greeks came to believe it referred to foam. Quite possibly this belief arose from the story of Aphrodite's

APHRODITE, *goddess of love and beauty, was born from the foam of the sea; she rose from the waves on a seashell, stepping ashore on Cyprus. At her side, the west wind, Zephyrus, and Flora, the spring, blow her gently ashore in a shower of roses, her sacred flower.* (THE BIRTH OF VENUS BY SANDRO BOTTICELLI, TEMPERA, C. 1482.)

birth. When the Titan CRONOS cut off the penis of his father Ouranos with a sharp sickle, he cast the immortal member into the sea, where it floated amid white foam. Inside the penis Aphrodite grew and was then washed up at Paphos on Cyprus. There were in fact sanctuaries dedicated to her on many islands, which suggests that she was a West Asian goddess who was brought to Greece by sea-traders.

Once she arrived, the ancient Greeks married her in their mythology to the crippled smith god HEPHAISTOS. But Aphrodite is not content to be a faithful wife and she bore children by several other gods, including DIONYSUS and ARES. When Hephaistos found out about Aphrodite's passion for the war god Ares, the outraged smith god made a mesh of gold and caught the lovers in bed together. He called the other gods from Mount Olympus to see the pair, but they only laughed at his shame, and POSEIDON, the god of the sea, persuaded Hephaistos to release Aphrodite and Ares.

Perhaps Aphrodite's greatest love was for the handsome youth Adonis, another West Asian deity. Killed by a wild boar, Adonis became the object of admiration for both Aphrodite and PERSEPHONE,

queen of the dead. Their bitter quarrel was only ended by ZEUS, who ruled that for a third of the year Adonis was to dwell with himself, for a third part with Persephone, and for a third part with Aphrodite. So it was that the ancient Greeks accommodated a West Asian mother goddess and her dying-and-rising husband. Indeed the Adonia, or annual festivals commemorating Adonis' death, were celebrated in many parts of the eastern Mediterranean.

Because of her unruly behaviour, Zeus caused Aphrodite to fall in love with Anchises, the father of AENEAS. In the Roman version of this myth Venus herself is deeply attracted to the Trojan, but warns him to keep the parentage of their son Aeneas a secret. This Anchises fails to do, and as a result suffers blindness or a disability of the limbs. While the Roman goddess provided, through the leadership of Aeneas, a means for some of the Trojans to escape and flourish anew in Italy, the Greek Aphrodite actually helped to cause the Trojan War. In order to ensure that he would name her as the most beautiful of the goddesses, Aphrodite promised PARIS, son of PRIAM the king of Troy, the hand of the most beautiful woman in the world. This fatefully turned out to be HELEN, wife of MENELAUS, king of Sparta.

APOLLO
was the son of ZEUS and the Titaness LETO, and the twin brother of the goddess ARTEMIS, the virgin huntress. He was one of the most important deities of both the Greek and

Roman religions, and was the god of prophecy, archery and music. The origin of his name is uncertain but it is probably non-European.

A fight with the gigantic earth-serpent Python at Delphi gave Apollo the seat of his famous oracle. Python was an offspring of GAIA, mother earth, which issued revelations through a fissure in the rock so that a priestess, the Pythia, could give answers to any questions that might be asked. After he slew the earth-serpent, Apollo took its place, though he had to do penance in Thessaly for the killing. Indeed, Zeus twice forced Apollo to be the slave of a mortal man to pay for his crime.

Apollo's interest in healing suggests an ancient association with the plague and its control. His son ASCLEPIUS was also identified

with healing and connected with sites in northern Greece. Indeed, so accomplished was Asclepius in medicine that Zeus slew him with a thunderbolt for daring to bring a man back to life. (See also FORCES OF NATURE)

ARES,
the son of ZEUS and HERA, was the Greek god of war, and was later identified with the Roman war god MARS. Although Ares had no wife of his own, he had three children by APHRODITE, the goddess of love. The twins, Phobos, "panic", and Deimos, "fear", always accompanied him on the battlefield. In Greek mythology, Ares is depicted as an instigator of violence, a tempestuous and passionate lover and an unscrupulous friend. The Roman god Mars, however, has nothing of Ares' fickleness.

APOLLO *(above), the sun god, urges the sun-chariot to rise in the sky. This unusual version of the myth has Apollo, rather than Helios, as rider, and lions, instead of horses, pull the chariot, recalling the link between Leo and the sun.* (PHOEBUS APOLLO BY BRITON RIVIERE, CANVAS, C. 1870.)

ARES *(below), in full armour, leads the gods into battle. However, in war, the gods were not impartial; Ares, Aphrodite (left), Poseidon and Apollo (centre) would often aid the Trojans, while Hera and Athena (right) supported the Greeks.* (ILLUSTRATION FROM STORIES FROM HOMER, 1885.)

LOVERS OF ZEUS

ASTRIKING ASPECT OF GREEK MYTHOLOGY is the marital conflict between the two chief deities, Hera, an earth goddess, and her husband, Zeus, supreme power on Olympus. One of the most amorous gods in mythology, Zeus loved countless women and he courted them in as many forms, sometimes as a bull, as a satyr, as a swan, sometimes as a mortal man, and even in the form of a golden shower. Hera was notoriously jealous and vengeful, pursuing without mercy his lovers and their offspring. The antagonism between the two could be viewed as a clash between different religious traditions or local cults, each cult recognizing a different lover who was often regarded as the ancestor of a ruling family.

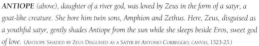

ANTIOPE (above), daughter of a river god, was loved by Zeus in the form of a satyr, a goat-like creature. She bore him twin sons, Amphion and Zethus. Here, Zeus, disguised as a youthful satyr, gently shades Antiope from the sun while she sleeps beside Eros, sweet god of love. (ANTIOPE SHADED BY ZEUS DISGUISED AS A SATYR BY ANTONIO CORREGGIO, CANVAS, 1523-25.)

CALLISTO (above), forest nymph and companion of Artemis in the chase, was loved by Zeus and bore him a son, Arcas. She was then changed into a bear either by Zeus, wishing to hide her from Hera, or by Hera herself. As a bear she was shot by Artemis in the forest and was placed among the stars as the She-Bear. Here, surrounded by the trophies of the chase, Artemis and her nymphs comfort Callisto possibly after her encounter with the overwhelming god, Zeus. (DIANA AND CALLISTO BY PETER PAUL RUBENS, CANVAS, 1636-40.)

EUROPA (right) was wooed by Zeus in the shape of a beautiful bull who emerged from the waves and carried her over the sea to Crete where she bore him three sons. The various stages of the drama are represented here: on the left, Europa mounts the bull encouraged by its tameness. On the right, she is borne sedately down to the sea, with many little Erotes (love spirits) hovering in the sky. Finally she floats happily away, waving to her maidens. (THE RAPE OF EUROPA BY PAOLO VERONESE, CANVAS, 1580.)

DIONYSUS (above), Zeus' child by Semele, appears here hugging his mother, while Apollo stands by with a bay tree. Once he became a god, Dionysus raised his mother to heaven and placed her among the stars as Thyone. This Etruscan mirror is bordered with ivy, which was Dionysus' sacred plant. (ILLUSTRATION FROM DR SMITH'S CLASSICAL DICTIONARY, 1895.)

DANAE (below) was confined in a brazen tower by her father who feared an oracle predicting that he would be killed by a grandson. In her tower she was visited by Zeus in the form of a golden shower, and bore him a son, Perseus. When her father discovered the baby, he cast both of them out to sea in a wooden chest, but they floated ashore on the Isle of Seriphos where they were rescued by Dictys. (ILLUSTRATION BY GEORGE SOPER FROM TANGLEWOOD TALES, C. 1920.)

SEMELE (left), encouraged by Hera, persuaded Zeus to show himself in all his splendour. When he appeared before her as the radiant god of thunder and lightning, Semele was consumed by the flames and, dying, gave birth prematurely to Dionysus, whom Zeus saved from the fire. In this powerful Symbolist version of the myth, the great god radiates fiery, blood-red lightning. A winged child hiding from the light could be Dionysus, while the dark, horned god seems to be a fusion of Hades and Pan. (JUPITER AND SEMELE, BY GUSTAVE MOREAU, CANVAS, 1896.)

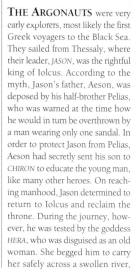

THE ARGONAUTS were very early explorers, most likely the first Greek voyagers to the Black Sea. They sailed from Thessaly, where their leader, *JASON*, was the rightful king of Iolcus. According to the myth, Jason's father, Aeson, was deposed by his half-brother Pelias, who was warned at the time how he would in turn be overthrown by a man wearing only one sandal. In order to protect Jason from Pelias, Aeson had secretly sent his son to *CHIRON* to educate the young man, like many other heroes. On reaching manhood, Jason determined to return to Iolcus and reclaim the throne. During the journey, however, he was tested by the goddess *HERA*, who was disguised as an old woman. She begged him to carry her safely across a swollen river,

THE ARGONAUTS (top) commissioned Argus to build the Argo, a ship with twenty oars. Here he carves out the stern, while Athena makes sails. Behind her, perched on a pillar, her sacred creature, the owl, symbolizes her wisdom. (ILLUSTRATION FROM DICTIONARY OF CLASSICAL ANTIQUITIES, 1891.)

JASON (above left), helps Hera, disguised as an old woman, across the stream. In the current he loses a sandal, fulfilling part of an oracle that a half-shod man would take Pelias' throne. The peacock beside Hera denotes her all-seeing vision. (ILLUSTRATION FROM TANGLEWOOD TALES, C. 1920.)

JASON (above), with Medea's help – she anoints him with a salve to protect him from fire and steel – ploughs the fields with the bulls of Aietes. He was the first hero to yoke the wild and fiery creatures. (ILLUSTRATION FROM TANGLEWOOD TALES, C. 1920.)

which Jason did at the cost of one of his sandals. Thus the prophecy was fulfilled: a man wearing only one sandal arrived at Iolcus to challenge Pelias. Because Jason made his intentions known at the time of a religious festival, Pelias could not kill his nephew without the risk of suffering divine disfavour. So the king told Jason that he could have the throne provided he obtained the Golden Fleece, which was an apparently impossible task. This miraculous fleece belonged to a ram which had flown to Colchis, a distant land identified with modern Georgia. It hung from a tree there, guarded by an enormous snake that never slept.

The *DELPHIC ORACLE* encouraged Jason to undertake the quest. Hera inspired a group of Thessalian

ARIADNE (above) hands the vital skein to Theseus, which allows him to track his way through the Labyrinth. After killing the bull-like beast, the Minotaur, in the Labyrinth, he sailed away with her, but then deserted her on Dia, possibly believing that she was destined to marry a god. (ILLUSTRATION FROM TANGLEWOOD TALES, C. 1920.)

warriors to join his expedition and they became known as the Argonauts, the crew of the ship *Argo*. Among their number were Castor and Polydeuces, *ORPHEUS* the poet, Calais and Zetes the sons of *BOREAS* and the hero *HERACLES*. Together they crossed a sea of marvels, visited strange lands and overcame many obstacles before reaching Colchis, where Hera used the goddess of love *APHRODITE* to make *MEDEA*, the second daughter

of King Aietes, fall in love with Jason. The king hated Greeks but he kept his feelings hidden from the Argonauts. He even consented to Jason's attempt to capture the Golden Fleece. But first Aietes set Jason a challenge that was intended to result in his death. The hero was required to yoke a team of fire-breathing bulls, plough and sow a field with dragon's teeth, and slay the armed men who would at once rise from the ground.

With the assistance of Medea's skills in the magic arts, Jason accomplished Aietes' task within a single day. But the king of Colchis was not prepared to give up the Golden Fleece so easily. He secretly planned to attack the Argonauts, who were warned by Medea, now Jason's lover. She employed her magic once again to deal with the unsleeping snake, and Jason seized the Golden Fleece. The Argonauts quickly rowed away from Colchis with the fleece and Medea, whom Jason had promised to marry once back in Thessaly.

The Colchian princess seems to have been associated with the rites of dismemberment as well as magic, for during the pursuit of the Argonauts across the Black Sea, Medea slowed the fleet of her father Aietes by killing and cutting up her own brother, Apsyrtus. Pieces of Apsyrtus' body were thrown overboard, forcing the Colchians to gather up the remains for a decent burial. Later, in Thessaly, Medea also persuaded the daughters of King Pelias to cut their father to pieces and boil him, so as to restore his youth. This they did, and in killing him avenged the disgrace of Jason's father Aeson.

Jason and Medea led an unsettled life in Greece. After a few years he deserted her for another woman, but Medea killed this rival and her own children by Jason. Jason died in Corinth as a result of a rotten piece of the *Argo* falling on his head. Afterwards the gods raised the ship to the sky and made

it into a constellation. The Golden Fleece also appears in the heavens as the first constellation of the Zodiac, Aries the ram.

ARIADNE, in Greek mythology, was the daughter of PASIPHAE and King MINOS, the ruler of Knossos on the island of Crete. When the Athenian hero THESEUS came to Knossos to pay the annual tribute of seven young men and seven girls, Ariadne gave him a sword and a skein of thread that allowed him to escape from Daedalus' Labyrinth after a bloody struggle with the dreaded bull-headed man, the MINOTAUR. Theseus and Ariadne then fled from Crete, but for some unknown reason the hero abandoned the princess on the nearby island of Dia. The deserted princess may then have become the wife of DIONYSUS, the god of ecstasy and wine. Local legend would suggest such a connection, although the whole story of the Minotaur was probably no more than a garbled

version of far older tales of the sport of bull-leaping, which dated from the pre-Greek era of Cretan history. Dionysus himself was known to the Greeks as "the roaring one", a "bull-horned god" who was full of power and fertility.

ARION see VOYAGERS

ARTEMIS was the daughter of the Titaness LETO and ZEUS, and the twin sister of APOLLO. She was in all likelihood a very ancient deity whom the Greeks adopted as goddess of the wild. Traces of human sacrifice could still be found in her worship. Most of all, Artemis liked to roam the mountains with a companion band of nymphs. Certainly the virgin goddess resented any kind of intrusion into her domain, or any harm done to her favourite animals. For killing a stag sacred to Artemis, the leader of the Greek expedition against Troy, King AGAMEMNON of Mycenae, found his fleet stranded by contrary winds

ARTEMIS, virgin goddess of the wild, always resisted the love or attentions of men. When the hunter Actaeon saw her in the nude, bathing with her nymphs, she indignantly turned him into a stag, which was set upon by his own hounds. (DIANA AND ACTAEON BY TITIAN, CANVAS, 1556-59.)

at Aulis. Only a promise to sacrifice his daughter IPHIGENIA was enough to appease the goddess, although there are differing accounts as to whether the girl was actually killed.

Another mortal punished by Artemis was ACTAEON. He had the misfortune while hunting to come upon the goddess as she was bathing. She changed him into a stag and he was chased and torn apart by his own hunting dogs. However, according to a different version, Actaeon actually tried to approach the naked goddess hidden beneath a stag's pelt.

To the Romans, Artemis was closely identified with their goddess Diana, who was also a goddess of light as well as of the wild.

ASCANIUS weeps beside his wounded father, Aeneas. Close by, in a mantle of mist, Aeneas' divine mother, Venus, descends from heaven with a sprig of healing dittany, while the Greek surgeon, Iapyx, pulls out the arrow-head with his forceps. (WOUNDED AENEAS, ANON, AD 62 AND 79.)

the Centaur CHIRON, whose knowledge was so great that ZEUS himself feared that Asclepius might learn a way of overcoming death. When he did succeed in resurrecting one of his patients, Zeus decided that Asclepius should be punished for threatening the gods' monopoly over immortality. Asclepius was slain by a thunder-bolt, but at Apollo's request the god of medicine was placed among the stars, as Ophiuchus, the serpent-bearer.

So impressed were the Romans with Asclepius' cult that during a time of plague they requested aid from Epidauros and a sacred snake was duly shipped to Rome.

ATALANTA, in Greek mythology, was the daughter of Iasus of Arcadia and was known as a famous huntress. As an unwanted daughter she was exposed and left to die on a mountainside, but was suckled by a bear and later brought up by hunters. This experience may have inclined her to manly pursuits. She even tried to enlist with the ARGONAUTS, but JASON refused her because the presence of one woman on the ship might cause jealousies amongst them.

Atalanta's most famous myth concerns the lengths to which she went to avoid marriage. She said that her husband must first beat her in a race and any man who lost would be put to death. Despite the awful consequence of losing, there were many who admired Atalanta's beauty and paid the price against her speed. None could catch her, although they ran naked while she was fully clothed. Finally, the love goddess APHRODITE took pity on a young man named Melanion and provided him with a way to delay

ASCANIUS was the son of AENEAS and Creusa. According to the Romans, he founded the city of Alba Longa thirty-three years after the arrival of the Trojan refugees in Italy. An alternative tradition makes Ascanius' mother Lavinia, a Latin princess whose marriage to Aeneas brought peace and unity to the Latin and Trojan peoples. It was in her honour that Aeneas founded Lavinium within three years of landing. This would mean that Ascanius was king of Lavinium following Aeneas' death, and before he left to take up residence in a new city at Alba Longa. Early rivalry between the two cities probably explains the removal myth.

The family of Julius Caesar, the Julii, claimed descent from Aeneas through Ascanius, who was also called Iulus Ilus ("made of Ilium"), Ilium being the old name for Troy.

ASCLEPIUS, the Greek god of healing, was the son of APOLLO, god of prophecy, and the lake nymph Coronis. In mythology he is a somewhat shadowy figure, which suggests his late arrival as a major deity. Asclepius would seem to have been a Thessalian healer whose skills became known throughout Greece: his cult eventually took over the sanctuary at Epidauros in the Peloponnese. Sacred snakes resident there were

believed to embody the god's healing power. The ancient association between snakes and medicine is probably due to the snake's apparent ability to renew its youth each year by sloughing off its own skin.

Only the stories of Asclepius' birth and death were ever well known to the Greeks and Romans. When Coronis dared to take in secret a mortal as a second lover, an enraged Apollo sent his sister ARTEMIS to kill the lake nymph with a disease. However, as the flames of the funeral pyre burned Coronis, Apollo felt sorry for his unborn son and removed him from the corpse. Thus was Asclepius born. He was taught medicine by

ASCLEPIUS, Greek god of healing, tends a man on his sickbed. A son of Apollo, the greatest healer, Asclepius was gifted with miraculous powers, once resurrecting a mortal from death. His attributes, staff and serpent, signify power and renewal of life. (ILLUSTRATION BY NICK BEALE, 1995.)

Atalanta. She gave him three golden apples, which he placed at different points on the course. Curiosity got the better of Atalanta, who stopped three times to pick up the apples. So Melanion won the race and Atalanta as a wife. But in his haste to make love to her, Melanion either forgot a vow to Aphrodite or consummated their union in a sacred place. To pay for the sacrilege both he and Atalanta were turned into lions.

ATALANTA, the gifted huntress and unusually athletic heroine, found her match in the equally resourceful and energetic Melanion. Here the heroic pair hunt and slay the monstrous wild boar which has been ravaging the plains of Calydon. (ILLUSTRATION FROM TANGLEWOOD TALES, C. 1920.)

ATHENA, sometimes Athene, the daughter of ZEUS and the Titaness Metis, was the Greek goddess of war and crafts. Although a fierce virgin like ARTEMIS, she did not shun men but on the contrary delighted in being a city-goddess, most notably at Athens. This city adopted her cult when an olive tree grew on its acropolis: the other divine rival for worship was the god POSEIDON, who produced only a spring of brackish water. Athena sprang into being fully grown and armed from the head of her father Zeus, after he had swallowed the pregnant Metis. The smith god HEPHAISTOS assisted the birth with a blow from his axe. Quite likely this intervention accounts for her title of Hephaistia, the companion of the smith god. Athena's symbol was the wise owl, which featured on Athenian coins. The Romans identified her with MINERVA, a goddess of wisdom and the arts.

An early myth relates how Hephaistos tried to rape Athena. To avoid losing her virginity, she miraculously disappeared so that the semen of the smith god fell to the ground, where it grew into the serpent Erichthonius. The three daughters of Cecrops, the semi-serpent who first ruled Athens, were given a box by Athena and told not to look inside. Ignoring this command, two of them looked inside, found themselves gazing upon Erichthonius, and went insane. However, Athena continued to protect Athens. Although the city fell into enemy hands during the Persian invasion of Greece in 480–479 BC, the Athenians later went on to achieve mastery of the sea and found their own empire. It was during this period that the Parthenon was built on the Athenian acropolis.

Athena was always regarded by the Greeks as an active goddess, involved in the affairs of men. She helped several heroes such as BELLEROPHON, JASON, HERACLES and PERSEUS. Also, it was she who eventually got ODYSSEUS back to the island of Ithaca, following his epic voyage home from the Trojan War. Perhaps Athena's most significant aid was given to the matricide ORESTES. Not only did she offer him protection, but she also arranged for him to be tried and acquitted of his terrible crime by the ancient court of the Areopagus, in Athens. The verdict meant an end to the blood-feud, not least because for the first time even the FURIES accepted Orestes' deliverance from guilt.

ATLAS was a TITAN, the son of Iapetus and the Oceanid Clymene. He was thought by the ancient Greeks to hold up the sky, and his name means "he who carries". His most famous encounter was with the hero HERACLES, one of whose labours was to obtain the golden apples of the HESPERIDES, female guardians of the fruit that mother earth, GAIA, presented to HERA at her marriage to ZEUS. Atlas offered to fetch them for Heracles if the

ATHENA, goddess of wisdom and crafts, guided and helped her favourites. Here she visits the hero Bellerophon with a gift – the bridle with which to tame and mount the winged horse, Pegasus. (ILLUSTRATION FROM STORIES FROM GREECE AND ROME, 1930.)

hero took over his job of holding up the sky. When Atlas returned with the apples he suggested that he should deliver them himself, as Heracles was doing so well. The hero pretended to agree and then asked if Atlas would take the world for a moment so that he could adjust the weight on his shoulder, so tricking Atlas into resuming his lonely duty. (See also GIANTS)

ATLAS, the great Titan giant, was condemned to shoulder the heavens forever, as punishment for fighting the sky god Zeus. (ILLUSTRATION FROM DICTIONARY OF CLASSICAL ANTIQUITIES, 1891.)

B

ATREUS

ATREUS was the son of *PELOPS*, an early king after whom the Peloponnese in southern Greece is named, and Hippodameia. The house of Atreus was infamous for the hereditary curse laid upon it by the son of *HERMES*, the messenger god. A terrible cycle of murder and revenge was ended only by the trial in Athens of Atreus' grandson *ORESTES* on a charge of matricide.

Family misfortune stemmed from the action of Pelops, the father of Atreus. He seems either to have brought about the death of Hermes' son Myrtilus, or to have caused him great grief by refusing to make a promised gift. Friction between the sons of Pelops, Atreus, Thyestes and Chrysippus, arose about the ownership of a golden ram, a wondrous animal placed in Atreus' flock by Hermes. First, Chrysippus was murdered by Atreus and Thyestes, then Thyestes seduced Aerope, the wife of Atreus, in order to gain her help in seizing the golden ram. An enraged Atreus slew Aerope and exiled Thyestes.

At a banquet supposedly for reconciliation, Atreus served his brother Thyestes with the flesh of his children. When Thyestes had

ATREUS, son of Pelops, cherished a golden ram, a double-edged gift of the god Hermes. The god gave the coveted treasure to Atreus, hoping to sow strife and discord in the house of Pelops, in revenge for the murder of his son, Myrtilus.
(ILLUSTRATION BY NICK BEALE, 1995.)

BELLEROPHON swoops down for the kill on his winged horse, Pegasus, diving through the smoke and flames of the fire-breathing Chimaera, a monster with the forepart of a lion, the hindpart of a dragon and its middle formed from a goat.
(ILLUSTRATION FROM TANGLEWOOD TALES, C. 1920.)

finished eating, Atreus showed his brother the hands and feet of his dead sons and told him what he had consumed. In horror the sun halted in its course. Thyestes' only surviving son, Aegisthus, may have slain Atreus in revenge for this outrage. Certainly he became the lover of *CLYTEMNESTRA*, whose husband *AGAMEMNON* was the eldest son of Atreus and his successor as king of Mycenae, or Argos. Not until Clytemnestra and Aegisthus had murdered Agamemnon, and were themselves killed by Agamemnon's son *ORESTES*, did the curse of Myrtilus come to an end.

BELLEROPHON

BELLEROPHON was a Greek hero from the city of Corinth and the son of Glaucus. He possessed a wonderful winged horse named *PEGASUS*, which had sprung out of the *GORGON* Medusa's blood when she was beheaded by *PERSEUS*. The goddess *ATHENA* gave Bellerophon a special bridle in order to help him tame Pegasus.

Bellerophon's problems began, as his own name indicates, with a murder. He evidently killed an important Corinthian because in exile he changed his name from Hipponous to Bellerophon ("killer of Bellerus"). Although he was given refuge in Argos by King Proteus, the passion of the local queen Stheneboea for him caused further difficulties, and not least because he steadfastly rejected her advances. Stheneboea accused him of attempted rape and the enraged

BOREAS, one of the four winds, blew from the north, whistling through his conch. He often helped sailors with a friendly breeze. Along with his brother winds, Eurus, Zephyrus and Notus, he was depicted in the Temple of Winds. (ILLUSTRATION FROM DR SMITH'S CLASSICAL DICTIONARY, 1895.)

Proteus dispatched Bellerophon to southern Asia Minor, where he was supposed to meet his end, but service in the local king's forces saved his life. Mounted on Pegasus, the hero was able to overcome the monstrous Chimaera, defeat neighbouring peoples, including the Amazons, and even become the champion of Lycia. A constellation was named after his fabulous winged horse.

Two tales cast a certain shadow over Bellerophon's character. In the first he is credited with a brutal revenge on the false Argive queen. By pretending that he really loved her, Bellerophon persuaded the queen to elope with him on Pegasus, only to push her off the winged horse's back in mid-air. The second tale almost ends in the hero's death when he attempted to fly to Mount Olympus, the home of the gods. *ZEUS* in anger caused Pegasus to unseat Bellerophon, who was lamed for life.

BOREAS

BOREAS, the north wind, was the son of *EOS*, the goddess of dawn, and the Titan Astraeus. His home was thought to be Thrace, which is situated to the north of the Aegean Sea. In contrast to Zephyrus, the

gentle west wind, Boreas was capable of great destruction. During the Persian invasion of Greece, he helped the Greek cause by damaging the Persian fleet at the battle of Artemisium in 480 BC.

Boreas abducted Orithyia, a daughter of King Erechtheus of Attica. Coming across Orithyia dancing near a stream, he then wrapped her up in a cloud and carried her off to Thrace. She bore Boreas twin sons, Calais and Zetes, who were known as the Boreades. At birth these boys were entirely human in appearance, but later they sprouted golden wings from their shoulders. They were killed by the great hero *HERACLES*.

Boreas was worshipped in the city of Athens, where an annual festival, known as the Boreasmi, was celebrated in his honour.

BRITOMARTIS fled from King Minos who pursued her for nine months, until at last, in despair, she leapt into the sea. Luckily, she became entangled in some fishing nets, and when Artemis changed her into a goddess she was known as Dictynna, which means "net".
(ILLUSTRATION BY NICK BEALE, 1995.)

BRITOMARTIS ("sweet maid") was said to be the daughter of *ZEUS*. She lived on the island of Crete, where she spent her time as a huntress. King *MINOS* of Knossos tried to make Britomartis his mistress. But she fled from him and in her desperation to preserve her virginity threw herself off a cliff into the sea. The king finally gave up the pursuit when the Cretan goddess sought sanctuary in the sacred grove of *ARTEMIS*, and became her close associate. The myth is almost certainly an account of the amalgamation of two ancient cults.

BRUTUS was said to be the son of Tarquinia, who was the sister of *TARQUINIUS SUPERBUS*. He was the founder of the Roman Republic. Like most Roman myths, the story of Lucius Junius Brutus lays emphasis on duty to the state, even though in this instance it involved the sacrifice of two sons. During the early part of his life Brutus was regarded as a simpleton, which his name implies. Indeed, he was something of a joke in the court of Tarquinius Superbus, the last Etruscan king to rule Rome. When a snake was found in the king's palace, two princes travelled to Delphi to ask the Oracle to explain this event and Brutus accompanied them almost in the role of a jester. The Oracle told the Romans that the first person in the delegation to kiss his mother would be the next ruler of Rome. The princes drew lots to decide who was to kiss their mother on their return home, but Brutus tripped and kissed the earth, much to their amusement.

BRUTUS, the first consul of the new republic of Rome, condemns his sons to death for rising against the government. Brutus, as his name implies, feigned idiocy but was no fool; wisely and dutifully, he led the trial against his rebel sons.
(ILLUSTRATION FROM STORIES FROM LIVY, 1885.)

Shortly after their return to Rome, the youngest prince raped *LUCRETIA*, a Roman matron. This act of violation was the last straw for the oppressed Roman aristocracy, especially when it was learned that Lucretia had stabbed herself to death. The outrage was cleverly used by Brutus as a means of overthrowing the monarchy and setting up a republic. The now eloquent Brutus was elected consul, one of the two highest offices of state. But this fulfilment of the Oracle was soon to cause him grief, when a conspiracy to restore Tarquinius Superbus to the throne was found to have the support of Titus and Tiberius, two of Brutus' own sons. As he was the chief magistrate, Brutus, with great dignity, oversaw their arrest, trial and execution. Thus, at the moment of the new Republic's triumph, the typically Roman idea of self-sacrifice appears as part of its foundation myth.

C

CACUS see GIANTS

CADMUS was the son of Agenor, king of Phoenicia, and Telephassa, and the brother of EUROPA. When Europa was forcibly taken to Crete by ZEUS, disguised as a bull, Cadmus and his four brothers were sent after her, with instructions not to return home without her. Although the five Phoenician princes failed in their task, they seem to have had an impact on the places where they eventually settled. Cadmus himself was told by the Oracle at Delphi to forget about Europa and instead find a cow with a moon-shaped mark on its flank. He was to follow the animal and build a city on the spot where it chose to lie down and rest. Having found the cow and followed it eastwards to Boeotia, where at last it sank in exhaustion, Cadmus then sent some of his men for water so that they might sacrifice the animal to ATHENA. But these men were attacked by a serpent sprung from the war god ARES. After Cadmus had killed the monster, the goddess Athena advised him to remove its teeth and sow half of them in the ground. Immediately, armed men arose, but wily Cadmus threw stones among them so that, suspecting each other, they fell upon themselves. It was later believed

CADMUS sows the teeth of a dragon he has slain, and instantly the soil bristles with armed warriors, who spring up to attack each other. Only five survived, to become ancestors of the Thebans, whose city Cadmus founded on the site.
(ILLUSTRATION BY NICK BEALE, 1995.)

that the Theban aristocracy was descended from the five warriors who survived the mutual slaughter.

After a period of penance for killing Ares' serpent, Zeus gave Cadmus a wife – none other than Harmonia, the daughter of Ares and APHRODITE, goddess of love. Since he was marrying a goddess, the gods themselves attended the wedding and gave wonderful gifts. The unusual union of mortal and immortal was not blessed by particularly successful offspring, however. One of their descendants, Pentheus, suffered a horrible fate. Having insulted DIONYSUS, he was torn to pieces by the god's female worshippers when he spied on their secret rites. Among the frenzied worshippers was Pentheus' own mother, Agave, the daughter of Cadmus and Harmonia.

The ancient Greeks always acknowledged the importance of Cadmus' reign, hence, his divine wife. He was credited with the introduction from Phoenicia of an alphabet of sixteen letters. There

are in fact a number of ancient accounts of Phoenician activity in the Aegean Sea. For instance, on the island of Cythera, which lies off the southern Peloponnese, a shrine to Aphrodite is known to have been erected based on the goddess's chief temple in Phoenicia.

CALCHAS see ORACLES AND PROPHECIES

CALLISTO see LOVERS OF ZEUS

CASSANDRA was the daughter of PRIAM, king of Troy, and his wife Hecuba. Her beauty was as remarkable as her power of prophecy, which was said to have been a gift from APOLLO, who loved her, but because she refused his advances he condemned her to prophesy the truth but never to be believed.

Cassandra foretold the Trojan War, the true purpose of the Wooden Horse and the murder of

CASSANDRA, frenzied seer, flees through burning Troy, aghast at the sight of her own predictions. Gifted with prophecy, she clearly foresaw the Trojan War and the trickery of the Wooden Horse, but no one believed her for she was fated to be ignored.
(ILLUSTRATION BY NICK BEALE, 1995.)

CERBERUS snarls and growls by the mouth of Hades. A three-headed hound with a snake for a tail, he allowed no shades to return from the dead, though a few slipped by with the help of the gods. His dark den opened onto the Styx along which Charon ferried the dead. (ILLUSTRATION BY GLENN STEWARD, 1995.)

AGAMEMNON, to whom she was awarded as part of his share of the spoils. But ultimately Cassandra had her revenge on the Greeks. When Troy fell, she had sought sanctuary in ATHENA's temple but was raped, and so the goddess punished this sacrilege by killing many of the Greeks during their voyage home. However, Cassandra met her own end at the hands of Agamemnon's wife CLYTEMNESTRA. (See also ORACLES AND PROPHECIES)

CECROPS see FOUNDERS

CENTAURS, according to Greek mythology, were said to be the descendants of IXION, son of ARES. These strange creatures had the head, arms and chest of a man but the legs and lower half of a horse. They lived in Thessaly, fed on meat and were given to riotous behaviour. They were usually depicted as drunken followers of DIONYSUS, except for wise CHIRON who was the tutor to several heroes, including ACHILLES. (See also MONSTERS AND FABULOUS BEASTS)

CERBERUS was a three-headed hound, the offspring of two monsters, TYPHON and Echidna. He was the watchdog of the Greek underworld and stopped anyone trying to return to the land of the living. One of HERACLES' labours was to fetch Cerberus, a challenge the god of the dead, HADES, allowed him to

CHIRON (left) *instructs the youthful Achilles in the arts of war, medicine, hunting, music and prophecy. Unlike his brother Centaurs, who indulged in riotous revelries, Chiron was noted for his wisdom and gentleness.* (THE EDUCATION OF ACHILLES BY POMPEO BATONI, CANVAS, C. 1770.)

CINCINNATUS

CINCINNATUS was a Roman hero who was instrumental in saving the early Republic. In 458 BC, Rome was in danger of being destroyed by the Aequi, a neighbouring Italian tribe. To defeat this threat, the Senate voted to appoint Cincinnatus as dictator, a temporary office vested with unlimited powers. A deputation was sent to his small farm, which was the smallest landholding allowed to qualify for citizenship. The senators found Cincinnatus at work tending his crops. He was told of the Senate's decision and was saluted as dictator. However, the plebeians, the ordinary people, feared that Cincinnatus might abuse his position. Their fears proved groundless and, after the defeat of the Aequi, they voted Cincinnatus a golden wreath at the end of his sixty days of office. He then returned to his fields and was remembered as the perfect example of a virtuous and dutiful Roman citizen.

CINCINNATUS, one of the most modest of Roman heroes and a model of Roman integrity. After 60 days in office, he quietly returned to his farm. (ILLUSTRATION FROM STORIES FROM LIVY, 1885.)

undertake, but only on condition that he was unarmed. Like the *GORGONS*, Cerberus was so dreadful to behold that anyone who looked upon him was turned to stone. He was brother to the Hydra and the Chimaera.

CHIRON was the son of Philyra, daughter of *OCEANOS*, and the Titan *CRONOS*, who had adopted the form of a horse to hide from his wife *RHEA* his passion for Philyra, which is why Chiron had the appearance of a typical *CENTAUR*, with the body and legs of a horse, and the arms and head of a man.

His unusual parentage explains why Chiron was so wise, unlike other Centaurs, for he was learned in music, medicine, hunting and warfare. He was a friend of *APOLLO* and the tutor to several Greek heroes such as *ACHILLES, ASCLEPIUS* and *JASON*. He lived in a cave on Mount Pelion in Thessaly, and when he died *ZEUS* set him in the sky as the constellation Centaurus.

HEROES

THE MYTHS OF ALL CULTURES contain inspiring individuals who express ideal traits and talents, such as the courage of Achilles, might of Heracles, wit of Odysseus and endurance of Oedipus. A classic hero is a champion in every sense, overcoming trials, ridding the world of troublemakers, blazing trails and winning through despite all the odds. Yet he is neither invulnerable nor immortal, though often helped, and sometimes hindered, by the gods. Greek mythology is unusually rich in heroes and heroines of every kind. Some, such as Achilles and Hector, are wartime champions; others, such as Odysseus or Theseus, are heroes for peacetime; some are positive and outgoing, such as Heracles or Perseus; still others are heroes of attitude rather than action, such as Oedipus, Antigone, or Hector, who, at the end, remained steadfast in the face of hopeless defeat.

HERACLES (below) shoots his poisoned arrows at his old foe, the Centaur Nessus, who raced away with his wife, Deianira, while ferrying her across the river Evenus. The dying Centaur offered Deianira the gift of his blood as a salve for preserving the love of Heracles. The love philtre proved to be a fatal trick by which Heracles died many years later, tragically, by the hands of his insecure but loving wife, Deianira, who in her sorrow killed herself. (HERCULES AND NESSUS BY FRANZ VON STUCK, CANVAS 1863-1928.)

HERACLES (above), best known for his mighty labours, was all his life a helper of gods and men, setting the earth free of many monsters and rascals. Worshipped as a hero and deity, he was invoked as a saviour; as the hero of labour and struggle, he was patron deity of the gymnasium. In art he appears as the ideal of manly strength, with massive muscles and grave expression. This celebrated Greek sculpture shows the hero in repose leaning on his club, draped with the famous lion's skin. (THE FARNESE HERCULES BY GLYCON, C. 200 BC.)

ACHILLES (above), godlike hero and peerless warrior was, paradoxically, disguised as a girl in his youth. His divine mother, Thetis, wishing to save him from the Trojan War, hid him amongst the daughters of Lycomedes on Scyros. There Odysseus went, disguised as a merchant, and showed the girls jewels, dresses and arms. Only Achilles seized the arms eagerly, suddenly realizing his true sex and role in life. He then accompanied Odysseus to Troy.
(ODYSSEUS RECOGNISING ACHILLES AFTER FRANS FRANCKEN THE YOUNGER, CANVAS, C. 1570.)

PERSEUS, guided and guarded by the gods, was able to slay the mortal Gorgon, Medusa, one of three frightful sisters who dwelt on the farthest shore of the ocean, and whose looks turned men to stone. By viewing Medusa in his shining shield, Perseus was able to cut off her head as she slept. Hidden by the invisible helmet of Hades he flew to safety on winged sandals given him by the nymphs. Medusa's head was placed on Athena's breastplate – a paralysing power in battle. (ILLUSTRATION FROM TANGLEWOOD TALES, C. 1920.)

CLOELIA (above), Roman heroine, was given as a hostage to the Etruscan, Lars Porsenna, during his campaign against Rome. But she escaped from his camp and swam across the Tiber to Rome. When the Romans sent her back to Porsenna, he was so taken by her gallantry, that he set her free with some other hostages and gave her a splendid horse. Here she rides triumphantly to freedom with her companions. (ILLUSTRATION FROM STORIES FROM LIVY, 1885.)

JASON (above), the celebrated captain of the Argonauts, embarked on a great adventure to bring back the Golden Fleece, which was suspended from a branch of an oak tree in the grove of Ares in Colchis. It was greatly cherished by Aietes, the king of Colchis. With the help of a potion from the sorceress Medea, daughter of the king of Colchis, Jason charmed to sleep the ever-watchful dragon that guarded the Golden Fleece. (ILLUSTRATION FROM TANGLEWOOD TALES, C.1920.)

HORATIUS (above), brave Roman hero, held the Sublician Bridge with two comrades against the Etruscan army. While he held off the Etruscans, the Romans hacked the bridge behind him until it collapsed. Having sent back his comrades, Horatius stood alone until the bridge fell, then he swam to safety across the raging Tiber, amid enemy arrows. The state erected a statue to his honour in the Comitium. (ILLUSTRATION FROM LAYS OF ANCIENT ROME, 1891.)

CIRCE (left), an enchanting nymph, invites Odysseus to drink from her magic cup, containing a potion which turns men into swine. But Odysseus has been forewarned and, immunized with the herb moly, he drinks without coming to harm. (ILLUSTRATION FROM TANGLEWOOD TALES, C.1920.)

CLYTEMNESTRA (above), the estranged wife of Agamemnon, watches and waits for the ships from Troy, bringing her husband home. Yet no hero's welcome awaits the returning warrior, only betrayal and murder by his wife and her lover. (ILLUSTRATION BY NICK BEALE, 1995.)

CIRCE, daughter of *HELIOS*, the sun god, was a powerful witch who had poisoned her husband, king of the Sarmatians, before going to the fabulous island of Aeaea. Her magical powers turned *ODYSSEUS'* men into swine when they landed on Aeaea on their way home from Troy. Aided by *HERMES*, the messenger god, Odysseus was immune to Circe's magic and restored his crew to human form, and also gained the witch's aid for the next part of his journey. For a year he stayed as her lover, before she told him how to navigate through the waters of the Sirens and between Scylla, a monster, and Charybdis, a whirlpool. Scylla had been a rival of Circe, who had turned her into a monster when one of her many lovers had shown an interest in the unfortunate girl. In some accounts, Circe eventually married Odysseus' son Telemachus.

CLOELIA see *HEROES*

CLYTEMNESTRA was the daughter of *LEDA* and Tyndarcos, king of Sparta, and the estranged wife of *AGAMEMNON*. Sometimes she is portrayed as a weak woman, easily persuaded by her lover Aegisthus to assist in the murder of her husband on his return from the Trojan War. Otherwise it is Clytemnestra who is the strong character, the instigator of the murder, while Aegisthus is little more than a weakling. Even before the the Greek force departed for Troy, Clytemnestra already had good reason to hate her husband. In order to gain a fair wind to Troy, he agreed to sacrifice her favourite child *IPHIGENIA*. Even though the champion *ACHILLES* had promised to defend the girl against all threats, the Greek host had its way and Iphigenia was offered to the god-

dess *ARTEMIS*, either as sacrificial victim or as priestess.

Like her sister *HELEN*, whose elopement with *PARIS* caused the Trojan War, Clytemnestra felt no loyalty towards her husband. She openly conducted an affair with Aegisthus, Agamemnon's cousin, and ruled Mycenae with him. The end of the war required desperate measures. When he returned home Agamemnon was butchered by Aegisthus, using a two-headed axe, while Clytemnestra had him entangled in a net. For this terrible crime, Clytemnestra was herself killed by her son *ORESTES*.

CORIOLANUS was a legendary Roman traitor of the fifth century BC. Conscious above all of his noble birth, Coriolanus objected to the Senate's wish to distribute free bread to poorer citizens, who were starving because of Rome's endless

wars. He said that unless the plebeians, the ordinary people, were willing to restore to the nobility its full ancient privileges they should expect no charity. Hounded from Rome for such an opinion, he joined the Volsci and eventually led a Volscian army against the city. All seemed lost until his mother Volumnia spoke to him, asking Coriolanus whether he saw her as his own mother or as a prisoner of war. As a result he quit the battlefield and went into exile.

CREON, in Greek mythology, was the brother of Jocasta and a reluctant ruler of Thebes. He was regent during the uncertain period after King *LAIUS*, Jocasta's husband, had been killed near the city. Creon offered the throne and the hand of Jocasta to any man who could solve the riddle of the *SPHINX* and thus rid Thebes of this bloodthirsty

CREON, reluctant king of Thebes, lost his son, wife and niece in a tragic cycle of suicides caused by his inflexible will. His crushing fate was to endure a life of solitary grief and remorse. (ILLUSTRATION BY NICK BEALE, 1995.)

CORIOLANUS, a Roman exile, marched against his old city with an army of Volscians, encamping just outside Rome. There, he ignored all entreaties for peace until visited by his mother (centre), his wife and the Roman matrons, whose tears softened his stern heart. (ILLUSTRATION FROM STORIES FROM LIVY, 1885.)

monster. OEDIPUS managed to achieve the apparently impossible task, then took over the kingdom, married Jocasta and raised a family. Not until a plague threatened Thebes and the Delphic Oracle was consulted about its cause, did it become known that Jocasta was Oedipus' mother and that he had killed Laius. Oedipus blinded himself, Jocasta committed suicide and Creon became regent once more.

A quarrel between Oedipus' sons, Eteocles and Polynices, caused another period of dismay, eventually leaving both of them dead and Creon on the throne. Whereas Eteocles was regarded by Creon as a patriot and properly buried, the body of the rebel Polynices was thrown outside the city walls and forbidden burial. Such a situation was unacceptable to ANTIGONE, Oedipus' daughter and companion during his wanderings around Greece, and on her return to Thebes she sprinkled Polynices' corpse with earth, so as to give her brother a token burial.

As a result of this act of defiance, Creon had Antigone walled up in a cave. The seer TIRESIAS told Creon to bury the dead and disinter the living, but he refused. The result was personal grief, when his own son committed suicide on learning of Antigone's death, and his own wife soon followed suit.

Although Creon was well known to the ancient Greeks, his own character seems less important in myth than his role as regent in the troubled city of Thebes.

CRONOS, in Greek mythology, was the son of Ouranos, the sky god, and GAIA, the earth mother. With the help of Gaia, Cronos emasculated Ouranos and seized control of the universe. He then married his sister RHEA and followed the example of Ouranos in disposing of his children by swallowing them, because he had been warned that he would be displaced by one of his sons. Rhea, however, gave him a stone wrapped in swaddling clothes instead of the infant ZEUS, his youngest son, who was taken secretly to Crete in order to grow up safely on the island. When Zeus came of age, he forced Cronos to vomit up his brothers and sisters – POSEIDON, HADES, HERA, HESTIA and DEMETER – and to release his uncles and aunts, especially the Titans, whom Cronos had chosen

to keep chained up. In gratitude, the Cyclopes, the single-eyed giants, fashioned for Zeus his famous lightning and thunderbolts.

In a subsequent struggle for power, Zeus and his brothers successfully dealt with all the might and power that Cronos could direct against them. After his defeat, Cronos was either banished to a distant paradise, or he simply slowly faded away as an unimportant deity. The Romans equated Cronos with their SATURN, who

was a corn god whom they associated with the Golden Age.

CUPID was the Roman god of love and son of the love goddess VENUS. He was depicted as a beautiful but wanton boy, armed with a quiver full of "arrowed desires". Some of his arrows, however, would turn people away from those who fell in love with them.

According to one myth, Venus was jealous of PSYCHE ("the soul") and told Cupid to make her love the ugliest man alive. But Cupid fell in love with Psyche and, invisible, visited her every night. He told her not to try to see him, but, overcome by curiosity, she did try and he left her. Psyche searched the world for him, until the sky god JUPITER granted her immortality so that she could be Cupid's constant companion. The couple's daughter was named Voluptas ("pleasure").

CUPID fishes playfully amongst the waves. He is usually portrayed as a cute, capricious child with wings and often with a quiver of arrows or a torch to inflame love in the hearts of gods and men. (CUPID FISHING BY GEORGE FREDERICK WATTS, SEPIA C. 1890.)

D

CURTIUS leaps into the chasm in the Roman forum. The seers declared that the chasm could only be filled by Rome's greatest treasure, and so Curtius jumped in, declaring that there was no greater treasure than a gallant Roman citizen. (ILLUSTRATION FROM STORIES FROM LIVY, 1885.)

CURTIUS is the subject of a strange incident in Roman mythology. Around 362 BC a great chasm appeared in the Forum in Rome, which led straight down to the underworld. It had appeared because the Romans forgot to make an appropriate sacrifice to the dead. Marcus Curtius therefore plunged on horseback into the bottomless pit and was seen no more.

CYCLOPES see GIANTS

DAEDALUS, according to Greek mythology, was said by some to be the son of Alcippe, the daughter of the war god ARES, and by others to be the son of Merope. It is agreed, though, that he came from Athens. He was a gifted craftsman and was employed by King MINOS at his palace of Knossos in Crete. Daedalus designed and built the Labyrinth for the dreaded MINO-TAUR. This was the offspring of PASIPHAE, Minos' wife, and a great bull. Daedalus had designed an artificial cow into which the queen could place herself and so be able to mate with the bull. Thus was the Minotaur conceived. Minos later imprisoned Daedalus for revealing the secret of the Labyrinth, but he managed to escape by constructing

DAPHNE, a river nymph, was loved by Apollo who pursued her until, on the banks of her father's river, she prayed for help and was at once changed into a laurel tree. Here, her father, the river god Peneius, weeps inconsolably, while Apollo strokes her leafy arms in wonder. (APOLLO AND DAPHNE BY NICOLAS POUSSIN, CANVAS, C.1627)

wings of wax and feathers for himself and his son Icarus. Despite his father's warning, Icarus flew too close to the sun, the wax of his wings melted and he fell into the sea and drowned. Daedalus managed to arrive safely in Sicily, where he amused the daughters of King Cocalos with his inventions. When Minos eventually caught up with the fugitive craftsman, a battle of wits ended in Daedalus' favour: Minos was killed by boiling water, or oil, which Daedalus persuaded Cocalos' daughters to pour down a pipe into the king's bath.

DANAE was the mother of the Greek hero PERSEUS and the daughter of Acrisius, king of Argos in the Peloponnese. It had been foretold that her son would cause the death of Acrisius, so he locked her in a bronze tower. But ZEUS visited her as a shower of golden rain and Perseus was conceived. The king banished the mother and her son, but after many adventures Perseus did accidentally kill Acrisius when throwing a discus. (See also LOVERS OF ZEUS)

DANAE (above) was imprisoned in a bronze tower by her father, because he feared a prophecy that he would be killed by his grandson. Yet even hidden away in her tower, she was still accessible to the god Zeus, who came to her as a golden shower. They had a son, Perseus. (DANAE AND THE GOLDEN RAIN BY TITIAN, CANVAS, 1554.)

DAPHNE, in Greek mythology, was the daughter of the river god Peneius. She was similar in many ways to the goddess ARTEMIS, in that she was also a virgin huntress who happily roamed the wilderness. One day, the love god EROS shot a flurry of arrows in response to taunts from APOLLO, the god of prophecy. The first of Eros' arrows

DAEDALUS (right) crafted wings of feathers, held together by wax, to escape from Crete, and taught his son, Icarus, how to fly, warning him that he must not fly too close to the sun. But Icarus was drawn to the light of the sun, so his wings melted and he fell into the sea, now named the Icarian. (DAEDALUS AND ICARUS BY CHARLES LANDON, 1799.)

was a gold-tipped shaft and when it struck Apollo it made him fall immediately in love with Daphne. The second one, however, had a lead tip and caused Daphne to become even more indifferent than she already had been to any lover. Apollo, however, pursued Daphne relentlessly until, in desperation, she turned herself into a laurel tree.

DEMETER, (left) goddess of the earth, and her daughter, Persephone, holding a mystic torch, consecrate the young Triptolemus, the first man to sow corn. This relief was found at Eleusis, site of the Eleusian mysteries which centred on Demeter and her worship. (MARBLE RELIEF, C. 490 BC.)

dead she pined and refused to eat any food, while in the world of the living her mother lost all interest in fertility, so that plants languished, animals ceased to multiply and people feared for their future. Eventually, Zeus had to intervene and rule that Hades must give up Persephone if she would not consent to stay with him. As she had by then eaten something in his realm, it was deemed that she had not completely rejected Hades, so henceforth Persephone would divide the year equally between her mother and her husband.

DIDO (below), exotic queen of Carthage, tragically stabbed herself when her lover Aeneas deserted her to fulfil his destiny, and lead his people to Rome. The heroine is portrayed by Virgil as a noble and generous soul who, in the classic tradition, endures her tragic fate alone.
(ILLUSTRATION BY NICK BEALE, 1995.)

DELPHIC ORACLE see
ORACLES AND PROPHECIES

DEMETER, the Greek goddess of vegetation and fruitfulness, was the daughter of *CRONOS* and *RHEA*. Like her Roman equivalent, Ceres, she was especially associated with corn. Demeter possessed mysterious powers of growth and even resurrection. She was the focus of

an important cult at Eleusis, just south of Athens, where rites were celebrated annually in the autumn when, through music and dancing, her worshippers recalled the loss and rediscovery of her daughter *PERSEPHONE*. Demeter means "mother earth" – the abundant soil as well as the resting-place of the dead (which were known by the Athenians as "Demeter's people").

Her myth turns on the disappearance of Persephone. When the girl was a child, her father, *ZEUS*, without even consulting Demeter, agreed to his brother *HADES*' request that Persephone should be his bride and rule the underworld with him. Hades was impatient and rose from the earth and abducted Persephone as she plucked flowers in a field. But in the world of the

The story of Demeter and Persephone is clearly ancient. It has parallels in the mythology of West Asia, where growth and decay were closely associated with a dying and reviving deity. For the Greeks, Persephone as Kore ("the maiden"), was identified as the power within the corn itself, which was a natural extension of her mother the corn goddess Demeter.

DIONYSUS, *the vital and beautiful Greek god of wine, whirls in a state of blissful euphoria induced by his own fruit, the grape. Entwined in his hair is a wreath of vine, and covering his shoulders the skin of a lynx, one of the creatures sacred to him.* (RED-FIGURE VASE, C. 400 BC.)

DIONYSUS was the son of ZEUS and SEMELE, who was a Theban princess. In Greek mythology, he is a youthful god of vegetation, wine and ecstasy, known as the "bull-horned god" because he often adopted the form of this powerful beast. In Roman mythology he is represented by the god Bacchus. Originally, he may have had a mythological role somewhat similar to that of the goddess DEMETER ("mother earth"). His cult in later times, however, developed into one of personal salvation, particularly for women worshippers who were known as maenads.

From the beginning, the ancient Greeks were well aware of the strange character of Dionysus, and in some city-states his wild, orgiastic rites were outlawed. The most famous attempt to prohibit his worship was by King Pentheus of Thebes. The king even tried to imprison Dionysus, but the chains fell off him and the prison doors could not be closed. Dionysus then told Pentheus that he could observe at first hand the secret rituals performed on a mountain close to the city, but only if he disguised himself as a woman. The king readily took the bait and spied on the maenads from a hiding-place in a tree. However, the maenads soon discovered him and, in their ecstatic frenzy, thought that he was a lion and tore him limb from limb. Afterwards his mother, Agave, who was also one of the leading maenads, realized to her horror that they had dismembered not a lion but her son. After his burial, Agave, together with her parents, CADMUS and Harmonia, left Thebes and went into exile. (See also LOVERS OF ZEUS)

DIDO, originally a princess of Tyre, in Phoenicia, became the tragic queen of Carthage and the abandoned love of AENEAS. Her husband had been murdered by her brother, when the latter ascended the throne of Tyre. Dido escaped from Phoenicia with a small band of followers and settled in present-day Tunisia, where she purchased enough land to found the city of Carthage. The local ruler agreed to sell her as much ground as a bull's hide might contain, so Dido cut the skin into strips in order to obtain an adequate plot.

When the Trojan hero Aeneas arrived in Carthage, having been blown off course on his way to Italy from Troy, Dido welcomed him and his fellow refugees with great understanding. Aeneas and Dido soon fell in love, but the Roman god JUPITER sent MERCURY with a message reminding Aeneas of his destiny to found a new Troy in Italy and ordering him to resume his voyage at once. When Aeneas sailed away, Dido became so overwhelmed by the loss of her lover that she stabbed herself and then leapt into the flames of a pyre. (See also FOUNDERS)

E

THE DIOSCURI, the mysterious twin sons of *LEDA*, queen of Sparta, were known to the Greeks as Castor and Polydeuces, and to the Romans as Castor and Pollux. They were brothers of *HELEN* and *CLYTEMNESTRA*. Around all these children, except Clytemnestra, there hung a definite sense of divine parentage, and it may well be that they were ancient deities whose worship had declined so that their exploits could be told as the mythological actions of mortal rulers. Castor and Polydeuces ("the heavenly twins whom the corn-bearing earth holds") were regarded as being both dead and alive. In one story, Polydeuces was the immortal son of *ZEUS* while Castor was the mortal son of King Tyndareos. At Polydeuces' request the twins shared the divinity between them, living half the year beneath the earth with the dead, and the other half on Mount Olympus with the gods. They are shown together in the constellation of Gemini.

In their youth the Dioscuri ("the sons of Zeus") were *ARGONAUTS*. During the expedition to retrieve the Golden Fleece, Polydeuces killed with his bare hands Amycus, king of the savage Bebryces, who were a people living in Asia Minor. On another occasion the twins were ranged against the Athenian hero *THESEUS*, who carried off the twelve-year-old Helen prior to her marriage to King *MENELAUS*. They brought their sister safely home to Sparta, and even set up a rival to Theseus on the throne of Athens.

THE DIOSCURI (above), twins Castor and Pollux, returned to earth to help the Roman ranks against the Latins in the fabled Battle of Lake Regillus. Adorned with gleaming armour, and mounted on snow-white steeds, they led the Romans to victory. (ILLUSTRATION FROM LAYS OF ANCIENT ROME, 1881.)

The Dioscuri were revered by the Spartans and the Romans in particular. Roman soldiers swore that the presence of Castor and Pollux on a battlefield secured for them victories against all the odds.

ELECTRA was the daughter of *AGAMEMNON*, king of Mycenae, and *CLYTEMNESTRA*, and the sister of the matricide *ORESTES*. Her name (which once may have meant "fire" or "spark") refers to amber. When Agamemnon returned from the Trojan War and was murdered by his wife and her lover Aegisthus, Electra rescued her young brother Orestes and ensured that he escaped Aegisthus' evil intentions. Years later, Orestes returned to Mycenae as a grown man. Electra met him at the tomb of their murdered father and gave him advice and encouragement. In at least one version of the myth Electra is portrayed as being so consumed by hatred for Clytemnestra that she participates in the act of revenge herself. Later she was overwhelmed by remorse, while her distraught brother fled before the *FURIES*, the deities who wreaked vengeance on murderers.

ENDYMION was the king of a small city-state in the Peloponnese,

ELECTRA (above), heroic daughter of Agamemnon and Clytemnestra, meets her exiled brother Orestes outside Agamemnon's tomb. It was Electra who rescued her brother from the evil intentions of Aegisthus by helping him escape. Having thought that she would never see him again, she is seen here rejoicing in his return. (ORESTE AND ELECTRA, MARBLE, C. AD 100.)

EOS (below), Greek goddess of the dawn, rises early each day to announce the coming of the sun. She was the daughter of Hyperion and Theia and sister to the sun god Helios. In works of art, she is often depicted hovering in the sky, her rosy form adorned in a golden mantle. She is accompanied here by her starry daughters. (ILLUSTRATION FROM STORIES FROM HOMER, 1885.)

ENDYMION (above) was loved by Selene who visited him in his eternal sleep. Here, the lovers part at dawn. In the sky, the goddess sprinkles dew before the sun-chariot, while on earth Nyx draws a curtain of darkness about her. (SELENE AND ENDYMION BY NICOLAS POUSSIN, CANVAS, C. 1594-1665.)

EUROPA (right) was a Phoenician princess borne away by Zeus, who assumed the form of a great white bull. He swam to the island of Crete with Europa riding on his back. She eventually married Asterius, the ruler of Crete. (ILLUSTRATION FROM DR SMITH'S CLASSICAL DICTIONARY, 1895.)

in all likelihood Elis. According to Greek mythology, he became the lover of the moon goddess Selene (frequently identified with Diana), who bore him fifty daughters. Because she could not endure the thought that Endymion would eventually die, Selene put her youthful lover into an everlasting, deep sleep. However, in another version of the myth, it is said that ZEUS granted Endymion his wish that he might be allowed to sleep forever in a cave without ageing

EOS was the Greek, winged goddess of the dawn and the third child of the TITANS Hyperion and Theia. She was seen as a charioteer riding across the sky just before sunrise, pulled by her horses Shiner and Bright. Her brother, the sun god HELIOS, had a four-horse chariot to indicate his greater status. The Romans called her Aurora.

Eos had a reputation for passion and fell in love with a large number of young men, including the particularly handsome Tithonus, son of Laomedon, king of Troy. When Eos asked ZEUS to make Tithonus immortal, she forgot about eternal youth and ended with a lover made helpless with age. Thereupon, according to different versions of the myth, she

locked him in a bedchamber or he became the cicada (an insect noted for its complaining sound).

ERINYES see FURIES

EROS, according to some Greek traditions, was the son of Erebos and the Night, while in others he was the son of ARES, god of war. As the youngest of the gods and the companion of APHRODITE, he appeared to enjoy making as much mischief as he could by firing his arrows of passion into the hearts of gods and humans alike. His connection with homosexual love may have derived from his supposed

relationship to Ares, for he was the patron divinity of the Sacred Band of Thebes, which was a group of one hundred and fifty pairs of lovers who were all killed by the Macedonian army at the battle of Chaeronia in 338 BC. After the battle King Philip of Macedon granted them a special burial.

EUROPA, in Greek mythology, was the daughter of Telephassa and of King Agenor of Tyre, a city in Phoenicia. Agenor's five sons, including CADMUS, were sent out to look for their sister after ZEUS, disguised as a white bull, swam to the island of Crete with Europa on his back. There she bore the god three sons, MINOS, RHADAMANTHYS and SARPEDON, before marrying the local ruler Asterius. By way of compensation for Europa's virginity, Zeus gave Asterius a mighty bronze man, Talos, to defend his realm. (See also LOVERS OF ZEUS)

41

ORACLES AND PROPHECIES

IN THE ANCIENT WORLD, a man's life was thought to be determined by fate or destiny. Even the gods themselves were, to a large extent, subject to fate, although it was Zeus who saw to it that fate took its proper course. As people believed that the future could be revealed, they frequently consulted oracles of every kind for personal and political purposes. The most famous was the Delphic Oracle where Apollo, the seer-god, spoke through a priestess. The future was also revealed by oracular signs, such as the fall of dice, lots, or burnt offerings. Dreams afforded another type of oracle, usually inspired by the gods, sometimes to mislead. Prophecies were also sought from seers, both living and dead. Although the Romans consulted lots (or sortes) for personal problems, they rarely, if ever, prophesied for political purposes.

DREAMS (below) could sometimes reveal the future and were often inspired by the gods, usually to guide a favourite mortal in distress. Here, Penelope is visited in her dream by Athena in the form of her sister Iphthime. The vision consoled Penelope in her troubles and predicted that her son, Telemachus, though in grave danger, would nonetheless return home safely. (ILLUSTRATION FROM STORIES FROM HOMER, 1885.)

CASSANDRA (above), fairest daughter of Priam and Hecuba, was a gifted but tragic seer, who was doomed to be ignored. She was endowed with prophecy by Apollo, in exchange for the promise of her love. When she broke her word, he punished her by decreeing that her prophecies, however true, would always be ignored. This powerful portrayal of Cassandra reveals the solitary, all-seeing world of the sorrowful seer, who accurately predicted the fall of Troy. (CASSANDRA BY MAX KLINGER, MARBLE, 1886-95.)

THE DELPHIC ORACLE
(left), ancient and fabled seat of
prophecy at Delphi, was
described as the "navel of the
earth". The oracle itself was a
cleft in the ground which
emitted cold vapours, inducing
ecstasy. Over the chasm the
seer sat on a gilded tripod
inhaling the vapours and
uttering enigmatic words which
were recorded by a priest and
interpreted as the revelations of
Apollo. (ILLUSTRATION FROM
TANGLEWOOD TALES, C. 1920.)

THE FATES (above), or Moerae, spun out a child's destiny at birth, symbolized by a thread which
was drawn, measured and cut off. Although Greek portrayals of the spinners reveal grave, busy
maidens, the Romantic Fatae can seem mean, denying humans their hopes and desires. Here they
appear as frightful old hags: Clotho, on the left, unravels a spindle in the shape of a helpless child,
while Lachesis squints through her glass and Atropos manically waves her scissors. The fourth figure
possibly symbolizes the general concept of destiny. (THE FATES BY FRANCISCO DE GOYA, CANVAS, 1819-23.)

SIGNS OR OMENS (below) foretold the future in a variety of ways. Sometimes
lots or dice were thrown; sometimes burnt offerings were inspected at the altar. In
some sacred precincts, the sound of a rustling oak or the clash of cymbals signified
a response to the seeker's question. Here, offerings are burnt at the altar, and
examined for signs of the future. (ILLUSTRATION FROM STORIES FROM HOMER, 1885.)

CALCHAS (above), celebrated seer, accompanied the Greeks on their expedition against Troy,
correctly predicting that the Trojan war would last ten years. It was prophesied that he would die
when he met a seer wiser than himself, and when the soothsayer, Mopsus, beat him in a match of
guessing riddles, Calchas died of grief. A temple was erected to him in Apulia where the votaries
received oracles in their sleep. (THE SACRIFICE OF IPHIGENIA BY GIOVANNI BATTISTA, TEMPERA, 1770.)

G

THE FATES, or the Moerae, were invoked at birth to decide a man's destiny. Often depicted as spinners, Clotho, at the right, with a spindle spins out the thread of life, while Lachesis, at the left, measures the length of a life, and Atropos, with the shears, cuts it off. (A GOLDEN THREAD BY J M STRUDWICK, OIL ON CANVAS, C. 1890.)

THE FATES, from the Roman, Fatae, were three goddesses known to the Greeks as the Moerae. Their origins are uncertain, although some called them daughters of night. It is clear, however, that at a certain period they ceased to be concerned with death and became instead those powers which decided what must happen to individuals. The Greeks knew them as Clotho ("the spinner"), Lachesis ("the apportioner") and Atropos ("the inevitable"). A late idea was that the Fates spun a length of yarn which represented the allotted span for each mortal.

Although ZEUS was the chief Greek god, he was still subject to the decisions of the Fates, and thus the executor of destiny rather than its source. Hence the great importance to both gods and humans of oracles which indicated the inevitable drift of events. In mythology, however, the Fates played little direct part. (See also ORACLES AND PROPHECIES)

FAUNUS was the Roman god of the countryside and identified with the Greek PAN, god of the mountainside. Faunus was said to be the grandson of SATURN and was credited with prophetic powers, which on occasion inspired the Romans to renew efforts on the battlefield in the face of defeat. Perhaps this is the reason for Faunus sometimes

FAUNUS, a spirit of the plains and fields, frolics along with a friendly goat. Faunus' children, known as Fauni, half-men, half-goats, were delightful but capricious creatures, who sometimes plagued men's sleep with nightmares. (ILLUSTRATION FROM DR SMITH'S CLASSICAL DICTIONARY, 1895.)

being seen as a descendant of the war god MARS. His mortal son, Latinus, was the king of the Latin people at the time of AENEAS' arrival in Italy after the long voyage from Troy.

FLORA see FORCES OF NATURE

THE FURIES, from the Roman name, Furiae, were the avenging goddesses of Greek mythology and were known as the Erinyes ("the angry ones"). They were born from the blood of Ouranos that fell into the womb of GAIA, when CRONOS, his son, castrated him. The Furies

A FURY, goddess of punishment, wields a torch, scourge and spears – the tools of her vengeance. The Furies pursued without mercy in life and in death all wrong-doers. Sometimes they were winged, symbolizing the swiftness of their vengeance. (ILLUSTRATION FROM DR SMITH'S CLASSICAL DICTIONARY, 1895.)

were portrayed as ugly women with snakes entwined in their hair, and were pitiless to those mortals who had wrongly shed blood. They relentlessly pursued ORESTES, who avenged his father AGAMEMNON's murder by killing CLYTEMNESTRA, his mother. The Furies were only persuaded to abandon their persecution of Orestes after his acquittal by the Areopagus, an ancient Athenian council presided over by the goddess ATHENA. The verdict calmed the anger of the Furies, whose name was then changed to the less-threatening Eumenides, ("the soothed ones").

GAIA, in Greek mythology, was the earth, who came out of Chaos and gave birth to Ouranos the sky god, who was her son and husband. So passionate was their relationship and so overwhelming Ouranos' embrace that their offspring could not emerge from her womb. One of these buried children, CRONOS, the youngest son, decided to overthrow Ouranos. Gaia conceived a great sickle which Cronos used to cut off his father's penis within the earth womb. The god was emasculated and the sky separated from the earth. From Ouranos' blood, Gaia conceived the FURIES, the avenging goddesses who pursued murderers.

Ouranos then faded from the mythological scene and Cronos ruled the universe, taking his sister RHEA as a wife. The Greeks regarded this as the golden age of the TITANS. Cronos, however, turned out to be as tyrannical to his own family as Ouranos had been before him. He had been warned by an oracle that he would be displaced by one of his sons, so he swallowed his children as soon as they were born. Rhea, on Gaia's advice, gave him a stone wrapped in swaddling instead of the infant ZEUS, who was secretly taken to Crete in order to grow up there in safety. When Zeus was grown, he compelled his father to disgorge his brothers and sisters, including his future wife HERA, the sea god POSEIDON, the god of the underworld HADES and DEMETER, the goddess of vegetation.

Gaia may have saved Zeus from a fate similar to that of Ouranos and Cronos when she warned him that a child of his born by Metis

GAIA, the great earth mother, pushes through the fruitful earth with her gifts of fertility and abundance. Not only was she the mother of all and the nourisher of children, but she was also a goddess of death who, like the earth, calls her creatures back to her. (ILLUSTRATION BY NICK BEALE, 1995.)

("thought") would replace him as the supreme god. So Zeus swallowed Metis and later the goddess ATHENA sprang from his head.

The story of the separation between sky and earth is an ancient one. It is found in a variety of forms in West Asian mythology. The Hurrians, who lived on the borders of modern Turkey and Iraq, had in their myths the most violent version of the sky's emasculation. Kumarbi, the equivalent of Cronos, bit off and swallowed his father's penis. As a result of his unusual action, however, Kumarbi became pregnant with terrible deities, one of whom at last overthrew him.

GANYMEDE, in Greek mythology, was the son of Tros, the king of Phrygia, and brother of Ilus. He was such a beautiful young man that ZEUS abducted him and took him to Mount Olympus to be his cupbearer. It was believed that Ganymede also became Zeus' lover, and gained his immortality as the constellation Aquarius, the water-carrier.

GANYMEDE, a handsome boy, excited the passion of Zeus who, in the guise of an eagle, bore him away to Mount Olympus. (THE RAPE OF GANYMEDE, BY PETER PAUL RUBENS, CANVAS, 1577-1640.)

HADES (above), lord of the underworld, with his wife, Persephone, receives the souls of the dead, who are guided by Hermes. Hades appears with typically dark looks and unruly hair over which he often wore a magic helmet. (ILLUSTRATION FROM DR SMITH'S CLASSICAL DICTIONARY, 1895.)

HECTOR (below), the Trojan champion, snatches a moment of peace with his loving wife and small son. He was portrayed as both a raging warrior and a gentle family man who had taught himself to be valiant out of duty rather than any natural courage. (ILLUSTRATION BY ALAN LEE, 1994.)

THE GIANTS (above) were gigantic creatures with snake-like tails. After they were defeated by the gods, they were buried beneath volcanoes. Here we see the hound of Artemis killing a giant at the battle of the Giants and the gods. (ZEUS ALTAR OF PERGAMON, MARBLE, C. 180 BC.)

THE GIANTS

THE GIANTS, from the Roman name, Gigantes, in Greek mythology, had human shape, except for the snake-like tails that were attached to their legs. They were born at the same time as the FURIES, from the blood that fell into GAIA's womb from Ouranos' severed penis. When the Giants attacked Olympus, the gods stood their ground, but knew that they would not be able to defeat them, because the Giants could not be killed by divine hands. ZEUS therefore fathered the great hero HERACLES through a mortal woman. During the great battle between the gods and the Giants, Heracles played a decisive part, finishing off each opponent with poisoned arrows. It is important to realize that the Giants are quite different from the TITANS, who were the oldest generation of the gods and were led by CRONOS, Zeus' father.

THE GORGON MEDUSA (above) was once a beautiful woman whose locks were turned to writhing snakes by a vengeful goddess. The image of her frightful face was carved, like an evil eye, on warriors' shields, city walls, charms and amulets. (ILLUSTRATION FROM DR SMITH'S CLASSICAL DICTIONARY, 1895.)

THE GORGONS

THE GORGONS were three sisters named Stheno ("strength"), Medusa ("queen") and Euryale ("wide-leaping"), and were the children of Phorcys, son of GAIA. The only mortal of the three was Medusa, the victim of the Greek hero PERSEUS. Like her immortal sisters, she had snakes for hair and one look at her face could turn any living man or thing to stone.

THE GRACES

THE GRACES, from the Roman name, Gratiae, were the daughters of ZEUS and Eurynome, and were minor goddesses to both the Greeks and the Romans. According to the most widely accepted myth, their names were Aglaia, Euphrosyne and Thalia. They were attendants to APHRODITE and VENUS, the love goddesses of Greece and Rome respectively. A favourite subject for artists, the Graces were thought to represent beauty, gentleness and friendship.

THE GRACES, or Charities, graced the world with beauty, bloom and brilliance, lifting the spirits of gods and men. In the earliest works of art, the Graces appear in flowing chitons, veiling their beauty, but later on they were depicted as nudes. (THE THREE GRACES BY RAPHAEL, WOOD, C. 1501.)

HADES (whose name means "the unseen") was the Greek god of the underworld, the realm of the dead. He was the son of *CRONOS* and *RHEA*, and the brother of *ZEUS, POSEIDON, HERA, DEMETER* and Hestia. He forcibly married *PERSEPHONE*, Demeter's daughter. At the division of the universe after the overthrow of their father, Zeus took the sky, Poseidon the sea, and Hades the underworld; the earth was to be shared among them. Another name for Hades was Polydegmon ("receiver of many guests") on account of the multitudes who had died and come to his kingdom. The ghosts of the dead were escorted by *HERMES*, the messenger god, to the boatman Charon who ferried across the Styx, a subterranean river, only those ghosts who could pay the fare. *CERBERUS*, the three-headed dog, guarded the entrance to the underworld and prevented anyone from returning to the world of the living.

As in Egyptian mythology, the Greeks associated the underworld with the west, the place where the sun sets. Neither the Greeks nor the Romans, however, ever thought of Hades as an evil force like Satan in Christianity. He was certainly a grim and implacable deity, and worshippers always averted their eyes when making a sacrifice. In order to avoid any reference to the nature of the underworld it was usual to call Hades by the title of Pluto ("the giver of wealth").

Hades' chief myth concerns the abduction of Persephone, who was the daughter of Demeter and his brother Zeus. Persephone was abruptly taken underground by Hades when she beheld a special narcissus planted by the earth mother *GAIA* to please the god of death. The conflict between Hades and Demeter over Persephone's fate was decided by Zeus, who gave the husband and the mother equal shares of her time. As a dying-and-rising goddess, Persephone sank and rose annually from the underworld, in tune with the natural cycle of sowing and harvesting.

Although usually a faithful husband, Hades at one time became enamoured of the nymph Minthe. When Persephone discovered this, however, she became so jealous that she turned the nymph into the sweet-smelling herb, mint.

HARPIES see *MONSTERS AND FABULOUS BEASTS*

HECATE was believed by some to be descended from the *TITANS*. A Greek goddess with two quite separate aspects, in the day she was supposed to have a benign influence on farming, but during the hours of darkness she was interested in witchcraft, ghosts and tombs. In many ways similar to the vegetation goddess *DEMETER*, Hecate uncomfortably combined fertility with death as a power of the earth. The witch *MEDEA*, *JASON*'s rejected Colchian princess, used to invoke Hecate in her magic arts. Hecate is usually portrayed with three faces. The Athenians were particularly respectful towards her, and once a month they placed offerings of food at crossroads, where her influence was said to be felt.

HECTOR was the eldest son of *PRIAM*, the king of Troy during the Greek siege. The bravest of the Trojan warriors, he was unbeaten on the battlefield. He mistakenly killed Patroclus, the squire and lover of *ACHILLES*, the Greek hero. Achilles had quarrelled with *AGAMEMNON* and refused to fight, but Patroclus borrowed his divine armour in order to rally the Greeks, only to be slain by Hector. Roused from his lethargy, Achilles sought out Hector and compelled him to fight to the death. Such was Achilles' anger that for twelve days he dragged Hector's corpse round Patroclus' tomb. In the end *ZEUS* himself intervened, by sending Achilles' mother *THETIS* to stop this humiliation. So in exchange for a great treasure, Hector's body was returned and properly buried.

HELEN was the daughter of *LEDA* and *ZEUS*, the wife of the Spartan king *MENELAUS*, and the cause of the Trojan War. Her immortality as the daughter of the supreme Greek deity suggests that Helen was once a goddess and that her incorporation into myth as an unfaithful queen only occurred when her worship was largely forgotten.

Zeus mated with Leda, wife of the Spartan king Tyndareos, in the guise of a swan. Leda laid an egg, and when Helen hatched from it she brought her up as a member of the royal family. Helen's brothers were Castor and Polydeuces, the mysterious *DIOSCURI*, and her sister was King *AGAMEMNON*'s unfaithful wife *CLYTEMNESTRA*.

At the time of her marriage to Menelaus, the younger brother of Agamemnon, Helen was the most

HELEN (above) paces the walls of Troy. The most beautiful woman of the ancient world, she was also, according to Homer, a thoughtful heroine, given to self-mockery and ever aware of the misery caused by her beauty. (HELEN ON THE WALLS OF TROY BY LORD LEIGHTON, CANVAS, C. 1880.)

desirable bride in Greece. At first Menelaus and Helen were very happy, but then *PARIS*, one of the many sons of King *PRIAM* of Troy, visited Sparta and, with the help of the love goddess *APHRODITE*, gained Helen's affection. They even eloped with a part of Menelaus' treasury. When the Trojans refused to return Helen and the stolen treasure, Agamemnon assembled a great army to help his brother Menelaus. For ten years the city of Troy was besieged and then only captured through the trick of the Wooden

Horse. Throughout this long war the sympathies of Helen were mainly with the Greeks, although she was treated as the proper wife, and not merely the mistress, of Paris. After the fall of Troy, Helen and Menelaus were reconciled and they lived undisturbed at Sparta.

HELIOS was the Greek sun god and son of the *TITAN* Hyperion. To the Romans he was known as Sol. It was thought that Helios, after crossing the sky, sailed during the night around the earth in a golden bowl on the encircling waters of *OCEANOS*, and so arrived back in the east just before dawn. Both the Greeks and the Romans held that the inhabited world was a large

HELIOS, god of the sun, appears in works of art as a strong and beautiful youth with gleaming eyes, and a crown of flaming rays. Just as the sun's rays penetrate everywhere, so Helios saw everything, and was invoked as a witness of oaths. (ILLUSTRATION FROM DR SMITH'S CLASSICAL DICTIONARY, 1895.)

island surrounded by an ocean. Although Oceanos was sometimes described as a river, it stretched into the unimaginable distance and far from any shore.

One myth of Helios concerns the death of his son *PHAETHON*. Once this impetuous youth tried to steer his father's radiant chariot, but he quickly lost control. Only the timely action of *ZEUS* steadied its runaway horses and prevented the earth from catching fire. Phaethon fell from the vehicle and was drowned. However, Helios had

many other children, among them Augeas, *CIRCE* and *PASIPHAE*. A gigantic statue of the sun god was erected at the harbour of Rhodes, an island sacred to him. This so-called Colossus was one of the seven wonders of the ancient world, but was toppled by an earthquake around 226 BC.

HEPHAISTOS was the son of *ZEUS* and *HERA*, and was the Greek smith god. His Roman equivalent was *VULCAN*, whose smithy lay beneath the crater of Mount Aetna in Sicily. Hephaistos was lame as a result of having interfered in a quarrel between his parents. So angry did Zeus become that he flung his son from the top of Mount Olympus and let him fall heavily on the volcanic island of Lemnos, in the northern part of the Aegean Sea. In another version, Hera tried to drown her imperfect child, only to be thwarted by sea nymphs who took him to a beach. A sequel to this tale has the smith god gain his revenge as a fully grown man by making a golden throne for his mother which was actually a trap. None of the gods could release Hera, so Hephaistos was invited to return permanently to Mount Olympus. There, under the influence of drink, he was persuaded by his friend *DIONYSUS* to unlock the cunning device and let his mother escape.

Hephaistos seems to have come originally from Asia Minor, where iron mines date from a very early period. His cult was strong in Caria and Lycia, along its south-western shore. His marriage to the love goddess *APHRODITE* may have something to do with this eastern connection, as she also came to Greece from West Asia. Their relationship was almost as tumultuous as that of Zeus and Hera. Once Hephaistos fashioned a trap to catch his unfaithful wife in bed with the war god *ARES*. The Olympian gods merely laughed at Hephaistos' situation; the sea god *POSEIDON* only

HEPHAISTOS, god of fire, fashions exquisite golden works in his fiery forge. Lame, he leans on one leg. By him stands Apollo, who reveals that his wife, Aphrodite, loves Ares, and Hephaistos resolves to trap the guilty pair. (THE FORGE OF VULCAN BY DIEGO VELASQUEZ, CANVAS, 1630.)

promised some remedy if he agreed to release Aphrodite and Ares.

A myth about *ATHENA's* birth recounts how Hephaistos split open Zeus' head with an axe in order to release the fully grown goddess. Apparently, Zeus had swallowed Athena's mother, Metis, once he realized she was pregnant with a powerful deity. Later, Hephaistos fell in love with Athena, but was rejected by her and his semen fell to earth where it gave birth to the serpent Erichthonius. (See also *FORCES OF NATURE*)

HERA means "lady" and was undoubtedly the title of a powerful mother goddess whom the Greeks inherited from the earlier inhabitants of Argos, which was a major city in the Peloponnese. It was claimed that she was the daughter of *CRONOS* and *RHEA*; however, her addition to the Greek pantheon was not an easy or straightforward matter, as the ceaseless conflicts between her and her husband *ZEUS* readily bear witness. Often her fits of jealousy and quarrelsomeness led to disaster for gods, heroes and men, when she relentlessly persecuted Zeus' mistresses and their children. For example, against the baby *HERACLES*, whom Zeus had fathered in order to help in the coming battle against the *GIANTS*, she sent two serpents to kill him, but the infant hero strangled them

HERA, queen of heaven, directs Helios across the sky. She is crowned with a diadem and veil, symbolizing her status as Zeus' bride. Her sceptre is tipped with a cuckoo, sacred to her as the messenger of spring, the season in which she married Zeus. (ILLUSTRATION FROM STORIES FROM LIVY, 1885.)

in his cradle. However, later in his life, Hera succeeded in driving Heracles temporarily mad.

There are a number of myths about Zeus' courtship of Hera. In one of them he disguised himself as a cuckoo and took shelter inside her clothes during a heavy downpour. Once out of the rain, Zeus resumed his normal shape and promised to marry Hera. Later she bore him the war god *ARES*, the goddess of birth Eileithyia, and Hebe, the cupbearer of the gods. Another child was the smith god *HEPHAISTOS*, who is said in some myths to have been the son of Zeus and Hera, but in others the offspring of Hera alone. Hera was worshipped with particular reverence in Crete and at Samos, where a great temple was said to have been built for her by the *ARGONAUTS*.

HERACLES wrestles with Antaeus, a giant who draws his strength from the earth. To weaken the giant's might, Heracles lifts him high above the earth, and crushes him in mid-air. This bronze expresses the classical ideal of heroic skill and might. (HERCULES AND ANTAEUS BY PIER ANTICO, BRONZE, 1460-1528.)

HERACLES, the son of *ZEUS* and *ALCMENE*, was the greatest of all the Greek heroes. To the Romans he was known as Hercules, and they added various encounters in Italy to his already large cycle of adventures. The name Heracles means "Hera's glory" – a circumstance that firmly ties the hero to Argos, the site of the goddess *HERA's* temple. It remains a mystery that Heracles should have been persecuted so much by Hera, even going mad at one point during his life.

Because Zeus needed a mortal champion in the forthcoming battle between the gods and the *GIANTS*, he fathered Heracles at the court of Thebes. The chosen mother was Alcmene, the Theban queen. Zeus intended Heracles to be ruler of Mycenae or Tiryns,

HERACLES slays the Hydra, while a crab, sent by the vengeful goddess Hera, nips at his heels. After burning away the Hydra's eight mortal heads, Heracles buried its ninth immortal head under a huge rock in the swamp. (HERCULES AND THE HYDRA, A F GORGUET, CANVAS, C. 1920.)

strongholds close to Argos, but Hera frustrated this plan so well that the hero became the slave of Eurystheus, king of Tiryns. She struck Heracles with a fit of madness, in the course of which he killed his wife and their three sons with arrows. To atone for this terrible deed he had to become Eurystheus' dependent and undertook his famous twelve labours.

These labours began with the killing of the Nemean lion, which could not be harmed by arrows.

Heracles had to fight it with his bare hands and a wooden club. After overcoming the lion, he cured the skin and wore it as a trophy. His next opponent, the Hydra, was a nine-headed serpent sacred to Hera. It lived in a swamp at Lerna, not far from Argos. The problem that the hero encountered when fighting with the Hydra was that for every head he cut off with his sword two new ones grew in its place. But with assistance from his nephew Iolaus he was able to triumph, for Iolaus burned the stumps of the necks as soon as Heracles severed each head. When he returned to Eurystheus, the king refused to count the exploit as a labour, because Heracles had received help from his nephew.

The next labour was not quite so bloody. Heracles had to capture the Ceryneian hind, which was a beast sacred to *ARTEMIS*, goddess of the wild. According to different accounts, he returned to Tiryns with either its golden antlers or the hind itself. Another labour required

him to capture the Erymanthian boar, which plagued the countryside of Arcadia. He trapped it with a net, and during the hunt Heracles encountered a band of *CENTAURS*, beast-like men who lived in woodlands. One of them, Nessus, was later to cause the hero's death.

The fifth labour was the cleansing of Augeas' stables. The son of the sun god, Augeas had vast herds of animals, which he pastured in the kingdom of Elis in the western Peloponnese. King Eurystheus told Heracles to remove the immense piles of dung from the stables, a feat he achieved by diverting the course of a nearby river. The last labour that the hero performed in the Peloponnese was the removal of the Stymphalian birds. Although they had steel-tipped feathers with which they killed both men and animals, these birds were frightened away by the noise of a rattle, which the goddess *ATHENA* had specially made for Heracles.

On the island of Crete the hero tracked down the bull that *MINOS* had failed to sacrifice to the sea god *POSEIDON*. The bull had mated with Minos' wife, *PASIPHAE*, who then gave birth to the *MINOTAUR*, the bull-headed man slain by the Athenian hero *THESEUS*. Heracles captured Poseidon's bull alive and brought it back to Tiryns, where he let it go free at the end of this seventh labour. The eighth labour was more gruesome. It took Heracles to Thrace in pursuit of the man-eating mares of Diomedes, which he subdued after feeding them on their master's flesh.

The last four labours were quite different in nature. First of all Eurystheus had Heracles fetch the girdle of Hippolyta, queen of the fierce *AMAZONS*. Then he captured the cattle of Geryon, a western king who had three heads, three bodies and six hands. After this labour Heracles brought back the golden apples of the *HESPERIDES*, female guardians of the fruit that the earth goddess *GAIA* gave to Hera on her

HERMAPHRODITOS, the beautiful son of Aphrodite and Hermes, inspired the love of the water nymph Salmacis. Here, the golden boy bathes in a shower of sunlight, unaware of his beautiful admirer on the river bank. (SALMACIS AND HERMAPHRODITOS BY BARTHOLOMEUS SPRANGER, CANVAS, C. 1581.)

wedding to Zeus. The last exploit of Heracles was the most testing, for it meant a descent into the underworld, the realm of the dead. From there the hero managed, with some help from *PERSEPHONE*, queen of the underworld, to bring briefly back to Tiryns the three-headed hound *CERBERUS*. As a result of this labour, hard-working Heracles attained immortality for himself. No other hero gained this honour.

Heracles' death on earth, an event that the Greeks expected to precede his translation to Mount Olympus as a god, was the work of the Centaur Nessus, who gave the hero's second wife a poisoned garment for him to wear. Realizing that his death was near, Heracles

consulted the Delphic Oracle, which told him to build a funeral pyre in Thessaly. When the dying hero climbed on to it, there was a great flash of lightning and Zeus took his son to join the immortals.

Some of the labours of Heracles are reflected in the names of certain constellations, such as Leo, which represents the Nemean Lion, and Cancer, the crab that was allegedly sent by Hera to help the Hydra. (See also *HEROES*)

HERMAPHRODITOS was the

bisexual offspring of the messenger god *HERMES* and *APHRODITE,* the goddess of love. According to one Greek myth, this handsome boy excited the passion of Salmacis, who was a nymph of a fountain near to the city of Halicarnassus in Asia Minor. When the young Hermaphroditos ignored her attentions, Salmacis prayed to the gods that she might be eternally united with him. The wish was granted

when he bathed in some waters and she merged with him physically. The result was a female boy, hence the term hermaphrodite. But Hermaphroditos was not emasculated like Attis, the lover of the Phrygian mother goddess Cybele, for this West Asian god intentionally cut off his own manhood.

HERMES was the Greek messen-

ger god, and the son of *ZEUS* and Maia. He enjoyed playing tricks and games. During the Trojan War, it was Hermes who was always sent to steal something that was otherwise unobtainable. Before the sea nymph *THETIS* persuaded her son *ACHILLES* to stop mutilating the corpse of *HECTOR*, the gods considered that the simplest solution might be to let Hermes steal the broken body. Hermes was the god who most easily crossed the line between the living and the dead, for the Greeks believed that he guided the dead to the realm of *HADES*, the underworld. This duty helps to explain the later identification of the Germanic god Odin

with the Roman equivalent of Hermes, *MERCURY*. Odin was the champion of warriors and the father of the slain.

Hermes is usually depicted as a young man with a wide-brimmed hat and winged sandals, carrying a herald's staff crowned with two snakes. In ancient Greece this staff assured the messenger safe passage even during time of war. Hermes' greatest passion was for the love goddess *APHRODITE*.

The two sons that are attributed to them were both renowned for their unusual sexuality. *HERMAPH-RODITOS* was the first female boy, while the gnome-like Priapus was famous for his enormous penis. Like that of Hermaphroditus, the cult of Priapus originated in Asia Minor, though some distance farther north at Lampascus, near the Black Sea.

HERMES leads Eurydice (centre) and Orpheus (right) through the underworld. As psychopomp, Hermes conducted souls from life on earth to death in Hades. (ILLUSTRATION FROM DICTIONARY OF CLASSICAL ANTIQUITIES, 1891.)

VOYAGERS

THE LURE OF THE UNKNOWN prompts all restless heroes to strike out on a new path in search of a fabulous treasure or shining dream, or for the sheer joy of discovery and adventure. Three intrepid explorers stand out in Classical mythology: Jason, Aeneas and Odysseus. Jason set sail with his fearless crew of Argonauts in search of the Golden Fleece; while Aeneas' seven-year voyage after the fall of Troy led him to the site of future Rome. Most famous and appealing, perhaps, was the fabled Odyssey of the shipwrecked wanderer, Odysseus. Tossed from shore to shore by the angry sea god, Poseidon, he found his way home after ten years' wandering through fabulous lands. The lure of the underworld, or a foray into a monster's den, attracts many heroes, too, such as Theseus who went into the Labyrinth to slay the Minotaur, and found his way out again. Aeneas and Odysseus both journeyed to the underworld in search of prophetic counsel.

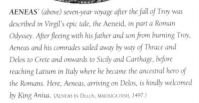

AENEAS' (above) seven-year voyage after the fall of Troy was described in Virgil's epic tale, the Aeneid, in part a Roman Odyssey. After fleeing with his father and son from burning Troy, Aeneas and his comrades sailed away by way of Thrace and Delos to Crete and onwards to Sicily and Carthage, before reaching Latium in Italy where he became the ancestral hero of the Romans. Here, Aeneas, arriving on Delos, is kindly welcomed by King Anius. (ÆNEAS IN DELOS, MAIOLICA DISH, 1497.)

ORPHEUS (left) went down into Hades, the underworld, to bring back his wife, Eurydice. Charming the shades and even Persephone with his music, he was allowed to take Eurydice back to the upper world as long as he did not look back until clear of Hades. Just as they were about to step out into the light, Orpheus turned round only to see Eurydice slip back into the world of shades forever. Here, Orpheus bids farewell to Eurydice, while Hermes (left), waits to lead Eurydice back through the world of shades. (HERMES, EURYDICE AND ORPHEUS, MARBLE, C. 420 BC.)

ARION (right), a lyrical poet and cithara player, sailed to Sicily to take part in a magical contest which he won. On his way home in a Corinthian ship, he was robbed by the sailors, and forced to leap overboard where he was borne away to safety by song-loving dolphins. Here, Arion plays his cithara on the prow of the ship, invoking the gods of the sea, before leaping overboard. (ILLUSTRATION FROM TANGLEWOOD TALES, C.1920.)

ODYSSEUS (above), celebrated traveller, was renowned for his wits and silver tongue, for his cunning, craft and curiosity. On his way home from Troy, he beached at Sicily, home of the lawless race of one-eyed giants, the Cyclopes. Bold and inquisitive, Odysseus wandered into a Cyclops' den where he and his comrades became trapped by the hostile giant. To escape, they blinded the giant and slipped out, hidden under sheeps' bellies. Here, Odysseus and his comrades pierce the giant's single eye with a sharpened stake. (THE BLINDING OF POLYPHEMUS BY ALESSANDRO ALLORI, FRESCO, 1580.)

JASON (below) sailed across the seas on a perilous voyage in his famous ship, the Argo, accompanied by all the heroes of the age. They went in search of the Golden Fleece, guarded by a watchful dragon at Colchis. After snatching the treasure from under the dragon's eye, Jason and his Argonauts sailed away, finally arriving at Iolcus. Here, Jason steals past with his trophy, casting a furtive glance at a statue of Ares in the sacred grove of the god. (JASON AND THE GOLDEN FLEECE BY ERASMUS QUELLINUS, CANVAS, C. 1670.)

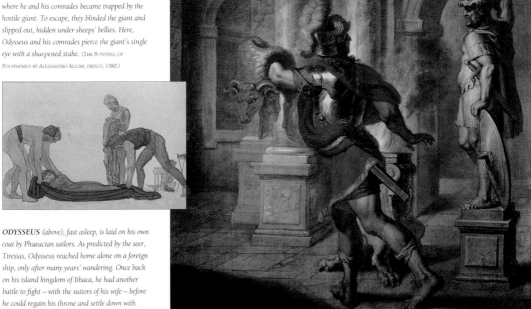

ODYSSEUS (above), fast asleep, is laid on his own coat by Phaeacian sailors. As predicted by the seer, Tiresias, Odysseus reached home alone on a foreign ship, only after many years' wandering. Once back on his island kingdom of Ithaca, he had another battle to fight – with the suitors of his wife – before he could regain his throne and settle down with Penelope. (ILLUSTRATION FROM STORIES FROM HOMER, 1885.)

HERO AND LEANDER were one of the great pairs of lovers in Greek mythology. Hero was a priestess of *APHRODITE* at Sestos in the Dardanelles, while Leander lived on the Asian side of the channel at Abydos. They met and fell in love, but because of her religious calling Hero was barred from marriage. In order to keep their affair secret, they arranged that Leander should swim across to Hero each night, guided by a light that she placed in her tower. Next morning he would swim back at dawn. One stormy night the light blew out,

Leander lost his sense of direction and he drowned in the cold waters. When his body was washed ashore at Sestos, Hero threw herself from her tower and died.

THE HESPERIDES were supposedly the daughters of Hesperus, the evening star. Their names were Hespera, Aegle and Erytheis, and they were the guardians of a tree of golden apples given by *GAIA*, mother earth, to the goddess *HERA* on her marriage to *ZEUS*, chief of the Greek gods. This tree stood in the Garden of the Hesperides on the

HERO (below) looks for her Leander, who usually swam to her across the Hellespont guided by a light in her tower. But her light blew out in a storm and Leander was drowned. (THE LAST WATCH OF HERO BY LORD LEIGHTON, CANVAS, 1880.)

THE HESPERIDES (right) guarded the golden apples in the garden of the gods. The serpent recalls the myth of the dragon Ladon who guarded the apples until he was slain by Heracles. (THE GARDEN OF THE HESPERIDES BY EDWARD BURNE-JONES, CANVAS, 1869-73.)

slopes of Mount Atlas in the far west. For one of his labours the hero *HERACLES* tricked the Titan *ATLAS* into getting him the golden apples, offering to hold up the heavens in his stead.

HORATIUS (below), a Roman hero, held the Sublician Bridge, with two of his comrades, against the Etruscan army. While other Romans hacked down the bridge, he held off the enemy until the last moment when he leapt into the stream and swam to safety. (ILLUSTRATION FROM STORIES FROM LIVY, 1885.)

HORATIUS was a Roman hero who saved the early Republic from the Etruscans, when they tried to restore *TARQUINIUS SUPERBUS* to the Roman throne by force of arms. The Etruscans mounted a surprise attack and attempted to capture Rome by crossing a poorly defended bridge over the River Tiber. With two comrades, Horatius held the enemy back until the Romans had destroyed the wooden bridge. As the final supports were sawn away, he ordered his comrades

INO rescues shipwrecked Odysseus by throwing him her veil which saves him from drowning. She was honoured along the Greek shores as a marine deity who aided sailors in distress and guided ships through storms. (ODYSSEUS AND THE GODDESS INO BY ALESSANDRO ALLORI, FRESCO, 1580.)

back to the Roman bank. They just made it, but Horatius was obliged to swim back in full armour. Only prayer saved the hero as he dodged the Etruscan arrows and struggled across the waters of the Tiber.

His full name was Horatius Cocles ("Horatius the one-eyed"). Whether he was wounded in the eye remains uncertain, though tradition says that an ancient statue of a lame, one-eyed man was erected near the bridge in his honour. He was also given as much land as he could drive a plough over in a day. (See also HEROES)

HYPNOS ("Sleep"), in Greek mythology, was the son of Nyx, the night goddess, and the brother of Thanatos ("Death"). Morpheus, the god of dreams, was his son. Hypnos lived in the underworld, the realm of HADES, and never saw the sun. On several occasions HERA asked Hypnos to lull her husband ZEUS to sleep so that she could attack his son HERACLES. Hypnos usually refused to anger Zeus, possibly because he had already come close to having a thunderbolt hurled at him. He was saved by taking refuge with Night, whose power Zeus always respected.

ILUS see FOUNDERS

INO was the daughter of CADMUS, the Phoenician king of Thebes, and Harmonia. In Greek mythology, she brought up DIONYSUS, the son of ZEUS and Semele, who was Ino's dead sister. Semele had been tricked by the goddess HERA, the jealous and vengeful wife of Zeus, who advised her to test the divinity of her lover by telling him to come to her in his true form. This Zeus was also tricked into doing, and the unfortunate result was that he appeared to Semele as lightning and thunderbolts, and she was killed. The unborn Dionysus, however, was taken from her womb and placed in Zeus' own thigh until it was time for his birth. Then, at the suggestion of HERMES, the messenger god, Ino suckled the divine child and kept him safe from Hera. However, such a powerful goddess could not be thwarted without great personal cost. When she discovered the deception, Hera made Ino kill her own children. After she had done this Ino killed herself by jumping off a cliff into the sea. In another myth, she and her infant son Melicertes leapt into the sea and became marine deities.

IO was the daughter of the river god Inachus, and was one of the mortal women who bore children by ZEUS. Although Io was a virgin priestess of HERA, Zeus's wife, at her temple in Argos, this did not prevent Zeus from having her expelled from Argos so that he could make love to her without any difficulties. According to one version, he turned Io into a beautiful heifer, and would have mated with her at once had not Hera guessed his intentions and sent a gadfly to prevent the animal from standing still. It seems that Zeus eventually made love to Io on a cloud over Egypt, where she was returned to her human form. Surprisingly, she was forgiven by Hera. Because Io had been bovine in shape on her arrival, she became identified with the Egyptian cow goddess Hathor.

IO, "the wanderer", was loved by Zeus who changed her into a heifer in order to avoid his jealous wife Hera. Hera ordered all-seeing Argus to watch Io, but Zeus, in his turn, sent Hermes to lull Argus to sleep by the dreamy notes of his flute. (MERCURY AND ARGUS BY PETER PAUL RUBENS, CANVAS, C. 1635.)

J

IPHIGENIA was the eldest daughter of King *AGAMEMNON* and Queen *CLYTEMNESTRA* of Mycenae. When Agamemnon and the Greek fleet were about to sail for Troy, contrary winds caused by *ARTEMIS* kept the ships at Aulis. The goddess of the forest and wild animals had been offended, either by Agamemnon himself or by an action committed by his father *ATREUS*. In any event, Artemis demanded that Iphigenia should be sacrificed. To bring the sacrificial victim all the way from Mycenae to the port of Aulis in Boeotia, without his wife Clytemnestra's becoming suspicious, Agamemnon pretended that Iphigenia was to be married there to the Greek hero and champion *ACHILLES*. After she discovered her true intention, Clytemnestra never forgave her husband, and years later on his return from the Trojan War helped her lover Aegisthus to murder him.

IXION was a Thessalian king of Larissa and supposedly the son of Phlegyas, though some say his father was *ARES*, god of war. In order to avoid paying a bride-price to Eioneus for his beautiful daughter Dia, Ixion prepared a trap for his unsuspecting father-in-law – a pit filled with fire. Eioneus fell into it on a visit to Larissa and died, and Ixion thus became the first man to shed the blood of a kinsman.

IXION, chained to a rolling wheel, expiates his sins in Tartarus, a hell beneath Hades. Alongside him, fellow prisoners Sisyphus and Tantalus endure their own ordeals – Sisyphus condemned to endless toil and Tantalus to endless thirst. (ILLUSTRATION FROM DR SMITH'S CLASSICAL DICTIONARY, 1895.)

IPHIGENIA, the young daughter of Agamemnon and Clytemnestra, was offered as a "sacrificial lamb" to appease Artemis who was angry with Agamemnon. Here, while the high priest Calchas raises his arms in prayer, Agamemnon (right) bows his head sorrowfully. (ILLUSTRATION FROM STORIES FROM HOMER, 1885.)

Because he was polluted by this unprecedented act, the Thessalian king could not properly rule his land. Perhaps a secret passion for Dia prompted *ZEUS* himself to devise special rites of purification for Ixion. At first Ixion was grateful to the god, but it was not long before he took an interest in *HERA*, Zeus' wife. It was therefore Ixion's turn to be trapped, when Zeus made an exact copy of Hera from a cloud and enticed the unwary king to rape it. The punishment for such sacrilegious crime was to spend eternity in Tartarus, the prison beneath the underworld.

JANUS was a very old Italian god whom the Romans associated with beginnings. In Rome, his double-gated temple in the Forum was always kept open in time of war and closed in time of peace. The month of January – a time for people to look backwards and forwards – was sacred to Janus. There are few myths concerning him, although his extra eyes did on one occasion enable him to catch the nymph Carna, who liked to tease her lovers with sexual advances before suddenly running away. Their son became a king of the important city of Alba Longa.

JASON, the son of Aeson and Philyra, was a Greek hero and voyager, born in Iolcus, a town in Thessalian Magnesia. However, difficulties arose when Aeson, ruler of Iolcus, was deposed by his half-brother Pelias. Either because Philyra distrusted Pelias' intentions towards Jason, or simply because it would better for the boy if he were educated elsewhere, she placed him in the care of the wise Centaur *CHIRON*, who lived in the Thessalian woodlands. Chiron was skilled in many things, including medicine, and may have given the boy the name Jason ("healer").

The Delphic Oracle warned Pelias that he would be turned off the throne of Iolcus by a man wearing only one sandal. So the usurping king was amazed and frightened when a mature Jason arrived

JANUS, a dual-faced god, presided over all that is double-edged in life. His image was found on city gates, which look both inwards and outwards, and he was invoked at the start of each new day and year when people look both backwards and forwards in time. (ILLUSTRATION FROM DR SMITH'S CLASSICAL DICTIONARY, 1895.)

in the city with only one of his sandals. The hero had lost it while carrying what seemed to be an old lady across a swift stream; it was in fact the goddess *HERA* in disguise. Unable to harm the unwelcome guest because he had arrived at the time of a religious festival, Pelias decided to rid himself of the threat he represented by sending Jason on an impossible quest. He offered to name Jason as his successor provided he should bring home from Colchis the Golden Fleece belonging to a wonderful ram which had flown there from Iolcus.

Jason gathered together his companions, who became known as the *ARGONAUTS*, and crossed a sea of marvels, overcame difficult tasks, defeated a guardian serpent and returned with the magic fleece. Part of his success was due to the aid of the Colchian princess and witch, *MEDEA*, whom Jason made his wife with the assistance of the goddess *ATHENA*. On returning to Iolcus, the Argonauts found that Pelias had assumed that they had died in a shipwreck and murdered Jason's father Aeson. Two versions of the myth exist from this point onwards. In one of them Pelias is destroyed by means of Medea's magic. In another the Argonauts, seeing that Pelias will not honour his promise to Jason, sail off to Corinth after failing to capture Iolcus. Jason seems to have accepted exile in Corinth with Medea, where for some ten years they lived happily together and had three sons. Then the hero was offered the hand of a princess named Glauce. When he deserted Medea for her, Jason brought down on his own head the full fury and magical powers of the Colchian princess. For Medea not only killed Glauce but she also destroyed her sons by Jason. Alone and depressed, the hero lingered at Corinth until one day, as he sat in the shade of the *Argo*, his old ship, a piece of rotten timber fell and crushed his skull. (See also *HEROES; VOYAGERS*)

JASON (left), the celebrated hero of the Argonauts, was loved by the dark sorceress Medea, whose magic arts helped him slay the dragon guarding the Golden Fleece. With salves and invocations, she protected him from harm by fire, demon or sword. (JASON BY GUSTAVE MOREAU, CANVAS, 1865.)

JUNO was the Roman equivalent of *HERA*, the wife of *ZEUS*, the chief god of the Greeks. Juno was the queen of the sky and the wife of *JUPITER*. She was always associated with the Greek goddess of birth, Eileithyia, and was called by the Romans "the one who makes the child see the light of day". At the touch of a magical herb specially grown by Flora, the goddess of flowering and blossoming plants, Juno became pregnant with the war god *MARS*. Juno's own warlike aspect is apparent in her attire. She often appears armed and wearing a goatskin cloak, which was the garment favoured by Roman soldiers on campaign. In Rome she was worshipped on the Capitol hill along with Jupiter and *MINERVA*, goddess of wisdom and the arts. The festival of Matronalia was held in her honour on 1 March.

JUNO (below), the Roman queen of heaven and of womanhood, accompanied every woman through life from birth to death. She is here portrayed in classical style, with a regal diadem, severe hairstyle, and tranquil, majestic air. (JUNO WITH DIADEM, MARBLE, C. 200 BC.)

L

JUPITER *and Mercury, who is wearing his travelling hat, enjoy a wholesome meal with the kindly rustics, Philemon and Baucis, who alone among mortals welcomed the gods as they wandered in human form through Phrygia.* (JUPITER AND MERCURY WITH PHILEMON AND BAUCIS, BY PETER PAUL RUBENS, CANVAS, 1620-25.)

JUPITER was the Roman sky god, the equivalent of *ZEUS*. The cult of Jupiter Optimus Maximus ("the best and greatest") began under the Etruscan kings, who were expelled from Rome around 507 BC. At first, Jupiter was associated with the elements, especially storms, thunder and lightning, but he later became the protector of the Roman people and was their powerful ally in war. The games held in the circus in Rome were dedicated to him.

LAIUS, son of Labdacus, king of Thebes, was the father of *OEDIPUS* and one of the most tragic figures in Greek mythology. The fate that destroyed his family was due to a curse uttered by *PELOPS* in revenge for Laius carrying off Pelops' young son Chrysippus, who later hanged himself for shame.

In Thebes, Laius took Jocasta as his wife, but they had no children, which the Delphic Oracle told them was fortunate, because Laius was destined to be killed by his own son. For a time Laius and Jocasta did not share the marriage bed. Then one night, full of wine, Laius slept with her and Jocasta

conceived a son. So as to overcome the prophecy, the baby was left to die on a distant mountainside, his feet having been cut through with a spike. This action may have been intended to hasten death, but it is not impossible that Laius was also concerned to prevent the child's ghost from walking freely. But the effect was quite the opposite. A shepherd heard the baby's screams and took him to Corinth, where the childless King Polybus adopted him and gave him the name of Oedipus ("swell-foot").

When Oedipus reached manhood he went to Delphi to ask about his parentage. He was told that he would be reunited with his parents in a terrible manner, for he was destined to kill his father and marry his mother. Concluding incorrectly that Corinth was his place of birth, Oedipus travelled towards the north and approached Thebes. On the road he encountered Laius, who was on his way to consult the Delphic Oracle about the *SPHINX*, a monster with the face and breasts of a woman, the body of a lion and wings, which was causing havoc in the Theban coun-

tryside. Oedipus refused to stand aside for the king, a fight ensued and Laius was killed. Thus was Laius' destiny, and the first part of his son's, fulfilled.

LAOCOON was a Trojan, said by some to be the brother of Anchises, and a priest of the sea god *POSEIDON*. Both the Greeks and the Romans remembered him as the man who warned the Trojans not to accept the so-called Greek gift of the Wooden Horse. He even drove a spear into its side to show his fellow countrymen that inside the hollow belly could lurk a terrible danger to Troy. However, like the prophetess *CASSANDRA*, Laocoon was ignored. Worse than the fate of Cassandra was that of Laocoon and his two sons, for no Trojan lifted a hand to help when two great sea-serpents suddenly arrived and crushed them to death.

There was no agreement, however, among the Greeks or the Romans about why Laocoon and his sons were killed by the sea-serpents. One opinion was that Laocoon's punishment was not connected with the Trojan War at

all. The god of prophecy, *APOLLO*, was simply punishing the priest for disobeying a divine command. An alternative view was that the death of Laocoon and his sons was the work of *ATHENA* or Poseidon for causing damage to the dedicatory horse. A Greek named Sinon had informed the Trojans that it was an offering to the goddess Athena: if they destroyed it, then Troy would fall, but if they dragged it inside the city walls, then the Wooden Horse was a guarantee of Troy's safety. In the event the cunning plot worked for the benefit of the Greeks, as those warriors hidden within the horse began a slaughter that led to the eventual overthrow and destruction of the besieged city.

As for the two serpents, once they had crushed Laocoon and his sons to death, they hid themselves in either the temple of Apollo or the temple of Athena.

*LAOCOON *and his sons were crushed to death by a pair of giant sea-serpents. The ancient poets differed as to the serpents' origin, whether they were sent by Athena or Apollo, and whether Laocoon was innocent or guilty and of what sin.* (ILLUSTRATION FROM DICTIONARY OF CLASSICAL ANTIQUITIES, 1891.)

LEDA was loved by Zeus in the shape of a swan. From their union, Leda produced two eggs, one containing the twins, Castor and Polydeuces. As young men, the twins are often depicted with egg-shaped helmets, recalling their unusual parentage. (LEDA AFTER LEONARDO DA VINCI, CANVAS, C. 1515-16.)

LETO was the daughter of the *TITANS* Coeus and Phoebe, and she was one of the few Titanesses to be worshipped in ancient Greece. However, her cult was commonly associated with those of her more famous son and daughter *APOLLO* and *ARTEMIS*, whose father was the sky god *ZEUS*. Leto may have given birth to her divine children on the sacred island of Delos, which a helpful *POSEIDON* is said to have fastened permanently to the bottom of the sea with a huge pillar. Later, one of Apollo's most important temples was built on the island. Even the invading Persians respected this sanctuary, when in 490 BC their fleet passed by on its way to punish the Eretrians and Athenians for providing aid to the Greek rebels who were fighting Persia in Asia Minor.

LETO (below), clutching her tiny twins, children of Zeus, flees a giant serpent sent by the vengeful Hera who relentlessly plagued her husband's lovers. The boy, Apollo, plucks a cithara, his attribute as god of the arts, while Artemis clutches a tiny bow, symbol of her role as goddess of the wild. (ILLUSTRATION BY NICK BEALE, 1995.)

LEDA was the daughter of King Thestius of Aetolia, which was a state in north-western Greece. Her husband was King Tyndareos of Sparta. Two of Leda's children were *CLYTEMNESTRA*, the murderous wife of *AGAMEMNON*, and *HELEN*, who was the unfaithful wife of *MENELAUS*, Agamemnon's brother, and the cause of the Trojan War. Leda was also the mother of the *DIOSCURI*, the twin sons Castor and Polydeuces. Various accounts are given of the fathers of her children, for Leda was loved by *ZEUS* who came to her disguised as a swan. Some say that as a result of their union Leda produced two eggs, one contained Clytemnestra and Helen, and the other the Dioscuri, but that Helen's and Polydeuces' father was Zeus while Tyndareos was the father of the mortals Clytemnestra and Castor. In the case of Helen there is little doubt that the myth of the Trojan War turned a goddess into a Queen. She clearly has a connection with older Aegean goddesses who were associated with birds and eggs.

MONSTERS AND FABULOUS BEASTS

CLASSICAL MONSTERS come in all shapes and colours, sometimes hideous, but sometimes bewitchingly fair, sometimes half-human and sometimes entirely demonic. Monsters generally symbolize the dark and unresolved forces in life and in human nature. Greek mythology is full of composite creatures, such as the Chimaera, Sphinx and Scylla, symbolizing complex evil. Not all monsters were cruel, and some, such as Ladon, guarded a precious treasure, while the Sphinx guarded the pass to the city of Thebes. Other monsters ravaged the land, such as the Hydra and Chimaera. Still others were raised by a curse, as when Poseidon sent a sea monster in response to Theseus' rage. Savage beasts, such as satyrs and Centaurs, part human and part animal, represent man's unruly, instinctive nature. Although less awesome than demons, they still harassed and haunted humans.

PYTHON (above), a monstrous serpent, son of Gaia, haunted the caves of Parnassus until slain by Apollo with his first arrows. Apollo founded the Pythian games to commemorate his victory and was afterwards named Apollo Physius. The monster's defeat was celebrated every nine years at the festival of Stepteria at Delphi and involved an enactment of the whole event. (ILLUSTRATION BY GLENN STEWARD, 1995.)

SCYLLA (above), a six-headed sea monster, fished for dolphins, sea-dogs and sailors from her cavern in the Strait of Messina. According to one myth, she was originally a beautiful sea nymph, loved by Zeus and Poseidon in turn, until changed by the jealousy of Circe into a snapping, barking monster. Here, she snatches up the crew of Odysseus as his ship sails past her cavern. (ILLUSTRATION FROM STORIES FROM GREECE AND ROME, 1930.)

THE SIRENS (right) were beautiful sea nymphs who charmed sailors by their alluring songs. Although initially depicted as bird-maids, they later became fair temptresses. Here, Odysseus sails past with his crew; having advised his men to stop their ears with wax, he had himself bound to the mast so that he could hear the sirens' magic song without being lured away. (ODYSSEUS AND THE SIRENS BY FRANCESCO PRIMATICCIO, CANVAS, 1505-70.)

SATYRS (above), wild spirits of the forest, appeared as goat-like creatures with puck noses, bristling hair, budding horns and goat's ears, tails and sometimes hooves. Usually portrayed as wanton and crafty, they frolicked in the forest, chased after nymphs and played impish tricks on men. Here, Diana's forest nymphs are plagued by licentious old satyrs. (DIANA'S NYMPHS CHASED BY SATYRS BY PETER PAUL RUBENS, CANVAS, C. 1670.)

CENTAURS (below), apparently the offspring of Ixion and a cloud, were man-horse beasts who led a wild and savage life in Thessaly, and were fond of riotous revelries. They came to symbolize the dark, unruly forces of nature. The wise Centaur, Chiron, who instructed heroes, was a unique case. Here, the centaurs, writhing in a fierce battle, symbolize the blind and brute force of human nature. (BATTLE OF THE CENTAURS BY ARNOLD BÖCKLIN, CANVAS, 1873.)

HARPIES (left), storm goddesses, were feared as robbers and spoilers who raged over battlefields and carried away the weak and wounded or stole children without warning. Originally they were imagined as winged goddesses with beautiful hair. Later on, they appear as awful monsters and spirits of mischief, half-birds, half-maids. (ILLUSTRATION BY GLENN STEWARD, 1995.)

61

M

LUCRETIA, after her suicide, returned to haunt Sextus Tarquinius, "false Sextus", the high-handed Etruscan who had raped her, incensing the whole of Rome. She appears as a pale, shrouded phantom who sings as she spins through the watches of the night.
(ILLUSTRATION FROM LAYS OF ANCIENT ROME, 1881.)

LUCRETIA was the wife of Tarquinius Collatinus and represented the ideal of Roman womanhood. When Sextus, youngest son of the Etruscan king *TARQUINIUS SUPERBUS*, raped her at dagger point around 507 BC, she made her father and her husband promise to avenge her honour before she stabbed herself to death. According to Roman legend, Lucretia's funeral roused the people and their anger was channelled by the inspiring eloquence of Lucius Junius *BRUTUS* into a desire for the overthrow of the monarchy.

MARS, the son of *JUNO* and a magical flower, was originally the Roman god of fertility and vegetation but later became associated with battle. As the god of spring, when his major festivals were held, he presided over agriculture in general. In his warlike aspect he was offered sacrifices before combat and was said to appear on the battlefield accompanied by Bellona, a warrior goddess variously identified as his wife, sister or daughter. Mars, unlike his Greek counterpart,

MARS, god of war, forces himself on gentle Pax and Abundanti, spirits of peace and plenty, while Minerva skilfully steers him away. The allegory dramatizes an age-old conflict, keenly felt in the warring Roman heart. (MINERVA DRIVING MARS BY JACOPO ROBUSTI TINTORETTO, CANVAS, C. 1576.)

ARES, was more widely worshipped than any of the other Roman gods, probably because his sons *REMUS AND ROMULUS* were said to have founded the city.

MEDEA was the daughter of Aietes, king of Colchis, a country adjoining the Black Sea, and the first wife of the voyager *JASON*. Medea means "the cunning one" – a suitable name for a princess skilled in the magic arts. In fact, to the Greeks she hovered somewhere between witch and goddess.

Medea fell in love with the Thessalian hero Jason as soon as he landed in Colchis with the *ARGONAUTS*, and she used magic to help him gain the Golden Fleece, the object of their expedition. On the hasty voyage back, when the Colchian fleet gave pursuit, Medea sacrificed her brother to slow the pursuers. On their return to Iolcus, Jason's birthplace, she managed to rejuvenate an old ram by boiling him in a magic pot whereupon he turned into a lamb. She also disposed of Jason's enemy, King Pelias of Iolcus, by persuading his daughters to give him a similar course of beauty treatment, but which killed him. As a result, Jason and Medea were banished to Corinth.

The relations between Jason and Medea went badly wrong. Jason put his first wife aside in order to marry Glauce, a Theban princess. Medea, feeling very insulted, took a terrible revenge on Jason. Glauce was burned alive in a poisoned wedding dress, and Medea saw to it that her own children by Jason were also killed. She then escaped to Athens in a magic chariot, which was said to belong to her grandfather *HELIOS*, the sun god.

In Athens, Medea married its king, *AEGEUS*, and bore him a son named Medus. At this time Aegeus believed he was childless, although he already had a son in the hero *THESEUS*. Through her wily skills, Medea prevailed upon Aegeus to reject Theseus when he came to Athens to claim his inheritance, and she may also have persuaded him to send Theseus to subdue the bull of Marathon. When Theseus succeeded in this dangerous task and at last Aegeus recognized him as his own successor, Medea fled with Medus to Colchis, where they avenged the recent overthrow and death of Aietes. Medus became a ruler of Colchis, but nothing else is known of Medea.

MENELAUS, king of Sparta, was the younger son of *ATREUS*. It was to recover Menelaus' wife *HELEN* that his older brother *AGAMEMNON*, king of Mycenae, led the Greek expedition against Troy. In spite of being warned, Menelaus not only entertained *PARIS*, the eldest son of King *PRIAM* of Troy, but he also

MERCURY (above), as the messenger god of the Romans, was closely identified with the Greek god Hermes. In works of art, he typically wears a winged helmet, or wide-brimmed traveller's hat, and carries a herald's staff, the emblem of peace. (MERCURY AND ARGUS BY PETER PAUL RUBENS, DETAIL, CANVAS, 1635.)

MEDEA, a ruthless sorceress, flees from Colchis with Jason and the Golden Fleece across the seas to Greece, with her father, Aietes, in pursuit. To slow him down, she cut up her brother and cast the parts into the sea, forcing Aietes to pick up the pieces for a pious burial. (THE GOLDEN FLEECE BY H J DRAPER, CANVAS, C. 1880.)

went off to Crete and left Helen alone at Sparta with the handsome visitor. Paris and Helen eloped, taking many of the treasures for which Menelaus was famous.

During the ten-year struggle against Troy, Menelaus played a secondary role to Agamemnon and the other Greek kings, although he was no coward. In single combat with Paris, Menelaus tried to settle the dispute between the Greeks and the Trojans. He won and was only prevented from killing his rival

by the intervention of the love goddess APHRODITE. She was indebted to Paris for judging her more beautiful than the goddesses HERA and ATHENA; in gratitude she had given him the love of Helen, the most beautiful woman alive.

After the fall of Troy, Menelaus could not bring himself to kill Helen because of her outstanding beauty. Once again the goddess Aphrodite cast her spell and they were reconciled and returned to Sparta, where they lived happily for many years. When Menelaus died he went to live in the Elysian Fields with his immortal Helen.

MERCURY was the Roman messenger god, and was also the deity who watched over trade and commerce, as his name suggests. He was associated with peace and

prosperity. He was apparently imported from Greece around the fifth century BC. Mercury is usually depicted in the same way as his Greek counterpart HERMES, with a winged hat and staff.

MIDAS was said to be the son of Gordius and Cybele, or to have been adopted by Gordius. He was the king of Phrygia and renowned for his wealth. According to the Greeks, his fabulous riches were the result of a kindness he showed to SILENUS, the old goat-like tutor of DIONYSUS, the god of vegetation, wine and ecstasy. So pleased was Dionysus with this behaviour that he offered Midas whatever he wished. The king asked for everything he touched to be turned into gold. At first Midas was overjoyed with the gift, but once he realized that even his food and drink were being transformed on touching his lips, he was horrified. Out of pity

Dionysus told him how to wash away his golden touch, which Midas did in the River Pactolus, thereafter famous for the gold dust to be found on its bed.

Another myth told about Midas concerns a musical competition between the gods APOLLO and PAN, the divine inventors of the lyre and pipes respectively. When the prize was awarded to Apollo, Midas incautiously expressed his surprise at the outcome and received from Apollo a set of ass's ears for his foolish presumption.

MIDAS, the fabled king of Phrygia, was fabulously rich, yet chose, when granted a wish by the gods, to become richer still, by asking for everything he touched to turn to gold. His wish was granted, but joy quickly turned to grief when he could neither eat nor drink. (ILLUSTRATION BY NICK BEALE, 1995.)

MENELAUS (left) was usually a gentle, even-tempered man, but here he fights fiercely over the fallen body of Patroclus who lies naked, for Apollo had struck off his helmet, splintered his ash spear and broken his corselet, stripping him bare so that he would be easily killed by Hector. (ILLUSTRATION FROM STORIES FROM HOMER, 1885.)

MINERVA (whose name may have originally meant "thought") was the Roman goddess of wisdom and the arts, the equivalent of the Greek goddess *ATHENA*. She was worshipped throughout Italy, though only in Rome did she take on a warlike character. Minerva is usually depicted wearing a coat of mail and a helmet, and carrying a spear. The Romans dedicated the spoils of war to her.

MINOS was the son of *ZEUS* and *EUROPA* and became the king of Crete, with his palace situated at Knossos. The Greeks regarded him both as a just lawgiver and as a cruel oppressor. To build his wonderful palace, Minos employed the Athenian craftsman *DAEDALUS*, whose creations were thought to be almost divine. So lifelike were his statues, for instance, that they had to be chained down in order to stop them running away. Minos was less pleased, however, with the hollow cow that Daedalus made for his queen, *PASIPHAE*, so that she might satisfy her desire for the white bull which *POSEIDON* had sent from the waves as a sign that Minos should ascend the Cretan throne. The *MINOTAUR*, a man with a bull's head, was the outcome of Pasiphae's unnatural union. This monstrous creature was housed in the Labyrinth, a special maze built by Daedalus at Minos' request.

Minos was known to the Greeks as an ancient ruler of the seas. His naval strength could well have owed something to Daedalus' inventiveness. Certainly he was not prepared for another ruler to enjoy the remarkable services of the craftsman. When Daedalus and his son Icarus left Crete without permission, Minos sailed to Sicily in hot pursuit. There, in the city of Kamikos, Minos met his death. Daedalus had arrived in Sicily as a refugee. He quickly went to ground and was hidden by King Cocalos of Kamikos. In order to find out where the craftsman was hiding,

MINERVA (above), the Roman goddess of wisdom, is depicted here taming a wild Centaur, who symbolizes the dark unruly side of human nature. His yearning expression suggests man's longing for divinity, despite himself. (MINERVA AND THE CENTAUR BY SANDRO BOTTICELLI, CANVAS, C. 1482.)

Minos carried a shell and promised to reward anyone who could pass a thread through it. Daedalus alone could solve the problem, which eventually he was unable to resist. When King Cocalos, on Daedalus' behalf, claimed the prize, Minos demanded that the craftsman be surrendered to him. But the daughters of Cocalos were unwilling to lose the inventive man who made them beautiful toys, and with his help they plotted Minos' death. When they took their royal guest to the bathroom, Daedalus led a pipe through the roof and boiling water, or oil, was poured down upon the

THE MINOTAUR (below) wrestles with Theseus in the Labyrinth, which is represented by the meander pattern at the sides. The bull-baiters above illustrate the sport of bull-leaping, part of the mysterious bull-cult of ancient Crete. (THE BULL-BAITERS BY JOHN DUNCAN, WATERCOLOUR, C. 1880.)

unsuspecting Cretan king. After his death Minos became a stern judge in the realm of *HADES*, the underworld, the land of the dead.

THE MINOTAUR was the monstrous son of a white bull, which was sent by the sea god *POSEIDON*, and *PASIPHAE*, the wife of King *MINOS* of Crete. When the child was born it had the head of a bull and the body of a man, and was given the name Minotaur ("Minos' bull").

The creature was fed on seven boys and seven girls sent annually as tribute by the Athenians. To free his countrymen of this terrible burden the hero *THESEUS* came to Knossos, entered the maze-like Labyrinth where the Minotaur lived and killed it. He was assisted by King Minos' daughter *ARIADNE*, who gave him a ball of thread, instructing him to unravel it on his way into the maze so that he could find his way out again. She also gave Theseus a sword.

In the strange story of the Minotaur the Greeks recalled in a garbled form the glories of the older inhabitants of Crete. It is now known that the bull games of the ancient Cretans involved young athletes leaping over bulls, even attempting somersaults holding the horns. Although some of them doubtless sustained serious injury, or may even have been killed, there is nothing to suggest that a man-eating creature was involved.

MOERAE see *FATES*

THE MUSES, from the Roman name, Musae, were the daughters of *ZEUS* and Mnemosyne, a *TITAN*, whose name means "memory". They used to dance and sing at parties held by the gods and heroes. For the Greeks, the Muses were the inspiration of poetry, music and dance. Later, other intellectual activities were added to their care. Although accounts of their number differ, it is generally accepted that

THE MUSES, guiding spirits of the arts, inspired all gifted artists, though they resented any serious competition and deprived the Sirens of their feathers for daring to be better than them in song. The nine Muses appear here amid the aspiring artists of the Renaissance. (THE REALM OF THE MUSES BY LORENZO COSTA, CANVAS, c. 1506)

there were nine Muses altogether – Clio, Euterpe, Thalia, Melpomene, Terpsichore, Erato, Polyhymnia, Urania and Calliope.

NAIADS see FORCES OF NATURE

NARCISSUS, according to Greek mythology, was the beautiful son of the River Cephissus in Boeotia and the nymph Liriope. Among the many who loved him, including immortals and mortals, was Echo, who slowly pined away, leaving just

NARCISSUS (right), a beautiful youth, was loved by the nymph Echo who, failing to attract him, died of grief. He, in his turn, fell in love with his own reflection and pined away until changed by the gods into the flower that bears his name. (ECHO AND NARCISSUS BY J W WATERHOUSE, CANVAS, 1880.)

the echo of her voice. Narcissus was then condemned by Nemesis, goddess of retribution, to spend the rest of his days admiring his own reflection in a pool. At last he died and was turned into the flower that bears his name.

NEPTUNE was an ancient Italian water god whom the Romans identified with *POSEIDON*. Compared to Poseidon, however, Neptune plays a minor role in Roman mythology.

NOTUS see FORCES OF NATURE

OCEANOS was a *TITAN*, the son of Ouranos and *GAIA*, but never an enemy of *ZEUS*. On the contrary, he protected Zeus' wife *HERA* and mother *RHEA* when the gods fought the Titans. As ruler of the encircling sea, which the Greeks believed surrounded the world, Oceanos married his sister Tethys and they produced three thousand rivers.

OCEANUS (left), father of the river gods, is depicted here with a typically tempestuous face, unruly locks and horned brow. Above him, Selene, the crescent moon, sheds a mild light; and on either side flash the stars, Phosphorus (left) and Hesperus (right). (ILLUSTRATION FROM DICTIONARY OF CLASSICAL ANTIQUITIES, 1891.)

ODYSSEUS *alights on the island of Aeaea where he is warned by Hermes of the horrors of Circe's enchanting wine, which turns men into swine. This fate has already befallen one comrade and so Odysseus must keep his guard.* (CIRCE WITH THE COMRADES OF ODYSSEUS *BY* ALESSANDRO ALLORI, *FRESCO, 1580.*)

Greek warriors under his own command. The Trojans dragged the Wooden Horse inside their walls when they learned from a Greek, deliberately left behind when the rest put to sea, that the offering would bring their city a guarantee of divine protection. But in the night the Greeks emerged from it, and surprised the Trojans. Hence, the ancient saying "Never trust the Greeks bearing gifts".

Although Troy fell, the wildness of the looting and the slaughter deeply offended the gods. In particular, the goddess ATHENA was enraged at the rape of CASSANDRA within the sanctuary of her own temple. Odysseus tried to appease Athena, and he escaped drowning in the great storm which the angry goddess sent to shatter the victorious Greek fleet on its homeward journey. But he could not entirely avoid blame, and POSEIDON saw to it that he was the last Greek leader to reach home, after a voyage lasting some ten years.

The long period of wandering that Odysseus suffered was a favourite story of both the Greeks and the Romans, who knew the voyager by the name of Ulysses. The exact route that he followed remains a mystery, not least because his travels took him beyond known territory and into strange and dangerous lands. From Troy Odysseus sailed first to Thrace, where he lost many of his

ODYSSEUS, king of Ithaca, was one of the Greek leaders who took part in the Trojan War. He was celebrated for both his part in this conflict and his remarkable voyage home to his island kingdom in the Ionian Sea.

A brave and clever man, Odysseus was sometimes thought to have been the son of SISYPHUS, the trickster of Greek mythology. But his real father was probably Laertes, whom he succeeded as king of Ithaca. His mother was named Anticleia and his faithful wife Penelope was the sister of King Tyndareos of Sparta.

From the start of the campaign against Troy it is clear that King AGAMEMNON, the Greek leader, placed great store upon Odysseus' cunning. He was sent with Nestor, the aged king of Pylos, to discover where the great warrior ACHILLES

was hidden. Again, at Aulis, where the Greek fleet was stranded by contrary winds, it was Odysseus who tricked Agamemnon's wife CLYTEMNESTRA into sending her daughter IPHIGENIA from Mycenae, supposedly to marry Achilles. Instead, however, Iphigenia was to be sacrificed to ARTEMIS, goddess of the wild, in order to obtain a fair wind to Troy. Throughout the ten-

year struggle against the Trojans, Odysseus was important not so much as a fighter but as a counsellor and a schemer. His eloquence was renowned, and it was probably Odysseus who thought of the Wooden Horse, which gave the Greeks victory.

Odysseus deceived the Trojans with this horse built of wood whose hollow belly was filled with

ODYSSEUS *raises his great bow and, with effortless might, stretches the bowstring which the suitors had struggled in vain to bend. He then slays the suitors who have devoured his wealth and plagued his wife during his long voyage home.* (ILLUSTRATION FROM STORIES FROM HOMER, *1885.*)

ODYSSEUS, on his way through the ghostly underworld, consults the shade of Tiresias, who warns him that if he offends Helios he will return home alone on a foreign ship only after many years' wandering. (TIRESIAS COUNSELS ODYSSEUS BY ALESSANDRO ALLORI, FRESCO, 1580.)

men in battle. After this bloody incident the places he touched upon are less easy to identify. Storms drove him to the land of the Lotophagi ("the lotus-eaters"), whose diet made visitors forget their homelands and wish to stay on forever. Then he encountered in Sicily, it was later believed, the Cyclops POLYPHEMUS, whose father was Poseidon. By putting out Polyphemus' single eye when the gigantic man was befuddled with wine, Odysseus and his companions managed to escape becoming his dinner. They then arrived on the floating island of Aeolus, who was the ruler of the winds. There Odysseus received a rare present, a sack full of winds. The idea appears in many different mythologies, but according to the Greeks, it was of little use on the voyage because the curiosity of Odysseus' men got the better of them and they opened the sack and the winds no longer blew in a helpful direction.

A tragedy overcame the squadron of ships that Odysseus led among the Laestrygones, a race of giant cannibals. Only his own ship survived the attack and reached Aeaea, the island of the enchantress CIRCE, later considered to be situated off Italy. Odysseus resisted her spells, with the aid of the messenger god HERMES, and made the enchantress restore to human shape his men who had been turned to swine. Afterwards, on Circe's advice, he sailed to the western edge of the encircling sea,

the realm of OCEANOS, where ghosts came from the underworld realm of HADES to meet him. The shade of the blind seer TIRESIAS gave Odysseus a special warning about his homeward journey to Ithaca. He told him that if the cattle of the sun god HELIOS on the isle of Thrinacia were harmed by him he would never reach his home. The ghost of Odysseus' mother also spoke of the difficulties being faced by Penelope in Ithaca at the time. The ghost of Agamemnon, his old comrade-in-arms, also warned him about his homecoming; when he returned home he had been murdered by his wife and lover in the bathroom.

Turning eastwards, Odysseus sailed back towards Greece and was the only man who dared to listen to the alluring song of the Sirens, bird-women of storm. He filled his men's ears with wax and had himself bound with strong cords to the mast. Odysseus then passed through the straits between Sicily and Italy, where six of his crew were seized by the six-headed monster Scylla. On the island of Thrinacia, as Tiresias had foretold, the voyagers were tempted by hunger to slay some of Helios' cattle. Despite his warning, the desperate men killed and cooked several cows when Odysseus was asleep. Later they deserted him, but were drowned in a storm sent by ZEUS at Helios' request.

Alone, Odysseus was almost swallowed by the great whirlpool

Charybdis. In an exhausted state he drifted to the wondrous island of the sea nymph Calypso, who cared for him and eventually proposed marriage. But not even immortality would tempt him, and after seven years the gods forced Calypso to let Odysseus set off again. Shipwrecked once more in the land of the Phaeacians, he was welcomed as an honoured guest and offered a passage back to Ithaca. So it was that he was secretly landed near his own palace, which he entered disguised with Athena's aid as a beggar.

Penelope had been patiently awaiting Odysseus' return from the war. Although pressed to marry one of her many noble suitors, she had put them off for a while by pretending that she could not marry until she had finished weaving a shroud for Laertes, her father-in-law. But Penelope unrav-

elled it each night, until one of her maids betrayed the trick. Finally, after ten years, Penelope agreed to marry the suitor who could bend and string Odysseus' great bow. This challenge was proposed on the advice of the goddess Athena. The only suitor who succeeded at the challenge was a beggar, who then threw off his disguise and revealed himself as Odysseus.

Assisted by his son Telemachus and two loyal retainers, Odysseus dispatched the suitors and hanged the treacherous maids. Reunited with his family at last, including his father Laertes, Odysseus then defeated an attack by the relations of the suitors and returned Ithaca to peace. Zeus himself threw down a thunderbolt to signal an end to the fighting. (See also VOYAGERS)

ODYSSEUS the wanderer returns home after twenty years and embraces Penelope at last. She had refused to acknowledge her husband until he had reminded her of the secret of their bed, which was carved out of a great olive tree grown in the courtyard. (ILLUSTRATION FROM STORIES FROM HOMER, 1885.)

OEDIPUS ("swell-foot") was the unlucky son of King LAIUS and Queen Jocasta of Thebes. Because, as a guest at the court of PELOPS, Laius had taken sexual advantage of Pelops' young son Chrysippus, a curse was laid on the ruling house of Thebes. Indeed, an oracle warned Laius that any son Jocasta bore him would kill him. For a long time the king and queen abandoned the marriage bed, but drink one night caused Laius to throw caution to the winds and a son was duly conceived. At birth, the infant was pierced in the feet and left to die on a distant mountainside, a fairly common practice for unwanted children in ancient Greece. However, a shepherd found the baby and took it to King Polybus of Corinth, who, having no children, adopted the boy and chose the name of Oedipus because of his damaged feet. When he grew up, Oedipus was taunted that he was not Polybus' son, so he went to ask

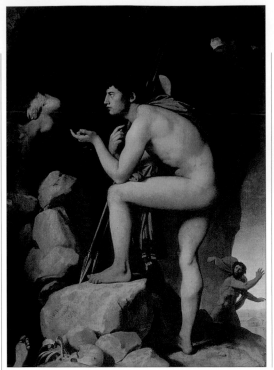

OEDIPUS puzzles over the Sphinx's riddle, which she challenges all travellers to Thebes to solve. When Oedipus outwits the Sphinx, she flings herself into the chasm below and destroys herself. Oedipus is portrayed here, as he is in ancient art, as a calm and pensive hero. (OEDIPUS AND THE SPHINX BY JEAN AUGUSTE INGRES, CANVAS, 1808.)

Jocasta, Oedipus decided to try or die in the attempt. By outwitting the Sphinx and causing its death, Oedipus unwittingly fulfilled his own destiny: he had killed his father, now he married his mother.

For a time Oedipus and Jocasta lived happily together, having a family of two sons, Polynices and Eteocles, and two daughters, ANTIGONE and Ismene. Then a dreadful plague settled on Thebes, and Creon was sent to ask the Oracle at Delphi for a remedy. The divine command he brought back to the city was to drive out the murderer of Laius. Although the famous seer TIRESIAS announced

OEDIPUS, after years of wandering since his exile from Thebes, leans on his loyal daughter Antigone; they travel to Colonus where it is destined that Oedipus will finally find peace and death in a sacred grove. (ILLUSTRATION BY NICK BEALE, 1995.)

the Delphic Oracle about his parentage. He was told that he was destined to kill his father and marry his mother, and in horror he fled north. En route he encountered Laius, whose charioteer deliberately ran over Oedipus' foot. The result was that Oedipus killed everyone there, except one of his father's servants who ran away.

Arriving in Thebes, Oedipus discovered its people were greatly distressed at the news of Laius' death and terrified of the SPHINX, an ugly monster causing havoc in the countryside. When the regent CREON announced that whoever rid the city of the Sphinx would be offered the throne and the hand of

ORESTES (right) finds some peace at the shrine of Apollo in Delphi where he has fled, pursued by the Furies, after murdering his mother. At Delphi, Orestes is partly purified by Apollo, and even the Furiae, asleep on the altar, find rest. In time, Orestes is acquitted by the Areopagus. (ORESTES, MARBLE, C. 200 BC.)

that Oedipus was the guilty one, the new king would not believe this was true until he traced those involved in his own exposure as a child. Convinced at last of his exceptional crime, Oedipus blinded himself and left Thebes. His mother and wife, Jocasta, had already committed suicide. In the company of his daughter Antigone, a broken Oedipus eventually found spiritual peace in a sacred grove at Colonus near Athens. His death there was considered to be a good omen by the Athenians, because in gratitude for the sanctuary he was given, Oedipus had foretold that his bones would save them from any future attack by the Thebans.

ORESTES was the son of King *AGAMEMNON* of Mycenae and *CLYTEMNESTRA* and is renowned for having committed matricide. In ancient Greece there were many places associated with his purification after such a terrible crime. For example, in front of the sanctuary of *APOLLO* in Troezen, there was a hut used by Orestes, which was said to have been built to avoid receiving the polluted murderer as a guest in a normal house.

When Agamemnon left to lead the Greek expedition against Troy, his wife Clytemnestra took a lover, Aegisthus. When Agamemnon returned, some ten years later, the two lovers murdered him, and it was to avenge this crime that Orestes killed his mother. The great horror felt by the Greeks over Orestes' actions runs deep in his myth. Correct though he was to seek vengeance for his father's murder, as the Delphic Oracle had advised him to, the killing of a mother by her son could not be expected to bring anything other than dire misfortune. The *FURIES* were avenging deities who tracked down all those with blood on their hands, and they now relentlessly pursued Orestes.

Wild-eyed and distraught, Orestes wandered as an outcast

throughout Greece. When finally he went to Delphi for help, since Apollo had advised him to slay his father's murderers, Orestes was told to go to Athens and stand trial by the Areopagus, an ancient council presided over by *ATHENA*. The verdict in his favour calmed the Furies, so they were renamed the Eumenides ("the soothed goddesses"). It is likely, however, that the Greeks called them by this euphemism because they were afraid to use their real name, the Erinyes, "the angry ones".

ORION see *GIANTS*

ORPHEUS was a Thracian singer much revered in ancient Greece. He was said to be the son of Calliope, *MUSE* of epic poetry. His chief myth concerns the death of his wife, the nymph Eurydice. One

day she died of a snake bite. Orpheus was so saddened and grief-stricken by this sudden loss that he no longer sang or played. Then he decided to risk his own life in a desperate journey to the land of the dead in the forlorn hope of bringing Eurydice home. By using his miraculous music, Orpheus was able to charm the boatman, Charon, who ferried him across the Styx, and the three-headed *CERBERUS* so that he could enter the underworld. Even the ghosts of the dead were greatly moved by his song, but the rulers of the underworld, *HADES* and his wife *PERSEPHONE*, granted Orpheus his only desire on one condition: under no circumstances was Orpheus to look back at Eurydice until both of them were completely returned to the land of the living. But so overcome was the singer by love for his

ORPHEUS, after his death, became an oracle, and is pictured here being consulted by a Thracian maid. His head rests on a lyre that is encrusted with seaweed because, ever musical, even in death his decapitated head had floated downstream calling for Eurydice. (A THRACIAN MAID WITH THE HEAD OF ORPHEUS BY GUSTAVE MOREAU, CANVAS, 1865.)

departed wife that just before they reached the surface of the ground, he could not resist a quick glance in the half-light. The result was that Eurydice turned into a ghost again and sank back to Hades' kingdom forever. Orpheus' own fate was to be dismembered by Thracian maenads, the female worshippers of *DIONYSUS*, the god of vegetation, wine and ecstasy. Apparently, they tore the singer to pieces except for his head, which was then cast into a river and went floating downstream calling out "Eurydice!"

Ancient fascination with this romantic story was probably connected with religious ceremonies and rituals that were aimed at securing personal salvation after death. The worshippers of both Orpheus and Dionysus believed in some form of afterlife. Paintings of Orpheus have even been found in the catacombs, the early burial chambers of Christians in Italy. (See also *VOYAGERS*)

ORPHEUS was pursued and torn apart by the frenzied maenads, who were the wild devotees of Dionysus. They were usually depicted, as they are here, whirling in ecstasy, with swirling robes, and dishevelled, snakebound hair. (ILLUSTRATION FROM DR SMITH'S CLASSICAL DICTIONARY, 1895.)

FORCES OF NATURE

T HE WONDERS AND MYSTERIES OF NATURE are explained in mythology through the will and actions of the gods. Sunrise and sunset, storms and tidal waves, summer and winter unfold as part of a divine drama. For the ancient Greeks, the sun rose and set because Phoebus Apollo drove the glittering sun-chariot on a fiery course across the sky, preceded by Eos who sprinkled morning dew from her vase. Springtime came when Persephone, who symbolized the seed-corn, rose from the underworld to live in the light of day with her mother, Demeter, goddess of corn. The tempestuous sea god, Poseidon, could stir up sea-storms, or soothe the waves; while mighty Zeus could strike from afar with a bolt of lightning or brighten the sky with rainbows. In addition to the great gods of sky, land and sea, nature spirits or nymphs infused the forests, fields and rivers.

APOLLO (above), god of light, symbolized not only sunlight – for originally Helios (the sun) radiated daylight and was only later identified with Apollo – but also the bright, life-giving, pure, healing light of divinity. Apollo's light underlies his other roles as god of healing, god of prophecy and god of the arts. He withdrew in winter to sunny Lycius and returned in spring to dispel winter. Here, he drives the sun-chariot on its course across the heavens. (ILLUSTRATION FROM STORIES FROM LIVY, 1885.)

POSEIDON (above), the turbulent god of the seas, symbolized the might of the sea-storm. He dwelt in a golden palace in the depths of the ocean, and rode the waves in his sea-chariot, drawn by sea-horses, speeding so fast that he passed from Samothrace to Aegae in three great strides. Beside him basks his wife, the sea nymph Amphitrite, while a school of tritons (part men, part fish) frisk around his chariot blowing their conches, which they used to raise or calm the waves. (POSEIDON AND HIS CHARIOT BY MIRABELLO CAVALORI, C. 1497.)

ZEUS (left), the chief deity, governed the winds and clouds, rain, thunder and lightning. By striking his aegis he caused storms and tempests to rage, but equally, he could calm the elements and brighten the sky. As the father of the hours, he governed the changing seasons. An awesome but benign god, he is seen here resplendent in fiery light, bearing his aegis, symbol of his sovereign power over all forces of nature and all other gods. (JUPITER AND SEMELE BY GUSTAVE MOREAU, CANVAS, DETAIL, 1896.)

FLORA (right), blooming Roman goddess of spring, was honoured every year at the time of the Floralia, a theatrical festival when the people decked themselves in flowers and enjoyed a great feast lasting for six days. Flora, serene and benign, is here honoured in a lavish parade. Poussin's atmospheric scene vividly revives the pagan splendour of the early Greek pastoral festivals. (THE TRIUMPH OF FLORA BY NICOLAS POUSSIN, CANVAS, C. 1627.)

HEPHAISTOS (below), the smith god, is typically depicted as a grave, intense man wearing a workman's cap and immersed in his fiery craft. He had forges beneath volcanoes but also on Olympus where 20 bellows worked at his bidding. Famed for his artistry, he crafted works of wonder, such as Achilles' shield, embossed with a dramatic scene of life and death, joy and grief, peace and war. (APOLLO IN THE FORGE OF HEPHAISTOS BY DIEGO VELASQUEZ, CANVAS, DETAIL, 1630.)

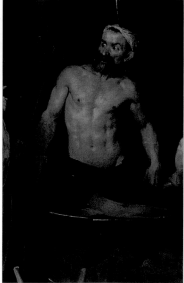

THE NAIADS (above), or water nymphs, dwelt beside running water. Like their cousins, the Nereids and Oceanids of the oceans, the Oreads of the hills and the Dryads of forests and trees, they were usually sweet, benign spirits. Naiads, especially, were helpful and healing, nurturing fruits, flowers and mortals. Yet the youth Hylas who went to draw water from a pool was lured by the nymphs into the water and never seen again. (HYLAS AND THE WATER NYMPHS BY J W WATERHOUSE, CANVAS, C. 1890.)

NOTUS (below), the south wind, brought with it fog and rain. Here, as a winged deity, Notus pours rain from a vase, much as his mother, Eos, goddess of dawn, sprinkles dew from a vase before the sun-chariot in the early morning. (ILLUSTRATION FROM DR SMITH'S CLASSICAL DICTIONARY, 1891.)

ZEPHYRUS (below), the west wind, dwelt with his brother wind, Boreas, in a palace in Thrace. He was father of the immortal horses, Xanthus and Balius, Achilles' battle steeds who galloped with the speed of wind. (ILLUSTRATION FROM DR SMITH'S CLASSICAL DICTIONARY, 1891.)

P

PAN (above) plays his pipes at dusk. As a spirit of the dark forest, he often startled solitary travellers, arousing sudden awe and panic. He is usually depicted with shaggy head, goat's horns and hooves, dancing or playing a syrinx. (ILLUSTRATION FROM TANGLEWOOD TALES, C. 1920.)

PAN was the son of the messenger god *HERMES*. As the Greek god of the mountainside, the pastures of sheep and goats, he was himself goat-horned and goat-legged. Pan was especially associated with Arcadia, the mountainous state in central Peloponnese. He was playful and energetic, but very irritable, especially if disturbed during his afternoon nap. He liked to play on a pipe, which was known as a syrinx after a nymph of that name who turned herself into a reed-bed to avoid his advances. For Pan could also be a frightening god when he blew on his conch. Our

PANDORA (below), "all-gifts", was the first woman to appear on earth, created by the gods to work mischief for men. Irrepressibly curious, she could not resist opening a sealed jar, containing the horrors of life: strife and sickness, sorrow and grief. (ILLUSTRATION BY NICK BEALE, 1995.)

word "panic" derives from this aspect of his divinity. His worship spread from Arcadia to Athens immediately after the Athenian and Plataean victory over the Persians at Marathon in 480 BC, because he made the Persians flee in panic. He rendered a similar service for *ZEUS* during the battle against *CRONOS* and the *TITANS*. His conch deeply worried Zeus' opponents.

PANDORA was the Greek Eve, the bringer of all sorrows for mankind. She was the first woman and was created by *HEPHAISTOS*, the smith god, on *ZEUS'* orders in order to upset *PROMETHEUS*, the Greek god of fire and friend of men. When she went to live among men, she was given a gift from the gods which was a sealed jar that contained all the misfortunes of existence. But soon Pandora's great curiosity overcame a natural fear of what might be inside, and she broke the seal, releasing sorrow, disease and conflict. As a result, the men who originally comprised the human race gained a mortal, female companion, but also untold woes. Appropriately, the name Pandora means "all gifts" – the bad as well as the good.

PARIS (above), the judge of a divine beauty contest, chose Aphrodite as the winner because she offered him the world's fairest woman. Behind her, wise Athena had promised him fame, while queenly Hera had offered him power. (THE JUDGEMENT OF PARIS BY JEAN REGNAULT, CANVAS, 1820.)

PARIS was one of the fifty sons of King *PRIAM* of Troy. According to the Greeks, he was responsible for causing the Trojan War. Paris was a very handsome young man and wooed *HELEN* so well that she left her husband *MENELAUS*, king of Sparta, and fled with her lover to Troy. His unusual attractiveness was believed to have been a gift from *APHRODITE*, the goddess of love. In return for choosing her as the fairest of goddesses, Aphrodite offered Paris the most beautiful woman in the world, Helen.

During the long siege of Troy Paris cut a poor figure as a warrior. His single combat with Menelaus, Helen's husband, was supposed to have settled the outcome of the whole war. Instead it revealed Paris as a coward, who only escaped with his life through the intervention of Aphrodite. As a result, the Trojan champion *HECTOR*, his eldest brother, treated him very badly. It was an irony of fate that a poisoned arrow shot from Paris' bow should have found the one vulnerable spot on the mighty Greek champion *ACHILLES*, his heel. Paris himself was killed by an arrow, prior to the fall of Troy.

PASIPHAE, in Greek mythology, was the daughter of *HELIOS*, the sun god, and wife of *MINOS*, king of Crete. The sea god *POSEIDON* sent a white bull as a sign of Minos' right to rule the island, but the king refused to sacrifice the animal when it emerged from the waves, and Poseidon pronounced a curse in anger at the lack of respect

PASIPHAE, queen of Crete, was drawn irresistibly to a mysterious white bull which emerged from the waves. She developed a strange passion for the bull, and from her union with the creature she bore a dreadful bull-man, the Minotaur, who was kept hidden in an underground maze. (ILLUSTRATION BY NICK BEALE, 1995.)

PEGASUS, a magnificent winged horse, dips and dives through the flames of the fire-breathing monster, the Chimaera. On his back, Bellerophon urges him on. The hero had successfully tamed Pegasus with a golden bridle given to him by Athena. (ILLUSTRATION FROM TANGLEWOOD TALES, C. 1920.)

shown to himself. Pasiphae was to be stricken with a passionate desire for the bull. In order to gratify her lust, the great craftsman *DAEDALUS* made a cow, into which Pasiphae fitted and so could mate with the bull. Later, she gave birth to the *MINOTAUR* ("Minos' Bull"), which was kept in the Labyrinth.

PEGASUS, in Greek mythology, was the flying horse belonging to the Corinthian hero *BELLEROPHON*. The winged steed was born from blood which spilled from the severed head of the *GORGON* Medusa, who was already pregnant by the sea god *POSEIDON* (a deity always associated with bulls and horses). Bellerophon was given a magic bridle by *ATHENA* to help him tame Pegasus. When the hero tried to fly to Mount Olympus, Pegasus threw him on the instruction of *ZEUS*.

PELOPS was the son of King *TANTALUS*, the ruler of a kingdom in Asia Minor. Pelops' name is still recalled in the Peloponnese ("the isle of Pelops"), which is the large peninsula of southern Greece.

The sea god *POSEIDON* so loved Pelops that he seized the youth and carried him off to Mount Olympus. Possibly because of this divine favour shown to his son, Tantalus was honoured by the gods as no other mortal. He was allowed to eat nectar and ambrosia, the immortal food served to the deities on their mountain home. But Tantalus fell from divine favour and suffered eternal torment as a result.

According to one version of the myth, Tantalus cut up, boiled and served his own son Pelops to the gods in order to test their omniscience. Only *DEMETER*, the goddess of vegetation, partook of the feast, inadvertently eating a piece of Pelops' shoulder. Later, when the gods returned the youth to life, the missing piece of his body was replaced by ivory.

By favour of Poseidon the restored Pelops became famous as a champion charioteer, which was an accomplishment that the ancient Greeks regarded as one of the greatest. So when Oenomaus, king of Elis, offered his daughter Hippodameia in marriage and also his lands to anyone who could defeat him in a chariot race, Pelops accepted the challenge. But he had to agree that Oenomaus could shoot an arrow at him if he caught up with his chariot. Thirteen contestants had already perished.

It was said that Pelops bribed a certain Myrtilus, the king's charioteer, to remove the linchpins from his master's chariot, but when he won Pelops refused to acknowledge this assistance. In different versions of the story, he either threw Myrtilus into the sea, or he spurned him. As a consequence, the father of Myrtilus, who was the messenger god *HERMES*, saw that a curse afflicted the descendants of Pelops. The consequences of this curse on the house of *ATREUS*, Pelops' eldest son and the father of *AGAMEMNON*, is the basis for that family's tragic story.

PELOPS, in the winning chariot, races along the Greek track, fast outstripping his rival Oenomaus, whose chariot swerves and crashes. Pelops' white shoulder was made of ivory, fashioned by the gods after he had been partly eaten by Demeter. (ILLUSTRATION BY GLENN STEWARD, 1995.)

PENELOPE was the daughter of Icarius, king of Sparta, and a nymph Peribaea. As the faithful wife of *ODYSSEUS*, the ruler of Ithaca, she was celebrated for her patience in waiting almost twenty years for his return from Troy. Beset by suitors, Penelope kept them at bay for a long time by pretending to weave a shroud for her father-in-law Laertes. Each night she would secretly unravel the day's work. Eventually, the return of Odysseus saved her from an enforced second marriage, but she remained cold towards her saviour until she was absolutely certain of his identity. Penelope refused to be convinced that the new arrival really was Odysseus until he described their bed, carved in part from a tree trunk still rooted in the ground.

PERSEPHONE was the daughter of *ZEUS* and *DEMETER*, the earth goddess, and became queen of the underworld as the abducted wife of *HADES*. According to the Greeks, Zeus promised his beautiful daughter to Hades without consulting her mother. When Hades rose from the underworld and took his bride by force, Demeter was beside herself with grief. The goddess wandered the earth searching for her daughter, two burning torches in her hands. As a result the land was no longer fertile. Plants wilted, animals

PENELOPE (right), patient wife of Odysseus, shared her husband's cleverness. During his long absence, she kept her many suitors at bay by refusing to marry until she had completed a shroud which she secretly unravelled each night, until the suitors discovered her ploy. (ILLUSTRATION FROM STORIES FROM HOMER, 1885.)

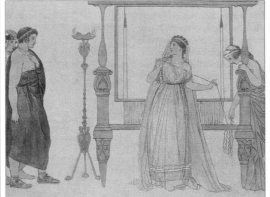

PERSEPHONE (far right), goddess of death, spent the winter in the underworld, rising each spring to live with her mother, the goddess of corn. She symbolizes the seed-corn that is buried, rises and falls again in a cycle of constant renewal – a theme central to the Eleusian mysteries. (PERSEPHONE, MARBLE, DETAIL, C. 490 BC.)

PERSEUS and Andromeda (above) peer gingerly at the face of Medusa, reflected in the water. Burne-Jones' Medusa recalls the tranquil air and death-like beauty of the Greek Medusas carved on amulets and charms, which remind us that she was once beautiful. (THE BALEFUL HEAD BY EDMUND BURNE-JONES, CANVAS, 1887.)

bore no offspring and death stalked mankind. In the end, Zeus was obliged to intervene and ruled that Persephone should spend time each year with both her husband and her mother. Persephone could never return entirely to the living world because she had eaten in Hades' realm: a very old idea that strictly divided the food of the dead from that of the living.

The story of Persephone's abduction, disappearance and return parallels the fertility myths of West Asia. She may well have been a pre-Greek goddess, a deity worshipped by earlier settlers of the country who was later incorporated into Greek religion. Her association with the dead may have a similar origin. The Athenians, who were originally a non-Greek speaking people, referred to the dead as "Demeter's people".

PERSEUS was the son of *ZEUS* and *DANAE*, daughter of Acrisius, king of Argos. Danae had been shut up in a bronze tower in order to thwart a prophecy that if she had a son he would kill Acrisius. But Zeus visited her as a golden shower and Perseus was born. A terrified Acrisius placed mother and son in a wooden chest and cast it on the sea. The protection of Zeus, however, was enough to bring them safely to the shores of the island of Seriphos, where Perseus grew up among fishermen.

On reaching manhood Perseus was sent by the local ruler, Polydectes, to fetch the head of the *GORGON* Medusa, a very dangerous task. Luckily for the hero the goddess *ATHENA* hated Medusa and instructed him how to proceed.

PHAEDRA, seen here with her sister Ariadne and husband Theseus, was the unfortunate daughter of King Minos and Queen Pasiphae of Crete. She fell in love with her stepson Hippolytus which eventually proved to be her downfall.
(THESEUS WITH ARIADNE AND PHAEDRA BY BENEDETTO GENNARI THE YOUNGER, CANVAS, 1702.)

First he visited the Graiae, three old hags who shared a single eye. Perseus seized the eye and obliged the Graiae to tell him about the nature of the Gorgons, their three dreadful sisters.

Most important of all, they informed him how a direct glance from Medusa's eyes would turn him to stone. He also received three useful gifts from some friendly nymphs: a cap of invisibility, winged shoes and a bag for Medusa's head. Ready for the exploit at last, Perseus put on the shoes and flew to the Gorgon's cave in the far west. Careful not to look at Medusa directly, he approached by watching her reflection in his shield. Having cut off Medusa's head and stowed it in his bag, Perseus flew away unseen by her two sisters.

The chilling powers of the head were used to good purpose by Perseus on his way home. Having

saved the beautiful *ANDROMEDA* from a sea monster, he married her, but several people had to be turned to stone before he and his bride returned safely to Danae. Having returned his magical equipment to *HERMES*, the messenger god, Perseus visited Argos only to find that Acrisius had already fled to Larissa on hearing of his grandson's arrival. The prophecy was fulfilled, nevertheless, when Perseus was invited to compete in the games at Larissa and his discus hit the old man on the head.

Because of the accident the hero chose to be king of Tiryns rather than Argos. On hearing of their deaths Athena placed both Perseus and Andromeda in the sky as constellations. (See also *HEROES*)

PHAEDRA was the daughter of King *MINOS* and Queen *PASIPHAE* of Crete. According to the Greeks, the Athenian hero *THESEUS* made

her his second wife. He seems to have abandoned her sister *ARIADNE* not long after she helped him kill the *MINOTAUR*, the bull-headed creature kept in the Labyrinth at Knossos. Like her mother Pasiphae, who gave birth to the Minotaur, Phaedra was soon overcome by an illicit desire. It was not for an animal this time, but for her stepson, Hippolytus, the son of Theseus' earlier marriage to the queen of the *AMAZONS*, Hippolyta. When she saw how Hippolytus was horrified by her passion for him, Phaedra hanged herself and left a message to Theseus saying that his son had tried to rape her. Theseus exiled his son, who was later killed in a chariot accident. In another version, Theseus cursed his son and asked *POSEIDON* to destroy Hippolytus, which he did by sending a sea-monster. Phaedra, filled with sorrow, then killed herself.

PHAETHON was the son of the sun god *HELIOS* and Clymene, daughter of *OCEANOS*. He drove his father's four-horse chariot so fast that he lost control and threatened the world with a terrible heat. *ZEUS* stopped him with a thunderbolt, which sent Phaethon crashing to the earth. The great god may have also flooded the earth in an attempt to reduce the temperature. It was believed that Phaethon's mad exploit could be traced in the shape of the Milky Way, while he was reflected in the constellation of Auriga, the charioteer.

THE PLEIADES were the seven daughters of the Titan *ATLAS*, and were named Maia, Electra, Taygete, Celeno, Merope, Asterope and Alcyone. They may have become stars, or doves, in order to escape from the passionate intentions of Orion, the giant hunter. Their appearance in the night sky in May coincides with the beginning of summer, and the constellation of Orion then appears to be in perpetual pursuit of them.

POLYPHEMUS, a one-eyed giant, was in love with the nymph Galatea, but she scorned him, loving instead the handsome Acis. In a jealous rage, the giant crushed Acis with a rock; but Galatea turned her beloved into a Sicilian river bearing his name. (POLYPHEMUS AND THE NYMPH GALATEA BY ANNIBALE CARRACCI, FRESCO, C. 1595.)

POLYPHEMUS was the son of *POSEIDON* and the sea nymph Thoosa. He was a Cyclops, a one-eyed giant, and was thought to have lived on the island of Sicily. *ODYSSEUS*, during his long journey home, came to the island and asked for hospitality, but called himself Nobody. Polyphemus indeed proved to be a dangerous host and treated the Greeks as part of his flock, shutting them up in his cave and eating them one by one for his evening meal. Odysseus dared not kill the Cyclops during the night because his men lacked the strength to move the boulder blocking the entrance to the cave. So Odysseus thought of a cunning plan to enable their escape. He got Polyphemus drunk on wine and then put out his single eye with a stake. The injured giant roared with

pain, but in response to the other Cyclopes' questions he cried out that he was being attacked by Nobody, so they went away, considering him drunk or mad. In the morning Polyphemus opened the entrance to the cave to let out his flock and felt the back of each animal as it passed to ensure no men escaped. But Odysseus and his men tied themselves to the undersides of the sheep and managed to leave undetected. For this crime against his son, Poseidon promised revenge on Odysseus.

POSEIDON was the son of *CRONOS* and *RHEA*. He was the Greek god of the sea, and the equivalent of the Roman *NEPTUNE*. He was particularly associated with horses and bulls. After the overthrow of Cronos, his three sons divided the world between them:

POSEIDON, god of the oceans, rode the waves in a chariot drawn by golden sea-horses. With his three-pronged trident, symbol of his power, he shattered the rocks, called forth storms and shook the earth. (NEPTUNE AND HIS HORSES BY E K BIRCE, CANVAS, C. 1880.) ؟ .

ZEUS took the sky, *HADES* the underworld and Poseidon the sea, while the land was ruled by all three. It was agreed that Zeus was the senior deity, though Poseidon frequently asserted his independence. Once he even chained up Zeus, with the aid of *HERA*, Zeus' wife, and his daughter *ATHENA*. Possibly because his element was the tempestuous sea, Poseidon was thought of as an unruly god. Earthquakes were attributed to his anger, and Hades was often afraid that the roof of the underworld would cave in because of the shaking Poseidon gave the earth.

Poseidon was pictured riding the deep in a chariot pulled by golden seahorses. In his hands was a mighty trident, a weapon capable of stirring the waters to fury, like the sudden violence of an Aegean storm. His wife was Amphitrite, a sea nymph whose name recalls that of the sea monster Triton. This fearful pre-Greek creature was turned by the Greeks into the merman. One of Poseidon's children by Amphitrite bore this name. However, the sea god had many other offspring by other partners. He even mated with the *GORGON* Medusa, much to the annoyance of the goddess Athena. From the severed head of Medusa sprang the winged horse *PEGASUS*, surely a favourite of Poseidon. Worship of the sea god was widespread among

PRIAM, the king of Troy, savours a moment of rare peace with Helen on the city walls, as she describes the kings and chieftains of the Greek host, who circle the city on the plains below. (ILLUSTRATION FROM STORIES OF GREECE AND ROME, 1930.)

the Greeks, although the maritime state of Athens did not always enjoy the best relations with him.

Because the Athenians chose Athena as the deity of their city, Poseidon flooded the countryside until Zeus brought about an understanding. The temple of Athena stood on the acropolis in Athens and Poseidon's own sanctuary was conspicuously sited on Cape Sunium, which majestically juts out into the Aegean Sea.

Another naval power that offended Poseidon was Crete. When its ruler, King *MINOS*, asked

PSYCHE was so beautiful that Aphrodite became jealous and sent her son, Eros, to inspire Psyche with a passion for an ugly man, but he was so entranced when he saw her that he dropped an arrow on his foot, and so fell in love with her himself. (CUPID AND PSYCHE BY FRANCOIS GERARD, CANVAS, 1798.)

the sea god for a sign, a white bull emerged from the waves. Religious custom required Minos to sacrifice the animal, but he chose not to do so, with the result that his own wife *PASIPHAE* became the bull's lover. Their strange union produced the *MINOTAUR*, the bull-headed man slain by Athenian hero *THESEUS*. (See also *FORCES OF NATURE*)

PRIAM was the son of Laomedon and the nymph Strymo, daughter of the River Scamander. By the time of the Trojan War Priam, the king of Troy, was already an old man, father of fifty sons, some by his queen Hecuba, the rest by other women. Although he disapproved of the conflict with the Greeks and its cause, Priam was always kind to *HELEN* throughout the long siege. She had eloped to Troy with his son *PARIS*. Priam was killed in the courtyard of his palace when the Greeks sacked Troy.

PROMETHEUS was a son of the *TITAN* Iapetus and one of the older Greek gods who sided with *ZEUS* in his fight against his father *CRONOS*. His fame was due to his affection for mankind, to whom he gave fire. Zeus, the leader of the new and stronger gods, had hidden fire away, but Prometheus stole it and brought it to earth with him. But this drew Prometheus into conflict with Zeus, who chained the rebellious Titan to a rock and sent an eagle to eat his liver. As this organ was immortal, it grew at night as fast as the bird could consume it by day. Prometheus was only released when he gave Zeus the information that the sea nymph *THETIS*, whom both Zeus and *POSEIDON* were pursuing, would give birth to a son

mightier than his father. By making sure that Thetis married a mortal ruler, the newly victorious gods protected themselves because her son turned out to be the warrior *ACHILLES*, an invincible but not immortal fighter.

Zeus' anger with mankind was on occasion explained by poor sacrifices. But Prometheus himself was not a straightforward helper either. He gave fire, an essential of civilized

life, but other gifts were perhaps less helpful. Out of the flaming forge came weapons of war, plus all the miseries that follow the disruption of a simple way of life.

PSYCHE in Greek religious belief was the "soul", but in mythology she was represented as a princess so beautiful that people adored her instead of *APHRODITE*. To put an end to this sacrilege, Aphrodite

sent her son *EROS* to make Psyche fall in love with the ugliest creature he could find. But when Eros saw her he fell in love and forgot his mother's command. They became lovers, though Eros forbade Psyche ever to look upon him. When at last she did, he fled in fear of what Aphrodite would do to him now the secret was out. In the end, however, *ZEUS* agreed that the lovers could be united for eternity.

GIANTS

GIANTS SYMBOLIZE IMMENSE PRIMAL forces, neither good nor bad, but larger than life. While Greek giants could be "gentle" guardians, such as Talos, the gigantic bronze man who defended the island of Crete, others, such as Geryon, were predators, preying on unwary travellers. Equally, the Cyclopes were orginally creative beings, making armour and ornaments in the forge of Hephaistos, and building the massive city walls of Tiryns. Later on they were also portrayed as moody, rebellious shepherds who ignored divine laws and preyed on mortals. The gods themselves are gigantic, especially the older gods, reflecting their primal nature, such as the Titans, and the Giants, who were beings with mighty torsos and snake-like legs. The Titans overthrew their father Ouranos, replacing him with Cronos, who was in his turn dethroned by his son Zeus. Such a cosmic struggle between older primal gods and a younger generation is a common feature in world mythology.

ATLAS (right), the "bearer" or "endurer", bore the heavens on his shoulders, as punishment for having fought against Zeus with the other divine Titans. The myth probably arose from the impression that great mountains bear the heavens. In another story, Atlas, because he refused Perseus shelter, was turned to a stony mountain, named after him. Here, the heavens are depicted as a celestial globe showing the constellations. (THE FARNESE ATLAS, MARBLE, C. AD 200.)

THE CYCLOPES
(left), fabulous race of one-eyed giants, were initially regarded as creative craftsmen who helped Hephaistos in his volcanic forge, crafting special armour, such as Hades' invisible helmet, Zeus' thunderbolt and Poseidon's trident. Yet they were also portrayed as lawless, man-eating shepherds. One such, Polyphemus, here looms over Odysseus and his comrades who have rashly strayed into his den. (ILLUSTRATION FROM STORIES FROM HOMER, 1885.)

ORION (above left), who was one of Poseidon's unruly sons, was a gigantic and handsome hunter, who could walk through the oceans with his feet on the seabed and his head above the waves. Like his giant brother, the one-eyed Polyphemus, Orion was blinded in a quarrel, but his eyes were healed by the radiance of the sun god Helios. There are many differing stories concerning his death, but according to one myth, the love that Eos, the goddess of the dawn, felt for Orion was such that it caused divine jealousy until Artemis was persuaded to shoot him with an arrow on behalf of the gods. He was then raised to the stars to form a constellation. (ILLUSTRATION BY NICK BEALE, 1995.)

CACUS (above), son of Hephaistos, and a goat-like giant, preyed on human beings who strayed by his cave near Rome. Cacus stole Geryon's red cattle from Heracles while he slept, and hid them in his cave. However, the cattle began to bellow and Heracles came and slayed Cacus, retrieving the cattle that he had originally stolen from Geryon. (HERACLES SLAYS THE GIANT CACUS BY GIAMBATTISTA LANGETTI, C. 1670.)

R

PYGMALION was a king of Cyprus. According to the Greeks, he commissioned an ivory statue of his ideal woman, since no real one measured up to his expectations. Not surprisingly, Pygmalion fell hopelessly in love with the statue, an even more unsatisfactory fate than he had previously suffered. Because of his obviously genuine disappointment, the love goddess *APHRODITE* brought the statue to life and made it love him. Some traditions tell how the couple had a daughter named Paphos, who gave her name to the town.

PYTHON see *MONSTERS AND FABULOUS BEASTS*

REMUS AND ROMULUS were the twin sons of *RHEA SILVIA* and *MARS*, and the two founders of Rome. Rhea Silvia had been the only child of King Numitor of Alba Longa. When Numitor's brother *AMULIUS* deposed him, he also forced Rhea Silvia to become a Vestal Virgin, thereby ensuring that there would be no other claimant to the throne. But the war god Mars raped her in his sacred grove, and Rhea Silvia gave birth to Romulus and Remus.

Amulius ordered his servants to kill the new-born twins, but instead they cast them on the Tiber. Their cradle was carried swiftly away and eventually came to rest on a mudbank. To look after his children Mars sent his sacred animal, the wolf. Later Romulus and Remus were discovered in the wolf's lair by a shepherd named Faustulus, who took the foundlings home. So they were raised as shepherds, although the ability of the brothers to lead others, and to fight, eventually became widely known. One day Numitor met Remus and guessed who he was and so the lost grandchildren were reunited with him, but they were not content to live quietly in Alba Longa. Instead, they went off and founded a city of their own – Rome. A quarrel, however,

REMUS AND ROMULUS (above) were set adrift on the Tiber by Amulius, but the cradle came ashore and was found by a shewolf. The twins (left) march triumphantly from Alba Longa. On the left, Romulus bears aloft the head of their treacherous uncle, Amulius. On the right, Remus carries the wild head of Camers, a priest who counselled the king to drown the twins. (ILLUSTRATIONS FROM LAYS OF ANCIENT ROME, 1881.)

RHEA SILVIA (below), a vestal virgin, was loved by Mars, and bore him twin sons, Romulus and Remus. For violating the laws of her holy order, she was thrown into the Tiber, but the god of the river, Tibernus, saved and married her. (MARS WITH RHEA SILVIA BY FRANCESCO DEL COSSA, FRESCO, 1476.)

S

SARPEDON *is lifted by Thanatos (Death) and Hypnos (Sleep) from the battlefield of Troy. This Lycian ruler, an ally of the Trojans, was later confused with Zeus' son of the same name.* (ILLUSTRATION FROM STORIES FROM HOMER, 1885.)

ensued and Romulus killed Remus, possibly with a blow from a spade. Though he showed remorse at the funeral, Romulus ruled Rome with a strong hand and the city flourished. It was a haven for runaway slaves and other fugitives, but suffered from a shortage of women, which Romulus overcame by arranging for the capture of Sabine women at a nearby festival. After a reign of forty years he disappeared to become, some of his subjects believed, the war god Quirinus.

The Romulus and Remus myth was as popular as that of *AENEAS*. From the beginning of republican times, around 507 BC, the she-wolf became the symbol of Roman nationhood. (See also *FOUNDERS*)

RHADAMANTHYS was the son of *EUROPA* and *ZEUS*, and the brother of *MINOS* and *SARPEDON*. According to one tradition he married *ALCMENE* after the death of her husband Amphitryon. Others say that he was one of the three Judges of the Dead and lived in the paradise of Elysium, in the far west.

RHEA was the daughter of Ouranos and *GAIA*. As the wife of *CRONOS*, she bore six children, the hearth goddess Hestia, the goddess of vegetation *DEMETER*, the earth goddess *HERA*, the underworld god *HADES*, the sea god *POSEIDON* and *ZEUS*, the sky god. Cronos, having learned that one of his children would depose him, swallowed all of them, except for Zeus, as they were born. Rhea substituted the baby Zeus with a stone wrapped in swaddling clothes. He was then taken to the island of Crete, where the worship of Rhea was notable, and was secretly raised.

RHEA SILVIA was the mother of *REMUS AND ROMULUS*. She was the only child of Numitor, the king of Alba Longa. When he was deposed by his younger brother *AMULIUS*, the new king forced Rhea Silvia to become a Vestal Virgin. However, Amulius could not guarantee Rhea Silvia's protection from the attentions of the gods and she was raped by *MARS* in his sacred grove. Her twin sons were then cast into the swollen Tiber, where she may have been drowned.

ROMULUS see *REMUS*

SARPEDON was the son of *ZEUS* and *EUROPA*. He was adopted by Asterius, king of Crete. Sarpedon quarrelled with one of his brothers, *MINOS*, over the throne of Crete and fled to Asia Minor, where he founded the Greek city of Miletus. It is said that Zeus allowed him to live to a great age.

SATURN was an ancient Italian corn god, the Roman equivalent of the Greek god *CRONOS*, though he had more in common with the goddess *DEMETER*. He was believed to have ruled the earth during a lost Golden Age. His festival, the Saturnalia, was celebrated in Rome over seven days and was held at the end of December.

THE SATYRS were the wild spirits of Greek and Roman woodlands. Their bestial nature was shown in their horse-like or goat-like appearance. They were mainly associated with *DIONYSUS*, the Greek god of vegetation, wine and ecstasy, and played a crucial role in his festivals. (See also *MONSTERS AND FABULOUS BEASTS*)

SATURN, *"the sower", was also regarded as an early king of Latium during a lost Golden Age. Here, with his daughter Juno, he is wearing exotic robes, reflecting the Roman belief that he was a foreigner who fled to Latium to escape Zeus.* (JUNO AND SATURN BY PAOLO VERONESE, CANVAS 1553–55.)

SCYLLA see *MONSTERS AND FABULOUS BEASTS*

SEMELE see *LOVERS OF ZEUS*

SIBYL, in Roman mythology, was the prophetess who dwelt near Cumae, in southern Italy. One tale explains how she became immortal but still grew old. She refused the favours of *APOLLO*, the god of prophecy, so he condemned her to an endless old age. She was already ancient when *AENEAS* consulted her about his visit to the underworld. Another story concerns the famous Sibylline Books, which were a collection of oracles that detailed Rome's destiny. These were offered for sale to Rome during the rule of the Etruscan kings.

SIBYL, the gifted seer, foretold the destiny of Rome as predicted in the Sibylline Books, which became a vital source of religious inspiration and guidance. (SIBYL AND THE RUINS OF ROME BY GIOVANNI PANNINI, CANVAS, 1750.)

SISYPHUS, the slyest and craftiest of men, was punished for his sins by being condemned forever to push a marble block up a hill only to see it roll down again. (ILLUSTRATION BY NICK BEALE, 1995.)

When the offer was refused, Sibyl burned three books and offered the other six at the same price, but the offer was still refused, so three more were burnt and then she offered the last three at the original price. In haste the Romans closed the deal before all the irreplaceable oracles were totally destroyed.

SILENUS was a jovial satyr, much given to sleep and drink. Bald but hairy, and as fat and round as his wine-bag, he was more often drunk than sober, but when drunk or asleep, he became an inspired and much sought-after prophet. (ILLUSTRATION FROM DICTIONARY OF CLASSICAL ANTIQUITIES, 1891.)

SILENUS

SILENUS was variously described as the son either of the Greek messenger god *HERMES*, or of *PAN*, the goat-like god of the pastures. He was usually portrayed as the elderly companion of *DIONYSUS*, the Greek god of vegetation, wine and ecstasy. In appearance Silenus was a fat, bald man with the tail and ears of a horse. Because of the kindness shown to Silenus by King *MIDAS* of Phrygia, Dionysus granted the king his famous and short-sighted wish for a golden touch.

SIRENS see *MONSTERS AND FABULOUS BEASTS*

SISYPHUS was the son of King Aelus of Thessaly and Enarete. He was known to the Greeks as the craftiest of men, and suffered for his trickery by endless labour in Tartarus, a place of punishment beneath the underworld. Sisyphus is credited with the foundation of Corinth. According to one tradition, he angered *ZEUS* by revealing that the god had abducted the daughter of a river god. Zeus therefore sent Thanatos, god of death, to take Sisyphus to the underworld. Somehow the ingenious king temporarily made Thanatos his own prisoner. When the gods again claimed him, Sisyphus tricked *HADES* into letting him return to earth. Having told his wife to do

nothing if he died, Sisyphus said that his body was unburied and the customary offerings to the dead had not been made. He must therefore see to the arrangements himself before he could be said to be truly dead. Finally, Zeus lost patience and condemned Sisyphus to Tartarus to pay for his lifelong impiety. For the rest of eternity he had to roll a block of stone to the top of a hill only to see it roll back again as it reached the crest.

THE SPHINX, according to Greek mythology, was the daughter of Echidna, either by *TYPHON* or by Orthus. A monster with the face and breasts of a woman, the body of a lion and the wings of a bird, she was sent as a curse on the city of Thebes by the goddess *HERA*. The Sphinx guarded a pass to the city and asked all who wished to pass a riddle. Those who failed to give the correct answer were eaten. The riddle was: "What thing walks on four legs in the morning, on three in the evening, and is weakest when it walks on four?" The correct answer was Man, because he walks on four as a baby and leans on a stick in old age. When *OEDIPUS* gave the correct answer, the Sphinx hurled herself over a cliff and died. As a reward for destroying the monster, he was made king of Thebes and married

THE SPHINX, or throttler, perched on a rock at a pass to the city of Thebes and challenged all travellers with a riddle, devouring all who failed the test. In Moreau's chilling scene, the queenly, feline Sphinx paws her victims. (THE TRIUMPHANT SPHINX BY GUSTAVE MOREAU, WATERCOLOUR, 1888.)

the widowed queen Jocasta, and so fulfilled his tragic destiny because the queen was his mother.

The Greek Sphinx should not be confused with the Egyptian Sphinx. The Great Sphinx at Giza was the protector of the pyramids and scourge of the sun god Ra.

TARPEIA was a Roman heroine, the daughter of Spurius Tarpeius, the commander of the Capitoline fortress at Rome. She may have played a role in saving the city. A war between Romans and Sabines, a people of central Italy, had been provoked by *ROMULUS*' abduction of Sabine women to provide wives for Rome's men. One tradition says that Tarpeia let the Sabines into her father's fortress after making them promise to give her what they wore on their left arms, their shields. Another mentions only their bracelets. In the first version the Sabines realized that they had been tricked and threw their shields at her and killed her. The Romans could not agree how Tarpeia died but, whatever her motive was, real traitors were always thrown from the Tarpeian Rock.

TARPEIA, a Roman heroine, was crushed to death by the shields of the Sabines as they stormed through the gates of the Capitoline fortress. According to one legend, she had lured the Sabines inside, to trap them, so giving her life for Rome. (ILLUSTRATION FROM STORIES FROM LIVY, 1885.)

TARQUINIUS SUPERBUS

was the seventh and last Etruscan king of Rome, who reigned in the sixth century BC. His youngest son, Tarquinius Sextus, caused the end of the monarchy by raping the Roman matron *LUCRETIA*, which caused *BRUTUS* to lead a rebellion. Tarquinius was defeated and the Roman republic was established.

TARQUINIUS SEXTUS, as he fled the battlefield of Lake Regillus, was struck from behind. His inglorious death was recounted in Macaulay's lays: "And in the back false Sextus felt the Roman steel./ And wriggling in the dust he died, like a worm beneath the wheel." (ILLUSTRATION FROM LAYS OF ANCIENT ROME, 1881.)

THESEUS

was the son either of *POSEIDON* or *AEGEUS* the king of Athens. His mother was Aethra. The childless Aegeus consulted the Delphic Oracle and was told not to untie his wine skin until he returned home. He did not understand what the oracle meant and so visited his friend King Pittheus of Troezen. Realizing that Aegeus was going to beget a powerful son immediately after the celebration feast for his safe return to Athens, Pittheus made his guest drunk and put him to bed with his daughter Aethra, and so Theseus was conceived. Before he left for home, Aegeus took the pregnant Aethra to a great boulder underneath which he placed his sword and sandals. He told her that, should she have a son, she must wait until he was strong enough to raise the boulder before she sent him to his father's court. After Aegeus' departure the wily Pittheus said his daughter's lover was really Poseidon.

When Theseus came of age, Aethra explained that he was heir to the Athenian throne and he retrieved the sword and sandals. On his journey to Athens he slew several desperate bandits, a fearsome son of *HEPHAISTOS,* and a dreadful sow, the daughter of the monster *TYPHON.* At Eleusis, then a kingdom separate from Athens, Theseus was forced to accept the challenge of a wrestling match with its king, Cercyon. The aggressive ruler died as a result of the contest, so Theseus became king of Eleusis, which he later added to the Athenian kingdom.

On his arrival in Athens, Theseus learned that his father Aegeus was hardly able to hold on to the throne. Not only was the apparently heirless king challenged by the fifty sons of his half-brother Pallas, but, worse still, Aegeus had fallen under the spell of *MEDEA*, the former wife of *JASON* and a powerful witch. She hoped that her own son Medus would succeed Aegeus. Although Theseus hid his true identity, Medea knew who he was and persuaded Aegeus to let her poison the mighty stranger at a banquet. Theseus was saved when

TARQUINIUS SUPERBUS, a cruel and tyrannical king, sired a no less cruel and ignoble son, Tarquinius Sextus, who raped the Roman matron, Lucretia. She, in shame, killed herself. The outrage provoked an uprising and Tarquinius was overthrown. (THE RAPE OF LUCRETIA BY PALO IL GIOVANO, CANVAS, C. 1570.)

the king recognized his sword as the hero carved the meat. The plot was revealed, Medea fled from Athens with her son, and Aegeus named Theseus as his successor.

The next cycle of Theseus' exploits was designed to secure the safety of Athens. First, he dealt with Pallas' sons. Then he killed a wild bull that was ravaging Marathon, to the north-east of the city. He also overcame the *MINOTAUR*, the strange offspring of *PASIPHAE*, the wife of King *MINOS* of Crete. An annual tribute of young Athenians was fed to the Minotaur, which lived in the Labyrinth that had been designed by *DAEDALUS*. No one had ever managed to find their way through this maze, so when Theseus volunteered to confront

THESEUS' exploits are illustrated on an intricate Roman mosaic. At the centre of the Labyrinth Theseus battles with the Minotaur. On the left, Theseus and Ariadne pledge their love at the altar, while at the top, Theseus sets Ariadne ashore, deserting the unfortunate maiden on Dia, on the right. (THE EXPLOITS OF THESEUS, MOSAIC. C. AD 200.)

the Minotaur his father despaired. It was agreed that if Theseus should, by some miracle, survive, he was to change the sail of the tribute ship from black to white on the homeward voyage.

At Minos' palace in Knossos the goddess *APHRODITE* gave Theseus an invaluable ally in *ARIADNE*, a daughter of the Cretan king who fell in love with the hero. Princess Ariadne knew that the Labyrinth was so complex that the only way out was to follow back a thread fastened to the entrance. After Theseus had promised to marry her, Ariadne gave him a ball of thread and a sword. The hero entered the Labyrinth, slew the Minotaur and then set sail for Athens with Ariadne and the rest of the Athenian party. He then left the princess on the nearby island of Dia. It is thought that he was in love with another woman, but whatever the reason he was soon repaid for his heartlessness. As the ship approached Athens, Theseus forgot to change the sail to indicate to his father that he was alive. Aegeus saw a black sail and, thinking his son dead, threw himself off the Athenian acropolis.

The suicide meant that Theseus was now king of Athens, and he joined all the communities of Attica into one state. Apart from enlarging Athens' territory, Theseus also undertook a number of heroic exploits. On one expedition he captured Hippolyta, the queen of the *AMAZONS*, who bore him a son, Hippolytus, but she died shortly afterwards. Theseus gave the accursed *OEDIPUS* and his daughter *ANTIGONE* sanctuary at Colonus,

near Athens. But discord entered his own house when his second wife *PHAEDRA*, another daughter of Minos, came to desire her stepson Hippolytus, to the young man's horror. Although he promised to keep her passion a secret, Phaedra was so humiliated by his rejection that she hanged herself and left Theseus a letter in which she accused Hippolytus of attempted rape. He was exiled and died in a chariot accident before his father discovered the truth. In another version, Hippolytus was killed by a sea monster that was raised by Theseus' anger, and Phaedra, filled with remorse, killed herself .

Theseus later seized the twelve-year-old *HELEN*, daughter of *ZEUS*, as a future wife. He claimed that only she was worthy enough to be his wife, possibly because of her divine father. But she had powerful kinsmen, and her two brothers, the *DIOSCURI*, defeated the Athenians and drove Theseus abroad. He died on the island of Scyros, when its king, fearing the presence of such a man, pushed him over a cliff as he admired the view. It was believed that in the fifth century BC, the Athenian admiral Cimon went to Scyros and brought the hero's bones back to Athens, where they were kept in a shrine.

THESEUS AND SINIS circle each other in a battle of wits and wills. Sinis, the pine-bender, was a robber who killed by tying his victim between two bent pine trees and then letting them spring upright, thereby tearing the man apart. (THESEUS AND SINIS, RED-FIGURE, C. 490 BC.)

FOUNDERS

THE ANCIENTS BELIEVED that many of their fabulous cities were founded by the pioneering heroes and heroines of legend, such as Cadmus of Thebes and Dido of Carthage. In Classical mythology, the heroic ethic combined with the Greek ideal of *polis,* or city-state, to create a variety of dynamic founders who built such celebrated cities as Athens, Mycenae, Sparta and Thebes. The Greek *polis* was an autonomous, independent community of citizens, slaves and foreigners who gathered within and around a fortified city. Each city honoured its own hero who was also often its legendary founder, such as Perseus of Mycenae and Lacedaemon of Sparta. Mythic founders were innovative, godlike heroes, guided by destiny and deity to create a fresh, vibrant culture. Apart from leading a tribe to a bright new land, and building a strong citadel, founders often developed helpful new ways and customs: Cecrops of Athens, for instance, encouraged religious worship, while Cadmus of Thebes introduced an alphabet of 16 Phoenician letters. A city or tribe sometimes honoured its founder hero by sharing his name, such as Ilium, named after Ilus, the Trojans after Tros, and Rome after Romulus.

CECROPS (above), one of the mythic founders of Athens, and the first king of Attica, is depicted with a serpent's tail, recalling his origin as an aborigine of Attica. He divided the natives into twelve communities and founded the Acropolis, the stronghold of Athens, which was also named Cecropia after him. An innovator, Cecrops abolished blood sacrifice, encouraged the worship of Zeus and Athena and introduced basic laws of property, politics and marriage. (ILLUSTRATION FROM DICTIONARY OF CLASSICAL ANTIQUITIES, 1891.)

ATHENS (right), the splendid capital of Attica, owed its origin both to Cecrops, who founded the ancient Acropolis, and to Theseus who united Attica's twelve states into one, and made Athens their capital. The city divided into the upper town, or Acropolis, and the lower walled town, as well as three harbour towns. The Acropolis, seen here, rises on a steep rock, its summit once crowned with sparkling temples. Most famous of all was the Parthenon, built of Pentelic marble in pure Doric style and adorned within and without with gilded and painted sculpture. North of the Parthenon rose a great statute of the city's goddess, Athena, whose helmet and spear were seen from the sea. Athens, the artistic centre of the ancient world, reached its greatest splendour in the time of Pericles (460-429 BC). (THE ACROPOLIS BY CARL HAAG, CANVAS, C. 1890.)

ROME (above), the world-ruling capital of Italy, situated on the River Tiber, was founded in c. AD 753 by the mythic hero, Romulus. The Colosseum, seen here, was one of the greatest monuments of the ancient city, initiated by the Emperor Vespasian and inaugurated by his son, Titus, in 80 AD. The gigantic amphitheatre was designed to accommodate 87,000 spectators around circular tiers, overlooking a central arena. In front of the amphitheatre rises the triumphal Arch of Titus, erected in AD 81, to celebrate Titus' victorious campaign in Judaea. (VIEW OF THE COLOSSEUM BY LIPOT KERPEL, CANVAS, 1846.)

ROMULUS (above), the mythic founder of Rome, was suckled at birth by a she-wolf, with his twin brother, Remus. The twins had been cast into the River Tiber by their great-uncle Amulius who coveted the throne of Alba Longa, but their divine father, Mars, sent his sacred animal, the wolf, to save his sons. Later the twins were rescued by the good shepherd Faustulus who raised them as his own. Once grown, they left Alba Longa to found Rome, but the belligerent brothers bickered over the site and name of the future city, and Romulus slew Remus, setting the warlike tone of the future city. (ILLUSTRATION BY PAUL WOODROFFE, C.1920.)

DIDO (above), legendary founder of Carthage, supervises a team of architects and masons on the left bank of the bay. Dido had fled to Africa from Tyre in Phoenicia where her husband, Sychaeus, had been murdered by her brother, Pygmalion, who coveted the throne of Tyre. On the coast of North Africa, the local king, Iarbus, sold Dido as much land as she might contain in a bull's hide. By artfully cutting the hide into narrow strips, Dido managed to secure enough land to build a citadel, named Byrsa, or "hide". Around this fort, the fabulous city of Carthage flourished from 853 BC. On the right bank, the still, calm tomb of Sychaeus rises beside a new sapling, symbolizing the growth of Carthage. The girls and boys playing on the bank represent the future power and generations of Carthage; while the rising sun, likewise, symbolizes the rising power of the bright new city. (DIDO BUILDING CARTHAGE BY J W TURNER, CANVAS, 1815.)

TROY (above) or Ilium arose on the grassy plain of Troas by the foot of Mount Ida. Founded by the mythic hero, Ilus, son of Tros, the ancient city was named Ilium and Troja after both father and son. The famous walls of Troy were built by the gods, Poseidon and Apollo, in the reign of Ilus' son, Laomedon. The next king, Priam, ruled during the tragic Trojan War, provoked by Paris' abduction of Helen, wife of the Greek chieftain, Menelaus. At a critical stage in the ten-year siege, the Greeks dreamt up the Trojan Horse, a massive wooden model hiding within its hollow belly an army of Greeks. (THE TROJAN HORSE BY NICCOLO DELL' ABBATE, TEMPERA, C. 1560.)

THETIS was a sea nymph and the daughter of Nereus and Doris. She was the mother of ACHILLES, the great Greek hero. Because it was known that she was fated to bear a son mightier than his father, both ZEUS and POSEIDON gave up all thoughts of possessing Thetis, who was much admired on Mount Olympus, the home of the gods. Instead, Zeus ensured that she became the wife of a mortal king, Peleus of Phthia. Thetis bore him seven sons, but she was dissatisfied with the mortality of her children. She tested them with fire and boiling water, but none could withstand such treatment, not even the youngest boy Achilles until Thetis dipped him in the Styx, the river of the dead. Even then, she forgot to wet the heel she held him by, with the result that he was not totally immortal. About this time Thetis left Peleus and returned to the sea, although she continued to assist Achilles as far as she could during his eventful life.

TIRESIAS, in Greek mythology, was the son of a nymph, Chariclo, and Everes, descendant of one of CADMUS' own men. The blind seer of Thebes, he was so wise that even his ghost had kept its wits, and not been overcome by forgetfulness like the other inhabitants of the underworld. At the edge of the world Tiresias advised ODYSSEUS that he would never return home to Ithaca if he harmed the cattle of HELIOS, the sun god.

During his lifetime Tiresias played a part in several myths. For instance, he warned King Pentheus in vain about the identity of DIONYSUS, when that powerful god

THETIS, although an immortal sea nymph, loved her mortal son, Achilles, with all the care and tenderness of a human mother. She shared his sorrows, and rushed to his aid, ever conscious of his mortality. Here she brings him some splendid armour as he mourns Patroclus' death. (ILLUSTRATION FROM STORIES FROM HOMER, 1885.)

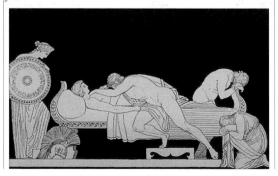

came in disguise to Thebes. As a result of Pentheus' refusal to listen to the seer, he gravely offended Dionysus and was torn to pieces by the god's frenzied worshippers, the maenads. Tiresias also confirmed the pronouncement of the Delphic Oracle that it was indeed King OEDIPUS who was personally responsible for the plague which troubled the Thebans.

The blindness of Tiresias was explained by two tales. One account states that the affliction was a punishment for seeing the goddess ATHENA bathing. The other story is a somewhat less traditional explanation. Tiresias one day saw snakes mating and struck them with a staff, whereupon he turned into a woman. After living as a woman for a period of time,

TIRESIAS, the legendary blind seer, advised many heroes. Some listened to him, but others, to their cost, ignored him, such as hard-headed Creon, or short-sighted Pentheus. His golden staff was a gift from Athena and enabled him to find his way like a sighted man. (ILLUSTRATION FROM DICTIONARY OF CLASSICAL ANTIQUITIES, 1891.)

the seer witnessed the same sight and became a man again. His unique experience led to Tiresias being asked by ZEUS and HERA, the chief Greek deities, to settle a dispute between them as to which sex got most pleasure out of love. When he said that it was the female, Hera blinded him, but Zeus awarded him a long life and the power of prophecy.

THE TITANS and Titanesses, according to Greek mythology, were the children of Ouranos, the sky, and GAIA, the earth. These gigantic beings were the older gods who ruled before the Olympian gods, who were the brothers, sisters and children of ZEUS. The Titans included CRONOS, RHEA, Coeus, Metis, Mnemosyne and Hyperion.

They came to power after Cronos emasculated his father Ouranos with a sickle provided by Gaia, his long-suffering mother. The eventual battle between the older generation of gods, the Titans led by Cronos, and the younger generation, the Olympians led by his son Zeus, lasted ten years and shook the universe like no other conflict. Afterwards Zeus threw those deities who had opposed him down to Tartarus, which was a land beneath the underworld.

The battle against the Titans should not be confused with the Olympian gods' later struggle with the GIANTS. In order to win this terrible confrontation, Zeus knew that he would require the help of a mighty, mortal champion, and so he fathered by ALCMENE the greatest of the Greek heroes HERACLES.

THE TITANS were gigantic beings who ruled the earth before the Olympian gods. They overthrew their tyrannical father, Ouranus, and put Cronos in his place. Cronos, in his turn, swallowed all his children, except Zeus, who was raised in secrecy. Here, Rhea presents Cronos with a stone wrapped in swaddling clothes instead of the baby Zeus who is safely hidden away. (RHEA AND CRONOS, RELIEF, C. 400 BC.)

supreme deity, but the recently victorious ZEUS destroyed him with a mighty thunderbolt. The volcanic activity of Mount Aetna in Sicily was believed to be caused by Typhon's imprisonment beneath the crater. The struggle between Typhon and Zeus was an evenly balanced fight, however. At one point Zeus was left helpless in a cave, weaponless and without his sinews. Fortunately the messenger god HERMES came to his aid on this occasion. Before his final defeat, Typhon sired the Chimaera, the huge sea monster killed by the hero PERSEUS.

VENUS was the Roman equivalent of APHRODITE, the Greek love goddess. Venus was originally a goddess connected with agriculture, but when she was identified with Aphrodite she took on a more active and different role in mythology. One of her most crucial actions was to return AENEAS' spear after it had stuck in a tree stump during his fight with the Italian champion Turnus. Indeed, in some versions Aeneas is her son.

TYPHON (left), a fire-breathing serpent, was imprisoned beneath the crater when the volcano at Mount Aetna erupted. Symbolizing the dark forces of earth, he sired monsters as hideous as himself: the flaming Chimaera and snarling Cerberus. (GREEK VASE, C. 600 BC.)

TYPHON was a terrible, serpent-like monster whose eyes shot out flames. He was conceived by GAIA, mother earth, when she was banished to Tartarus along with the other defeated TITANS.

According to the Greeks, Typhon endeavoured to establish himself as the ruler of the world, the

VENUS, the Roman goddess of love, is rarely portrayed without her capricious and cherubic son, Cupid. This graceful portrait of her (see right) by the French artist Boucher, full of light and charm, owes much to Venus of Arles. (ILLUSTRATION FROM DICTIONARY OF CLASSICAL ANTIQUITIES, 1891.)

Z

VESTA was the Roman equivalent of the Greek goddess Hestia, who was the goddess of the hearth. Vesta, however, was worshipped both as the guardian of the domestic hearth and also as the personification of the ceremonial flame. Ceremonies in her honour were conducted by the Vestal Virgins, who were young girls from noble families who took vows of chastity for the thirty years during which they served her. Vesta's chief festival, the Vestalia, was held on 7 June.

VIRGINIA was the daughter of a Roman centurion named Virginius and, as with *LUCRETIA*, she was a Roman connected with a major constitutional change. Whereas Lucretia's rape and suicide led to

VIRGINIA (above) dies in the arms of her father who killed her to release her from bondage to the corrupt Appius Claudius. He then cursed the Claudian line, who were overthrown by the outraged Romans. (ILLUSTRATION FROM STORIES FROM LIVY, 1885.)

VULCAN (below), Roman god of fire, presents Venus with glorious arms for her son, Aeneas. The golden sword was described in the Aeneid as loaded with doom. (VENUS IN THE FORGE OF VULCAN BY FRANCOIS BOUCHER, CANVAS, 1757.)

the dethronement and exile of the Etruscan monarchy, the death of Virginia was a major factor in the ending of an aristocratic tyranny in 449 BC.

The lust of a corrupt official, Appius Claudius, for Virginia knew no bounds. He even dared to claim that the girl was his slave and used the law to have her handed over to him. At the last moment her father stabbed Virginia through the heart, declaring that her death was less painful to suffer than her dishonour. The Roman army rose to support him, along with the poorer citizens not then bearing arms, and checks were placed thereafter on magistrates' powers.

VULCAN was the Roman smith god and the equivalent of the Greek *HEPHAISTOS*. He was widely associated with Maia and *VESTA*, who were both goddesses of the hearth. His smithy was believed to be situated underneath Mount Aetna in Sicily. At the Vulcanalia festival, which was held on 23 August, fish and small animals were thrown into a fire.

XANTHUS was said to be the off-spring of the *HARPY* Podarge and *ZEPHYRUS*, the west wind. He was one of two immortal horses belonging to the great Greek champion *ACHILLES* and had the power of human speech. Achilles inherited the horses from his father, King Peleus of Phthia, who had received them as a present from the gods on his wedding to the sea nymph *THETIS*. Achilles took Xanthus and Balius, the other wonderful steed, to Troy with him. They performed extremely well on the battlefield, although they seemed unnerved by the slaughter. When Achilles questioned them, Xanthus warned the champion that his own death was near, at which point the horse was struck dumb by the *FURIES*.

ZEPHYRUS see *FORCES OF NATURE*

ZEUS, all-powerful father of the gods, enthroned on Olympus, is begged by Thetis to help her son, Achilles; she tugs his beard and clasps his knee in her affectionate way, as described in the Iliad, and the great god nods his assent. (ZEUS AND THETIS BY JEAN-AUGUSTE INGRES, CANVAS, 1811.)

After the overthrow of Cronos, Zeus divided up the world between himself and his two brothers, HADES and POSEIDON. Zeus chose to rule the sky, Hades the underworld, and Poseidon the sea: the earth and Mount Olympus, which was the home of the gods, were regarded as common territory. A rare visitor to either of them was Hades, who preferred to be among the dead. Zeus' influence, however, was felt everywhere, although he had no control over destiny itself. Rather he was the god who saw that fate took its proper course.

The many lovers taken by Zeus, both mortal and immortal, form the very stuff of mythology. It is highly likely that they describe the coming together of several religious traditions, as Zeus incorporated the attributes of rival deities and gained credit for all important events. The continual antagonism between Zeus and his wife HERA, who was definitely an ancient, pre-Greek mother-goddess in origin, often broke out into major conflict. So jealous was Hera that she spent most of her time persecuting Zeus' lovers and their children. Once Zeus became so angry about Hera's cruelty to the hero HERACLES, his greatest son by a mortal woman, that he suspended the goddess from a pinnacle by her wrists and hung weights on her ankles. (See also FORCES OF NATURE)

ZEUS was the supreme deity in Greek mythology and the son of the Titans CRONOS and RHEA. The Romans identified Zeus with their JUPITER, an all-powerful sky god. The tyrannical Cronos insisted on swallowing all Zeus' older brothers and sisters as soon as they were born, but Zeus escaped this fate when his mother Rhea offered Cronos a stone wrapped up in swaddling clothes to swallow instead. In secrecy, Zeus was raised on the island of Crete. He grew to manhood determined to topple his father. The wise Metis, an early love and daughter of OCEANOS, gave Zeus the idea of a potion that would make his father vomit up all the children he had swallowed.

XANTHUS AND BALIUS, immortal horses and children of the west wind, "tore with the speed of wind". They were Achilles' battle steeds during the Trojan War, and wept for fallen heroes on the field. Here, Zeus leads them as a gift of the gods to Peleus on his wedding day. (ILLUSTRATION BY GLENN STEWARD, 1995.)

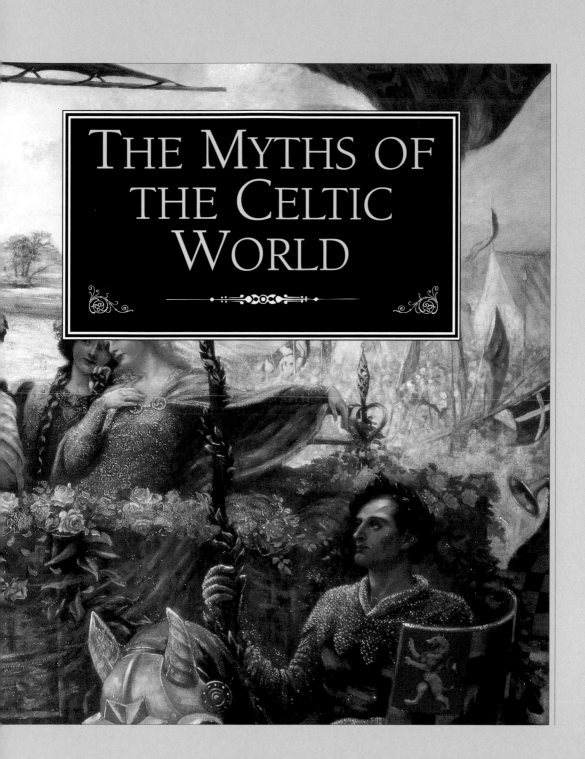

THE MYTHS OF
THE CELTIC
WORLD

INTRODUCTION

TODAY PEOPLE OF CELTIC DESCENT IN Europe are concentrated on its western shores. They live chiefly in Brittany, Cornwall, Wales, Scotland, the Isle of Man and Ireland. At one time, however, the Celts were spread over a large part of the Continent, and in 278 BC one roving band even penetrated as far east as Asia Minor, where they gave their name to Galatia. Until the rise of Roman power, the Celts were a force to be reckoned with. Rome itself had been sacked by them in 385 BC, a historical fact not forgotten by the legionaries who gave Julius Caesar victory between 59 and 49 BC over the Celtic tribes living in Gaul, present-day France. Although largely incorporated into the Roman Empire, the Celts continued to worship their own gods and goddesses right up to the time of the official adoption by the Romans of the Christian faith. Then their religion and mythology waned in importance, except where people remembered tales about the Celtic gods and heroes of the past. Even in distant Ireland, an island that was never under Roman control, the influence of Christianity was soon felt. But here conversion did not mean the wholesale destruction of the Celtic heritage, for monks took great care from the fifth century onwards to write down the ancient sagas.

To this remarkable effort of preservation we owe almost our entire knowledge of Celtic mythology. For except in Wales, where a small group of stories was recorded, nothing else was ever committed to writing. The Celts always distrusted script and preferred to rely on speech and properly trained memories.

In Ireland the poet was held in particular esteem. Possibly because there was a clear distinction there between druid and poet in pre-Christian times. The newly-founded monasteries could therefore undertake the work of recording the ancient texts without any fear of paganism. It seems that poets went on reciting the sagas long after St Patrick converted the Irish and cleared the country of snakes, because these tales were seen as entertainment. Irish folklore insists, however, that they kept something of their magic, since the Devil could never enter a house where the exploits of the heroes were being sung.

BRANWEN was a classic Celtic heroine who remained calm and dignified under pressure. A falsely slandered wife, she was forced to suffer unjustly, until rescued by her brother, Bran the Blessed. (BRANWEN BY G SHERRINGHAM, CANVAS, C. 1920.)

Irish myths nearly always include fighting, though the combat is undertaken more often by heroes than by gods. The fearless warrior Cuchulainn, the lone defender of Ulster during the invasion of forces raised by Queen Medb of Connacht, is very much the ideal. He was chosen as the Irish champion after a beheading contest with the water giant Uath. No other man had courage enough to receive the giant's return blow. Yet Cuchalainn, "the Hound of Culann", enjoyed but a brief life; his refusal to return the affections of Morrigan, the goddess of slaughter, sealed his fate. Not even the intervention of his father Lugh, the sun god, could save him.

The apparently endless conflict appears less terrible when it is recalled how the Celts believed in reincarnation. Their otherworld, unlike the Greek or Roman underworld, was not a dismal abode of the dead. Rather it was a paradise in which souls rested prior to their rebirth in the world. The warrior-poet Oisin, son of the Fenian leader Finn MacCool, spent three hundred years there before returning to Ireland. Oisin was warned that he would never be able to go back to the underworld if he dismounted from a magic steed. When the saddle slipped and he fell to the ground, Oisin was immediately changed from a handsome youth into a blind, grey-haired, withered old man. Only St Patrick is said to have bothered to listen to his fantastic story as it was being written down.

The interest of St Patrick in the adventures of Oisin and, indeed in the exploits of many other heroes of old, is obviously a later embellishment, but it does indicate a degree of tolerance not readily found elsewhere in Christian Europe. Yet saints in Ireland could curse as well as anyone else when the occasion demanded. For instance, the troublesome King Suibhne Geilt was cursed by St Ronan for his violence towards the faith, and

HEROIC combat was a feature of Celtic culture and myth. Champions, such as Cuchulainn, fought to the death, often defending their clan alone. The warriors here wear helmets with boar and raven motifs; symbols of ferocity and death. (GUNDESTRUP CAULDRON, GILDED SILVER, C. 100 BC.)

spent the rest of his life with the characteristics of a bird, leaping from tree to tree and eating at nights nothing but watercress.

In late Celtic mythology, especially the Arthurian myths, Christianity has become a central element. The quest for the Grail is the most obvious example. Although similar to a Celtic magic cauldron, this holy vessel was the cup used at the Last Supper and, at the Crucifixion, the one that received the blood which flowed from the spear thrust in Christ's side. It was brought to Britain by Joseph of Arimathea, but was later lost and its quest preoccupied King Arthur's knights. Only Sir Galahad was pure enough to be granted a full vision of the Grail, which he took as "Our Lord's body between his hands".

Whether or not Arthur was a historical

MERLIN AND NIMUE represent opposite poles of the Celtic otherworld. Merlin, in the tradition of Celtic druids, guided his king, Arthur, with wisdom and foresight; while Nimue, his enchantress, symbolized the threatening powers of the otherworld. (THE BEGUILING OF MERLIN BY E BURNE JONES, CANVAS, C. 1870–74.)

figure is still uncertain. It is quite likely that he may have been a successful warlord in the confused and violent period following the withdrawal of the Roman legions from Britain around 410 AD. That his myth blames the ultimate victory won by the Anglo-Saxon invaders on civil strife perhaps reflects a kernel of truth. The Celtic peoples were notorious for only rarely combining against an external, common foe, so deep-rooted were their own bitter quarrels. Thus British chivalry came to an end with King Arthur's disastrous battle against his nephew Modred near Salisbury. Hardly a knight survived and the King himself was badly wounded. His departure to Avalon, accompanied by three mysterious ladies, gave rise to the idea of his undeath. In an otherworld, it was believed, King Arthur lingered, awaiting reincarnation as a national saviour.

ARTHUR and his Christian Fellowship of Knights probably derived from the earlier Welsh warlord Arthur, who journeyed to the otherworld with his warband in search of a wondrous cauldron. Here, the Knights of the Round Table experience the Grail vision for the first time, amid divine light and splendour. (MANUSCRIPT ILLUSTRATION, C. 1470.)

CELTIC BRITAIN AND IRELAND

CALEDONIA

LINDISFARNE

TORY ISLAND

ULSTER

EMAIN MACHA

IRELAND   MEATH   ISLE OF MAN

CONNAUGHT   BRIGANTES   PARISI

KELLS

R. BOYNE   SETANTII

TARA   NEW GRANGE

R. LIFFEY   DUBLIN   ANGLESEY

R. SHANNON   BRITAIN

LEINSTER

IRISH SEA

MUNSTER

CORK   DYFED

R. SEVERN   CAMULOS

LONDINIUM

STONEHENGE

GLASTONBURY   SALISBURY

TINTAGEL

A

ABARTA, which probably means "doer of deeds", was, in Irish mythology, a mischievous god. He was one of the *TUATHA DE DANANN*, who ruled Ireland until they were overcome by the Milesians, war-like invaders from Spain. Driven underground, Abarta and his kin appear in the Irish sagas more like heroic mortals than gods, although in the tale of his trick on the Fenian warriors there remains a strong trace of his original divinity.

Abarta offered himself as a servant to *FINN MACCOOL*, one of the foremost Irish heroes, and hereditary leader of the *FIANNA*. Abarta tried to serve Finn MacCool shortly after the hero had succeeded his father as leader of the band. As a gesture of goodwill, tricky Abarta presented the Fianna with a wild, grey horse. Only after great effort did the warriors manage to get a bridle on the animal, and then it refused to move even one hoof when mounted. It was not until fourteen warriors had climbed on its powerful back that it would stir at all. Once Abarta had mounted behind them, it broke immediately into a gallop, even pulling along a fifteenth warrior who was unable to let go of the horse's tail. Abarta took them to the otherworld, for that was the reason for his appearance on earth. This wonderful land was thought by the Celts to be the home of the gods and goddesses, and the place where souls briefly rested before rebirth. The rest of the Fianna, or Fenians, acquired a magic ship to give chase to Abarta's steed. The best tracker among them was Finn MacCool's assistant Foltor. He succeeded in navigating a course to the otherworld for the rescue expedition. There Abarta was compelled to release the prisoners as well as to run back to Ireland himself holding on to the horse's tail. Honour being satisfied, the Fenians agreed to a peace with Abarta.

AILILL, who was the brother of Eochaidh, a High King of Ireland,

AINE, Irish goddess of love and fertility, was worshipped on Midsummer Eve by the local people who lit up her hill with torches. When some girls stayed late one night, Aine appeared among them and revealed the hill to be alive with fairies, which were only visible through her magic ring.
(ILLUSTRATION BY NICK BEALE, 1995.)

fell in love with his brother's wife, *ETAIN*, who was actually a goddess, one of the *TUATHA DE DANANN*. Etain had been the second wife of the proud and handsome god *MIDIR*, who lived under a mound in the middle of Ireland. She had been reborn as a human as punishment for her great jealousy of Midir's first wife, Fuamnach. When High King Eochaidh was looking for a bride himself, he heard reports that described Etain as the fairest maiden in Ireland. So he brought the beautiful former goddess back to his palace at Tara, the capital. There Eochaidh and Etain enjoyed a happy married life. Ailill, however, gradually succumbed to a terrible wasting disease because of his unrequited passion for the new queen.

Etain was steadfast in her love for Eochaidh, but she also

AMAETHON, though the fruitful rustic god of agriculture, was not always helpful. It was Amaethon that robbed Arawn, thereby provoking the Battle of Trees, and who refused to help hard-pressed Culhwch to plough, sow and reap a hill in a day – a task in his quest to win Olwen.
(ILLUSTRATION BY NICK BEALE, 1995.)

felt sorry for ailing Ailill and eventually promised to satisfy his desire as the only means of saving his life. It was arranged that they should meet secretly in a house outside Tara. However, Ailill never came because he fell into an enchanted sleep.

AILILL MAC MATA, according to some versions of the myth, was the king of Connacht and husband of the warrior-queen *MEDB*. He is generally portrayed as a rather weak character who was entirely under the influence of Medb. It was due to her taunting that he agreed to go to war with Ulster over the Brown Bull of Cuailgne. Ailill finally met his death at the hands of *CONALL*, who killed him in revenge for the death of *FERGUS MAC ROTH*.

AINE was the Irish goddess of love and fertility. She was the daughter of Eogabail, who was the foster son of the Manx sea god *MANANNAN MAC LIR*. Her main responsibility was to encourage human love, although one mortal lover of hers, King Aillil Olom of Munster, paid for his passionate audacity with his life. When he

brothers plunged the country once again into dreadful strife. The fighting came to an end only with the death of Eber. Amairgen then installed Eremon as High King of Ireland at Tara. Even then conflicts still occurred because of the ceaseless rivalries between lesser rulers.

AMFORTAS see *PELLES*.

ANNWN was a Welsh otherworld that was an idyllic land of peace and plenty. In Annwn there was a fountain of sweet wine and a cauldron of rebirth, which, it would seem, was the basis of the medieval Grail myth. In one Welsh tradition, *ARTHUR* lost most of his warriors in a disastrous attempt to seize this magic cauldron.

The lord of Annwn was the grey-clad *ARAWN*, with whom the Dyfed chieftain *PWYLL* agreed to exchange shapes and responsibilities for a year. Arawn had a pack of hounds, the Celtic "hounds of hell", which were believed to fly at night in pursuit of human souls. (See also *CELTIC OTHERWORLDS; WONDROUS CAULDRONS*)

attempted to force himself upon Aine and rape her, she slew him with her magic.

Aine's worship was always associated in Ireland with agriculture, because, as a goddess of fertility, she had command over crops and animals. Even as late as the last century, celebrations were still held in her honour on Midsummer Eve at Knockainy, or "Aine's hill", in County Kerry.

AMAETHON (whose name means "labourer" or "ploughman") was the god of agriculture and the son of the Welsh goddess *DON*. Amaethon was said to have stolen from *ARAWN*, the lord of the otherworld *ANNWN*, a hound, a deer and a bird, and as a result caused the Cad Goddeu or Battle of Trees. It was in this battle that Amaethon's brother, *GWYDION*,

magically transformed trees into warriors to fight in the battle.

AMAIRGEN, sometimes known as Amergin, was one of the first Irish druids, the ancient priests in Celtic lands. He came to Ireland with the Milesians. These children of *MILESIUS*, or Mil, who was a leader of the Celts who lived in Spain, were believed to be the ancestors of the present-day Irish. Having defeated the divine rulers of Ireland, the *TUATHA DE DANANN*, the Milesians could not agree on which of their leaders should be king. Two sons of Mil, Eremon and *EBER*, contested the throne and for the sake of peace the island was divided into two kingdoms, one in the north, the other in the south. However, peace was not to survive for long, and renewed fighting between the followers of the two

AMAIRGEN (above) was one of the first druids in Ireland. He possessed both spiritual and political authority, and pronounced the first judgement in the land, deciding who would be the first king. An inspired shaman and seer, he is credited with a mystical poem in the Book of Invasions. *(ILLUSTRATION ANON.)*

ANNWN (below), a Welsh otherworld, was a land of fruitfulness and rest, filled with the song of birds. Annwn's magical cauldron, guarded by nine maidens, healed the sick and restored the dead to life. A recurrent motif in Celtic myth, magic cauldrons feature in the tales of Bran and Dagda. (ILLUSTRATION BY NICK BEALE, 1995.)

ANU, *a great earth goddess and mother of all the heroes, was known as the "lasting one" and also as Dana, mother of the Tuatha De Danann. In Munster there are two hills known as the Paps of Anu because they symbolized her breasts.* (ILLUSTRATION BY GLENN STEWARD, 1995.)

ANU, sometimes called Danu or Dana, was the mother goddess of Irish mythology. The *TUATHA DE DANANN* ("the people of the goddess Dana") were her divine children and the gods and goddesses who ruled Ireland prior to the arrival of the Milesians. It is quite possible that the monks who wrote down the Irish sagas from the fifth century onwards underplayed the original role of goddesses in their compilations. Certainly, the stories they recorded show us a man's world, a place where warriors seem most at home. The cult of Anu was especially associated with Munster, and two hills in County Kerry are still known as Da Chich Anann ("The Paps of Anu").

AOIFA, sometimes known as Aoife, was the daughter of Ard-Greimne and an Irish warrior-princess in the Land of Shadows, an otherworld kingdom. Her sister *SCATHACH* instructed the Ulster hero *CUCHULAINN* in the arts of war. But when the sisters went to war Scathach was frightened to take the hero with her into battle in case Aoifa killed him. Undeterred by Aoifa's reputation as a fighter, Cuchulainn challenged her to single combat. Before the fight took place, Cuchulainn asked Scathach

what Aoifa loved best and Scathach told him that above all else she treasured her chariot. At first the combat went as expected in Aoifa's favour, but Cuchulainn distracted her attention at a critical moment by calling out that her chariot horse was in trouble. Afterwards, Aoifa became Cuchulainn's lover and bore him a son named *CONLAI*. It was, however, the boy's fate to be killed by his own father.

AONGHUS was the Irish love god. His father was *DAGDA*, the father of the gods and the protector of druids, and his mother was the water goddess *BOANN*. Rather like Zeus, Dagda deceived Boann's husband and lay with her. The monks

who wrote down the Irish sagas tried to legitimize the birth by making Boann the wife of Dagda, but it is obvious that Aonghus was a divine love-child.

Aonghus was handsome and four birds always hovered above his head which were said to represent kisses. Birds also feature in his courtship of *CAER*, a girl of divine descent who came from Connacht and lived as a swan. Her father, Ethal, was one of the *TUATHA DE DANANN*. He seems to have been reluctant about the marriage until Aonghus' father, Dagda, made Ethal his prisoner. It was finally agreed that Aonghus could marry Caer provided he could identify her and she was willing to be his bride. On the feast of Samhain, Aonghus found Caer swimming on a lake with a hundred and fifty other swans. He instantly recognized her and she agreed to marry him.

An interesting tale that has attached itself to Aonghus concerns his foster-son *DIARMUID UA DUIBHNE*, or "Diarmuid of the Love Spot". This attractive young man received a magic love spot on his forehead from a mysterious girl one

ARAWN, *king of Annwn, strides through his enchanted forest accompanied by his flying hounds, the Celtic "hounds of hell", one of whose duties was to escort souls on their journey to the otherworld. Like some other fairy creatures, they appear white with red ears, a token of the otherworld.* (ILLUSTRATION BY JAMES ALEXANDER, 1995.)

night during a hunt. From then on, no woman could ever see Diarmuid without loving him. This included *GRAINNE*, the princess who had been promised by the High King of Ireland to his Fenian commander *FINN MACCOOL*. Aonghus saved the lovers from the great warrior's wrath, but he could not protect Diarmuid from the fate given to him at birth by the gods, that he should be killed by a magic boar. Nevertheless, Aonghus brought Diarmuid's body back to his own palace at New Grange, on the banks of the River Boyne, where he breathed a new soul into it so that he could talk to his foster-son.

ARAWN was the ruler of the Welsh otherworld *ANNWN*, which was a paradise of peace and plenty. The Dyfed chieftain *PWYLL* became friends with Arawn and was allowed to claim in his title some authority over the otherworld. The two rulers met by chance. While out hunting, Pwyll encountered a strange pack of hounds chasing a stag, so he drove them off and set

AOIFA, *a warrior-princess from the Land of Shadows, spars with her young son, Conlai, instructing him in the martial arts. The tradition of warrior-women was strong in Celtic society, where women bore arms as late as AD 700, and where the fiercest gods were often women.*
(ILLUSTRATION BY JAMES ALEXANDER, 1995.)

AONGHUS *(left), an engaging god of love and courtesy, a Celtic equivalent of Eros, appears in this fanciful portrayal as a charming, if somewhat whimsical character, who calms the foamy sea with his fairy magic.* (AONGHUS, GOD OF LOVE AND COURTESY, PUTTING A SPELL OF SUMMER CALM ON THE SEA BY JOHN DUNCAN, CANVAS, DETAIL, 1908.)

ART *(above) confronts an army of savage and venomous giant toads on his perilous journey through the Land of Wonder, in search of Delbchaem. A taboo laid on the young hero by the jealous goddess Becuma, forced him to find and win the lovely girl imprisoned by her wicked parents.* (ILLUSTRATION BY ARTHUR RACKHAM, C. 1900.)

than she gave birth to DYLAN and LLEU. GWYDION, Arianrhod's brother, immediately took charge of Lleu and brought him up, but this did not prevent Arianrhod placing a series of taboos upon him, including the stricture that he was to have no wife in the human race.

ART, in Irish mythology, was the son of Conn of the Hundred Battles. In one myth, Conn's jealous mistress, the goddess Becuma Cneisgel, contrived to send Art off on a perilous journey through the Land of Wonder in search of Delbchaem ("Fair Shape"). After facing untold dangers, he managed to find and rescue Delbchaem. Art's son by another woman was CORMAC MAC ART. Art was killed by the rebel Lugaide Mac Con in the battle of Moy Muchruinne.

his own hounds on to the prey. Just as the stag was about to fall, a grey-clad figure appeared and rebuked Pwyll for this discourtesy in the field. It was Arawn. In order to placate Arawn and to gain his friendship, Pwyll accepted a proposal that he should exchange forms with him for a year and then slay Arawn's enemy, Havgan. It was also agreed that Pwyll would share the bed of Arawn's queen for the

same period of time, but without making love to her.

Arawn warned Pwyll that he must kill Havgan by a single blow, for if struck a second time he instantly revived. When Pwyll and Havgan fought, the Welsh chieftain dealt him a fatal blow and ignored Havgan's plea to finish him off with another strike. As a result of this service, Arawn and Pwyll became close allies and Dyfed prospered.

ARIANRHOD was the daughter of the Welsh goddess DON and niece of MATH, king of Gwynedd. Math could sleep only if his feet were held in a virgin's lap, and when Goewin, the virgin who usually acted this part for him was raped by his nephew Gilvaethwy, it was suggested that Arianrhod should take her place. To test her purity Arianrhod had to step over Math's wand. No sooner had she done so

ARTHUR is undoubtedly the best known of the Celtic heroes. He was most popular during the Middle Ages, when the exploits of his followers, the Knights of the Round Table, impressed the greater part of western Europe. It was with some misgivings that the Church permitted a Christianized version of these Celtic myths to occupy such an important place in the medieval imagination. It was never quite at ease with the story of the Grail, or SANGREAL, which JOSEPH OF ARIMATHEA was believed to have brought to Britain, since its miraculous properties were clearly derived from the Celtic cauldron, a vessel of plenty as well as of rebirth. The strength of popular feeling for the Arthurian myth can be appreciated by a riot that occurred in 1113 at the town of Bodmin in Cornwall because the French servants of visiting nobility denied Arthur's undeath.

Although some of the earliest stories concerning Arthur are found in Welsh poems of the seventh century, there can be little doubt that the warlike king belongs to the heroic traditions of both Ireland and Wales. He appears in several

ARTHUR, a child of destiny, was guarded and guided by spiritual forces from birth. Smuggled out of Tintagel Castle by Merlin, the mage, he was fostered in safety and secrecy, unaware of his destiny until his rightful time to draw the sword from the stone, thus proving his birthright. (MERLIN AND ARTHUR BY W HATHERELL, CANVAS, C. 1910.)

Irish sagas, one of which describes how he stole the hounds of the Fenian leader FINN MACCOOL on one of his daring raids. Indeed, as a warrior, hunter of magic boars, killer of giants, witches and monsters, and as leader of a band of heroes whose adventures led them into untold mysteries and marvels, Arthur had much in common with Finn MacCool. But according to the ninth-century monk Nennius, Arthur was a historical leader who rallied the people of Britain against Anglo-Saxon invaders after the Roman legions had gone. Nennius credits Arthur with twelve victories, but does not mention the account of his death recorded slightly later in a history of Wales, which states that Arthur and his sworn enemy MODRED both fell in 537 at the battle of Camluan.

Arthur was the son of the British king UTHER PENDRAGON and Igraine, wife of the Cornish duke Gorlois. He was conceived out of wedlock and brought up away from his parents by the wizard MERLIN. The resourceful Merlin had already designed for Uther Pendragon a wonderful stronghold and placed in it the famous Round Table, at which one hundred and fifty knights could be seated. This unusual piece of furniture may

ARTHUR, prompted by Merlin, asks the Lady of the Lake for the sword, Excalibur. The young king marvelled at the shining sword but Merlin insisted that the scabbard was worth ten of the swords because it prevented loss of blood in battle. (ILLUSTRATION BY AUBREY BEARDSLEY, C. 1870.)

have a connection with Joseph of Arimathea, not least because it had a special place reserved for the Grail. While Joseph of Arimathea was imprisoned in Palestine, the Grail is said to have kept him alive. Later he brought it to Britain, where it disappeared due to people's sinfulness. Thus the recovery of the Grail became the great quest of Arthur's knights.

When Uther Pendragon died, the Knights of the Round Table were at a loss to know who should be the next king. They decided that Merlin should guide them. The wizard told them that they would know who Uther's successor was when he drew a magic sword from a stone, which had mysteriously appeared in London. Many knights tried to pull the sword from the stone, but none could move it.

After a number of years Arthur journeyed to London to watch his first tournament. A knight who had been appointed by Merlin to act as the boy's guardian was taking part, but finding he was without a sword, he sent Arthur to get one. Without realizing the significance of the sword in the stone, Arthur pulled it out and gave it to the amazed knight. Thus was the heir of Uther Pendragon revealed.

Even then, there were knights who would not accept Arthur as

ARTHUR, at rest in an enchanted forest, gazes in wonder at the amazing Questing Beast at the well. It was a ferlie or bewitching otherworldly wonder, which defied capture. Sir Pellinore and later Sir Palomides spent years in futile pursuit of the tantalizing chimaera. (ILLUSTRATION BY AUBREY BEARDSLEY, C. 1870.)

ARTHUR'S *Round Table served many
purposes: it prevented quarrels over
precedence; symbolized wholeness; and
commemorated the Table of the Last
Supper, with the Grail at the centre.*

(KING ARTHUR AND THE KNIGHTS OF THE ROUND
TABLE SUMMONED TO THE QUEST BY A STRANGE
DAMSEL BY E BURNE-JONES, TAPESTRY, 1898–99.)

king. Only with Merlin's aid was
the young ruler able to defeat his
opponents and bring peace to
Britain. How much he depended
on magic became obvious to
Arthur early in his reign. Having
drawn his own sword without
cause against one of his knights,
Arthur was dismayed to see the
blade shatter. Merlin saved him by
putting the knight to sleep, for
Arthur was otherwise unarmed. In
despair the king wandered along
the shore of a lake when, to his
amazement, he saw a hand and
arm rise out of the water, holding
another magic sword. This was the
famous Excalibur, his sure support,
according to the Lady of the Lake,
who handed it to him.

Rearmed and reassured, Arthur
went on to be a great king. He
defeated the Anglo-Saxons, aided
King Leodegraunce of Scotland in
his wars against the Irish and even
campaigned as far away from his
kingdom as Rome. In return for the
aid given to Leodegraunce, Arthur
was betrothed to his daughter

GUINEVERE. At first Merlin objected to the match, since he knew of
Guinevere's love for Sir *LANCELOT*,
the most handsome of the Knights
of the Round Table. But he later
blessed the married couple and,
according to one version of the
myth, gave Arthur the Round Table
as a wedding gift. Nevertheless, the
queen and Lancelot were soon
lovers, and when Arthur found out
about his wife's unfaithfulness
Lancelot fled to Brittany.

Arthur pursued Sir Lancelot and
besieged him in his Breton stronghold. The siege had to be lifted,
however, because news reached
the king that his nephew Sir
Modred had seized Camelot and
even forced Guinevere to consent
to marriage, after spreading stories
of the king's death on campaign.
Returning to Britain, Arthur summoned his knights to do battle
with the rebels. Prior to the conflict, it was agreed that the king and
his nephew would meet between
the two armies to discuss the possibility of peace. Because neither
one trusted the other, each ordered
his forces to attack if they saw anyone draw a sword. When a knight
unsheathed his weapon to kill a
snake, a terrible battle was fought,
in which the flower of British
chivalry fell.

Only two of Arthur's knights
were left alive on a battlefield that

was covered by the dead and dying.
Although he had won, King Arthur
had to be carried away by these
knights, such was the severity of his
wound. Knowing his own end was
near, he had Excalibur thrown into
a lake, where a hand swiftly seized
it. Then Arthur boarded a magic
boat and disappeared. His last
words were that he was going to
AVALON to be cured of his wounds
so that he might return one day to
lead his people once more.

The inscription on Arthur's
tomb at Glastonbury picks up this
Celtic idea of reincarnation. It
reads: "Here lies Arthur, king that
was, king that shall be." Such an
undeath was not enough to save

his weakened kingdom from the
Anglo-Saxons, however. The whole
of the Arthurian myth turns on the
disintegration of the chivalric unity
that was established by the Round
Table, but which was finally
destroyed by the implacable hatred
between Arthur and Modred. (See
also *MAGIC AND ENCHANTMENT*,
HEROIC QUESTS)

*ARTHUR rests in peace in Avalon,
guarded by four fairy queens. Morgan le
Fay, cowled in black, consults her book of
magic crafts, to heal the wounds of the
"undead" king. The winged apparition
carrying the Grail symbolizes the hope and
future promise of Arthur's reign.* (LA MORT
D'ARTHUR BY JAMES ARCHER, CANVAS, 1860.)

B

AVALON was another name for the Welsh otherworld, *ANNWN*, and its name suggests that it was an island of apples. The mortally wounded *ARTHUR* was ferried there by three mysterious women in a black boat, following the terrible battle against Sir *MODRED*'s army. The undead king was expected to return from Avalon and lead the oppressed Celtic population of Britain to victory over their Anglo-Saxon and, later, Norman conquerors. According to one version of the myth, Excalibur was forged there. Traditionally, Avalon has been identified with Glastonbury, the supposed site of Arthur's tomb. (See also *CELTIC OTHERWORLDS*)

BADB (meaning "crow") was an Irish goddess of battle. She was one of a group of war deities who could influence the outcome of conflict by inspiring the combatants with fear or courage. The others were known as *MORRIGAN*, *NEMAIN* and *MACHA*. Myth connects Badb with the historical battle of Clontarf in 1014, when the High King Brian defeated the Viking invaders and Badb was said to have appeared over the warriors' heads.

BALOR, a formidable one-eyed god of death, led the misshapen Fomorii against the younger Tuatha De Danann. Here his grandson, Lugh, casts a fatal stone into Balor's deadly eye, forcing it back through his head where its lethal gaze destroys his warriors marching behind him. (ILLUSTRATION BY MIRANDA GRAY, 1995.)

BALOR was the Irish Cyclops. This one-eyed god of death was the most formidable of the *FOMORII*, the violent and monstrous sea gods who ruled Ireland before the arrival of the *TUATHA DE DANANN*. So dreadful was his one eye that he destroyed whoever he looked upon and his eyelid had to be levered up by four servants. It was prophesied that he would be slain by his own grandson. To avoid this fate he locked his only daughter *ETHLINN* in a crystal tower on Tory Island, off the north-west coast of Ireland. Even so, Balor was killed in battle with a sling-shot by the sun god *LUGH*, Ethlinn's son and the champion of the Tuatha De Danann.

Lugh's father was Cian, a lesser member of the Tuatha De Danann. With the assistance of a female druid, Cian had entered the crystal tower and slept with Ethlinn. When Balor learned that his daughter had given birth to three sons, he ordered that they be drowned in a whirlpool near Tory Island. Balor's servants duly rolled them up in a sheet, but on the way to the whirlpool one of the boys fell out unnoticed. Either the druid then handed the fortunate baby to the smith god *GOIBHNIU*, or alternatively *MANANNAN MAC LIR*, the god of the sea, decided to foster him. In either event, Lugh was saved and set on the road to his destiny as the slayer of Balor.

The fateful meeting between Lugh and Balor occurred at the second battle of Magh Tuireadh, a fierce contest between the Fomorii and the Tuatha De Danann. Nobody could stand Balor's lethal gaze, not even the Tuatha De Danann leader *NUADA*, the owner of a sword which previously none could escape. The battle was just turning into a Tuatha De Danann rout, when Lugh noticed that the

BANSHEE, or bean sidhe, women of the fairies, lived underground in sparkling sidhe – fairy heavens hidden beneath grassy mounds on Irish hillsides. Legend has it that a banshee attaches itself to a family and warns of impending death with an eerie wail. (ILLUSTRATION BY H J FORD, 1902.)

AVALON, Arthur's last resting place, was an otherworldly retreat of wonder, mystery and peace. Its nine guardian queens recall an actual, historical order of nine nuns who lived off the coast of Roman Brittany, as well as the nine mythical maidens guarding Annwn's magic cauldron. (KING ARTHUR IN AVALON BY E BURNE-JONES, CANVAS, 1894.)

single eyelid of Balor was slowly closing through weariness. Lugh crept near to him with a magic sling-shot in hand. The moment the eyelid opened again, he hurled the stone so hard that it forced the eyeball backward through Balor's head, with the result that it was the Fomorii who now suffered from the destructive effect of its paralysing stare. The Tuatha De Danann were able to defeat the Fomorii, who were driven from Ireland for ever. (See also *CELTIC OTHERWORLDS*)

BANSHEE is the modern name for the *bean sidhe* ("woman of the fairies"), the traditional fairy of the Irish countryside. After the arrival of the Milesians from what is now Spain (the ancestors of the present-day Irish) the gods and goddesses known as the *TUATHA DE DANANN* disappeared underground and dwelt in mounds, and over the centuries they were slowly transformed in the popular imagination into fairies. It was believed that the wailing of a banshee foretold the approach of a human death.

BEDIVERE see *BEDWYR*

BEDWYR, according to Welsh mythology, was a one-handed warrior who, together with his friend and companion *KAI*, played an important part in helping *CULHWCH* to procure the prizes he required to win the hand of *OLWEN*. They were both members of King *ARTHUR*'s court. In later Arthurian romance Bedwyr became Sir Bedivere, the faithful knight who remained with King Arthur after he was mortally wounded, threw the sword Excalibur into the lake on the king's instructions and bore his body to the boat which carried him to *AVALON*.

BEL see *BELENUS*

BELENUS, also known as Bel, was a Celtic sun god known to the Romans. Julius Caesar compared Belenus to Apollo, the god of prophecy. He appears in various forms across the Celtic world, as Beli to the Welsh, Bile to the Irish and Belenus to the Gauls. Beltaine,

one of the important festivals of the Celtic calendar, was celebrated on the first of May in his honour, and his name survives in a number of place names such as Billingsgate, "Bile's gate" (formerly a fish market in London). Although his worship was clearly widespread, little else is known about him.

BENDIGEIDFRAN see *BRAN THE BLESSED*

BILE see *BELENUS*

BLATHNAT was the wife of King *CU ROI* of Munster. She fell in love with *CUCHULAINN*, the great Ulster hero and enemy of Cu Roi, and betrayed her husband's people by showing the hero how he could enter her husband's apparently impregnable fortress. A stream flowed through the fort and when Blathnat poured milk into the

BELENUS, a Celtic sun god, was honoured on the eve of Beltaine when Celts lit bonfires, the "fires of Bel", symbolizing the rays of the sun and the promise of summer fruitfulness. Here, the fairies, once Celtic gods, ride out from their hollow hills to celebrate Beltaine. (THE RIDERS OF THE SIDHE BY JOHN DUNCAN, CANVAS, 1911.)

water, Cuchulainn was able to follow its course. In the fierce battle that followed Cu Roi was killed and Cuchulainn was able to ride off with Blathnat. He also took with him Cu Roi's bard, Fer Cherdne. When the party halted on a cliff top, however, Fer Cherdne took the opportunity to avenge his former master's death by grabbing hold of Blathnat and jumping over the edge with her in his arms.

BEDWYR guarded Arthur at the end of his life, as they waited by a lake for the ship that would ferry the king to Avalon. This evocative scene blends photographic realism with a ghostly backdrop to create an effective and convincing representation of an otherworldly realm. (MORT D'ARTHUR BY JOHN GARRICK, CANVAS, 1862.)

CELTIC OTHERWORLDS

THE GLITTERING OTHERWORLDS of Celtic myth are the invisible realms of gods and spirits, fairies, elves and misshapen giants. Some are sparkling heavens and some are brooding hells. The veil between the visible and invisible worlds is gossamer-thin and easily torn. Seers and bards pass in and out on spirit-flights or journeys of the soul, as do some privileged heroes, such as all-knowing Finn MacCool, or the intrepid voyagers, Bran, Brendan and Maeldun. Some heroes, such as Cuchulainn, pay only fleeting visits; while Oisin returned from his otherworldly trip 300 years after his time. Common gateways to the otherworld are by water and across narrow bridges, beneath mounds or wells which hide sparkling underground heavens, or dark purgatories. On the eve of Samhain, October 31, all the gates to the otherworld open and wondrous spirits emerge from under the hollow hills.

THOMAS THE RHYMER (above right), like all inspired bards, slipped in and out of the otherworld, drawing on divine sources of inspiration for his poetry. Bards, like druids, possessed supernatural powers of prophecy and inspiration when seized by Awen, the divine muse. Their power to satirize with the glam dicin, an undermining song, made them more feared than fierce warriors. Here, the poet is visited by a being from the otherworld, possibly his divine muse. (THOMAS THE RHYMER AND THE QUEEN OF FAERIE BY J N PATON, CANVAS, C. 1890.)

CELTIC FAIRIES (right) ride out from their underground palaces on the eve of Beltaine to celebrate Belenus' feast. The splendid riders bear treasures from the otherworld; on the left, a wand of intelligence and Tree of Knowledge, and on the right, the recurrent Cauldron of Plenty. The solemn mood and glittering Celtic jewellery and harness create a convincing and haunting portrayal of lordly beings from another world. (THE RIDERS OF THE SIDHE BY JOHN DUNCAN, CANVAS, DETAIL, 1911.)

CARBONEK (above), the Grail Castle of Arthurian legend, was an otherworldly heaven guarded by angels and wondrous spirits whose unearthly song was beautiful beyond imagining. The castle housed the Grail, a holy vessel, said to be the Cup of the Last Supper, which contained healing spiritual sustenance. Lancelot was ferried to Carbonek on a ghostly ship without captain or crew and permitted a distant vision of the sacred chalice because of his courageous spirit. His love of Guinevere forbade a complete vision. (ILLUSTRATION BY ALAN LEE, 1984.)

BALOR (above) and his misshapen people, the Fomorii, symbolize the dark forces of the otherworld. Before their defeat at the hands of the Tuatha De Danann, they oppressed the Irish with crushing tributes and cruelty. While the Tuatha De Danann lived underground in glittering sidhe, the Fomorii roamed beneath lakes and seas in bleak purgatories. Balor's single eye, poisoned in youth, paralysed his enemies with its deadly gaze. (ILLUSTRATION BY ALAN LEE, 1984.)

PWYLL, riding through a lush, wooded idyll, suddenly found himself in the otherworldly realm of Annwn. After driving off some shining white hounds from a fallen stag, he encountered Arawn, the grey-clad lord of Annwn. Like the Greek god of the underworld Hades, Arawn may possibly symbolize a Lord of Winter, because he fought an annual battle with Havgan ("Summer Song"). On one occasion, he asked Pwyll to swap places with him for a year, at the end of which Pwyll fought and won the seasonal duel. (ILLUSTRATION BY ALAN LEE, 1984.)

BLODEUEDD (whose name means "born of flowers" or "flower face") was a beautiful, magical woman. She was conjured by MATH and GWYDION from the blossoms of oak, broom and meadowsweet to be the wife of LLEU, Gwydion's nephew, because Lleu's mother, ARIANRHOD, had declared that he should marry no mortal woman. For a time the young couple lived together happily, but one day Lleu went to visit Math and while he was away Blodeuedd kindly offered hospitality to a passing huntsman, Goronwy, the lord of Penllyn. Blodeuedd and Goronwy fell in love and began to plot the murder of Lleu. This was no easy task, for Lleu could be killed only while standing with one foot on a goat's back and the other on the edge of a bath tub, and only by a spear which it had taken a full year to make. However, even though the pair finally succeeded in meeting all the conditions and attacked him, he did not die but flew into the air in the shape of an eagle. Math and Gwydion set out to avenge Lleu. When they found Blodeuedd, Gwydion turned her into an owl, the bird of the night.

BOANN was a water goddess and the mother of AONGHUS, the Irish god of love. According to the different versions of her myth, she was married either to NECHTAN or to Elcmar. DAGDA, the chief god of the TUATHA DE DANANN, was her lover and the father of Aonghus. He was able to seduce Boann by sending her husband on a nine-month journey that seemed but one day.

BRAN, son of Febal, is the hero of the most famous of the Irish voyage myths. Sea voyages fascinated the Irish storytellers, who would tell of strange adventures on remote islands, including those of other-worlds, such as the home of gods and goddesses, as well as the place where souls briefly rested before rebirth. Bran's great journey began

BLODEUEDD (above), the fairest woman in the world, was conjured out of blossoms by the magicians Gwydion and Math, so that she could be the wife of Gwydion's nephew, Lleu. But she betrayed her husband for another man. Gwydion, here, watches as his beautiful creation comes to life. (ILLUSTRATION BY ALAN LEE, 1984.)

BOANN, a water goddess and the mother of Aonghus, violated the sanctity of a sacred well of inspiration. In outrage the waters bubbled and swelled, forming a torrent which became the River Boyne, which is named after her. In its current swam the Salmon of Knowledge (below). (ILLUSTRATION BY ARTHUR RACKHAM, C.1910.)

when he found a silver branch that was covered with white flowers. Gathering his kinsmen together, Bran displayed the magic bough, only to be surprised by the sudden appearance of a woman dressed in very unusual cloth. She sang to the assembled company of the great wonders to be found in the lands beyond the sea, the otherworld islands, each larger than Ireland, and inhabited by beautiful women who had no knowledge of sorrow, sickness or death. Happiness, she sang to them, was the lot of all living in these wonderful lands. Then the strange woman stopped singing and vanished, taking the magic bough with her. Bran had been unable to hold on to it, even with both his hands.

The next day Bran sailed west-wards with twenty-seven kinsmen. Their first encounter was with the sea god MANANNAN MAC LIR, who was driving his chariot across the waves. Once again the Irish heroes were informed by the sea god of the marvels that awaited them. Even then the sea appeared to be a plain of flowers, with blossoming shrubs and an orchard of fruitful trees. That day Bran's boat came to the Isle of Merriment, where his crew could hardly stand up for laughing, and then in the evening they reached the Isle of Women. The beautiful women's leader called to Bran to step ashore, but he was afraid to land; so she threw a ball of thread that stuck to Bran's hand, and by magic drew the boat from the waves. When they came ashore the Irish heroes found soft beds and delicious food ready for them. The delightful stay seemed to them to last for only a year, but in fact many years had passed. When one of the crew grew homesick and persuaded Bran that it was time that they sailed home, he was warned by the chief woman not to set foot on soil again. Arriving off the Irish coast, Bran discovered that nobody recognized him, and he was known only as a legendary figure who had long ago embarked on a great voyage to the other-worlds, so he set sail again; but not before one desperate hero forgot the warning and jumped ashore, and immediately turned into a pile of ash, as though he had been dead for centuries.

The voyage of Bran is certainly an ancient myth, although it was not written down until the eighth century by monks. Even though the monks added certain Christian elements such as references to Jesus Christ and Adam's sin, they did not obscure the tale's original magical atmosphere. (See also *FABULOUS VOYAGES*)

BRAN (below), on his epic voyage, visited the Isle of Women, where the chief woman brought his ship to shore with magic thread. Here, she holds a cup of plenty, symbolizing the idyllic delights of the island. The voyagers stayed for what they thought was a year before they left for home.
(ILLUSTRATION BY DANUTA MEYER, 1993.)

BRAN THE BLESSED, the son of the sea god Llyr, played a different role to *BRAN*, son of Febal. In Welsh mythology, he was called Bendigeidfran and seems to have been an otherworld god, although he was also active as a British king in mortal affairs. He allowed his sister *BRANWEN* to marry the Irish king *MATHOLWCH*, without the consent of her half-brother *EFNISIEN*.

Because of this slight, Efnisien cut off the lips, ears and tails of Matholwch's horses during the wedding feast in Wales. Not unnaturally, hostilities almost broke out between the Irish and the Britons as a result, but Bran managed to

BRAN THE BLESSED (right), the mighty ruler of Britain, sailed to Ireland to rescue his beautiful sister, Branwen. In the ensuing battle, Bran was mortally wounded, but his head, cut from his body, lived on. His magical cauldron of rebirth is seen here, restored, along with his head.
(ILLUSTRATION BY ALAN LEE, 1984.)

avoid a war by presenting Matholwch with a magic cauldron. This otherworld vessel could bring men back to life, but without restoring their speech.

Back in Ireland, Matholwch was unable to convince his warriors that Bran's gift was adequate compensation for the damage done to the horses. So Branwen ceased to be the Irish queen and was made to work in the palace kitchens, even though she had already given Matholwch a son and heir, *GWERN*. When Bran learned of how she was being treated, he raised a great army and sailed to Ireland. In the ensuing battle the Britons slew every Irish man there was, but only seven of their own army survived. Even Bran was killed, by a wound caused by a poisoned arrow. On his deathbed he told his followers to cut off his head, which apparently was still able to eat and talk during the voyage home. A later addition to the myth says that the head was brought to London and buried facing Europe, to ward off foreign invaders. King Arthur is said to have used the head for its power.

The Celts believed that heads were the seat of the soul, which may partly explain their practice of head-hunting. Even more curious, was the medieval Christian claim that Bran was the first British man. (See also *WONDROUS CAULDRONS*)

*BRANGAINE (above) and Iseult peer
quizzically at the shy young stranger in the
palace garden, puzzling over his identity.
But as soon as the dog leapt fondly onto his
lap, they recognized the stranger as Tristan,
who had been assumed dead. They were
confused at first because he was much
changed after his wanderings in the
wildwood. (ILLUSTRATION BY EVELYN PAUL, C. 1920.)*

BRANGAINE was the maid of
ISEULT, princess of Ireland and
lover of *TRISTAN*. Iseult had been
promised in marriage to King *MARK*
of Cornwall. Tristan, his nephew,
came to Ireland to escort her across
the sea. Before the ship sailed,
Iseult's mother gave Brangaine a
love potion for Iseult and Mark on
their wedding night, as it caused
those who drank it to love only
each other for the rest of their lives.
However, during the voyage, Tristan
became thirsty and unwittingly
drank the potion, and then offered
some to Iseult.

Through all the ensuing difficulties Brangaine was always loyal,
sharing their secrets, such as when
Tristan was brought to Mark's
castle mistaken for a wild man,
even taking Iseult's place in Mark's
bed on the wedding night.

*BRANWEN (right) releases a starling,
bearing a plea for help, across the sea to
her giant brother, Bran. When he reads
of her plight in Ireland, he sets sail
immediately with a fleet to rescue her.
(ILLUSTRATION BY ALAN LEE, 1984.)*

BRANWEN was the daughter of Llyr, the Welsh equivalent of the Irish sea god LIR, and sister to BRAN THE BLESSED, and MANAWYDAN. When High King MATHOLWCH of Ireland came to Bran's court at Harlech it was agreed that Branwen should be given to him in marriage. But her half-brother EFNISIEN was not consulted and, feeling insulted, he cut off the lips, ears and tails of Matholwch's horses. To restore peace Bran offered the Irish king replacement horses and a magic cauldron. Matholwch returned to Ireland with Branwen, who was at first received with great rejoicing for she was generous with gifts, and before long she gave birth to a son, GWERN. But after a few years Matholwch's friends and family began to complain that the compensation he had received from Bran was not enough. To satisfy them, Matholwch insisted that Branwen relinquish her position as queen and become a cook for the court.

During the next three years, as Branwen worked in the palace kitchens, she reared a starling and taught it to recognize her brother Bran. Then she sent it across the sea with a letter tied to its leg, telling of her treatment. When Bran and the Britons learned of her fate they brought an army to Ireland.

BRENDAN the Navigator was the title given to a sixth-century Irish saint. Indeed, the account of the two voyages undertaken by St Brendan was just as popular in the Middle Ages as the stories told about the Knights of the Round Table. This wonder tale is in the same tradition as that of BRAN, son of Febal, although its direct inspiration was the voyage of the Aran hero MAELDUN. Having taken holy orders, Brendan prayed to go on a pilgrimage into unknown lands. An angel then showed him an island in a vision. In search of this beautiful land, St Brendan set sail twice, first in a craft made from skins, and

BRENDAN, the Irish saint and navigator, returns to Ireland after his wondrous voyage in search of the Land of Promise. His tour of twelve mysterious islands included a land of birdlike spirits, which was possibly the Land of Promise. His amazing tale seems to be a blend of earlier voyages. (ILLUSTRATION BY JAMES STEPHENS, C. 1920.)

second in a boat made of wood. Miraculous events took place due to the saint's faith. One Easter a whale appeared so that St Brendan and his followers could hold a service on its broad back. After the service, the whale plunged under the waves and swam away. This great animal was made docile by St Brendan, as were numerous whirlpools. Even the Devil was unable to disturb the saint's serenity when he showed him the pain of Hell. St Brendan also restored to life one of the monks who were his companions after he had insisted on seeing this forbidden sight for himself.

On the voyages he also encountered a heathen giant, whom he baptized, terrifying mice and an enormous sea cat. Finally, they reached the island in St Brendan's vision. Inhabited by a hermit clothed in feathers, it was probably the Land of Promise, a place of Christian resurrection similar to the Celtic otherworlds. On his return to Ireland, St Brendan refused to stay in his old monastery but moved instead to a retreat near Limerick, where he died. (See also FABULOUS VOYAGES)

BRES, in Irish mythology, was briefly the leader of the TUATHA DE DANANN, the implacable enemies of the FOMORII, the sea gods who ruled Ireland long before them. Bres was an unusual leader of the Tuatha De Danann because his father was ELATHA, who was a Fomorii king of a land that lay under the sea. Elatha had met a Tuatha De Danann goddess named Eri on the sea-shore and made love to her on the sand. Bres was born as a result, although Eri was careful to say nothing to her husband about the boy's real father.

When Bres grew up, he fought against the existing inhabitants of Ireland, the FIRBOLG, at the first battle of Magh Tuireadh. In this engagement NUADA, the leader of the invading Tuatha De Danann, lost a hand and in consequence he retired for a time. Nuada tried to use a silver replacement without success, until Miach, son of the healing god DIAN CECHT, made him a hand of flesh and blood. However, until Nuada was fully recovered and able to resume his

BRIAN and his brothers set out on a perilous voyage across the world to fulfil eight tasks, set by the sun god Lugh. With daring and resource they sought and found wondrous treasures, such as an invincible sword and healing pigskin, which helped the De Danann in their battle with the Fomorii. (ILLUSTRATION BY STEPHEN REID, 1912.)

leadership, the De Danann were under the command of Bres. But Bres had no gift for leadership and became something of a tyrant. On the restoration of Nuada, Bres and his mother Eri fled to Elatha in order to seek Fomorii assistance. This caused the second battle of Magh Tuireadh, in which Nuada was killed. Through the bravery of the sun god LUGH, however, the Fomorii were routed and Bres was taken prisoner. One version of the myth explains how, in return for his life, Bres promised to instruct the Tuatha De Danann in the arts of planting and sowing crops. It is possible that Bres, like his wife, the fertility goddess BRIGID, was a deity connected with agriculture.

BRIAN was one of the three sons of TUIREANN, whose family were engaged in a feud with the family of Cian, father of the god LUGH. When Lugh sent Cian to summon the warriors of the TUATHA DE DANANN to battle, Brian and his brothers, Iuchar and Iucharba, killed him during his journey. To atone for this act of murder they were given by Lugh eight tasks to perform. Among the objects they had to retrieve were three apples from the Gardens of the Sun, a healing pigskin from the king of Greece, a poisoned spear from the king of Persia, a cooking-spit belonging to the nymphs of an undersea kingdom and the seven pigs of King Asal of the Golden Pillars, which could be cooked and eaten one day and found alive the next. Finally, they were to shout three times on the Hill of Mochaen. Having successfully brought back to Lugh all the magical objects he required, they then set out to perform their last duty. However, they were mortally wounded by Mochaen and his sons. Tuireann therefore asked Lugh if he might borrow the magical pigskin and so heal his sons, but the god refused and Brian and his brothers died. (See also FABULOUS VOYAGES)

BRICIU was one of the trouble-makers of Irish myth. An Ulster lord, he arranged a great feast to which he invited all the Ulster heroes, and ordered that the hero's portion be given to the greatest among them. At which point the three great warriors, *CUCHULAINN*, *CONALL* and Laoghaire, sprang up at once and began fighting each other for the honour. In order to settle the argument it was agreed that a monster should be sum-moned to test the courage of the three heroes. Briciu did this by challenging each one to cut off the demon's head, on the understand-ing that the following day that man should then lay his own head on the block. Cuchulainn stepped up first and beheaded the monster, whereupon the creature rose, took up its head and departed. The next day Cuchulainn offered his own head and the monster pronounced him the bravest man in Ireland.

BRIDE see *BRIGID*

BRIGANTIA ("High One" or "Queen") was the chief goddess of the Brigantes, the dominant tribe in the north of England before the invasion of the Romans. She was associated with water, war and healing, and also with prosperity. A widely revered goddess, she was worshipped throughout the Celtic world. In Ireland she was known as *BRIGID* and in France as Brigindo.

BRIGID, sometimes known as Brigit, was a goddess of healing and fertility who was believed to assist women in labour. She seems to have been widely worshipped in Ireland and Britain, where she was most likely known as *BRIGANTIA*. In Irish mythology, she was the wife of *BRES*, the half-*FOMORII* god who briefly led the *TUATHA DE DANANN* after the first battle of Magh Tuireadh against the *FIRBOLG*. Bres was handsome but also oppressive, like all Fomorii, so his reign was short. Brigid, however, bore him three sons. She often appears as an alternative for her mother *ANU*, which suggests that they were probably different aspects of the same mother goddess.

ST BRIDE is ferried by angels from Iona to Bethlehem on the eve of Christ's birth to foster the infant Christ. Celtic and Christian motifs merge in this scene, while the angels' soaring flight beyond the frame enhances the powerfully spiritual effect.
(ST BRIDE BY JOHN DUNCAN, CANVAS, C. 1913.)

St Brigit, or St Bride, one of Ireland's patron saints, may have been a priestess of the goddess Brigid prior to her conversion to Christianity. It was said that she was able to feed animals without reducing the available food for the people, and this also links her with Brigid, who was celebrated at the Celtic festival of Imbolc on the first of February, at the same time as the ewes came into milk.

CAER was a fairy maiden who was loved by Aonghus. She chose to live as a swan for part of her life. When the swans gathered on the Lake of the Dragon's Mouth, Aonghus went to find Caer and win her love. As he reached out to her he was also turned into a swan, and they flew away together. (ILLUSTRATION BY GLENN STEWARD, 1995.)

BRIGIT see BRIGID

CAER was a fairy maiden loved by AONGHUS, the Irish love god. Her father Ethal was one of the TUATHA DE DANANN. Aonghus became aware of Caer in a dream and so attracted was he to her beauty that he fell into a deep sickness. When the identity of Caer was discovered, Aonghus immediately asked her father for her hand, but Ethal said it was not in his power to grant this because his daughter had taken the form of a swan. It was agreed, however, that Aonghus could ask Caer to marry him but only if he was able to recognize her from among the large flock of swans with whom she lived.

When the swans arrived at the Lake of the Dragon's Mouth, Aonghus went to the shore and, recognizing Caer, called out her name. Afterwards Aonghus and Caer were married.

CAMELOT, a mythical castle-city named after Camulos, was the heart of Arthur's kingdom, the seat of his power, symbol of his golden age and his most beloved home. Its shining towers drew knights from all over the world. Part of the mystique of Camelot is its elusive location which has yet to be found. (ILLUSTRATION BY ALAN LEE, 1984.)

CAILTE, son of RONAN, was a Fenian warrior and poet, and a cousin of FINN MACCOOL, leader of the FIANNA, the warrior bodyguard of the High King of Ireland. Cailte, though exceptionally thin, was a formidable fighter and is credited with killing LIR, the sea god who was the father of MANANNAN MAC LIR. But it was as a poet that he was most admired, and his most famous audience was St Patrick. Possibly after returning from an otherworld, Cailte was said to have travelled through Ireland recounting to the saint the legends of the hills, woods and lakes that they encountered, and also the great exploits and battles of the Fianna.

CALATIN, in Irish mythology, was a misshapen druid of FOMORII origin who was said to have studied sorcery for seventeen years. Queen MEDB of Connacht dispatched Calatin along with his numerous sons to fight the Ulster hero CUCHULAINN. All of them had their left hands and right feet missing, but they never missed with their poisoned spears, and Cuchulainn only succeeded in beating them with the assistance of a Connacht warrior who disapproved of such a one-sided contest. The destruction of the male Calatins did not spell the end of Cuchulainn's troubles, however, for not long afterwards Calatin's wife gave birth to three daughters, who were blinded in one eye, like the Germanic god Odin, so as to learn the magic arts. Soon the three Calatin sisters became powerful witches, and they deceived Cuchulainn with their spells, and so assisted Queen Medb's invasion of Ulster. When Cuchulainn rode out in his chariot against the invaders, he came across these hideous women cooking a dog next to the road. Either

CAILTE, a Fenian warrior and bard, was renowned for his songs and legends. Bards or lyric poets played a central role in Celtic society, perpetuating the mysteries, praising their leaders and satirizing their enemies. Bardic schools flourished in Ireland right up to the seventeenth century. (AQUATINT BY R. HAVELL c 1890.)

because the dog was his namesake, or because it would have been discourteous to refuse a piece of the cooked meat, Cuchulainn stopped and took hold of the dog's shoulder. As a result, his own hand and shoulder withered. Gravely weakened, he still advanced with his faithful charioteer LAEG.

CAMELOT see HEROIC QUESTS

CAMULOS was the god of the Remi, a Celtic tribe living in what is now Belgium, although there is evidence that he was also worshipped as a divinity of war in northern Britain and at the town of Camulodunum ("The Fort of Camulos"), modern Colchester, in Essex. The name of the town formed the basis for the mythical city of Camelot. The Romans associated Camulos with their god Mars. He was said to wield an invincible sword.

CARADAWC, in Welsh mythology, was the son of BRAN (son of the sea god, Llyr). When Bran sailed with his army to Ireland to avenge the ill-treatment of his sister BRANWEN by the High King MATHOLWCH, he left Caradawc as chief steward. When news of Bran's death arrived, Caradawc was overthrown by Caswallon, son of the death god Beli.

CARBONEK see CELTIC OTHERWORLDS

CATHBAD (above), the inspired druid and seer, predicted Deirdre's tragic destiny at her birth. Druids, both male and female, held high rank in Celtic society. They were counsellors, judges, teachers and ambassadors. Even a high king could not speak at an assembly before his druid. (ILLUSTRATION BY NICK BEALE, 1995.)

CATHBAD, in Irish mythology, was a seer and druid, and advisor to *CONCHOBHAR MAC NESSA*, the king of Ulster. Cathbad prophesied that though *DEIRDRE* would have great beauty she would bring destruction to Ulster. He also foretold that the hero *CUCHULAINN* would have a glorious but short life. When King Conchobhar Mac Nessa became cruel towards the end of his reign, Cathbad cursed the king and his stronghold at Emain Macha. Cathbad had three children, *DECHTIRE*, the mother of Cuchulainn, Elbha, the mother of *NAOISE*, and Findchaem, mother of *CONALL* Cearnach.

CERIDWEN was a Welsh goddess of fertility and the mother of Afagddu, reputedly the ugliest man in the world. To compensate for his looks Ceridwen boiled a cauldron of knowledge for a year and a day so that Afagddu could become wise and respected, and she set Gwion Bach, the second son, to watch over the pot. But Afagddu was denied the prophetic gift when a drop fell on Gwion Bach's finger and he unthinkingly sucked it. In fury, Ceridwen chased and ate Gwion Bach, only later to reincarnate him as *TALIESIN*, who was the greatest of all the Welsh bards. Ceridwen had another equally ugly son, Morfan, who was also a fearsome warrior. He fought with King

CERIDWEN boils a magical brew hoping to endow her ill-favoured son with wisdom. At the end of a year, the broth would yield just three precious drops of inspiration; but these splashed on to the hand of Gwion Bach, who became all-knowing. (ILLUSTRATION BY JAMES ALEXANDER, 1995.)

ARTHUR in his last battle, at Camlan. At first none of Sir *MODRED*'s men would fight Morfan because they thought he was ugly enough to be a devil.

CERNUNNOS was a Celtic god worshipped in both France and Britain. He is usually depicted sitting cross-legged and wearing a sleeveless tunic and bead necklace. He has an impressive pair of antlers, and the name Cernunnos means "the Horned One", which suggests that he was a god of wild animals and the forest, although he has also been seen as a god of plenty. The Romans identified him with their god Mercury, the messenger god and the guide of the dead to the underworld. In medieval Ireland the antlers of Cernunnos were transferred to the Devil.

CESAIR was the daughter of Bith, son of Noah and one of the earliest arrivals in Ireland. In her myth, Celtic and Hebrew traditions were brought somewhat uncomfortably together by the monks who wrote down the sagas and who suggested that the first settlers had reached Ireland before the Flood. Although Bith was denied a place in the Ark, he was fortunate to be advised by a god to build his own boat. Cesair appears to have guided him to this decision as well. They sailed for seven years and eventually reached

CESAIR, granddaughter of Noah, set sail with her father, Bith, to escape the Flood. After a seven-year voyage, they reached the shores of Ireland. Yet neither Cesair nor her father survived the Flood when it engulfed the land, although her husband, Fintan, escaped by changing into a salmon. (ILLUSTRATION BY JAMES ALEXANDER, 1995.)

CERNUNNOS, *a Celtic hunter god of beasts, is typically depicted in a lotus position. The "horned one" was a lord of animals and is here surrounded by wild creatures such as the stag, boar and lion. In one hand he clasps a warrior's torc, in the other a serpent, demonstrating his power.* (GUNDESTRUP CAULDRON, GILDED SILVER, C. 100 BC.)

Ireland, where Cesair was married to FINTAN. When the rising waters of the Flood engulfed the land, Fintan saved himself by changing into a salmon, but the rest of Bith's family drowned. This myth is known as the first invasion of Ireland. Subsequent invasions were by the PARTHOLON and Nemed, the FOMORII and TUATHA DE DANANN, who were all more or less supernatural in nature. The final invasion of Ireland was by the sons of MILESIUS, who came from Spain and brought human rule to the island.

CLIODHNA, in Irish mythology, was an otherworld goddess of beauty. It was said that her three magical birds could sing the sick to sleep and cure them. Cliodhna was passionately in love with a mortal named Ciabhan, a youth with wonderful curling locks. One day on the shore near Cork, while Ciabhan went hunting inland, Cliodhna was put into a magic sleep by the sea god MANANNAN MAC LIR, who then sent a wave to pull her back to the Land of Promise.

CONAIRE MOR was a High King of Ireland. He was the son of a cowherd's foster-daughter named Mess Buachalla and the bird god NEMGLAN. His mother was actually

the daughter of Etain Oig and CORMAC king of Ulster. However, Cormac was so disappointed not to have a son that he ordered Mess Buachalla to be thrown into a pit. According to the myth, the baby girl was saved by two kind-hearted servants, who could not bring themselves to carry out the king's order. Instead they gave Mess Buachalla to a cowherd. When she grew up, her beauty was so remarkable that Eterscel, the High King of Ireland, decided to marry her. He was also persuaded by a prophecy which said that an obscure woman would bear him a famous son. But on the night before the wedding, Mess Buachalla slept with the god Nemglan, who had magnificent plumage. From this union was born Conaire Mor, whom Mess Buachalla passed off as the son of Eterscel. The one instruction that Nemglan told Mess Buachalla to give to their child was that he was never to kill a bird.

When Conaire Mor was a young man, Eterscel died and the right of succession was raised in Tara, the Irish capital. It was agreed to follow the ancient custom of the dream. After a feast, one of the court would have a spell of truth sung over him as he slept. The man the courtier dreamed about would then be the next High King. In the succession dream a naked man was revealed, walking along the road to Tara with a sling in his hand.

At this time Conaire Mor was some distance from Tara. As he headed back to the palace in his chariot, a flock of birds descended upon him. They had such wonderful plumage that Conaire Mor forgot the taboo about killing birds and got out his sling. The birds shed their feathers and attacked the charioteer as warriors. But one of the birdlike fighters, who was more handsome than the rest, protected Conaire Mor. He introduced himself as his father Nemglan and reminded the young man that he must never cast stones at birds for they were his own kin. As a penance, Nemglan told his son to walk naked along the road to Tara, carrying only his sling. If he did this, and promised to rule Ireland in peace, Conaire Mor would be made High King.

So it was that Conaire Mor was received at Tara as the High King. Peace and prosperity at first marked his reign, although the lure of plunder gradually drew the Irish back to their old habit of cattle-raiding. Since Conaire Mor was reluctant to punish severely those who took

CONAIRE MOR *was burdened by more geis (taboos) than any other Irish warlord. Violation of geis led to misfortune or death and marked a tragic turning-point in the hero's life. Despite his wisdom, Conaire Mor was lured by his enemies into breaking his geis one by one.* (ILLUSTRATION BY STEPHEN REID, 1910.)

part in the growing disorder, the country soon slid back into clan warfare. Eventually, the High King had to forgo the ways of peace and break his promise to his father. Conaire Mor soon realized that this would bring about his own downfall. While on campaign, he came to a roadside hostel where he was greeted by three strange horsemen, whose clothes, weapons, bodies and horses were all red. A hideous old woman told Conaire Mor that during his stay in the hostel "neither skin nor flesh of you will escape from the place to which you have come, save what the birds will take in their claws." The same night a rebel force surrounded the hostel and attacked. Three times the building caught fire and three times the flames were brought under control, but all the water had now been used. When a druid accompanying the rebels laid a spell of thirst on the High King, he sent one of his companions to fetch some water. On returning, the warrior saw that the fight was over and Conaire Mor's severed head lay on the floor. So he poured the water into the king's head, at which Conaire Mor's decapitated head praised him for his sense of duty.

CLIODHNA *fled to Glandore to live with her mortal lover, Ciabhan, but the sea god, Manannan Mac Lir, sent a great wave to scoop her up and bring her home. Here, lulled to sleep by fairy music, she drifts back to fairyland. The Wave of Cliodhna is still one of the three great waves of Ireland.* (ILLUSTRATION BY JAMES ALEXANDER, 1995.)

SAGES AND SEERS

THE SPIRITUAL SEERS and shamans of Celtic myth were endowed with extraordinary gifts of prophecy, wisdom and healing. They enjoyed a profound rapport with natural and supernatural forces, and acted as intermediaries between the realms of the living and the dead, between the visible world of men and the invisible otherworld, a realm of wondrous spirits. Most famous of all was Arthur's wise counsellor, Merlin; but other inspired druids – Amairgen, Taliesin and Cathbad – feature in Celtic myths as prophetic bards and counsellors to clan chiefs and kings. Some lived as hermits in the wilderness, while remaining powerful in Celtic society. Although on the whole helpful to mortals, some dark sorceresses, such as Morgan, Nimue or the Calatins, used their supernatural gifts to bewitch and manipulate mortals for their own ends.

MORGAN LE FAY (above right), Queen of Avalon, the otherworldly Isle of Apples, bears an apple bough, the Celtic symbol of peace and plenty. A gifted sorceress, she is often portrayed as a dark soul, thwarting Arthur and manipulating heroes. At a deeper level, she is a winter goddess of darkness and death, opposing Arthur, the Lord of Summer. She reveals the redeeming aspect of her character in her role as sovereign healer of Avalon and guardian of Arthur's body in death. (ILLUSTRATION BY STUART LITTLEJOHN, 1994.)

MERLIN (right) is best remembered as the fatherly and spiritual guardian of Arthur. A wise seer, Merlin counselled the young king, sometimes sternly and sometimes gently, but always with wisdom. Merlin was also a peerless sage, credited with the design of the Round Table, the plan for Camelot and the stone ring at Stonehenge. He learnt his craft from a master, Bleise, portrayed here as an historian recording the deeds of Arthur's reign, as reported by Merlin. (MANUSCRIPT ILLUSTRATION, C. 1300.)

HELLAWES (below) was a sorceress in the Arthurian myths who had set her heart on the noble knight Sir Lancelot, whom she had loved from afar for some seven years. Eventually, she managed to lure him into her Chapel Perilous and there she tried all the methods she knew to inspire his love for her. But it was to no avail because the steadfast and loyal knight loved one woman only, Arthur's queen, the fair Guinevere, and he had come to the chapel with but one mission in mind, which was to collect healing talismans for the wounded knight Sir Meliot. When Lancelot left with the talismans, he was completely untouched by Hellawes' love and even her magical craft. The sorceress finally realized that he would never love her and she died of a broken heart. (ILLUSTRATION BY AUBREY BEARDSLEY, C. 1870.)

DRUIDS (above) held both political and spiritual power in Celtic society and were gifted not only as shamans and seers but also as legal and moral advisors. Druids underwent a long apprenticeship of at least twenty years, learning the mysteries and laws by heart. Here, druids on a snowy hill celebrate the winter solstice by gathering a bough of mistletoe, cut with the sacred golden sickle borne by the foremost druid. (THE DRUIDS BRINGING IN THE MISTLETOE BY G HENRY AND E A HORNED, CANVAS, 1890.)

TALIESIN (left), a prophetic poet and shamanistic seer, was gifted with all-seeing wisdom after consuming a "greal" of inspiration from Ceridwen's cauldron. Wales's greatest bard, he foretold the coming of the Saxons and the oppression of the Cymry as well as his own death. He appears here as an eagle, the bird often chosen by shamans on their spirit-flights or trance journeys to the otherworld. The eagle's gold nimbus symbolizes Taliesin's radiant brow. (ILLUSTRATION BY STUART LITTLEJOHN, 1994.)

SIR. LAVNCELOT. AND. THE. WITCH. HELLAWES.

CONALL, in Irish mythology, was the foster-brother of the Ulster hero CUCHULAINN. As children, they swore that if either was killed first the other would avenge him. When Queen MEDB of Connacht invaded Ulster, Cuchulainn faced her army single-handed, but he was doomed because he had offended the war goddess MORRIGAN. After Cuchulainn had been killed, and his head and sword-hand cut off by the enemy, the warriors of Ulster were stirred by Conall to wreak bloody revenge. They caught up with Queen Medb's army and Conall slew those who had killed his foster-brother. Later, Conall went on to ravage the whole of Ireland as he punished Queen Medb's allies one by one. In doing so he earned his title, Caernach ("of the Victories").

CONCHOBHAR MAC NESSA,

in Irish mythology, was an Ulster king. He was the son of Fachtna Fathach and NESSA, a local beauty who, according to one tradition, conceived Conchobhar on the eve

CONCHOBHAR MAC NESSA, a high king of Ireland, granted arms to the young Cuchulainn, but when the boy grasped his spears, they splintered in his hand; next, a chariot shattered beneath his stamp. No weapons withstood the hero's mighty grasp until he was given the king's own arms.
(ILLUSTRATION BY STEPHEN REID, 1910.)

of her royal marriage through a secret affair with a druid. When her husband died shortly after the wedding, Nessa had courted by his half-brother and successor, FERGUS MAC ROTH. But she would only agree to become his wife on the condition that he would first let her son Conchobhar rule as king of Ulster for a year. An ambitious and determined woman, Nessa instructed her son how to be a great ruler so that when the time arrived for Fergus Mac Roth to return to the throne, the people of Ulster simply refused to let Conchobhar step down.

Although he was married, King Conchobhar fell deeply in love with DEIRDRE, who was sometimes called Derdriu ("of the Sorrows"). She was the daughter of an Ulster chieftain, and at her birth the druid CATHBAD had warned that, though Deirdre would be the most beautiful woman in Ireland and would marry a king, she would be the cause of death and destruction throughout the land. By the time Deirdre grew up, Conchobhar was an old man, and she in disgust

refused his advances and eloped with a handsome young warrior named NAOISE. But the king never gave up his passion, and so eventually he had Naoise killed and was married to Deirdre. She found her situation so intolerable that she committed suicide by throwing herself from a speeding chariot. Fergus Mac Roth, appalled by Conchobhar's behaviour, offered his services to Ulster's enemies and a long war ensued. Conchobhar was himself killed by a magic sling-shot. It was the famous "brain ball" made by Conall out of the brains of a slain Leinster king. The ball lodged in the king's skull, and his doctors advised him to avoid any strenuous exercise and excitement. Some years later Conchobhar Mac Nessa got into a rage and the "brain ball" caused his death.

CONLAI, sometimes known as Connla, was the doomed son of the great Ulster hero CUCHULAINN. According to one Irish tradition, Cuchulainn had visited the Land of Shadows in order to challenge the warrior woman AOIFA to single combat. After the fight, which the

hero just managed to win by the use of cunning, they became lovers and Conlai was conceived. When he left, Cuchulainn gave Aoifa a gold ring. Years later Conlai wore this ring on a visit to Ulster, where he challenged the local heroes to combat. Just like his father, Conlai was quick to anger and soon over-came CONALL, Cuchulainn's foster-brother. Despite the misgivings of his wife EMER, Cuchulainn could not resist fighting the young stranger himself. Too proud to announce his own identity when challenged by Cuchulainn, Conlai accepted the possibility of death and drew his sword. Although Cuchulainn was impressed by sword-play that matched his own, he lost his temper the moment Conlai cut off one of his locks of hair. The terrible combat only

CONLAI, the ill-starred son of Aoifa and Cuchulainn, grew up in Skye, a stranger to his father. When he went to Ulster to challenge the local heroes, he met Cuchulainn in single combat and was killed. Recognizing his son too late, Cuchulainn was overwhelmed with grief.
(ILLUSTRATION BY JAMES ALEXANDER, 1995.)

CONALL of the Victories, a veteran warlord, avenged Cuchulainn's death by slaying his killers one by one. From the brain of one of his victims, Mac Da Tho, he made a magic brain ball, a lethal weapon. Conall here is welcomed by his Ulstermen at a feast in Mac Da Tho's dun.
(ILLUSTRATION BY STEPHEN REID, 1910.)

ended when Cuchulainn drove his spear through Conlai's stomach. Only then did Cuchulainn notice on his young opponent's finger the gold ring he had given to Aoifa. Cuchulainn, overwhelmed with remorse and grief, carried the dying Conlai to his house and afterwards buried his forgotten son.

CORMAC was the son of the Ulster king *CONCHOBHAR MAC NESSA*. An Irish myth tells of his distaste at his father's treachery in killing *NAOISE*, the husband of *DEIRDRE*, and of his going into voluntary exile with the deposed Ulster ruler *FERGUS MAC ROTH*. Not until he received an invitation from his father Conchobhar, when the dying king had nominated Cormac as his successor, did he consider returning home. However, a druidess had warned Cormac that if he went back to Ulster he would be killed, but he set out anyway and on the journey he fell into a deep magic sleep and was slain by a group of warriors. The attack was said to have been arranged by a jealous husband, whose wife had fallen in love with Cormac.

CORMAC (below), returning home after his long, voluntary exile, stopped by a roadside hostel where he was lulled to sleep by the soft notes of a harp. Defenceless in his enchanted sleep, he was slain by assassins, sent by the harpist, Craiftine, in revenge for Cormac's affair with his wife. (ILLUSTRATION BY NICK BEALE, 1995.)

CORMAC MAC ART'S (above) reign was distinguished by peace and plenty. A wise and good man, he was favoured by the Tuatha De Danann who invited him to their hidden world, and gave him a curative apple branch. In tune with Christian kindness, he warmly welcomed St Patrick at his court. (ILLUSTRATION BY JAMES ALEXANDER 1995.)

CORMAC MAC ART was the High King of Ireland during the period that *FINN MACCOOL* led the Fenian warrior band. He was the most famous of the early rulers of Ireland, his reign being tentatively dated from 227 to 266. Cormac Mac Art was the Irish Solomon, a wise and powerful king, who was well served by the brave exploits of Finn MacCool. His wisdom seems to have impressed the *TUATHA DE DANANN*. These gods and goddesses invited Cormac Mac Art to their home in the otherworld, where they gave him wonderful presents. One of these was a silver branch that bore golden apples, and when shaken produced music that could cure the sick and wounded. On his own death Cormac Mac Art had to hand back this incredible talisman. One of Cormac's sons, Cellach, raped the niece of Aonghus of the Terrible Spear. In the ensuing fight, Cellach was slain and Cormac lost an eye. As a High King could have no imperfection Cormac had to step down and his son Cairbe took his place. The reputation of the High King remained so strong that later the Irish Christians also adopted him. It was claimed that Cormac Mac Art learned of the Christian faith before it was actually preached in Ireland by St Patrick, with the result that he ordered that he should not be buried at the royal cemetery by the River Boyne because of its pagan associations.

CREIDHNE was the goldsmith of the *TUATHA DE DANANN* and the brother of *GOIBHNIU*, the smith god, and Luchtar, the carpenter. During the second battle of Magh Tuireadh, when the De Danann finally defeated the *FOMORII*, the three brothers could be seen on the battlefield making and repairing spears with magical speed. As Goibhniu fashioned a blade with three blows of his hammer, Luchtar carved a handle in a flash, and Creidhne crafted rivets that flew into place and bonded at once.

CUCHULAINN as a youngster lived at the court of the High King, where he trained with other sons of chieftains, whom he soon outstripped in arms and might. Although small, he glowed with an inner divine light and warmth, which he inherited from his father the sun god Lugh.

(ILLUSTRATION BY STEPHEN REID, 1912.)

CUCHULAINN, in Irish mythology, was the champion warrior of Ulster. His name means "the Hound of Culann", although he was usually called the Hound of Ulster. Cuchulainn was the Irish Achilles, a larger-than-life fighter whose bouts of temper often caused grief to himself and others. Anger certainly made him slay his son CONLAI, when the young man travelled from the Land of Shadows to visit Ulster. The fifteen-year-old warrior was Cuchulainn's son by the warrior-princess AOIFA. Neither father nor son would identify themselves, so a tragic fight ensued. A gold ring on Conlai's finger revealed too late that he was Cuchulainn's own offspring.

Cuchulainn's mother was DECHTIRE, the daughter of the druid CATHBAD, an advisor to the King CONCHOBHAR MAC NESSA. It was Cathbad who foretold that Cuchulainn would become a great warrior but die young. Shortly after her marriage to SUALTAM MAC ROTH, who was the brother of the deposed Ulster ruler FERGUS MAC ROTH, Dechtire along with fifty of her kinswomen flew to the otherworld in the form of a flock of birds. During the wedding feast she had swallowed a fly and dreamed as a result of the sun god LUGH, who told her to make this journey. Cathbad reassured his son-in-law by saying that Dechtire had merely gone to visit her otherworld relations, for her mother was a daughter of the god AONGHUS. In fact, Lugh kept Dechtire there for his own pleasure for three years.

When Dechtire and her women returned to Emain Macha, the stronghold of the Ulster kings, in the form of brightly coloured birds, Dechtire was expecting Lugh's son, Setanta. Sualtam Mac Roth was so pleased to have his wife home again that when the boy was born he accepted him as his own child.

As a youth, Setanta quickly learned the ways of the warrior, but it was not obvious to everyone just how strong and brave he was until he killed an enormous hound with his bare hands. One day, arriving late at the gate of a house where King Cochobhar Mac Nessa was being entertained by the Ulster smith CULANN, the young hero was attacked by the ferocious guard dog and only saved himself by dashing out its brains on one of the gate's pillars. Their host had now lost a faithful guardian, so Setanta offered to take the hound's place while a replacement was found. When Culann thanked the young warrior but declined his offer, it was decided that henceforth Setanta would be known as Cuchulainn ("the Hound of Culann").

Even though Cathbad warned that anyone going to battle for the first time on a certain day was destined for a short life, Cuchulainn could not wait to deal with Ulster's enemies and he soon took up arms against three semi-divine warriors named Foill, Fannell and Tuachell, as well as their numerous followers, all of whom he killed. In this combat Cuchulainn displayed for the first time the dreadful shape of his battle-frenzy. His body trembled violently; his heels and calves appeared in front; one eye receded into his head, the other stood out huge and red on his cheek; a man's head could fit into his jaw; his hair bristled like hawthorn, with a drop of blood at the end of each single hair; and from the top of his head arose a thick column of dark blood like the mast of a ship. Returning to Emain Macha in his chariot, "graced with the bleeding heads of his enemies", and with the battle-frenzy still upon him, Cuchulainn was only stopped from circling the defences and screaming for a fight through a ploy of the Ulster queen Mughain. She led out of Emain Macha some hundred and fifty naked women carrying three vats of cold water. An embarrassed or amazed Cuchulainn was swiftly womanhandled into the vats. The first one burst its sides. The second boiled furiously, but the last vat whose water became only very hot. Thus was the young hero tamed after his first taste of blood.

In his calm, everyday state of mind Cuchulainn was a favourite of womenfolk. But he fell in love with EMER, the daughter of Fogall, a wily chieftain whose castle was close to Dublin. Cuchulainn asked for Emer's hand but Fogall, who was against the match, pointed out that Cuchulainn had yet to establish his reputation as a warrior and suggested that he should go and learn

CUCHULAINN, the Irish Achilles, performed many mighty deeds in his brief years. The hero's dreamy eyes reflect his idealism, which is expressed in the inscription beneath this portrait, "I care not though I last but a day if my name and my fame are a power forever."

(CUCHULAINN BY JOHN DUNCAN, CANVAS, 1913.)

CUCHULAINN, *mortally wounded in his final combat but determined to fight to the end, lashed himself to a pillar and died on his feet. At the end a crow settled on his shoulder, signifying death. This memorial symbolizes all those who fought for Irish independence.* (THE DEATH OF CUCHULAINN BY O SHEPPARD, BRONZE, 1916.)

For a year and a day Cuchulainn was taught by Scathach, and became the lover of her daughter *UATHACH*. Scathach seems to have feared for the safety of Cuchulainn, and she warned him without success not to challenge her sister Aoifa. But Cuchulainn beat Aoifa by cunning, and afterwards she became his mistress, conceiving the unfortunate Conlai. Cuchulainn finally returned to Fogall's stronghold and claimed Emer, but only after a heated battle with Fogall and his warriors, during which Fogall leapt to his death escaping the hero.

Acclaimed as the champion of Ireland in a beheading contest, Cuchulainn was soon unbeatable in combat, a skill he was to need dearly in his last campaign, which was a single-handed defence of Ulster against the invading army of Queen *MEDB* of Connacht. The main reason for this large-scale cattle raid was a famous brown bull which was kept in Cuailgne. But the tyrannical ruler of Ulster, King Conchobhar Mac Nessa, also played a part in gathering rebellious Ulstermen and others from many parts of Ireland to Queen Medb's side. One prophecy told the queen that there would be "crimson and red" upon her forces because of Cuchulainn's prowess, but she was determined to invade and she also had three advantages. First, the great hero had made bitter enemies of the *CALATIN* family, whose daughters were witches. Just prior to his last stand along with his faithful charioteer *LAEG*, they cast a spell on Cuchulainn which withered a shoulder and a hand. Second, Medb attacked when Ulster's heroes were laid low by *MACHA*'s curse, and were unable to fight for five days and nights. Finally, Cuchulainn had lost the support of the goddess *MORRIGAN*, because he had rejected her passionate advances. Yet he still managed to conduct a successful single-handed defence and was able to slow the advance of Queen

from the Scottish champion Domhall. Domhall told Cuchulainn that his best trainer in arms would be *SCATHACH*, a warrior-princess in the Land of Shadows. So he travelled to this mysterious land and served Scathach. She taught the young hero his famous battle leap.

CUCHULAINN journeyed to the Isle of Skye to train in the martial arts. On the Isle he met a man who gave him a flaming wheel to guide him through the deadly quagmire. The guide was his father, the sun god, Lugh. (ILLUSTRATION BY STEPHEN REID, 1912.)

Medb's forces by the use of clever tactics and lightning attacks, until the effects of Macha's curse had almost worn off, and the dazed warriors were able to respond to Sualtam Mac Roth's call to arms. But their help came too late for Cuchulainn. Pressed on all sides by his enemies, the Ulster champion was overcome in spite of aid from his divine father, the sun god Lugh. His only companion, Laeg, was laid low with a spear, then Cuchulainn himself suffered a terrible stomach wound that even Lugh could not heal. Finally, Cuchulainn tied himself to an upright stone in order to fight till his last breath. As soon as he died Morrigan, in the form of a crow, settled on his shoulder and his enemies cut off his head and right hand, leaving his body for the carrion birds. Conall, his foster-brother, managed to recover the missing parts, but Ulster wept for the loss of their champion. Indeed, so widespread was Cuchulainn's fame that his exploits influenced the development of the Arthurian myths in Britain and France. (See also *MAGIC AND ENCHANTMENT; CELTIC ROMANCE*)

CULANN, in Irish mythology, was an Ulster smith who was thought to be a reincarnation of the sea god *MANANNAN MAC LIR*. It was his enormous guardian dog that young Setanta killed with his bare hands. Culann was angry about this so Setanta offered to become his hound until a new one was trained. Thereafter the young man was known as *CUCHULAINN*, "the Hound of Culann".

CULHWCH, in Welsh mythology, was the son of Cildydd, one of King *ARTHUR's* knights. His stepmother hated Culhwch so much that she placed a curse on him that he could marry only *OLWEN*, the daughter of the giant Yspaddaden. This fate, however, seemed less dreadful once Culhwch found Olwen, a task which took over a year, for they fell deeply in love. Culhwch's next problem was how to persuade her giant father to agree to the match. Like the Irish Cyclops *BALOR*, Yspaddaden's eyelids needed to be levered up with supports in order for him to see

CULANN (below), the Ulster smith, and the High King Conchobhar gaze in amazement at the young Cuchulainn who slew Culann's fierce hound outright when the great guard dog had attacked the hero at the gate. To compensate for killing his hound, Cuchulainn offered to take its place. (ILLUSTRATION BY STEPHEN REID, 1912.)

CU ROI and his comrade, Cuchulainn, on one wild escapade, raided Inis Ter Falga, carrying off the king's booty and beautiful daughter, Blathnat. When the heroes fell out over the girl, Cuchulainn was at one point beaten and buried up to his arms while Cu Roi galloped off with Blathnat. (ILLUSTRATION BY JAMES ALEXANDER, 1995.)

Culhwch. Also like Balor, the Welsh giant did not favour the idea of his daughter marrying a man. At interviews held on successive days Yspaddaden threw a poisoned spear at Culhwch and his companions, but they managed on each occasion to catch it and throw it back. When Culhwch finally put out one of the giant's eyes with a return throw, Yspaddaden agreed to the marriage on condition that Culhwch perform a whole series of difficult tasks. With the assistance of King Arthur's men and a couple of divine allies, Culhwch successfully completed these trials, then killed Yspaddaden and married Olwen. (See also *HEROIC QUESTS*)

CUMAL (whose name means "sky") was the father of the Fenian hero Finn Mac Cumal, more commonly known as *FINN MACCOOL*, who was born after his father's death. Cumal was also a renowned leader of the *FIANNA* and chief of the Clan Bascna. He was killed by Jadhg, a druid, who had been enraged when Cumal eloped with his daughter.

CU ROI (whose name means "hound of Roi") was a Munster king. It was King Cu Roi who transformed himself into *UATH*, the dreadful giant, in order to choose the champion of Ireland. The three

CULHWCH (right), on his quest for Olwen, arrives at Arthur's court, seeking help and counsel. This Victorian painting evokes a medieval mood, portraying the hero as a courtly hunter from the Age of Chivalry. The surly steward could be Arthur's brusque seneschal, Kay. (KILHWYCH, THE KING'S SON BY ARTHUR GASKIN, WOOD, C. 1900.)

D

contenders for the championship – Laoghaire, Cuchulainn's foster-brother CONALL, and CUCHULAINN himself – were invited by Cu Roi to a beheading contest, which only Cuchulainn had enough courage to go through with. Later, Cu Roi and Cuchulainn carried off BLATHNAT, a beautiful woman. Although she expressed her love for Cuchulainn, Cu Roi took her to his castle in Munster. When Cuchulainn laid siege to the stronghold, Blathnat betrayed Cu Roi by showing how the place could be entered.

CYNON, according to a late Arthurian myth, was a knight who encountered a black man with one foot and one eye, and bearing a large wooden club. This Fomorii-like fighter, doubtless a cousin of the violent and misshapen Irish sea gods, ordered Cynon to go to a fountain and fill with water a silver bowl that he would find there , and then to throw the water against a marble slab. Sir Cynon did as he was instructed and a Black Knight appeared to the sound of thunder and the singing of magic birds. Sir

CYNON, an Arthurian hero, battles with the Black Knight, a mysterious warrior who appeared by magic. Although defeated, Cynon returned home on foot to tell the tale, and thus inspired Owain to set out on his memorable quest. Years later Cynon retraced his steps in search of Owain. (ILLUSTRATION BY H THEAKER, 1920.)

Cynon then fought his mysterious opponent but was defeated.

DAGDA means "the good god". He was in fact the great god of Irish mythology, and was usually depicted as a man in rustic clothes dragging an enormous club on wheels. With one end of this weapon he could slay his enemies and with the other he could restore the dead to life. Dagda was believed to be wise, full of knowledge and well versed in the magic arts. He was a chief of the TUATHA DE DANANN.

Dagda was a great fighter and the lover of MORRIGAN, the war goddess. The bones of his enemies were described as "hailstones under horses' hooves" when he wielded his mighty club. Like an all-powerful chieftain, Dagda led the Tuatha De Danann on the battlefield, slaying all those who dared to confront him. Yet he was also associated with abundance, being able to satisfy the hunger of every-body by means of an inexhaustible cauldron. That Dagda took great pleasure in eating was apparent, when just before the second battle of Magh Tuireadh he visited the camp of the FOMORII, his bitter enemies, during a truce at the time of the New Year festival. There they made for him a porridge of milk, flour, fat, pigs and goats, enough for fifty men.

On pain of death Dagda was

ordered by the Fomorii to consume this massive meal, which he readily did with a huge wooden ladle "so big that a man and a woman could have slept together in it". This test turned Dagda temporarily into a gross old man, but it did not prevent him from making love to a Fomorii girl, who promised to use her magic on behalf of the Tuatha De Danann. The story may recall, in a distorted form, a holy marriage between a chieftain and a maiden at the beginning of each year; similar to

DANA, the great mother goddess, gave her name to the Tuatha De Danann, a race of wonderful, beautiful but often vulnerable gods who lived in the sparkling otherworld. Here, they gather to hear the poignant song of Lir's children, ill-starred gods who were turned into swans. (ILLUSTRATION BY STEPHEN REID, 1912.)

DAGDA, father of the gods, owned a wondrous cauldron of plenty and a double-edged magic club, carried on wheels. This bronze relief of a powerful Celtic deity, with a wheel, is regarded by some to be Dagda, with the wheel symbolizing his treasures. (GUNDESTRUP CAULDRON, GILDED SILVER, C. 100 BC.)

the sacred rite that was performed by a Sumerian ruler and a priestess in Mesopotamia. This union was meant to ensure prosperity, strength and peace.

Although the eventual defeat of the Fomorii at the second battle of Magh Tuireadh was really due to the sun god LUGH, it was Dagda who was held in the greatest respect, even after the Tuatha De Danann were in their turn overthrown by the sons of MILESIUS, the ancestors of the present-day Irish.

To Dagda fell the important task of settling the defeated Tuatha De Danann underground. Just as the Fomorii had retreated beneath the waves, so the vanquished De Danann disappeared underground. Over the centuries these powerful deities were gradually transformed into fairies – the bean sidhe or BANSHEES of Irish folklore. (See also WONDROUS CAULDRONS)

DANA, another name for ANU, was the goddess after whom the TUATHA DE DANANN were named – "the people of the goddess Dana".

DECHTIRE, in Irish mythology, was the mother of *CUCHULAINN*. She was a daughter of Maga, the child of the love god *AONGHUS* and of the druid *CATHBAD*, advisor to King *CONCHOBHAR MAC NESSA* of Ulster. When Dechtire married *SUALTAM MAC ROTH*, a fly flew into her cup during the wedding feast and she swallowed it. She fell into a deep sleep and dreamed that the sun god *LUGH* insisted that she and fifty of her kinswomen follow him to the otherworld as a flock of birds. Three years later a flock of brightly coloured birds reappeared at Emain Macha, the capital of Ulster. The Ulstermen went after them with slings, but were unable to hit any of them. It was decided, therefore, to surprise the birds at night as they rested. So it was that the warriors came upon Dechtire, her women and Lugh sleeping in a hut on a site renowned for its magical properties. When Conchobhar was told of of this he sent for Dechtire at once, but she told her captors that she was too ill to be able to travel for another day. The next morning she showed them her new-born son, a gift to Ulster.

DECHTIRE, who had disappeared mysteriously on her wedding day, returned three years later with the shining sun god, Lugh. Dechtire brought with her a gift from the otherworld – her child, Setanta, who became Ulster's greatest hero, Cuchulainn. (ILLUSTRATION BY G DENHAM, C. 1900.)

DEIRDRE was the cause of Ulster's sorrows, according to Irish mythology. The druid *CATHBAD* foretold this before she was born, as well as telling of how beautiful she would become. When she grew up, King *CONCHOBHAR MAC NESSA* wished to marry her, even though he was already advanced in years, but Deirdre would have none of this. She persuaded *NAOISE* and his brothers to run away with her to Alba. After living for many years in their voluntary exile, they were tricked into returning to Ulster on the understanding that they would come to no harm. But Conchobhar arranged to have Naoise killed and then forced Deirdre to agree to marry him. Once married, however, Deirdre remained sad and kept her distance from the king, with the result that he handed her over to the killer of Naoise. Rather than sleep with this man, she threw herself from his speeding chariot and smashed her brains out on a rock. From each of the graves of Naoise and Deirdre grew a pine, which eventually intertwined and grew as a single tree.

DERBFORGAILLE was the daughter of a ruler of Lochlann. When her father left her on the shore as a tribute for the *FOMORII*, she was rescued by the Ulster hero *CUCHULAINN* and fell in love with him. In order to follow him, she turned herself into a swan. However, unaware of the bird's true identity, Cuchulainn brought her down with a sling-shot. She returned to human form and he sucked the stone out of the wound, but now they were linked by blood and so he could not marry her.

DIAN CECHT was the Irish god of healing. It was said that with his daughter Airmid, he had charge of a spring whose waters restored the dying gods to life. After *NUADA*, the leader of the *TUATHA DE DANANN*, lost his hand fighting the *FIRBOLG* at the first battle of Magh Tuireadh, Dian Cecht gave him a silver hand, thus earning him the title Nuada "of the Silver Hand". Impressed though the Tuatha De Danann were by Dian Cecht's handiwork, Nuada was felt to be no longer fit to be a war leader and *BRES*, who was

DEIRDRE grieves for the death of her beloved Naoise and his brothers, slain by the jealous King Conchobhar. Over the brothers' grave, she sang her pitiable lament, "May my heart not break today for the sea-tides of our everyday sorrows are strong, but I am sorrow itself..." (DEIRDRE OF THE SORROWS BY JOHN DUNCAN, C. 1912.)

half *FOMORII*, took his place. But Bres was a tyrant and became very unpopular, so Nuada was restored to the leadership, once Dian Cecht's son Miach had made him a new hand of flesh and blood. Apparently the god of healing grew jealous of his son's medical skills and so killed him.

DIARMUID UA DUIBHNE, or Diarmuid "of the Love Spot", was the foster-son of the Irish love god *AONGHUS*. His mortal father gave him to the god as a child, a gift that was returned when Diarmuid received the famous love spot as a young Fenian warrior. One night, when out hunting, Diarmuid and three companions took shelter in a small hut in a wood. There a beautiful young woman received them but chose to sleep only with Diarmuid. She told him that she was Youth, and that the love spot she put on his forehead would make him irresistible to women. As a consequence, Diarmuid's life was almost continuously troubled by desperate women, the worst being *GRAINNE*, the passionate daughter of High King *CORMAC MAC ART*. Grainne was betrothed to *FINN MACCOOL*, the Fenian commander, but she wanted Diarmuid and forced him to elope with her. For sixteen years the Fenians pursued them until, at the request of the king and the love god, a peace was grudgingly made.

It seemed that Diarmuid and Grainne would settle down to a contented family life and they had several children. But Diarmuid's own destiny was about to catch up with him. His mortal father had killed his brother at birth because

he believed that Aonghus' steward, Roc, was responsible for the pregnancy. However, Roc revived the infant as a magic boar and told it to bring Diarmuid to his death. When hunting one day with Cormac Mac Art and Finn MacCool, Diarmuid came face to face with this creature. His hounds fled in terror, his slingshot had no impact on the charging boar's head and his sword broke in two, so the irresistible Diarmuid was left bleeding to death on the ground. Finn MacCool refused to fetch the dying Diarmuid a drink of water, and by the time the other hunters arrived on the scene, he was too near to death to be saved. Grainne was devastated by the loss, although she was moved by the way that Aonghus took care of Diarmuid's corpse. He took the body to his own palace by the River Boyne, where he breathed a new soul into Diarmuid so that they could converse each day. This was how the young man came to live with the TUATHA DE DANANN, who had by this time left the upper world and lived beneath the soil of Ireland.

DIARMUID, gored by a wild boar, was denied healing water by Finn, still smarting over Diarmuid's love affair with Grainne. A Celtic Adonis, the hero was loved by women often against his will, and, like Adonis, was killed by a boar, but enjoyed some form of immortality. (ILLUSTRATION BY H J FORD, 1912.)

DON was the Welsh equivalent of the Irish mother goddess DANA and was the daughter of Mathonwy, sister of MATH, and the wife of Beli, the god of death. She had many children, including AMAETHON, ARIANRHOD, Govannon, GWYDION, Gilvaethwy and NUDD.

DIAN CECHT (above), god of healing, guards the sacred spring of health with his daughter, Airmid. Its miracle waters cured the sick and restored the dead to life. Known as the father of medicine, Dian Cecht is credited with a remarkable sixth-century Brehon Law tract on the practice of medicine. (ILLUSTRATION BY NICK BEALE, 1995.)

DON (below), the Welsh mother goddess, was as popular as her Irish counterpart, Dana. This female figure, surrounded by birds and children, is widely assumed to be a Celtic mother goddess. She is one of several Celtic deities embossed on the gilded panels of the Gundestrup Cauldron. (GILDED SILVER, C. 100 BC.)

DIARMUID (below), a gifted Fenian warrior, was lured underground by the De Danann who often recruited champions to fight in their otherworldly battles. To test his skill, they sent a mysterious warrior to challenge him as he drank from their forest well. (ILLUSTRATION BY STEPHEN REID, 1912.)

MAGIC AND ENCHANTMENT

ENCHANTMENT PERMEATES Celtic myth, shrouding the tales in a haunting, dreamlike quality. The all-pervasive otherworld lies behind much of the mystery and magic, penetrating the forests and lakes, and crafting charmed rings and weapons. Yet spells and magic also arose in the visible world where bards, druids and some privileged heroes, such as Finn MacCool, possessed magical powers. Bards could weaken the enemy with satire or enchanted sleep, while druids bewitched the host with magical illusions. Off the battlefield, love and romance were also subject to spells, love philtres or magical

trickery, as in the romances of Sadb, Rhiannon and Iseult. On the brighter side, many heroes enjoyed the gifts of the otherworld, such as Arthur's sword, Excalibur, or Fergus Mac Roth's *sidhe* sword; while Fergus Mac Leda's water-shoes afforded underwater adventures; and countless heroes were nourished or reborn from magical cauldrons.

FERGUS MAC LEDA, (above), a high king of Ulster, owned a pair of water-shoes with which he enjoyed underwater travel. He never tired of exploring the depths of the lakes and rivers of Ireland until he encountered a fierce river-horse in Loch Rury. The incident so terrified Fergus that his face became permanently distorted with fear. As only an unblemished king could rule Ireland, Fergus returned to the loch to slay the monster before going down himself, but with a face at last restored and serene. (ILLUSTRATION BY STEPHEN REID, 1912.)

THE ENCHANTED FOREST (left) of Arthurian legend, was alive with beguiling fairy maidens, who often taunted errant knights. One such, La Belle Dame Sans Merci, described by the poet Keats, was a banshee who attracted mortal lovers for her own amusement, inspiring them with a hopeless infatuation and then leaving them bereft of will or purpose until they withered on the lake, "alone and palely loitering". As the languishing knight here sleeps, he dreams of the pale kings and warriors whom La Belle Dame holds in thrall. (LA BELLE DAME SANS MERCI BY H M RHEAM, CANVAS, 1897.)

EXCALIBUR (above), Arthur's enchanted sword, shone with the light of thirty torches and dazzled his enemies. The precious scabbard prevented the loss of blood in battle, but Arthur rather rashly handed this talisman over to his half-sister Morgan Le Fay for safekeeping; she instantly made a duplicate for Arthur, passing the original on to her lover, Accolon. Here, Arthur marvels at the sword rising from a white-clad arm in the enchanted lake. (ILLUSTRATION BY AUBREY BEARDSLEY, C. 1870.)

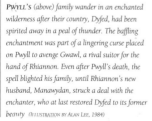

PWYLL'S (above) family wander in an enchanted wilderness after their country, Dyfed, had been spirited away in a peal of thunder. The baffling enchantment was part of a lingering curse placed on Pwyll to avenge Gwawl, a rival suitor for the hand of Rhiannon. Even after Pwyll's death, the spell blighted his family, until Rhiannon's new husband, Manawydan, struck a deal with the enchanter, who at last restored Dyfed to its former beauty. (ILLUSTRATION BY ALAN LEE, 1984.)

MERLIN (right), wise and thoughtful though he was, was enchanted by the ravishing Lady of the Lake, Nimue, and despite his foresight, he allowed himself to be lured deep beneath a stone and bound there by his own magic spells. In another legend, Nimue put Merlin into a trance beneath a thorn tree and then trailed her veil around him, creating an invisible tower of air in which he was trapped forever. It is said that his voice can still be heard in the plaintive rustling of leaves. (ILLUSTRATION BY ALAN LEE, 1984.)

E

DONN ("the Dark One") was the Irish god of the dead. He is sometimes confused with *EBER* Donn, one of the leaders of the sons of *MILESIUS*, who insulted *ERIU*, one of the *TUATHA DE DANANN*, and was drowned off the south-west coast of Ireland. Donn's home, the House of Donn, was thought to be an assembly point on the journey to the otherworld.

DRUIDS see *SAGES AND SEERS*

DUBH was a druidess. According to one Irish tradition, her anger at her husband Enna's passion for another woman ultimately led to the name of Dublin. Dubh used magic to drown her rival, but her husband in turn drowned her in what became known as Dubhlinn ("Dubh's pool").

DYLAN ("Son of the Wave") was a Welsh sea god whose parents were *ARIANRHOD* and her brother *GWYDION*. As soon as he was born

DYLAN, a Welsh sea deity, leapt from his mother's arms at birth and plunged straight into the sea and swam as well as any fish. Beloved by the sea, all the waves wept when he was killed, and his death-groan can still be heard in the roar of the incoming tide. (THE BAPTISM OF DYLAN, SON OF THE WAVE BY GEORGE SHERRINGHAM, CANVAS, C. 1900.)

DONN, god of the dead, gathers souls around him as they assemble on his stormy island before setting out on their journey to the otherworld. Inevitably, he became associated in popular folklore with shipwrecks and sea storms, and was often confused with Eber Donn, who died at sea. (ILLUSTRATION BY JAMES ALEXANDER, 1995.)

he headed straight to the sea, where he immediately swam as well as a fish. When his uncle, the smith god Govannon, killed him, all the waves of Britain and Ireland lamented his death.

EBER was the name of two of the three leaders who led the Milesians in their conquest of Ireland. They were Eber Donn, or Eber "the Brown", and Eber Finn, or Eber "the Fair". The third was named Eremon. Eber Donn failed to reach the Irish coast because his ship foundered in a storm caused by, it was said, his bloody war cry. The

druid *AMAIRGEN* had only just succeeded in casting a spell over the turbulent waves, when Eber Donn was seized by a battle-frenzy and the charm was broken by his wild cries. After the defeat of the *TUATHA DE DANANN*, the advice of Amairgen was ignored by Eber Finn, who refused to acknowledge the right of his older brother Eremon to be king of the whole island. So it was that Ireland was partitioned into two kingdoms, with Eremon ruling the north and Eber Finn the south. But Eber Finn invaded Eremon's territory and laid waste to his lands until he fell in battle. Eremon then became the first High King of all Ireland.

EFNISIEN, in Welsh mythology, was the troublesome half-brother of *BRAN THE BLESSED* who caused the rift between Bran and King *MATHOLWCH*. Because Efnisien had not been consulted by Bran over the marriage of his half-sister *BRANWEN* to the Irish king, he proceeded to cut off the lips, ears and tails of Matholwch's horses during the wedding feast. To compensate for this act, Bran gave Matholwch a magic cauldron that was capable of restoring dead warriors to life, but with one small imperfection – they came back to life without the power of speech. However, the

Irish did not consider this gift a sufficient redress for Efnisien's act of mutilation, and some time after her arrival in Ireland Branwen was demoted from being queen to just a lowly cook in the palace kitchens. Efnisien accompanied the army that was sent against Matholwch to avenge this insult. It was fortunate for Bran that his half-brother did come, because Efnisien foiled a cunning trap that had been laid for the Britons by Matholwch in his hall. He had placed behind each of Bran's strongest warriors a sack hung from the wall containing an armed Irishman, and at a signal they were to fall upon the Britons during what was supposed to be a feast of welcome. When Efnisien inspected the hall beforehand, he asked what was in the bags. On being told it was corn, Efnisien laid hold of the sack and felt about till his fingers closed on the head of the warrior within it, then he squeezed and cracked his skull. One by one Efnisien asked about the contents of the sacks and each time repeated his squeezing.

The feast took place therefore not as Matholwch had planned. An even more unexpected turn of events occurred when Efnisien threw Matholwch's three-year-old son by Branwen on to the fire. Branwen would have leapt after her

ELATHA (above), a Fomorii king, lived beneath the waves with his violent and misshapen people. Unlike the other Fomorii, Elatha was a godlike being with long golden hair. Emerging from the sea one day in his silver ship, he met the lovely goddess, Eri, who fell immediately in love with him. Soon after, they had a handsome but troublesome son, Bres. (ILLUSTRATION BY NICK BEALE, 1995.)

EBER DONN (above) and the Milesian chiefs drift in the fairy sea mists off the Irish coast. On board Eber's ship, the druid Amairgen charmed the sea with magic of his own, but Eber let out his great war cry which broke the druid's spell and stirred up a storm in which he was drowned.

(ILLUSTRATION BY JAMES ALEXANDER, 1995.)

EFNISIEN (below) inspects sacks in Matholwch's hall. In each sack he felt a warrior's head, which he crushed between his fingers. The moody trickster went on to provoke a deadly contest, but then, in remorse, sacrificed himself to save his comrades. (ILLUSTRATION BY STEPHEN REID, 1910.)

son, but Bran held her back. In the fight that took place afterwards the Britons were almost defeated by the magic cauldron that Bran had given Matholwch, because at night it restored to life the Irish warriors who had been slain during the day. The Britons were in a desperate predicament and so Efnisien, at the cost of his life, destroyed the magic cauldron. He hid among the Irish dead and was thrown into the boiling cauldron, where he stretched and burst its sides, but the great effort involved killed him.

ELATHA, in Irish mythology, was the son of Delbaeth, the leader of the *FOMORII* and father of *BRES*, who was briefly the leader of the *TUATHA DE DANANN*. Unlike the other Fomorii, who were described as being hideous and deformed, Elatha was fair and had golden hair. He met the goddess Eri on the sea shore and there they conceived their child Bres. When Bres was removed from the leadership of the De Danann, he and his mother went to Elatha to ask for help, but the Fomorii were defeated at the second battle of Magh Tuireadh and driven from Ireland.

EMER, in Irish mythology, was the daughter of Fogall and the wife of *CUCHULAINN*, who first saw her when he was at the court of the High King of Ireland at Tara. She appeared "dark-haired almost as himself, and her skin white as mare's milk, and her eyes wide and proud and brilliant like the eyes of Fedelma, his favourite falcon". Emer's father was a chieftain from Meath and was against the match. He told Cuchulainn to travel to improve his fighting skills and only then would he consider him as a son-in-law. Cuchulainn survived and returned to claim his bride. Indeed, Cuchulainn was forced to attack the reluctant Fogall's fortress before the wedding could take place. Although Emer was totally enraptured by her handsome husband, their marriage was not without its troubles, not least because many other women also found the Ulster hero attractive. Just before his final battle, when he fought the army of Queen *MEDB* alone, Emer tried to persuade him to remain in the fortress of Emain Macha, the seat of King *CONCHOBHAR MAC NESSA*. However, he got on his chariot when it was brought

around to the front of his house. Even then, he thought of Emer's request, but his enemies the witches of *CALATIN* cast a spell to harden his resolve to fight single-handed.

ENID see *CELTIC ROMANCE*

EMER, a peerless Irish maiden, inspired the love of Ulster's great hero, Cuchulainn. She was blessed with the six gifts of womanhood: beauty, chastity, wisdom, sweet speech, song and needlecraft. When the hero courted her, she smiled at his youth, and said that he had "deeds to do". (ILLUSTRATION BY STEPHEN REID, 1912.)

F

ETAIN (right), one of the High Queens of
Ireland, appears with her peers in power
and beauty: from left to right, Etain, Greek
Helen, Medb and Fand, the fairy queen.
The jewelled cup of plenty recalls Etain's
links with the otherworld. (ETAIN, HELEN,
MEDB AND FAND BY HARRY CLARKE, GLASS, C. 1900.)

EPONA, the Celtic horse goddess, won the favour of the Roman
army and was depicted in monuments set up at its cavalry barracks
as a woman riding a fast steed, her
cloak billowing with air behind her.
She was even given her own festival
in Rome on December 18. Originally, Epona was almost certainly
seen by the Celts as a mare, possibly like the great white horse carved
in the chalk downs near Wantage,
in southern England. The fact that
she is often depicted riding a horse
with a foal suggests that she was
also a goddess of fertility. In the
Welsh myth of *PWYLL* there is a
connection between Epona and his
wife *RHIANNON*, who is made to
carry visitors into her husband's
palace.

ERIU, or Erinn, was the wife of
Ma Greine, son of *OGMA*, and herself one of the *TUATHA DE DANANN*.
When the Milesians invaded, she
and her two sisters, Banba and

EPONA (below), the Celtic horse goddess,
was adopted by the Roman cavalry who
spread her cult across Europe. Her effigy,
often placed in stables, portrayed her riding
side-saddle, sometimes with a foal, which
reflected her role as a fertility goddess,
symbolized here by the wheat and birds.
(ILLUSTRATION BY MIRANDA
GRAY, 1995.)

ETHNE, a gentle Tuatha De Danann maiden, was lost to the otherworld when she mislaid her Veil of Invisibility, key to the Realm of Fairy. She was rescued by monks and, according to a later legend, became a nun, but she was disturbed by "voices", the cries of her fairy folk, seeking her in vain. (ILLUSTRATION BY STEPHEN REID, 1910.)

Fotla, went to greet them. All three asked that the newcomers would name the island after her. AMAIRGEN, druid and advisor to the sons of MILESIUS, promised that Ireland would be named after Eriu.

ETAIN, in Irish mythology, was one of the TUATHA DE DANANN and was reincarnated several times. She was the second wife of the god MIDIR. His first wife was jealous of Etain and by a druid's spell Etain was reborn as a mortal, the daughter of the Ulster warrior Etar. To hinder Midir's search for her, Etain was turned first into a pool of water, then a worm and finally a fly. When Etar's wife accidentally swallowed the fly she became pregnant with Etain. Unaware of her previous existence, Etain was loved both by the High King Eochaidh, whom she married, and by his brother AILILL. This potentially difficult situation was solved by her sudden discovery that she was already married to Midir, who had awakened her memories. High King Eochaidh lost Etain to the god at a game of chess, but although she lived once again with Midir for a period of time, Etain decided in the end to return to Tara and finish her mortal life as Eochaidh's queen.

ETHLINN, sometimes Ethnea, was the only daughter of BALOR, the one-eyed giant of Irish myth. Balor imprisoned Ethlinn in a crystal tower on Tory Island, off the north-western coast of Ireland, because of a prophecy that said he would be killed by his own grandson. However, a certain Cian, brother of the smith god GOIBHNIU, managed to reach Ethlinn, and so the sun god LUGH was conceived. Despite Balor's attempts to have the baby killed, he survived to be brought up either by Goibhniu or, according to another version of the myth, by the sea god MANANNAN MAC LIR, and so fulfilled his destiny by killing Balor at the second battle of Magh Tuireadh.

ETHNE was the daughter of Roc, steward of the love god AONGHUS, and acted as maid to the daughter of MANANNAN MAC LIR. After a chieftain of the TUATHA DE DANANN tried to rape her, she refused to eat or drink. Aonghus and Manannan searched for a remedy and found two magic cows whose milk never ran dry and she lived on their milk.

ETHNEA see ETHLINN

EXCALIBUR see MAGIC AND ENCHANTMENT

FAND, in Irish mythology, was the wife of MANANNAN MAC LIR. One day she quarrelled with her husband and he left her. When she was attacked by the FOMORII, Fand sent for CUCHULAINN, who came to her island and defeated her enemies, and remained for one month as her lover. Before he returned home, they arranged to meet again in Ireland. But Cuchulainn's wife, EMER, found out about this secret meeting and took fifty of her maidens armed with sharp knives to kill Fand. A confused argument then took place between Fand, Emer, Cuchulainn and Manannan Mac Lir, who had also learned of the arrangement. But in the end, Fand

FAND's maidens appeared to Cuchulainn in a vision, beating him with rods, which left him sore for a year. Having gained his attention, they explained that the goddess, Fand, needed his help to fight the Fomorii. After defeating her attackers, Cuchulainn stayed on Fand's island for a month. (ILLUSTRATION BY STEPHEN REID, 1912.)

decided to stay with her husband and forget Cuchulainn. Manannan Mac Lir then shook his magic cloak between Fand and Cuchulainn so they would never see each other again, and druids gave Cuchulainn and Emer drinks of forgetfulness. (See also CELTIC ROMANCE)

FEDLIMID the story-teller was the father of DEIRDRE. One day, when CONCHOBHAR MAC NESSA and some fellow Ulstermen were drinking at his house, the unborn Deirdre cried out from her mother's womb. The druid CATHBAD then foretold that the child would cause nothing but doom and destruction.

FERDIA son of Daman the FIRBOLG, was a friend and comrade of CUCHULAINN. As young men, they were both taught to fight by SCATHACH. During the war of the brown bull of Cuailgne, Ferdia fought on the side of Queen MEDB and against Cuchulainn and the men of Ulster. Ferdia did his best to avoid coming up against his friend, but eventually Medb taunted him into fighting the great hero in single combat and he was killed.

FERGUS MAC LEDA see MAGIC AND ENCHANTMENT

FERGUS MAC ROTH, a king of Ulster, according to one myth fell in love with his predecessor's widow, NESSA. She would only marry him if her son, CONCHOBHAR MAC NESSA, was allowed to rule for a year. Conchobhar, with help from his mother, proved to be a popular king and the people refused to let him stand down. At first Fergus accepted this but, later, when Conchobhar lost the support of several leading Ulstermen, he led them in revolt. Conchobhar's love for DEIRDRE was the cause of his unpopularity, especially after he had her lover NAOISE killed in order to marry her. Fergus with three hundred Ulster warriors joined Queen MEDB in her invasion of Ulster. The great CUCHULAINN lost his life in this war, but not at the hands of Fergus. They had been friends before the war and had sworn not to fight each other. During the final battle, Fergus pretended to retreat and the next time they met Cuchulainn would do the same. It was due to Fergus' retreat that CONALL, Cuchulainn's foster-brother, was able to defeat Medb's army and rally the Ulstermen after the death of Cuchulainn.

FERDIA is borne from the battlefield by his lifelong friend, Cuchulainn. The two were goaded into single combat by Medb and fought grimly to the death. At Ferdia's death, Cuchulainn fell exhausted, lamenting, "Why should I rise again now he that lies here has fallen by my hand?" (ILLUSTRATION BY E WALLCOUSINS, 1912.)

THE FIANNA (right), a fierce band of free warriors, guarded the High King of Ireland and roved up and down the countryside on various ventures. Hand-picked, they were gifted in both arms and the arts. Although close-knit, occasional rivalry broke out and there was the odd brawl, as shown here.
(ILLUSTRATED BY ARTHUR RACKHAM, C. 1910.)

THE FIANNA was the famous band of warriors responsible for the safety of the High King of Ireland. Popularly called the Fenians, their greatest leader was *FINN MACCOOL* and the majority of their members came from one of two clans, the Bascna and the Morna. Many of the adventures of the Knights of the Round Table recall the exploits of the Fenians. To join, "no man was taken till in the ground a hole had been made, such as would reach the waist, and he put into it with his shield and a forearm's length of a hazel stick. Then must nine warriors, having nine spears, with a ten furrows' width between them and him, assail him and let fly at him. If he sustained injury, he was not received into the band."

FINEGAS, the aged seer and poet, humbly offers Finn the Salmon of Knowledge, fulfilling the prophecy that a man named "Fionn" would benefit from the miraculous fish. On eating the salmon, Finn became as wise as he was strong, with instant insight into the past and future.
(ILLUSTRATION BY H R MILLAR, 1912.)

FINEGAS, in Irish mythology, was a druid. Hoping to become supremely wise, he caught the Salmon of Knowledge, but unfortunately for his own ambitions he gave it to the young *FINN MACCOOL* to cook. Finn burnt his thumb on the flesh of the fish and sucked the burn. Realizing that his pupil Finn was the one destined to gain the wisdom, Finegas generously let the boy eat the whole fish.

FINN MACCOOL, sometimes called Finn Mac Cumaill or Fionn MacCumal, was the leader of the *FIANNA*, or Fenians, the select band of warriors which guarded the High King of Ireland. His father, *CUMAL*, a previous leader of the Fenians, was killed by Goll, a Fenian warrior. Cumal had eloped with a girl named Hurna and her father urged Goll to avenge this dishonour. Goll slew Cumal, but later Cumal's son Finn was born and brought up secretly. One of his tutors was the druid *FINEGAS*, who lived beside the River Boyne and caught the Salmon of Knowledge. He gave the fish to his pupil to cook, but Finn burnt his thumb on the flesh and in sucking it obtained wisdom.

So great was Finn MacCool's prowess as a warrior that he was soon appointed over the head of Goll to lead the Fenians, as his father had done. Goll accepted this decision with good grace, a gesture that may explain why Finn MacCool did not challenge Goll over his father's death. Indeed, Goll eventually married one of Finn MacCool's daughters, though he also slew his son. This last act of violence was too much and the Fenians pursued him. Trapped, Goll chose to starve to death rather than surrender. Finn MacCool used to quote a saying of Goll: "A man lives after his life but not after his dishonour."

Under Finn MacCool's leadership, the Fenians reached the high point of their fame as a warrior band. The pursuit of *DIARMUID UA DIUBHNE*, the foster-son of the love god *AONGHUS*, alone took sixteen years. He had taken *GRAINNE*, the daughter of High King *CORMAC MAC ART*, but she was betrothed to Finn MacCool at the time. The Fenians were relentless in the chase, but a peace of sorts was begrudgingly agreed. However, Finn never forgave Diarmuid for

FINN MACCOOL (below), a precocious and gifted child, enjoyed a special affinity with the creatures of the woods. He was raised on the slopes of Bloom Slieve by two warrior women, who helped him develop the heroic virtues of wisdom and strength.
(ILLUSTRATION BY ARTHUR RACKHAM, C. 1910.)

the elopement, and he exulted over his rival's mortal wound, which he had received when hunting.

The account of Finn MacCool's own death is unclear. Some sagas tell how he fell attempting to quell an uprising among the Fenians

FINTAN, the Salmon of Knowledge, basks in Nechtan's well of inspiration, overhung with the Nuts of Knowledge. Fintan gained his wisdom from eating the nuts which fell into the well, causing bubbles of inspiration. The well is decorated here with Celtic heads, symbols of spiritual power.
(ILLUSTRATION BY STUART LITTLEJOHN, 1994.)

THE FOMORII, a misshapen race of sea gods, oppressed Ireland with cruelty and crushing tributes. This imaginative and powerful scene portrays the Fomorii as repellent and alien creatures, who are driven by a sick and menacing frenzy. (THE FOMORS OR THE POWERS OF EVIL ABROAD IN THE WORLD BY JOHN DUNCAN, 1912.)

themselves, while others refer to an *ARTHUR*-like undeath in a cave. There he was supposed to remain in a deep sleep until such time as Ireland needed his aid.

FINTAN was the husband of Noah's granddaughter *CESAIR*. It is likely that the monks who first recorded the Irish sagas altered the original myth in order to link it with Noah's descendants, because of the deluge that only Fintan managed to survive by becoming a salmon. The monks wanted to tidy up the Irish myth of Fintan's mysterious transformation. The same name was also given to the Salmon of Knowledge, which was so called because it had eaten the nuts of a hazel tree that grew over the waters of *NECHTAN*'s well.

THE FIRBOLG, or bag-men, arrived in Ireland after escaping a life of slavery in Thrace, where they had been forced to cultivate the land by heaving heavy bags of fertile earth up rocky hills. In revolt, they turned their bags into boats and sailed to Ireland. (ILLUSTRATION BY NICK BEALE, 1995.)

THE FIRBOLG, or "bag men", in Irish mythology were said to have acquired their name from a time when they were enslaved in Thrace and made to carry bags of earth. They lived in Ireland just before the arrival of the *TUATHA DE DANANN*. But they were already being hard pressed by the *FOMORII*, the sea gods whom the Tuatha De Danann eventually overcame. At the first battle of Magh Tuireadh the Tuatha De Danann defeated the Firbolg, though the De Danann leader, *NUADA*, lost a hand. In the second battle of Magh Tuireadh the Fomorii were thoroughly beaten, due mainly to the bravery of the sun god *LUGH*, and were driven from Ireland for ever.

THE FOMORII were sea gods in Irish mythology. Violent and misshapen, the Fomorii emerged from the waves to challenge two rulers of Ireland: the *FIRBOLG* and the *TUATHA DE DANANN*. The Tuatha De Danann were younger gods, and they seized control of Ireland from the Firbolgs at the first battle of Magh Tuireadh, only to have to defeat the Fomorii at a second battle there in order to secure their conquest. Often the Fomorii were described as having only a single hand, foot or eye.

FORBAI was the son of the Ulster king *CONCHOBHAR MAC NESSA*. According to one myth, Queen *MEDB* of Connacht fell back before the fury of the Ulster warriors after her invasion of the kingdom. In Galway, however, Forbai caught up with her as she was bathing in a lake. A shot from his sling fatally struck the old warrior-queen in the centre of her forehead.

FRAOCH ("wrath" or "fury"), in Irish mythology, was a warrior who defeated a fearsome water monster in order to marry Findbhair, who was the daughter of Queen *MEDB* of Connacht. The terrible struggle with the monster left Fraoch very badly wounded and he recovered fully only after a timely visit to the

otherworld. His mother Be Find (who was a goddess and sister of the river goddess *BOANN*) nursed him back to health so that he could claim the hand of Findbhair. The account of Fraoch and the water monster is thought to have had some influence on the Danish legend of Beowulf's battle with Grendel, a monster invulnerable to weapons who lived in an underwater cavern.

FINN MACCOOL stands guard on the ramparts of Tara awaiting a fiery goblin whose magic music usually disarms his foes. Armed with a fairy spear, Finn breaks the spell and slays the unsuspecting demon. For his valour he was made captain of the Fianna. (ILLUSTRATION BY STEPHEN REID, 1910.)

WONDROUS CAULDRONS

MIRACULOUS CAULDRONS feature as a recurrent motif in Celtic myth. Some overflow with plenty, others restore the dead to life, while still others contain a special brew of wisdom. Dagda's gigantic Cauldron of Plenty overflowed with abundant, delicious meats; no hero left his bowl hungry, though cowards never had their fill. From Bran's massive Cauldron of Rebirth warriors emerged alive but dumb; another Cauldron of Rebirth in Annwn was guarded by nine maidens. Cauldrons of Inspiration provided "greals" or brews of wisdom. The most famous belonged to the goddess Ceridwen, whose magical broth endowed Taliesin with all-knowing insight. Some cauldrons, such as Dagda's, combined the magical properties of both plenty and rebirth. Similar mystery bowls or cups feature in Greek and eastern myths as holy vessels of spiritual insight. Ultimately, the early Celtic cauldrons find expression in the Arthurian Grail, which overflows with spiritual sustenance and leads the hero from death to immortality.

CAULDRONS OF PLENTY (left) glittered in bronze, copper, silver or gold, embossed with exquisite craftsmanship. The gilded Gundestrup Cauldron, here, found in a bog in Denmark, is a magnificent surviving example of a Celtic cauldron. Embossed in silver gilt, it is beautifully decorated in the La Tene style with Celtic deities and ritual activities, such as hunting or fighting. (GUNDESTRUP CAULDRON, GILDED SILVER, 100 BC.)

BRAN'S (above) Cauldron of Rebirth restored warriors to life, but without the power of speech. Bran received his wondrous cauldron from two martial giants, in gratitude for his kindness. Here, the great and gloomy giants brood over their bubbling cauldron, flanked by armed warriors on either side, for the warlike giants produced a grown warrior every six weeks. (ILLUSTRATION BY ALAN LEE, 1984.)

luue de   iowmessue

THE GRAIL, *or Sangreal, (above) appeared to the knights of the Round Table amid dazzling light in which they saw each other more wisely and generously than ever before. The vision rendered them speechless, much like the Celtic warriors who emerged from their Cauldron of Rebirth alive but dumb. The Grail itself, shrouded in white samite, appears in the form of a Chalice of the Mass, recalling the Cup of the Last Supper. The chalice filled the hall with spicy odours and the knights ate and drank as never before, which all recalls the earlier Celtic Cauldrons of Plenty. (MANUSCRIPT ILLUSTRATION C. 1400.)*

CAULDRONS OF REBIRTH *(below), such as Annwn's or Bran's, must have been as large as tubs to contain the bodies of fallen warriors. In this section, a towering god appears to be dipping warriors into a mighty bucket or bowl, probably a cauldron of rebirth. Foot soldiers march in procession towards the cauldron, while a line of mounted infantry gallop off at the top, after their renovating dip. (CELTIC CAULDRON, GILDED SILVER, 100 BC.)*

CELTIC CAULDRONS *(below right) varied greatly in size, but such legendary cauldrons as Dagda's were so huge that they had to be conveyed on wheels or by chariot; while Bran's mighty cauldron was carried on the back of the giant Llaser. This cult wagon depicts just such a monumental cauldron. Mounted heroes in their peaked helmets, possibly hunters, travel triumphantly either to or from the hunt. The two stags, plus the hunters, suggest that the deity bearing the cauldron of plenty could well be the hunter god Cernunnos. (CULT WAGON, BRONZE, 100 BC.)*

135

G

GALAHAD (left), the pure and peerless knight, stands resplendent in a blaze of holy light, armed as a Christian Crusader. His snow-white shield, marked with the blood of Joseph of Arimathea, was designed in Sarras for Galahad alone. (GALAHAD BY W HATHERELL, GLASS, C. 1910.)

GALAHAD (right), robed in red, entered Arthur's court escorted by a hermit, and took his place at the Round Table, filling the Siege Perilous. Completing the circle of knights, his arrival sparked off the Grail Quest. (GALAHAD ENTERS ARTHUR'S COURT BY W HATHERELL, CANVAS, C. 1910.)

GALAHAD was unique at the court of King *ARTHUR*, for he alone saw the entire Grail, or *SANGREAL*. He may even have handled the sacred vessel, as one version of the Arthurian myth states that Sir Galahad took "Our Lord's body between his hands" and then died. The quest for the Grail was an important preoccupation of the Knights of the Round Table. One of the seats was always left vacant as it was the place reserved for the knight who would find the Grail. Until Sir Galahad sat there, no knight had earned the right to occupy the place without being instantly swallowed by the earth.

The worthy young Sir Galahad was the son of Sir *LANCELOT*, the secret lover of Queen *GUINEVERE*, Arthur's wife. From the beginning of Galahad's manhood, however, it is made clear that he is without blemish. Twelve nuns, who had raised Galahad, told his father that he should "make him a knight, for there is no man alive more deserving of the order of knighthood". As soon as Sir Galahad had taken his rightful place at the Round Table, the presence of the Grail was felt in

GALAHAD receives spiritual nourishment from the Grail, followed by Percival and Bors. The idea of an all-sustaining and all-inspiring "greal" or brew is rooted in Celtic myth. (HOW SIR GALAHAD, SIR BORS AND SIR PERCIVAL WERE FED WITH THE SANC GRAEL BY DANTE ROSSETTI, CANVAS, 1864.)

Camelot. A mysterious lady then announced how the sacred vessel would come and feed all the knights. This happened, although none at the wonderful meal saw or touched the Grail. When Sir Gawain vowed to find its home in order to see the Grail for himself, most of the Knights of the Round Table followed suit, despite the efforts of King Arthur to dissuade them from undertaking what might prove to be their final quest. Although they set off in different directions, Sir Galahad was in the company of Sir *PERCIVAL* and Sir

Bors when he encountered the Grail. Together they had received the sacrament from the long-dead *JOSEPH OF ARIMATHEA*, who told Sir Galahad to take a bleeding spear to the castle of the "Maimed King" and rub it on this crippled ruler's body and limbs. Once this task was carried out, and the strange king restored to health, Sir Galahad saw the Grail in a vision. When he prayed that "he might leave the world", a voice told him how his soul would live in the next life with Christ the moment his request could be granted.

After this, various miracles took place and Sir Galahad was even obliged to become a king for a time while he waited patiently for his request to be fulfilled. When Joseph of Arimathea eventually returned, Galahad was at last granted his wish to leave the world. Joseph first allowed the pure and humble knight to hold the Grail for a few moments, then, as Sir Galahad knelt down to pray for his deliverance, his soul was suddenly released from his body and "a great multitude of angels bore it up to heaven".

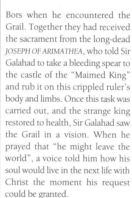

GAWAIN, in Welsh Gwalchmai, was the most courteous knight at ARTHUR's court. He was a strict upholder of chivalry and the enemy of Sir LANCELOT. Sir Gawain's most extraordinary adventure concerned the Green Knight. Rather like the hazard faced by the Ulster hero CUCHULAINN, when a water giant came to test the courage of Irish warriors, the gigantic Green Knight strode into King Arthur's hall at Camelot one New Year's Eve and challenged the Knights of the Round Table to a beheading contest. Sir Gawain accepted and cut off the stranger's head in a single blow. As the severed head rolled around the hall, the royal court relaxed and thought the challenge over. But to the amazement of all present, the giant behaved as if nothing had happened. Calmly stooping, he picked up his head and mounted his green charger. Then, from the saddle, the Green Knight pointed his severed head in Sir Gawain's direction and told him to be at a lonely chapel a year from that day in order to take a turn at receiving a blow from an axe. On the journey to this dangerous appointment Sir Gawain stayed with Sir Bercilak de Hautdesert who had a beautiful wife. He was sorely tempted by Sir Bercilak's wife but managed to resist her advances for two days. However, on the third day Sir Gawain accepted from her a green sash, which was the usual token worn by a knight to show his love for a lady.

At the meeting between Sir Gawain and his fearful opponent, the Green Knight turned out to be none other than Sir Bercilak himself. Three times the axe was swung at Sir Gawain's neck. Twice it was deflected because he had not abused his host's hospitality by making love to his wife. The third time it made a slight cut, at which Sir Gawain flinched. It did not cut off his head because Sir Gawain had only accepted the green sash out of good manners. Yet Sir Gawain realized that courtesy was no equal to moral purity, and thereafter he always wore the green sash as a reminder of his lapse.

This late British version of the Celtic beheading contest was quite clearly influenced by Christianity.

GAWAIN, an active and restless knight, lost interest in the Grail Quest quite early on. Although one of the first to set forth, inspiring the rest of the Knights, he lost heart, lacking the necessary discipline, patience and humility. (THE FAILURE OF SIR GAWAIN BY W MORRIS, TAPESTRY, 1895–96.)

Unlike Sir Gawain, Cuchulainn had no hesitation in slipping away from the battlefield in order to keep a secret meeting with a lover, even during Queen MEDB's invasion of Ulster. The magical transformation of Sir Bercilak de Hautdesert into the Green Knight was explained as the work of the witch MORGAN LE FAY, King Arthur's half-sister.

GERAINT see CELTIC ROMANCE; SINGLE COMBAT

GOIBHNIU was the Irish smith god and one of the *TUATHA DE DANANN*. He could make a perfect sword or spear with three blows of his magic hammer. Just before the second battle of Magh Tuireadh, a *FOMORII* spy came to see how Goibhniu made such impressive weapons, and even wounded the god. Goibhniu was said to preside over an otherworld feast called *Fled Goibnenn*, for which he brewed the ale. His Welsh counterpart was named Govannon.

THE GRAIL see *SANGREAL*; see also *WONDROUS CAULDRONS*; *HEROIC QUESTS*.

GRAINNE, in Irish mythology, was the daughter of *CORMAC MAC ART*, the High King of Ireland. She was promised to *FINN MACCOOL*, leader of the *FIANNA*, the body-guard of the High King. Although still powerful, Finn MacCool was quite old and Grainne preferred *DIARMUID UA DUIBHNE*, who was

GOIBHNIU, the Irish smith god, was an outstanding craftsman and armourer. Along with his gifted brothers, Creidhne the goldsmith, and Luchtar, the carpenter, he repaired the Tuatha De Danann armour with miraculous speed on the battlefield. (ILLUSTRATION ANON.)

the foster-son of the love god *AONGHUS*. By using magic, Grainne managed to escape from Tara, the Irish capital, with a rather reluctant Diarmuid. Gradually, however, he came to love Grainne, although for sixteen years they had to keep moving in order to avoid capture

by the Fenians. But Diarmuid was killed by a magic boar in a hunting accident after Cormac Mac Art and Finn MacCool had finally accepted his marriage to Grainne. Although Grainne blamed Finn MacCool for Diarmuid's death and swore to obtain vengeance through her four sons, the wily Finn wooed her until she agreed to marry him.

GUINEVERE, whose Welsh name, Gwenhwyfar, probably means "white spirit", was the wife of *ARTHUR* and the secret lover of Sir *LANCELOT*. In the stories about the Knights of the Round Table, Guinevere is always compared with Helen of Troy, the famous beauty of Greek mythology. Such a comparison is not unjustified, for both these women brought disaster to those who loved them. In Guinevere's case the love affair with Sir Lancelot weakened the unity of the Round Table. It was her beauty that also attracted Arthur's nephew Sir *MODRED*, who seized Camelot

GRAINNE (above), a passionate and wilful maiden, fell for the irresistible Diarmuid. As she was betrothed to Finn MacCool, Diarmuid politely refused her advances. But she persisted until he agreed to elope, with the Fianna in hot pursuit. Here, the guilty pair hide in a magic tree. (ILLUSTRATION ANON.)

GUINEVERE (below), in her original role as Flower Bride, is crowned May Queen in a bower of petals. On May Morning, Arthur and his knights celebrated with sports and contests. Lancelot, her champion, always excelled. (LANCELOT AND GUINEVERE BY HERBERT DRAPER, CANVAS, 1900.)

GUINEVERE (above), condemned to death for her affair with Lancelot, was rescued by him. In the bloody contest that ensued, Lancelot slew many knights. Arthur wept at the loss of "the fairest fellowship of noble knights". (LANCELOT RESCUES GUINEVERE BY W HATHERELL, CANVAS, C. 1910.)

and forced Guinevere to consent to marry him during the king's absence abroad. The confrontation between Arthur and Modred at the battle of Camlan brought to a bloody end the golden age of British chivalry, as hardly a knight was left alive. Arthur, mortally wounded, was taken to AVALON, while Guinevere became a nun at Amesbury, where she later died. It is believed by some that her body was buried at Glastonbury, not far from Arthur's tomb. (See also CELTIC ROMANCE)

GWERN, according to Welsh mythology, was the son of the Irish king MATHOLWCH and the Welsh princess BRANWEN. A dispute between the two royal families led to Branwen becoming a cook, which caused her brother, BRAN THE BLESSED, to sail to Ireland to avenge the insult. Matholwch suggested a compromise to settle the

quarrel. He proposed that Gwern, though only three, should be placed on the Irish throne. But Branwen's half-brother EFNISIEN would not agree and threw the child on to a fire.

GWYDION was the nephew of MATH, lord of the Welsh kingdom of Gwynedd. In order to help his brother, Gilvaethwy, sleep with Gowein, the young woman who was Math's footholder, Gwydion stirred up a quarrel between Math and PRYDERI, which meant that the king went away to war. When Math returned and discovered the deception, he turned his nephews into a stag and a hind for one year, into a boar and a sow for the next, and into a pair of wolves for the third. Later, Gwydion took charge of his sister ARIANRHOD's son LLEU.

GWION BACH see TALIESIN.

GWYN AP NUDD, in Welsh mythology, was an otherworld king who crossed swords with King ARTHUR. Gwyn abducted Griddylad, the daughter of Lludd Llaw Ereint, on her wedding day. According to one late myth, Lludd Llaw Ereint was the son of the death god Beli

and the builder of London. King Arthur set out after Griddylad and demanded that Gwyn ap Nudd return her to her rightful husband, his loyal follower Gwythyr. The siege of the otherworld king's castle proved to be long and difficult, so a strange compromise was agreed by both sides. Gwyn ap Nudd and Gwythyr agreed to meet in combat each May Day until the end of time; whoever was the winner on doomsday could have Griddylad.

HELLAWES see SAGES AND SEERS.

IRNAN, in Irish mythology, was a witch who once spun a magic web to catch some members of the FIANNA, or Fenians, the bodyguard of the High King of Ireland. When this plan failed, Irnan changed herself into a monster and challenged any one of the Fenians to single combat. FINN MACCOOL, the leader of the Fenians, stepped forward but was persuaded that it would not be heroic enough for a warrior of his stature to fight a hag, even if she was in the form of a monster. So another Fenian, Goll, slew Irnan and as a reward Finn allowed him to marry his daughter

GWYDION (above) and Gilvaethwy flee from Pryderi's castle with his precious swine. The daring theft was part of an ingenious plan to help Gilvaethwy win Gowein. A resourceful magician, Gwydion had tricked Pryderi into exchanging his swine for some illusory horses. (ILLUSTRATION BY ALAN LEE, 1984.)

IRNAN (below) was one of three sister witches. She spun a magic web to snare the Fenian warriors. The warriors were rescued by Goll who slew two of the sisters, but spared Irnan when she begged for mercy. However, Irnan instantly changed into a monster and Goll killed her. (ILLUSTRATION BY STEPHEN REID, 1910.)

ISEULT, sometimes Isolde, was an Irish princess, and the story of her love for TRISTAN was extremely popular in medieval times. The Celtic myth of Tristan and Iseult originated in Brittany and was retold in almost every European country. It became attached to the Arthurian stories by the later addition of ARTHUR to the myth.

Iseult, a beautiful woman with wonderful golden hair, cured the orphan Tristan of a wound in the side; a lingering ailment similar to the one afflicting the "Maimed King" in the story of the Grail. On Tristan's arrival in Cornwall, his uncle King MARK wanted to name the young man his successor, but the nobles objected to this arrangement, so the king said that he would marry only the girl to whom belonged the golden hair a swallow had just dropped. Sir Tristan, recognizing the hair as belonging to Iseult, suggested to his uncle that he should go on his behalf to ask for her hand.

Disguised as a Cornish trader, Sir Tristan arrived in Ireland to find the country terrorized by a dragon,

ISEULT (below), an Irish beauty, was also a gifted healer, and cured the Cornish knight Tristan of a lingering wound. While nursing him to health, they fell in love, but their bliss was shortlived as Tristan was forced to leave the Irish court for political reasons. (ILLUSTRATION BY EVELYN PAUL, C. 1900.)

an enormous "crested serpent". Realizing that the best way to advance King Mark's suit would be to slay this monster, Sir Tristan sought out its lair and fought it. Although he just managed to overcome the dragon, its poisonous breath weakened him temporarily and an imposter claimed to have won the contest. Iseult and her mother, however, suspected trickery and discovered the injured young knight. While they were nursing Sir Tristan back to health, Iseult noticed that his sword had a piece missing exactly like the fragment of metal found in the head of MORHOLT, the Irish champion. Sir Tristan had mortally wounded him on the last occasion the Irish tried to collect tribute from Cornwall.

Iseult wanted to kill Sir Tristan in revenge, but she found that her heart would not let her wield the sword against him. It came as a shock then, on his recovery, that Sir Tristan asked for Iseult on behalf of King Mark. When her own father readily agreed to the marriage as a means of restoring good relations between Ireland and Cornwall, Iseult was deeply upset. But her mother gave Iseult's maid BRANGAINE a love potion which, if drunk on their wedding night, would make the couple love each other forever. All would have been well had not Tristan accidentally drunk the potion and given some to Iseult on the journey to King Mark's court. Although Iseult did marry the Cornish king, on the wedding night, under the cover of darkness, Brangaine took her place in the royal bed so that he would suspect nothing. For a time the lovers managed to meet in secret, but, like the love of GUINEVERE and LANCELOT, they were eventually discovered. It happened one day

ISEULT and Tristan unwittingly drank a love philtre which heightened their already awakened passion, forging an unbreakable and finally tragic bond. Duncan's strongly Celtic portrayal captures the intense and undying nature of their love. (TRISTAN AND ISOLDE BY JOHN DUNCAN, CANVAS, 1912.)

that King Mark found them asleep with Sir Tristan's sword between them, but he decided not to slay them there and then. Instead he exchanged Sir Tristan's sword for his own and left them sleeping. Overcome by the mercy shown by his uncle, Tristan persuaded Iseult to return to her husband and he left for voluntary exile in Brittany.

In Brittany Sir Tristan married but without happiness. On several occasions he returned to Cornwall in disguise and secretly met Iseult again, but war took up most of his energies. A serious wound forced Sir Tristan to send for Iseult. It was agreed that Iseult should indicate her imminent arrival with a white sail. Jealous of the reunion of the lovers, Sir Tristan's Breton wife said a ship with a black sail had been sighted. Tristan lost the will to live and threw himself on his sword before Iseult could land and reach his bedside. Iseult followed him into death shortly afterwards.

Stories about elopements, courtships and ill-fated lovers were always popular with the Celts, for whom this story of frustrated passion held great appeal. (See also CELTIC ROMANCE)

ITH was said to have dwelt in a great tower in Spain, from which he was able to see Ireland and so decided to go there. He landed with ninety followers just after the TUATHA DE DANANN had defeated the FOMORII at the second battle of Magh Tuireadh. The Tuatha De Danann suspected Ith of harbouring invasion plans and so killed him. When his body was returned to Spain, his sons swore to conquer the island. The leader of this

IUBDAN (below), one of the Wee Folk, was inclined to brag of his greatness, inciting his bard to cut him down to size by insisting that far greater men lived in Ulster, a veritable race of giants. To prove his valour, Iubdan ventured off to the dun of the "giant", Fergus Mac Leda. (ILLUSTRATION BY STEPHEN REID, 1910.)

invasion of Ireland, the last to be recorded in Irish mythology, was Ith's uncle Mil, or MILESIUS.

IUBDAN was a ruler of tiny people. According to Irish mythology, King Iubdan liked to boast a lot; to put a stop to this annoying habit his court poet told him that Ulster was a land of giants. He even made King Iubdan and his wife, Queen Bebo, travel there in secret and try the porridge of the king of Ulster, Fergus Mac Leda. Unfortunately, Iubdan fell into the porridge and, along with his wife, was taken prisoner by Fergus. No ransom offer proved acceptable to the king of Ulster, although the tiny people offered him an abundant crop of corn. So they went on to the offensive: milk became scarce, rivers and wells were made foul and polluted, mills burned and during the nights the

JOSEPH OF ARIMATHEA (above), the man who interred Christ's body in his own tomb, is believed to have brought the Grail to Glastonbury. After building a church for it where Glastonbury Abbey now stands, he founded a family of Grail Guardians. (MANUSCRIPT ILLUSTRATION C. 1450.)

hair of men and women was entirely cut off. After a year and a day of this harassment Fergus Mac Leda eventually agreed to release Iubdan and Bebo, but only on the condition that in return he was given the king's most valuable and treasured possession, a pair of magic shoes. Whoever wore these shoes was able to travel underwater or across the surface as if walking on dry land; when Fergus Mac Leda put them on they grew to fit his feet exactly. Echoes of the tiny people in this Irish myth can be found in Jonathan Swift's novel, *Gulliver's Travels*.

KAI (above), Arthur's steward, was a knight of legendary might and prowess. Endowed with unusual skills, he could go for nine days underwater and could grow as tall as a forest tree at will. He was very gruff, thwarting both Peredur and Culhwch at the gate. (MANUSCRIPT ILLUSTRATION C. 1450.)

JOSEPH OF ARIMATHEA was a biblical figure who was included in Arthurian mythology because of the Grail story. Joseph allowed Christ's body to be placed in his own tomb. His own long life was said to have been due to the Grail. Either Joseph, or his brother-in-law Bron with his son Alan, brought the Grail to Glastonbury. Later, it disappeared and its recovery was the greatest quest for the Knights of the Round Table. Only GALAHAD was granted a complete vision of the Grail. It was handed to him by Joseph of Arimathea, a "bishop already dead for more than three hundred years"; this "good man took Our Lord's body between his hands, and offered it to Sir Galahad, who received it with humble joy".

KAI, in Welsh mythology, was one of the senior warriors of ARTHUR's court. In medieval romance, he became the steward Sir Kay. In one tradition, he is a Cornishman and Arthur's foster-brother. He was said to have magical powers: he could go nine days and nine nights without sleep and breathe for nine days and nine nights under water.

KAY see KAI

141

CELTIC ROMANCE

T HE LIVELY AND COMPELLING character of Celtic romance stems from the heated rivalries and passions of the lovers. Most, if not all, tales involve a love triangle with two men contesting one desirable woman. Sometimes one of the rivals is young and handsome, while the other is an oppressive guardian, as in the tale of Naoise and Conchobhar; elsewhere, the two suitors are simply rival admirers, one loved and the other despised, as in the case of Pwyll and Gwawl. This recurrent rivalry probably symbolizes a seasonal battle between a Lord of Summer and a Lord of Winter for the Spring Maiden. Celtic love triangles create tension, drama and colourful characters of timeless appeal. The attractive young heroes, such as raven-haired Naoise, or Diarmuid of the Love-Spot, are quite as irresistible as the ravishing Celtic beauties, Deirdre and Fand. While all the characters are portrayed with touching flaws, the heroines emerge as strong and independent women, expressing warmth and wisdom.

LANCELOT (above) and Guinevere's abiding love for each other wounded Arthur, shook his court and split the Fellowship of Knights. Yet both lovers are portrayed by Malory as essentially good but tragic characters. Even Arthur realized that Guinevere had been true to him in her way as a generous and faithful consort, and he was never lessened by their love. Here, the couple kiss at their first meeting, contrived by Galleot in an embroidered medieval setting. Although their love grew out of the courtly tradition, it went far beyond what the courtly code would have allowed. (MANUSCRIPT ILLUSTRATION C. 1400.)

TRISTAN (above) and Iseult snatch a tense moment together in their clandestine romance. They had grown obsessively attached to one another after accidentally drinking a love philtre intended for Iseult and her betrothed, King Mark of Cornwall. The doomed lovers embarked on a desperate and tragic romance, fraught with guilt and unrequited longings. (TRISTAN AND ISOLDE BY A W TURNBALL, CANVAS, 1904.)

THE LADY OF THE FOUNTAIN (right), a shining vision in
gold, appeared to young Owain as the fairest, wisest, noblest,
most chaste, most generous woman in the world. But, as
Owain had just slain her husband, the Black Knight, he had to
press his suit with care. The Lady's faithful handmaiden,
Luned, helped Owain woo her mistress by reminding her that
the realm required a strong guardian. Luned here escorts
Owain to her Lady's chamber. (ILLUSTRATION BY ALAN LEE, 1984.)

FAND (above), a breathtaking beauty from the otherworld, set
her heart on the Ulster hero, Cuchulainn, and lured him to her
realm to fight a Fomorii giant. After a month in her delightful
company, the two arranged a tryst where the hero's wife, Emer,
joined them, lamenting, "What's new is sweet, what's well-
known is sour…" Her heartfelt plea inspired the generous
Fand to give up her beloved Cuchulainn, realizing that he had
a worthy mate in Emer. (ETAIN, HELEN, MAEV AND FAND BY HARRY
CLARKE, GLASS, DETAIL, C. 1900.)

GERAINT (right), suspecting his wife of infidelity, forced her to
accompany him on a gruelling journey of errands, and so
tested her love and obedience every step of the way. Like other
strong-minded Celtic heroines, Enid endured her ordeal calmly,
remaining loyal and loving throughout. Geraint, for his part,
finally felt "two sorrows" of remorse for having mistrusted and
mistreated her so. At one stage in their journey, the pair passed
through a wonderful walled tower, as seen here.
(ILLUSTRATION BY ALAN LEE, 1984.)

L

LAEG was *CUCHULAINN*'s charioteer. The Celts were renowned in the ancient world for their skill in handling chariots on the battlefield, and Laeg's skill was crucial to many of Cuchulainn's victories. He was also a great friend and companion. When *FAND* invited Cuchulainn to the Land of Promise, he sent Laeg before him to survey the place. During Cuchulainn's final and mortal combat, Laeg threw himself in front of a spear aimed at his master. Id, Laeg's brother, was charioteer to *CONALL* Caernach.

LANCELOT was one of the greatest and noblest knights in the Arthurian tales. He was known as Lancelot of the Lake because the Lady of the Lake had plunged him into a magic pool when he was a child. Sir Lancelot, described as "the flower of knights", was very attractive to women, not unlike the handsome Irish warrior *DIARMUID UA DUIBHNE*. Once King *ARTHUR*'s half-sister and enemy *MORGAN LE FAY* cast a spell over the sleeping knight and shut him in a dungeon. There she demanded that he must choose among four enchantresses who would be his "paramour", or

LAEG, charioteer of Cuchulainn, drove the hero on all his adventures, acted as scout and comrade and finally cast himself in front of a spear meant for his master. War chariots played a key role in Celtic battle, with driver and warrior acting as a single unit. (ILLUSTRATION BY J LEYENDECKER, 1916.)

LANCELOT, most handsome and gifted of Arthur's knights, attracted both mortal and immortal queens. Four fairy queens here kidnap the sleeping knight and hold him in their castle, demanding that he choose one of them to be his mistress. (HOW FOUR FAIRY QUEENS FOUND LANCELOT SLEEPING BY W F CALDERON, CANVAS, C. 1900.)

mistress. When he turned them all down, including Morgan Le Fay, the knight admitted his love for *GUINEVERE*. All of Sir Lancelot's great adventures and exploits were indeed informed by this secret love. For a time Queen Guinevere would not allow Sir Lancelot to come to her, but they eventually became lovers. Sir Meliagaunt, however, was suspicious and confronted Sir Lancelot in the presence of King Arthur and Queen Guinevere. A tournament was held to discover the truth. "With such great force Sir Lancelot smote Sir Meliagaunt on the helmet that the stroke carved the head into two parts."

LANCELOT, after much fasting and praying, came at last to Carbonek, the Grail Castle. Being tainted with sin, he could not enter but was granted a vision. When he stepped too close he was struck by fire and left dazed for 24 days. (LANCELOT REFUSED THE GRAIL BY E BURNE-JONES, CANVAS, 1870.)

Honour seemed satisfied and the reputation of Arthur's queen also appeared unblemished, but there were other Knights of the Round Table who could not accept this judgement by arms. So Sir Agravain and Sir *MODRED* led twelve knights to Guinevere's chamber and surprised the lovers. Although Sir Lancelot managed to make a fighting exit and several days later saved Queen Guinevere from being burnt to death, his actions effectively split the Round Table and weakened the strength of King Arthur's realm. First, Arthur conducted an unsuccessful siege of Sir Lancelot's castle in Brittany. Then a second and more deadly challenge to the king's authority came from Sir Modred, his nephew. In the subsequent battle at Camlan, near Salisbury, most of the Knights of the Round Table were slain. King Arthur was mortally wounded and taken by a magic boat to *AVALON*. Queen Guinevere retreated from the world and became a nun at Amesbury, where she died. Sir Lancelot and Guinevere met only once more before the knight renounced the ways of war to lead the life of a hermit. (See also *CELTIC ROMANCE*)

LLEU (right) had to turn into an eagle to escape his murderous wife, Blodeuedd. He hid in the forest, wounded and starving, until Gwydion lured him down and restored him to health. Blodeuedd was turned into an owl. (ILLUSTRATION BY ALAN LEE, 1984.)

LIR, or Llyr in Welsh, was the father of *MANANNAN MAC LIR*, the Manx sea god, magician and god of healing. Although Lir was also a sea god he is hardly mentioned in mythology, despite giving his name to many places, including Leicester in England. Shakespeare probably had the Welsh Llyr in mind when he wrote his tragedy *King Lear*.

LLEU, named Lleu of the Skilful Hand, in Welsh mythology was the son of *ARIANRHOD*. His mother laid a series of curses upon him, including the promise that he was to have no name unless she gave him one, no weapons unless she provided them and no wife of the human race. With the help of his uncle *GWYDION*, who raised him, Lleu overcame all these taboos, though the wife conjured by Gwydion and the magician *MATH* was nearly his undoing. For this woman, *BLODEUEDD*, fell in love with

LIR'S four lovely children were turned into swans by their jealous stepmother. For 900 years they endured cold and hunger in icy waters, charming listeners with their poignant song. When at last restored to human form, they were bent and bony. (LIR'S CHILDREN BY JOHN DUNCAN, CANVAS, 1912.)

another man and plotted Lleu's death. When the guilty lovers struck him, Lleu rose into the air in the shape of an eagle. After a long search, Gwydion found him, restored him to human form and healed his wounds.

LLUD see *NUDD*

LUGH was the Irish name for the Celtic sun god, who was known as Lleu in Wales and as Lugos in France. He was always described as a young and handsome warrior.

Lugh was himself part *FOMORII*, since his grandfather was the Irish one-eyed god *BALOR*, the Fomorii champion. The Fomorii were sea gods who challenged the *TUATHA DE DANANN* for control of Ireland; they were sometimes described as having only a single hand, foot or eye. Lugh's mother was *ETHLINN*, the only daughter of Balor. Because a prophecy had said that Balor would be killed by his own grandson, he locked Ethlinn in a crystal tower on Tory Island, off the northwestern coast of Ireland. But Cian, son of the Tuatha De Danann healing god *DIAN CECHT*, succeeded in reaching Ethlinn and she bore Lugh as a result. Either the sea god *MANANNAN MAC LIR* or the smith

god *GOIBHNIU*, Cian's brother, saved Lugh from Balor's wrath and raised him to manhood.

Well before the final battle between the Tuatha De Danann and the Fomorii, Lugh's prowess as a warrior had been recognized. The De Danann leader *NUADA* stepped down in his favour, and at the second battle of Magh Tuireadh Lugh fulfilled the prophecy of Balor's death when he killed him with a sling-shot. Before delivering this decisive blow Lugh had circled the enemy host on one foot and with one eye closed, a magic circuit that copied the single-leggedness of the Fomorii in general and one-eyed Balor in particular. It would seem that, like the Ulster hero *CUCHULAINN* and the berserkers of Germanic mythology, the battle-frenzy gripped Lugh in such a way that one eye disappeared into his head while the other expanded into a hideous, paralysing stare. Balor's own single eyelid had to be raised by four servants, and Lugh sent his shot smashing into the eye the moment it was opened. Balor's eye was forced back through his head, with the result that its terrible gaze fell upon the Fomorii ranks behind. Thus Balor died and the Fomorii scattered. Lugh became known as

Lamfhada ("of the Long Arm"). Quite possibly this great victory represented the rise of younger gods amongst the Tuatha De Danann themselves, for the youthful Lugh felled Balor with a more modern weapon than *DAGDA*'s ancient club. Indeed, an alternative name for Lugh was Samildanach ("the many-skilled"). This ingenuity may account for Lugh's introduction as the father of Cuchulainn in the more historical sagas. The sun god was believed to have fought alongside his hard-pressed son during Queen *MEDB* of Connacht's invasion of Ulster. After Cuchulainn's death his foster-brother *CONALL* claimed to have received help from Lugh when he chased Cuchulainn's killers. On one occasion the sun god appeared in a magic mist.

Lugh's final claim to fame is that his name became part of the term used to describe the fairy in Irish folklore, because over time "Little stooping Lugh", or Luchorpain, turned into the leprechaun, the tiny guardian of hidden treasure and the expert cobbler.

LUGH, the resplendent Celtic sun god, led the Tuatha De Danann against the Fomorii led by his grandfather, Balor, whom he slew with his magic sling-shot. As god of arts and crafts, he invented the popular board game of fidchell, in which he excelled. (ILLUSTRATION BY E WALLCOUSINS, 1912.)

M

LUGUS was the name used in Britain and France for a god very similar to the Irish *LUGH* and the Welsh *LLEU*. His importance can be judged from the old name for Lyon, Lugdunum ("the fortress of Lug"). The Roman emperor Augustus made it the capital of the provinces of Gaul, and ordered the inhabitants to celebrate this choice each August, the month in which the feast of the Celtic sun god Lugus occurred. The god's name was used for many other place names, possibly even London: the Roman Londinium may have derived from Lugdunum.

MABON, son of the Welsh divine mother Modron, was said to have been abducted when only three nights old and imprisoned in Gloucester. However, since only he was able to control the hound which *CULHWCH* needed to win the hand of *OLWEN*, an expedition was mounted to release Mabon. Once free, he duly helped to capture the wild boar *TWRCH TRWYTH* with the aid of the hound and to take from between the boar's ears the razor

MACHA cursed the Ulstermen to suffer the pain of childbirth for five days, at the time of Ulster's greatest need. The bitter curse stemmed from her ill-treatment by the Ulstermen when, though near her term, she was forced to race on foot to prove a bet.
(ILLUSTRATION BY STEPHEN REID, 1910.)

MABON, or Maponos, was the youthful Welsh love god. A gifted musician, he was also equated with the classical god Apollo. Although forgotten as a god, Maponos survived in Welsh myth as Mabon, a skilled hunter among Arthur's champions.
(ILLUSTRATION BY MIRANDA GRAY, 1994.)

that Olwen's father had demanded. Apart from adventures like this, the actions of Mabon are uncertain, suggesting that he may have been a former god, possibly Maponos, a Celtic god of youth, who was incorporated in Welsh mythology as a warrior once his worship was all but forgotten. The Romans knew of Maponos, whom they equated with Apollo, the god of prophecy.

MAC CECHT was the Irish god of eloquence and the son of *OGMA*. After *NUADA* had been killed at the second battle of Magh Tuireadh, Mac Cecht and his brothers could not decide whether to divide Ireland between them and so they consulted a stranger named *ITH*. Suspecting from his response that he had designs on conquering the island himself, they killed him, thus provoking the invasion of the sons of *MILESIUS*.

MAC DA THO was king of Leinster at the time that *MEDB* was queen of Connacht. He owned a fine hound and a huge boar, and many of his neighbours coveted these animals, including Medb and *CONCHOBHAR MAC NESSA*, king of Ulster. Mac Da Tho promised both these rulers that they could have the hound, and slaughtered the boar to provide a feast, to which he invited them. Fighting broke out between the Ulster king and the men of Connacht, but the latter soon retreated. When the hound, over which they had been quarrelling, ran past the king's chariot his charioteer cut off its head.

MACHA was one of the Irish war goddesses, often identified with *BADB*, *MORRIGAN* and *NEMAIN*. She first married Nemed, a Scythian ruler who defeated the *FOMORII*, the sea gods who slew her second husband *NUADA* and herself at the second battle of Magh Tuireadh. A later Macha laid a curse on Ulster after her boastful husband said that, though heavy with child, she could outrun all the king's horses and chariots. When the king of

Ulster threatened to execute her husband if she did not race, Macha cursed all Ulstermen to suffer the pain of childbirth for five days and five nights whenever the kingdom was in danger. Macha won the race and gave birth to twins, which is said to be the reason for calling the fortress of the Ulster kings Emain Macha ("Macha's Twins").

MAELDUN, or Mael Duin, was one of the great Irish voyagers. The late saga that describes his voyage is a mixture of Christian and pre-Christian ideas, in contrast to the fundamentally pre-Christian mythical voyage of the earlier *BRAN*.

Maeldun's father was a chieftain of the Aran Islands who attacked the Irish mainland, looted a church and raped a nun. He was killed shortly afterwards by raiders from overseas, in all likelihood Vikings. The nun gave birth to Maeldun and the child was fostered by the local ruler's wife, who was the sister of the unfortunate nun. It was only when children taunted Maeldun that he was not really well born that his foster-mother took him to see his true mother and his parentage was revealed. He then set out with three of his foster-brothers to find his father, only to learn that he had been murdered.

Determined to avenge his father's death, Maeldun was advised by a druid as to which were the favourable days for him to build, launch and sail a three-skinned coracle. Then, still accompanied by his foster-brothers and also a crew of seventeen warriors, he sailed on his long and strange voyage of revenge.

The first island Maeldun came to was inhabited by murderers, but apparently not the killers of his father. Next they landed upon an isle of enormous ants; as large as horses, the ants almost devoured the crew and the boat. Large birds living on another island were found to pose no threat, however. They even provided the voyagers with

on top of a pedestal; the offer of eternal youth on one island which was inhabited by a queen and her daughters; intoxicating fruits; contagious laughter; revolving fire; and a hermit who lived on salmon that was given by an otter and half a loaf provided each day by angels.

Eventually, Maeldun caught up with his father's killers, but they pleaded for mercy and a peace was agreed. Thus ended the voyage that was said to contain "the sum of the wisdom of Ireland". (See also FABULOUS VOYAGES)

MAEVE see MEDB.

MAELDUN (below) and his sailors found a wondrous silver column rising straight from the sea. Its summit, lost in the sky, was draped with a silver net, flung far out to sea. As they sailed through the mesh, Diurnan hacked off a piece as proof of the tale. (ILLUSTRATION BY DANUTA MEYER, 1994.)

MAELDUN, on his epic voyage, stopped by the bleak island of the mill (above) where lived a gloomy miller grimly grinding mounds of corn. He observed dourly that the corn symbolized all that men begrudged each other. The voyagers, aghast, sailed away. (ILLUSTRATION BY ALAN LEE, 1984.)

meat. Two subsequent islands of monstrous, gigantic horses proved to be even more dangerous, so it was with some relief that Maeldun and his companions landed on the Island of the House of the Salmon. There they discovered an uninhabited house with food and drink, as well as comfortable beds, awaiting them. A regular supply of fresh salmon was provided by a device that periodically threw fish into the house from the sea. Similar luxury was encountered on the next isle, which was covered with orchards of delicious apples.

Danger was soon encountered again, however, on islands that were populated by revolving beasts, fighting horses, a mysterious cat and fiery swine. The ground on one of them was hot like a volcano. Among other strange creatures and encounters on the voyage were gigantic swine and calves so huge that they could not be cooked whole; sheep that changed the colour of their wool apparently at will; a sombre miller who ground everything that was begrudged in the world; a population of mourners; an island divided into four kingdoms by fences made of gold, silver, brass and crystal; a castle with a glass bridge where there lived a beautiful girl who rejected Maeldun's advances; crying birds; a solitary pilgrim on a tiny island that was enlarged every year by divine providence; a wonderful fountain that gushed milk, beer and wine; giant smiths; a sea of glass; a sea of clouds in which castles, forests, animals and a fearsome monster suddenly appeared; an underwater island of prophecy; an amazing water-arch; a gigantic silver column and net, from which the voyagers cut off a small piece as a souvenir; an inaccessible island

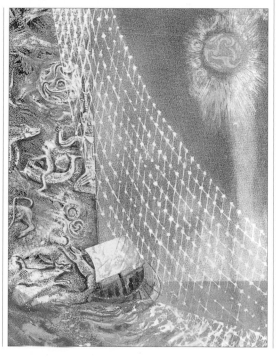

MANANNAN MAC LIR, son of the Irish sea god LIR, took his name from the Isle of Man, which is situated in the Irish Sea about halfway between Ireland and Britain. Manannan was a sea god, magician and healer, and the ruler of the Land of Promise, where he lived in Emhain ("of the Apple Trees"). His home was imagined to be sited off the western coast of Ireland, somewhere in the Atlantic Ocean. His wife was the renowned beauty FAND, who fell in love with the Ulster hero CUCHULAINN but finally chose to stay with her sea god husband. Manannan therefore shook a magic cloak between Fand and Cuchulainn in order to make sure they would never meet again.

Manannan Mac Lir was a noble and handsome warrior, who drove a chariot as easily over the waves as over a plain and was said to have a ship that sailed itself. He had both divine and mortal children, and one of his mortal sons, MONGAN, was conceived by way of a deception similar to the ruse used for ARTHUR's conception. Manannan slept with an Ulster queen when disguised as her husband. Mongan did, however, inherit supernatural gifts, including the ability to shape-change, and he went on to become a great king and mighty warrior.

MANANNAN, (below), the Irish sea god, rode the waves in a self-propelled boat called "Wave Sweeper". As a sea god, Manannan could stir up or soothe the sea, and help or hinder ships. He often appeared to voyagers, such as Bran, at the outset of their trip. (ILLUSTRATION BY MIRANDA GRAY, 1994.)

MANAWYDAN (above) tried to grow wheat after a mysterious blight had devastated his land. One field was ripe for harvest when overnight it was stripped to the stalks by mice. In despair, he planned to hang one of the mice, until dissuaded by a stranger. (ILLUSTRATION BY ALAN LEE, 1984.)

MARK (below) watches sadly as his wife, Iseult, kneels before a drawn sword, beside herself with grief at Tristan's death. Mark, who was often portrayed as a merciful man, gathered her up and bore her off to a tower where she was restored to health. (ILLUSTRATION BY RUSSELL FLINT, C. 1900.)

MANAWYDAN, son of Llyr, was the Welsh equivalent of the Irish sea god MANANNAN, though his links with the sea were far less well defined. The brother of BRAN THE BLESSED and BRANWEN, he married RHIANNON on the death of her husband PWYLL. One day he and Rhiannon, along with Rhiannon's son PRYDERI and his wife Cigfa, were enveloped in a magical mist. When it cleared, their palace was deserted and the land around it desolate, so they travelled to England, where Manawydan and Pryderi made a living as leatherworkers. So successful were they that the local craftsmen forced them to leave. On their return to Wales, both Pryderi and Rhiannon disappeared by magic, leaving Cigfa and Manawydan alone. He then tried to support them by growing a crop of wheat, but his fields were stripped by mice. He caught one of the mice and would have hanged it, but a passing stranger offered him whatever he wanted in return for the mouse's life. Manawydan asked for the return of Rhiannon and Pryderi. The stranger agreed and revealed himself to be Llwyd, a magician and friend of Gwawl, the suitor whom Rhiannon had refused in order to marry Pwyll. (See also MAGIC AND ENCHANTMENT)

MAPONOS see MABON.

MARK was the king of Cornwall in the Breton myth of TRISTAN and ISEULT. He was the guardian of his orphaned nephew Tristan and the husband of Iseult, an Irish princess. Although jealous of Tristan and Iseult, he was not entirely unsympathetic, and even when he came upon the lovers sleeping together with Tristan's sword between them he did not kill them. He exchanged the sword for his own and left without waking them. Shamed by this act of mercy, the lovers knew that they must part. Tristan solemnly returned Iseult to his uncle and went into exile in Brittany.

MATHOLWCH'S (left) convoy of ships glides up to the ragged Welsh shore in the prelude to a doomed marriage between himself and Branwen, the beautiful sister of Bran the Blessed. The ships had ensigns of brocaded silk and an uptilted shield as a sign of peace. (ILLUSTRATION BY ALAN LEE, 1984.)

MEDB (above), the magnificent but malevolent queen of Connacht, was a warrior who fought as fiercely as Morrigan. A wild and wilful woman, she precipitated and perpetuated the bloody war with Ulster in which Cuchulainn and other heroes lost their lives. (ILLUSTRATION BY J LEYENDECKER, 1916.)

MATH was the brother of the Welsh mother goddess *DON* and a great magician. At the time that *PRYDERI* ruled over Dyfed in the southern part of Wales, Math was the lord of Gwynedd in the north. Except during war, Math could only live if his feet were held in the lap of a virgin. When Gilvaethwy, one of his nephews, fell in love with the young woman who held Math's feet in her lap, his brother, *GWYDION*, tricked Math into going to war with Pryderi so that the girl might be left behind. On discovering that he had been deceived, however, the furious Math turned his nephews into animals.

MATHOLWCH, in Welsh mythology, was the Irish king married to *BRANWEN*, the sister of *BRAN THE BLESSED* and half-sister of *EFNISIEN*. Efnisien, because he claimed that he had not been consulted over Branwen's wedding, "cut off the lips of Matholwch's horses at their teeth, their ears to their heads, and their tails to their bodies". Later, when Bran took his army to Ireland to avenge the insult of Branwen being made a cook, Efnisien tossed Matholwch's three-year-old son *GWERN* into a fire. In the battle that followed, nearly all the Britons were killed and all of the Irish except for five pregnant women.

MAXEN see *FABULOUS VOYAGES*

MEDB, also known as Maeve, was the warrior-queen of Connacht. According to Irish mythology, no king could reign in Connacht unless he was married to Medb, who was believed to hold the kingdom's sovereignty in her person. It was also said that she "never was without one man in the shadow of another". Medb's most famous action was the invasion of Ulster, when her forces captured the great brown bull of Cuailgne and killed the Ulster hero *CUCHULAINN*. She was herself slain by Forbai, the son of King *CONCHOBHAR MAC NESSA*, while she was bathing in a pool. Forbai had discovered that Queen Medb was in the habit of regularly taking her bath in a Galway pool. He very carefully measured the exact distance between the spot where she bathed and the shore, then he returned to the Ulster stronghold of Emain Macha and practised with a sling-shot until he was able to knock an apple from the top of a pole over the same distance. Satisfied at last that his aim was perfect, he stealthily made his way back to the pool and hit Queen Medb in the centre of her forehead using his sling-shot. Thus was Ulster revenged.

SINGLE COMBAT

I N WAR, THE ANCIENT CELTS relied on heroic single combat, rather than all-out warfare, as a means of settling disputes. Shortage of manpower forbade multiple pitched battles. Instead, chosen champions, such as Cuchulainn or Morholt, duelled to the death. Even in a large-scale epic war, like the campaign of Cuailgne, the Ulster champion fought in single combat every day with a different warrior. In the Arthurian legends, single combat continued in the form of knightly jousts. While the Celtic heroes wore scant armour, Arthur's mounted knights encased themselves in glittering iron. In addition to the basic weapons of spear, sword, sling and shield, the hero of legend had recourse to magical skills and a range of enchanted weapons, such as Arthur's Excalibur or Fergus Mac Roth's Caladcholg, the original Excalibur.

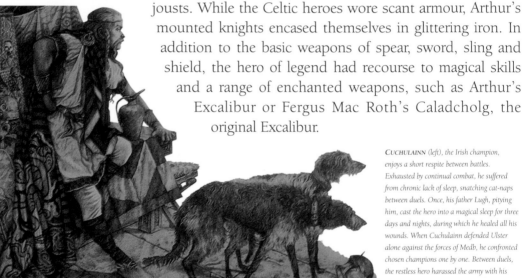

CUCHULAINN (left), the Irish champion, enjoys a short respite between battles. Exhausted by continual combat, he suffered from chronic lack of sleep, snatching cat-naps between duels. Once, his father Lugh, pitying him, cast the hero into a magical sleep for three days and nights, during which he healed all his wounds. When Cuchulainn defended Ulster alone against the forces of Medb, he confronted chosen champions one by one. Between duels, the restless hero harassed the army with his sling. (ILLUSTRATION BY YVONNE GILBERT, 1994.)

CELTIC CAVALRY (right) ride their battle horses to war, armed with spears and crested helmets. Their comrades on foot wear breeches and caps, and bear spears and long bossed shields, while trumpeters bring up the rear. The Celts were heavily reliant on their long shields, which were usually made of wood and sometimes covered with decorative bronze work. Other sharp-rimmed shields could also be used as missile weapons. (GUNDESTRUP CAULDRON, GILDED SILVER, C. 100 BC.)

GERAINT (left) and the Knight of the Kestrel engage in single combat with such ferocity that they shatter each other's armour. Ostensibly, the duel was over the kestrel, but really Geraint was intent on avenging an insult to Guinevere's handmaiden, made by the knight's dwarf. Goaded on by their seconds, both champions fought tirelessly, until Geraint's rage gave him the edge and he overcame, but spared, the knight. (ILLUSTRATION BY ALAN LEE, 1984.)

OWAIN'S (below) kindness to a lion earned him a faithful friend who proved to be a valiant comrade-in-arms. In this unequal match, the giant was winning until Owain's lion leapt to Owain's defence. When the giant complained that he could handle Owain well enough if it were not for his lion, Owain pushed his pet back into the fortress, but the irrepressible creature leapt over the fortress walls and mauled the giant to death. (ILLUSTRATION BY ALAN LEE, 1984.)

HOW MORGAN LE FAY GAVE A SHIELD TO SIR TRISTRAM

MORGAN LE FAY (above) charmed the unsuspecting Tristram into accepting a beautiful gold shield decorated with a strange motif. The shield's design portrayed a knight, Lancelot, enslaving a royal couple, Arthur and his wife. Innocent of the shield's true motif or motive, Tristram rode to Arthur's court and jousted in the royal tournament. When he duelled with Arthur, the king's spear shattered on the enchanted shield. Such enchanted weapons could help or hinder the best of heroes. (ILLUSTRATION BY AUBREY BEARDSLEY, C. 1870.)

MERLIN, sometimes Myrddin, was the famous wizard of Arthurian mythology. So powerful was his magic that one medieval tradition credits him with the magical construction of Stonehenge, the outstanding British monument that has survived from ancient times. Another of his works was supposed to be King ARTHUR's famous Round Table, a late copy of which can still be seen at Winchester today.

Merlin's birth was the subject of a strange story. Apparently, the Britons were told that a great fortress they had built on Salisbury plain, possibly near Stonehenge, would never be safe until the ground there had been soaked by the blood of a child who had no

MERLIN (below), for all his wisdom, was bewitched by the Lady of the Lake who turned his love to her own ends. She sapped his power and plundered his store of secret knowledge, and when done, she bound him in stone by his own spells. (MERLIN AND NIMUE BY E BURNE-JONES, CANVAS, C. 1870.)

mortal father. Such a half-human sacrifice seemed impossible to achieve, until it was learned that a beautiful girl was with child by a demon. The child turned out to be Merlin, who, though baptized as a Christian, still possessed fabulous powers inherited from his demon father. Somehow the boy did not need to be sacrificed for the sake of the fortress because it is likely that Merlin was able to deal with the

MERLIN (left), sage from another world, was an inspired seer and mystic mage, a wise counsellor and faithful friend to three able kings. This powerful portrayal captures the mystical and visionary nature of Celtic bards, rooted in a deep affinity with nature. (MERLIN BY ALAN LEE, CANVAS, 1984.)

MIDIR (right), one of the Tuatha De Danann, appeared at the palace of Tara to carry off Etain, the Ulster woman he loved, long since lost to him by enchantment. The pair drifted upwards and disappeared through a palace window, and flew to an otherworld. (ILLUSTRATION BY STEPHEN REID, 1910.)

problem by means of magic. Two dragons were, in fact, responsible for the problem.

This mixture of pre-Christian and Christian ideas sits strangely with Merlin's later assistance to King Arthur, whose father UTHER PENDRAGON was said to have successfully invaded Britain about this time. Merlin sided with Uther and employed his powers to enable him to sleep with Igraine, the wife of a Cornish nobleman, by disguising him as her husband. Due to this deception Arthur was conceived. Once he ascended the throne, King Arthur had Merlin as his trusted advisor and often used the wizard as a messenger because, as with many of the Celtic gods and goddesses, he could assume any shape he pleased.

There are various accounts of Merlin's death. One tells how the wizard forgot about the seat at the Round Table that only GALAHAD could use, being the only knight worthy enough to see the GRAIL. Merlin sat down and was at once swallowed up by the earth, like other sinful men who had tried it before him. Another story blames the wizard's death on his passion for women. Either Viviane, possibly the Lady of the Lake, or Nimue, the daughter of a Sicilian siren, imprisoned him in an enchanted wood after Merlin had explained all about the secrets of his own magic. As Merlin told Sir GAWAIN, who once

passed by: "I am also the greatest fool. I love another more than I love myself, and I taught my beloved how to bind me to herself, and now no one can set me free." (See also SAGES AND SEERS; MAGIC AND ENCHANTMENT)

MIDIR, in Irish mythology, was the proud son of DAGDA, father of the gods. Unlike his father, who is usually portrayed as a rough, coarse figure, Midir always appeared as a splendidly dressed young man. Midir's first wife was Fuamnach, the daughter of Beothach. She became furious with jealousy when Midir married a second wife, ETAIN, from Ulster. With a druid's aid, Fuamnach turned Etain first into a pool, then into a worm and finally into a fly in order to keep her away from Midir. As a fly Etain was swallowed by the wife of Etar, an Ulster warrior, and reborn as the wife of the High King of Ireland. Although Midir recovered Etain, he had to accept in the end that she was the High King's consort and leave her alone. Midir also had some difficulty in accepting his father's successors as leaders of the TUATHA DE DANANN. The conflict that started seems to have had a dangerously weakening effect on this generation of gods just before the invasion of the Milesians, who then went on to defeat the gods.

MIL OR MILE see MILESIUS

MILESIUS sails for Ireland to avenge the death of his nephew, Ith, who was slain by the Tuatha De Danann, rulers of Ireland. Although Milesius did not reach shore himself, his family succeeded, defeating the De Danann who retreated into an invisible otherworld. (ILLUSTRATION BY STEPHEN REID, 1910.)

MILESIUS, sometimes Mil or Mile, was the name given to a Spanish soldier whose sons were said to have organized the final invasion of Ireland. The murder there of their kinsman ITH caused the Milesians to take revenge by conquering the island. This they achieved by defeating the TUATHA DE DANANN, "the people of the goddess Dana", the existing rulers. Following the final decisive battle between the two forces, which the Milesians won, the Tuatha De Danann retired to an otherworld beneath the soil of Ireland.

MODRED was the treacherous nephew of King ARTHUR. While he was away waging war in Brittany, Arthur had appointed Modred his regent, but his scheming nephew tried instead to take the throne and force GUINEVERE to marry him. On the king's return, a terrible battle was fought near Salisbury and most of the Knights of the Round Table were killed, including Modred. Arthur, who had been mortally wounded during the battle, was then taken to AVALON in a black boat by three mysterious women.

MONGAN was the son of the Manx sea god MANANNAN MAC LIR. According to Irish mythology, his conception had been made possible by the use of a deception akin to the one used by MERLIN so that UTHER could sleep with Igraine and so conceive ARTHUR. Manannan Mac Lir had assumed the shape of an Ulster king in order to sleep with his beautiful queen. When Mongan was three days old, his father took him to one of his otherworld realms, the Land of Promise, where the boy remained until he had grown to manhood. It is claimed by some traditions that Mongan then returned to Ireland reincarnated as FINN MACCOOL, the famous leader of the FIANNA, but in other accounts he retained his own identity. The stories about Mongan describe how he used his shape-changing ability to get his own way, and mention in particular the recovery of his wife Dubh Lacha. He had inherited the divine ability of metamorphosis from his father.

MORGAN LE FAY was King ARTHUR's half-sister and in some versions of the story she is said to have been the mistress of Sir Accolon of Gaul. Throughout all the British myths that tell of Arthur's incredible reign Morgan Le Fay is always depicted as the king's implacable enemy, often plotting his downfall. According to one story she is supposed to have stolen the magic sword Excalibur and sent it to Accolon, who then challenged Arthur to single combat. When Accolon dropped the sword Arthur recognized it and the other knight admitted his guilt and surrendered. However, after the bloody battle against Arthur's rebellious nephew Sir MODRED, Morgan le Fay was one of the three women who took the grievously wounded king in a black boat to AVALON. The other two were "the Queen of Northgales and the Queen of Wastelands". (See also SAGES AND SEERS; SINGLE COMBAT)

MORGAN LE FAY'S (below) paradoxical nature is reflected in her dual role as both healer and dark magician, as Arthur's thorn in life, yet also his guardian in death. Although educated at a convent, she managed to emerge as a gifted magician. (MORGAN LE FAY BY A SANDYS, WOOD, 1864.)

MODRED (above), Arthur's treacherous nephew, abused his role of regent and usurped the throne, forcing Arthur to quash the rebel forces. Both perished in the final battle that ended the war and so came to an end the Arthurian golden age. (ARTHUR AND MODRED BY W HATHERELL, CANVAS, C.1910.)

N

MORHOLT was the gigantic brother of the king of Ireland, to whom King Mark and Cornwall were expected to pay an annual tribute. Mark's nephew *TRISTAN* was determined to put an end to this practice. He therefore sailed to Ireland and succeeded in killing Morholt, but not before he had been wounded by the giant's great poisoned sword. Before he died, Morholt told Tristan that only his sister *ISEULT* would be able to cure his poisoned wound.

MORRIGAN, sometimes known as Morrigu, was an Irish goddess of death on the battlefield who helped the *TUATHA DE DANANN* at both battles of Magh Tuireadh. She was associated with the other war deities *MACHA*, *BADB* and *NEMAIN*. Her favourite form was the crow, and as such she settled in triumph on the shoulder of the Ulster hero *CUCHULAINN* when he was finally killed in the war against Queen *MEDB*'s forces. Cuchulainn had not only refused Morrigan's love, but in anger he had even wounded her. For such a deed his fate was sealed.

MORRIGAN, the terrible goddess of war, appeared sometimes as a warrior in a battle, siding with her favourites. Most often she soared overhead as a raven or crow, shrieking and flapping her wings to scare the host, or to signify imminent death, as here. (ILLUSTRATION BY STEPHEN REID, 1910.)

MORHOLT, the Irish champion, confronts Tristan, the Cornish newcomer, in a duel over Irish taxes. Despite Morholt's greater power and skill, the young Tristan fought like a mighty lion and dealt the older knight a mortal blow to his helm, lodging a piece of sword in his brain. (ILLUSTRATION BY EVELYN PAUL, C. 1900.)

NAOISE was the eldest son of Usna and his wife Elbha, daughter of *CATHBAD*. When *DEIRDRE* persuaded him to run away with her so that she could avoid marriage to the Ulster king *CONCHOBHAR MAC NESSA*, Naoise and his two brothers fled with her to Alba. Conchobhar sent *FERGUS MAC ROTH* to bring them all home. Suspicious of Conchobhar, but trusting Fergus' promise that no harm would come to them, Naoise agreed. In the event, Conchobhar had Naoise killed, and so enraged was Fergus Mac Roth that he joined the forces of Conchobhar's great enemy, Queen *MEDB* of Connacht.

NECHTAN was an Irish water god and, according to some versions, the husband of *BOANN*. On Nechtan's hill there was a holy well that was the source of all knowledge, to which only Nechtan and his three cup-bearers had access. When Boann found her way to the well, the waters rose from the ground and chased after her, becoming the River Boyne.

NEMAIN (whose name means "dreadful" or "venomous"), in Irish mythology, was a goddess of war. Along with *BABD*, *MORRIGAN* and *MACHA*, she formed one of a group

of war deities who sometimes appeared as beautiful young women and sometimes as crows, screeching over the battlefield. Nemain was said to have been the wife of *NUADA*, the leader of the *TUATHA DE DANANN*.

NEMGLAN, an Irish bird god, fell in love with Mess Buachalla, the betrothed of Eterscel, High King of Ireland. On the eve of the wedding, Nemglan came to her in a bird skin and seduced her, and this was how she conceived *CONAIRE MOR*. The child was passed off as High King Eterscel's son, but Mess Buachalla was careful to warn the boy that he must never, whatever the circumstances might be, kill a bird. When Conaire Mor was a young man, Eterscel died and the question of the succession was raised in Tara, the Irish capital. Unknown to Conaire, there was a prophecy to the effect that Eterscel's successor would be a naked man walking along the road to Tara with a sling in his hand. It happened one day that Conaire was driving his

NAOISE elopes with the great Irish beauty, Deirdre. They fled across the sea to Scotland, pursued by Fergus Mac Roth. By Loch Ness, they found refuge and hunted deer and salmon, living in pastoral bliss until they were lured back to a deadly trap in Ireland by an unsuspecting Fergus Mac Roth. (ILLUSTRATION ANON.)

NEMAIN, one of the dreadful goddesses of war, appeared sometimes as a washer at the ford, presaging doom. Before his last combat, Cuchulainn saw a washer weeping and wailing as she rinsed a heap of bloody raiment belonging to the great hero. (ILLUSTRATION BY STEPHEN REID, 1910.)

chariot down this very road when a flock of birds with beautiful plumage descended upon him. Forgetting his mother's instruction never to harm any bird, he loaded his sling, at which point the birds immediately turned into armed warriors. The leader of these incredible warriors, however, introduced himself to Conaire as his real father Nemglan. To make up for his misconduct towards the birds, Conaire was told to undress and return home to Tara on foot, carrying only his sling. He thus became the next High King of Ireland.

NESSA, in Irish mythology, was the mother of *CONCHOBHAR MAC NESSA*, the Ulster ruler during the lifetime of the hero *CUCHULAINN*. Nessa's husband was King Fachtna of Ulster and when the king died his half-brother, *FERGUS MAC ROTH*, succeeded to the throne and proposed marriage to Nessa.

However, she would agree to the match only on the condition that her son should be allowed to rule Ulster for one year. Fergus Mac Roth was so in love with her that he readily agreed, but at the end of the year the people of Ulster refused to let Conchobhar step down from the throne, so excellent was his rule.

NEMGLAN, a bird god from an other-world, came to Mess Buachalla before her wedding to the High King. As he flew in, his plumage moulted to reveal a beautiful youth. Like Leda and Danae before her, she loved the god and bore him a son, Conaire Mor. (ILLUSTRATION BY NICK BEALE, 1995.)

NIAMH was the wife of *CONALL* Caernach. While *CUCHULAINN* was recovering from wounds sustained during the war against the men of Connacht, Niamh nursed him and became his mistress. She then tried to prevent him returning to battle. But the witch *BADB*, one of the daughters of *CALATIN*, cast a spell on Niamh so that she wandered away into the countryside. Badb then assumed the form of Niamh and told Cuchulainn that he must return to the war and fight.

NIAM OF THE GOLDEN HAIR was a daughter of the sea god *MANANNAN MAC LIR*. She fell in love with the poet *OISIN* and they lived happily together in the Land of Promise, which was one of the otherworld realms. Niam bore the poet a daughter, Plur nam Ban ("Flower of Woman").

NODENS was a British god of healing, whose magic hounds were also believed to be able to cure the sick. Nodens was worshipped during the Roman occupation; the ruins of a great temple have been found on the banks of the River Severn. In Ireland, he became *NUADA* of the Silver Hand and in Wales *NUDD* of the Silver Hand, also known as Llud to the Britons.

NUADA, also known as Nuada Airgetlamh ("Nuada of the Silver Hand"), because of a temporary replacement for a hand he lost at the first battle of Magh Tuireadh, was an important Irish god and leader of the *TUATHA DE DANANN*. He was married to *NEMAIN*. The De Danann were a younger generation of gods than the *FOMORII*, the sea gods who were soon to challenge them at the second battle of Magh Tuireadh. For a while between the two battles, Nuada appointed *BRES* as leader because of the loss of his hand. The silver replacement was made by *DIAN CECHT*. But Nuada was dissatisfied with it and turned to Dian Cecht's son Miach, who made him a new hand of flesh and blood. Dian Cecht slew Miach out of jealousy. Nuada's restoration as leader caused the second battle of Magh Tuireadh, because the half-Fomorii Bres complained to his kinsmen about his treatment.

At the second battle the lethal eye of *BALOR* killed both Nuada and Nemain before the sun god *LUGH* destroyed it with a sling-shot. Their victory saved the Tuatha De Danann, but later they in turn were defeated by the sons of *MILESIUS*. That Nuada was the great De Danann leader, there is no doubt. He is described as sitting on his throne "with a white light about him as it had been a fleece of silver, and round his head a wheel of light pulsed and beat with changing colours". Nuada is cognate with the Welsh *NUDD*.

NUDD, known as Llud to the British, is the Welsh equivalent of *NUADA*. He also had a silver hand, and in one tale was known as Llud Llawereint ("silver-handed").

NUDD, or Llud, ruled Britain at a time when it was plagued by a strange May Eve scream. It transpired that two subterranean dragons caused the scream during an annual battle. They were soothed by sinking mead into a pit dug through the centre of the earth. (ILLUSTRATION BY ALAN LEE, 1984.)

O

OGMA was the Irish god of eloquence and the inventor of Ogham, the earliest system of writing used in Ireland. Ogham is made up of a series of vertical or sloping lines inscribed on a base line. The sagas tell of vast libraries of Ogham writing, though only inscriptions in stone carvings have survived, and the sagas themselves were later recorded by monks using the Roman alphabet.

Ogma was a son of DAGDA, who was a god described as the "Lord of Knowledge". Besides having a truly remarkable skill as a poet, Ogma was a fighter like other Irish gods and also, like the the Greek god Hermes or the Roman Mercury, he was responsible for conveying souls to the otherworld. Whereas for the Greek and Roman messenger gods this was a sad duty, not least because the kingdom of Hades was not an inviting place, Ogma's task was a happier one since the Celtic otherworld was a delightful and peaceful resting-place for the soul prior to its next rebirth in the world. It is thought that Greek colonists in the western end of the

OGMA, god of eloquence, invented the Ogham script, consisting of vertical lines crossing a lateral baseline. Ogham messages were carved on stone and inscribed on barks and wands of hazel or aspen. Over 400 ancient messages have survived. (ILLUSTRATION BY NICK BEALE, 1995.)

OISIN and the fairy maiden, Niamh, flew away on a snow-white steed through golden mist to the Land of Promise, which was a delightful otherworld beyond all dreams, filled with birdsong and scented flowers, with overflowing mead and wondrous creatures. (ILLUSTRATION BY STEPHEN REID, 1910.)

Mediterranean first encountered the idea of the transmigration of souls from their Celtic neighbours. In the sixth century BC the famous and unusual Greek philosopher Pythagoras left the Aegean island of Samos and went to live in the city of Croton in southern Italy. He became extremely interested in the theory of reincarnation. His followers, who believed that the soul was immortal, accepted transmigration through animals and plants as well, and as a result proposed the kinship of all living things.

In some Irish myths Ogma is said to have married ETAIN, who was the daughter of the god of healing DIAN CECHT. At the second and final battle of Magh Tuireadh Ogma slew Indech, son of the FOMORII goddess Domnu. Indech was one of the leaders of the Fomorii, who were the older sea gods who had challenged the TUATHA DE DANANN, the younger generation of gods of which Ogma was one. After the terrible battle was over and the De Danann were victorious, Ogma claimed as his prize a magic Fomorii sword that was capable of recounting all the deeds it had performed.

OISIN, sometimes Ossian, was the son of the Fenian, or FIANNA, leader FINN MACCOOL. According to Irish mythology, Oisin was the greatest poet in Ireland, perhaps not a surprising achievement considering how as a young man his father had eaten the Salmon of Knowledge. Oisin's mother was none other than the goddess SADB, the granddaughter of DAGDA. This made OGMA, the god of eloquence, Oisin's uncle.

One day, as Finn MacCool with his companions and dogs was returning homewards, a beautiful deer started up on their path and the ensuing chase took them towards Tara, the Irish capital and the base of the Fenians. At last the exhausted animal stopped and crouched down on the ground, but instead of attacking their quarry the hounds began to play round her, and even to lick her head and limbs. So Finn MacCool ordered that no harm should be done to the deer, which followed them on the way home until sunset.

That same night Finn MacCool awoke to find the most beautiful woman he had ever seen standing next to his bed. It was Sadb. She

explained how a spell had been placed upon her, but that she had learned that if Finn MacCool came to love her, then all the enchantments would cease to have power and she could resume her normal shape. So it came to pass that Sadb lived with Finn MacCool as his mistress, and for months neither of them stirred from their dwelling. Then news arrived of invaders in ships off Dublin, most likely a Viking raid, and the Fenians were called to arms. For only one week Finn MacCool was absent dealing with the Vikings. On his return, however, he discovered that Sadb had been lured away by someone disguised as himself (a common trick among shape-changers in Irish mythology). Realizing that it must be the enchanter whom Sadb had rejected, Finn MacCool organized a search of every remote hill, valley and forest in the country, but without success. Eventually he gave up all hope of finding his mistress and returned to his pleasure of hunting. It happened, by chance, that his dogs tracked down a very strange quarry and Finn MacCool came upon them surrounding a naked boy with long hair. His two best hounds were, in fact, keeping the pack from seizing the child.

Having driven off the dogs, Finn MacCool and the other huntsmen regarded the boy with curiosity. He told them that he did not know the identity of his father, but that his mother was a gentle hind, with whom he lived in a quiet valley safely shut in by steep cliffs. To their home a tall, dark stranger came every now and again to see his mother, but she always shrank away in fear and the man left in anger. When the stranger finally

OISIN returned from the otherworld after his time and found himself an old man, alone and bereft, the sole survivor of a magical age. With his lyre he sang of the heroes and gods of his era, conjuring up the magical phantoms of that bygone age.
(OSSIAN BY FRANÇOIS GERARD, CANVAS, 1800.)

His famous adventure concerns *NIAMH*, the daughter of the sea god *MANANNAN MAC LIR*. Oisin met her while on a hunt by the shores of a lake. She suddenly appeared riding a horse with silver hooves and a golden mane. When Niamh told Oisin how she had travelled a great distance to invite him to her father's otherworld realm, the Land of Promise, he readily mounted the magic steed and was never seen by his father again. In the otherworld kingdom he fought against a *FOMORII* giant in an undersea combat worthy of his father. But after a number of other exploits Oisin began to miss his own land of Ireland. Niamh gave him her magic horse so that he could visit his home, but told him not to dismount otherwise he would never be allowed to return. Ireland appeared to Oisin almost a strange land, for everyone he knew had died long before. The people seemed far sadder and more careworn than the heroes he had grown up with. By chance he came upon a ragged group of men attempting to move a boulder, which he easily lifted for them while still seated on his mount. However, his saddle slipped and he fell to the ground. In an instant the magic horse vanished and the valiant young warrior was turned into a blind and frail old man.

A Christian addition to the end of this myth includes St Patrick. Because everyone took Oisin to be mad he cried out: "If your god has slain Finn MacCool, then I would say that he is a strong man." So he was taken to the saint, who recorded his strange tale and explained the changes to Ireland since the arrival of Christianity.

struck her with a magic hazel wand, the hind was forced to follow him, although she tried to comfort her son as she left.

As soon as the boy finished this account, Finn MacCool embraced him as his own son by Sadb, and immediately named him Oisin ("Little Fawn"). He was trained as a Fenian warrior, which involved one of the most difficult courses of training imaginable, and became a skilled fighter like his father, but he also inherited the gentler ability of eloquence from his mother, and his songs and poetry were admired throughout Ireland.

OISIN, on his return from the otherworld, found Ireland bleak and cold, the people sad and small, and himself a weary and withered old man. After passing on the magic legends, he quietly slipped away, his end as strange as his beginning.
(ILLUSTRATION BY STEPHEN REID, 1910.)

HEROIC QUESTS

THE THRILLING PURSUIT of a real or visionary goal forms the plot of many compelling tales of adventure. The goal is not always the most tantalizing part of the venture and might seem like a tedious or even trivial task, but serves to spur the traveller on his way. Other goals, such as the Grail, seem barely attainable, but serve as shining symbols of aspiration. The impetus is sometimes romantic, as when Culhwch set out to find fair Olwen; or retributory, as when Geraint went forth to avenge a wrong; while Peredur, Owain and the Grail Knights were inspired by otherworldly visions and ideals. Whatever the goal, the quest usually takes on a magic of its own, leading the hero down unexpected bypaths of adventure and discovery. *En route* he meets new friends and travelling companions, learns much-needed lessons and catches sight of even more tantalizing quests ahead.

OWAIN (above), inspired by the tale of Cynon, set off in search of the Castle of the Fountain, which was guarded by the Black Knight. He passed through the fairest vale until he saw a shining castle on the hill. After entering its otherworldly domain Culhwch defeated the Black Knight, and went on to woo his widow. After a rather difficult beginning, he overcame her resentment, and guarded her realm until his yen for adventure lured him off again. (ILLUSTRATION BY ALAN LEE, 1984.)

CAMELOT (left), Arthur's shining city-castle, drew knights from far and wide to join the Fellowship of the Round Table, inspired by ideals of courage, honour and vision. From Camelot, the questing knight set forth on journeys of adventure and discovery, to seek honour, to avenge wrongs and to win ladies and renown. The figure of the questing knight became a symbol of aspiration. (ILLUSTRATION BY ALAN LEE, 1984.)

THE GRAIL QUEST (right) proved to be the hardest, highest and greatest of all quests. Many knights set forth but few returned. When Arthur's warriors resolved to undertake the Grail Quest, Arthur wept, lamenting that the fairest fellowship of noble knights would never meet again around the table at Camelot. He was right, for few of his company were fitted for the quest and many perished. (THE ARMING AND DEPARTURE OF THE KNIGHTS BY E BURNE-JONES AND W MORRIS, TAPESTRY, 1895–96.)

CULHWCH'S (left) quest for the fair Olwen involved thirty-nine impossible tasks, the longest series of tasks in Celtic mythology. En route the hero enlisted the help of Arthur's war-band who assisted Culhwch in one of his hardest tasks, which was the retrieval of a comb, razor and scissors from between the ears of the terrible, enchanted boar, Twrch Trwyth. (ILLUSTRATION BY ALAN LEE, 1984.)

PEREDUR'S (above) quest for adventure led him through many wondrous lands. At one point he passed through a lovely river valley, filled with colourful pavilions and a wondrous multitude of windmills and water-mills. He lodged with the head miller and jousted in the tournament, defeating countless warriors with such skill and might that he impressed the local empress. After fighting her battles, he ruled with her for fourteen years before continuing his search for new adventures. (ILLUSTRATION BY ALAN LEE, 1984.)

OLWEN, in Welsh mythology, was the daughter of the giant Yspaddaden and her suitor was CULHWCH, one of King ARTHUR's warriors. Culhwch's stepmother hated him so much that she cursed him to marry only Olwen, a girl whom the warrior came to love dearly. Yspaddaden was so upset by the obvious affection between Olwen and Culhwch that he set his daughter's lover a series of tasks in order to prevent the marriage. Among other things, Culhwch had to uproot a forest, burn the wood for fertilizer and plough the cleared land in one day; force AMAETHON, the god of agriculture, to nourish its crops; make the smith god Govannon forge tools for the work; bring four strong oxen to help; obtain magic seed; provide honey nine times sweeter than that of a virgin swarm; get a magic cup and a hamper of delicious meat; borrow the drinking-horn of the underwater king Gwyddbwyll and the magic harp belonging to Teirtu (an instrument that played itself); capture the birds of RHIANNON, whose song could wake the dead and lull the living to sleep; provide a magic cauldron; a boar's tusk for the giant to shave with and shaving cream made from a witch's blood;

OWAIN and Arthur (below) appear in a warrior's dream, playing gwyddbwyll. During the game, Arthur's knights battle with Owain's ravens, but the players simply play on, until Arthur smashes the pieces. The game symbolizes a battle, possibly for sovereignty. (ILLUSTRATION BY ALAN LEE, 1984.)

steal a magic dog, leash and collar; hire as a huntsman MABON, son of Modron, who had first to be released from prison; find a wonderful steed and swift hounds; steal a comb, scissors and a razor from between the ears of a fierce boar; and persuade a number of unlikely guests to come to Yspaddaden's stronghold. Undaunted by the

OLWEN (left), in flaming red, wanders through the otherworld, depicted here as a vibrant, brooding wooded idyll. Olwen was loved by Culhwch, a warrior of King Arthur's court, who had to go to great lengths to secure his bride.
(ILLUSTRATION BY ALAN LEE, 1984.)

sheer size and complexity of the challenges, Culhwch said that "King Arthur will provide horses and men to help him win Olwen". He also informed the giant that he would return to slay him. Culhwch succeeded and married Olwen "and she was his only wife as long as he lived". The giant was killed by one of Culhwch's fellow knights.

OWAIN (below) peers through the tangled branches of the wildwood, like a shy, wild creature. Overcome with shame after wronging his wife, he fled into the wilderness and lived as a wild man, wasting away until rescued by a noblewoman.
(ILLUSTRATION BY ALAN LEE, 1984.)

PARTHOLON (above) found a lush, primal country when he first landed in Ireland. The forests and plains were alive with strange, shy and beautiful creatures. Partholon cleared the land for cultivation and in his time three new lakes appeared, one of which was named after his son.
(ILLUSTRATION BY ARTHUR RACKHAM, C. 1910.)

OSCAR, in Irish mythology, was the son of OISIN and the grandson of FINN MACCOOL. His name means "deer lover" and recalls his grandmother, the goddess SADB, whom Finn MacCool first encountered while he was hunting. Sadb had been changed into a hind by a spell, which Finn MacCool briefly lifted. Oscar's mother was Eibhir, who was said to be "a yellow-haired maiden from a warm country".

Oscar was a mighty fighter, one of the best of all the FIANNA, or Fenians, the warriors who acted as a bodyguard to the High King of Ireland. But he lived during a time when the ruler, Cairbe, felt that the Fenians had too much power, and

a bloody struggle ensued. High King Cairbe refused to pay the Fenians for their services and raised another band of fighters to replace them. In a battle fought at Gabhra, near present-day Dublin, Oscar killed Cairbe in single combat but was himself mortally wounded. According to one version of the myth, Finn MacCool returned briefly from the otherworld to mourn Oscar's death.

OWAIN, in Welsh mythology, was the son of URIEN and one of King ARTHUR's warriors. When a fellow warrior named CYNON was defeated by a mysterious Black Knight, Owain set out to find this stranger. He severely wounded the Black Knight but did not unseat him, and when the knight galloped off to a nearby castle, he gave chase only to find himself almost a prisoner once he entered its walls. Owain was saved by a lady named Luned, who gave him a ring of invisibility. Soon the lord of the

castle, the Black Knight, died of the wound Owain had inflicted on him. Not deterred by her grief, Owain persuaded Luned to plead his cause with such success that his widow consented to marry him. Thus he became master of the Castle of the Fountain, as the Black Knight's stronghold was called. But the long absence of Owain worried King Arthur a great deal, so he sent out a party of knights to find him. Owain returned with them to King Arthur's court, and he gradually forgot about his wife.

When a very angry lady arrived at court to accuse Owain of deceit, treachery and unfaithfulness, he was overcome with shame. A remorseful Owain fled to the forest and pursued the solitary life of a hermit. There he would have died but for a well-born lady who used a magic potion to restore his health. Sir Owain took up his arms, slew a dragon and befriended a lion. The knight and the lion had numerous adventures, which included saving Luned from death by burning and slaying a giant. Owain returned to the Castle of the Fountain, where he was reconciled with his wife. They seem to have spent the rest of their lives together in King Arthur's court. (See also CELTIC ROMANCE; SINGLE COMBAT; HEROIC QUESTS)

PARSIFAL see PERCIVAL

PARTHOLON, son of Sera, was believed to have led one of the early invasions of Ireland. Together with twenty-four men and their wives, he is said to have come out of the west after the waters of the Flood had receded and cleared the island of trees ready for cultivation. According to the myth, after living in Ireland for some five thousand years, the race of Partholon were stricken by disease and they all died within the space of a week.

PELLES was one of the names given to the "Maimed King" of the GRAIL story in whose castle of Carbonek the holy vessel was kept. In other versions of the tale he is known as Amfortas. Pelles was said to have been the father of Elaine, who fell in love with Sir LANCELOT and bore him the pure knight Sir GALAHAD, who was the only one of ARTHUR's knights granted a vision of the Grail and allowed to hold it.

PELLES, the Grail King, guarded the Grail in Carbonek, the Grail Castle. Maimed by an incurable wound, symbolizing some spiritual imperfection, he lived in a twilight state, while his country wasted, awaiting the coming of Galahad, the redeeming knight. (ILLUSTRATION BY ALAN LEE, 1984.)

PERCIVAL, the Perfect Fool, attained a glimpse of the Grail through his innocence. Returning from Sarras, he became Grail King, heading the Order of Grail Knights, sometimes known as Parsifal, sometimes as Templeisen, after the Knights Templar.

(PARZIVAL BY MARTIN WIEGAND, CANVAS, 1934.)

PERCIVAL, who was also sometimes called Perceval or Parsifal in different traditions, was in later Arthurian mythology something of an outsider. He was brought up in a forest far from the court of Camelot and was completely ignorant of courtly manners. However, he travelled to King *ARTHUR*'s court and was duly made a knight, and then set off in quest of the Grail, the holy vessel that was used at the Last Supper and which received the blood that flowed from the spear thrust in Christ's side at the time of the Crucifixion. The Grail had been brought to Britain by *JOSEPH OF ARIMATHEA*, the rich man who had allowed Christ's body to be placed in his tomb. However, the Grail was later lost and its recovery became the great quest for the Knights of the Round Table.

The purity of Sir Percival may have meant that he was permitted a brief glimpse of the Grail, but he was denied the complete vision and heavenly release that was eventually granted to Sir *GALAHAD*, Sir *LANCELOT*'s son. Only Galahad was allowed to touch the Grail, "Our Lord's body between his hands", and then to die in the company of angels. The mysterious Queen of the Wastelands, one of the three ladies who took the dying King Arthur to *AVALON* after he had been wounded in the battle against *MODRED*, was Sir Percival's aunt. On his personal quest for the Grail, Sir Percival unfortunately fell somewhat short of the high standard of conduct required for recovering the Grail. One day on his journey he encountered a wondrous and mysterious ship and at once fell in love with its beautiful owner. Indeed, he was on the point of entering her bed when, "by chance and grace, Sir Percival saw his unsheathed sword lying on the ground, and on its pommel was a red cross, the sign of the Crucifixion, which reminded him of his knightly duty to behave as a good man. So he made the sign of the cross on his forehead, at which the boat was upended, then changed into a cloud of black smoke." So annoyed and filled with remorse was Percival by this moral lapse that he felt obliged to inflict a punishment on the weakness of his own flesh by wounding himself in the thigh. Meanwhile, the enchantress who had attempted to waylay him and divert him from his quest "set off with the wind roaring and yelling, that it seemed all the water was burned after her".

PEREDUR, in Welsh mythology, was the seventh son of Evrawg and the only surviving male. His father and brothers were killed before his own coming of age. This did not prevent Peredur from becoming one of *ARTHUR*'s warriors and his many adventures formed the basis for the later stories about *PERCIVAL*. Possibly because of his position as a seventh son, always a significant

PEREDUR, raised in rustic secrecy, grew up strong and agile but devoid of courtly manners. When he saw three shining knights, he was entranced. Devising a saddle of twigs, and armed with a sharpened stake, he set forth for Arthur's court. (ILLUSTRATION BY ALAN LEE, 1984.)

number, Peredur was particularly adept at defeating witches, who in Wales took to the field like knights attired in full armour. Indeed, his myth as it is told in the *Mabinogion* ends with a terrible duel between him and a leading witch. "For the third time the hag slew a man of Arthur's before Peredur's eyes, and Peredur drew his sword and smote the witch on the crest of her helmet so that the helmet and all the armour were split into two. And she raised a shout, and ordered the rest of the witches to flee, and said it was Peredur who was destined to slay all the witches of Caer Loyw." (See also *HEROIC QUESTS*)

PRYDERI, in Welsh mythology, was the son of *PWYLL*, a notable chieftain of Dyfed in south Wales, and of *RHIANNON*. Pryderi was snatched from his cot by one of

Rhiannon's rejected suitors and brought up by *TEIRNON*, a chieftain who discovered the infant in his stable. The chieftain's wife named the child Gwri, or "Golden Hair", but when, after seven years, he was finally returned home, Rhiannon renamed him Pryderi, "Care", because during the child's absence her life had been very careworn. She had been falsely accused of killing her son and was made to do penance by sitting at the gate of Pwyll's fortress and telling strangers of her crime, then offering to carry them on her back into his hall.

When Pwyll died, Pryderi succeeded him as lord of Dyfed and gave his mother in marriage to *MANAWYDAN*, son of the Welsh sea god Llyr, although in Pryderi's myth Manawydan appears as a mortal warrior rather than a god. At their wedding banquet there was a peal of thunder and a mist fell. "No one could see the other, although the great hall was filled with light." When the mist cleared, the land was desolate. People, animals and crops were gone. Pryderi, his wife Cigfa, Manawydan and Rhiannon were the only people left. After two

years eking out an existence on wild honey, fish and game, they finally decided to travel across the border to Lloegyr, present-day England. But the skill of Manawydan and Pryderi as craftsmen made them many enemies and they returned to Wales. In a ruined castle, Pryderi came across a golden bowl fastened by four chains on a marble slab. Pryderi went to pick it up, but his hands stuck to the bowl and he found that he could not move or let it go. He was also struck dumb. When his mother tried to save him, Rhiannon and Pryderi disappeared in another mist.

It later emerged that all the strange events had been caused by a spell laid on the household by an enemy of Pwyll, Pryderi's father. Manawydan discovered the truth as he was about to hang a mouse for eating their corn. The creature turned out to be the wife of Llwyd, the old enemy of Pwyll. Other mice helping to devour the crops were his warriors transformed by magic. During their temporary disappearance, Pryderi and his mother had been forced to work as donkeys.

PEREDUR aroused the rage of the Pride of the Clearing when he supped with his wife. The arrogant knight assumed his wife's guilt and punished her until Peredur finally challenged and overthrew him. Here, splendid as a peacock, the proud one rides out to joust with Peredur. (ILLUSTRATION BY ALAN LEE, 1984.)

PRYDERI, lord of Dyfed, marched into Gwynedd to avenge the theft of his swine by the resourceful magician, Gwydion. The dispute was to be decided by single combat, but the match was unequal as Gwydion bewitched Pryderi with magical illusions. (ILLUSTRATION BY ALAN LEE, 1984.)

R

at last, because when the baby was stolen her maids were so afraid of Pwyll that they blamed Rhiannon. They laid bones next to their sleeping mistress and smeared her face and hands with blood. When Rhiannon awoke in amazement, the maids told Pwyll how she had devoured the baby in the night.

Pwyll imposed a humiliating penance upon her. Every day she had to sit by his gate, tell her tale to every stranger who came and offer to carry them on her back to the great hall. Not until the eventual return of her son, whom she called PRYDERI ("Care"), was Rhiannon excused from her penance. (See also CELTIC OTHERWORLDS; MAGIC AND ENCHANTMENT)

RHIANNON, in Welsh mythology, was the daughter of Hereydd, and the long-suffering wife of PWYLL, a chieftan of Dyfed. All of Rhiannon's troubles stemmed from her rejection of Gwawl, the man to whom she had been promised, and as a result his enraged father had laid a spell on Pwyll's household.

Because of this curse, Rhiannon suffered years of barrenness and, after the birth of a son, she was unjustly accused of eating the baby. Even after the boy, whom she named PRYDERI, which meant "Care", had been restored and grown up, the spell continued to dog Rhiannon. At one stage she and Pryderi were changed into donkeys. Rhiannon herself had her own magical aspect, however, for the singing of her birds was said to be able to wake the dead and send the living to sleep.

Rhiannon is a singular figure in Welsh mythology. She bore her suffering and injustice with a patience that still seems remarkable. But her real nature was in all likelihood originally connected

RHIANNON (below), as first seen by Pwyll, was a vision in white and gold, riding a pearly steed, and clad in brocaded silk. The two seemed made for each other, but a curse clouded their love and marriage. As patient as she was beautiful, Rhiannon endured her lot without complaint. (ILLUSTRATION BY ALAN LEE, 1984.)

PWYLL was a chieftain of Dyfed whose authority even reached into ANNWN, the Welsh otherworld. Indeed, he boasted the title Pen Annwn ("Lord of Beyond"). One day Pwyll was hunting in the forest when he saw an unusual pack of hounds running down a stag. These hounds were snow-white in colour and had red ears. Pwyll drove them off and was setting his own pack on the cornered stag when a grey-clad horseman rode up and accused him of discourtesy for chasing away his hounds. Pwyll accepted the charge and promised to make amends, at which the stranger revealed himself to be ARAWN, the ruler of Annwn. Arawn told Pwyll that he was being harried by a rival named Havgan, who could be slain only by a single blow, since a second one immediately revived him. Pwyll agreed to change places and shapes with Arawn for a

PWYLL (above), disguised as a beggar, lies in wait with 100 horsemen to trick Gwawl, a rival suitor for the hand of Rhiannon. Once overpowered, Gwawl agreed to leave the two in peace, but his bitter curse blighted their marriage with strange misfortunes. (ILLUSTRATION BY ALAN LEE, 1984.)

year, and to slay Havgan. During the period of exchange it was understood that Pwyll would not make love to Arawn's wife, even though he would share her bed.

Pwyll, having successfully killed Havgan and fulfilled his promise to Arawn, returned home. He then wooed and won RHIANNON for his wife, although a rival suitor never forgave him and laid a curse upon his household, both before and after Pwyll's death. For years no child was born and, angered at her barrenness, Pwyll treated Rhiannon unkindly. His attitude became worse after she gave birth to a son

S

RHIANNON'S singing birds were heralds of the otherworld. Their beautiful and enchanting song was said to be able to wake the dead and to lull the living into a deep sleep. Celtic art and myth are alive with birds of every kind. While some, such as ravens, presage doom, swans and singing birds heal with their magical song.

(ILLUSTRATION ANON.)

RUADH, an intrepid voyager, discovered a secret island beneath the waves, on which lived nine beautiful women who slept on nine bronze beds. Their eyes shone with rainbow light, bewitching Ruadh for nine blissful nights before he grew restless again.

(ILLUSTRATION BY NICK BEALE, 1995.)

with horses. When Pwyll first set eyes on her, Rhiannon was riding "a big fine pale white horse, covered with a garment of shining gold brocaded silk". Also, Rhiannon's stolen son was found in a stable and her punishment for losing him was to act as a beast of burden to visitors who came to her husband's palace. It is tempting to link her with the horse goddess *EPONA*, one of the few Celtic gods or goddesses to be worshipped by the Romans.

RONAN, king of Leinster, was, in the tangled relations of his second marriage, the Irish equivalent of the great Greek hero Theseus. Just like Theseus' second wife Phaedra, the king's second wife Eochaid loved Ronan's son more than her husband. When the stepson showed his horror of her passion, Eochaid told her husband that the young man had attempted to rape her. Ronan ordered his son's execution and died of remorse when he later learned the truth. Eochaid ended her own life with poison.

RUADAN, in Irish mythology, was the son of the goddess *BRIGID* and of *BRES*, the half-*FOMORII* ruler

of the *TUATHA DE DANANN*. At the second battle of Magh Tuireadh Ruadan was sent to spy on the Tuatha De Danann smith god *GOIBHNIU* who was busily making spears. Ruadan seized one of these weapons and thrust it into the god, but Goibhniu merely pulled it out again and drove it into Ruadan, mortally wounding him. When the goddess Brigid came to the battlefield to bewail her son, her weeping was said to have been the first keening in Ireland.

RUADH was a voyager whose ship became becalmed off the north coast of Ireland. According to Irish mythology, when he swam away to find help for his dying crew, he chanced upon a magical underwater island. On the island there lived nine beautiful women, and for nine wonderful nights Ruadh slept with all of them. The women then informed him that together they would bear him a son. Although Ruadh promised faithfully to return at the end of his voyage, he unfortunately forgot about his underwater lovers, and they, in their fury, pursued him, kicking the severed head of his son before them like a football,

SADB, a gentle goddess, was compelled by an evil druid to live much of her life as a deer. However, she bore Finn MacCool a lovely son, from whose tiny forehead grew a tuft of deer hair where she had licked the boy, giving rise to his name, "Little Fawn".

(ILLUSTRATION BY ARTHUR RACKHAM, C. 1910.)

SADB, in Irish mythology, was the mistress of *FINN MACCOOL*, the great leader of the *FIANNA*, popularly known as the Fenians, the bodyguard of the High King. She first appeared to the hero while he was out hunting, but although a goddess herself, Sadb had been placed under a powerful spell by a wizard and was compelled to take the form of a deer. That night, however, Sadb came to Finn as a woman and for a time they lived happily together. Then, when Finn was away from home, the wizard returned and turned Sadb into a deer again. Finn searched the whole of Ireland for his lost mistress, but the only trace he found of her was a naked boy who had been raised in the wild. The hero recognized him as his own son by Sadb, so he called him *OISIN*, meaning "Little Fawn". Oisin grew up to become one of the most famous of all Irish poets.

FABULOUS VOYAGES

THE EPIC VOYAGES of Celtic myth are fabulous tours of the otherworld, usually through an archipelago of wonder isles. The yen to travel itself was often inspired by tales of the otherworld, and the epic trips of both Bran and Brendan were sparked off by otherworldly visions. Like another intrepid voyager, Maeldun, they sailed across the oceans, exploring a myriad of dreamlike isles, some of timeless delights and some of deadly perils. Like time travellers, Celtic voyagers experienced a time warp, either returning home long after their time or condemned to wander on a journey without end. Another feature of the restless Celtic voyager was his eventual disenchantment with otherworldly delights, and a yearning for the changing seasons of his homeland.

MAELDUN (left) set sail to avenge his father's murder and, en route, passed through a fabulous archipelago. In one striking episode, he reached an island surmounted by a fortress with a brazen door and a glass drawbridge which threw the travellers backwards – a telling sign of the otherworld. When they struck the bronze door, a soporific sound sent them to sleep until they awoke to the welcoming voice of the castle's enchantress. When Maeldun tried to woo her, the whole castle dissolved, and the sailors found themselves at sea again. (ILLUSTRATION BY ALAN LEE, 1984.)

BRAN'S (above) voyage was sparked off by a blossoming and scented silver fairy bough, left beside him as he slept. Later a beautiful woman clad in otherworldly robes came to reclaim the bough; she sang a lay about her lovely home across the sea which inspired Bran and his kinsmen to set sail. Far out to sea, they reached her wondrous isle of blossoming trees, just one of 50 such delightful heavens where people lived in timeless joy and plenty. Yet all too soon, Bran's crew craved the changing seasons of their homeland. (ILLUSTRATION BY DANUTA MEYER, 1994.)

A DREAM (below) of a fabulous voyage inspired the Roman ruler, Maxen, to set off on an epic voyage from Rome to Britain, in search of the lovely isle and even lovelier woman of his dream. He passed through river valleys and scaled mountains with their summits lost in heaven. Beyond, he reached a great harbour filled with beautiful ships. Picking the loveliest, crafted in silver, gold and ivory, he sailed across the wide sea until he reached the sparkling shores of Cornwall. Within a jewelled fortress, he found the lovely woman of his dream. (ILLUSTRATION BY ALAN LEE, 1984.)

BRIAN (above) and his brothers set off on a perilous mission to find eight objects deposited around the world. They voyaged in "Wave Sweeper", the self-propelled boat of Manannan, across the oceans to Greece and Persia. One task was to find an inexhaustible cooking spit, which was kept by sea nymphs on the sunken isle of Finchory. Brian, in a magical water suit, sank down among 150 maidens and seized the golden spit from the hearth of their underwater castle. (ILLUSTRATION BY STEPHEN REID, 1912.)

BRENDAN (above), an intrepid Irish monk inspired by tales of the Land of Promise, set sail on an epic voyage. Like Maeldun, he reached an island of bird-like spirits, possibly the Land of Promise, and crossed a translucent sea. Unlike Maeldun, he landed on an island which moved when he lit a fire and turned out to be the giant whale, Jasconius. Here, the dauntless saint tames a siren or merman of the sea. (ILLUSTRATION FROM THE MARVELLOUS ADVENTURES OF ST BRENDAN, 1499)

SANGREAL, or Grail, was the holy vessel of Arthurian mythology during the Middle Ages. It was said to be the cup that Christ drank out of at the Last Supper. It was also believed to have received the blood which flowed from the spear thrust in Christ's side at the Crucifixion. Brought to Britain by JOSEPH OF ARIMATHEA, the rich man who buried Christ, or by his brother-in-law Bron and his son Alan, the Grail was always associated with the early Christian settlement at Glastonbury. Another miraculous object connected with the Grail was a bleeding lance or spear. Sir GALAHAD used its magic power to cure a mysterious ruler, the "Maimed King", who lay between life and death in his castle. It seems, however, that Sir PERCIVAL was originally the knight who saw the Grail, and that it was only in later versions that Galahad took his place as the only knight worthy of such a vision.

The Grail was lost, but it was thought not to have left Britain, rather that it was hidden somewhere in the country because of the

SANGREAL (below) was guarded by angelic women, the Grail Maidens. Here, the dove of heaven bears a gold censer from which arose "a savour as if all the spice of the world had been there", recalling the spicy "greal" of Celtic myth. (THE DAMSEL OF THE SANC GRAIL BY DANTE ROSSETTI, CANVAS, 1874.)

SANGREAL (left), after inspiring the great quest in Britain, was borne back to Sarras by the three good knights, Galahad, Percival and Bors, and was celebrated in a Eucharistic Mass before ascending to heaven. (HOW THE GRAIL ABIDITH IN A FAR COUNTRY BY WILLIAM MORRIS, GLASS, C.1890.)

sinfulness of the times. Indeed, the mere presence of the holy vessel was enough to act as a challenge to most knights to pursue a path of goodness. On its unseen arrival at Camelot, the chivalrous Sir GAWAIN immediately vowed to seek out its home in order to see the Grail for himself. Many of the Knights of the Round Table made similar vows, much to the distress of King ARTHUR, who feared the loss of his best fighting men. But only Sir Galahad successfully completed the quest and died contented. After holding the Grail in his own hands, the young knight's soul was released from his body and "a great multitude of angels bore it up to heaven". That the Grail was the representation of the body and blood of Christ there can be no doubt, for Joseph of Arimathea administered it as part of the sacrament to Sir Galahad, "who had trembled when his mortal flesh beheld spiritual things". It is even stated that Sir Galahad was a descendant of the same Joseph, "the first Christian bishop".

There remains, nevertheless, a powerful charge of Celtic magic in this Christian myth. When "the Holy Grail covered with a white cloth" appeared at Camelot, the vessel filled King Arthur's hall with the most tasty smells, so that the Knights of the Round Table ate and drank as never before. It was, in fact, nothing less than a Celtic cauldron of plenty. When, at the end of the quest, the Grail became "Our Lord's body", the draught that Sir Galahad took from it at Joseph of Arimathea's request ensured his spiritual survival. Like a Celtic cauldron of rebirth, it allowed Sir Galahad to live on in a Christian otherworld. This obvious debt to Celtic mythology meant that the Church never fully embraced the Grail as a Christian symbol. The great popularity of Grail stories forced a degree of toleration, but clerics were always aware of its links with pre-Christian rites. (See also WONDROUS CAULDRONS; HEROIC QUESTS)

SCATHACH (whose name means "shadowy") was a warrior-princess in the Land of Shadows and tutor in the martial arts. One myth recounts that her most famous pupil was the Ulster hero CUCHULAINN. She taught him his famous battle leap and gave him the spear named Gae-Bolg ("Belly-spear"). Although it made a single wound on entry, once inside the body of one of Cuchulainn's enemies, thirty barbs opened to tear the stomach apart. UATHACH, the daughter of Scathach, was Cuchulainn's mistress during his year of training, and was unhappy that he wanted to fight her sister AOIFA. In the event, Cuchulainn was able to defeat Aoifa by trickery and made her his next mistress.

SANGREAL *(above) was attained by three very different knights. Galahad, the purest, beheld its contents; Bors, the most worldly, returned to tell the tale; Percival, the simplest, became its guardian.* (THE ATTAINMENT BY WILLIAM MORRIS, TAPESTRY, C. 1870.)

SCOTA

SCOTA was said to be the earliest known ancestor of the Scots. According to one version of the myth, she was the daughter of an Egyptian pharaoh. A wise teacher named Niul, who had settled in Egypt, became her husband and they had a child, Goidel, who gave his name to the Gaels. In another tradition, she was the wife of *MILESIUS* and was killed fighting the *TUATHA DE DANANN*.

SEARBHAN

SEARBHAN, in Irish mythology, was a *FOMORII* warrior, one of the ancient sea gods. This one-eyed, one-armed and one-legged fighter

SEARBHAN (left), the surly one-eyed Fomorii giant, guarded a magic tree, squatting at its foot all day. The eloping lovers, Diarmuid Ua Duibhne and Grainne sheltered in its branches, but Grainne developed a craving for the tree's magic berries. This so enraged the giant that he and Diarmuid fought and the mighty Searbhan was slain with his own club. (ILLUSTRATION ANON.)

SUALTAM MAC ROTH'S (right) head rallied the Ulstermen to battle, even after his death. He had exhorted them in life without success, as they were weakened by Macha's curse. The cries of the severed head at last broke the spell and roused the men to fight. (ILLUSTRATION BY STEPHEN REID, 1910.)

guarded a magic tree, which no one dared approach. However, during the sixteen-year flight of *GRAINNE* and *DIARMUID UA DUIBHNE* from the *FIANNA*, the hard-pressed lovers managed to become friends with Searbhan and he allowed them to shelter in the branches of the magic tree, which made it difficult for *FINN MACCOOL* to find them. However, Searbhan and Diarmuid came to blows when Grainne attempted to eat some of the magic berries that grew on the tree, and the Fomorii warrior was slain.

SETANTA see CUCHULLAIN.

SUALTAM MAC ROTH

SUALTAM MAC ROTH, in Irish mythology, was the brother of *FERGUS MAC ROTH*. An Ulsterman, he accepted *CUCHULAINN* as his own son, although the hero's real father was the sun god *LUGH*. On the night of her wedding to Sualtam Mac Roth, *DECHTIRE* had swallowed a fly and fallen into a deep sleep. In this state she went to the otherworld with Lugh and there conceived Cuchulainn. While Cuchulainn was single-handedly defending Ulster against the invading forces of Queen *MEDB* of Connacht, Sualtam Mac Roth attempted to gather the men of Ulster who had been weakened by *MACHA*'s curse. So desperately did he turn his horse that Sualtam cut off his own head with the sharp edge of his shield. But the severed head continued the call to arms long enough to rouse the warriors.

SUIBHNE GEILT, "the mad one", in late Irish mythology was a king cursed by St Ronan. One day King Suibhne was outraged to learn that, without his permission, Ronan was founding a church on his land. Although his wife, Eorann, tried to restrain him, the king rushed to the new foundation, seized the saint's psalter and threw it in a nearby lake. He then laid hands on St Ronan, when a messenger arrived to summon him to an ally's aid on the battlefield. Next day an otter returned the psalter unharmed. St Ronan thanked heaven for this and cursed Suibhne, who assumed the characteristics of a bird, leaping from trees for seven years before his reason returned.

When St Ronan heard about this recovery, he prayed that the king would not return to persecute Christians. So Suibhne was once again on the brink of madness as headless bodies and severed heads harried him. Another priest took pity on the tormented man and wrote down his sad tale, after which Suibhne "died a Christian and his soul ascended to heaven".

TARANIS, "the thunderer", was a Celtic sky god whom the Romans equated with their supreme deity Jupiter. The wheel, which is sometimes used as a symbol of the sun in Celtic art, here represents the electric light of a thunderbolt, symbolized by the trident, a three-pronged spear.
(ILLUSTRATION BY MIRANDA GRAY, 1994.)

TAILTU was the daughter of a ruler of the FIRBOLG and wife of Eochaidh Mac Erc, another Firbolg king. She was said to have cleared the forest of Breg so that it became a plain, a task which killed her. Because she was the foster-mother of the sun god LUGH, he declared that the festival of Lughnasadh be held in her honour, which took place on the first day of August. It was originally the occasion of a national sporting competition, not unlike the Olympic Games.

TALIESIN ("Shining Brow") was a Welsh wizard and bard and according to Welsh mythology he was the first person to acquire the skill of prophecy. In one version of his story he was the servant of the witch CERIDWEN and was named Gwion Bach. Ceridwen prepared a magic brew that, after a year of boiling, was to yield three drops of knowledge. Whoever swallowed these precious drops would know all the secrets of the past, the present and the future. As Gwion Bach was tending the fire beneath the cauldron, some of the hot liquid fell on his finger and he sucked it to relieve the pain (much like FINN MACCOOL when he was cooking the Salmon of Knowledge). The furious Ceridwen employed all her magic powers to pursue the boy. During the chase he transformed himself into a hare, a fish and a bird before being eaten by the witch in the form of a grain of wheat. Later Gwion Bach was thrown into the sea and was caught in a fish-trap and renamed Taliesin because of his radiant forehead. "I am old, I am new," he said. "I have been dead, I have been alive." (See also SAGES AND SEERS)

TALIESIN was a prophetic bard who was gifted with all-knowing vision, which was symbolized by his shining brow. At the young age of thirteen, he already surpassed all of Arthur's bards in spiritual insight. He is portrayed here as a visionary spirit who was at one with the forces of nature.
(ILLUSTRATION BY STUART LITTLEJOHN, 1994.)

TARANIS (whose name means "Thunderer") was one of the few Celtic gods with whom the Romans identified and he was often equated with Jupiter. Monuments to Taranis have been found all over the Celtic world, from the Adriatic coast to the northern regions of Britain. Taranis is usually depicted with his symbol, the wheel. The word "taran" is still used in modern Welsh and Breton to mean thunder.

TEIRNON was lord of Gwent Is Coed and foster-father of PRYDERI. Teirnon owned a beautiful mare, and every year on the eve of the first of May the animal gave birth to a foal, which mysteriously disappeared. One year Teirnon decided to keep watch to see what would happen. A giant clawed hand came through the stable window and took the new-born foal. He hacked off the hand but heard a crying coming from outside and found a three-day-old baby boy lying on the doorstep.

Teirnon and his wife took the child in and raised him as one of their own, but as he grew, the resemblance to PWYLL became increasingly marked until they knew that he was the missing son of Pwyll and RHIANNON.

TEUTATES, also called Toutatis, was one of the Celtic gods mentioned by the Roman historian Lucan and is often equated with the god Mars. His name means "a people" or "a tribe" and so it may well be that the many inscriptions to him are actually dedicated to local deities of a region rather than to a single pan-Celtic figure.

THOMAS THE RHYMER see
CELTIC OTHERWORLDS

TRISTAN, the nephew of King
MARK of Cornwall, was one of the
great lovers of medieval mythology.
His name is said to have been given
to him after his mother's death in
childbirth. Of Breton origin, the
story of Tristan and ISEULT was
popular in Cornwall, Ireland and
Brittany. A love potion prepared by
Iseult's mother, the Irish queen,
was the cause of their great love.
Tristan and Iseult drank it accidentally when Tristan was escorting her

*TRISTAN and Iseult (left), enchanted by a
love potion, gaze at each other in rapture.
In one legend, the two had fallen in love
before sipping the potion, which only served
to quash their scruples. The Victorian
design captures the extreme nature of
courtly love. (ILLUSTRATION BY EVELYN PAUL, 1900.)*

*TEIRNON, watching the birth of a foal,
was shocked to see a vast hairy arm thrust
through the stable window. After hacking at
the arm with his sword, Teirnon found a
beautiful baby boy outside, whom he raised
and who turned out to be the lost son of
Rhiannon and Pwyll, rulers of the realm.
(ILLUSTRATION BY ALAN LEE, 1984.)*

to Cornwall, where King Mark waited to marry her. The ensuing tale
relates the sad course of their love,
separation and their deaths. The
lovers' end was particularly touching. Having agreed to part, Tristan
went to Brittany, but later was
gravely wounded and sent for help
from Iseult, who had once before
cured him of a serious wound. So
she sailed to Brittany with a magic
cure. It had been agreed that the
ship carrying Iseult would hoist a
white sail to indicate that she was
aboard. However, an incorrect
report of a black sail caused Tristan
to lose the will to live and he died
of his wound. When Iseult was told
of her lover's death she too quickly died, but of a broken heart. (See
also *CELTIC ROMANCE; SINGLE
COMBAT*)

*TRISTAN humbly sought the Grail, even
though he doubted his chances because of
his illicit love for Iseult. At one stage in his
quest, he found a splendid castle all alight
and alive with song. Sadly, however, he
was struck back by a burning beam of light,
for only the purest could attain the Grail.
(ILLUSTRATION BY EVELYN PAUL, C. 1900.)*

TUATHA DE DANANN were "the people of the goddess Dana" in Irish mythology. They were the last generation of gods to rule Ireland before the invasion of the sons of *MILESIUS*, the ancestors of the present-day Irish. The Tuatha De Danann overcame the *FOMORII*, violent and monstrous sea gods, at the second battle of Magh Tuireadh largely because of their superior magic. They were said to have learned magic, crafts and knowledge in four marvellous cities of the north, Falias, Gorias, Finias and Murias. From these cities the Tuatha De Danann brought to Ireland four talismans: the Stone of Fal, which screamed aloud when the rightful king of Ireland placed his foot upon it; the magic sword of *NUADA*, their great war-leader, which was a weapon that could only inflict fatal blows; the spear or

TWRCH TRWYTH (below) was a boar that guarded three treasures between his ears which Culhwch sought to retrieve. Arthur's war-band hunted the boar, and here Mabon, the renowned hunter, skilfully snatches one treasure from between the boar's ears. (ILLUSTRATION BY ALAN LEE, 1984.)

TUATHA DE DANANN (above), an ancient race of Irish gods, went to live underground after their defeat by the Milesians. Beneath grassy mounds, each had his own sparkling sidhe, a subterranean court which glittered with wonders within. (ILLUSTRATION BY ALAN LEE, 1984.)

sling-shot of the sun god *LUGH*, who, as the slayer of *BALOR*, was the bringer of victory over the Fomorii; and the cauldron belonging to *DAGDA*, father of the gods, which was an inexhaustible pot that was capable of satisfying every appetite.

It is clear that the gods known in Ireland as the Tuatha De Danann were common to all Celtic peoples. Their names can be found in Welsh myths and in inscriptions on the continent of Europe. In Ireland they were not entirely lost with the advent of Christianity. Apart from having their exploits recorded by the monks who wrote down the Irish sagas, the Tuatha De Danann took up residence underground as the fairies. On the ancient Celtic feast of Samhain, celebrated on the last day of October to mark the new year, the De Danann were believed to allow mortals to enter their realm.

TUIREANN was the Irish father of three sons who killed Cian, father of the son god *LUGH*. To atone for this crime, Lugh demanded that the sons of Tuireann should perform a series of near impossible tasks, bringing back to Ireland such magical objects as a healing pigskin belonging to a king of Greece and a cooking spit from an undersea kingdom. When fulfilling their final labour they were badly wounded and Tuireann begged Lugh for the pigskin to cure his sons, but the god refused and they died.

TWRCH TRWYTH, in Welsh mythology, was a king who was turned into a gigantic boar for his sins. Between his ears he kept a comb, a pair of scissors and a razor. The retrieval of these objects was one of the hardest of the tasks that the giant Yspaddaden set *CULHWCH* who wanted to marry his daughter *OLWEN*. The boar was an important animal to the Celts and appears in many myths, as well as in statues and carvings. It represented both war and feasting.

UAITHNE was the god Dagda's inspired harpist. He had three equally gifted sons who played such sad music that on one occasion twelve men died weeping from sorrow. The Celtic bards accompanied their music with lyrics which perpetuated the legends down the generations. (ILLUSTRATION ANON.)

UATH submitted three Irish heroes to a beheading contest to test their courage and find the champion of Ireland. The rules allowed a hero to behead the giant but only if he could return the favour on the next day. Only Cuchulainn had the courage to behead the giant and place his head on the block. (ILLUSTRATION BY JAMES ALEXANDER, 1995.)

UAITHNE, in Irish mythology, was the magic harp of the *TUATHA DE DANANN* god *DAGDA*. It was stolen by the *FOMORII*, the enemies of the De Danann. When Dagda discovered where it was, he called out to the harp to free itself. The harp responded by killing nine Fomorii and then singing Dagda's praises. Uaithne was also the name of Dagda's harpist.

UATH ("Horror") was the name of the water giant who challenged the three Irish heroes *CUCHULAINN*, Laoghaire and *CONALL* to a beheading contest. Each was invited to take an axe and chop off the giant's head, provided that he would then lay his own head on the block for the giant to decapitate. Only Cuchulainn rose to the challenge, and was proclaimed by the giant as the Irish champion. After the announcement Uath revealed himself to be *CU ROI*, the Munster king.

UATHACH was one of the lovers of the great Ulster hero and champion *CUCHULAINN*, and, according to Irish mythology, the daughter of the female warrior *SCATHACH*, who had been Cuchulainn's tutor in the martial arts. When Uathach served

UTHER PENDRAGON, Arthur's father, hit upon the incredible idea of having a round table at which 150 knights could see each other and sit without quarrelling. Turning to Merlin, he asked him to design a table "round in the likeness of the world". (ILLUSTRATION ANON.)

the hero food, he forgot his own strength and accidently broke her finger while taking a dish from her hand. Her scream brought her previous lover to Uathach's immediate aid, but Cuchulainn easily slew him in the fight that followed and afterwards Uathach transferred her affection to the victor.

VORTIGERN, a fifth-century ruler of Britain, tried to build a grand castle, but the walls kept crumbling. The boy Merlin, a precocious seer, was consulted and revealed that two dragons battled beneath the site every night, destroying the castle walls. (ILLUSTRATION BY ALAN LEE, 1984.)

URIEN, father of *OWAIN*, ruled Rheghed in north-west Britain. His courage and skill as a warrior were celebrated in many songs, including the work of *TALIESIN*. When the Angles invaded, Urien is said to have fought a successful campaign against them and besieged them on the island of Lindisfarne.

UTHER PENDRAGON (whose name means "dragon head") was *ARTHUR*'s father. According to late-British mythology, Uther was able to sleep with Igraine because he was disguised as her husband, Gorlois, Duke of Cornwall, and the result of their union was Arthur. The wizard *MERLIN* helped in this deception and later Uther killed Gorlois and married Igraine, while Arthur was taken by Merlin.

VORTIGERN was a British ruler who hired Jutish mercenaries, but as increasing numbers of Saxons came into Britain he fled to Wales. Here he tried to build a stronghold, but it kept collapsing. When *MERLIN* was consulted he said that a red dragon (the Saxons) battled with a white dragon (the Britons) beneath the fort and that the red dragon would eventually win.

V

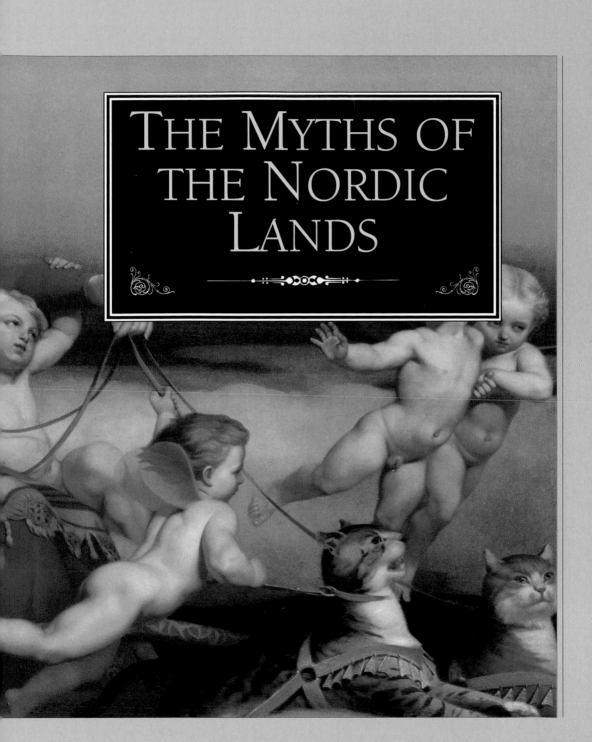

THE MYTHS OF
THE NORDIC
LANDS

INTRODUCTION

THE MYTHOLOGY OF NORTHERN AND eastern Europe is essentially that of two main groups, peoples of Germanic and of Slavic descent. Today the former group includes Germans, Dutch, Danes, Swedes, Norwegians, Icelanders, English, and any of their extraction, while the Slavs are made up of Russians, Serbs, Croats, Bulgarians, Rumanians, Slovacs and Poles. Other peoples have also contributed to the mythological tradition of the region, such as the inhabitants of the Baltic shore: the Prussians, Lithuanians and Letts. Further north there are contributions from the Finns and the Lapps of Sweden and Norway. The northernmost people of all, the Lapps of Finland and their cousins, the Samoyeds of Russia, are actually the scattered remnants of the Uralians, an ancient group once spread right across the tundra of Europe and Asia. Their beliefs remained similar to those held by the tribespeople of Siberia until quite recent times. For the purpose of this book these traditions have been grouped together under the generic term, Norse.

It is a fact that the overwhelming bulk of mythology surviving from northern and eastern Europe is Scandinavian and Icelandic in origin. Most Slavic gods are not much more than names, and the little we know about their worship is usually as a consequence of its Christian termination. In Russia the conversion of Vladimir in 989 to the Orthodox faith involved the ransacking of pagan temples at Kiev. Fortunately, chroniclers of this event noted the strange worship accorded to the thunder god Perunu or Veles, the god of flocks. Without such passing testimony our scant knowledge would be almost nonexistent. Even so, there are difficulties with Vladimir's own pagan beliefs prior to his conversion to Christianity. He was of Swedish descent and the "Rus" state he ruled on the

River Dnieper was a by-product of Viking exploration. It is therefore likely that the Slavic thunder god Perunu had already absorbed much of Thor's mythology. Although a native hammer-god undoubtedly existed before the Vikings arrived in the 860s, the importance of northern warriors in Novgorod and Kiev made it inevitable that the Russian god would be identified with his Germanic counterpart. The strength of the Viking presence can be judged from the Arab traveller Ibn-Fadlan's account of the ship cremation of a "Rus" leader on the Volga river in 922.

In the Balkans the Slavs not only encountered Orthodox Christianity, but were later for a time under Islamic rule also. This long

isolation from such Slavonic influences did not bode well for Balkan mythology. As the myths were never written down, the influence of Christianity and Islamic rule replaced the native story-telling. Of Baltic mythology next to nothing now exists, although some idea can be formed of the pantheon. The brutal truth is that European mythology has escaped the Baltic fate only where by historical accident it was written down. In the case of Celtic

ODIN, the leading warrior god of the Vikings, at left, bears the weapons of his warcraft, an axe and spear. The stylized tree depicted beside him symbolizes Yggdrasil, the World Tree. At centre is the thunder god Thor, wielding his fiery thunderbolt, Mjollnir; while at right, Freyr bears an ear of corn to represent his fertility. (TAPESTRY, 12TH CENTURY.)

mythology we are fortunate in the care taken by Christian monks in Ireland to record the ancient sagas. The classical heritage of Greece and Rome was preserved like that of the Celts in monastic libraries, after the Germanic peoples overran the western provinces of the Roman empire. And much of Germanic mythology would have been lost in its turn without the efforts of the Icelandic scholar and statesman Snorri Sturluson.

At the turn of the thirteenth century Snorri Sturluson wrote a handbook for poets on the world of the Germanic gods, providing detailed explanations of the old myths. He was recalling the sagas of the Viking era, approximately 750–1050, when a vigorous tradition formed around the heroic deeds of Odin, Thor and Freyr. Still untouched by Christianity, the restless and adventurous Northmen – the Danes, Norwegians and Swedes – put to sea in search of plunder and land. Viking warriors were largely organized in small bands or ships' crews, only joining together in temporary alliances for military expeditions, trading voyages or piracy. They might serve under a famous leader for a while, and then break up again, although on occasion they built up armies or large fleets of warships, like the forces that attacked France in 842 or invaded England in 866. Their magnificent ships and expert seamanship gave them mastery of rivers and seas, and enabled them to travel far and wide.

The Irish lamented the Viking onslaught most. "The sea spewed forth floods of foreigners over Ireland," noted the *Annals of Ulster*, "so that no harbour, no beach, no stronghold, no fort, no castle, might be found, but it was sunk beneath waves of northmen and pirates." In 836 the Vikings had decided to set up a permanent raiding base on the site of present-day Dublin.

It is hardly surprising that aggressive Viking

SIGURD roasts the heart of the terrible dragon, Fafnir, and sucks his thumb which was splashed with the dragon's blood. On tasting the otherworldly blood, Sigurd gained the power to understand birdsong and learnt from the birds that Regin, his tutor sleeping by the fire, planned treachery. (WOOD CARVING, 12TH CENTURY.)

warriors loved hearing about the exploits of one-eyed Odin. This chief of the Germanic gods exerted a special fascination as "father of the slain". He shared those who fell on the battlefield with Freyja, the goddess of fertility. He also inspired the frightful berserkers, the shield-biting fighters who rushed unheeding and naked into the fray. When the Danish king Harald Wartooth complained about Odin's fickleness, the way he gave luck in battle and then suddenly withdrew it again,

the war god said "the grey wolf watches the halls of the gods". Gathering to Valhalla the heroic warriors slain in battle was the only policy Odin felt he could sensibly follow under the constant threat of Ragnarok, the doom of the gods. These dead warriors, the *Einherjar*, were desperately needed for the final battle on the Vigrid Plain, where nearly all would fall in an encounter between the gods and the frost giants. Odin himself was destined to be killed by the wolf Fenrir, the monstrous offspring of the fire god Loki and the frost giantess Angrboda. Whether Harald Wartooth accepted this as an adequate answer is uncertain, since Odin, who was acting as his charioteer, flung the old king down and slew him with his sword as he fell.

177

VALHALLA (below), the splendid, many-spired Hall of the Slain, housed Odin's phantom army of heroic warriors, gathered to fight at Ragnarok the preordained doom of the gods. On the right, the massive World Serpent, Jormungand, was destined to overwhelm the world at Ragnarok. (ILLUSTRATION FROM THE PROSE EDDA, 1760.)

The "axe-age, sword-age", which was the age that would lead up to the catastrophe of Ragnarok, must have seemed like a description of contemporary times to the footloose Vikings. But for those who settled down as colonists, either as farmers or traders, an alternative god to worship was Thor, Odin's son. Although "allergic" to frost giants, Thor is represented in the sagas as an honest and straightforward person. He was very popular with Icelandic colonists, who had fled southern Norway to avoid the Odin-like activities of leaders like Erik Bloodaxe. Thousands of them revealed their allegiance in the choice of family name: Thorsten or Thorolf were most common. Thor was indeed a reassuring supernatural presence in both divine and human crises, be they encroachments by frost giants on gods, or local tyrants on farmers, or even overzealous Christian missionaries on pagan temples. Ever handy was his thunder-hammer Mjollnir, a magic instrument with powers of destruction, fertility and resurrection. It was hardly surprising then that Thor became a greater god than Odin at the close of the Viking era, just a century or so before Scandinavia was converted to Christianity.

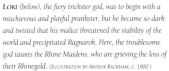

LOKI (below), the fiery trickster god, was to begin with a mischievous and playful prankster, but he became so dark and twisted that his malice threatened the stability of the world and precipitated Ragnarok. Here, the troublesome god taunts the Rhine Maidens, who are grieving the loss of their Rhinegold. (ILLUSTRATION BY ARTHUR RACKHAM, C. 1900.)

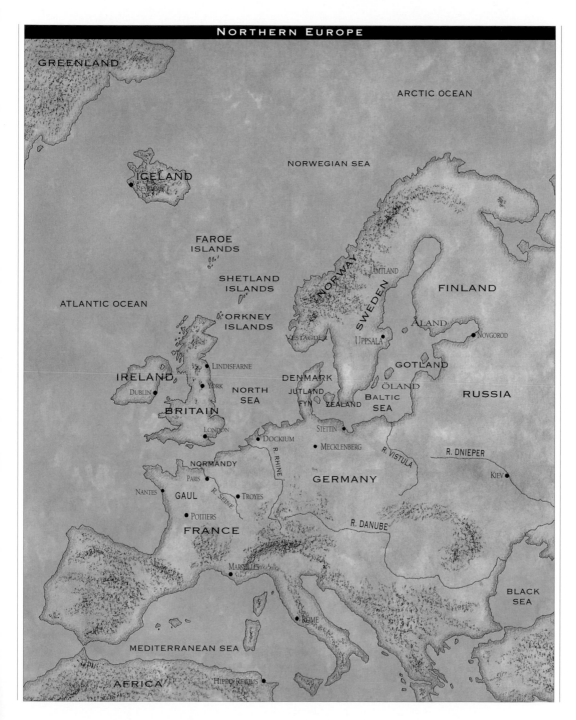

NORTHERN EUROPE

GREENLAND

ARCTIC OCEAN

NORWEGIAN SEA

ICELAND
Reykjavik

FAROE
ISLANDS

SHETLAND
ISLANDS

ATLANTIC OCEAN

ORKNEY
ISLANDS

NORWAY

SWEDEN

Jämtland

FINLAND

Åland

Vestagder

Uppsala

Novgorod

GOTLAND

IRELAND

Lindisfarne

Dublin

York

NORTH
SEA

DENMARK

JUTLAND

ÖLAND

RUSSIA

BRITAIN

FYN

ZEALAND

BALTIC
SEA

London

Stettin

Dockium

Mecklenberg

R. VISTULA

R. DNIEPER

Kiev

NORMANDY

R. RHINE

GERMANY

Paris

Nantes

GAUL

R. SEINE

Troyes

Poitiers

R. DANUBE

FRANCE

Marseilles

BLACK
SEA

Rome

MEDITERRANEAN SEA

AFRICA

HIPPO REGIUS

A

AEGIR, or Eagor, was a Germanic sea god, the husband of *RAN* and father of nine daughters, the waves. He seems to have belonged to an older generation of the gods than either the *AESIR* or the *VANIR*, although no details of his descent survive. Aegir was sometimes depicted as a very old man with white hair and claw-like fingers. Whenever he rose from his underwater hall, he broke the surface of the sea for a single purpose, the destruction of ships and their crews. To ensure a calm voyage, prisoners would usually be sacrificed to Aegir before a Viking raiding party set sail for home.

One myth tells how the proud sea god was outwitted by *THOR*. Aegir had been ordered by Thor to brew some ale for the gods, but he pretended that he had no cauldron large enough for the task. In fact he disliked being told what to do. But undaunted, Thor acquired a vast cauldron from the frost giant *HYMIR*. It was so big that when he hoisted it onto his shoulders, the

AEGIR (above), a tempestuous and powerful god of the sea, resided in a glistening underwater palace from where he directed the swirling waves through his nine daughters, who were known as the billow maidens. The hissing, seething Nordic sea was called "Aegir's Brewing Kettle". (ILLUSTRATION BY JAMES ALEXANDER, 1995.)

AEGIR'S sister-wife, Ran, was famous for her drowning net, which she used to snatch unsuspecting sailors from the decks of ships and drag them down to the seabed. She entertained them in her coral caves, which were lit by gleaming gold and where mead flowed as freely as in Valhalla. (ILLUSTRATION BY PETER HURD, 1882.)

handles reached his ankles. Hymir tried to stop Thor leaving with the cauldron, but the god's hammer saw off Hymir and his gigantic friends. As a result, a humiliated Aegir had to accept the cauldron and supply *ASGARD*, the home of the gods, with ale.

It was at a subsequent feast for the gods held by Aegir that *LOKI* showed how evil he had become when he insulted the assembled company and stabbed Aegir's servant Fimafeng.

THE AESIR, in Germanic mythology, were one branch of the family of the gods; the other branch were the *VANIR*. At one time there was a war between the younger Aesir and the older Vanir, which ended in a peace that left the Aesir dominant. Both branches had in fact grown weary of fighting, and were pleased to come to terms. In order to cement the peace, several of the leading Aesir went to live among the Vanir, while a number of important Vanir went to *ASGARD*, the Aesir's home.

The Aesir, under the leadership of *ODIN*, included his sons *BALDER* ("the bleeding god") and *BRAGI*, the god of eloquence; the justice god *FORSETI*, who resolved quarrels in a splendid hall supported by pillars of red gold and covered with a roof inlaid with silver; the fertility god *FREYR*, once a leading Vanir; the vigilant *HEIMDALL*, whose duty it would be to summon every living creature to *RAGNAROK*, the day of doom, with his horn; blind *HODR*, the unwitting killer of Balder; the trickster *LOKI*, god of fire and ally of the frost giants; the sea god *NJORD*, one of the gods exchanged with the Vanir; another of Odin's sons, *THOR*, whose mighty magic hammer was the only weapon the frost giants feared; the god of war *TYR*, a son of Hymir; *VILI* and *VE*, the brothers of Odin; and *VIDAR*, a son of Odin who was destined to avenge his father's death at Ragnarok.

The goddesses of the Aesir were *FREYJA*, the fertility goddess and twin sister of Freyr; *FRIGG*, Odin's wife; *SIF*, the wife of Thor; and *IDUN*, who was the keeper of the apples of youth.

Almost all the Aesir were to be killed at Ragnarok (the doom of the gods), when a terrible battle was destined to take place between the forces led by Odin, and the forces led by Loki.

ALBERICH see *ANDVARI*

ALVIS ("All Wise"), in Germanic mythology, was a dwarf who was outwitted by *ODIN*'s son *THOR*, the possessor of a magic hammer of irresistible force. In payment for the weapons Alvis had forged for them, the gods promised that he could marry Thor's daughter *THRUD*. However, Thor was displeased with the arrangement and so devised a test of knowledge to stop the dwarf from marrying his daughter. When Alvis came to *ASGARD*, Thor questioned him all night long because sunlight turned dwarfs to stone.

ALVIS, a dwarf famed for his wisdom, hoped to marry Thor's giant daughter, Thrud, but first he had to prove that his great wisdom made up for his small stature. Thor quizzed him and prolonged the test until sunrise when the first ray petrified Alvis who, like all dwarfs, turned to stone in daylight. (ILLUSTRATION BY JAMES ALEXANDER, 1995.)

THE AESIR *(left) were warrior-gods worshipped by heroes and kings. Very like Norsemen, they loved, fought and died with human feelings for, though divine, they were not immortal. Odin, seen here in horned helmet, behind the Vanir twins, led the heroic Aesir.* (THE NORTHERN GODS DESCENDING BY W COLLINGWOOD, CANVAS, C. 1890.)

ANDVARI'S *(above) treasure trove was stolen by the gods Odin and Loki in order to pay a ransom. When they took his gold-making ring too, Andvari danced with rage and cursed the ring. At top, the three Norns examine the dark thread of destiny, while below, Hel awaits a new inmate.* (ILLUSTRATION BY F VON STASSEN, 1914.)

ANDVARI, or Alberich, as he was known in later German legend, was a craftsman dwarf who lost his hoard of treasure to the fire god *LOKI*. On an expedition to Midgard (the land of men), Loki killed a sleeping otter with a stone. Carrying the dead otter, he, *ODIN* and *HONIR* came across a farm and offered to share the otter's meat with the household in return for a night's lodgings. To the horror of *HREIDMAR*, the farmer, the offering was none other than his own son *OTTER*. First of all, Hreidmar chanted a spell to weaken his guests and then his two surviving sons, *FAFNIR* and *REGIN*, bound them hand and foot. Odin protested their innocence and pointed out that they

would not have come straight to the farm had they known the otter was the farmer's son. So, eventually, Hreidmar settled on a death-price: enough gold to cover Otter's skin, inside and out. Because the flayed skin was endowed with magic powers, it was capable of being stretched to a great size and so no ordinary amount of gold could be accepted in compensation.

Loki was allowed by Hreidmar to seek this great treasure, while Odin and Honir (in some versions just Honir) remained at the farm as hostages. The fire god was not permitted to wear his sky-shoes, however, and these were also kept as security against Loki's return. Having borrowed the drowning-net

of Ran, wife of the sea god *AEGIR*, Loki descended through a maze of dripping tunnels to an underground lake, where he caught a large pike. This fish, like the otter before, turned out to be more than it first seemed. For it was in fact the dwarf Andvari, who was the richest of those who dwelt underground. Only because of Loki's terrible threats, Andvari surrendered all his immense hoard of gold, including his magic gold-making ring. But in his anger the dwarf laid a terrible curse on the ring which would cause the doom of whoever wore it. When Loki returned to the farm with the gold and Odin and Honir were released, he told Hreidmar of Andvari's curse and in this way

passed it on to the farmer. Indeed, Hreidmar was soon after killed by his son Fafnir, who then ran away with the cursed treasure.

The hero *SIGURD* was later persuaded by his foster-father Regin to pursue Fafnir, who had by this time become a dragon. The hero duly searched for the creature and eventually found it in its lair and slew it. However, when Sigurd realized that for the sake of the treasure Regin intended to kill him in turn, he made sure that he slew his foster-father first. Thus it was that Andvari's curse continued to cling to the stolen gold and brought about the death of all those who attempted to possess it. (See also *RINGS OF POWER*)

ANGRBODA (left) mothered a dreadful
brood of monsters – a rotting girl, Hel; a
savage wolf, Fenrir; and a giant serpent,
Jormungand – who were banished by the
gods. Here, Odin flings the serpent into the
icy deep, while Angrboda guards her wolf-
child. (ILLUSTRATION BY JAMES ALEXANDER, 1995.)

the sun and the moon, as his price
for the eighteen-month task. At
LOKI's suggestion, ODIN set the
seemingly impossible limit of six
months for the construction of
Asgard's walls. As a concession the
stonemason was allowed to use his
horse, the magic Svadilfari, to help
him in the work. To the horror of
the gods he had finished all the
walls, except a gateway, three days
before the time was up. So Loki
transformed himself into a mare
and beguiled the stonemason's
stallion, thus preventing the com-
pletion of the job. The stonemason
then revealed himself as a frost
giant and THOR broke his skull with
his hammer. It is ironic that the
defences of Asgard should have
been built by the labour of a frost
giant, given the bitter enmity
between the gods and the giants.
Indeed, at RAGNAROK these two
enemies were destined to meet in a
battle of mutual destruction.

The idea of city walls that were
built by giants is a widespread
myth in Europe. The walls of
Tiryns in southern Greece, for
example, were believed to have
been constructed by the Cyclopes,
who were giant, one-eyed beings.
There is also a story of a dispute
over payment for the strengthening
of Troy's walls by the gods Apollo
and Poseidon and King Laomedon,
which is not dissimilar to the above
story concerning Asgard's walls.
(See also RAGNAROK)

ANGRBODA, or Angerboda
("Distress-bringer"), in Germanic
mythology, was a frost giantess.
She was the mistress of LOKI and
the mother of three monstrous
offspring: the wolf FENRIR, the serpent JORMUNGAND, and a daughter
named HEL. When the gods heard
about this brood, they agreed that
such creatures must be dealt with
quickly. A group of gods broke into
Angrboda's hall at night, bound
and gagged her, and took her and
Loki's children to ASGARD.

ODIN first banished Hel to the
"world beneath the worlds" and
there he put her in charge of all the
inglorious dead. He then hurled
Jormungand into the ocean, where
the huge snake smashed through
the ice and sank down into the
depths. Odin was less certain what
to do with Fenrir, so at first he
decided that the gods should keep
an eye on him at Asgard. However,
when the NORNS, the goddesses of
destiny, warned that the wolf
would bring about Odin's death
action was finally taken to bind
Fenrir securely with a magic chain
and keep him in captivity.

Although Angrboda's children
were thus contained, Odin knew
that the wolf Fenrir would break
free at RAGNAROK, the day of doom,
and destroy him. The sea serpent
Jormungand also awaited the final
conflict, like his sister Hel "surrounded by corpses and swirling
death-mist" in the netherworld. A
tenth-century Danish complaint
about Odin's withdrawal of luck
from brave warriors is answered in
terms of Angrboda's brood. Odin
is supposed to have said that "the

grey wolf watches the halls of the
gods". With this threat in mind, he
had no choice but to gather to his
side the greatest champions.

ASGARD, in Germanic mythology, was the divine stronghold of
the AESIR, who were the younger
and stronger branch of the family of
gods. The other branch, the VANIR,
lived in Vanaheim. Asgard's mighty
walls were built by a stonemason,
Hrimthurs, who named the hand
of the fertility goddess FREYJA, plus

ASGARD (left), the stronghold of the Aesir
gods, shimmered above Midgard. Within,
there were countless shining, glittering halls
for each of the gods. Asgard was linked to
Midgard by an ethereal pathway for the
gods, a wondrous rainbow bridge called
Bifrost. (ILLUSTRATION BY H HENDRICH, C. 1890.)

B

AUDHUMLA was the primeval cow in Germanic mythology. This creature was the first animal to emerge from *GINNUNGAGAP* ("the yawning emptiness") at the start of creation. From Audhumla's teats "flowed four rivers of milk", nourishment enough for *YMIR*, the first frost giant and the first live thing of all. From Ymir's children descended the frost giants, the implacable enemies of the gods. The cow herself seems to have survived on the goodness that she obtained from an icy salt lick. As she licked, first some hair appeared, then a head, and finally the whole body of a man, *BURI*. In time Buri had a son named *BOR*, who married Bestla, the daughter of a frost giant. Their sons were the first gods, *ODIN*, *VILI* and *VE*. These three battled against the frost giants and finally slew Ymir. As the giant fell the blood from his wounds flooded the land and drowned all his frost children, except for *BERGELMIR* and his wife who managed to escape.

BABA YAGA, sometimes Jezi Baba, is the hideous man-eating female demon of Slavonic tradition. According to some versions of her myth, her mouth is said to stretch from earth to the gates of hell. She lived in a strange house which had legs like a chicken's at each corner, and stood inside a fence made of human bones. When she wished to travel, it was believed that she flew in an iron kettle.

ASGARD'S (above) walls were built by a giant stonemason, Hrimthurs, aided by his wondrous horse, Svadilfari. The gods gave him only six months to complete the work, hoping to avoid payment. He nearly finished on time but was thwarted by Loki's trickery. (ILLUSTRATION BY ALAN LEE, 1984.)

AUDHUMLA (below), the original cow, emerged from the primal ice at the dawn of time, and nourished the first frost giant, Ymir. She survived by licking ice from which she freed the first man, Buri. Here, while Ymir suckles her milk, Audhumla licks Buri free of the ice. (AUDHUMLA BY N A ABILGAARD, CANVAS, C. 1790.)

BABA YAGA (bottom right) was a Slavonic witch of monstrous size who preyed on travellers, devouring their flesh with a mouth that stretched from earth to hell. She was seen as a hunched hag, bearded, part woman, part-tree. Here, perched on a rolling log, she propels herself forward with a pole. (ILLUSTRATION BY I BILIBIN, 1900.)

BALDER, sometimes Baldr or Baldur, was the son of *ODIN* and *FRIGG* and the "bleeding god" of Germanic mythology. His wife was Nanna and their son, *FORSETI*, was the god of justice.

As a young man, Balder was tormented by night-mares, all of which indicat-ed that he was about to die. A sense of foreboding, therefore, settled over *ASGARD*, the home of the gods, as the divine inhabitants tried to understand the meaning of Balder's dreams. They were deeply puzzled because the gentle god least deserved to suffer such tor-ments. So Odin rode his eight-legged steed *SLEIPNIR* to the land of the dead and by means of magic learned from a seeress there that Balder was to be killed by the blind god *HODR*, his own brother, with a branch. Although depressed by this news, Odin returned to Asgard and found that his wife Frigg had a plan to save Balder. The goddess travelled through the nine worlds and got each and every thing to swear an oath that it would do her son no harm. To Odin's relief this plan seemed to work. When the

BALDER, a loving and gentle soul, spread light and goodwill wherever he went but, inevitably, evoked the envy of the bitter god Loki, who plotted his tragic death and imprisonment in Hel. This romantic portrayal captures the sacred, Christ-like goodness of the god.
(BALDER BY B FOGELBERG, MARBLE, 1840.)

gods decided to test Balder's new invulnerability by throwing stones and spears at him with great force, he remained unharmed. All in Asgard were delighted except *LOKI*, the god of fire. He was so annoyed by Balder's escape from danger that he transformed himself into an old woman and visited Frigg's hall. In conversation with the goddess, Loki learned that she had received a promise of harmlessness from all things except the mistletoe, which was a plant too small and too feeble to bother about.

Armed with this information, Loki went off to cut some mistle-toe. In his normal shape the fire god returned to the assembly of the gods and found everyone throwing things at Balder, except blind Hodr. Pretending to help Hodr enjoy the sport, Loki gave him the branch of mistletoe and directed his throw, with the result that the branch passed right through Balder, who immediately fell down dead. At Frigg's entreaty *HERMOD*, Balder's brother, was sent to *HEL* in order to offer a ransom for Balder. He used the eight-legged Sleipnir for the journey. While Hermod was away, the bodies of Balder and Nanna, who had died of grief, were placed on a pyre in a longship which was allowed to drift burning out to sea.

BALDER's body was laid on a pyre in his longship and he was then covered in treasure and decorated with flowers and thorns, the emblems of sleep. His ship was set aflame and pushed out to sea where it shone brightly, before sinking into darkness.
(FUNERAL OF A VIKING BY F DICKSEE, CANVAS, 1893.)

In the netherworld the brave Hermod found his brother Balder seated in a high position. When he asked for his release, Hel said Balder could leave only on condition that "everything in the nine worlds, dead and alive, wept for him". Messengers were sent out and soon even the stones were weeping. But THOKK, an old frost giantess, refused, saying, "Let Hel hold what she has." So upset were the gods at this refusal to mourn that it took some time for them to realize that Thokk was none other than Loki in disguise. Nevertheless, Balder remained with Hel.

Balder's good looks and early death recall the myths of the Egyptian Osiris and the Sumerian Tammuz, as well as that of Adonis, who was the dying-and-rising god the ancient Greeks adopted from the Phoenicians. For the Germanic peoples believed that the return of the wounded, dying Balder would occur in a new world, a green land risen from the sea, after RAGNAROK, the doom of the gods. Like the undead Celtic King Arthur, Balder was expected to return and rule over a world cleansed by catastrophe. It would seem that some of the initial appeal of Christianity in northern Europe was connected with the triumphant return of the risen Christ on Judgement Day. (See also RAGNAROK)

BALDR see BALDER

BALDUR see BALDER

BEOWULF was the Germanic hero who slew two water monsters. He was said to be the nephew of the king of Geats, whom some interpret as the Jutes. His story is set in Denmark. One night a dreadful creature known as GRENDEL came to the hall of King Hrothgar and ate one of the warriors sleeping there. Although invulnerable to weapons, Grendel was seized by Beowulf and held in a powerful grip, from which it could only

BEOWULF, seen here with raised drinking horn, gazes up at the gory trophy hanging from the splendid vault of Denmark's Victory Hall. The giant hairy hand belonged to the fearsome sea monster, Grendel, who had continually terrorized and devoured the Danes, until Beowulf tore the creature's arm right out of its socket. (ILLUSTRATION BY ALAN LEE, 1984.)

BEOWULF wrestles with a monstrous merwoman in the crystal cavern of her underwater den. Grieving for the death of her son, Grendel, slain by Beowulf, the merwoman fought with frenzy, but Beowulf battled calmly and took her by surprise. (ILLUSTRATION BY JAMES ALEXANDER, 1995.)

break away by losing an arm. Mortally wounded, the water monster fled to its home, deep in a nearby lake, and bled to death.

Delighted by this feat of courage and strength, King Hrothgar loaded Beowulf with gifts, since his kingdom had been rid of a menace. But neither the king nor the warrior reckoned on Grendel's mother, an even more dreadful creature. She returned to the attack and ate another sleeping warrior. In pursuit, Beowulf followed her into a lake and dived down to her cavernlike lair. A desperate struggle then took place and Beowulf lost his

trusty sword. Like Arthur, he was fortunate to find another magic weapon in the water and he used this to finish off Grendel's mother.

Having once again saved King Hrothgar's kingdom from danger, Beowulf returned home to southern Sweden, where his father ruled. Towards the end of his popular reign a dragon attacked his land. Going out with twelve followers to slay the fiery beast, Beowulf soon found himself almost on his own, for all his companions but one ran away in terror. Although he managed to kill the dragon, it was at the cost of his own life.

In contrast to the Celtic myths that describe combat with watergiants, the Germanic stories tell of heroes who face actual monsters rather than magical opponents. This is quite unlike the great Ulster hero and champion Cuchulainn's beheading contest with Uath, or Sir Gawain's with the Green Knight, for in these traditions their monstrous opponents were able to restore themselves to life after they had been decapitated.

BEOWULF, even in his old age, tackled firebreathing dragons. Yet neither his might nor his fabled armour, crafted by Wayland, could withstand the dragon's crushing teeth. Beowulf was mortally wounded in the combat, but he did not die before seeing the dragon's treasure released for his people. (ILLUSTRATION BY JAMES ALEXANDER, 1995.)

BERGELMIR, according to Germanic mythology, was the son of Thrudgelmir and the grandson of *YMIR*. When *ODIN*, *VILI* and *VE* killed Ymir and threw his body into the middle of *GINNUNGAGAP*, all the frost giants drowned in the giant's blood except Bergelmir and his wife. By using a hollowed tree trunk as a boat, they escaped to

BIFROST (above) was a gigantic rainbow causeway, reaching from the shining citadel of Asgard to the earthly realm of Midgard. Composed of fire, water and air, it shimmered with rainbow-coloured light in hues of red, blue and green. Over the ethereal arch, the gods moved to and fro.
(ILLUSTRATION BY ALAN LEE, 1984.)

continue the race of giants, who never lost their hatred for the gods. At *RAGNAROK* the frost giants and the dead of *HEL* were destined to settle the final account for Ymir's dismemberment.

BIFROST, in Germanic mythology, was the flaming three-strand rainbow bridge between *ASGARD* and Midgard (heaven and earth respectively). It was said to have been built by the gods out of red fire, green water and blue air, and was guarded by the watchman god *HEIMDALL*. Every day the gods rode across the bridge to hold meetings at the well of *URD*.

BILLING, in Germanic mythology, was the father of *RIND*. According to some traditions, he was king of the Ruthenians, or Russians. So strong-willed was Rind that *ODIN* could not woo her, even though Billing approved of the god's suit. On the contrary, she treated the chief of the Germanic gods with undisguised contempt. Eventually, however, she gave way to his advances and she bore a son, *VALI*, who killed *HODR* with his bow and arrow.

BERGELMIR (below) and his wife were the only frost giants to escape drowning in the torrent of Ymir's blood that flowed from his mortal wounds. They journeyed in a hollowed-out tree trunk to the edge of the world where they founded the realm of Jotunheim and bred a new race of giants.
(ILLUSTRATION BY NICK BEALE, 1995.)

BILLING (above) gazes in wonder at the glittering trinkets fashioned by the dwarf goldsmith Rosterus. Unknown to King Billing, the dwarf is Odin in disguise, who was intent on wooing the king's daughter, Rind. She was destined to bear Odin a son, Vali, who would avenge Balder's death.
(ILLUSTRATION BY NICK BEALE, 1995.)

BOR was the son of *BURI*, husband of the giant Bestla and father of *ODIN*, *VILI* and *VE*. An ancient god, Bor lived in the time before the world had been made, when there was no earth, sky or sea, only mist, ice, fire and the gaping pit of *GINNUNGAGAP*. Bor's father-in-law, the giant Bolthur, also had a son who imparted his wisdom to his nephew Odin.

BRAGI was the son of *ODIN* and Gunnlod, a female giant, and was the Germanic god of poetry and eloquence. He was married to *IDUN*, the goddess who kept the magic apples of youth. When *LOKI* returned to *ASGARD*, after being instrumental in causing *BALDER*'s death, Bragi, who was never at a loss for words, told him that he was

BRAGI (above) was born in a glittering stalactite cave, where his mother, Gunnlod, guarded the Mead of Poetry, until seduced by Odin. The dwarfs gave the fair child a magical harp and set him afloat on one of their fine-crafted vessels from which he sang his poignant Song of Life which rose to the heavens. (ILLUSTRATION BY PETER HURD, 1882.)

THE BRISINGAMEN (below) was an exquisite necklace crafted by dwarfs so finely that it shone like liquid flame. The goddess Freyja, beside herself with longing, paid dearly for possessing the treasure. An emblem of the stars, it so enhanced her beauty that she wore it continually, night and day. (ILLUSTRATION BY J PENROSE, C. 1890.)

unwelcome company at their feast. Enraged, Loki called Bragi "the bragger", whereupon Bragi threatened to twist off Loki's head as the only sure method of stopping his lies. Although Odin tried to calm the gathering, the effect of Bragi's words on Loki was to make him even more threatening. He finally prophesied the destruction of the gods and then fled from Asgard.

Possibly Bragi was a late addition to the Germanic pantheon. It is not unlikely that Bragi was added through the divine elevation of a poet, since in Germanic courts poets were venerated second only to kings. Bragi was portrayed as an old, bearded man carrying a harp, and when oaths were sworn they were solemnized by speaking over a vessel called the Cup of Bragi.

BRISINGAMEN see *RINGS OF POWER*

THE BRISINGS, also known as the Bristlings, were the mysterious owners of a golden necklace, called the Brisingamen, that the fertility goddess *FREYJA* craved. To *ODIN*'s disgust she slept on four successive nights with the dwarfs Alfrigg, Dvalin, Berling and Grer in order to acquire it. When she returned to *ASGARD*, Odin accused her of debasing her divinity by paying such a price. As a penance he made her stir up war in Midgard, the world of men. Freyja and Odin shared those slain on the battlefield.

No agreement exists about the meaning of this strange myth, not least because the identity of the Brisings is unknown. It has been suggested that necklaces were the special adornment of mother goddesses, but this hardly does more than explain Freyja's attraction to this particular one. What seems more likely is that the sexual price Freyja paid for it represents the other side of love, namely, blind passion and lust. Nothing could stop her, not even Odin's great disapproval, when she desired something badly enough. The Brisingamen came to be identified so closely with Freyja that when *THOR* wished to disguise himself as the goddess to retrieve his hammer from *THRYM*, she lent it to him to make his costume convincing. (See also *TREASURES AND TALISMANS*)

THE BRISTLINGS see *BRISINGS*

BRUNHILD see *BRYNHILD*

BRYNHILD was a *VALKYRIE* who defied *ODIN* and so was banished to earth and imprisoned within a ring of fire. When *SIGURD* braved the fire and broke her charmed sleep, they fell in love. He gave her his ring, Andvarinaut, unaware of its curse. On his travels he was bewitched by Grimhild into betraying Brynhild, first by marrying Gudrun and then by helping Gunner win Brynhild. On discovering Sigurd's betrayal, Brynhild planned his death, but then killed herself in despair. (See also *THE VALKYRIES*; *TRAGIC LOVERS*)

BURI, in Germanic mythology, was the ancestor of the gods. He was released from the ice by *AUDHUMLA*, the primeval cow. One day Buri's hair appeared where she licked; on the second day, his head was free of ice; and, on the third, his entire body. He had a son, *BOR*, who married a frost giantess, and their sons were *ODIN*, *VILI* and *VE*.

BRYNHILD, one of the leading Valkyries, was punished by Odin for meddling with his will in warfare. The god put her to sleep and imprisoned her in a ring of fire, where she would remain until a peerless hero freed her. Only Sigurd braved the scorching fire, waking her from her enchanted sleep. (ILLUSTRATION BY ARTHUR RACKHAM, C.1900.)

NATURE SPIRITS

THE DRAMATIC LANDSCAPE of Scandinavia, with its electric skies, icy wastes and seething springs, was easily peopled with nature spirits. Such spirits roamed the mountains and snow slopes as fearsome frost, storm and fire giants, personifying the mysterious and menacing forces of nature. So great were the terrors of crushing ice and searing fire that the giants loomed large in the Norse myths as evil and ominous forces. Yet other less dramatic but no less important spirits were the invisible *landvaettir*, or land spirits, who imbued the land and guarded its welfare. Helpful and timid, the *landvaettir* easily took fright, shying away from Viking dragon ships. In the underground caverns, dark dwarfs unearthed glittering gems and metals, while light elves inspired the forests and lakes. In Slavonic myth, a host of vital forces filled the world and imbued the forests, fields and rivers with whirling spirits of nature.

THE FROST GIANTS (below) personified the icy terrors of the Nordic landscape. Mighty, menacing and numbing, the ice masses of the North were a constant threat to the Norsemen, much like the frost giants, whose undying enmity would overwhelm the gods at Ragnarok. In the interim, the frost giants sent freezing blasts to nip the buds of spring, or shook avalanches from their icy shoulders and brows. (RONDANE AT NIGHT BY H SOHLBERG, CANVAS, C. 1890.)

THE SUN (above), in one myth, was fashioned by the gods from a bright spark of fire. Its glowing orb was placed in a chariot, drawn by two white steeds and driven by the sun-maid, Sol. Fearing that the sun's heat might be harmful, the gods placed a shield, Svalin, or Cooler, in front of the golden car. In another myth, the gods gave a giant, Day, a chariot and horses to drive round the earth once every 24 hours. Day's horse, Shining Mane, lit up the earth and sky with the radiance of his shining hair. (SUN DISC, GILDED BRONZE, C. 1000 BC.)

THE RHINE MAIDENS (above) were ethereal sprites who dwelt in lakes and rivers during the winter, emerging from the water to flit through the forests in summer. The river's colours reflected the nymphs' moods, turning black with grief when the Rhine Maidens lost their gold. Here, the Rhine Maidens bemoan their loss to the gods crossing the rainbow bridge above. (ILLUSTRATION BY ARTHUR RACKHAM, C.1900.)

ROCK AND STORM GIANTS personified the vast craggy mountains and storm clouds. Rocky chasms and outcrops were created by giants treading too heavily at the dawn of time. Best suited to mist and fog, the mountain giants, like dwarfs, were petrified by the light of day, which explains some fantastic rock formations, such as the Riesengebirge (right), formed by foolish giants who were caught outside at sunrise. Similarly, in Iceland the highest peaks are named Jokul which derives from Jotun or Giant.

(ILLUSTRATION BY NICV BEALE, 1995.)

RAN (left), a stormy spirit of the sea, reflected the shifting moods of the ocean, sometimes helpful, sometimes harmful. She gathered sailors in her drowning net and dragged them down to the depths of the sea. There, with her husband, Aegir, she entertained her victims in her gleaming coral caves, which were lit by the shining gold of the sea. Ran loved gold, named the Flame of the Sea, after the fluorescent quality of Nordic waves. Sailors seeking Ran's favour wisely pocketed some gold for the trip.

(ILLUSTRATION BY ARTHUR RACKHAM, C. 1900.)

DARK DWARFS (below) were formed from maggots in the rotting flesh of the slain giant, Ymir. The gods thought them too ugly to be seen, however, and condemned them to a life underground. Like giants, they turned to stone in daylight, thus explaining the many smaller stones and rocks scattered across the Nordic landscape. The twin peaks of Trold Tindterne, for example, are two bands of warring dwarfs who forgot to retreat before sunrise. As dwarfs had a habit of whispering behind rocks, the mountain echoes were known as "dwarfs' talk". (ILLUSTRATION BY ALAN LEE, 1984.)

F

DAZHBOG was the Slavic sun god, known as Dabog to the Serbs and Dazbog to the Poles. Son of Svarog, the god of the sky, and brother of *SVARAZIC*, god of fire, he was born again every morning and rode through the sky on his dia-mond chariot until he became an old man in the evening. In some versions he is married to *MYESYATS*, the moon, and quarrels between them are said to cause earthquakes.

DRAUPNIR see *RINGS OF POWER*

DIETRICH see *RINGS OF POWER*

EAGOR see *AEGIR*

THE EINHERJAR were the "heroic dead" of Germanic myth-ology. They were gathered from the battlefields by the *VALKYRIES*. In *VALHALLA*, the Einherjar formed *ODIN*'s private army, which he raised to fight at *RAGNAROK*, the doom of the gods. This was the final battle between the gods and the frost giants on the *VIGRID* Plain. Until then, these dead warriors would fight every day and feast every night, and any wounds they sustained were magically healed. (See also *THE VALKYRIES*)

FAFNIR slays his father, Hreidmar, because he is bewitched by the treasure trove stolen from the dwarf Andvari. The dwarf's cursed ring can be seen glittering on Hreidmar's forefinger as he writhes in the dust. Behind the warring pair, the gods gaze on in numb dismay. (ILLUSTRATION BY F VON STASSEN, 1914.)

THE EINHERJAR, or "heroic dead", were gathered up from the battlefield by the Valkyries who galloped over the fray, choosing the bravest heroes for Odin's ghostly army. A chosen hero saw a soaring Valkyrie just before the fatal blow. (THE RIDE OF THE VALKYRIES BY W T MAUD, CANVAS, C. 1890.)

FAFNIR, son of the magician *HREIDMAR*, was corrupted by the cursed ring Andvarinaut. Lusting after the fabulous ring-hoard, he slew his father, helped by his brother *REGIN*. Greed made him monstrous in nature and form, as he turned into a dragon to guard his hoard. The legend of his trea-sure drew many aspiring heroes to his lair in search of fame and for-tune. Most met their deaths on the blasted heath outside his lair, but the youthful *SIGURD*, armed with his father's sword and guided by Regin, outwitted the dragon and won his ill-fated treasure.

FARBAUTI ("Cruel striker") was a giant and father of the fire god *LOKI*. According to one tradition, his wife was another giant, Laufey ("Tree island") who gave birth to Loki when hit by a lightning bolt unleashed by Farbauti. Little else is known of Loki's parents.

FENRIR, or Fenris, according to Germanic mythology, was the son of the mischief-making god *LOKI* and the frost giantess *ANGRBODA*. He was the devouring wolf, the beast of *RAGNAROK*, the doom of the gods. His was "an axe-age, a sword-age, a wind-age, a wolf-age, before the wrecking of the world". *ODIN*, the chief of the gods, was destined to become his victim.

Kidnapped by the gods and brought to *ASGARD* where they could keep an eye on him, Fenrir was so savage that only the war god *TYR* dared to feed him. At first Odin was uncertain about the wolf, but when the *NORNS*, the goddesses of destiny, warned him about his own fate, he decided that Fenrir should be restrained. No chain, however, was strong enough to hold the ani-mal. Finally, the dwarfs made a magic fetter called Gleipnir from strange materials such as the roots of a mountain and bird's spittle. Although it seemed to be a silken ribbon, Fenrir would not have it round his neck unless one of the gods put his hand between his jaws as a pledge that it was as harmless as it seemed. Tyr was the only one prepared to risk his hand, and the other gods laughed when the wolf bit it off on finding that the chain could not be broken. Fenrir was then secured to a rock and his mouth was kept open by a sword so he could not bite.

When freed from captivity at Ragnarok, Fenrir was a fearsome spectacle. His vast mouth gaped so wide that the lower jaw touched the ground and the upper one reached the sky, and Odin was swallowed by him.

FENRIS see *FENRIR*

FJALAR and his brother Galar, in Germanic mythology, were the wicked dwarfs who killed the wise man *KVASIR* in order to gain his magic powers. They mixed his blood with honey in a cauldron and made a mead that bestowed wisdom. But Fjalar and Galar lost the wonderful drink to Suttung, a frost giant whose parents they had also killed. Unlike the dwarfs, Suttung was boastful about his

FORSETI, the fair god of justice, was a Solomon-like force for peace. He sat in judgement in his golden hall, Glitnir, and settled the disputes of gods and men, allaying strife and resolving feuds. He never failed to reconcile even the bitterest foes. (ILLUSTRATION BY NICK BEALE, 1995.)

acquisition and it was not long before the gods heard about the mead. ODIN himself decided that he would go to JOTUNHEIM, the land of the frost giants, and lay hold of the magic drink. Disguised as evil Bolverk, he journeyed to Jotunheim and persuaded the frost giant Baugi to tunnel through a mountain to where Suttung kept the mead under the care of his daughter Gunnlod. Once the hole was drilled, Odin changed his shape from Bolverk's to a snake, and slithered downwards to the hidden treasure as quickly as he could. Reaching the secret cave, he changed himself into a handsome one-eyed giant and for three days and nights he was Gunnlod's lover. The passionate giantess let Odin drink up every drop of the mead, before he turned himself into an eagle and flew back to ASGARD, the home of the gods. There he spat the mead into jars left empty for his return. Suttung gave chase as another eagle, but just failed to catch Odin.

In the account of Kvasir's death, it is clear that this is a myth about fermentation. To put the seal on their peace agreement the two branches of the gods, the AESIR and the VANIR, had spat into a jar, and it was from the spittle that Kvasir had been formed. Spittle, like yeast, causes fermentation, and so when Fjalar and Galar mixed Kvasir's blood with honey in a cauldron they created a magical mead. The connection between inspiration, poetry and wisdom and some form of potent drink occurs in several mythological traditions.

FORSETI was the Germanic god of justice, and was known to the Frisians as Forsite. He was the son of BALDER and Nanna. Both of his parents were killed, his father stabbed by a piece of mistletoe, thrown unwittingly by the blind god HODR, and his mother with a broken heart shortly after this tragic event. Although Forseti plays only a relatively small role in Germanic mythology, we are told in detail that his hall of Glitnir "had pillars of red gold and a roof inlaid with silver." There he sat in judgement and resolved strife.

FREA see FREYJA

FREY see FREYR

FREYA see FREYJA

FENRIR (above), the wolf fathered by Loki, was so savage that the gods chained him to an underground rock. Only a magical cord was strong enough to bind him. Here, the brave god Tyr fetters Fenrir at the cost of his own hand, which he placed in the wolf's mouth as a sign of trust. (DIE, 8TH CENTURY.)

FJALAR (below) and his brother Galar slew the wise Kvasir and drained his blood to extract his wisdom. Two glistening bowls and the Kettle of Inspiration contained the magical fluid, which the brothers mixed with honey to produce the golden Mead of Poetry. (ILLUSTRATION BY JAMES ALEXANDER, 1995.)

FREYJA, the voluptuous, blue-eyed goddess of love, rode in a chariot drawn by cats, which were symbols of her warm affections. Accompanied by a flock of airborne love spirits, she toured heaven and earth in search of her roving husband, Odur, shedding tears of gold all the while. (FREYJA BY N J O BLOMMER, CANVAS, 1852.)

FREYJA ("Lady"), sometimes known as Freya or Frea, was the daughter of the sea god NJORD in Germanic mythology and sister of FREYR. She was an important fertility goddess and a member of the VANIR, one of the two branches into which the Germanic gods were divided. After a war the Vanir seem to have been supplanted by the younger AESIR, who were led by ODIN. When peace was agreed between the two sides, Njord went with Freyr and Freyja to ASGARD, where they lived with the Aesir as a token of friendship.

Freyja's greatest treasure was the BRISINGS' necklace, which she obtained by sleeping with its four dwarf makers. Her beauty won her many admirers, including OTTAR, whom she changed into a boar. She was said to be a sorceress who could fly in a falcon's skin. Some traditions state that, on her arrival in Asgard, she taught the gods the spells and charms of the Vanir.

Both Odin and Freyja took an interest in the heroic dead, dividing the slain between them at the end of every battle. Odin's share went to live in VALHALLA, while Freyja's lived in her hall, Sessrumnir. It is possible that Freyja's lost husband Odur, or Od, of whom nothing is known but his name, was Odin. For she was the goddess of lust as well as love, a suitable partner for Odin who was the father of battles and the lover of destruction. (See also SORCERY AND SPELLS)

FREYR ("Lord"), sometimes Frey, was the twin brother of the Germanic fertility goddess FREYJA. Their father was NJORD, the god associated with the wind and the sea. Freyr, with ODIN and THOR, was one of the principal gods. He was mainly concerned with fertility, having control of sunlight, rain, fruitfulness and peace. His title of Skirr means "shining", and the name of the frost giantess he married, GERDA, derives from "field". As late as 1200, Freyr's statue in his temple at Uppsala, Sweden was noted for the size of its penis. Possibly for this reason the Romans had always identified him with Priapus, the virile son of Dionysus and Aphrodite. Although a member of the VANIR by descent, Freyr moved to ASGARD to live with the AESIR, the younger branch of the gods under the leadership of Odin, along with his father Njord and his

FREYJA (below) flew over the earth, sprinkling morning dew and summer sunlight behind her. She shook spring flowers from her golden hair and wept tears which turned to gold, or to amber at sea. She was so beautiful that she was wooed and pursued by all living creatures. (ILLUSTRATION BY F VON STASSEN, 1914.)

FREYR (right), a gentle god of summer sun and showers, was lord of the fairy realm of Alfheim, home of the Light Elves. Here, he is sailing his ship, Skidbladnir, personifying the clouds. His flashing sword, symbolizing a sunbeam, fought of its own accord. (ILLUSTRATION BY JAMES ALEXANDER, 1995.)

sister Freyja, as a gesture of good-will that had been agreed at the end of the war between the Vanir and the Aesir.

Freyr's myth is about his wooing of Gerda, the daughter of the frost giant Gymir. When Freyr first saw Gerda he immediately fell in love with her, and because he did not know how to gain her affection he became ill. Njord became so worried about him that he asked his faithful servant Skirnir to find out what was amiss. Having learned of this love, Skirnir went to JOTUNHEIM, the land of the giants, taking two of Freyr's greatest treasures, his magic horse and his magic sword. The servant was instructed to bring Gerda back to Asgard, whether her father liked it or not. On reaching Gymir's hall, Skirnir tried to persuade Gerda to

FRIGG (below), a deity of the atmosphere, spun long pearly webs of cloud from her jewelled distaff which shone in the night sky as the constellation of Frigg's Spinning Wheel. Her heron plumes symbolize her discretion, while her keys signify her divine housewifery. (ILLUSTRATION BY NICK BEALE, 1995.)

declare her love for Freyr in return for "eleven of the apples of youth". She refused both this gift and Skirnir's second offer of one of Odin's arm-rings. Gerda's resolve was only strengthened further when Skirnir then threatened to decapitate her with Freyr's sword. Finally, Skirnir said that he would impose on her an unbreakable spell that would make her a permanent outcast and it was this that persuaded Gerda to pledge herself to

the fertility god with an agreement to meet Freyr in a forest in nine days' time. In this way the passion of Freyr was fulfilled, though it cost him his horse and sword which he gave to Skirnir. At RAGNAROK, the doom of the gods, he sorely missed his mighty magic weapon, since it could fight giants on its own. (See also TREASURES AND TALISMANS; TRAGIC LOVERS)

FRICKA see FRIGG

FRIGG, also known as Frigga, Frija and Fricka, in Germanic mythology, was the daughter of Fjorgyn, goddess of the earth and atmosphere, wife of ODIN, the chief of the gods, and mother of BALDER. She has given her name to Friday. Frigg was a fertility goddess who "will tell no fortunes, yet well she knows the fates". When Balder dreamed of impending danger, Frigg extracted a promise from each and every thing, except the mistletoe, that no harm should happen to him. Apparently, the mistletoe appeared such a harmless

plant that she did not bother about it. This proved to be a mistake because the fire god LOKI got the blind god HODR to throw a branch of mistletoe at Balder which killed him. Frigg's subsequent effort to have her son released from the land of the dead also failed, because Loki refused to mourn on behalf of Balder. Thus it would seem that Frigg was a fertility goddess not unlike the Sumerian deity Inanna, though she lacked that goddess's ability to enter the netherworld.

Frigg has much in common with FREYJA. Although her role as consort of Odin shows her to be a devoted wife and mother, she too possesses a falcon skin and has a great passion for gold. It is quite possible that the two goddesses had their origins in a single earth-mother deity.

FRIGGA see FRIGG

FRIJA see FRIGG

FRITHIOF see TRAGIC LOVERS

GEFFINN see GEFION

FRIGG enjoyed the privilege of sitting beside her husband, Odin, on his fabulous throne, Hlidskialf, from where the divine pair could view the nine worlds, witnessing events present and future. A paragon of silence, she never revealed her foreknowledge. (ILLUSTRATION BY H THEAKER, C. 1920.)

GEFION, also known as Gefinn and Gefjon, was a Germanic goddess of fertility akin to *FREYJA*, the sister of the fertility god *FREYR*, and *FRIGG*, the wife of *ODIN*. Appropriately for a goddess of agriculture, Gefion's name is connected with "giving". She was usually imagined as a virgin and as the protector of virgins after their deaths. However, *LOKI* accused Gefion of selling herself, like Freyja, for a necklace.

Her myth concerns ploughing and doubtless recalls the ancient ritual of ploughing a token strip of land each spring. Gefion, disguised as an old beggar, managed to trick King Gylfi of Sweden out of a great tract of land. In return for her hospitality, the king offered Gefion as much of his kingdom as she could plough with four oxen during one day and one night. With the aid of her four giant sons, transformed into oxen, she cut from the mainland the whole island of Zealand, part of present-day Denmark.

GEIRROD was a frost giant, the father of two daughters, *GJALP* and Greip, and was one of *THOR*'s most formidable enemies. It happened that *LOKI*, a constant companion of Thor, had taken the form of a hawk and was captured by Geirrod. The only way Loki could avoid death was to promise to bring Thor to Geirrod's hall without his magic belt and magic hammer which protected the god against frost giants.

Because Thor trusted Loki he went with him to Geirrod's hall. Fortunately, they rested on the way at the home of a friendly giantess named *GRID*, and she warned Thor about the plan while Loki was asleep. She also lent the god her own magic belt of strength, magic iron gloves and magic staff. Thus equipped, Thor arrived at their destination, with Loki hanging as usual on his belt. Geirrod was not at home, but the giant's servants received the visitors. It was not long, though, before Geirrod's two

GEIRROD's (left) immense body, slain by Thor, lay in the City of the Not-Dead, shrouded in cobwebs. Beyond the sleeping giant sparkled the Chamber of Treasures full of jewels and weapons. Here came the Danish hero, Thorkill, years later, on a raid for his king. (ILLUSTRATION BY NICK BEALE, 1995.)

GEFION (above), disguised as a beggar, ploughed a vast field in Sweden with four giant oxen, her supernatural sons. They dragged the tilled field to the coast and floated it across the sea to Denmark, where it formed the island of Zealand. (ILLUSTRATION BY JAMES ALEXANDER, 1995.)

daughters tried to kill the slumbering Thor by lifting up his chair and dashing out his brains on the ceiling. But with the aid of Grid's staff, Thor succeeded in driving the chair downwards and crushed the frost giantesses instead. However, Geirrod himself then appeared in the hall and using a pair of tongs he picked up a red-hot iron ball and threw it at Thor, who caught it in Grid's iron gloves. Angered beyond measure by this extremely discourteous action, Thor threw the still hot and smoking ball back down the hall, straight through an iron pillar and deep into Geirrod's stomach. After this, the thunder god laid about the frost giant's servants with the magic staff.

GERDA, in Germanic mythology, was a beautiful frost giantess and daughter of the giant Gymir, who reluctantly became the wife of *FREYR*, the fertility god. Although initially resistant to the idea, she was persuaded to marry by Freyr's faithful servant *SKIRNIR*, when he threatened to recite a terrible spell. This spell would have made Gerda so ugly than no man would ever come near her again. She would be transformed into "a sight to make the blood run cold". So it was that Gerda met Freyr in a forest after nine nights, representing the nine months of the northern winter. The Aurora Borealis was believed by some to be the radiance of Gerda. (See also *TRAGIC LOVERS*)

GINNUNGAGAP, in Germanic mythology, was a "yawning emptiness" at the time of creation, which lay between the realms of fire and cold. As the warm air from the south met the chill of the north, the ice of Ginnungagap melted and from the drops was formed YMIR, the frost giant, and AUDHUMLA, the primeval cow. By licking the ice, Audhumla uncovered BURI, ancestor of the gods. Buri's three grandsons, ODIN, VILI and VE, killed Ymir and took his body to the centre of Ginnungagap. There they made Midgard, the world of men, from his body. Ymir's flesh became the earth, his bones the mountains, his teeth rocks and stones, his hair the trees and his blood turned into the lakes and seas. The brothers used his skull to form the sky, with four dwarfs named Nordi, Sudri, Austri and Westri holding up the corners.

GJALP ("Howler") was a frost giantess, daughter of GEIRROD, who, along with her sister Greip, tried to kill THOR, the Germanic thunder god. When Thor, accompanied by the fire god LOKI, came to the hall of Geirrod, Gjalp did what she could to harm the visitors. Even before their arrival she added a torrent of her menstrual blood to a river in order to drown Thor and Loki. A well-aimed stone stopped Gjalp and sent her howling home. However, she and Greip then tried to ram the head of sleeping Thor against the rafters by suddenly raising his chair. The thunder god woke just in time to force the chair downwards by using a magic staff. Its massive weight broke the backs of the two giantesses and they died in agony on the floor.

GERDA (above), a frosty beauty, inspired the love of Freyr who sent Skirnir to win her hand. Although he offered her the apples of youth, and revealed his master's glowing portrait reflected in water, she remained unmoved until forced by threat of magic to consent. (ILLUSTRATION BY H THEAKER, C. 1920.)

GJALP (right) stirs up a river into a great flood, engulfing Thor as he wades across. Thor managed to stem the torrent by striking Gjalp with a boulder. He then heaved himself ashore by grasping a mountain ash named "Thor's Salvation". (ILLUSTRATION BY JAMES ALEXANDER, 1995.)

GINNUNGAGAP (right), the primal abyss at the dawn of creation, lay between the icy north and fiery south. Twelve swirling streams gushed into its vacuum and froze into massive ice blocks. In the south, fiery sparks slowly melted the ice, and from the icy droplets slowly emerged a frost giant (ILLUSTRATION BY NICK BEALE, 1995.)

GRENDEL, a man-devouring monster, met his match in the fearless warrior Beowulf, who seized the creature's hairy limb in a vice-like grip and wrenched it from its socket. Howling with pain and rage, Grendel fled back to his watery lair and bled to death. (ILLUSTRATION BY ALAN LEE, 1984.)

GRENDEL was the name of a water monster which was invulnerable to weapons and troubled the kingdom of King Hrothgar of Denmark. One night Grendel, "grim and greedy, brutally cruel", came to the royal hall and ate a sleeping warrior, but a visiting warrior, BEOWULF, held one of the monster's arms in a vice-like grip. In the fierce struggle that ensued, Grendel's arm was torn off and he ran away and bled to death in his watery lair. It was in this lair that, later, Beowulf killed the monster's mother. Grendel's head was so large that when Beowulf brought it back as a trophy to King Hrothgar, he needed the assistance of four men to carry it.

GRID was a kindly frost giantess who helped the Germanic thunder god THOR in his struggle against GEIRROD. Thor had been lured by LOKI, the fire god, into danger without the protection of his magic belt of strength and his magic hammer. Grid loaned Thor her own belt, iron gloves and unbreakable staff to face Geirrod. In some traditions she is said to have borne ODIN a son, the silent god VIDAR, and to have made for him a special shoe which enabled him to stand in the mouth of the wolf FENRIR.

GRIMHILD see *SORCERY AND SPELLS*

GROA, according to Germanic mythology, was a seeress and the wife of Aurvandil, whose frozen toe THOR turned into a star by throwing it up into the sky. Exactly who this Aurvandil, or Aurvandill, was remains uncertain, though it has been suggested that he may have been a fertility god of the wetlands. Groa herself tried by magic to remove whetstone fragments from Thor's head after his fight with the frost giant HRUNGNIR. They had come from Hrungnir's sharp-edged, three-cornered stone when it had collided with Thor's hammer in mid-air. So excited was Groa, however, by Thor's news about the star and the return of her lost husband that she unfortunately failed to finish the spell, and this was why a few fragments of whetstone remained in Thor's head. Some time after her death, Groa was roused from the grave by her son, Svipdrag, who needed her advice on how he could win the love of the beautiful Menglad.

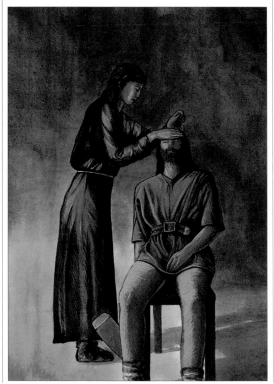

GUNGNIR was the magic spear belonging to ODIN, the leader of the Germanic gods. It was forged by dwarfs, the sons of Ivaldi, at the same time as a wig of spun gold, which the fire god LOKI ordered as a replacement for the golden hair of THOR's wife SIF. Mischievous Loki had cut off her beautiful locks as a joke. Having made the wig, the dwarfs decided to please the gods by using the furnace to make a ship for FREYR and, for Odin, a spear that managed to be both strong and slender, and never missed its mark. It was required in Viking custom that a spear should be thrown over the heads of an enemy before battle commenced, as an entreaty for Odin's aid. When the god hung himself on the cosmic tree YGGDRASIL for nine nights in order to obtain wisdom, he was, just like Christ, stabbed with a spear. (See also *TREASURES AND TALISMANS*)

GUDRUN see *THE VALKYRIES*

GUNNER see *NORSE HEROES*

HARBARD ("grey-beard"), in Germanic mythology, was a surly boatman. Wishing to cross a deep river, the god THOR summoned Harbard to ferry him over, only to be met by insults. Thor could think of no response to Harbard's abuse other than anger, but the boatman remained away from the bank. In his fury, Thor failed to notice that Harbard was his father ODIN. The meeting between the two gods reveals their different characters: Odin, the deceitful troublemaker and braggart; while Thor is hot-tempered but honest.

GROA, a gifted healer, chants charms over Thor in order to loosen the stone splinters lodged in the god's forehead. Feeling relief and gratitude, Thor rashly revealed that her long-lost husband was alive. The happy news so excited Groa that she forgot her spells and so left a splinter in Thor's head. (ILLUSTRATION BY NICK BEALE, 1995.)

HEIMDALL (right), bright guardian of the Bifrost Bridge, was ever alert, sleeping less than a bird. Gifted with special sight and hearing, he could see for 100 miles by night or day, and hear grass growing on the hillside. With his curved herald's horn, he would summon the gods to Ragnarok. (ILLUSTRATION BY NICK BEALE, 1995.)

GUNGNIR'S (below) spear shaft was carved from the sacred wood of Yggdrasil. After gaining wisdom at the World Tree, Odin broke off a bough, and fashioned a perfect staff from its holy wood. Here, the one-eyed, all-seeing god peers through the boughs of the sacred ash. (ILLUSTRATION BY ALAN LEE, 1984.)

GUNGNIR (above) was the name of Odin's spear; both slender and strong, it was unswerving in its flight. The weapon was so sacred that oaths were sworn on its point. Dvalin, the dwarf, forged its head, and Odin made the staff, carving it with magic runes. (ODIN BY R FOGELBERG, MARBLE, C. 1890.)

HEIMDALL, or Heimdalr, was

the son of nine mothers and the watchman for the Germanic gods. Originally, he may have been an omniscient sky god. He could hear the sound of grass and wool growing, and see for over a hundred miles. He stood upon BIFROST, the three-strand bridge that linked ASGARD and Midgard (heaven and earth respectively). There he stood ready to blow his horn Gjall at the onset of RAGNAROK, during which he was to be the last to fall in single combat with LOKI. Heimdall's name may be related to the concept of a "world tree", as he was thought to be the supreme watchman perched at its top, above the highest rainbow. He disguised himself as RIG, the mortal who established the three social groups: the nobles, the peasants, and the enslaved. Disguised as Rig, the god visited in turn three houses in Midgard and fathered handsome children for the nobility, sturdy children for the peasants and ill-favoured children for the slaves.

HEIMDALR see *HEIMDALL*

TREASURES AND TALISMANS

THE MOST CELEBRATED CRAFTSMEN of the Norse world were wise and gifted dwarfs who laboured underground in caverns studded with gems. With superhuman artistry and secret wisdom, they fashioned fabulous treasures and talismans for gods and heroes. Some of their creations were exquisitely beautiful, such as the Brisingamen necklace; others were supernaturally powerful, such as the silken thread which fettered the fierce wolf, Fenrir. Most indispensable were the gods' wondrous weapons – Thor's boomerang hammer, Mjollnir, and Odin's infallible spear, Gungnir. The tireless dwarfs were also innovative engineers who crafted a collapsible, flying ship for Freyr and a sword that fought of its own accord once drawn. Most amazing of all, perhaps, were their living treasures, the gold-bristled boar, Gullinbursti, and Sif's golden hair which grew naturally. Some precious marvels were created by nature, such as the golden apples of youth. Among mortals, only Volund the smith could match the dwarfs in artistry and craft while, among sorcerers, the Finnish Ilmarinen excelled in magical craft and produced a peerless talisman, the Sampo.

IDUN'S (left) golden apples kept the gods eternally young. The fabulous fruit tree was tended and guarded by the three wise Norns who allowed only Idun, the deity of Spring, to pick the magic fruit. Yet such precious gifts were coveted by the giants who sought to strip the gods of their vigour and youth. Here, the giant Thiassi, disguised as a bird, carries Idun and her apples off in an ill-fated attempt to steal the gods' elixir of life. (ILLUSTRATION BY H THEAKER, C. 1920.)

THE BRISINGAMEN (above) necklace was crafted by four dwarfs with such artistry that it glittered like a constellation of stars in the night sky. Around Freyja's lovely neck it became an emblem of the fruits of the heavens and earth. She, in her turn, produced treasures for the earth whenever she cried, and Freyja wept profusely, especially during her search for her husband, Odur. When her tears fell on rock, they turned to gold, but tears shed at sea turned to amber. (FREYJA BY N J O BLOMMER, DETAIL, CANVAS, 1852.)

MJOLLNIR (left), Thor's wondrous hammer, was never far from his grasp, as seen here in this characteristic pose of the god with his hammer clutched close to his heart. The Mjollnir was used as a fiery thunderbolt, launching shafts of lightning, and as a weapon for smashing giants' skulls. It was a talisman of both creativity and destruction, and was used to hallow both birth and death ceremonies. (BRONZE, 10TH CENTURY.)

GUNGNIR (right), Odin's great spear, never missed its mark. The spear shaft was fashioned by Odin from the sacred ash of Yggdrasil and carved with the god's magic runes. Just as valuable was Odin's fabulous ring, Draupnir, which produced eight similar gold rings every nine days, an everlasting source of wealth and power. (ILLUSTRATION BY H HENDRICH, C. 1906.)

THE SAMPO (below) was forged by Ilmarinen, the Eternal Hammerer of Finnish myth, who hammered out the sky at the dawn of time. Over three days, the talisman was fashioned mysteriously from one swift quill, milk of the fertile cow, a grain of barley and the fleece of a summer lamb. So out of the magical flames of the forge the Sampo was created; it consisted of a flour mill, salt mill and money mill, ensuring lasting prosperity and power. Here, the master smith looks intently into the furnace to see what the fire has produced. (THE FORGING OF THE SAMPO BY A GALLEN-KALLELA, CANVAS, C. 1852.)

WONDROUS LONGSHIPS (above) belonged to both Freyr and Thorstein. The god's ship, Skidbladnir, was crafted by the dwarfs. A personification of the clouds, it glided across land, sea and air. Although massive enough to convey all the gods and an entire host, it could be folded up and pocketed like a handkerchief. Thorstein's fabulous dragon boat, Ellida, was a gift from the sea god, Aegir. Shaped by swelling planks which grew together in the form of a winged dragon, Ellida raced with the whistling wind and outstripped the eagle. The floating fortress was famed far and wide. (ILLUSTRATION BY I J BILIBIN, C. 1900.)

HEL was the daughter of trickster LOKI, the fire god, and the frost giantess ANGRBODA. She was ruler of the Germanic netherworld (also called Hel), to which she had been banished by ODIN, the chief god. Once there, however, her powers were stronger than Odin's, for when Odin's son BALDER was killed Hel refused to return him to his parents. Her brothers, FENRIR the wolf and JORMUNGAND the serpent, were as terrifying as she, though it was Hel and her ghastly home which were adopted by the Christians as the name for their realm of eternal damnation.

The unpleasantness of Hel's realm stands in marked contrast to the pleasurable and enviable afterlife that was enjoyed by the heroic dead who dwelt in Odin's wondrous hall VALHALLA. However, Hel's subjects were little more than silent attendants of the semidecomposed queen. She was only partly decomposed because she had the face and body of a living woman, but her thighs and legs were those of a corpse. Hel's throne was known as the Sick Bed and her subjects were "all who died through sickness and old age".

HEL, the grim goddess of the dead, listens unimpressed to Hermod's plea to release the much-loved god Balder from her dismal realm. Behind her, kneeling, there are rows of her sad subjects – souls of the old, sick or criminal who suffered ceaseless cold, pain and hunger in their cheerless, dreary home. (ILLUSTRATION BY JAMES ALEXANDER, 1995.)

HERMOD, in Germanic mythology, was the son of ODIN and FRIGG, and brother of BALDER. Rather like the Greek god Hermes and the Roman Mercury, he acted as a divine messenger. Hermod also shared these gods' interest in the dead, for it was he who was sent to HEL after Balder's death to ask for his brother's release. He rode there on Odin's famous horse, the eight-legged SLEIPNIR. When Hel refused to let Balder go until everything wept for him, Hermod was allowed to take back to ASGARD the armring which Odin had fastened to Balder's body as a memento.

Hermod nearly met his own death on a journey to Midgard, the land of men. He was sent there by Odin to consult a Finn named Rossthiof about his worries concerning the future. He was saved by magic, however, and returned to reassure his father as best he could.

HIMINBRIOTER see HIMINRJOT

HIMINRJOT, or Himinbrioter, ("Sky Bellower") was the head of a gigantic black ox. The ox belonged to HYMIR with whom THOR went fishing for JORMUNGAND, the sea serpent. Thor had no trouble in breaking Himinrjot's neck, despite

HERMOD leaps bravely into misty Hel on his vain mission to seek Balder's release from death. The great noise made by the hero and his eight-hoofed horse Sleipnir when they crossed the crystal Gioll Bridge, provoked the grim guardian, Modgud, to complain irritably that Hermod must be alive. (ILLUSTRATION BY PETER HURD, 1882.)

the animal's vast size, and used its head to bait his hook. Jormungand rose for this delicacy, but the head stuck in his throat. Thor would have landed the prize had not the sight of the serpent rising from the depths of the sea terrified Hymir. In the confusion that ensued Hymir was able to cut the great sea serpent free.

HOD see HODR

HODR, sometimes Hodur or Hod, the son of ODIN and FRIGG, was the blind god of Germanic mythology. In the Icelandic tradition, Hodr unintentionally killed his brother BALDER. When Balder was troubled by dreams of his coming death, his mother Frigg exacted a promise from each and every thing not to do her son any harm. A sole exception was the mistletoe, a plant the goddess considered to be too insignificant. The trickster god LOKI learned about the mistletoe, however, and guided Hodr's hand when he threw it at his brother. The branch of mistletoe went straight through Balder, who fell down dead. Once it became clear that Balder would have to stay in the land of the dead, Hodr was sent to join him as a punishment. In a very different version of the story, Hodr and Balder are rivals for the hand of Nanna, and Balder is portrayed as a hateful figure. Their conflict is finally resolved when Hodr kills Balder with a magic sword. This Danish version shows the brothers in a very different light.

HERMOD (below) spurs his fabulous steed to assail the barred gate of Hel. Within, Balder can be seen waiting stoically beside an alarming creature, who is possibly one of the starved inmates of Hel. Balder, who knew the future well, knew that he was destined to remain in cheerless Hel for ever. (ILLUSTRATION FROM THE PROSE EDDA, 1760.)

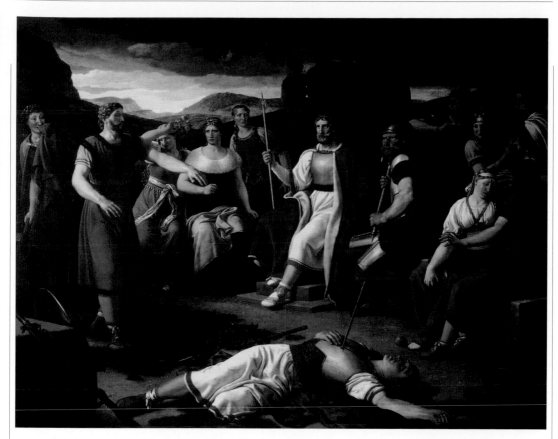

HODR (above), who was blind from birth, unwittingly slew his beloved brother, Balder, prompted by the twisted god, Loki. Here, Loki gleefully guides Hodr's hand to aim a deadly dart of mistletoe at Balder, while the other gods look on in shocked dismay. (THE DEATH OF BALDER BY C ECKERSBERG, CANVAS, C. 1840.)

After *RAGNAROK*, the doom of the gods, "Balder and Hodr return from the world of the dead", reconciled, to a new earth. That these two sons of Odin are mentioned together here shows their importance in Icelandic mythology. First there is Balder, handsome and kind, almost too good for the world. He represents the positive side of his father's nature, as the god of magic and inspiration. The second brother, Hodr, is the opposite of Odin's foresight. Instead, he represents his blind spot, the side of his nature that takes delight in

death. Not for nothing was Balder slain by his blind brother in a game that involved throwing potentially dangerous objects.

HODUR see *HODR*

HOENIR see *HONIR*

HOGNI and his brother, Gunner, befriended the hero *SIGURD*, who owned a famous but ill-fated fortune generated by a magic ring called Andvarinaut. Under the ring's spell, Sigurd had unwittingly betrayed the Valkyrie *BRYNHILD*. She asked the brothers for help, and, bewitched by the curse, they arranged Sigurd's death. However, when Hogni and Gunner inherited Sigurd's fortune, they in turn were doomed and suffered at the hands of the Atli who coveted the gold. (See also *NORSE HEROES*)

HONIR, or Hoenir, according to Germanic mythology, was a member of the *AESIR* group of gods and brother of *ODIN*, the chief god. Apart from a terrible inability to make up his mind, his other prominent characteristic was said to be his long-leggedness. Sent to live among the *VANIR* as a token of goodwill after peace was agreed between the two warring branches of the gods, Honir unfortunately proved to be a grave disappointment to his new companions, who became increasingly angry at the way he appeared always to rely on his fellow Aesir, the wise *MIMIR*, when it came to making decisions of any kind. The Vanir therefore killed Mimir and sent his head back to the Aesir. In some versions of the Germanic creation story, it was believed that Honir was the god who gave humans their senses.

HOGNI (below) listens suspiciously to Brynhild's passionate plea for vengeance on her lover, Sigurd, who had unwittingly betrayed her love. Although refusing to kill Sigurd himself, he persuaded Guttorm to undertake the awful deed. Brynhild was later filled with remorse and killed herself. (ILLUSTRATION BY ARTHUR RACKHAM, C. 1900.)

HREIDMAR, or Reidmar, according to Germanic mythology, was a magician-farmer and the father of *REGIN*, *FAFNIR* and *OTTER*. When Otter, who was a shape-changer, was killed accidentally by *LOKI*, Hreidmar demanded to be compensated and told Loki to obtain enough gold to cover Otter's flayed skin, inside and out. The wily fire god seized the dwarf *ANDVARI*'s treasure, but the dwarf placed a curse upon it. Hreidmar was so pleased with the gold that he did not worry about the curse. But his second son, Fafnir, came to covet the treasure and killed him for it. Fafnir changed into a dragon to guard the gold and Regin asked *SIGURD* to slay him and recover the treasure, but he was killed as well.

HRUNGNIR, in Germanic mythology, was the strongest of the frost giants and owner of a powerful stallion named Gullfaxi, or Golden Mane. He encountered *ODIN* on one of the god's journeys through the nine worlds and challenged him to a horse race. Mounted on eight-legged *SLEIPNIR*, Odin won a narrow victory over Hrungnir on Golden Mane. By this time, the two had ridden to *ASGARD*, the divine stronghold, where Hrungnir was invited to rest before returning to *JOTUNHEIM*, the land of the giants. But Hrungnir drank too much strong ale and became arrogant. He even threatened to carry *VALHALLA*, the hall in which the honoured dead lived with Odin, off to Jotunheim on his back and to kill

HRUNGNIR (left), a mighty frost giant with a stony heart and skull, foolishly balances on his stone shield, believing that his expected foe, Thor, plans to attack him from below. Fully exposed to the impact of Thor's crushing hammer, the giant tries to deflect the hammer with his whetstone. (ILLUSTRATION BY JAMES ALEXANDER, 1995.)

HUGI (above) outstrips his rival Thialfi, an athletic warrior, competing in a contest of skills between gods and giants. Try as he would, Thialfi could not outrun his frosty rival who gathered speed at every step for, unknown to Thialfi, Hugi was an illusion symbolizing Thought, ever faster than action. (ILLUSTRATION BY JAMES ALEXANDER, 1995.)

all the gods, except *FREYJA* and *SIF*. At this point the giant-slayer *THOR* returned and waved his magic hammer at Hrungnir, but the frost giant, understanding that he would be easily killed without his own weapons, challenged Thor to a duel on the border between Asgard and Jotunheim. No one had met the thunder god in single combat before. Thor accepted eagerly, even though Hrungnir's head, heart and shield were made of stone.

When the frost giants heard about the forthcoming duel, they were both proud and anxious: proud that Hrungnir had challenged Thor, but anxious lest the god slay the most powerful of their number. So they made out of clay a man so huge that the thunder god would shake with fright when he first caught sight of him. The heart of a dead mare was used to animate the clay giant, whom they called Mist Calf. Alongside Mist Calf stood Hrungnir, awaiting the arrival of Thor. The frost giant knew that he had to avoid his opponent's hammer, and he held his sharp whetstone in readiness. As soon as Thor was in range, he hurled his magic weapon at Hrungnir, who swiftly launched his own sharp-edged, three-cornered stone in Thor's direction. The weapons met in mid-air. Although the hammer shattered the whetstone and went

on to crush Hrungnir's skull, a number of stone fragments lodged in Thor's head and he was also pinned beneath one of the fallen Hrungnir's legs. After this heroic incident, Thor became known as "Hrungnir's skull splitter".

HUGI ("Thought"), in Germanic mythology, was a young frost giant who outran THOR's human servant THIALFI in a race. The story of Thor's journey to the stronghold of UTGARD in the land of the frost giants is full of magic. The race between Hugi and Thialfi was but one incident in this strange adventure, which shows Thor to be an ineffectual strong man in the face of cunning spells. Throughout the journey the trickster LOKI, the god of fire, had cause to remind Thor of the superiority of brain over brawn. At one point Thor, Loki, Thialfi and his sister ROSKVA inadvertently slept in the thumb of an empty glove belonging to the enormous frost giant SKRYMIR, mistaking it for a vast hall. When he woke, Skrymir warned them that at Utgard there were giants even greater than he. Sure enough, when the travellers reached Utgard, they were unable to see the top of its battlements

without pressing the crowns of their heads on the napes of their necks. Inside the great fortress Thor and his companions failed in a number of tests, the thunder god himself being wrestled down on one knee by an "old, old woman". He also failed to empty a drinking horn, only to learn afterwards how its other end was in the sea. At the end of their adventure, however, the travellers saw that Skrymir and Utgard were no more than magic creations sent out by the frightened frost giants to mystify mighty Thor.

HUGINN ("Thought") and Muninn ("Memory") were the ravens of ODIN, the chief Germanic god. In order to be informed about events in the nine worlds, Odin sent the ravens out every day to see and hear all that happened there. They would then return to rest on Odin's shoulders and tell him what they had observed.

HYMIR ("Dark One") was a frost giant and, according to some traditions, father of the war god TYR. Hymir had an enormous cauldron, so deep that it could brew ale for all the gods. Without this huge vessel, there was no way that the sea god

AEGIR could offer hospitality to ODIN and his companions, so Tyr and THOR were sent to fetch it. When they arrived at Hymir's hall, Tyr's mother advised them to hide until she had explained their presence. Hymir found them and offered them a meal, though he felt uneasy. Thor astonished the assembled company by eating two whole oxen by himself. The next day their host suggested they go fishing if they wanted to eat again. Together they put to sea in Hymir's boat, Thor baiting his colossal hook with the head of HIMINRJOT, the giant's black ox. When the sea monster

JORMUNGAND took this bait and Thor set about its head with his hammer, Hymir shook with terror. In the confusion Jormungand tore itself free of the great hook and sank bleeding beneath the surface of the waves. Two whales had to suffice for food instead.

Back in Hymir's hall, relations between host and guest quickly deteriorated into violence. Goblets were thrown before Thor left with the gigantic cauldron. When Hymir and some frost giants attempted to follow him in order to regain the cauldron, Thor used his hammer to such effect that all were killed.

HUGINN (left), one of Odin's fabulous ravens, whose name means Thought, was an airborne gatherer of news. Along with his brother raven, Muninn, or Memory, he flew through the nine worlds collecting information. They would then fly back to Odin and whisper the latest news into his ear. (ILLUSTRATION FROM THE PROSE EDDA, 1760.)

HYMIR and Thor (below) forage for food on a fated fishing trip. Thor's tantalizing bait attracted the monstrous water serpent, Jormungand, which delighted the god who battled furiously with his giant catch. When the struggle threatened to capsize the boat, however, Hymir, in fear, cut the line. (ILLUSTRATION FROM THE PROSE EDDA, 1760.)

IDUN, Idunnor or Iduna, was, in Germanic mythology, the goddess who guarded the apples of youth. She was the wife of *BRAGI*, the god of poetry. When *LOKI*, the fire god, was captured by the frost giant *THIASSI*, he had to promise to steal the apples from Idun to secure his release. On his return to *ASGARD*, therefore, Loki told Idun that he had discovered apples of much better quality growing nearby, and so the goddess trustingly accompanied him into the forest, where, in the shape of an eagle, Thiassi awaited his prey. He took Idun and her apples in his claws and flew to *JOTUNHEIM*, the land of the frost giants. The loss of the apples at first caused the gods to become weak and old, with bleary eyes and loose

IDUN guarded a fabulous fruit tree, which produced life-giving apples. Here, she hands out her precious gifts to the ever-youthful gods from her inexhaustible casket. The mythic tradition of the golden apple, symbolizing immortality and fertility, can be found in both ancient Greek and Celtic cultures. (ILLUSTRATION BY J PENROSE, C. 1890.)

skin. Then their minds began to weaken, as a general fear of death settled on Asgard. At last *ODIN* gathered his remaining strength and found Loki. By threat of magic he compelled Loki to bring back Idun and her apples.

Loki flew to Jotunheim as a falcon, changed Idun into a nut and carried her home. The frost giant gave chase as an eagle, but he was burned to death by fires placed along the tops of Asgard's mighty walls. Loki then restored Idun to her true shape and she gave magic apples to the ailing gods. (See also *TREASURES AND TALISMANS*)

IDUNA see *IDUN*

JORMUNGAND (left), the serpent son of Loki, was hurled into the icy ocean by Odin. There he grew to such a monstrous size that he encircled Midgard and threatened sailors throughout the oceans. Here, the World Serpent rises to a bait of ox head, dangling from Thor's fishing line. (ILLUSTRATION FROM THE PROSE EDDA, 1760.)

JOTUNHEIM (right), the home of the frost giants, was a snow-covered wasteland on the ocean edge, possibly near the North Pole. It was a realm of mists, blizzards and roaring winds. From here the frost giants directed blasts of wind to nip the buds of spring. (ILLUSTRATION BY NICK BEALE, 1995.)

IDUNNOR see *IDUN*

INGEBORG see *TRAGIC LOVERS*

JEZI BABA see *BABA YAGA*

JORMUNGAND, in Germanic mythology, was the serpent son of *LOKI*, god of fire, and the frost giantess *ANGRBODA*, and brother of *FENRIR* and *HEL*. *ODIN* arranged for these monstrous children to be kidnapped and brought to *ASGARD*. He then threw Jormungand into the ocean, where he grew so long that he encircled the earth, and was known as the Midgard Serpent. At *RAGNAROK* Jormungand was to come on to the earth and be slain by *THOR*. (See also *RAGNAROK*)

JOTUNHEIM was the land given to the frost giants by *ODIN* and his brothers at the Creation. With its stronghold of *UTGARD*, it was one of the nine worlds sheltered by the cosmic tree *YGGDRASIL*. The others were *ASGARD*, the home of the

AESIR, one branch of the gods; Vanaheim, the home of the *VANIR*, the other branch of the divine family; Alfheim, the land of the light elves; Nidavellir, the land of the dwarfs; Midgard, the home of humankind; Svartalfheim, the land of the dark elves; *HEL*, the realm of the unworthy dead; and cold Niflheim beneath Yggdrasil's roots. A mountainous region of freezing cold, Jotunheim was variously described as being inside Midgard, the land of mortals, or over the sea.

JUMALA was the creator god of Finnish mythology and their supreme deity. Very little is known about him, except that the oak tree was sacred to him. He was later replaced by Ukko, also a supreme god, but a deity of the sky and the air, who allowed the rain to fall. Ukko's wife was Akka, which suggests a link with *MADDER-AKKA*, the creator goddess of the Lapps.

KIED KIE JUBMEL was a stone god worshipped by the Lapps, the northernmost people of Europe. Reindeer were sacrificed to Kied Kie Jubmel as late as the seventeenth century to ensure success in the hunt. He seems to have been regarded as "lord of the herds". Among the Swedes he was known as Storjunka, or "Great Lord".

KREIMHILD see *TRAGIC LOVERS*

LEMINKAINEN (above) was slain and dismembered during one of his exploits. But his magician mother gathered him up and restored him to life. Here she calls upon a bee to bring life-giving honey from beyond the highest heaven. (LEMINKAINEN'S MOTHER BY A GALLEN-KALLELA, CANVAS, C.1890.)

KULLERVO see SORCERY AND SPELLS

KVASIR was a wise man in Germanic mythology. His name means "spittle" and recalls his creation when the gods spat into a jar to mark the end of conflict between two branches of the divine family, the *VANIR* and the *AESIR*. The Aesir then took the jar and Kvasir was made from the spittle. Renowned for his great wisdom, he travelled the world and wherever he went people stopped what they were

doing to listen to him. He was killed by two dwarfs, *FJALAR* and Galar, who wanted his wisdom. They mixed his blood with honey in order to make a wonderful mead which gave the gift of poetry to everyone who drank it.

LEIB-OLMAI ("Alder man") was
a Lapp bear god. At bear festivals hunters used to sprinkle their faces with an extract of alder bark. As the protector of bears, Leib-Olmai required certain prayers before he would allow any man to kill a bear.

LEMINKAINEN ("Lover") was
one of the heroes in Finnish epics. As a child, he was bathed by his mother three times in one summer night and nine times in one autumn night to ensure that he would become a wise adult, gifted

KVASIR (right), a character endowed with wondrous wisdom, was created from the spittle of the gods. He travelled the world inspiring gods and mortals with his sense and wisdom. After his death his blood was used to make a mead of inspiration. (ILLUSTRATION FROM THE PROSE EDDA, 1760.)

with a talent for song. A carefree young man, many of his adventures involve the pursuit of women and he accompanied *VAINAMOINEN* on a journey to the land of Pohja in search of wives. His most dangerous exploit was an attempt to kill the swan of *TUONI*, the god of the dead. Failing to protect himself with magic, he was torn apart by Tuoni's son and his remains were scattered in the river. But his magician mother put his body back together again and restored him to life. (See also *NORSE HEROES*)

NORSE HEROES

THE VIKINGS were famed for their fighting spirit, facing death and doom with vigour and courage. Their hardy heroism was doubtless shaped by the crushing Nordic climate, but also by a stoic fatalism. While accepting the inevitability of death on the field and doom at the end of the world, the Norsemen fought with undiminished spirit. For the Vikings, word-fame was everything, redeeming and surviving a hero's death. After death, the bravest heroes went to Valhalla where they awaited the fated and fatal showdown at Ragnarok. No less than the heroes, the Norse gods were heroic, facing doom at Ragnarok with fighting spirit. Finnish heroes were quite as determined and brave in their way, though perhaps less grand and stoic. Armed with magical forces, they battled with incantations rather than force of arms. For the Finns, death was not always final: Leminkainen had more than one life, while aged Vainamoinen could always slip out of a tight corner by shifting shape.

GUNNER AND HOGNI (left), the Nibelung brothers, died gallantly though neither lived a flawless life. Drawn into the web of tragedy woven by a cursed ring, they slew the peerless hero Sigurd, and hoarded his gold. When seized by Atli, who coveted their gold, they refused to surrender under threat of death. Hogni died laughing as his heart was cut out; and Gunner, here, cast into a serpent's pit with bound hands, played his harp with his feet, defying death to the last. (WOOD CARVING, 12TH CENT.)

THOR (right), supernaturally strong and armed with the magical Mjollnir, was a formidable foe. Being neither immortal nor invulnerable, he fought with a fearless spirit, slaying giants with effortless ease and reckless rage. Along with some of the other gods, Thor was destined to die heroically at Ragnarok, after putting up a fierce fight and slaying his arch-foe, the World Serpent. (THOR AND THE GIANTS BY M E WINGE, CANVAS, DETAIL, c. 1890.)

SIGURD (above), the most famous of Iceland's heroes, slew the terrible dragon, Fafnir. Armed with his father's invincible sword, Sigurd hid in a hole in the dragon's slime track and, as Fafnir slithered across on his daily trip to the foul forest pool, thrust his sword into its belly. The bloated creature had grown increasingly monstrous in shape and character; all the better to guard his cursed treasure. Although Sigurd's heroic deed won him fame and fortune, his life from then on was blighted by the curse that came with the ill-fated treasure. (ILLUSTRATION BY ALAN LEE, 1984.)

SIGMUND THE VOLSUNG (right) proved his heroic status by drawing forth a magical sword thrust into the Branstock oak by Odin. With this sword he won fame throughout Scandinavia, but also provoked the envy of his brother-in-law, Siggeir, who resolved to slay all the Volsungs. All ten sons were tied to forest trees, prey to the beasts of the forest. Only Sigmund escaped, by biting off a wolf's tongue, and sought vengeance for his kinsmen. (ILLUSTRATION BY P WILSON, C. 1900.)

LESHY (left), spirit of the forest, though he appeared in the shape of a man, cast no shadow where he walked and could easily camouflage himself among his forest trees, sometimes as small as a leaf, sometimes as tall as the tallest tree. A jealous guardian of his leafy realm, he loved to lead trespassers astray. (ILLUSTRATION BY M VON SCHWIND, C. 1860.)

LIF (right) and her mate, Lifthrasir, took shelter at the end of the world in the sunlit branches of the cosmic ash tree, Yggdrasil. After the earth had been purged by fire and flood, the young couple climbed down and a new age dawned, a fresh green age in which they were destined to repopulate the world and so renew the human race. (ILLUSTRATION BY NICK BEALE, 1995.)

THE LESHY, also known as Lesovik and Lesiye, was the Slavonic spirit of the forest who led travellers and hunters astray in the woods. Although human in form, he had a long green beard and cast no shadow. His chief attribute, however, was his ability to change size: he could become as small as a mouse or as tall as the highest tree. Every October the Leshy went into a kind of hibernation, disappearing from his woodland home until the following spring, when he would return wilder and noisier than ever.

LESIYE see *THE LESHY*

LESOVIK see *THE LESHY*

LIF and Lifthrasir ("Life" and "Eager for Life") were the man and woman who were to hide in the cosmic ash tree *YGGDRASIL* at *RAGNAROK*, the doom of the gods. They were destined to survive this catastrophe and then repopulate a new world, which would rise from the sea like a volcanic island. "The bellowing fire will not scorch them; it will not even touch them, and their food will be the morning dew. Through the branches they will see a new sun burn as the world ends and starts again."

LIFTHRASIR see *LIF*

LODDFAFNIR, in Germanic mythology, was a man who learned the wisdom of the gods. He visited the Well of *URD*, where the gods held their daily assembly, and stayed in *VALHALLA*, *ODIN*'s hall. His myth comprises a retelling of the knowledge he gathered there. It is an interesting mixture of commonsensical advice about good conduct and superstitions concerning the avoidance of witchcraft.

LOKI, sometimes Lopt, was the Germanic fire god and son of the giants *FARBAUTI* and Laufey. He was a mischief-maker, trickster and shape-changer, and grew progressively more evil until eventually the gods bound him in a cave until the coming of *RAGNAROK*, the end of the world. Boredom was a problem for Loki, who "was tired of the string of days that unwound without a knot or a twist in them".

The fact that his parents were giants may help to explain his tendency towards evil deeds. He

LOKI helped to precipitate a cycle of violence by callously slaying Otter for his fur. To appease Otter's father, Loki stole a dwarf's treasure, invoking his bitter curse. Here, Loki helps Odin quieten the raging dwarf, while at the top, Otter's brothers see a weeping Norn, which was an omen of doom. (ILLUSTRATION BY F VON STASSEN, 1914.)

M

simply could not help playing tricks and exposing the gods to danger, although it was often his quick-wittedness that afterwards saved them. Loki, for instance, brought about the loss and return of *IDUN* and her apples of youth. Without these magic fruit, the gods were subject to the ravages of time like everyone else. On occasion Loki was even prepared to risk serious harm to his companion *THOR*, the thunder god. When Loki led Thor unarmed to the hall of the frost giant *GEIRROD*, only the loan of weapons from the kindly frost giantess *GRID* saved the thunder god. Loki tricked his friend because the price of his own release by Geirrod had been delivery of the thunder god into his power.

Yet it was Loki who devised the novel scheme to get back Thor's magic hammer after it was stolen by dwarfs and passed into the hands of the frost giant *THRYM*. The price for the hammer's return, Loki discovered, was the hand of *FREYJA*, the fertility goddess. He therefore persuaded Thor to go to Thrym dressed in Freyja's clothes. When Thrym took out the magic hammer, Thor seized it and laid low all the frost giants present.

Loki was married twice, first to the giant *ANGRBODA* and then to *SIGYN*, with whom he had two sons, *VALI* and Narvi. His monstrous children by Angrboda were *FENRIR*, *JORMUNGAND* and *HEL*, ruler of the underworld: all fearsome representatives of the evil side of his nature. Even after he brought about the death of *ODIN*'s son *BALDER*, the gods continued to tolerate his presence in *ASGARD*. But when he arrived at *AEGIR*'s feast and began to torment everybody present with insults and sneers, their patience came to an end.

To escape their wrath Loki changed himself into a salmon. From his high seat in Asgard, however, Odin located the fish and mounted an expedition to catch it. Loki was then placed in a dark cave. His son Vali was changed into a wolf, who immediately attacked his brother Narvi and killed him. Narvi's intestines were then used to bind Loki beneath the dripping mouth of a venomous snake. In this dreadful prison, the god awaited Ragnarok. Then he was to emerge to lead the army of evil in their final battle with the gods, when Loki would meet his own end at the hands of *HEIMDALL*. (See also *RAGNAROK*)

LOPT see *LOKI*

LUONNOTAR (which probably

means "Daughter of Nature") was the creator goddess of the Finns. At the beginning there was only Luonnotar "all alone in a vast emptiness". Later she floated for centuries on the cosmic ocean, until one day a bird made a nest on her knees and began to hatch some eggs. But the goddess became excited and upset the nest, with the result that from the broken shells of the eggs the heavens and the earth were formed. The yolks became the sun, and the whites the moon. Scattered fragments of these eggs were transformed into the stars. Afterwards Luonnotar fashioned the continents and the seas, and gave birth to *VAINAMOINEN*, the Finnish hero.

MADDER-AKKA and her male

companion Madder-Atcha were, according to the Lapps, the divine couple who created humankind. Madder-Atcha was responsible for the soul and Madder-Akka for the body. The child they made was then placed in the womb of its earthly mother. Their three daughters were involved with procreation as well. Sarakka supported women during childbirth; if a male child was to be born, Juksakka ensured that the baby changed from its originally female gender, while Uksakka, who lived underground, looked after the interests of the new-born child. See also *JUMALA*.

LOKI (above), the trickster god, was at first just a playful prankster, but became so dark and twisted that the gods realized he was evil and resolved to imprison him. Loki was eventually bound to a rock, with his face exposed to the fiery drops of a snake's venom. (ILLUSTRATION BY D PENROSE, C. 1870.)

LUONNOTAR (below), a primal goddess, grew restless in the heavens and slipped into the cosmic sea, where she drifted until an eagle built a nest on her knee. When she accidentally upset the nest, its eggs broke and formed the earth and sky, sun, moon and stars. (ILLUSTRATION BY NICK BEALE, 1995.)

MAGNI ("Mighty") was the son of *THOR*, the Germanic thunder god, and the giantess Jarnsaxa, and brother of Modi. After his duel with *HRUNGNIR*, the strongest of the frost giants, Thor fell wounded to the ground, as fragments of whetstone had lodged in his head. He was also unable to move because one of Hrungnir's lifeless legs pinned him to the ground. Even worse, Thor wetted himself when he noticed the clay giant Mist Calf. Insult was nearly added to injury when, at the age of three years, Magni proved strong enough to free his father Thor, even though none of the gods had been able to shift Hrungnir's leg. "It's a pity I didn't come sooner," Magni commented. "If I had met this giant first, he would be fallen to my bare fists." Although *ODIN* was rather put out by young Magni's intervention, Thor showed his gratitude by giving the young frost giant Hrungnir's magnificent horse, Golden Mane. After *RAGNAROK*, the doom of the gods, Magni and Modi together would inherit Thor's magic hammer, *MJOLLNIR*.

MATI SYRA ZEMLYA ("Moist Earth Mother") was the Slavonic earth goddess. Archaeological evidence suggests that her worship may have originated in the basin of the River Don as much as 30,000 years ago. Believed to possess the ability to predict the future and to settle disputes wisely, she was an object of veneration up to the early years of the twentieth century, when Russian peasant women were still performing elaborate rites in order to summon her presence to protect them from disease.

MENU, or Menulis, was the Baltic moon god. The sun was imagined as the goddess *SAULE*, the patroness of green snakes. The Letts believed that the stars were the children of Menu and Saule. The Morning Star, however, was said to have been the child of a love affair between Saule and *PERKUNO*, the thunder god. For this reason the moon god, in shame and anger, avoided his spouse, and appeared only by night, while the sun goddess was happy to be seen all through the day.

MAGNI and his brother, Modi, stride across the sunlit Plain of Ida at the dawn of a fresh green age, after the world destruction of Ragnarok. Magni ("Mighty") swings Thor's sacred hammer, while Modi ("Courage") follows behind. (ILLUSTRATION BY JAMES ALEXANDER, 1995.)

MATI SYRA ZEMLYA was invoked by Slavic farmers at harvest time. They entered their fields at dawn and blessed the earth with libations of hemp oil. Bowing to the east, west, north and south, they invoked the primal deity, each time soaking the earth with oil. (ILLUSTRATION BY NICK BEALE, 1995.)

MENULIS see *MENU*

MIMIR, in Germanic mythology, was a wise god sent by the *AESIR* to the *VANIR* in order to seal the peace after these two branches of the divine family tired of war. Because the Vanir felt that they had been cheated, they cut off Mimir's head and sent it back to the Aesir. *ODIN*, however, smeared the severed head with herbs so that it would never rot. He then recited a charm over it to restore its power of speech. Later, Mimir's head was placed by Odin to guard a magic well under the root of the cosmic tree *YGGDRASIL*. To gain Mimir's wisdom, which comprised "many truths unknown to any other person", Odin gave one of his eyes for permission to drink at the well.

MJOLLNIR was the magic hammer of the Germanic thunder god *THOR*. Made by the dwarfs Brokk and Eitri, it was an instrument of destruction, fertility and resurrection. In Thor's hands Mjollnir was the gods' certain protection against their enemies, the frost giants. That is why the gods were so worried when the frost giant *THRYM* stole it. The price for its return was the hand of *FREYJA*, the fertility goddess. Dressed in Freyja's clothes and accompanied by the trickster god *LOKI*, Thor went to Thrym's hall. Since it was customary to ask a blessing on any marriage by placing the hammer on the knees of the bride, Thrym ordered it to be brought out. But no sooner had Thor got hold of Mjollnir than he jumped up and crushed the frost giant's skull with a mighty blow.

Mjollnir's powers as a restorer of life were revealed on a journey made by Thor to the frost giants' stronghold of *UTGARD*, when he used it to reconstitute from skin and bones two goats which had been eaten the night before. The magic hammer was also used at funerals. When the fire was lit round the pyre of *BALDER* and

*MIMIR serves Odin a draught from his
wondrous Fountain of Wisdom. The price
demanded for this privilege was one eye,
symbolizing the sacrifice of one view for
another, greater vision. Odin's eye floated
in the fountain, a symbol of the full moon,
beside the crescent moon of Heimdall's
horn. (ILLUSTRATION BY NICK BEALE, 1995.)*

Nanna, Thor raised his hammer
and chanted certain magic words
to consecrate the ceremony.

After *RAGNAROK*, the day of
doom and the end of the world,
ownership of Mjollnir passed to
Thor's sons *MAGNI* and Modi. (See
also *TREASURES AND TALISMANS*)

MOKKURALFI, or Mist Calf,
was a gigantic clay giant. He was
made from the clay bed of a river by
frost giants in order to terrify *THOR*,
the thunder god. This occurred just
before Thor met *HRUNGNIR*, the
strongest of the frost giants, in
single combat. Mist Calf was animated by the heart of a mare, but it
proved inadequate for the task.
Though the creature towered into
the clouds, it was very slow-moving

and its legs were vulnerable to
attack. On the day of the duel,
Thor killed Hrungnir but wet himself at the sight of Mist Calf. His
human servant *THIALFI* was less
impressed, however, and swung
his axe at the clay giant's legs.
When Mist Calf toppled backwards, his fall shook *JOTUNHEIM*,
the land of the frost giants.

MUNDILFARI was a man who
offended *ODIN*. When Odin, along
with his brothers *VILI* and *VE*,
carved the world out of the carcass
of *YMIR*, the original frost giant,
they solved the problem of its illu-
mination by using sparks and glowing embers from the sun, moon
and stars. Mundilfari, who lived in
Midgard, had a son and a daughter
so handsome and beautiful that he
called one Moon and the other
Sun. The gods were angered by this
comparison. Odin snatched the
brother and sister from Midgard
and turned them into constellations to guide the real heavenly
bodies on their daily and nightly
journeys across the sky.

*MJOLLNIR (left), symbolizing Thor's
thunderbolt, glowed red-hot at the mallet
end, and could only be held by an iron
gauntlet. It was not just destructive, but
also creative and hallowed weddings and
births. The exquisite, whirling patterns of
Viking art beautifully depict the blazing
eyes of the god. (SILVER PENDANT, 10TH CENTURY.)*

*MUNDILFARI (below) named his lovely
children after the sun and moon, angering
the gods with his arrogance. The children
were made to drive the heavenly chariots
across the sky. At left, the moon is drawn by
All-Swift, while two eager steeds, Early
Waker and Rapid Goer, pull the larger sun
chariot. (ILLUSTRATION BY GLENN STEWARD, 1995.)*

N

MYESYATS was the moon deity of Slavonic myth. Some traditions represent him as the cold, bald-headed uncle of the sun god *DAZHBOG*. In others, Myesyats is a beautiful woman, the consort of Dazhbog and mother by him of the stars. Every spring the divine pair are remarried, but in the autumn Dazhbog leaves his bride and only returns to her after the cold winter months have passed.

NERTHUS was a Germanic goddess, whose cult was described by the Roman writer Tacitus in the first century AD. According to him, she was an important mother goddess who had a sacred grove on a Frisian island. At regular intervals Nerthus travelled inland along a recognized route, her image placed in an ox cart and attended by a priest. During these sacred journeys peace was expected to prevail because "all iron was put away". At a certain lake the goddess bathed,

NERTHUS rides in a triumphal procession, during her biannual fertility festival. Bedecked with flowers, her chariot was drawn by two heifers, which symbolized primal motherhood and abundance. The people honoured her by laying aside all iron tools and weapons and donning festive dress. (ILLUSTRATION BY JAMES ALEXANDER, 1995.)

and afterwards slaves who had helped in this ritual were drowned in Nerthus' honour. Sacrifice by drowning was a practice also favoured by the ancient Slavs in eastern Europe. The name of the goddess may have meant "power-ful one" because it refers to strength. Quite possibly Tacitus was describing a local cult of *FREYJA*. Some versions of the myths of *ASGARD*, home of the gods, sug-gest that Nerthus was sister and wife to *NJORD*, the sea god, and mother of Freyja and *FREYR*.

NIDHOGG, in Germanic myth-ology, was the dragon living at one of the three roots of the cosmic tree *YGGDRASIL*. The freezing mist and darkness of Niflheim, which was the lowest of the nine worlds, was

NIDHOGG (left), a gruesome dragon, dwelt in icy Niflheim and, when not devouring corpses, it habitually nibbled the root of Yggdrasil, the cosmic tree. Here, a stag browsing on the leaves of Yggdrasil is in its turn nipped by Nidhogg, reflecting the life and death struggle at the root of the universe. (WOOD CARVING, 8TH CENTURY.)

where the dragon lived, ripping corpses apart and eating them. Between mouthfuls he would send the squirrel Ratatosk up the cosmic tree on an errand of insult, for the agile animal periodically disturbed two birds, an eagle and a hawk, who were perched at the very top. When momentarily tired of the taste of dead flesh, Nidhogg would gnaw at the root of Yggdrasil itself, presumably hoping to inflict dam-age on the cosmos in some way. Both Yggdrasil and Nidhogg were destined to survive the final cata-strophe of *RAGNAROK*, the doom of the gods and the end of the world. Neither fire nor flood could deter the dragon from its ceaseless feast-ing on the vast and inexhaustible supply of dead.

NJORD was the Germanic sea god, a member of the divine race of *VANIR* and father of the fertility gods *FREYR* and *FREYJA*. When peace was agreed between the *AESIR* and the Vanir, the two branches of the divine family, Njord, Freyr and Freyja came to live with the Aesir as a sign of goodwill. According to some versions of the myth, the mother of Freyr and Freyja was Njord's own sister *NERTHUS*, but

NJORD (below) lines up with the gods to have his feet inspected by Skadi, who was obliged to choose a husband from the shape of his feet. When Skadi picked Njord, she found that she had won a sweet, old sea god with passions quite opposite to her own, and so she soon took to her chilly hills alone. (ILLUSTRATION BY J HUARD, 1930.)

NJORD *calmed the storms raised by the tempestuous god, Aegir. A gentle soul, Njord loved his sunlit coves and creeks, home of his sacred seagulls and swans. Popular with sailors and fishermen, he aided ships in distress, blew favourable winds and caused summer showers.*

(ILLUSTRATION BY JAMES ALEXANDER, 1995.)

since the Aesir disapproved of marriage between brother and sister, Nerthus did not accompany her husband and children to Asgard.

Njord's second marriage was to the frost giantess SKADI, who chose him on the basis of his beautiful feet. However, the couple could not agree about where they should live. Njord found Skadi's home in JOTUNHEIM, the land of the frost giants, too cold and barren, while Skadi disliked the noise and bustle of shipbuilding around Njord's hall of Noatun in Asgard. After nine

nights in each place they decided to live apart. Skadi went back to her favourite pastime of hunting on skis and the weather-beaten Njord returned to a life at sea. The apparently unbridgeable gap between them probably reflects more than personal taste. Njord was certainly seen as a god of fertility, since he provided to those who worshipped him not only safe voyages at sea, but also wealth and good fortune in the form of land and sons. Skadi's associations were quite different, however. She came from a range of frozen mountains, where heavy clouds masked the sun and harsh rocks made the ground as barren as death. In her wild and unforgiving land, where nothing was able to grow or prosper at all, there was hardly any scope for humankind.

NORNIR see THE NORNS

THE NORNS, *also known as the Nordic Fates, decided the destinies of both gods and mortals as they wove the Web of Fate. Here, at left, wise old Urd reads from the scroll of the past, while young Verdandi symbolizes the present, and veiled Skuld clasps her closed scroll of the future.*

(ILLUSTRATION BY JAMES ALEXANDER, 1995.)

THE NORNS,

or Nornir, were the Germanic fates, the goddesses of destiny. The original Norn was undoubtedly URD ("Fate"). The Well of Urd, which was situated under one of the roots of the great cosmic tree YGGDRASIL, was the site where the gods held their daily assembly. The two other Norns known by name are Verdandi ("Present") and Skuld ("Future"). It was believed that the Norns decided the destinies of gods, giants and dwarfs, as well as of humankind. The Anglo-Saxons

called Urd by the name of Wyrd, and in England there was maintained a belief in the tremendous powers of the three sisters long after the arrival of Christianity. For instance, in Shakespeare's tragic play *Macbeth*, the Three Sisters on "the blasted heath" obviously owed something to the Norns.

A clear parallel of the Norns are the Moerae, or "Fates", encountered in Greek mythology. As in the Germanic mythic tradition, they were seen as three sister goddesses: Klotho ("The Spinner"), Lachesis ("The Decider") and Atropos ("The Inevitable"). It would seem more than possible that the Norns were also originally thought of as spinners. However, in Germanic mythology the Greek and Roman concept of the Fates spinning an individual length of yarn for each mortal life does not appear.

213

THE VALKYRIES

VALKYRIES WERE ORIGINALLY SINISTER SPIRITS of slaughter, dark angels of death who soared over the battlefields like birds of prey, meting out fate in the name of Odin. Chosen heroes were gathered up and borne away to Valhalla, the heavenly abode of Odin's ghostly army. In later Norse myth, the Valkyries were romanticized as Odin's shield-maidens, virgins with golden hair and snowy arms who served the chosen heroes everlasting mead and meat in the great hall of Valhalla. On the battlefield, they soared over the host as lovely swan-maidens or splendid mounted Amazons. This far more appealing portrayal was further developed in the Volsung Saga and *Niebelungenlied*, where the heroine, Brynhild or Brunhild, was a beautiful, fallen Valkyrie. Idealized Valkyries were infinitely more vulnerable than their fierce predecessors, and often fell in love with mortal heroes. Swan-maidens, especially, were at risk as they might easily be trapped on earth if caught without their plumage.

MOUNTED VALKYRIES (left) soared over the battlefield through storm clouds on flying steeds. Their pearly mounts personified the rain clouds, spraying dew and hoar frost over a thirsty earth. The flying Amazon, here, expresses the swift, irrevocable force of fate and the finality of death. (THE VALKYRIE BY STEPHEN SINDRING, MARBLE, C. 1900.)

VALKYRIES (left) were originally demons of death who ravaged the battlefields or stormy seas, weaving the web of war, like the bloodthirsty Morrigu of Celtic myth. Behind the grisly image lay the ghastly necessity of death and revenge. The Valkyries' grim mission was reflected in their menacing names, such as Shrieking, Screaming or Raging. This striking modern portrayal captures the ancient vision of the Valkyries as wild and gleeful spirits of disorder and destruction, astride bat-like dragons. (THE RIDE OF THE VALKYRIES BY KARL ENGEL, CANVAS, C. 1860.)

ODIN (above) commanded the Valkyries, who dispatched his will on the battlefield without question. In a unique case of rebellion, the heroic Valkyrie, Brynhild, defied Odin by helping her half-brother, Siegmund, against his will. In penance, Brynhild was condemned to lie defenceless on a hilltop until claimed by a mortal. Later the god relented and softened his punishment by putting Brynhild to sleep in a ring of fire, protected against all but the bravest hero. (ODIN AND BRUNHILD BY F LEEKE, CANVAS, C. 1890.)

GUDRUN (above) fell in love with a mortal hero, Helgi. When Helgi died, Gudrun wept so much that he called from his grave, imploring her to stop crying, for each tear she shed so his wounds flowed. Soon after, Helgi's spirit rose to Valhalla where the lovers dwelt. Here, Gudrun gathers up the slain to swell the ghostly army which Helgi led at Ragnarok. (ILLUSTRATION BY K DIELITZ, C. 1890.)

A SERVING VALKYRIE (above) holds out a horn of plenty to welcome the chosen heroes to Valhalla. By the sixth century, the Valkyries were already being portrayed in a softer light as helpful handmaidens of Odin, gathering up the slain and serving the heroes in Valhalla. Clad in flowing robes and with long golden hair caught up in a bun, this gracious maiden helpfully offers a brimming horn of mead – a welcome sight for the weary warrior. (SILVER GILT, PENDANT, 6TH CENTURY.)

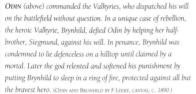

VALHALLA, (left), the glittering and magnificent Hall of the Slain in Asgard, the home of the gods, was built to house Odin's huge army of heroes who were gathered to fight at Ragnarok, the preordained doom of the gods. A Viking's paradise in every way, the splendid hall gleamed with walls of polished spears and vaults of shining shields. At the long benches, decorated with glowing chain mail, warriors wined and dined everyday on ever-flowing mead and everlasting meat, served by the lovely Valkyries. The heroic host, which was amassed over the centuries, must have been massive; to feed such an army the cook, Andhrimnir, stirred a mighty cauldron, called Eldhrimnir, in which he prepared an inexhaustible boar stew. (VALHALLA BY MAX BRUCKNER, CANVAS, 1896.)

ODIN, also known as Woden or Wotan, was the chief god of Germanic mythology, the son of *BOR* and grandson of *BURI*. He was particularly favoured by the Vikings and rose to prominence in the eighth and ninth centuries. These seafarers and raiders were attracted by Odin's love of battle as the "father of the slain", for in *VALHALLA*, an immense hall in the divine fortress of *ASGARD*, the one-eyed god was said to preside over the *EINHERJAR* ("glorious dead"). At this period it seems that Odin displaced *TYR*, whom the Romans had identified as the sky god of the north European peoples. Tyr retained his interest in war, but

Odin was looked upon as the inspiration for hard-bitten warriors. He alone had the power to inspire men in battle to a state of berserk rage in which they feared nothing and felt no pain. The terrible berserkers would rush naked into the fray, biting the edges of their shields in a maddened frenzy. Odin's name means something akin to "fury" or

ODIN (left), the highest of gods, sits on his exalted throne, Hlidskialf, which was a mighty watch-tower overlooking the nine worlds. Hovering nearby are his tireless ravens, the airborne news reporters, Huginn and Muninn, while at his feet crouch his pet wolves, Geri and Freki, omens of good luck. (ODIN BY E BURNE-JONES, C. 1870.)

"madness". It indicates possession, as in the battle-frenzy exhibited by the Irish hero Cuchulainn.

That Odin became the foremost god shows how important warfare always was in Germanic tradition. It should be noted, however, that he did not embody martial ecstasy himself; rather he inspired it in a devious manner. Odin was ever

ODIN (below), as the Wild Huntsman, leads the heroic host on a ghostly hunt through the stormy midnight sky. In the roar and rumble of the storm clouds, Norsemen fancied they heard Odin's phantom riders sweep across the sky, dark omens of doom. (THE WILD HUNT OF ODIN, BY P N ARBO, CANVAS, 1872.)

ready to stir up strife, and on one occasion commanded the fertility goddess FREYJA to "find two kings and set them at each other's throats" so that their vassals would wade through torrents of blood on the battlefield. The Danish King Harald was supposed to have been instructed in tactics by the god and granted many victories. In his final battle, though, Odin took the place of the king's charioteer and drove Harald to his death. When asked about such withdrawals of luck, Odin used to reply that "the grey wolf watches the halls of the gods". Gathering to Valhalla heroic warriors slain in battle was the only policy he could adopt under the constant threat of RAGNAROK, the doom of the gods. These Einherjar were desperately needed for the final battle on the VIGRID Plain, where nearly all would fall in a struggle between the gods and the frost giants. Odin himself was to be killed by the wolf FENRIR, the monstrous offspring of the fire god LOKI and the frost giantess ANGRBODA.

Besides his authority over the battlefield and the glorious dead, Odin was a god of magic and wisdom. As the oldest of the gods, the first-born son of Bor, he was treated by the other gods as their father. Shifty-eyed and flaming-eyed he might be, but Odin also had a strongly positive side to his character as the most learned god. His conflicting negative and positive aspects are indeed very similar to those of the Hindu god Shiva, the great destroyer-saviour of Indian mythology. For Odin's love of wisdom was so profound that he was prepared to sacrifice himself to plumb its depths. Odin was often portrayed as a grey-bearded old man with one eye, his face hidden by a hood or a broad-brimmed hat, because he had cast an eye into MIMIR's well in return for a drink of its "immense wisdom". He gained insight in another way by hanging himself for nine days from YGGDRASIL, the cosmic tree. This

voluntary death, and his subsequent resurrection by means of magic, gave Odin greater wisdom than anyone else.

It is possible that the obvious parallel between this myth and the Crucifixion gave Christianity a head-start in northern Europe. Odin's own worship appears to have gone into decline in the early eleventh century, at the close of the Viking age. Violent times were passing as Viking colonists settled down as peaceful farmers and traders. But during the Vikings'

ODIN (above), a god of vision, sacrificed one eye for a draught of Mimir's Fountain of Wisdom. His single eye symbolized the radiant all-seeing sun, while his lost eye, floating in Mimir's well, signified the full moon. Odin hung himself from Yggdrasil, the cosmic tree for nine days, to learn the secrets of the dead. (BRONZE RELIEF, c. 1950.)

heyday, hanging formed an important part of Odin worship, even being regarded as a shortcut to Valhalla. The great Viking raid of 842 on Nantes in north-western France can thus be seen as the outcome of a barbarous pledge to the god. Most of the city's inhabitants were slain and hanged naked or clothed from trees. It was "an axe-age, sword-age", a violent interlude prior to the end of the world that would come at Ragnarok.

In addition to FRIGG, his wife in Asgard, Odin had many other wives, and he fathered a number of children. Among those said to be his sons were THOR, BALDER, HODR, and VALI.

Odin kept himself informed about the affairs of the nine worlds with two faithful ravens. As Vikings at sea sent out ravens in search of land, Odin's own ravens HUGINN and Muninn flew about and then "whispered into his ears every scrap of news which they saw or heard tell of". The birds' names mean "thought" and "memory" respectively. Because of his wisdom and his knowledge of events, Odin was oppressed by the approach of Ragnarok. Just as the cycle of Germanic mythology started with a cosmos awash with the blood of the original frost giant YMIR, when Odin and his brothers VILI and VE carved the world of men out of his dead body, so the final scene was to be a battlefield, where the gods were predestined to gush out their own blood. Ragnarok, the doom of the gods, began with the death of Odin's son Balder and the realization by the gods that in Loki, the god of fire, they had tolerated the growth of evil. There was nothing that Odin could do to prevent the catastrophe. His only consolation was the foreknowledge that his resurrected son Balder would be worshipped in his stead in a new age and a new land which would rise from the sea. (See also THE VALKYRIES; SORCERY AND SPELLS; RINGS OF POWER; RAGNAROK)

ODIN (below), in a timeless battle scene, clasps his wife longingly, before diving into the fray. Armed for battle in eagle helmet and blue tunic, symbolizing the sky, he is armed with his infallible spear, Gungnir, and his wondrous ring Draupnir, which was the symbol of his power and wealth. (ODIN'S LEAVE-TAKING BY F LEEKE, CANVAS, C. 1875.)

P

OTTAR was disguised as a boar by his divine lover, Freyja. Here, Freyja rides him to the seer Hyrdla, seeking proof of Ottar's kingship. The seer imparted to Ottar his family tree with some Memory Beer to help him recite it correctly in a contest for the throne. (ILLUSTRATION BY JAMES ALEXANDER, 1995.)

OTTAR was the human lover of *FREYJA*, the Germanic fertility goddess, and was said to be a distant descendant of the hero *SIGURD*. The warrior caught the goddess's attention through grand sacrifices. He built a stone altar and turned it into glass by the constant heat of the fire he used in preparing his bloody offering. Freyja transformed him into a boar so that she could keep him with her in *ASGARD*, the home of the gods. She even used the disguised Ottar as a mount. Ottar may have been a leader of a warrior band, a lover pleasing to Freyja who shared those fallen in battle with Odin. In the myth it is suggested that he is related to the berserkers, warriors who, "howling and foaming in frenzy, left a trail of terror and leaped like wildfire over land and sea".

OTTER, in Germanic mythology, was the son of the magician-farmer *HREIDMAR*. When the fire god *LOKI* killed him by mistake, for he had taken the shape of an otter, Hreidmar demanded compensation. The otter's flayed skin was to be covered inside and out with gold. Loki succeeded in taking as much gold as he needed from the dwarf *ANDVARI*, and insisted that he also be given a ring which

Andvari tried to conceal. Andvari cursed both the ring and the gold, saying that whoever owned them would be destroyed by them. Loki put the ring on his own finger and returned to Hreidmar with the gold. There was enough to cover the whole skin, except for one whisker; so Loki was compelled to hand over the ring as well, and the curse passed to Hreidmar.

PATOLLO was the Baltic war god, the equivalent of Germanic *ODIN*, the one-eyed god of battle, magic, inspiration and the dead. He was depicted as an old man with a long green beard and death-like pallor, wearing a turban. His sacred objects were the skulls of a man, a horse and a cow.

Patollo was the chief god of the Baltic region. He bestowed good fortune and, like Odin, he took it away whenever he had a desire to taste human blood. At some point before the advent of Christianity Patollo seems to have taken on a more pronounced role in respect of the dead. This would explain why Christian missionaries immediately identified him with the Devil.

PERKONIS see *PERKUNO*

PERKONS see *PERKUNO*

PERKUNAS see *PERKUNO*

PERKUNO (which probably meant "striker"), known as Perkunas in Lithunia, Perkons or Perkonis in Latvia, was the Baltic thunder god. He was obviously connected with the Slavic god *PERUNU*, although Perkuno was the standard European god of the storm. He was depicted as an angry-looking middle-aged man with a fiery face and a curly black beard. An order of priests is known to have maintained a perpetual fire as part of Perkuno's worship.

Baltic mythology appears to have possessed three main gods, not unlike the Germanic trio

OTTER was turned into an otter by his father to catch fish for dinner. Here, he nibbles a salmon with his eyes closed to avoid seeing his dinner diminish with each mouthful. Blind to the world, he was easy prey for Loki who coveted the otter's fine fur. (ILLUSTRATION BY NICK BEALE, 1995.)

worshipped at Uppsala in Sweden. There the war god *ODIN*, the thunder god *THOR* and the fertility god *FREYR* were revered, whereas at Romowe in Prussia, Baltic peoples gave worship to *PATOLLO*, Perkuno and *POTRIMPO*. The young, beardless god Potrimpo was the Baltic Freyr; grim Patollo was the Baltic Odin; and the Baltic Thor was Perkuno, as quick to anger as the giant-killing Germanic thunder god. A late account of the Balts even supposes a migration from Sweden in the sixth century.

Unfortunately, next to nothing of Baltic mythology has survived, apart from the names of gods and goddesses. It is of considerable interest, therefore, that Perkuno

appears in a surviving myth about *SAULE*, the sun goddess, and the moon god *MENU*. According to this tale, the moon chose not to appear in the sky with the sun because of Perkuno, who had an affair with Saule. Their love-child was the Morning Star. Whereas the sun goddess carried on as if nothing had happened and continued to show herself to all humankind during the day, Menu made himself visible only by night.

PERUN see *PERUNU*

PERUNU, known as Pyerun in Russia, Piorun in Poland and sometimes Perun, was the Slavic thunder god. He was the chief god and a creator god. At Kiev in Russia he had an important temple until the tenth century. Perunu's supremacy was ended by Vladimir, the ruler of Kiev who was later raised to the sainthood. After living the typical life of a Slavic prince, with numerous wives and mistresses, Vladimir

"tired of the desire for women" and sought a new way of living. He sent out ambassadors to witness the religious ceremonies of both the Catholic and Orthodox churches, as well as those of the Jews and

PERUNU roamed the thundery sky on his millstone, flashing shafts of lightning from his thunderbolt. In his effigy at Kiev, he appeared with a silver head and golden moustache. He was transformed into St Elijah with the arrival of Christianity,
(ILLUSTRATION BY NICK BEALE, 1995.)

Moslems. His choice fell on the Byzantine form of Christianity and thereafter the Russians and the Greeks shared the same form of Christian worship.

Prior to this conversion in 988 though, the "Rus" owed more to north-western Europe, for the establishment of the Russian state resulted from Viking trade and settlement on its great rivers. The Viking leader Oleg had captured Kiev in 882 and raised its status to "mother of Russian cities". With this Germanic influx, it is hardly surprising that there are obvious parallels between Perunu and THOR. Oleg was referred to as a "wizard". It seems quite likely that Thor provided the native Slavic thunder god with a developed mythology, since surviving details of Perunu's worship suggest that he was originally believed to be an aid to agriculture. Indeed, rain-making ceremonies are known to have involved a chaste girl, naked and decked with flowers, dancing in a magic circle. Whirling and drinking seem to have been impor-tant in his Russian worship.

PERKUNO can be seen here riding with his divine companions: on the left, young Potrimpo, crowned with fruitful wheat; next, veteran Patollo bears a skull symbolizing his affinity with war and death, while his horned turban recalls his sacred cow. Perkuno, at right, flashes his lightning.
(ILLUSTRATION BY JAMES ALEXANDER, 1995.)

PERUNU, as a fertility god, wandered over the earth, spreading summer sun, chasing away clouds and melting the snow. A god with a social sense, he bombarded the lands of the wicked with hailstorms. The oak, his sacred tree, was burned in his honour.
(ILLUSTRATION BY NICK BEALE, 1995.)

Elsewhere in Europe the Slavic peoples also revered Perunu, as place names still indicate. In Slovenia there is Perunji Ort, in Croatia Peruna Dubrava, in Bulgaria Perin Planina, and in Poland Peruny as well as Piorunow. According to Procopius, secretary to the Greek general Belisarius in the sixth century, the Slavs wor-shipped above all the god of light-ning, and sacrificed cattle and other animals to him. In Russian folklore the memories of Perunu's great skill with the thunderbolt can doubtless be found in stories that tell of dragon-slaying and other supernatural deeds that required enormous strength.

PIORUN see *PERUNU*

POTRIMPO was the Baltic god of fertility and the equivalent of the Germanic fertility god *FREYR*, though he was also associated with rivers. He was depicted as a happy young man without a beard and crowned with ears of grain.

PYERUN see *PERUNU*

219

R

RAGNAROK was the doom of the Germanic gods. After a terrible winter lasting three years, a final battle would be fought between the gods and the frost giants on the *VIGRID* Plain. On the side of *ODIN* and the gods were ranged the "glorious dead" who had fallen in battle and were taken to live in *VALHALLA*; while with the fire god *LOKI* and the frost giants fought the "unworthy dead" from *HEL* (the Germanic netherworld), plus the fearsome wolf *FENRIR* and the sea monster *JORMUNGAND*. There was nothing that the chief god Odin could do to prevent this catastrophe. His only consolation was the foreknowledge that Ragnarok was not the end of the cosmos. After he had been killed by Fenrir, *THOR* had been overcome by Jormungand, and most of the other gods had died in the mutually destructive encounter with the frost giants, a new world was destined to "rise again out of the water, fair and green".

Before the battle two humans, *LIF* and Lifthrasir, had taken shelter in the sacred tree *YGGDRASIL* and they emerged after the carnage was over to repopulate the earth. Several of the gods also survived, among them Odin's sons *VIDAR* and *VALI*, and his brother *HONIR*, Thor's sons Modi and *MAGNI*, who inherited their father's hammer, and *BALDER* who came back from the dead.

Ragnarok held a great appeal for the Vikings, whose onslaught on western Europe is still the stuff of legend. Once they understood the effectiveness of the *standhogg*, the short, sharp shore-raid against the richer lands to the west and south, then, as Alcuin remarked in the eighth century, "no one is free from fear". In 793 the British offshore monastery of Lindisfarne was sacked and St Cuthbert's church was spattered with the blood of the monks. "Never before in Britain," Alcuin lamented, "has such terror appeared as this we have now

suffered at the hands of the heathen." But for the Vikings it was like Ragnarok, "an axe-age, a sword-age". It was a rehearsal for the "wind-age and wolf-age before the world is wrecked". Although Christianity did eventually come to the Germanic peoples of northern Europe, their preoccupation with a cosmic catastrophe did not fade altogether. The Last Judgement exercised their minds during the Middle Ages. It may well have been that behind the Nazis' resolve to fight on in World War Two lay a folk memory of Ragnarok.

RAN see *NATURE SPIRITS*

REGIN and his brother *FAFNIR* slew their father, the magician *HREIDMAR*, while under the spell of a cursed ring, Andvarinaut, which made them covet their father's gold. While Fafnir turned into a dragon in order to protect his gold, Regin settled down as a smith in the royal Danish household. There he tutored the young hero *SIGURD* and urged him to overcome Fafnir, which he did. But, equally as corrupted by the curse as his brother, Regin then plotted to murder Sigurd. However, he reckoned without the young hero's insight: Sigurd was forewarned by the birds and killed Regin first.

RAGNAROK *(above) was foreshadowed by a chilling Fimbul winter. Sol and Mani grew pale with fear; blizzards swept down from the peaks and icebergs towered over the frozen earth. Loki broke free from his bonds and set sail with the fiery host.* (ILLUSTRATION BY JAMES ALEXANDER, 1995.)

RAGNAROK'S *(left) war raged on the icy Plain of Vigrid. Here, Odin wrestles with the snarling wolf, Fenrir, while Thor slays the monstrous world serpent, Jormungand, though dying from its fatal venom. At left, Loki wrestles with the bright god, Heimdall, and both gods die in the conflict.* (ILLUSTRATION BY JAMES ALEXANDER, 1995.)

REIDMAR see *HREIDMAR*

RHINE MAIDENS see *NATURE SPIRITS*

RIG was the name assumed by the Germanic god *HEIMDALL* when he created the three categories of men: the slave or *thrall*; the free peasant or *karl*; and the noble or chieftain, known as *jarl*. Though usually imagined as the watchman of the gods, scanning the horizon for the final frost giant attack at Ragnarok, Heimdall was also identified with Rig, or "king". According to Rig's myth, the god once approached the lowly dwelling of an old couple,

Ai and Edda (literally "great-grandfather" and "great-grandmother"). After introducing himself as a lone wayfarer, Rig was given coarse food to satisfy his hunger and a place in the bed between them when it was time to sleep. Rig stayed three nights and gave them good advice. Nine months afterwards Edda bore a son, Thrall, who was black-haired and ugly, with rough skin, thick fingers, short nails, swollen knuckles, long heels and bent back; but he was strong. Thrall took as his wife an equally ungainly person, a drudge with crooked legs, dirty feet, sunburned arms and a big nose. Their many children included boys like Noisy, Roughneck and Horsefly, as well as girls such as Lazybones, Fatty and Beanpole. From these ill-favoured children descended the thralls, the enslaved labourers of the oppressed class. Eddar's son Thrall himself perfectly sums up the back-breaking toil of his oppressed class, weighed down with generations of hard labour.

Rig visited a second house, warm and better furnished. Inside

RIG wandered throughout the earth, visiting its people and fathering three classes of men, the thralls or serfs, karls or freemen and jarls or earls. Here, Rig sups with aged rustics in their seashore hut, gazing with pride at his first mortal child, Thrall, who was a born labourer and father of the serfs. (ILLUSTRATION BY NICK BEALE, 1995.)

he encountered an industrious couple, Afi and Amma (literally "grandfather" and "grandmother"). The well-dressed pair were spinning and weaving: Afi prepared a loom, Amma spun a thread. Once again Rig shared their table and bed, gave good advice and departed after three nights. Nine months afterwards Amma bore a son, Karl, who was red and fresh and bright-eyed. Karl took to wife Snor (meaning "daughter-in-law") and their children included boys named Strongbeard, Husbandman and Smith, and girls called Prettyface, Maiden and Capable. Together they ran farms and were free.

A third dwelling Rig stayed at was a splendid hall belonging to Fadir and Modir ("father" and "mother"). While Fadir attended to his bow and arrows, Modir saw to her own looks and clothes. After a large meal, accompanied by fine conversation and drink, Rig slept between his well-off hosts. He stayed three nights and gave good advice. Nine months afterwards Modir bore a son, Jarl, who was fair-haired and handsome, with a bright cheek and an eye as piercing as a serpent's. When he grew to manhood, Jarl could use bow, spear, sword and shield; he could ride and swim and hunt expertly. One day Rig returned and greeted Jarl as his special son, imparting wisdom and telling him how to claim his lands. In obedience to the

REGIN reforges the shards of Sigurd's wondrous sword, Gram. Once mended, the sword was so strong and sharp that it split the iron anvil in two. With it, Sigurd slew Regin's brother, Fafnir, who had turned himself into a dragon so that he could guard his gold. (WOOD CARVING, 12TH CENTURY.)

RIG next visited a thrifty farmhouse where he was hospitably entertained by Amma and Afi. Rig stayed for three days and fathered a fine sturdy, blue-eyed boy, named Karl, who grew up to be a natural farmer. Here, Karl and his wife, Snor, can be seen working their fruitful land. (ILLUSTRATION BY NICK BEALE, 1995.)

god, Jarl rode through the world, fighting and slaying, seizing booty and distributing treasure to his free followers. At last he married Erna ("lively"), a fair and wise noblewoman, and she bore him twelve sons. One of these learned magic so well that he could prevent forest fires, control storms and cure the sick. It was said that he excelled even Rig in understanding and almost became a god. The implication is that in his person he combined the roles of priest and king.

The myth of Rig sheds light on the structure of Viking society. In contrast with the Celts, the other main tribal people of pre-Christian Europe, the Germanic tribes of Scandinavia and northern Europe had already lost a priestly class by the time we encounter their mythology. As Julius Caesar noted, the ancient Germans had no equivalent of the druids and cared little for ritual. They found religious significance in the depths of forests. But the Romans, and later the Vikings' victims, were in no doubt about the Germanic love of warfare and the role of the armed retainer, the sturdy free peasant, in battle.

SORCERY AND SPELLS

ORCERY AMONG THE NORSEMEN was a unique and precious art practised essentially by Odin and the Vanir deities of nature, but also by dwarfs and some privileged mortals, usually women. Although distinguished heroes, such as Sigurd, were blessed with magical weapons, they usually lacked any magical powers. Odin, the arch-sorcerer, developed his skills over a lifetime of search and sacrifice, much like a mortal shaman. Ever thirsty for wisdom and power, he wandered the nine worlds as a vagrant, clad in a blue mantle and slouch hat, gathering and garnering every snippet of information he could find. After hanging himself on the World Tree, he learnt the secrets of the dead and restored himself to life. By contrast, the heroes of Finnish myth were often gifted from birth with astounding magical powers and arcane wisdom. The wise wizard, Vainamoinen, was a born sage and sorcerer, while debonair Leminkainen was bathed as a baby to imbue him with wisdom and sorcery. Equipped with a repertoire of sacred songs, the Finns penetrated to the roots of life. Finnish sorcerers were so famous that in medieval times Norwegian kings forbade people to sail to Finnmark for the purpose of consulting magicians.

KULLERVO curses Ilmarinen's wicked wife who had taunted him beyond endurance, giving him a dry loaf for his lunch, stuffed with a rock which shattered his family knife. In response, he turned her gentle cows into bears which devoured her at the milking. Kullervo, a tortured soul, unloved from birth, responded to the world's sleights with distorted malice. Gifted with powerful sorcery, he punished his enemies beyond their crime. (THE CURSE OF KULLERVO BY A GALLEN-KALLELA, CANVAS, C. 1850.)

VAINAMOINEN (above) fends off the griffin perched on his ship. The monster was the sorceress, Louhi, who had turned herself into a metallic bird. She was after the talisman, the Sampo. Just as she reared to strike the final blow, Vainamoinen raised his rudder and crushed her talons. The Sampo was broken and scattered, but Vainamoinen gathered some fragments and partly restored its power. (DEFENCE OF THE SAMPO BY A GALLEN-KALLELA, CANVAS, 1852.)

KULLERVO (above), doomed from birth, set out on his last journey, piping loudly on his cow horn, his mother's Blackie dog running behind. En route he passed a blasted stretch of green where he had unwittingly despoiled his long-lost sister. Here the meadow grasses bemoaned the maiden's terrible fate. Feeling the crushing weight of guilt and a lifetime of bitterness, Kullervo eventually threw himself on his sword. Although a powerful sorcerer, Kullervo was denied love throughout his life and never learnt the way of things. (KULLERVO BY A GALLEN-KALLELA, CANVAS, C. 1850.)

FREYJA (right) was renowned for her magical crafts, along with the other Vanir deities of fertility and nature. She was the first to teach the warrior Aesir the practice of seior or magic. Seior was useful but could be dangerous, giving its practitioners foreknowledge and power over life and death, love and intelligence. Odin quickly learnt all that Freyja could teach him and, ever thirsty for knowledge, surpassed the Vanir in magic arts. In later myth, Freyja was identified with Idun, goddess of Spring who guarded the magic apples of youth, seen here. (ILLUSTRATION BY ARTHUR RACKHAM, C. 1910.)

A RING OF FIRE (far left) encircled the Valkyrie, Brynhild, protecting her in an enchanted sleep from all but the bravest. Only Sigurd dared the fiery circle of flames to win the sleeping beauty. His fearless spirit carried him through, mysteriously unharmed, as predicted by the birds whose song he understood. (ILLUSTRATION BY H THEAKER, C. 1920.)

GRIMHILD (left), Queen of the Niebelungs, was famed and feared for her magic. With her spells and potions, she could erase a person's memory and control his will. When she offered unsuspecting Sigurd her magic mead, he forgot his love for Brynhild and instead fell in love with Grimhild's daughter, Gudrun. (ILLUSTRATION BY ARTHUR RACKHAM, C. 1910.)

S

RIND (above), a cool Nordic princess, became ill with a mystery malady and was nursed back to health by Odin in disguise. The old nurse, Vecha, restored Rind to health, first by bathing her in a hot bath. The warm water thawed her frozen heart and symbolized the melting of the frozen rind of earth. (ILLUSTRATION BY NICK BEALE, 1995.)

THE RUSALKI (right) dwelt in rivers and lakes. The southern sprites were pearly beauties who lured travellers with their sweet song. During Rusalki Week, which was at the start of summer, they emerged from the rivers to dwell and dance in the forests, enriching the grass in their wake. (ILLUSTRATION BY ALAN LEE, 1984.)

RIND, in Germanic mythology, was the daughter of King *BILLING* and the mistress of *ODIN*, who pursued her in various disguises. Their love led to the birth of *VALI*, the child who was to avenge the death of *BALDER*. In one version, Odin was deposed as king of the gods for forcing Rind to submit simply in order that he might father a son.

ROSKVA was a farmer's daughter who became a servant of the god *THOR*. When Thor stopped at her father's house and asked for food and shelter they were too poor to provide meat, so Thor offered his own goats on the condition that no bones were broken. But Roskva's brother *THIALFI* broke one of the thigh bones and when Thor came to resurrect the goats one of them had a limp. The enraged god was only pacified by the promised service of Roskva and Thialfi, who travelled with him thereafter.

THE RUSALKI were water nymphs and can be found in both Slavonic and Russian mythology. They were thought to be the spirits of drowned girls. During the winter months, they lived in the great rivers of eastern Europe, taking on different forms in different regions. For instance, in the Rivers Dnieper and Danube, in south-eastern Europe, they were commonly pictured as beautiful, siren-like creatures who would attempt to lure unsuspecting passers-by into the water with their magical song. In the northern regions, in contrast, the water nymphs were considered to be malevolent, unkempt and unattractive creatures, who would grab travellers from the river banks and drag them down into the river and drown them. During the summer, when the rivers were warmed by the sun, the Rusalki came out of the water on to the land and lived in the cool of the forests.

SAMPO see *TREASURES AND TALISMANS*

SAULE was the Baltic sun goddess and, according to one tradition, the mistress of the thunder god *PERKUNO*. She was worshipped by Lithuanians, Prussians and Letts before they were converted to Christianity. Her worship took the form of looking after a harmless green snake. Every house kept one: under the bed, in a corner, even under the table. Apart from ensuring a household's wealth and fertility, the kindness shown to the snake was regarded as a guarantee of Saule's generosity. To kill a snake was an act of sacrilege. The sight of a dead one was believed to bring tears to the eyes of the sun goddess. Even after the conversion of the Lithuanians to Christianity in the fifteenth century – they were the last people to be Christianized on the continent – the peasants continued to revere green snakes. It was long held that seeing one in the countryside meant that either a marriage or birth would follow.

Saule was imagined as pouring light from a jug. The golden liquid which she generously gave to the world was the basis of life itself, the warmth so necessary after the cold north-eastern European winter. Another fragment of myth about Saule concerns the Baltic equivalent of the Greek Dioscuri, who were the divine twins Castor and Polydeuces. The unnamed Baltic twins are said to have rescued Saule from the sea and built a barn in which the goddess could rest.

SIEGFRIED see *SIGURD*

SIEGMUND see *TRAGIC LOVERS*

SIF was the wife of *THOR*, the Germanic thunder god, and the mother, by a previous marriage, of Uu, god of archery and skiing. She is the subject of a strange myth in which the trickster *LOKI*, the god of fire, one night cut off her beautiful golden hair, probably a representation of ripe corn and therefore fertility. Next morning Thor was beside himself with rage at Sif's distress. When Loki protested that it was only a joke, Thor demanded to know what he was going to do about it, and the fire god said he would get the dwarfs to weave a wig as a replacement.

So Loki asked the sons of Ivaldi to make a wig from spun gold. The completed piece of work was quite remarkable, for it was so light that a breath of air was enough to ruffle its skeins and so real that it grew on her head by magic. Thinking to get the gods even more into their debt, the sons of Ivaldi used the remaining heat in their furnace to construct a collapsible ship named *Skidbladnir* for the fertility god *FREYR* and a magic spear called *GUNGNIR* for *ODIN*. On his way back to *ASGARD*, the stronghold of the gods, crossing the underground

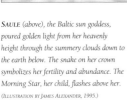

SAULE (above), the Baltic sun goddess, poured golden light from her heavenly height through the summery clouds down to the earth below. The snake on her crown symbolizes her fertility and abundance. The Morning Star, her child, flashes above her. (ILLUSTRATION BY JAMES ALEXANDER, 1995.)

SIF (above right) was famous for her gold, flowing hair, symbolizing ripe harvest corn. When Loki cut off her locks her misery represented the winter season when the cornfields are reduced to stubble. Here, Loki lurks menacingly behind the dreaming beauty. (ILLUSTRATION BY NICK BEALE, 1995.)

SIGNY (right) Queen of Gotaland, rushes down the glacial fjord to greet her kinsmen. She warns them of an ambush planned by her vengeful husband, Siggeir, a sore loser, who bitterly resented her brother Sigmund's victory in a magical sword contest. (ILLUSTRATION BY JAMES ALEXANDER, 1995.)

caverns where the dwarfs lived, Loki also met the dwarf brothers Brokk and Eiti. They were so jealous of the workmanship that had gone into the wig, the boat and the spear that Loki persuaded them to make something better; he even staked his own head on their inability to do so. As a result, the dwarf brothers fashioned the magic hammer known as *MJOLLNIR*, the scourge of the frost giants.

The gods were delighted with the treasures Loki and Brokk had brought back. However, Brokk demanded Loki's head. The gods would not agree, but they had no objection to Brokk sewing up Loki's lips with a thong when Thor dragged the god back home after he tried to flee, which caused Loki to plan a revenge against Thor. (See also TREASURES AND TALISMANS)

SIGMUND see NORSE HEROES

SIGNY, in Germanic mythology, was the unfortunate daughter of *VOLSUNG*, supposedly a descendant of *ODIN*. Married against her will to the Gothic king Siggeir, she tried to warn her father and her ten brothers about Siggeir's plot against them, but they were ambushed in a forest and bound to a fallen tree. Each night a wolf devoured one of them in turn, until only her youngest brother Sigmund was left alive. Signy got a slave to smear Sigmund's face with honey so that the wolf would lick him instead of biting him. Sigmund was thus able to catch the wolf's tongue in his teeth and overcome the beast.

Signy helped Sigmund to plot revenge. She even slept with him in disguise and bore a son named Sinfiotli. When Sinfiotli grew up she placed him in Sigmund's care, but they were both captured by Siggeir. A magic sword freed them and killed Siggeir and his sons. Signy chose to die herself in the burning Gothic palace, but not before she had told Sigmund the truth about Sinfiotli's parentage.

SIGRYN see *SIGYN*

SIGUNN see *SIGYN*

SIGURD, or Siegfried as he was known in German, was a northern Germanic hero similar to the Celtic King Arthur. He was the foster-son of *REGIN*, the smith at the court of King Hjalprek in Jutland, who sent him to recover a fabulous hoard of gold. Regin's father *HREIDMAR* had first acquired this treasure, which once belonged to the dwarf *ANDVARI*. To get their hands on the gold Regin and his brother *FAFNIR* had then killed Hreidmar, but Fafnir wanted the treasure for himself and turned into a dragon to guard it. By cunningly stabbing the monster from underneath, Sigurd succeeded in slaying Fafnir, thus apparently gaining both dwarfish wealth and wisdom, since Fafnir was said to have understood the language of birds. When he realized that Regin intended to kill him for the gold, Sigurd slew him before carrying it away himself. (See also *NORSE HEROES*; *TRAGIC LOVERS*; *RINGS OF POWER*)

SIGYN, also known as Sigunn or Sigryn, in Germanic mythology, was the faithful wife of the fire god *LOKI* and mother of his sons Narvi and *VALI*. Once the gods realized that in Loki they had allowed the growth of evil in their midst, they

SIGURD (above) watches with fascination as Regin forges the broken shards of his father's wondrous sword, a gift from Odin. The conquering sword would help Sigurd in his destined mission to slay the dragon, Fafnir, guardian of a fabulous but ill-fated treasure. (SIEGFRIED IN THE FORGE OF REGIN BY W VON HANSCHILD, FRESCO, 1880.)

SIGURD (right) confronts the fire-breathing dragon, Fafnir, and slays him, winning fame and a fateful fortune. On the advice of his mentor, Regin, he roasted the creature's heart, licking some spilt blood from which he learnt the speech of birds. (SIEGFRIED AND FAFNIR BY H. HENRICH, CANVAS, 1906.)

SIGURD (above) exults in his wondrous new weapon, anticipating victory over his frightful foe, Fafnir. Equipped with the sharpest blade and nerves of iron, the eager hero set off excitedly on his first quest. This striking portrayal highlights the youthful idealism of the zealous Nordic hero. (ILLUSTRATION BY ARTHUR RACKHAM, C. 1900.)

SKIRNIR (above) gallops through a fiery ring guarding the icy home of Gerda, a frost giantess. On a mission to win Gerda for his gentle master, Freyr, Skirnir bears gifts of life-giving apples, a multiplying ring, Draupnir, and a glowing portrait of Freyr, captured in his drinking horn. (ILLUSTRATION BY GLENN STEWARD, 1995.)

bound him in a cave. First they took hold of three slabs of rock, stood them on end and bored a hole through each of them. Then the entrails of Loki's son Narvi were employed as a rope which bound the fire god to the stones. When the gods had tied the last knot, the entrails became as hard as iron. To ensure Loki's discomfort the frost giantess SKADI, NJORD's wife, fastened a snake to a stalactite above the god's head and there he was to remain until RAGNAROK.

SIGYN (above), the devoted wife of Loki, stood by him even after he had been banished to an icy prison. There she lessened his pain by catching the fiery venom dribbled by a serpent tied above his face. When she went to empty the bowl, he writhed in agony, shaking the earth. (LOKI AND SIGYN BY M E WINGE, CANVAS, C. 1890.)

Despite all that her husband had done, Sigyn remained true to him and did what she could to lessen his suffering by catching the venom dripping from the snake in a wooden bowl. However, whenever she went away to empty its poisonous contents, the venom fell on Loki's head and caused him to twitch violently. According to the Vikings, it was these compulsive movements that accounted for earthquakes.

SKADE see SKADI

SKADI, a cool and independent huntress, roamed the mountains on her snow shoes. A spirit of winter, she was far happier on her icy slopes than in her husband's sunlit coves. A deity of hunters and mountain climbers, she guided their sleighs over the snow. (ILLUSTRATION BY JAMES ALEXANDER, 1995.)

SKADI, or Skade (which means "destruction"), was a figure in northern Germanic mythology. She was the wife of the sea god NJORD and daughter of the frost giant THIASSI. When the gods of ASGARD killed her father for stealing IDUN's apples, Skadi armed herself and went to the gods' stronghold to seek compensation. Refusing an offer of gold, she demanded a husband and a bellyful of laughter. This agreed, provided that Skadi chose her husband by his feet only. Thinking that the most shapely feet must surely belong to handsome BALDER, ODIN's son, Skadi made her choice only to discover that she had picked Njord. The merriment was provided by LOKI, who tied his testicles to a goat. As the couple were unable to stand the conditions in each other's homes, Njord and Skadi decided that it was best to live apart. Her relationship with the gods continued, however, and it was she who placed the venomous snake above Loki's head when the gods eventually imprisoned the troublesome god in a cave.

SKIRNIR ("Shining") was a servant of FREYR, the Germanic god of fertility. When Freyr wished to marry the frost giantess GERDA, he promised Skirnir his horse and his sword and sent him to JOTUNHEIM, the land of the frost giants. Skirnir had some difficulty in persuading Gerda to agree to the match, however. Eleven apples of youth, the magic fruit that kept the gods young, were no temptation to her. Nor was one of Odin's arm-rings. Gerda showed no fear when Skirnir threatened to behead her, but she began to panic the moment he started to recite a powerful spell. It promised to deny her any joy or passion, for the beautiful frost giantess was to be transformed into a loveless outcast, a companion of the "unworthy dead". As a result of this threatened fate, Gerda at last consented to meet Freyr and so Skirnir received his promised rewards. On another occasion, Skirnir acted in his role as messenger by going to the dwarfs on Odin's behalf to order a magical fetter so that Odin could restrain the terrible wolf FENRIR.

227

SKOLL, in Germanic mythology, was a wolf that pursued the sun in her flight across the sky. At RAGNAROK, the doom of the gods, Skoll was destined to seize the sun between his jaws and swallow her. Just before this happened, though, the sun would give birth to a daughter as beautiful as herself and this new sun would warm and illuminate the new earth risen from the sea, "fresh and green", following the catastrophe. Another wolf, named Hati, chased after the moon. Both creatures were said to be the sons of a giantess living in Iron Wood.

Ravenous dogs often threatened to eat the heavenly bodies in the myths of northern parts of both Europe and Asia. Chinese families today still bang cooking utensils to frighten "the dog of heaven" during a lunar eclipse.

SKOLL (below), a fierce wolf, symbolizing Repulsion, chased the sun across the sky, from dawn to dusk. Skoll's sole aim in life was to overtake and devour the heavenly orb, plunging the world into primordial darkness. (ILLUSTRATION BY GLENN STEWARD, 1995.)

SKRYMIR, a massive frost giant, acts as mountain guide to Thor and his party, pointing out the shortest route to Utgard, the citadel of the frost giants. The travellers struggled on through snow drifts, unaware that Skrymir was in fact only a giant illusion sent to thwart and mislead them. (ILLUSTRATION BY NICK BEALE, 1995.)

SKRYMIR ("Vast") was an extra large frost giant in Germanic mythology. So huge was he that on a journey through the land of giants THOR and LOKI, along with their servants THIALFI and ROSKVA, inadvertently slept in the thumb of Skrymir's empty glove, thinking it was a hall. When Thor later tried to hammer in the skull of the sleeping Skrymir, the frost giant awoke in the belief that either a leaf or an acorn had dropped on his brow. Afterwards it dawned on Thor and his companions that Skrymir was a gigantic illusion, a magic creation sent out by the frost giants in order to prevent them from reaching UTGARD, the giants' citadel.

SLEIPNIR ("Glider"), was the eight-legged horse ridden by ODIN, the chief of the Germanic gods. This fabulous creature was the offspring of an unusual union between Svadilfari, a stallion of great strength, and LOKI, the shape-changer, who had disguised himself as a mare. Sleipnir could travel over sea and through the air, and was swift enough to beat any other horse in a race. At RAGNAROK, Sleipnir was the horse that carried Odin into battle.

SOL see NATURE SPIRITS

SURT ("Black"), in Germanic mythology, was a fire giant with a flaming blade who would set the cosmos alight at RAGNAROK. He was identified with the fire god LOKI. At Ragnarok Surt was to rise from Muspell, the land of flame, and fling fire in every direction. The nine worlds were to become raging furnaces as gods, frost giants, the

SLEIPNIR (above), the fabulous eight-hoofed (or some say, eight-legged) steed of Odin, certainly deserved his name "Glider" for he slipped through cloud, sea or earth with equal ease. Sleipnir's hooves rumbled in the storm clouds when Odin travelled across the sky as god of the winds. (ILLUSTRATION BY GLENN STEWARD, 1995.)

SVANTOVIT (right), the four-headed war god of the Slavs, guarded the world on four sides. His stone effigy at Rugen was worshipped before battle. As a deity of fertility, plenty and destiny, he bore a horn of plenty and rode a horse of divination. A white horse was kept in the temple for ritual divination. (ILLUSTRATION BY NICK BEALE, 1995.)

SURT (below), a fierce fire giant, rose from the furnace of Muspell at Ragnarok to lead his fiery hordes against the divine host. With his flaming sword, he set the nine worlds ablaze, burning them to blackened cinders which sank beneath the boiling ocean only to rise again fresh, green and new. (ILLUSTRATION BY JAMES ALEXANDER, 1995.)

dead, the living, monsters, dwarfs, elves and animals were all to be reduced to ashes. Then the earth would sink into the sea, before rising again, fresh and green. It may be that the view of the end of the world as an immense conflagration was influenced by the volcanic nature of Iceland, from where many of the written myths originated. In 1963–7, a new island, formed by a volcanic eruption off the coast of Iceland, was named Surtsey after the god Surt.

SVANTEVIT see *SVANTOVIT*

SVANTOVIT, also known as Svantevit, was the war god of the Slavic peoples of central Europe. His temple at Arcona on the Baltic island of Rugen was destroyed by King Valdemar of Denmark and his Christian adviser Absalon in 1169.

The building contained a four-headed statue of Svantovit that was nearly thirty feet in height. Multiple heads were indeed a feature of the Slavic pantheon. It is thought that Svantovit may also have been worshipped as a supreme deity and seen as a father to other gods.

Prior to the Danish destruction of the temple in the Christian era, the worshippers of Svantovit at Arcona believed that the god would mount a sacred white horse and ride out at nights against those who denied his divinity. In the morning the horse was often discovered to be covered in sweat. Omens for success in war were read from the behaviour of the sacred horse as well. Human sacrifices, which were a widespread custom throughout the Germanic and Slavic peoples, were made to Svantovit before any great undertakings.

SVARAZIC, sometimes Svarozic or Svarogich (which probably meant "hot" or "torrid" – a meaning that can still be found today in the Romanian language), was the Slavic fire god, especially of the fire that was used to dry grain. He was the son of Svaroz, or Svarog (who was identified with the Greek smith god Hephaistos) and the brother of *DAZHBOG*. The fire god was depicted wearing a helmet and carrying a sword, and on his breast was a black bison's head. Human sacrifices were made to Svarazic, including, after his capture in 1066, the German bishop of Mecklenburg. In some traditions, Svarazic was identified with the flame of lightning.

SVAROGICH see *SVARAZIC*

SVAROZIC see *SVARAZIC*

TRAGIC LOVERS

TIMELESS TALES OF TRAGIC LOVE are common everywhere, yet rarely so stark and bleak as in Norse mythology. Sometimes a curse lies at the root of the trouble, as in the tale of Sigurd and Brynhild, where a cursed ring wrecks the lives of several pairs of doomed lovers. Sometimes the trials of love symbolize the battles of nature. Sigurd, for instance, might be seen as a sun lord who, armed with a sunbeam, dispels darkness; while his lover, Brynhild, symbolizes the dawn-maiden whose path he crosses only at the start and close of his shining career. In other tales, obstacles simply serve to test the lovers' honour and courage, as when Frithiof faithfully guards his sleeping rival, Sigurd Ring. In their love affairs, the gods seem luckier than mortals, though friction is rife, if short-lived, as when Odur flees Freyja or Skadi lives apart from Njord. Such conflict might symbolize seasonal changes: Njord's sunny love can only hold wintry Skadi for three months of the year. By contrast, in the heart-warming tale of the summer god, Freyr, he wins his frosty bride by sheer warmth of love which melts her icy heart.

SIEGMUND and Sieglinde (left), were siblings who grew up apart, both enduring tragic fates, before meeting by chance and falling in love. Here, the lovers exchange secret glances while in the company of Sieglinde's suspicious husband, Hunding, who plans to slay Siegmund in a duel. When Siegmund wins, he and Sieglinde enjoy brief love before dying, one on the battlefield, the other in childbirth. The child of their sad union is the great hero, Sigurd. (ILLUSTRATION BY F LEEKE, C. 1895.)

INGEBORG (above), in the sanctuary of Balder's temple, stops spinning and pines for her lover, Frithiof. Cloistered by her watchful brothers, she was denied contact with Frithiof, who was considered beneath her royal status. Yet when Frithiof broke the sanctity of the temple to rescue Ingeborg, she refused to flee with him, believing herself honour bound to obey the wishes of her royal brothers. (INGEBORG'S LAMENT BY F N JENSEN, CANVAS, C. 1830.)

FREYR (left), a gentle summer god, caught a glimpse of the radiant frost giantess, Gerda, from afar and at once fell in love, but doubted his chances until his decisive servant, Skirnir, set off to woo the girl for his master. Gerda remained unmoved until she was forced by threat of magic to at least consent to a meeting with Freyr. Once in the company of the fiery god, Gerda's icy heart thawed. Freyr appears here as a dreamy summer god, bearing his wheat, with his boar at his feet, emblems of fruitful harvest. (FREYR BY E BURNE-JONES JONES, CANVAS, C. 1870.)

KREIMHILD (right) wakes from a nightmare in which she dreamt that a lovely white falcon was struck in flight by two black eagles. Her mother interprets the dream to mean that Kreimhild will eventually fall in love with a peerless prince – who is symbolized by the white bird – and that he will be killed by two murderers – the black eagles. Indeed, some years later the dream came true as Kreimhild fell in love with the great hero Sigurd, later slain by her two brothers, Gunner and Hogni, who were acting under the influence of a curse. Here, Kreimhild is depicted telling her mother about her dream, while below a bard, a poet and a Christian pontiff ponder the meaning of the Teutonic epic, the Niebelungenlied. (THE LEGEND OF SIEGFRIED BY F PILOTY, WOOD, C. 1890.)

FRITHIOF and Ingeborg (left) are at last united in Balder's temple. The childhood sweethearts had been thwarted by Ingeborg's hostile brothers. While Ingeborg was forced into a marriage with an old chieftain, Sigurd Ring, Frithiof roamed the high seas in misery. When his undying love drove him home, he waited honourably until the old king died before at last winning his bride. (FRITHIOF AND INGEBORG BY J A MALMSTROM, CANVAS, C. 1840.)

BRYNHILD and Sigurd (above) find peace together at last after a romance wrecked by a web of intrigue and vengeance. After pledging his love to Brynhild, Sigurd was bewitched into marrying Gudrun. Brynhild, in her turn, was unwittingly tricked by Sigurd into marrying Gunner. When Brynhild discovered Sigurd's apparent betrayal, she cried out for vengeance. Sigurd was slain and Brynhild, overcome by grief, killed herself to be laid to rest beside him. (THE FUNERAL PYRE BY C BUTLER, CANVAS, 1909.)

T

TANNGNOST (meaning "Tooth-gnasher"), in Germanic mythology, was the name of one of the two billy goats which pulled *THOR*'s chariot. The other was named Tanngrisnir ("Tooth-grinder"). The rumble of the chariot was heard by people on earth as the sound of thunder. Like the magic boar of *VALHALLA*, which could be eaten one day and reappear alive the next, Thor's goats provided an endless supply of meat as long as, after cooking, all their bones remained intact. Thor would then wave his magic hammer over the skin and bones and the goats came alive.

TAPIO was the Finnish forest god, who, along with his wife Meilikki and his son Nyyrikki, was believed to ensure that woodland game remained in plentiful supply. He had a dangerous side to his nature, however, as he enjoyed tickling or smothering people to death. His daughter Tuulikki was a spirit of the wind. Tapio is often portrayed as wearing a cloak of moss and a bonnet of fire.

THIALFI and his sister *ROSKVA* were the children of a farmer and servants of the Germanic thunder god *THOR*. When Thor and *LOKI* were travelling through Midgard they stopped at the farmhouse and Thor provided goats for supper on condition that all the bones be kept intact. Because Thialfi had not had a satisfying meal for a long time, he ignored this instruction and split a thigh bone to get at the marrow. Next morning, when Thor used his magic hammer to restore the goats to life, the thunder god noticed

*TANNGNOST and Tanngrisnir (left) were a pair of goats who pulled Thor's chariot across the sky, creating the clatter and rumble of storm clouds. Thor alone among the gods never rode, but either strode or drove his goat-drawn chariot. (*THOR AND THE GIANTS BY M E WINGE, CANVAS, C. 1890.*)*

*TAPIO (above), a green god of the Finnish forests, dwelt in the depths of the greenwood, clad in moss, and growing a fir-like beard. Along with other sylvan deities, he was lord not just of forest plants, but also of forest beasts and the herds of woodland cattle. (*ILLUSTRATION BY JAMES ALEXANDER, 1995.*)*

that one animal was lame. He was so enraged that he threatened destruction of the farm and demanded compensation. He was placated only when Thialfi and Roskva were given to him as his servants. Although Thialfi lost a running contest to *HUGI* during Thor's visit to the frost giant stronghold of *UTGARD*, his master was outwitted by magic in several challenges too. In another myth Thialfi deserved Thor's gratitude when he toppled the enormous clay giant Mist Calf, which had caused Thor to panic with fear. He also fetched aid for the wounded thunder god after his duel with *HRUNGNIR*, the strongest of the frost giants.

THIASSI, or Thiazi, in Germanic mythology, was a frost giant and the father of *SKADI* who stole from the goddess *IDUN* the apples of youth. It was really *LOKI*'s fault that this event occurred. Disguised as an eagle, the giant grabbed hold of the god and, to secure his own release from Thiassi, Loki promised to deliver the goddess and her magic apples into the frost giant's hands. The effect upon the gods was immediate. Without Idun's apples to eat each day, they grew anxious and old. In this crisis Odin alone had the determination to rally enough strength to plan a recovery. The gods captured the trickster Loki, and made him fly as

THIALFI *(left) and his sister, Roskva,
accompanied Thor on a fabulous journey to
Jotunheim. En route, they sheltered in a
giant's glove, until woken by his gusty
snores. Here, Thor batters the giant's head,
hoping to silence his snores, while Thialfi
and Roskva gaze on in dazed disbelief.
(ILLUSTRATION BY NICK BEALE, 1995.)*

THIAZI see *THIASSI*

THOKK was the callous frost
giantess of Germanic myth. After
the popular god *BALDER's* unfortunate death, *HEL,* the queen of the
"unworthy dead", said that she
would allow him back to the land
of the living on the condition that
"everything in the nine worlds,
dead and alive, weeps for him".
Messengers were therefore sent out
to ensure that everything mourned
and were satisfied that they had
achieved their aim. On their way
back to *ASGARD*, however, they
found Thokk in a cave, and when
they explained their mission the
giantess replied that she had no use
for Balder and added, "Let Hel
keep what she holds." Some versions of the myth maintain that
Thokk was none other than *LOKI.*

THIASSI *(left), a frost giant, disguised as
an eagle, pestered Odin, Honir and Loki on
a trip to Midgard. At one point Thiassi
swooped down and scooped up the gods'
dinner pot. Enraged, Loki lunged at the
eagle with his staff but became stuck fast to
the bird. (ILLUSTRATION BY PETER HURD, 1882.)*

THOKK, *alone among all the creatures in
the nine worlds, refused to shed a single
tear for Balder, so destroying his one chance
of escape from Hel. Around bitter Thokk all
creation weeps – the leaves, stones and
snow itself – mourning the loss of the much-
loved Balder. (ILLUSTRATION BY NICK BEALE, 1995.)*

a falcon to Thiassi's hall in order to
bring back Idun and her apples.
This Loki was able to accomplish,
but the frost giant almost thwarted
the plan by turning himself yet
again into an eagle and flying after
the god. He very nearly caught up
with Loki, but as Thiassi flew over
ASGARD his wings were set alight by
fires that the gods had placed on
top of the stronghold's high walls.
The giant could no longer fly and
so fell to the ground, burned to
death by the flames.

Eventually, Thiassi's daughter
Skadi came to Asgard to seek compensation for her father's death.
When her demands had been satisfied, Odin took Thiassi's eyes
from his cloak and threw them into
the sky as stars. "Thiassi will look
down on all of us," he said, "for as
long as the world lasts."

233

THOR was the Germanic thunder god. He was the son of *ODIN*, the chief god, and Fjorgyn, the goddess of earth. When the Anglo-Saxons eventually adopted the Roman calendar, they named the fifth day Thursday after Thor, for this was the day belonging to Jupiter, the Roman sky god and peer of the hot-tempered, red-headed Thor, along with the Greek Zeus and the Hindu Indra. His name means "thunder" and his magic hammer, *MJOLLNIR*, may once have meant "lightning". Among Icelanders and Norwegians family names like Thorsten recall the name of the god, for these farmers had little sympathy with the footloose Vikings who worshipped Odin, the father of the slain. The Icelandic colonists, who had fled southern Norway to escape the aggression of Danish and Swedish rulers, preferred honest Thor, the powerful but straightforward opponent of the frost giants.

Yet Thor, the bitter enemy of the frost giants, was in many aspects not unlike a giant himself. He was exceptionally strong, very

THOR, in his most popular guise as champion of the gods, was a tireless warrior and giant-slayer. With his red-hot hammer and belt of strength, which doubled his power, he was a formidable foe. Here, the thunder god swings his fiery missile. (ILLUSTRATION BY ARTHUR RACKHAM, C. 1900.)

large – his frequent companion *LOKI*, the fire god, usually attached himself to Thor's belt – energetic and had an enormous appetite, which allowed him to eat a whole ox at one sitting. And, of course, there was his relish for a contest, a trial of strength. Two goats drew Thor's great chariot across the sky: their names were Tooth-grinder and Tooth-gnasher. His magic weapons were a hammer, really a thunderbolt; iron gauntlets, which he used to handle the red-hot hammer shaft; and a belt that increased his strength. *MJOLLNIR*, the hammer, was the handiwork of two dwarfs, the sons of Ivaldi. It had a huge head and a short handle and always hit its target.

Thor was the mightiest of the Germanic gods and their staunch protector against the frost giants. At *RAGNAROK*, the doom of the gods,

he was destined to be killed by the poisonous venom of the sea serpent *JORMUNGAND*, although not before Thor had killed the monster. Before he was slain by this terrible son of Loki, however, Loki and he had many adventures together.

These adventures were often dangerous for Thor, especially when Loki led the thunder god into danger as a price for his own freedom. Such was the case with their visit to the hall of the frost giant *GEIRROD*. Having been captured by Geirrod when Loki was in the shape of a hawk, he could avoid death only by making a promise to deliver an unarmed Thor into the frost giant's hands. Because Thor enjoyed Loki's company and was so trusting, he let the fire god lead him to Geirrod's hall without the protection of his hammer, gloves and belt. But on the

THOR (left), as a headstrong child, proved too much for his mother and was raised by two saintly guardians, Vingir and Hlora, spirits of lightning. Here, the fiery youngster displays both impressive temper and might by whirling bearskin bales in a fit of rage, while his guardians soothe his anger. (ILLUSTRATION BY JAMES ALEXANDER, 1995.)

edge of *JOTUNHEIM*, the land of the frost giants, Thor and Loki spent the night with *GRID*, a friendly giantess. Grid warned Thor about Geirrod's hatred of the gods. She told him that he would be especially pleased to avenge the death of *HRUNGNIR*, the strongest of the frost giants whom Thor had killed in a duel. The thunder god still had a piece of this dead frost giant's throwing stone stuck in his head to prove it, so Thor was most grateful at Grid's loan of her own belt of strength, iron gloves and unbreakable staff.

Crossing a torrent of water and blood near the frost giant's hall proved difficult, until Thor blocked the source of the blood with a well-aimed stone. It struck *GJALP*, Geirrod's daughter, whose menstrual outpouring had swollen the river. Even then, the two gods were swept away, as Thor lost his footing and Loki clung desperately to the belt of Grid that the thunder god was wearing. Happily, Thor succeeded in grabbing a mountain ash overhanging the flood and scrambled ashore on the opposite bank.

Soon Thor and Loki arrived at Geirrod's hall, where servants grudgingly received them. The owner was nowhere to be seen, so Thor sat down in a chair to await his return. Snatching a nap, he was surprised when he dreamed he was floating in the air. Thor opened his eyes and saw that his head was about to be rammed against the ceiling. Quick as a flash, he used Grid's staff to push against the ceiling, with the result that the chair came down hard enough to crush Gjalp and Greip to death. These two daughters of Geirrod had been

of such enormous size that Thor would be struck by terror on seeing him. Named MIST CALF, the clay giant was animated by the heart of a mare and, slow moving though he was, clouds gathered round his towering head. On the day of the duel Thor wet himself at the sight of Mist Calf, although his charioteer had the good sense to topple the clay giant by attacking his legs with an axe. Mist Calf's fall shook Jotunheim, the land of the frost giants. In the fight with Hrungnir it was Thor who came off best, although the thunder god was left

THOR's (left) hammer was a symbol of creative and destructive power and a source of fertility, renewal and good fortune. As Christianity swept north, the sign of the cross often fused with the sign of the hammer, as in this charm, containing a cross within a hammer. (SILVER, 10TH CENT.)

pinned to the ground by one of the dead frost giant's legs and with a piece of whetstone lodged in his head. None of the gods could release Thor and it was fortunate that his own three-year-old frost giant son MAGNI turned up after the fight. The son of the frost giantess Jarnsaxa, a mistress of Thor, Magni also told his flattened father how he could have dealt with Hrungnir with his bare fists. Thor was delighted to see Magni's strength and gave him the dead frost giant's steed Golden Mane as a reward, much to Odin's

THOR (below), the thunder god, ruled the storms and tempests. With eyes ablaze and hair aflame, he bears his red-hot hammer in its iron gauntlet. As his bronze chariot made a racket like the clash and clatter of copper kettles, he was nicknamed the Kettle Vendor. (ILLUSTRATION BY JAMES ALEXANDER, 1995.)

thrusting it upwards. Then the frost giant returned and tried to kill Thor as well. Using a pair of tongs, he launched a red-hot iron ball at Thor, but the thunder god caught it deftly in the iron gloves he had been given by Grid, and returned the compliment by throwing it back at the giant. The iron ball passed through an iron pillar before tearing a hole in Geirrod's belly. Afterwards Thor smashed the skulls of all the servants.

The frost giant mentioned by Grid, the powerful Hrungnir, had fallen in single combat with Thor. Foolishly, the frost giant challenged Odin to a horse race but then, as a guest at the gods' stronghold of ASGARD, he drank too much and insulted the gods. When Thor returned at this point the giant challenged Thor to a duel.

The frost giants did what they could to aid Hrungnir in the forthcoming fight. They built a clay giant

THOR battles with his arch enemy, the Jormungand, caught on his fishing line. A lurking evil coiled around the earth, the serpent was destined to overwhelm the world at Ragnarok. Here, while Thor struggles to overcome the beast, Hymir, in fear, cuts him free. (THOR IN THE BOAT OF HYMIR BY H FUSELI, CANVAS, 1790.)

annoyance. "You should not give a horse to the son of a giantess instead of your own father," complained Odin.

Another famous adventure in Jotunheim concerns the visit of Thor and Loki to the stronghold of *UTGARD*. On the way the thunder god passed through Midgard, the land of people, and gained two human servants named *THIALFI* and *ROSKVA*, a brother and sister. It happened that Thialfi disobeyed an instruction of Thor when they dined together at his parents' farm. Thor told everyone to be careful with the bones of some goats they were eating. But hungry Thialfi split a thigh bone to get at the marrow, before throwing the bone on the goat skins in a corner. Next morning, when Thor used his magic hammer to restore the eaten goats to life, the thunder god noticed that one of them was lame. As compensation and in order to prevent him from slaying the household, Thialfi and Roskva pledged themselves as Thor's servants.

As Thor, Loki, Thialfi and Roskva neared Utgard, they spent one night in an empty hall. It was so big that several of the halls in Asgard, the home of the gods, could have fitted inside it at the same time. Later they realized that the hall was in fact the thumb of a frost giant's empty glove. It belonged to *SKRYMIR*, whose name means "vast". Blows delivered by a frustrated Thor to Skrymir's sleeping head were dismissed by the giant as either a leaf or a twig brushing his brow during the night. On their arrival at Utgard, the travellers were just as amazed at the stronghold's dimensions. While Thor

said that size was of no importance – "the bigger they are, the heavier they fall" – Loki was more thoughtful. Inside Utgard huge frost giants eyed the four guests. Their leader at first ignored them, but finally acknowledged "little" Thor. Then he devised a series of games in which Loki, Thialfi and Thor all

failed to shine. First the fire god lost an eating contest. A second event saw Thialfi easily outpaced in a foot-race. Then successively Thor lost a drinking contest, managed to lift only one paw of a cat, and, most embarrassing of all, was easily wrestled down on to one knee by "an old, old woman".

Once Thor admitted on leaving Utgard that they had come off second best, the leader of the frost giants revealed that he had used spells to gain the advantage. He told them how Loki had actually been pitted against wildfire, and Thialfi against his own thought, while Thor had tried to swallow the

THOR (above) impulsive as ever, confronted mighty Skrymir with his tiny hammer, bashing him over the head to silence his snores, but to no avail. Each time the giant woke he scratched his brow and nodded off again. Later, Thor learnt that Skrymir had been an illusion. (ILLUSTRATION BY J HUARD, 1930.)

ocean, lift the massive sea serpent Jormungand and wrestle with old age. As soon as this message was delivered, Utgard vanished. Only then did it dawn on Thor that Skrymir and Utgard were illusions, vast creations sent out by frightened frost giants. But it gave Loki some satisfaction to learn that brain had indeed triumphed over brawn.

Even Thor had to admit that on certain occasions Loki's cleverness was necessary to hold the frost giants in check. Such a moment in time was when Mjollnir, Thor's magic hammer, fell into their hands after it was stolen by the dwarfs. Its new owner, the frost giant THRYM, demanded as the price of the hammer's return the hand of FREYJA, the fertility goddess. Loki got Thor to dress in Freyja's clothes and go to Thrym's hall instead. Despite his god-like appetite, Thor was passed

THOR (left) and his party visited the icy citadel of Utgard, the stronghold of the frost giants, where they underwent a series of allegorical tests. Thialfi was outstripped by the speed of Thought, Loki out-eaten by Wildfire, and Thor overcome by Age. Here, Thor fails to drain a horn brimful of the ocean. (ILLUSTRATION BY JAMES ALEXANDER, 1995.)

THOR (above) wrestles with Jormungand in their final combat at Ragnarok. Trapped within the serpent's crushing coils, Thor smashed its ugly head with a fatal blow of his hammer; he then staggered back nine paces and drowned in the flood of venom flowing from the beast's gaping jaws. (ILLUSTRATION BY JAMES ALEXANDER, 1995.)

off by his "bridesmaid" Loki as a blushing bride, and an excited Thrym handed over Mjollnir. The ensuing massacre did a great deal to restore Thor's fierce reputation, which had been tarnished by the god having to dress like a woman.

Mjollnir was the sole protection of the gods against the frost giants. It was the thunderbolt which terrorized them prior to the catastrophe of Ragnarok. Apart from its destructive side, the hammer had other magic powers over fertility and death. It seems to have had the ability to restore animal life. It also hallowed marriage, for otherwise Thrym would not have been so ready to place Mjollnir between

Thor's knees when the thunder god was disguised as Freyja. But throughout the myths relating to Thor we are never unconscious of its unlimited destructive powers. For it was the thunder god's purpose to quell the enemies of the gods – "to smash their legs, break their skulls, and crush their backs". Like his Hindu equivalent Indra, Thor was the scourge of evil and in Germanic mythology this could only mean frost giants. Loki's eventual siding with these grim opponents is therefore one of the saddest events to befall Thor, for the two gods "both enjoyed each other's company". (See also *NORSE HEROES; RAGNAROK*)

RINGS OF POWER

Among the Vikings, the ring was a potent symbol of power, fortune and fame. A gift of honour and form of currency, it was also sometimes a royal heirloom, such as the Swedish Sviagriss. The magical rings of Norse myth were also symbols of destiny and, in their bleakest form, symbols of doom. One famous example was the cursed ring, Andvarinaut, which blighted many lives. Another ring of doom was Thor's Domhring, formed by a circle of stone statues surrounding a punishment pillar in front of his temple. The Domhring possibly symbolized the inevitability of retribution. Much more joyous and fabulous rings were Odin's astounding Draupnir which literally dripped eight similar gold rings every nine days; or Thor's Oath Ring, a symbol of fair play and good faith. The rings of heroes inevitably brought wealth and power, but not always happiness and sometimes tragedy, if corrupted by greed. Yet the pure rings of Orthnit, Wolfdietrich and Dietrich were symbols of a ring-lord's circle of power and everlasting fame.

DRAUPNIR,
Odin's fabulous ring,
was an emblem of abundance
and power. Precious beyond compare, it
dripped eight similar gold rings every ninth night, consolidating
his vast wealth and dominion over the nine worlds. Draupnir
was crafted by the dwarf, Sindri, while his brother, Brokk,
pumped the bellows. In an extravagant gesture of grief, Odin
cast the ring upon Balder's funeral pyre, but later retrieved it
when Hermod ventured to Hel. The return of the ring symbolized
the promise of fertility after winter bleakness. Here, the dwarf
Sindri fashions the magnificent ring with fire and arcane magic
in his underground forge. (ILLUSTRATION BY ALAN LEE, 1984.)

THE GOLD RING among the Vikings was a precious token of power, fame and fortune. Sometimes bequeathed as an heirloom, it was also often buried with the ring-lord for the journey to the otherworld, such as this burial treasure. Exquisitely wrought, the ring's clear, bold lines express the vigour and strength of Viking craft. (GILT SILVER, 10TH CENTURY.)

ALBERICH (above), a dwarf in the Niebelungenlied, forged a ring of power from the Rhinegold stolen from the Rhine Maidens. News of the gold robbery and ring of power incited gods and giants alike to action. The giants Fafner and Fasolt demanded the ring in payment for building Valhalla, and carried off Freyja as a hostage. In the border, the gods, Odin, Frigg, Loki, Freyr and Thor all search despairingly for the hidden treasure. (ILLUSTRATION BY F VON STASSEN, 1914.)

DIETRICH (above), a Gothic hero, won a wondrous ring from the dwarf, Laurin, who ruled a fabulous underground kingdom lit by gems. After various battles and intrigues, Dietrich overcame the wily dwarf, and claimed his magical gold ring as well as a girdle of strength, a cape of invisibility, a magical sword and a vast ring-hoard. Laurin's ring was the very one owned by Dietrich's great-grandfather, the Emperor Wolfdietrich. Here, Dietrich breaks into Laurin's enchanted, ever-flowering rose garden, before winning the ring treasures. (ILLUSTRATION BY ALAN LEE, 1984.)

THE RING ANDVARINAUT wove a fortune of gold much like Draupnir, but was tainted by the bitter curse of Andvari. Heidmar, who had demanded the ring as wiergold from Loki, was the first to suffer from the curse by falling at the hands of his son, Fafnir, who lusted after the gold. Next, Fafnir turned himself into a monstrous dragon to guard the ring-hoard. When the youthful hero Sigurd (above) slew the dragon, he inherited the fabulous ring-hoard, but with it a terrible curse. (WOOD CARVING, 12TH CENTURY.)

SIGURD (right) won the cursed ring, Andvarinaut, after slaying its dragon guardian, Fafnir. Although innocent himself, he suffered from the ring's web of doom. After falling in love with the splendid Valkyrie, Brynhild, he was bewitched by Grimhild into betraying Brynhild by marrying Gudrun. When his memory returned, he suffered from guilt and grief. Sigurd's gold in turn evoked the envy of the Nibelung brothers who slew him, urged on by a vengeful Brynhild, seeking to assuage her honour. As the hero breathed his last, he died calling to Brynhild. (ILLUSTRATION BY ARTHUR RACKHAM, C. 1900.)

THRUD, in Germanic mythology, was the daughter of the thunder god *THOR* and his wife *SIF*. She was promised to the dwarf *ALVIS* as a payment for his handicraft. But Thor prevented the dwarf from claiming Thrud by keeping him talking until morning, when the sunlight turned Alvis into stone.

THRYM, in Germanic mythology, was the frost giant who came to acquire *THOR*'s magic hammer. The gods were at a loss because only this weapon could protect them against the frost giants. When Thrym said he would exchange the hammer for the fertility goddess *FREYJA*, the fire god *LOKI* persuaded Thor to go to the frost giant's stronghold disguised as the bride in order to recover the hammer. Loki also went along in the form of a maidservant. Thus the unusual pair arrived at Thrym's hall. Even though the frost giant was quite suspicious about his bride-to-be, Loki cleverly managed to talk him into producing the hammer, which Thor then used to lay low all the frost giants in sight.

THRYM (*left*), *a daring storm giant, stole Thor's sacred hammer, causing panic at Asgard. Here, the giant broods on his rocky hilltop overlooked by Loki, disguised as a falcon, and scouting the icy wastes in search of the hammer, buried eight fathoms down.* (ILLUSTRATION BY JAMES ALEXANDER, 1995.)

TIR see *TYR*

TIWAZ see *TYR*

TRIGLAV was a three-headed god of the Slavs living in central Europe. At Stettin in present-day Poland, Triglav once boasted four separate temples. These were maintained by war booty, one tenth being the amount due to the god at the end of a campaign. The best temple at Stettin housed a black horse for Triglav's use. In the twelfth century Christianity arrived and Triglav's statues were broken and their multiple heads sent to the Pope in Rome as curiosities.

TUONI was the Finnish god of the dead, who lived in the dark land of Tuonela, from which few travellers return. With his wife Tuonetar he had several children who were deities of suffering, including Kipu-Tytto, goddess of illness. One of the few heroes who managed to escape from Tuonela was *VAINAMOINEN*. After successfully crossing the river that marked the border of Tuonela, he was received there by Tuonetar, who gave him beer to drink. But while her visitor slept, her son created a vast iron mesh across the river so that Vainamoinen could not return that way and would be trapped forever. But when he woke, the hero changed into an otter and swam easily through the net.

TUONI *guarded the dark realm of Tuonela on the banks of a black river. When Vainamoinen visited Tuoni in search of magic charms, he was trapped by a vast iron net, flung across the river; but the hero changed into an otter and slipped through.* (ILLUSTRATION BY NICK BEALE, 1995.)

TYR (left), famed for his bravery and might, was assigned the task of feeding Fenrir, the fierce wolf-son of Loki. Yet Fenrir kept on growing, stronger and fiercer every day, until all-seeing Odin realized the danger and the gods decided to bind the beast underground. (ILLUSTRATION BY J HUARD, 1930.)

TYR (above left), a popular sword god, was invoked before battle, honoured with sword dances, and had his rune engraved on blades. He lost his right hand in a fight with Fenrir, but was just as skilful with his left, and at Ragnarok slew the hell-hound Garm. (ILLUSTRATION BY JAMES ALEXANDER, 1995.)

URD (above), a wise Norn, personified the past, while her sisters represented present and future fate. The Norns warned the gods of future evil and drew lessons from the past. Urd fed two swans on the Urdar pool who gave birth to the swans of the world. (ILLUSTRATION BY JAMES ALEXANDER, 1995.)

TYR, also known as Tiv and Tiwaz, was the Germanic war god, and the son of *ODIN* and his wife *FRIGG*. The Anglo-Saxons usually called him Tiw and gave his name to Tuesday (Tiwesdaeg in Old English). He was closely associated with Odin and, like that god, received sacrifices of hanged men. It is not unlikely that Tyr was an early sky god whose powers were later passed to Odin and Thor. *GUNGNIR*, Odin's magic spear, may once have belonged to Tyr, since it was customary for the Vikings to cast a spear over the heads of an enemy as a sacrifice before fighting commenced in earnest, and over recent years archaeologists have found numerous splendidly ornamented spears dedicated to Tyr.

The myth of Tyr relates to the binding of the wolf *FENRIR*. This monstrous creature had grown so powerful that the gods decided to restrain it. No ordinary chain was strong enough, and before Fenrir would consent to a magic one being placed round his neck, Tyr had to put his hand in the wolf's mouth as a sign of goodwill. When the wolf discovered the chain could not be broken, he bit off Tyr's hand. Although Tyr was in agony, the other gods just laughed. The downgrading of Tyr may not be unconnected with the loss of a hand. A Celtic god by the name of Nuada was forced to give up the leadership of the Irish Tuatha De Danann ("the people of the goddess Dana") after he lost a hand at the first battle of Magh Tuireadh. But Tyr was still able to fight at *RAGNAROK*, during which it was destined that the hound Garm, which stood at the gates of *HEL*, acting as watchdog to the land of the dead, was to leap at Tyr's throat and they would kill each other.

URD, or Wyrd (meaning "Fate" or "Past"), was one of three sisters who were the Germanic fates and were known as the *NORNS*. The two other sisters were Verdandi ("Being" or "Present") and Skuld ("Necessity" or "Future"). Urd gave her name to the well that was situated beneath one of the roots of *YGGDRASIL*, the cosmic tree, and that was where the gods would hold their daily meeting. As was also the case in Greek mythology, the gods were not superior or beyond the influence of the fates. Indeed, Urd warned the chief of the Germanic gods, *ODIN*, that he was destined to be killed by the terrible wolf *FENRIR* at *RAGNAROK*, the doom of the gods.

V

UTGARD ("Outer Place"), in Germanic mythology, was the huge giants' stronghold in *JOTUNHEIM*, where *LOKI*, *THOR* and Thor's servant *THIALFI* found themselves in contests against unequal opponents. Loki failed to consume more food than wildfire; Thialfi could not keep pace as a runner with thought; and Thor was unable to drink the sea dry, pick up the sea serpent *JORMUNGAND* or wrestle old age. When they left, the gods realized that Utgard was an illusion made by the frightened frost giants to deter Thor, their greatest enemy.

VAFTHRUDNIR, in Germanic mythology, was a wise frost giant. He was believed to have gained his impressive store of wisdom by consulting the dead. Possibly like *ODIN*, the chief of the gods, who voluntarily hanged himself for nine nights on *YGGDRASIL*, the cosmic tree, in order to become wise, Vafthrudnir had also temporarily died. Seeking to test his knowledge against the giant's, Odin decided to journey to Vafthrudnir's land in disguise. There he challenged the gigantic "riddle-master" to match their knowledge of the past, the present and the future. After an impressive display on the part of both Odin and Vafthrudnir, the giant was eventually defeated by a quite unanswerable question, when the god asked the giant what he had whispered to his dead son *BALDER* before he lit the pyre on which he lay. It is implied in the story that Odin's foreknowledge allowed him to assure Balder of future resurrection and worship on the new earth, "risen out of the water, fresh and green", after *RAGNAROK*, the doom of the gods and the end of the world.

UTGARD, the icy citadel of the frost giants, was carved out of snow blocks and glittering icicles. The Norse poets, who knew all about the terrors of the ice of their northern homes, inevitably portrayed the evil giants in just such a harsh realm, where numbing cold froze the muscles and paralysed the will. (ILLUSTRATION BY ALAN LEE, 1984.)

Now Vafthrudnir recognized Odin and admitted that no one could tell what the god had whispered into the ear of the dead Balder. The frost giant's last words were: "So I have pitted myself against Odin, always the wisest."

VAFTHRUDNIR spars with Odin in a friendly contest of wits. Ever thirsty for knowledge, Odin had resolved to test the wise frost giant and learn any new snippets of wisdom. Yet, after quizzing each other on every aspect of life and death, Odin emerged as the wisest of the wise.
(ILLUSTRATION BY JAMES ALEXANDER, 1995.)

VAINAMOINEN

VAINAMOINEN, the chief hero of Finnish epic, was the son of a primal goddess, *LUONNOTAR*. He was always depicted as a vigorous and sensitive old man, who from birth possessed the wisdom of the ages, for he was in his mother's womb for at least thirty years. As the champion of the Kalevala (which means "the fatherland of heroes"), Vainamoinen was gifted with extraordinary magical powers. He was less lucky in love, however. When he sought a bride from among the women of Pohja, he was promised one of Louhi's daughters if he made the magic talisman, the Sampo. He gave the task to his comrade Ilmarinen and so Louhi's daughter was married to Ilmarinen instead. But the bride was killed and the magic talisman stolen, so Vainamoinen and Ilmarinen, joined by *LEMINKAINEN*, set off to find the Sampo. After several great adventures, they succeeded in recovering it. However, Louhi raised a great storm and, in the form of a griffin, descended onto their ship. Only the swift action of Vainamoinen saved them, but during the storm the Sampo was lost to the winds. When the storm had passed, Vainamoinen collected all the scattered pieces together and was able to restore some of the talisman's former power. With his mission completed, Vainamoinen built a ship and embarked on an endless voyage. (See also *TREASURES AND TALISMANS*; *SORCERY AND SPELLS*)

VAINAMOINEN (above), a peerless mage, was also a gentle, humane hero. A tireless explorer, he journeyed across the known world and, alone among heroes, returned from the underworld. At the end of his life, he set sail in a copper boat and embarked on a voyage without end. (VAINAMOINEN BY A GALLEN-KALLELA, CANVAS, C. 1890.)

VAINAMOINEN (below) courts reluctant Aino in her father's grove. Promised to the old man against her will by her brother, she drowned herself rather than marry, only to wind up as a salmon on his fishing line, before leaping back into the river and returning to her human form. (THE AINO TRIPTYCH BY A GALLEN-KALLELA, CANVAS, C. 1890.)

The newly fallen joining the residents in Valhalla had to enter by a door called Valgrind ("the sacred barred-gate of the slain"). Even before they reached this entrance, they must pass several obstacles, including a fast-running river of air. Once in Valhalla "the men killed in war" were miraculously cured of their wounds and were able to indulge endlessly in the pleasures of feasting and fighting. The meat of a magic boar was prepared as wonderful stew in an inexhaustible cauldron. The same boar was eaten day after day through a process of resurrection. Mead was provided from the teats of a goat. It was said that every day the Einherjar put on their armour, went to the practice ground and fought each other. If killed, they were restored to life. At midday they returned to Valhalla and started drinking. Such an existence for a Viking helps to explain Odin's popularity in Denmark, southern Norway and Sweden, the regions where most of the raiding expeditions came from.

VALHALLA'S Valkyries – beautiful battle-maidens – welcomed the chosen slain with open arms. At other times, Odin's sons, Hermod or Bragi, received the heroes, conducting them to the foot of Odin's throne; while Odin himself rose to greet the bravest Vikings at the gate. (ILLUSTRATION BY E WALLCOUSINS, C. 1920.)

VALHALLA was a Viking's paradise where chosen heroes fought and feasted from dawn to dusk. Wounds healed overnight, and mead and meat flowed freely. The hectic round of combat ensured that heroes stayed in fighting form, fit for the final battle at Ragnarok. (ILLUSTRATION BY W B DRACK, 1900.)

VALHALLA (above), the Hall of the Slain, was built in the shimmering grove of Glesir. Encircled by strong outer walls, the magnificent hall glittered with precious metals, its walls were built of spears and its roof of shining shields. This starlit scene evokes a sense of the untold wonders that lie within. (ILLUSTRATION BY F VON STASSEN, 1914.)

VALHALLA, or Valholl, in Germanic mythology, was the hall of the *EINHERJAR* ("heroic dead"), those warriors slain on the battlefield and chosen by *ODIN* himself as his followers. Built in *ASGARD* by Odin, Valhalla was enormous. It had over five hundred doors, each wide enough to allow up to eight hundred men to march through abreast. These wide doors were designed to allow the chosen warriors to pour forth at the first sign of *RAGNAROK*, the doom of the gods. Then they were destined to fall again, alongside the gods, in a great battle on the *VIGRID* Plain.

Odin was known as the father of the slain and he was the host who presided over Valhalla, and daily sent out the VALKYRIES to add to the number of the dead. In Valhalla the Valkyries would carry food and drinks for the Einherjar.

Ragnarok was always given as the reason for creating Valhalla. When asked about his habit of giving luck to a warrior in a battle and then suddenly taking it away, Odin said that "the grey wolf watches the halls of the gods": that is to say, the gods were constantly threatened by Ragnarok, the catastrophe in which they would die in mutual destruction with the frost giants and the forces of evil. The gathering of the "heroic dead" in Valhalla was the only way the gods could prepare to face their own fate, no matter how vain the attempt would prove to be. At least Odin's men, caught up in a berserk fury, could be guaranteed to tear into the enemy ranks in one last battle. (See also THE VALKYRIES)

VALHOLL see VALHALLA

VALI was one of the few bright young gods to survive Ragnarok. Destined from birth to avenge Balder's death, he grew at an amazing rate, reaching manhood in a single day and rushing off with uncombed hair to slay Hodr. Here, he is portrayed striding across the new earth after Ragnarok. (ILLUSTRATION BY NICK BEALE, 1995.)

VALI was the son of *ODIN* and *RIND* and was destined to kill blind *HODR* in revenge for his unwitting murder of *BALDER*. Fulfilling a prophecy, he grew from a baby to manhood in a single day and rushed off to kill Hodr. Along with his half-brother *VIDAR*, he survived *RAGNAROK*. Another Vali was one of the unlucky sons of *LOKI*.

THE VALKYRIES ("female choosers of the slain") were *ODIN*'s battle- or shield-maidens. They rode over battlefields and selected the *EINHERJAR* ("heroic dead") who would go to *VALHALLA*. They probably derived from something more dreadful than the attendants of Valhalla, and must have originally been the goddesses of slaughter itself, wild Amazon-like creatures who took great delight in the severed limbs and bloody wounds of battle. Something of this early terror can be imagined in an account of the battle of Stamford Bridge, King Harold's victory over the Norwegians shortly before his defeat by the Normans at Battle in 1066. A soldier in the Norwegian army dreamt of a Valkyrie before the battle. He thought he was on the king of Norway's ship, when he beheld a great witch on an island, with a fork in one hand to rake up the dead and a trough in the other to catch the blood. (See also *THE VALKYRIES; RAGNAROK*)

VALKYRIES (above), Odin's martial maidens, alighted on the battlefield to select the bravest warriors for Valhalla, the idyllic abode of Odin's ghostly army. Although quite charming in Valhalla, on the battlefield the Valkyries became sinister spirits of slaughter, goading heroes to their death. (THE VALKYRIES BY G VON LEEKE, 1870.)

VALKYRIES (below) rode through the stormy sky on magnificent pearly steeds, personifying clouds, and whose soaking manes sprayed the earth with fertile frost and dew. They also scoured the seas, snatching sailors from ships, or sometimes beckoning from the strand. (THE RIDE OF THE VALKYRIE BY H HERMAN, CANVAS, C. 1890.)

RAGNAROK

RAGNAROK WAS THE preordained doom of the gods, and the climax of the cosmic drama. The seeds of doom were sown at the dawn of time when the world and its first creatures emerged from the violent extremes of ice and fire. Inherently fragile, the universe was beset by forces of destruction and flawed from the outset. The inevitable climax was precipitated by a series of disasters. Loki, a catalyst of evil, spawned three fearsome monsters against whom the gods were ultimately powerless. Consumed with hate, Loki went on to slay Balder, symbol of goodness and beauty. Beyond Asgard, the enmity of the hostile giants gathered momentum until, at Ragnarok, all the world's destructive forces burst forth in cataclysmic disaster. Apocalypse is a common mythical theme, but the Norse vision is starker than most and unique in the loss of its gods. In one hopeful version, some gods survive and the earth emerges fresh and green, purged by flood and fire. Ragnarok casts a dark shadow over the Norse myths, yet also highlights the heroism of gods and heroes.

LOKI (left), ever envious of anyone who was good and beautiful, guided blind Hodr to slay his brother, Balder, with a dart of mistletoe. The wanton destruction of the best of the gods marked a turning-point in Loki's downward spiral of evil. Yet even after the crime, the gods allowed Loki to roam unrestrained, growing ever more bitter and twisted. (LOKI AND HODR BY C QVARNSTROM, MARBLE, C. 1890.)

THE MIGHT OF THOR (above) and his hammer, Mjollnir, symbolized the foremost defence of the gods against the threat of the giants and the doom of Ragnarok. Yet Thor's sustained might proved ultimately inadequate to withstand the combined onslaught of giants and monsters. At the end, however, Thor rid the world of the giant monster, Jormungand, before dying himself from its venom. (THOR BY B FOGELBERG, MARBLE, C. 1890.)

JORMUNGAND (above) was one of the evils threatening the survival of the Norse world. Along with his monster siblings, Fenrir and Hel, Jormungand epitomized darkness and destruction. The massive serpent lurked in the ocean depths, circling the world in a stranglehold. Coiled in upon itself, this striking snake motif recalls the World Serpent curled around Midgard with its tail in its mouth, until it burst forth at Ragnarok. (BROOCH, 7TH CENTURY.)

LOKI (above) gate-crashes Aegir's feast and ridicules the gods with his sardonic wit, undermining and humiliating each in turn. None can either match or silence him, until Thor enters and threatens Loki with his hammer. Odin, at the right, looks on in speechless sorrow, recognizing the signs of Ragnarok. (AEGIR'S FEAST BY C HANSEN, CANVAS, C. 1861.)

ODIN (left), despite all his wisdom and power, was powerless to prevent the imminent doom of the gods. Yet he tried everything to fend off the fateful moment. Here, he carves magic runes on his spear, setting out rules of conduct for giants and dwarfs, gods and mortals. Odin learnt the wisdom of the runes from the dead when hanging from the sacred Yggdrasil in voluntary self-sacrifice. He also paid for wisdom with one eye at Mimir's well. Yet all his spies and sources only reinforce his own foreknowledge of doom. (ILLUSTRATION BY F VON STASSEN, 1914.)

AT RAGNAROK (above) the mighty walls of Asgard, home of the Aesir gods, were destroyed and the heavenly Bifrost Bridge was set alight by Surt, the fearsome flame giant. Jormungand, the gigantic World Serpent, burst from the seething ocean and engulfed the Vigrid Plain, spewing venom in all directions. Fenrir broke his bonds and roamed the earth with his savage brood, spreading death and destruction. The wolves swallowed the sun and moon, and even Yggdrasil itself shuddered. Over the whirling seas, Loki sailed with his giant host, while his daughter Hel rose from misty Niflheim with her pale army of the dead, and the assembled host issued forth over the Vigrid Plain. At the very end, Surt set all the nine worlds ablaze and the earth sank beneath the boiling ocean. (ILLUSTRATION BY ALAN LEE, 1984.)

THE VALKYRIES (left), Odin's formidable martial shield-maidens, gathered up the heroic slain from the battlefield and ferried them to Valhalla where they kept in fighting form until Ragnarok. By raising a heroic army, Odin determined to put up a fighting stand against the enemy host at Ragnarok. (THE RIDE OF THE VALKYRIES ANON.)

THE VANIR were the older of the two branches of the Germanic family of gods and were fertility deities. They lived at Vanaheim, far from *ASGARD*, the fortified residence of the *AESIR*, the younger branch, who were primarily war gods. Myth relates how the Vanir and the Aesir fought for supremacy not long after creation. After the Aesir had won, peace was sealed by an exchange of gods and goddesses. The Vanir sent to Asgard the sea god *NJORD* and his twin son and daughter *FREYR* and *FREYJA*, and also *KVASIR*, who was believed to be second to none in his wisdom. The Aesir despatched to Vanaheim long-legged *HONIR* and wise *MIMIR*.

At first Honir and Mimir were welcomed and accepted by the Vanir, but the gods gradually came to the conclusion that they had got the worst of the exchange with the Aesir. The problem was the terrible indecisiveness of Honir, which reached embarrassing proportions whenever Mimir was absent. To the Vanir it seemed that Mimir was not only Honir's voice but also his brain, so in anger they cut off Mimir's head and sent it back to Asgard. Although this did not rekindle the conflict, it effectively caused a rift between the Aesir and the Vanir which greatly reduced the mythological significance of the Vanir, so they slowly faded into the background.

The distinction between the older Vanir and the younger Aesir was uncertain even in Viking times. When the sagas were collected in the late twelfth century, there was speculation about the origins of the two groups. The Icelander Snorri Sturluson thought that the name of the Aesir recalled their homeland in Asia, and that *THOR* was the grandson of King Priam of Troy and *ODIN* his descendant in the twentieth generation, while the Vanir were originally inhabitants of the land by the River Don, formerly called Vanaquisl. Today, however, these theories have been discounted.

THE VANIR, deities of fertility, wealth and health, were worshipped by farmers. The three main Vanir gods, Njord (centre) and his lovely twins, Freyja and Freyr, were all gentle, benign spirits of nature, who nourished the earth and seas, and granted fair weather and good harvests. (ILLUSTRATION BY JAMES ALEXANDER, 1995.)

VE, in Germanic mythology, was one of the sons of *BOR* and the brother of *ODIN* and *VILI*. At the beginning of creation the primeval cow *AUDHUMLA* sustained herself by licking the ice and from her ample teats flowed enough milk to feed the frost giant *YMIR*, the first living creature. He is described as being utterly evil. However, Audhumla's licking also uncovered *BURI*, the grand-father of Ve. All the gods were descended from Buri, because his son Bor married the frost giantess Bestla and had three sons – Odin, Vili and Ve.

Although the blood of the frost giants and the gods intermingled, the implacable enmity between them could not be denied or resolved, for it went right back to the killing of Ymir. Odin, Vili and Ve disliked Ymir and his growing band of frost giants. Eventually, their dislike turned to hatred and they slew Ymir, making the world in *GINNUNGAGAP* (the "yawning emptiness") from the giant's body.

Afterwards the three brothers found on the seashore two fallen trees, an ash and an elm. From the wood they made first man and then woman. Odin breathed into them the spirit of life; Vili gave them intelligence and emotion; and Ve added the ability to see and hear. In some versions of the creation myth, Ve is known as Lodur or Lothur.

THE VANIR were famed for magic and foresight of which the macho Aesir were a little suspicious, except for Odin who, ever eager to increase his knowledge, rapidly absorbed the Vanir arts. Here, the fruitful Vanir twins follow Odin and Frigg over the Bifrost Bridge, with Thor and Loki in the rear. (ILLUSTRATION BY F VON STASSEN, 1914.)

VIDAR *(above), a strong, silent and solitary god, lived alone in a leafy palace deep in his primal forest. He personified the imperishable forces of nature, and was one of the few gods destined to survive Ragnarok. He slew the wolf Fenrir with his iron-shod foot.*
(ILLUSTRATION BY NICK BEALE, 1995.)

VE *(above) and his brothers, Vili and Odin, fashioned human forms from two pieces of driftwood lying on the cosmic beach at the dawn of time. Odin created a man from the ash, while his younger brothers formed a woman from the elm, and then Odin breathed life into them.*
(ILLUSTRATION BY JAMES ALEXANDER, 1995.)

VELES *guarded cattle and flocks for the Slavs. Especially popular with farmers, he survived into the nineteenth century, when Russian farmers still honoured him in the harvest fields by curling the ears of one sheaf of corn (see right), symbolizing the god's curly hair and beard.*
(ILLUSTRATION BY NICK BEALE, 1995.)

VELES, or Volos, was the Russian god who had authority over flocks and herds. It was customary to swear oaths in the names of Veles and *PERUNU*, who was the thunder god. When Vladimir, ruler of Kiev, was baptized into the Orthodox faith in 988, he had a statue of Veles thrown into the River Dniepner. In Russian folklore, however, the god of flocks survives. For instance, at harvest time the ears of the last sheaf of corn are still woven into a plait known as "Veles' beard". Also in Russian Orthodox tradition, Veles was incorporated into the Christian faith by identifying him with St Blasius, who was a shepherd and martyr from Cappadocia. Prayers offered to this saint are expected to protect and increase flocks of sheep and goats.

VIDAR was the silent and solitary god of Germanic mythology. He was the son of *ODIN* and the frost giantess *GRID*, and lived in a place called Vidi, where all was quiet and peaceful. It was Vidar's destiny to avenge his father's death at *RAGNAROK*, the doom of the gods and the end of the world. When the terrible wolf *FENRIR* had overcome Odin in a fierce and bloody struggle and swallowed him, Vidar stepped forward, smashed one of his well-shod feet against the wolf's lower jaw, and then with both hands he forced the upper jaw open till the ravenous beast's throat was torn asunder. It is more than likely that the meaning of Vidar's own name refers in some way to this ripping in half of evil.

W

VIGRID, in Germanic mythology, was the name of a plain that was destined to be the scene of the final conflict between the gods and the frost giants. There at *RAGNAROK* the two sides and their allies would engage in mutual destruction. A huge expanse of land, Vigrid was said to stretch 120 leagues in every direction. Even so, it was predicted that the assembled hosts would cover it completely.

VILI, in Germanic mythology, was the son of *BOR* and Bestla and the brother of *ODIN* and *VE*. At the beginning of creation he helped his brothers to slay the frost giant *YMIR* and form the world from his carcass. When they later created the first man and woman from wood, Vili's contribution was sharp wits and feeling hearts. Odin gave them the breath of life, while Ve added the powers of sight and hearing. In one Icelandic poem Vili is given the name *HONIR*.

VLKODLAK was the Slavic wolfman. More a figure of folklore than mythology, he exists because of the ancient respect accorded to the ravenous wolf, which in the forests of northern and eastern Europe was the animal most feared. According to Germanic mythology, the chief god *ODIN* was destined to be killed by the wolf *FENRIR* at *RAGNAROK*, the doom of the gods.

VOLOS see *VELES*

VOLSUNG was the subject of a late Germanic myth. He was said to be a descendant of *ODIN*. When Signy, Volsung's only daughter, was married against her will to the Gothic king Siggeir, a one-eyed stranger appeared among the wedding guests. It was Odin, chief of the Germanic gods. He stuck a sword deep into an oak and told the company that the weapon would belong to the man who pulled it out. Whoever wielded the sword could never be defeated.

THE VIGRID PLAIN (above) was mapped out as the battlefield of Ragnarok. When Heimdall sounded the call to battle, the warring hosts converged from all corners of the earth; gods and heroes poured over the Bifrost Bridge, while Loki and the fiery host swarmed in from the swirling seas.
(ILLUSTRATION BY JAMES ALEXANDER, 1995.)

Out of courtesy Volsung invited his son-in-law Siggeir to try his luck first. But Siggeir did not succeed. Nor was anyone else able to pull out the sword, except the youngest of Volsung's sons, Sigmund. When Siggeir offered to buy the magic weapon, Sigmund refused to part with it at any price.

This refusal made the Gothic king really angry. Despite Signy's

VOLSUNG's (below) great hall, built around a sacred oak, was the scene of a magical event when Odin appeared one night and thrust a sword, hilt-deep, into the great oak. He challenged the heroes to pull it out, offering the divine gift to the winner. Sigmund was the much-envied champion.
(ILLUSTRATION BY ALAN LEE, 1984.)

warning, Volsung and his ten sons walked into Siggeir's trap when they accepted an invitation to visit his court. They were ambushed on the way and left in the forest, bound to a fallen tree. Each night a wolf came and ate one of them, until only Sigmund was left alive. Signy succeeded in rescuing him.

As a result, Siggeir wrongly believed that no one had escaped the attentions of the wolf. He relaxed his guard and Signy was able to bury her family and help Sigmund. It took a long time to prepare a revenge, however. First of all Signy tried to have her own sons trained by Sigmund, but they lacked courage. A second attempt to reinforce her brother involved incest. Without his knowledge, Signy slept with him and bore Sinfiotli, a warrior with double Volsung blood. When Sinfiotli grew up, Signy sent him to her brother to be trained as a warrior.

Although Sigmund and Sinfiotli were captured by Siggeir, the magic sword secured their release and allowed them to take revenge on the king and his sons. Afterwards Sigmund returned home, and had another son, *SIGURD*, known in German legend as Siegfried.

VOLUND see *WAYLAND*

WAYLAND was the smith god of the Anglo-Saxons. The son of a sailor and a mermaid, he was renowned for making coats of mail and swords. In Scandinavia he was known as Volund, or Volundr, and in Germany as Wielund.

Wayland's myth is a story of revenge. King Nidud of Sweden cut Wayland's leg sinews and placed him and his forge on a remote island. The smith god avenged this mutilation by killing Nidud's two sons, who came to see his treasures, and sending their heads studded with precious jewels and mounted on silver to King Nidud. He may also have raped Nidud's daughter, but this is not certain.

WAYLAND's (above) smithy was visited not just by warriors seeking arms, but by noblewomen wanting dainty trinkets of purest gold. Wayland was also a craftsman on the grand scale, designing a fabulous Icelandic maze, known as Volund's House. (WHALEBONE CARVING, 8TH CENTURY.)

WAYLAND (below), captive on a desolate island, laboured in his underground forge, fashioning wondrous ornaments and weapons for his oppressive master, Nidud of Sweden. Like Daedalus, Wayland fashioned wings and flew away to freedom. (WIELAND BY MAX KOCH, WATERCOLOUR, 1904.)

WAYLAND (above right) and his brothers chanced upon three Valkyries bathing in a lake. They took their plumage left on the bank and kept them on earth for nine years, until they escaped. Fashioning wings for himself, Wayland flew after his wife, Alvit, to Alfheim. (ILLUSTRATION BY H THEAKER, 1900.)

Afterwards Wayland is said to have flown to *VALHALLA*, like the Greek inventor Daedalus, on wings he had made for himself. Near Uffington in Wiltshire, a long barrow has ancient associations with Wayland, and is locally known as his smithy. His lameness parallels that of Hephaistos, the Greek smith god whose injury had two different explanations. In one version it was claimed that his limp was the result of his having interfered in a violent quarrel between his parents, Zeus and Hera. So annoyed did Zeus become that he flung his son out of Olympus and let him fall heavily on the island of Lemnos. A second explanation tells how Hephaistos was born a dwarfish figure with a limp. Hera even tried to drown him, but he was saved by sea nymphs. The latter version of the myth is most relevant to Wayland. In Germanic mythology the master craftsmen were mainly dwarfs, and Wayland's own mother was a mermaid. It is interesting to note that Lemnos was an island with volcanic activity, like the remote island to which Wayland had been banished.

WIELAND see *WAYLAND*

WODEN see *ODIN*

WOTAN see *ODIN*

Y

YGGDRASIL, or Yggdrasill, (which means something like "dreadful mount") was the cosmic ash tree in Germanic mythology. Its name is a reference either to the gallows or ODIN's horse. Not only did Odin hang himself on Yggdrasil for nine nights in order to learn wisdom, but sacrificial hangings from gallows trees were also a favourite Viking way of worshipping the god. An archaeological find that reveals the extent of this ghastly ritual is the Tollund Man, found in a Jutland peat bog in 1950. The corpse was so well preserved that it was possible to deduce that he was a prisoner of war who had been sacrificed as a thank-offering after a battle.

The parallel between Odin's voluntary death on Yggdrasil and

YGGDRASIL (right) the World Tree, lay at the heart of the universe. Here, the whirling patterns of Viking art strikingly capture the swirling vitality at the centre of life. A stag browses on its evergreen foliage while a serpent nips the stag's neck, reflecting the life and death struggle at the root of life.
(WOOD CARVING, 8TH CENTURY.)

YMIR (below) was the first creature to emerge from the primal wastes of ice in the yawning abyss of Ginnungagap at the dawn of creation. As fire from the south melted ice from the north, the icy droplets fused to form a massive frost giant. As he slept, his sweat formed other frost giants.
(ILLUSTRATION BY NICK BEALE, 1995.)

the Crucifixion remains striking. Odin was also pierced with a spear and, like Christ, cried out before he died. Although it is possible that the Crucifixion was known at the time that the Odin myth was recorded, there is little doubt that his hanging on the cosmic tree had pre-Christian origins and derived from ancient pagan worship. Odin had long been the god of the spear, the god of the hanged.

Yggdrasil is described as the largest and most stately tree ever to have grown. Its branches overhung the nine worlds and spread out above the heavens. It was supported by three great roots: one descended to JOTUNHEIM, the land of the giants, where MIMIR's well stood; the second ended in foggy Niflheim, close by the spring of Hvergelmir, where the dragon NIDHOGG gnawed the root from below whenever it tired of chewing corpses; the last root was embedded near ASGARD, the stronghold of the gods, beneath URD's well, where the gods held their daily assembly. Water was taken from the well each day by the NORNS, the three fates, Urd, Skuld and Verdandi, and mixed with earth as a means of preventing Yggdrasil's bark from rotting. An eagle perched on the very top of the cosmic tree was daily harassed by a squirrel named Ratatosk, who brought unpleasant comments and insults up from the dragon Nidhogg. Another bird in its branches was a cock, sometimes referred to as "Vidofnir the tree snake".

The idea of a cosmic tree is common in the myths of the northern parts of both Europe and Asia. It was thought of as the backbone of the universe, the structural support of the nine worlds. In Ireland, however, the sacred tree acquired a different role. Although always associated with otherworld splendour, the musical branches of Irish mythology acted as cures for

YGGDRASIL's mighty limbs held up the nine worlds of the Norsemen. Seen here (above) are the three highest realms of gods and light elves, lying under the rainbow bridge; next, the worlds of mortals, dwarfs and dark elves rise from the ocean, with the frost giants' land at the icy edge.

(ILLUSTRATION FROM NORTHERN ANTIQUITIES, 1847.)

YGGDRASIL (right) filled the known world, taking root not only in the dark depths of NIFLHEIM (bottom), but also in Midgard and Asgard. Its topmost boughs reached heaven, while its lowest root touched hell. It was generally thought of as the structural support of the universe.

(ILLUSTRATION BY ALAN LEE, 1984.)

sickness and despair. In a number of tales these magic branches of silver or gold were brought by messengers from otherworld lands. Thus the fabulous voyage of Bran began with the sound of music that caused him to fall asleep. It came from a branch of silver with white blossoms, which a beautiful lady took away after telling of the delights of her world beyond the sea. Hints of such magic are also present in Germanic mythology. The obvious example must be the apples belonging to the goddess *IDUN*. Only this magic fruit prevented the gods from growing old. They were clearly the gift from

another sacred tree. How much trees were once revered can be seen from the reactions to early Christian missionaries like St Boniface. In the eighth century he cut down sacrificial trees, to the terror of the Frisians, until he himself was felled at Dockum by an outraged pagan.

YGGDRASILL see *YGGDRASIL*

YMIR, in Germanic mythology, was the first living creature. He was a frost giant who emerged from the ice in *GINNUNGAGAP* ("the yawning emptiness"). He was evil and the father and mother of all frost giants, who first came from the sweat of

his armpit. Ymir fed on the milk of the primeval cow *AUDHUMLA*. He was slain by the brothers *ODIN*, *VILI* and *VE*, who were the grandsons of *BURI*, whom Audhumla had licked free of the ice.

Growing tired of the brutality of Ymir and his ever-increasing band of frost giants, Odin, Vili and Ve took up arms. They slew Ymir and then drowned all the frost giants in his blood, with the exception of *BERGELMIR* and his wife, who managed to escape by sailing on a hollowed tree trunk.

Odin, Vili and Ve then threw Ymir's carcass into Ginnungagap. His flesh became the earth, his

unbroken bones mountains, his teeth and jaw rocks and boulders, his blood rivers, lakes and the sea, and his skull the sky, which was held up at its four corners by dwarfs. Sparks were used to make the sun, the moon and the stars.

Such an extremely violent creation myth is by no means unique. The Babylonian champion of the gods, Marduk, slew the chaos-dragon Tiamat with raging winds and an arrow, before splitting her carcass into two parts. One he pushed upwards to form the heavens, the other he used to make a floor above the deep, the emptiness at the bottom of the universe.

THE MYTHS OF EGYPT AND WEST ASIA

INTRODUCTION

THE ANCIENT MIDDLE EAST, the so-called "cradle of civilization", was the birthplace of Judaism, Islam and Christianity, the three faiths that came to have such an immense impact on human culture and, by tradition, originated amongst the descendants of Shem, one of the sons of Noah. Zoroastrianism, probably the most powerful religion of its time, also arose in the Middle East, whereas the wider area of West Asia witnessed the rise of the powerful Egyptian and Hittite empires.

What was it about this region that enabled it to bear witness to such remarkable achievements? One answer at least lies in the geography of the area: it was here that crop farming first began, and with it the beginnings of a settled, civilized way of life, which proceeded to bear rich cultural fruits.

The annual flooding of the Nile inspired many of the myths of ancient Egypt. The people there depended on the revival of the parched land for their livelihood, a concern that was reflected in the myth of Osiris, their dying-and-rising vegetation god, who finally retired from life to rule over the underworld. A preoccupation with death haunts Egyptian mythology, prompted by this sense of man's vulnerability in the face of forces beyond his control. Even the great sun god, Ra, was believed to die each evening and be born again at dawn.

It was on the fertile land produced by the Nile's annual floodings that Egypt's first city states grew up, each with its own gods. Eventually, around 3100BC, these separate states were unified under a succession of pharaohs. Many of the local gods were admitted into the national pantheon, giving

SYMBOLIZING the divine relationship between pharaohs and the gods, Horemheb, the last Egyptian pharaoh of the 18th dynasty, sits beside the god Horus, son of Isis and Osiris. (C. 1320BC.)

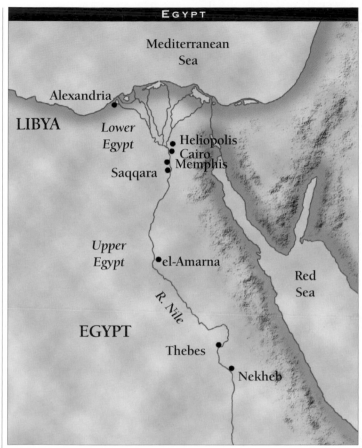

EGYPT

Mediterranean
Sea

Alexandria

LIBYA   Lower
Egypt   Heliopolis
           Cairo
Saqqara   Memphis

Upper
Egypt   •el-Amarna

Red
Sea

R. Nile

EGYPT

Thebes

Nekheb

featured dying and rising gods. The Mesopotamians' existence was, however, much more precarious than that of the Egyptians. Not only could the flooding of their rivers be sudden and unpredictable, but the people were also under constant threat from marauding tribes and foreign invaders. Their myths, therefore, tended to portray life as a constant battle against the forces of chaos.

Despite its political instability, ancient Mesopotamia produced an extensive written literature. As a result, the Mesopotamian deities and myths were transmitted to other West Asian peoples, including the Assyrians and Hittites. The Hittites, who originally hailed from Anatolia, came to be known in the Old Testament as one of the peoples occupying Canaan, the promised land of the Israelites. Many of the ancestors of the Israelites had themselves migrated from Mesopotamia to Canaan soon after 2000BC; some of them continued into Egypt where, at a date which is uncertain, they were taken into slavery by a pharaoh. However, in the

BAAL, an ancient fertility god, is a dying and rising god whose actions symbolized the growth and decay of vegetation. (BRONZE AGE, 1400–1300BC.)

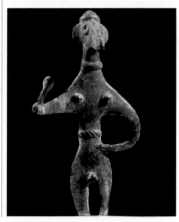

rise to a vast and splendid array of deities who flourished virtually unopposed by alien beliefs. Seen as divinely appointed mediators between the world of men and the gods, the pharaohs gave a political and religious focus to Egyptian civilization and culture. Their power was such that it came to extend into Canaan and Syria. However, in about 1387BC the pharaoh Akhenaten instigated vast religious reforms, which, though eventually overturned when he died, began to weaken Egyptian power.

Like the Egyptians, the Mesopotamian settlers were attracted to the rich land left by the flooding of rivers. The Sumerians, a non-Semitic people (not descended from Shem), had settled in Mesopotamia, the area lying between the rivers Tigris and Euphrates, around 4000BC. Some 2,000 years later, Babylon was made the region's capital and Sumer was gradually absorbed into Babylonia. The livelihood of these Mesopotamians, like that of the Egyptians, depended on the agricultural cycle, and their pantheon likewise

MOSES delivered the tribes of Israel from slavery in Egypt and led them through the desert to freedom. Here he strikes the rock to produce water. (19TH CENTURY ENGRAVING.)

13th century BC, Moses led the Israelites out of slavery in Egypt and back towards Canaan. On this journey, they made a solemn promise to worship only one god – Yahweh.

The Canaanite pantheon, which the Israelites encountered at the end of their journey, was dominated by the god of rain, fertility and storms, Baal. Many other gods also went under this name, which translates as "Lord", but the chief Baal was a warlike dying and rising god. His attributes reflected the Canaanite way of life which, like that of all the other peoples of the region, was closely bound up with the agricultural cycle.

As the tribes settled in Canaan, they united in their worship of Yahweh, who became the supreme god, although rites associated with

ZOROASTER, the great religious reformer of ancient Iran, receives fire and the law of reform, which is brought to him by Ahura Mazda, the principle of good. At the age of 30, Zoroaster received numerous revelations from the Amesa Spentas, or holy immortals. (19TH CENTURY ILLUSTRATION.)

other gods persisted for some time. The followers of the new faith were based around Jerusalem. In 587BC, the city was conquered by the Babylonians, and the leading Israelites were taken into exile in Babylon. Nearly 50 years later, the Achaemenids of Iran, whom the Greeks called Persians, conquered Babylon in turn.

The Persian conquerors introduced the Babylonians to their Zoroastrian faith, which, though often loosely adhered to, saw the world as in the grip of the forces of good and evil. Zoroaster, who founded the religion and who is now believed to have lived around 1200BC, had preached of his vision of a single, supreme god. Faced with encroaching monotheism, and sometimes directly overthrown, the Mesopotamian gods finally began to lose their power. In 525BC the Persians also occupied Egypt. Since the pharaoh Akhenaten had tried to bring about religious reform back in 1367BC, the country had never quite recovered its harmony or strength, and its glorious pantheon of gods was becoming increasingly threatened by outside beliefs.

Monotheism, as preached by both the Israelites and the Zoroastrians, was thus beginning to threaten the vast and dramatic array of gods and goddesses until then prevalent across West Asia, and the region was to see yet more turmoil. Over the following centuries it was overrun by the Greeks and Romans. However, Cybele, the great mother goddess of Asia Minor, Isis, the great mother goddess of Egypt, and Mithra, originally an ancient Iranian sun god, all arrived in Rome. There they became the focus of mystery cults, which flourished in the early centuries of the Christian era. When many of the old gods of West Asia were losing their power, these ancient deities were believed to renew the spirit and put their devotees in touch with the divine.

Monotheism eventually triumphed in West Asia. By the time the prophet Muhammad was born, around AD 570, Judaism and later Christianity had already spread throughout the region, and had also encroached on the Arabian peninsula. With the arrival of the strictly monotheistic Islam, the days of the old gods were numbered.

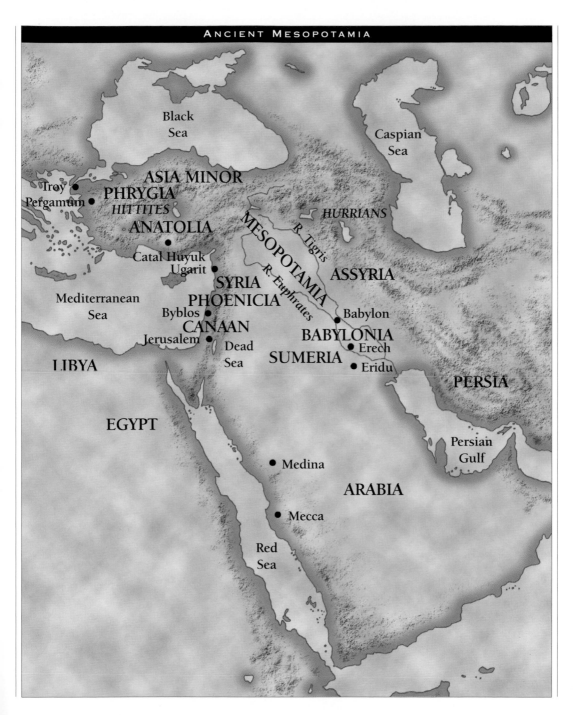

ANCIENT MESOPOTAMIA

Black
Sea

Caspian
Sea

ASIA MINOR

Troy
Pergamum

PHRYGIA

HITTITES

HURRIANS

ANATOLIA

MESOPOTAMIA

R. Tigris

Catal Huyuk

Ugarit

ASSYRIA

SYRIA

R. Euphrates

Mediterranean
Sea

PHOENICIA

Byblos

Babylon

CANAAN

Jerusalem

BABYLONIA

Dead
Sea

Erech

LIBYA

SUMERIA

Eridu

PERSIA

EGYPT

Persian
Gulf

Medina

ARABIA

Mecca

Red
Sea

A

ABRAHAM, whose name means "Father of a Multitude", is a major character in the Old Testament, and is referred to in the earliest sources simply as "the Hebrew". The founder of the Hebrew people, he was the first patriarch, the husband of Sarah and the father of Isaac. He lived around 2000–1800 BC and was a devout believer of and subservient to God, representing an ideal for Hebrews to emulate. In Islam, Abraham, or Ibrahim, is known as the "Friend of God". He is regarded as the propagator of the original pure monotheism, the "religion of Abraham", which was restored and perfected by the Prophet Muhammad. Abraham is also said to have rebuilt the *KA'ABA*, the sacred shrine at Mecca, after it had been destroyed by the flood.

ABRAHAM (below), the father of the Israelite tribes, prepares to sacrifice his son, Isaac. (STAINED GLASS, ENGLAND.)

ABRAHAM (above) is known in Islam as Ibrahim, the "Friend of God". His son, Isaac, bears wood for the fire on which he is to be sacrificed. (19TH CENTURY ENGRAVING.)

ABZU see *APSU*.

ADAD was the Akkadian-Babylonian god of the wind, rain and thunder. He was usually said to be the son of *ANU*, and he was one of the deities who inflicted a deluge on humanity. However, he also brought helpful winds and rain and caused the annual flooding of the rivers, thereby bringing fertility to the land. As a result, Adad was often referred to as "Lord of Abundance". He could also see into the future. Adad was often represented standing on a bull and holding thunderbolts or lightning flashes in each hand.

ADAD (right), stands on the back of a bull, holding a bundle of thunderbolts in his hand. He is the Akkadian-Babylonian god of wind and rain. (NEO-ASSYRIAN BASALT RELIEF ON A STELE, 8TH CENTURY BC.)

ADAM, according to the Old Testament story, was the first man. God made him from dust and gave him a beautiful garden in which to live. Everything in the garden belonged to Adam, except for the fruit of one tree. Together with his consort *EVE*, Adam ate the forbidden fruit. As a result, the couple immediately lost their innocence and incurred the wrath of God. They were thrown out of the garden and had to work to survive.

According to the Jewish mystical system known as the Kabbalah, Adam both symbolized and embraced cosmic perfection. With Adam's fall, the material world was created and the light of his divine nature was broken up into countless minute sparks. These sparks are the lights that illuminate human souls. At the end of time, they will be reunited into perfection once more. (See also *SERPENTS AND DRAGONS*)

ADAPA, a wise man of Babylonian mythology, was created by the great god *EA* in order to be his priest in the holy city of Eridu and to rule over the people. Ea gave Adapa numerous good qualities, including wisdom and prudence, but did not make him immortal. Adapa spent much of his time fishing in the waters of the Persian Gulf.

One day, the south wind blew so strongly that it overturned his boat, sending him plunging into the depths. Adapa was furious and cursed the wind, causing it to cease blowing. Hearing what had happened, the supreme god *ANU* grew troubled that a mere mortal should have so much power. He summoned Adapa to his court and planned to send him to the land of the dead by giving him the food of death.

Ea, however, heard of Anu's plot and warned Adapa to accept no food or drink from the supreme god. Ea also told Adapa how to placate both Anu and the deities who lived with him. Adapa followed

ADAM and EVE were tempted by the serpent to eat the forbidden fruit. God banished them from the garden, and they had to work. (SPANISH SCHOOL, 12TH CENTURY.)

Ea's advice so punctiliously that Anu, rather than offering the food of death, offered him the food of life. However, Adapa remembered Ea's warning and refused the food, thereby losing his chance of becoming immortal.

Adapa, who was also credited with having invented speech, laid the foundations of civilized life.

ADONIS was a Phoenician deity who was later assimilated into the Greek pantheon. His name comes from the Semitic word *adoni*, meaning "My Lord, My Master". His worship was prevalent throughout Phoenicia, but it was most fervent in the city of Byblos, where his greatest temple stood.

Adonis symbolizes vegetation scorched by the heat of the summer sunshine. According to Greek legend, he was born from a myrtle or myrrh tree. His mother, Myrrha, had been changed into the tree by the gods who had sought to protect her from the wrath of her father, the king. Unbeknown to the king, Myrrha had seduced him and had conceived a child. Soon after Adonis was born, Aphrodite, the goddess of love, discovered the

young deity. She hid him in a chest which she gave for safekeeping to Persephone, the goddess of the underworld. However, Persephone opened the chest and was so struck with the beauty of the child that she decided to keep him. Aphrodite appealed to Zeus, who decided that Adonis should spend a third of each year with himself, a third with Persephone and a third with the goddess of love.

When Adonis grew up, Aphrodite fell passionately in love with him. Out hunting one day, the god was killed by a boar. It is at this point, in some versions of the myth, that Aphrodite, mad with grief, managed to secure his release from the underworld for half of each year. In Byblos, it was said that he returned from the dead when the river ran red with soil brought down from the hills by rain.

The Adonia, the annual festivals that commemorated the god's death, were beautiful and opulent affairs in which the Phoenician women would ceaselessly repeat the word *adoni*. When the Greek writer Lucian visited Byblos in the second century AD he recorded the

ADONIS was killed and consigned to the underworld, but Aphrodite secured his release for half of each year, symbolizing the renewal of vegetation. (VENUS AND ADONIS BY ANTONIO CANOVA, MARBLE 1794.)

local belief that Adonis had been killed in a gorge. He also wrote that at the time of the god's return to the land of the living, pots of plants outside each house were tended to quickly blossom and wither, symbolizing Adonis's life and death. (See also *DYING AND RISING GODS*)

AGDISTIS was a hermaphrodite monster of Phrygian mythology. According to one tradition, he was born when some semen dropped from the great god Zeus on to Mount Ida, next to where the Great Mother *CYBELE* lay asleep.

The gods made Agdistis drunk by adding wine to the pool in which he bathed. The monster fell asleep, whereupon the gods tied his genitals to a tree. When he

awoke and moved, he castrated himself and an almond or pomegranate tree grew from his sexual organs. One day Nana, the daughter of the river god gathered the fruit into her lap. One of the pieces of fruit disappeared, and the young woman discovered that she was pregnant. In due course, the nymph gave birth to *ATTIS*.

In one story, the adult Attis fell in love with a beautiful maiden. On the day of their wedding, Agdistis appeared at the feast in the form of the goddess Cybele. The maiden was furious to see Attis professing love to another woman and caused havoc. As a result, the bride died of self-inflicted wounds and Attis, mad with grief, castrated himself beneath a pine tree.

AGLIBOL with Baal and the sun god Yarhibol, other members of the heavenly pantheon. (STONE, PALMYRA, 1ST CENTURY AD.)

AGLIBOL was a moon god from Palmyra in northern Arabia. He was depicted with a sickle moon either on his forehead or on his shoulders. His name is sometimes said to mean "Bull of Bol", suggesting that the sickle was originally intended to represent bull's horns.

AHAT, or Aqhat, according to Phoenician mythology, was the son of a local ruler, Daniel. Daniel had no children, but, prompted by the rain and fertility god *BAAL*, the supreme god *EL* gave him a son. When Ahat grew up, the divine craftsman *KOTHAR* gave him a splendid bow made from twisted horns. The goddess *ANAT* longed to possess the weapon and tried to persuade Ahat to give it to her. When Ahat refused, the goddess promised him immortality but Ahat replied that humankind's destiny was to die. Anat then sent Yatpan, her attendant, to kill Ahat. Though Yatpan killed the hero, the bow was lost in the struggle. In punishment, Baal stopped the rains falling, and so the crops failed.

Daniel mourned his son's death for seven years. Although the end of the myth is lost, it is believed that Ahat was resurrected and fertility was restored to the land. Ahat thus probably came to be regarded as a dying and rising god.

AHRIMAN see *ANGRA MAINYU*.

AHURA MAZDA, or Ohrmazd, was the supreme god and "Wise Lord" of ancient Iran. He was regarded as the all-encompassing sky. Until the time of the great religious reformer *ZOROASTER*, who lived around 1200BC, the Iranians worshipped numerous gods. Zoroaster denounced the old gods and Ahura Mazda came to be regarded as the one true creator god who was constantly beleaguered by *ANGRA MAINYU*, or Ahriman, the principle of darkness.

After creating the *AMESA SPENTAS* and *YAZATAS*, Ahura Mazda made people, cattle, fire, earth, sky, water and plants. Zoroaster taught that Ahura Mazda made light visible, so the god was often depicted as the sun.

Sometimes, however, the sun and moon are described as Ahura Mazda's eyes. Using the purifying quality of fire, Ahura Mazda was able to distinguish good from evil, and he bestowed fire, the symbol of truth, on his followers.

Under the Achaemenians, who ruled from 558 to 330BC, Ahura Mazda was adopted as the patron of the royal house and was represented as a pair of vast wings. In the centuries following Zoroaster, a movement known as Zurvanism developed. Both Ahura Mazda and Angra Mainyu came to be regarded as descendants of *ZURVAN AKARANA*, or "Infinite Time". This helped to circumvent the problem of Ahura Mazda having created evil or, at least, having allowed it to exist. At the end of time, it was said that, "Ohrmazd will reign and will do everything according to his pleasure." (See also *ANGELS AND DJINN*)

AL-LAT, or Allat, was a pre-Islamic goddess of central and northern Arabia. Her following was

AHURA MAZDA was the supreme god of ancient Iran, worshipped by Zoroaster and his followers. The world is the stage for the battle between Ahura Mazda and Angra Mainyu, the spirit of darkness; a battle in which Ahura Mazda will finally prevail. (ASSYRIAN RELIEF, 9TH CENTURY BC.)

particularly pronounced at Ta'if near Mecca, where she was worshipped in the form of a block of white granite. Women in particular would circle the stone in Al-Lat's honour, perhaps because she was regarded as a type of mother goddess. Al-Lat represented the earth and was said to be one of the three daughters of *ALLAH*, the supreme god. She is also believed to have been associated with the sun, moon or the planet Venus.

AL-UZZA, or El-'Ozza, was an Arabian goddess of pre-Islamic times who was regarded by the Bedouin tribes of central Arabia as the youngest daughter of *ALLAH*, the supreme deity. She was worshipped in the form of a black stone, on the surface of which lay a mark or indentation called the "Impression of Aphrodite". Al-Uzza was said to live in a tree and was identified with the morning star. She formed the centre of a sacrificial cult, and archaeologists have discovered recent evidence that human sacrifice was offered to her.

The tribe to which the prophet Muhammad belonged showed particular reverence for the goddess. The prophet himself was said to have taken the sacred Black Stone of Islam and placed it in the *KA'ABA*, the shrine in Mecca, Islam's holiest city. The cult of Al-Uzza was served by priestesses and, even after the arrival of Islam, the Ka'aba's guardians still continued to be called "Sons of the Old Woman".

According to the Qur'an, the sacred book of Islam, Al-Uzza, together with Arabia's other principal goddesses, *AL-LAT* and *MANAT*, "are not names which ye have named, ye and your fathers, for which Allah hath revealed no warrant. They follow but a guess and that which they themselves desire." In northern Arabia, Al-Uzza was known as Han-Uzzai.

ALALU, according to the Hittites, was the first king of heaven who came from south of the Black Sea. One myth tells how Alalu sat upon his throne and "the mighty *ANU*, the first among the gods, stood before him, bowed down at his feet and handed him the cup to drink". After nine years, Alalu was deposed by Anu and fled to the earth – possibly the underworld. Anu was in turn dethroned by *KUMARBI*, who was overthrown by his son *TESHUB*, the weather god.

ALLAH was the supreme, though not sole, deity in Arabia before the arrival of Islam. He lived, together with other deities, in the heavens and was said to have created the earth and bestowed water on it. In pre-Islamic times, animism was prevalent throughout Arabia: trees and springs were worshipped and certain stones were believed to contain sacred power. However, the prophet Muhammad (c. AD 570–632) adopted Allah as the one true god, to whom total submission was due, and proclaimed it blasphemous to worship any other deity. According to the Qur'an, polytheism is the greatest sin.

Allah is said to be supreme and transcendent; he is regarded as the creator of all life, the controller of all nature, the bestower of bounty and the judge of humankind in the last days. Although Allah can be terrifying, he is none the less righteous, just and merciful.

Because Allah is believed to be completely different from everything he has created, it is forbidden for anyone to attempt to portray him. In the Qur'an, he is given 99 names. The hundredth and greatest name is known to no mortal.

ALLAT see *AL-LAT*.

THE AMESA SPENTAS, or the Amesha Spentas, are the holy immortals of Zoroastrianism. They probably belonged to the pantheon of ancient Iranian gods which

existed before *ZOROASTER*'s time. It is possible that, although the religious reformer denounced the old gods, he assimilated the Amesa Spentas into his teachings as aspects of *AHURA MAZDA*, the one and only true spirit set in opposition to *ANGRA MAINYU*, the spirit of evil.

The Amesa Spentas were said to serve Ahura Mazda, the "Supreme Lord". Otherwise known as Amshaspends or Ameshas Spenta, each of them ruled over a particular aspect of reality, such as a category of beings or a part of the year. *VOHU MANO* reigned over useful animals, including cattle. Asha-Vahishta looked after fire; Khshathra-Vairya moved the sun and heavens and ruled over metals; *SPENTA ARMAITI* ruled over the earth; Haurvatat governed the waters; and Ameretat governed plant life. Spenta Mainyu, who ruled over humanity, is either numbered among the Amesa Spentas or identified as Ahura Mazda himself.

AMON, wearing his plumed headdress, protects the young pharaoh, Tutankhamun, who reinstated him at the head of the Egyptian pantheon. (1350BC.)

AMESHA SPENTAS see *AMESA SPENTAS*.

AMON, the Egyptian "King of the Gods", first came to prominence as the god of Thebes in Upper Egypt, where he was worshipped as a fertility deity. He grew in importance to become the god who looked after the most splendid of the *PHARAOHS*. Amon was often depicted wearing a headdress surmounted by two plumes, or sometimes with the head of a ram.

By the 18th dynasty, in the second millennium BC, Amon had become the supreme god of the whole of Egypt and was identified with the sun god as Amon-Ra, although *RA* continued to have his own separate following. The pharaohs Thuthmosis III and Amenhotep III described themselves as "Sons of Amon" and claimed that the god brought them victory over their enemies.

During the reign of Amenhotep's son, Akhenaten, worship of Amon was forbidden while *ATEN* was declared the true god. However, in 1361BC, the succeeding pharaoh reinstated Amon and called himself Tutankhamun or "Living Image of

Amon". Worship of Amon eventually spread beyond Egypt into Ethiopia and Libya. Amon's wife was Mut, whose son was called Khons.

AN see *ANU*.

ANAHITA, the Iranian goddess of water and fertility, was widely worshipped in Achaemenian times (558–330BC) and was often associated with the great god *MITHRA*. In the fourth century BC, the ruler Artaxerxes II ordered that images of Anahita should be erected in all the principal cities of the empire. Her following later spread throughout Asia Minor and the West.

Anahita assisted *SPENTA ARMAITI* and was associated with *HAOMA*, the god who conferred immortality. Occasionally identified with the planet Venus, she is said to have originated from *ISHTAR*, the Babylonian fertility deity who is associated with the same planet. Her name means "Immaculate".

Anahita was often represented dressed in gleaming gold with a crown and jewels. The dove and peacock were her sacred creatures, and sacred prostitution formed part of her cult.

ANAHITA, the Iranian patroness of women and fertility, and an aspect of the "Great Goddess", crowns the ruler Narses. (BAS-RELIEF, LATE 3RD CENTURY BC.)

ANGRA MAINYU *was the Zoroastrian
principle of darkness, the antagonist of
Ahura Mazda. He tried to thwart Ahura
Mazda's plans to create an earthly paradise
by sowing doubt and discord in the world,
and even sought to destroy humanity.*
(GOLD MEDALLION FROM THE OXUS TREASURE,
C. 5TH CENTURY BC.)

ANAT, or Anath, was a goddess of
the Canaanites and Phoenicians,
and was the sister, and sometimes
the consort, of BAAL. Her name is
usually translated as "Providence"
or "Precaution".

The goddess had a reputation
for violence. According to one
myth, she slaughtered Baal's worshippers and only ceased her attack
when Baal promised to reveal the
secret of lightning to her. Anat later
asked the supreme god, EL, to give
Baal a house, but it was the great
mother goddess ASTARTE who eventually persuaded him to do so.
After moving into the splendid
palace, Baal boasted that he was
now omnipotent and challenged
MOT, the god of death, to a contest.
However, it was Anat who eventually destroyed Mot, by killing,
thrashing and burning him.

Anat was later assimilated into
the Egyptian pantheon, where she
was regarded as a goddess of war
and a daughter of the sun god RA.

The Egyptians usually depicted her
carrying a spear, axe and shield,
and wearing a tall crown surmounted by two ostrich feathers.

ANATH see ANAT.

ANBAY was a pre-Islamic god of
southern Arabia who was known as
the "Lord of Justice". Famed for his
oracle, he spoke on behalf of the
moon god, Amm, who ranked
above him in the pantheon.

ANGRA MAINYU, or Ahriman,
was the principle of darkness in
ancient Iranian mythology. He was
set in opposition to AHURA MAZDA,

the principle of goodness and
truth. Ahura Mazda planned to
make Iran into an earthly paradise,
but Angra Mainyu interfered, creating harsh weather conditions,
smoke, darkness, sickness, disease
and all manner of other evils. His
was a world of death in which summer lasted for only two months
whereas winter lasted for ten.
Where people had faith, Angra
Mainyu sowed the seeds of doubt,

*ANAT, the sister and sometimes the
consort of Baal, was a Phoenician goddess
with a reputation for violence. She later
became a part of the Egyptian pantheon as
a goddess of war.* (ASSYRIAN SEAL.)

and where there were riches, he
created laziness and poverty. Such
was the extent of his evil-doing that
he was sometimes accused of having killed GEUSH URVAN, the
primeval bull. Angra Mainyu's symbol was the snake.

In later times, during the reign
of the Sassanian kings (AD
226–652), the idea of ZURVAN
AKARANA, or "Infinite Time" was
developed. Both Angra Mainyu and
Ahura Mazda were regarded as the
offspring of Zurvan Akarana, who
was said to have promised authority to the firstborn. As a result,
Angra Mainyu tore his way out of
the womb before his brother and
held the reins of power for several
thousand years. However,
Zoroastrians believe that there will
come a day when Ahura Mazda will
succeed to power and Angra
Mainyu will be destroyed, sinking
into eternal darkness.

ANSHAR was the male principle
in Babylonian mythology. In the
Babylonian epic *Enuma Elish*
("When on High"), he and Kishar,
the female principle, are described
as the second pair of deities, following Lahmu and Lahamu, the
first divine couple. Both these couples originated when APSU, the
primeval sweet water, mingled with
TIAMAT, the primeval salt water. It
is generally believed that the name
Anshar means "Horizon of
Heaven" and that the god represented the celestial world; Kishar,
on the other hand, is thought to
have been a terrestrial deity whose
name means "Horizon of Earth".

Anshar and Kishar begat ANU,
the sky god, and EA, the god of
fresh water and wisdom. They also

ANSHAR was a primordial deity of Babylonian mythology who represented the male principle. He was eventually equated with Ashur, a warrior god who ensured the victories of the Assyrians.

begat the Igigi, the deities who inhabited the sky, and the Anunnake, the gods who lived on earth and in the underworld. From the ninth century BC onwards, Assur or Ashur, the national god of Assyria, was equated with Anshar.

ANU was the son of *ANSHAR* and Kishar, the male and female principles of Babylonian mythology. He formed one of a triad of creator gods which also included *EA*, the god of sweet and fertilizing waters, and *ENLIL* or Bel, lord of the wind.

The god of the sky, Anu was the supreme deity who reigned over the heavens. He was known as the father of the gods and had the power to judge those who committed misdeeds after summoning them before his throne, in front of which were placed the sceptre, the diadem, the crown and the staff of command. The stars were Anu's soldiers, whom he had created in order to destroy the wicked. He never descended to earth and had little to do with human beings. Rather, he stayed in the heavens and busied himself with the fate of the universe. In Sumerian mythology, Anu was known as An. He was sometimes represented by a crown on a throne.

Anu was introduced into the Hittite pantheon from Mesopotamia by way of the Hurrians. In the story of the divine kingship, *ALALU*, the king of heaven, was served by Anu, the first among the gods. Alalu reigned for nine years until Anu deposed him. After another nine years, Anu's minister *KUMARBI* seized the throne. Anu immediately flew up into the sky, but Kumarbi seized him by the foot and bit off his penis. However, Anu's semen impregnated Kumarbi and gave rise to three mighty gods, who are believed to be different aspects of the weather god, *TESHUB*.

ANUBIS was originally said to be the fourth son of the Egyptian sun god, *RA*. However, in later times, he came to be regarded as the child of the vegetation god, *OSIRIS,* and *NEPHTHYS*, the sister of *ISIS*. When Anubis was born, Nephthys hid the child in the marshes of the Nile delta in order to protect him from her consort *SETH*. The infant god was discovered there by Isis, the mother goddess, who subsequently brought him up.

When Osiris left Egypt in order to spread his teachings throughout the world, Anubis accompanied him on his travels. Later, when Osiris was killed by Seth, Anubis organized his burial, binding him with cloth and thereby creating the first mummy. As a result, Anubis came to be regarded as the inventor of funeral rites and was referred

to as "Lord of the Mummy Wrappings". The god also assisted in the judgment of the dead and guided the honest dead towards the throne of Osiris. Anubis was depicted either as a jackal or as a man with the head of a jackal. (See also *GATEWAYS TO THE GODS; UNDERWORLDS*)

APEP was the eternal enemy of *RA*, the supreme god of the Egyptian pantheon. A terrifying serpent, Apep symbolized chaos and destruction. Each day, as the sun god, Ra, crossed the sky in his boat, Apep would viciously attack the vessel and occasionally, during a total eclipse, he was believed to have swallowed it whole.

Despite his ferocity, Apep never gained total victory over his enemy. However, at the same time, he himself was never believed to have been finally and completely conquered. However, the reddening of the sky at dusk was said to demonstrate that the serpent had been overcome by the sun's strength. According to one story, Apep was

ANU, Babylonian god of the sky, and Enlil, god of the earth, are symbolized by horned crowns on stylized thrones. (DETAIL OF BABYLONIAN BOUNDARY STONE, C. 1120BC.)

created when *NEITH*, the "Great Mother" associated with war and hunting, spat into *NUN*, the primal watery chaos. In later times, Apep came to be identified with *SETH*. He is often known by the Greek name of Apophis. (See also *SERPENTS AND DRAGONS*)

APEP was the Egyptian symbol of chaos, a giant snake who occupied the Duat or underworld. The sun god, Ra, represented here as a falcon, battled daily with the snake. (SMALL LIMESTONE PYRAMID, 19TH DYNASTY.)

SACRED ANIMALS

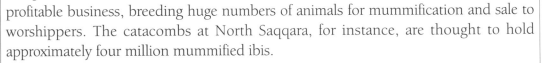

SURROUNDED BY A HOSTILE, DESERT landscape, people and animals alike depended on the great rivers that provided water and fertile soil. The ancient Egyptians were forcefully reminded of their close kinship with the animal world, as they had to share the fertile flood plain of the Nile with dangerous, powerful creatures such as lions, crocodiles, hippopotamuses and snakes. The association of these animals with the life-giving force of the river, and the fear and respect they commanded, gave rise to animal cults, which reached their peak during the Late and Ptolemaic Periods from 664–30BC. Devotees did not worship the animals themselves but associated their qualities with a particular deity, who was portrayed in animal form. At shrines, offerings consisted of small animal figurines or mummified creatures. The temple officials turned this into a profitable business, breeding huge numbers of animals for mummification and sale to worshippers. The catacombs at North Saqqara, for instance, are thought to hold approximately four million mummified ibis.

THE COBRA (left), or uraeus, rearing defensively, was a symbol that was both protective and potentially dangerous. The snake accompanied the deceased on his or her journey to the underworld in the sacred boat, and similar images were also placed protectively around shrines. A rearing female cobra formed part of the pharaoh's regalia, worn on the forehead, where it symbolically guarded both the pharaoh and the country. The Eye of Horus, a god often depicted with the head of a falcon, was another guarantee of protection in the afterlife. (DETAIL FROM A BOOK OF THE DEAD, 21ST DYNASTY, HERUBEN PAPYRUS, C. 1000BC.)

BASTET (above) was the daughter (or sometimes sister and consort) of the Egyptian sun god, Ra. She was originally a fierce and vengeful goddess, portrayed as a lioness, but from around 1000BC she became more peaceable and took on the shape of a cat. She was a goddess of fertility and love, and protected her devotees against disease and evil spirits. Her principal place of worship was at Bubastis, where thousands of mummified cats were dedicated to her. In the name of the goddess, cats were loved and respected by the Egyptians, to the extent that the killing of a cat was an offence punishable by death. (EGYPTIAN BRONZE, 6TH CENTURY BC.)

RA-HERARHTY (below), god of the rising sun, symbolized by his falcon wings and sun-disc headdress, is carved on the polished granite capstone of the pyramid of Amenemhet III. Coiled around the sun disc is the symbol of the cobra goddess Wadjet, representing the pharaoh's royal authority and power over the life and death of his people. The carvings below include a bee and an ibis, representing Thoth, the wise counsellor of the gods and the judge of the dead. (PYRAMIDION, C. 1818–1772BC.)

APIS (above), the sacred bull, was worshipped as a living animal believed to be the reincarnation of the god Ptah at his temple at Memphis. Mythical bulls, symbols of strength and potency, occurred in many belief systems from the earliest times. Hathor, the Egyptian goddess of maternal and sexual love, took the form of a cow (above right) who nourished humankind with her milk. She was the protector of women, helping them to conceive and give birth, and was regarded as the mother of the pharaohs. (EGYPTIAN BRONZE, 7TH–6TH CENTURY BC.)

DRAGONS (right) symbolized Marduk, the tutelary god of the fabled city of Babylon. These composite creatures had the head and tail of a serpent, the body and forelegs of a lion and the hind legs of a falcon, and were emblazoned on the monumental Ishtar Gate at the climax of the ceremonial route through the city. The processional way was lined with rows of lions sacred to Ishtar, the goddess of love and fertility. (GLAZED BRICK RELIEF, 6TH CENTURY BC.)

KHNUM (above), the ram-headed god, took mud from the life-giving Nile and used it to create humanity on his potter's wheel. He was also responsible for supervising the annual flooding of the river. At his sanctuary near its mythical source, offerings of mummified rams decorated with gold leaf were buried in stone tombs. His consort was Satis, who was depicted pouring water on to the dry earth.

SEBEK (left), the crocodile god, represented the skill and strength of the pharaoh in battle. The qualities he needed to display could be seen in the crocodiles of the Nile, which inspired awe with their speed and agility in catching their prey and the fearsome strength of their jaws. The mortuary goddess Serket took the form of a scorpion, though she was sometimes depicted in human form with a scorpion headdress. Her role was to guard the canopic jars containing the vital organs of the dead, and to protect the throne of the pharaoh. (EGYPTIAN BRONZES, 6TH CENTURY BC.)

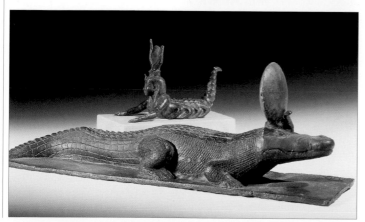

267

APIS, or Hapi, was the most renowned of Egypt's sacred animals. He was worshipped at Memphis, where his temple lay opposite that of the great creator god *PTAH*. Apis, in the form of a real black bull, was believed to be the reincarnation or "glorious soul" of Ptah, who was said to have inseminated a virgin cow in the form of fire, and to have been born again as a black bull.

Each day, Apis was let loose in the courtyard attached to his temple, and the priests would use his movements as a means for divining the future. Usually, the Apis bull was allowed to die of old age, but he was drowned in a fountain if he reached the age of 25. The bull was twice assassinated by the Persians.

Ptah's priests were said to be able to recognize the next holy bull by discovering certain markings on the creature's body, including a white triangle on his forehead and a crescent moon on his right side. The extent of the reverence with which the sacred bulls were regarded can be gauged by the fact that their mummified bodies were buried with great ceremony in huge underground burial chambers. (See also *SACRED ANIMALS*)

APSU, in Mesopotamian mythology, was the watery abyss or primordial, fresh-water ocean, which existed at the beginning of time and which circled and supported the earth. Apsu spread happiness and abundance over the earth and was the source of knowledge and wisdom. Eventually, the waters of Apsu merged with those of *TIAMAT*, the primordial, saltwater ocean, and gave rise to Mummu, the waves, and the primal couple, Lahmu and Lahamu. *ANSHAR* and Kishar, the next divine couple to arise from the waves, were the male and female principles who bore the great gods *ANU* and *EA* as well as the other divinities who peopled the sky, the earth and the underworld.

In time, Apsu became troubled by the gods and plotted with Tiamat to destroy them. Tiamat was at first unwilling to take part in the battle, but, when Apsu was slain by the god Ea, she was prompted to seek revenge. Ea's son, the great god *MARDUK*, who had been born in the waters of Apsu, was chosen to challenge Tiamat. The bloody battle that ensued gave rise to the creation of the world and the sky. According to one tradition in Sumerian mythology, the goddess Nammu formed the first men from clay dug out of the waters of Apsu. In the epic of *GILGAMESH*, the hero descended into the waters of Apsu to find the plant of eternal life.

AQHAT see *AHAT*.

ARINNA was the name of a Hittite town. Its chief goddess was known as the "Sun of Arinna", or Ariniddu. The "Queen of Heaven and Earth", the goddess Arinna became the supreme patroness of the Hittite kingdom, protecting it from enemies and helping out in time of war. Her symbol was the sun disc. Arinna was identified with the Hurrian goddess *HEPAT*; both deities were said to be married to the weather god *TESHUB*.

The sun goddess Arinna was sometimes addressed as a masculine deity, the "Inspired Lord of Justice". The sun god was also an important figure in Hittite mythology, although his actual name has been lost. He was regarded as the king of the gods and a dispenser of truth and justice. In one prayer he was addressed as "Sun god of heaven, my lord, shepherd of mankind! Thou risest, O sun-god of heaven, from the sea and goest up to heaven. O sun-god of heaven, my lord, daily thou sittest in judgment upon man, dog, pig, and the wild beasts of the field." There was also a sun god of the water and a sun god of the underworld, through which the sun was believed to travel during the night.

ARSU see *RUDA*.

ASHERAT; ASHTORETH see *ASTARTE*

ASHUR see *ANSHAR*.

ASTARTE was the principal goddess of the Phoenicians and Canaanites. She was incorporated into Egyptian mythology as a daughter either of the sun god *RA*, or of *PTAH*, and she was often depicted naked, bearing weapons and riding a horse.

According to one story from Egyptian mythology, Ptah and the other great gods were forced to pay tributes to the sea. Gifts of silver, gold and precious stones were brought to the seashore, but the sea wanted more. The gods then

ASTARTE was the principal goddess of the Phoenicians and the Canaanites. This figurine shows her, perhaps, as a fertility deity. She was associated with love and procreation. (CERAMIC FIGURINE, GATH, 8TH–7TH CENTURIES BC.)

told Astarte to take more offerings to the sea. When she arrived at the shore, Astarte mocked the sea, who responded by insisting that he have Astarte herself as a gift. The great gods covered Astarte with jewels and sent her back to the shore, but this time *SETH* accompanied her in order to fight the sea. Although the end of the story is missing, it is usually presumed that Seth fought the sea, and saved Astarte.

The name Astarte is sometimes translated as "Womb", or "That Which Issues from the Womb",

ATEN, the sun god, is symbolized by a sun disc whose rays fall on the pharaoh Akhenaten and queen Nefertiti as they perform a sacrifice to him. (FLAT RELIEF, AMARNA, C. 1350BC.)

and Astarte the light, heavenly aspect. In one text, they are both described as the daughters of *NEITH*, an Egyptian mother goddess. Moreover, they were both known as "Lady of Heaven". Aphrodite is widely believed to have developed from Astarte.

ATAR, or "Fire", was said to be the son of the Iranian deity *AHURA MAZDA*, although fire worship probably existed long before the naming of the supreme being. According to the teachings of Zoroastrianism, fire was one of Ahura Mazda's seven creations. Atar was said to bring men comfort and wisdom, and to defend the world from evil. It represented the light of truth and the divine spark in humankind, which signified the presence of the supreme god.

The monstrous dragon *AZHI DAHAKA* sought to extinguish the divine fire in a bloody battle, which took place across land, sea and air. Eventually, Atar caught the dragon and chained it to a mountain.

ATEN was a sun god who came to pre-eminence in the 14th century BC under Amenhotep IV, a *PHARAOH* of the 18th dynasty. He was regarded as none other than the sun god *RA* himself.

Amenhotep IV built temples to Aten close to those of the supreme god *AMON* and, to the disgust of Amon's priests, piled Aten's temples high with gifts. Four years into his reign, the pharaoh pronounced that the religion of Aten was the only official faith and that the god was to be worshipped as the exclusive creator of humankind. Worship of all other gods – especially Amon – was forbidden.

In an attempt to spread the religion of Aten throughout the empire, Amon's temples were closed and his images defaced. The pharaoh changed his name from Amenhotep, meaning "Amon is Satisfied", to Akhenaten, "Glory of Aten" or "He Who is Devoted to Aten", and relocated his capital from Thebes to a city known today as el-Amarna, which he had built specifically to glorify Aten.

Aten is always depicted as an enormous red disc, from which rays of light emanate. The rays, ending in hands, were believed to extend the beauty of Aten to the ruler. When Akhenaten died, Amon and the other gods were reinstated, and Aten's rays were sliced through to prevent his beauty reaching Akhenaten.

ATEN, the sun-disc, was worshipped by the pharoah Akhenaten as the embodiment of the supreme force of light, and, during his reign, worship of all the other deities of the Egyptian pantheon was forbidden. His successor, Tutankhamun (below) restored the old gods. (CARVED WOOD, 14TH CENTURY BC.)

suggesting that the goddess was primarily a fertility deity. Astarte was also associated with love and procreation, and her cult included the practice of temple prostitution among her devotees.

In the Old Testament of the Bible, she appears as Ashtoreth, and *SOLOMON* had a temple built in her honour near Jerusalem. Indeed, the Israelites sometimes revered the goddess as the queen of heaven and wife of *YAHWEH*.

The goddess Asherat, or Ashera-of-the-Sea, tends to be viewed as identical with Astarte. She was called "Mother of the Gods" and was said to have had 70 children. According to texts dating from the 14th century BC, the supreme god *EL* took two women, generally believed to be Asherat and *ANAT*, as

his consorts, and by them fathered *SHACHAR* and Shalim, "Dawn" and "Dusk", and many other deities.

It is still not certain whether Anat and Astarte were two separate goddesses or different aspects of the same goddess. Anat may have been the dark aspect of the goddess

ATTAR was worshipped in southern Arabia in pre-Islamic times. A god of war, he was often referred to as "He who is Bold in Battle". One of his symbols was the spear-point, and the antelope was his sacred animal. He had power over Venus, the morning star, and was believed to provide humankind with water.

ATTIS was the consort of *CYBELE*, the great mother goddess of Phrygia in Asia Minor. A vegetation god, he was sometimes known as Papas, or "Father". One of the oldest stories concerning the birth of Attis tells how the hermaphrodite *AGDISTIS* fell asleep, whereupon the gods tied its genitals to a tree. Agdistis awoke with a start, and the severed genitals fell to the ground. An almond tree grew up on the spot, and in due course Nana, the daughter of the river god, became pregnant by one of its fruits. The girl eventually gave birth to Attis. Other legends say that the god was a foundling or the son of a king.

The best-known story of Attis is that in which his desperate love for Cybele drove him insane, leading him to castrate himself under a pine tree. Flowers and trees grew up from his blood. Although he died, the god was reborn and united with Cybele.

The cult of Cybele spread to Greece and Rome, and with it, that of Attis. Cybele was said to have fallen in love with Attis, who was regarded as a handsome young shepherd. She chose him as her priest and imposed a vow of chastity upon him. However, Attis fell in love with a river nymph, so Cybele caused him to suffer a fit of madness, during which he mutilated himself. When the god recovered, he was about to kill himself when Cybele changed him into a fir tree. In another version of the story, Attis was gored to death by a boar sent by Zeus.

Each spring, at the end of March, a five-day festival was held in honour of Attis. The first day was

ATTIS was a vegetation god in Phrygia in Asia Minor. His death and rebirth symbolized the natural cycle. In a Roman legend, Attis was gored to death by a boar sent by Zeus. (MARBLE BUST, IMPERIAL ROME.)

one of mourning. The god, represented by a sacred fir tree taken from the grove near Cybele's temple, was bound with bandages, decorated with ribbons and flowers, and carried through the streets. On the second day, Cybele's priests performed frenzied dances, and on the third day they castrated themselves, sprinkling the altar and effigy of Attis with their blood. The fourth day was that on which the resurrection of Attis was celebrated. The fifth day was one of rest. A ritual marriage between Cybele and Attis formed part of the ceremony, with Cybele's high priest taking the role of the god.

The Romans generally represented Attis as a shepherd, usually holding a shepherd's crook and sometimes carrying a sheep on his shoulders. He plays a pipe and wears a pointed cap on his head. The rays of the sun, or ears of corn, protrude from the cap, symbolizing his function as a god of regeneration and rebirth. (See also *DYING AND RISING GODS*)

AZHI DAHAKA, the monstrous dragon of ancient Iranian mythology, was said to have had three heads, six eyes and three pairs of fangs. He was sometimes regarded as a mythical king of Babylon, Iran's

B

enemy, or as the enemy of YIMA, the great king. Originally, Azhi Dahaka was believed to kill cattle and men. One story tells how the hero FERIDUN cut the creature open with his sword and was horrified to find lizards and toads pouring out of its insides.

In time, Azhi Dahaka came to be seen as the embodiment of falsehood and the servant of ANGRA MAINYU, the principle of darkness. ATAR, the fire god, went into battle against the monster and harried him through land, sea and air before finally catching him and chaining him to a mountain.

It was believed that at the end of time Azhi Dahaka would succeed in breaking free from his chains and ravage the earth again. Eventually, the hero KERESASPA would kill the monster. (See also SERPENTS AND DRAGONS)

THE BA AND KA were believed by the ancient Egyptians to be the soul and spirit, or vital essence, of a dead person. The Ba hovered over the deceased and was usually depicted as a bird with a human head. The Ka was said to appear to the deceased in the form of a blue phoenix and was believed to return to the tomb, where it ate food left by relatives and priests. So deeply entrenched was this belief that menus were sometimes inscribed on the walls of tombs.

BAAL was the name given by many Canaanite tribes to their chief gods. In the Bible his name is used as a synonym for "false god, and sacrifice to him is there condemned". (ILLUSTRATION FROM MYTHS OF BABYLONIA AND ASSYRIA BY LEWIS SPENCE.)

BAAL, meaning "Lord" or "Owner", was the name given by many Canaanite tribes to their chief god. When the Israelites entered the land of Canaan, they took up the word and used it to describe any alien god – it is as a general term for a "false god" that the name Baal is used in the Bible. The most renowned Baal of Canaanite mythology was the rain and fertility god associated with the storm god, Hadad. He lived on a mountain in the north of the region and was sometimes referred to as "Lord of the North".

One story tells how this Baal defeated YAM, the sea deity. Yam asked the supreme god EL to crown him king. El agreed but warned him that first of all he would have to defeat Baal. Learning of the forthcoming battle, Baal equipped himself with magic weapons made by the gods, and as a result, he succeeded in killing Yam and scattering his remains. Baal then proclaimed himself king, built a sumptuous dwelling place on Mount Saphon and took control of several cities.

After this victory, Baal became so proud that he decided to challenge MOT, the god of death. He forced Mot to live in the barren wastelands and barred him from all fertile regions. In response, Mot challenged Baal to come to his underground dwelling and eat mud, the food of the dead. Baal took up the challenge and died.

BAAL was said to have a voice like thunder, and that he watered the earth through a hole in the floor of his palace. In the Greco-Roman period, Baal became assimilated in the Palestine region with Zeus and Jupiter. (GILDED BRONZE, SYRIA, C. 14–15TH CENTURY)

All the gods mourned Baal's death. His wife, the ferocious ANAT, descended to the underworld to retrieve his corpse. However, she was unable to revive Baal and so appealed to Mot for help. When Mot refused to come to her aid,

Anat burst into a frenzy and slaughtered him, whereupon Baal returned to life. Baal is thus seen as a dying and rising god. He is often depicted wielding a thunderbolt, or a flash of lightning. (See also DYING AND RISING GODS)

C

BASAMUM was worshipped in southern Arabia in pre-Islamic times. His name may come from the Arabic word for a balsam bush, suggesting that he was a god of healing. One ancient text tells how the god cured two wild goats.

BASTET was the local goddess of Bubastis, or "House of Bastet", the capital of a province of Lower Egypt. She was usually regarded as the daughter of the sun god *RA*, although she was sometimes said to be his sister and consort. Later, she became the wife of the creator god *PTAH*. According to some accounts, it was Bastet, rather

than *NEPHTHYS*, who was the mother of the jackal-headed god *ANUBIS*.

Originally a lioness goddess symbolizing both the warmth of the sun and the rage of the sun god's eye, from about 1000BC Bastet came to be represented as a cat, or a cat-headed woman. However, in some stories she continued to possess the qualities of Sekhmet (see *HATHOR*), the lion-headed goddess. Usually a benevolent goddess, Bastet protected humanity from diseases and evil spirits. Most importantly, she was a goddess of fertility, sex and love, and enjoyed music and dancing. In the fourth century BC fertility festivals were held in her honour at her temple at Bubastis. Cats were venerated as Bastet's sacred animals, and their mummified bodies were buried at her sanctuaries. (See also *SACRED ANIMALS*)

BEHEMOTH was a terrifying monster of Hebrew mythology, the dry-land equivalent of the monstrous sea serpent *LEVIATHAN*. According to the Old Testament

BASTET (left) was usually portrayed as either a cat or a cat-headed woman. Originally a local goddess of Bubastis, her cult reached its height in the Late and Ptolemaic periods (c 660–30BC) when animal cults became a major feature of popular religion. Bronze figurines and mummified cats were given as offerings. (BRONZE, C. 5TH CENTURY BC.)

BEHEMOTH (left) and the sea monster Leviathan were used in the Book of Job as examples of the largest and strongest animals imaginable. (HAND-TINTED ENGRAVING BY WILLIAM BLAKE, C. 1793.)

Book of Job, Behemoth was associated with the hippopotamus. The monster is sometimes said to have developed from *TIAMAT*, the fearsome Babylonian goddess.

BEL see *ENLIL*.

BELILI see *TAMMUZ*.

BORAK (below) with a human head, the body of a winged horse and a peacock's tail, carries the prophet Muhammad to heaven, surrounded by winged peris. (QAJAR LACQUERWORK, C. 1870.)

BORAK was a fabulous beast of Islamic mythology. Part human, part animal, the prophet Muhammad was said to have ridden on its back on the night of his ascension to heaven. The creature's name means "Lightning".

CORYBANTES see *KORYBANTES*.

CYBELE was the great mother and fertility goddess of Phrygian mythology. She probably originated as a mountain goddess and was sometimes referred to as the "Lady of Ida", a mountain in western Anatolia. She inhabited the wild and dangerous regions of the earth and ruled over the fiercest of wild animals. Cybele's origins have

CYBELE (above) was the great mother of Phrygian mythology. She was associated with the earth and with a black stone – believed to be a meteorite – which was enshrined at Pergamum. (2ND CENTURY AD.)

CYBELE's (right) priests, the Galli, celebrated rites in her honour which included music, convulsive dances, sacrifices and voluntary self-mutilation. (ROMAN CARVING, 1ST–3RD CENTURY AD.)

sometimes been traced back as far as Çatal Höyük, a large Neolithic site in southern Anatolia. There, archaeologists unearthed a terracotta figure believed to be the mother goddess in the act of giving birth.

Cybele was primarily associated with the earth, and in particular with a black stone enshrined at Pergamum. Other cities where worship of the great mother was particularly fervent were Troy and Pessinus. In Phrygia, Cybele may originally have been known as *KUBABA*, or "Lady of the Cube". She is sometimes associated with an ancient goddess of that name who was worshipped at Carchemish in the Hittite empire. The shrines of both goddesses were situated in caves or near rocks.

The cult of Cybele eventually spread from Asia Minor to Greece. In the fifth century BC, a magnificent statue of the goddess flanked by lions was placed in her temple in Athens. In 204BC, the black stone sacred to Cybele was brought from Phrygia to Rome. An oracle had foretold that if the "Phrygian Mother" were brought from Pergamum, she would aid the Romans in their war against the Carthaginians.

At Cybele's annual celebrations, held in spring, a chariot harnessed to lions would be drawn through the streets of Rome. According to the historian Lucretius (99–55BC): "Borne from her sacred precinct in her car she drove a yoke of lions; her head they wreathed with a battlemented crown, because

embattled on glorious heights she sustains towns; and dowered with this emblem even now the image of the divine mother is carried in awesome state through great countries. On her the diverse nations in the ancient rite of worship call as the Mother of Ida, and they give her Phrygian bands to bear her company, because from those lands first they say corn began to be produced throughout the whole world."

The public rites of Cybele were orgiastic and ecstatic. Her priests, the Galli or Galloi, would beat and castrate themselves in mad frenzies of passion, using whips decorated with knuckle bones. The celebrations were accompanied by the sacrifice of a bull or ram, during which the initiate, or high priest or priestess of Cybele, stood beneath

a platform and was drenched in the blood of the sacrificed animal. Cybele's followers believed that her mysteries would lead them to be reborn after death in a new life.

Cybele's attributes are a mirror, a pomegranate and a key. The great myth attached to the goddess is that in which she takes vengeance on *ATTIS* for his infidelity and causes him to go mad, to castrate himself and to die. Eventually, however, she gives him back his life. According to another story, Cybele and Gordius, the king of Phrygia, had a son whom they called Midas. This was the Midas who, after wishing that everything he touched might turn to gold, found himself unable to eat or drink until the god Dionysus took pity on him.

D

THE DAEVAS were gods in the Indo-Aryan period of ancient Iran. The religious reformer *ZOROASTER* initially regarded them as unimportant, but he later came to view them as enemies of the true religion. Whereas the *DRUJS* were usually female, most daevas were male. *ANGRA MAINYU* or Ahriman, the principle of darkness, was said to rule over the demons. They specialized in trickery and deceit, and in putting obstacles in the way of all efforts to achieve good.

Many of the daevas stood in direct opposition to one of the *AMESA SPENTAS,* or "Holy Immortals". One demon would lie in wait on the Chinvat Bridge, which souls had to cross in order to reach *AHURA MAZDA*'s paradise. If the creature caught them, he would throw them into the depths below. Another demon attempted to persuade rulers to be tyrannical, and a third promoted pride and rebellion. Some demons brought about old age and senility, and others caused rage and devastation.

The great hero *RUSTEM* constantly fought demons. In one story, a demon called Arzang attacked, captured and blinded the king. Rustem finally managed to release the ruler and to restore his eyesight using the heart of a demon as medicine.

In Armenian mythology, the daevas were known as devs. The daevas continued to be revered as good spirits in India.

DAGAN, the chief god of the Philistines, may have been a sea god and was represented with the tail of a fish.

DAGAN was a god of corn and fertility who was worshipped in both Canaan and Mesopotamia. The deity was often regarded as the father of *BAAL*, the god of rain and fertility. Several kings of Akkad and Babylonia declared themselves to be "Sons of Dagan", including King Hammurabi and Ashurnasirpal II.

In the Old Testament, a god called Dagon is described as the chief god of the Philistines. Samson destroyed Dagon's temple at Gaza by pulling down its two main pillars. This Dagon may have been a sea god, and he was represented with the tail of a fish. However, there continues to be some dispute as to whether Dagan and Dagon are one and the same deity.

DAGON see *DAGAN*.

DANIEL appears in the Old Testament as a prisoner in the sixth century BC of the Babylonian king Nebuchadnezzar. In 597BC, the king seized Jerusalem. A decade later, the city was attacked, and the Hebrews were taken to Babylon where they were held in captivity until the city fell. Daniel was one of these Hebrew exiles. He gained a reputation for interpreting dreams and visions, earning the title "Master of Magicians", and was made a provincial ruler. However, Nebuchadnezzar commanded all his subjects to worship an image of gold. Shadrach, Meschach and Abednego, Daniel's friends, refused to do so, insisting on remaining true to *YAHWEH*. The king threw the men into a fiery furnace but astonishingly, they remained unharmed.

Nebuchadnezzar had many troubling dreams and called on Daniel to interpret them for him. According to Daniel, the dreams meant that Nebuchadnezzar would be banished from Babylon. The prophecy came true, and in the king's absence, his son Belshazzar ruled the kingdom. One evening, during a magnificent feast that Belshazzar was holding for a thousand of his lords, mysterious writing appeared on the palace wall: "In the same hour came forth fingers of a man's hand and wrote over against the candlestick upon the plaister of the wall of the king's palace." Daniel took the message to mean that Babylon would be conquered by the Medes and Persians. In due course, Darius the Median did indeed take the kingdom from Belshazzar.

DANIEL was preserved in the lions' den by an angel sent from Yahweh. (MOSAIC, HOSIOS LOUKAS, GREECE, 11TH CENTURY.)

Members of the new court became envious of Daniel's position and powers. They devised a plot whereby the king was forced to have Daniel thrown into a den of lions. Darius sealed the entrance of the den with a stone, but Yahweh sent an angel to Daniel's aid, forcing the lions to close their mouths: "So Daniel was taken up out of the den, and no manner of hurt was found upon him, because he believed in his God."

THE DEVIL see *SATAN*.

THE DJINN, according to Arabic and Islamic belief, are usually ugly and evil demons with supernatural powers. In pre-Islamic belief, the djinn were nature spirits who were said to be capable of driving people mad. They roamed the wild and lonely desert areas and, though usually invisible, they were able to take on any shape, whether animal or human.

In Islamic lore, the djinn were modified. They were an intermediate creation, coming between

E

humankind and the angels. Those that refused to believe in Islam became demons, whereas others became beautiful and good spirits.

King *SOLOMON* was said to have tamed numerous djinn and to have become their ruler with the help of his magic ring. He allegedly carried them on his back when he travelled and ordered them to build the Temple at Jerusalem, as well as beautiful gardens and palaces.

There were several kinds of djinn, each with different degrees of power. The ghouls were female spirits who lived in the wilderness and manifested themselves as animals. *IBLIS*, or *SATAN*, is often regarded as the chief djinnee.

Djinn are born from smokeless fire. They are often said to live with other supernatural beings in the Kaf, a mythical range of mountains that encircles the earth. (See also *ANGELS AND DJINN*)

THE DRUJS, according to

ancient Iranian mythology, were the enemies of the *asha*, the universal law. The monstrous, demonic beings, usually female, made every effort to further the course of evil. The horrific dragon or snake *AZHI DAHAKA* was one of their number, as was Nasu, who was said to settle on dead bodies in the form of a fly with the intention of hastening their decay. The druj Jahi was a symbol of the evil within women. According to one tradition, *ANGRA MAINYU*, the principle or spirit of darkness, kissed Jahi and thus introduced the impurity of menstruation to women.

DUMUZI was the husband of *INANA*, the goddess of love and queen of heaven. He is the Sumerian equivalent of the Babylonian god *TAMMUZ*. In the Babylonian version of the goddess's journey to the underworld, *ISHTAR* descended into *ERESHKIGAL*'s kingdom in order to rescue Tammuz and awaken him from his sleep. However, in the Sumerian version of the myth, Dumuzi was seized by the demons of the underworld as a substitute for Inana on the goddess's own orders.

When Inana returned from the underworld to her city of Uruk, to find Dumuzi sitting happily on a throne rather than mourning her, she fastened the eye of death on him and elected that he should go to the underworld in her place. Dumuzi prayed to the sun god for help. The sun god turned Dumuzi into a snake and he escaped.

Dumuzi told his sister, Geshtinanna, about a dream in which he saw his own death, and Geshtinanna was overcome with grief. When the demons approached once more, Dumuzi changed into a gazelle. However, the demons found Dumuzi and again attacked him. This time, they succeed in dragging him away.

Dumuzi was mourned by Inana, his mother, and his sister Geshtinanna. Inana was so moved by Geshtinanna's grief that she eventually agreed that her husband need spend only half of each year in the underworld, with Geshtinanna taking his place for the other half.

EA, the Babylonian god of the earth, was tempted in a story reminiscent of that of Adam and Eve. (ILLUSTRATION FROM MYTHS OF BABYLONIA AND ASSYRIA BY DONALD A MACKENZIE.)

EA, or Enki, a Babylonian deity, was one of a trinity of creator gods that also included the sky god *ANU* and the wind god *ENLIL*. He corresponds to the Sumerian god Enki. *EA* lived in *APSU*, the primordial ocean that surrounded and supported the earth. He was the son of *ANSHAR* and Kishar, the male and female principles.

A god of the fresh waters, as well as of wisdom and magic, Ea had the power of an oracle and would advise and reason with human beings. When Apsu was plotting the destruction of the gods, Ea killed him, prompting *TIAMAT*'s fury. Later, when the god Enlil decided to destroy humanity, the wise Ea warned humankind of the conspiracy and advised Enlil to

EA was a Babylonian god who helped people survive by teaching them how to plough and till the land. With the sky god Anu and the wind god Enlil, he formed a trinity of creator gods. (BABYLONIAN SEAL.)

temper his fury. On earth, Ea lived in the city of Eridu, on the southern edge of Sumer. His home was the Ezuab or "House of the Apsu". Ea is usually represented as a goat with a fish's tail or as part human, part fish. His consort was Ninki, the "Lady of the Earth", or sometimes Damkina or Damgalnunna.

Ea was introduced into the Hittite pantheon by the Hurrians. In the story of the weather god *TESHUB*'s battle with *ULLIKUMMI*, Teshub seeks advice from Ea the wise. The gods are dismayed at Ullikummi's power, but Ea decides to visit Upelluri, on whose shoulder Ullikummi had been raised. Upelluri says, "When heaven and earth were built upon me I knew nothing of it, and when they came and cut heaven and earth asunder with a cutting tool, that also I knew not. Now something is hurting my right shoulder, but I know not who that god is." The god was Ullikummi, who was made of diorite stone. Ea used the ancient saw that had been used to separate heaven from earth to cut the stone creature's feet, thereby destroying Ullikummi's power.

MYTHS OF THE FLOOD

A LIMITLESS OCEAN FEATURED IN MANY creation myths as the primeval state of the world. A flood of global proportions was also a common theme, in which an inundation was sent to wipe out sinful humankind and thus restore the world to its pristine original state, so that it could be repopulated by a nobler race. The Egyptians believed that their creator god, Ra, would one day tire of humanity and return the world to the watery abyss of Nun before beginning a new cycle of creation. Stories of overwhelming floods reflected the ambiguous nature of humanity's relationship with water, which was vital to life but also carried the threat of violence and devastation. The Tigris and Euphrates, the two rivers on

which the civilizations of Mesopotamia depended, flooded unpredictably, and their fearsome nature is expressed in several versions of the flood myth, which was to find its way into the Hebraic tradition as the familiar story of Noah's ark.

ENLIL (above), as Sumerian god of the air, controlled the terrifying forces of nature. Angered by the noise rising from overpopulated cities, he determined to destroy the inhabitants of the earth, and sent a flood so great that even the other gods were frightened. Warned by the water god, Ea, the wise man Utnapishtim weathered the cataclysm in his boat and was rewarded by Enlil with the gift of eternal life.
(ILLUSTRATION BY E. WALLCOUSINS FROM MYTHS OF BABYLONIA AND ASSYRIA BY DONALD MACKENZIE.)

NOAH (left) and his family were the only human survivors of the flood that covered the earth for 150 days before its level began to fall, and it deposited Noah's ark on Mount Ararat. Noah released a dove who failed to find dry land and came back to take refuge on the ark. Seven days later he released her again, and this time, though she was forced to return, she carried an olive branch as a sign that the flood was abating at last.
(CATALAN BOOK ILLUSTRATION, C. AD970.)

NOAH (above) released his dove a third time, seven days after her return carrying the olive branch. This time, she left the ark for good. Noah, looking out, saw dry land once more and was able to disembark. God promised him and his family that they were safe, and as a token of his covenant, he set a rainbow in the sky, which would appear when rainclouds threatened as reassurance that the flood would not return. (THE DOVE SENT FORTH FROM THE ARK BY GUSTAVE DORÉ, 19TH CENTURY.)

NOAH (above right) was given a precise specification for the ark by God, detailing the dimensions of the boat, its roof and door, the number of decks, the type of wood to use and how it should be waterproofed. Noah was already an extremely old man at the time of the flood and lived on for many more years after it – his longevity recalls the eternal life granted to the survivors in the Mesopotamian versions of the myth. (DETAIL OF THE VERDUN ALTAR, 1181.)

UTNAPISHTIM's (right) boat eventually came to rest on Mount Nisir and, as the water began to subside, he sent out a dove and a swallow. Both returned to the boat unable to find food or a place to perch. However, when a raven was released, it did not come back, and Utnapishtim concluded that it had found dry land. He offered a sacrifice on the summit of the mountain, which placated the gods. (ILLUSTRATION FROM GILGAMESH BY ZABELLE C. BOYAJIAN, 1924.)

EL, a Canaanite deity, was referred to as the "Father of the Gods". He caused the rivers to flow, thus making the land fertile, and made his home near the seashore. Sometimes referred to as "Creator of the Earth", he was also known as "Bull", or "Bull-El", to signify his strength and powers of fertility. His name is usually translated as "Mighty One" or "First One". In 1929, stories about El were found on clay tablets at Ras Shamra in Syria, the site of the ancient city of Ugarit. The tablets dated from the 14th century BC.

Although El was usually regarded as the consort of Asherat (see ASTARTE), one myth found at Ras Shamra tells how he had intercourse with two women, probably representing Asherat and ANAT. The women subsequently gave birth to the deities SHACHAR, "Dawn", and SHALIM, "Dusk". According to the story recorded on the clay tablets, El walked along the shore, then plunged into the waves. His hands reached out like the waves, and he made his wives fruitful. He kissed their lips, which tasted as sweet as grapes, and in the kiss, and the conception and the embrace, Dawn and Dusk were

EL, the creator god, sits on his throne and listens to the prayer of a supplicant. (RELIEF ON A STELE, SYRIA, 13TH CENTURY BC.)

born. El went on to father many more deities. He was depicted as an old man, sitting on a throne and wearing bull's horns.

EL-'OZZA see AL-UZZA.

ENKI see EA.

ENLIL was originally worshipped in Sumer as "Lord of the Wind", the god of hurricanes who represented the power of nature. He was believed to have absolute power over humans and was represented among men by the earthly kings.

Long before humankind was created, Enlil was said to have supervised the gods in their task of digging out the beds of the Tigris and Euphrates rivers. In time, the gods became exhausted by their ceaseless toil and decided to rebel. Enlil was devastated, but the god Enki (see EA) came to his aid, suggesting that the goddess Nintur create humankind in order to take over the work from the gods. For hundreds of years, all went smoothly, but then the cities

became so overpopulated that the clamour made by the men and women kept Enlil awake. Enlil decided to solve the problem by sending a plague down to earth. However, Enki warned the people of the impending disaster, and they made huge efforts to keep quiet.

In time, the men and women forgot Enlil's threat and reverted to their noisy ways. This time, Enlil threatened to send a drought down to earth. Once again, Enki warned the people and they became quiet. The next time that Enlil was disturbed by the people's clamour, the god threatened to instigate a famine, but again Enki warned humankind and they were quiet.

Finally, when the men and women again began to create a huge clamour, Enlil lost all patience and sent down a massive flood. However, Enki had advised a wise man to build a ship and to save himself and his family from the flood. In some versions of the myth, the wise man was called Atrahasis, in others, Ziusadra. For seven days and seven nights, the rains lashed down, and the world was submerged by a massive flood. When the waters finally subsided, only Atrahasis (or Ziusadra), his

ENLIL, Sumerian "Lord of the Wind", receives worshippers at his throne. Son of the sky god, Anu, he represented the power of nature and threatened to destroy humankind because the clamour they made kept him awake. (CYLINDER SEAL, MESOPOTAMIAN, 3RD MILLENNIUM BC.)

family and the animals on the boat remained alive. In another version of the flood myth, which forms part of the epic of GILGAMESH, the hero UTNAPISHTIM survives the flood with his family.

In earliest times, Enlil's consort was believed to be NINHURSAGA, the "Lady of the Great Mountain". Later, however, he was associated with the grain goddess, NINLIL.

The Babylonians often equated Enlil with the great god MARDUK, calling him Bel, or "Lord". He was also assimilated into the Hittite pantheon, by way of the Hurrians. There, he features in the myth of the monstrous being ULLIKUMMI. (See also MYTHS OF THE FLOOD)

ENNUGI see UTNAPISHTIM.

ERESHKIGAL was the queen of the underworld in both Akkadian and Babylonian mythology. The underworld lay beneath the waters of APSU, the primordial ocean. It was a dry and dark realm, sometimes referred to as a mountain, sometimes as enemy territory. According to the epic of GILGAMESH, Ereshkigal, rather than having chosen her kingdom, was "given the underworld for her domain." Enthroned therein, she ate only clay and drank dirty water.

The goddess had an insatiable sexual appetite and never let compassion for others stand in the way of her desires. According to one story, when the war god Nergal entered the underworld, Ereshkigal

EVE was created by God, who placed her in paradise as a companion for Adam.
(*NUREMBERG BIBLE, 1483.*)

copulated with him for six days and nights. None the less, when he left, she remained unsatisfied.

In order that no one should return to the land of the living, the underworld was guarded by seven walls. At each of its seven gates, people had to take off an item of clothing, each representing one of their earthly attributes. When they finally reached the centre, they found themselves naked and imprisoned forever in eternal darkness. According to one tradition, Ereshkigal was the sole ruler of the underworld until Nergal invaded her territory, posting two demons at each gate. In order to achieve peace, Ereshkigal agreed to marry Nergal and to give him authority over the underworld. Ereshkigal was the sister of the fertility goddess *ISHTAR*, the counterpart of the Sumerian goddess *INANA*.

ETANA was the 12th king of the city state of Kish after the flood. King Etana grew miserable because he had no children and appealed to the sun god *SHAMASH* for help. Shamash told Etana to go to a particular mountain. There, on the mountain, an eagle and a serpent had recently had a terrible quarrel. Each of the creatures had children but the eagle had eaten all the serpent's offspring. The serpent complained to Shamash, who told him to trap the eagle and leave him to die. Etana found the dying eagle and asked him for a special herb that would enable him to have a son. The eagle promised Etana that he would bring him the herb if he would cure him. For several months, Etana brought the eagle food and drink until finally the bird was fully recovered. Then, the eagle told Etana to sit on his back so that he could carry him up to the sky of *ANU*, the supreme god. The eagle flew up to the gods and continued flying upwards towards the dwelling place of *ISHTAR*, the fertility goddess. In some versions of the tale, Etana seems to succeed in his quest and is given the herb by Ishtar. In another version, Etana grows dizzy and begs the eagle to return to earth. However, the eagle's strength suddenly runs out, and the two of them fall to the ground with a mighty crash.

EVE was the first woman, according to the Hebrew creation story. She was said to have been formed from her husband *ADAM*'s rib. A serpent tempted Eve to eat the one fruit which God had forbidden the couple, and she persuaded Adam to join her. As a result, both Adam and Eve were expelled from paradise. Eve was seen as responsible for the Fall and for bringing death, sin and sorrow into the world.

Christians have often viewed Eve's sin as a sexual failing. However, the Fall also opened the way for growth and learning. Adam refers to Eve as Hawwah, which is usually translated as "Mother of All Living", or "She who gives Life". According to one tradition, Adam was buried in paradise and was promised resurrection, whereas Eve was buried with her son, Abel. (See also *SERPENTS AND DRAGONS*)

EVE bears the apple, traditionally the forbidden fruit that led to the Fall and expulsion from paradise. (EVE BY LUCAS CRANACH THE ELDER, OIL ON WOOD, C. 1528.)

G

EYE see *HATHOR*.

FATIMA, the prophet Muhammad's daughter, is regarded by Isma'ilis as the "Mother of the Holy Imams". The Imams are the semi-divine leaders of Shi'ism, one of the two great forms of Islam of which the Isma'ilis form a subsect. Fatima is revered within esoteric Islam and is seen as symbolizing the "supra-celestial earth". She is considered to be the source of the Imams' wisdom because she is the "hidden tablet; upon which God has written."

FERIDUN, according to ancient Iranian mythology, was the hero destined to overthrow *ZOHAK*, the evil king sometimes regarded as the embodiment of the terrifying monster *AZHI DAHAKA*.

Zohak was warned in a dream that he would be deposed by someone called Feridun, and consequently ordered the massacre of all children. However, Feridun's mother, Firanak, saved her baby by hiding him in a garden, where he was suckled by a miraculous cow called Purmajeh. Firanak then hid the baby in Hindustan.

Throughout Feridun's childhood years, Zohak was obsessed with the thought that his destroyer was alive somewhere. Sure enough, Feridun grew up determined to overthrow the evil king.

One day, a man whose children had been killed by Zohak led a group of rebels to Feridun's palace. Feridun decided that the time was ripe for action. As he marched towards the king, an angel taught him magic and comforted him with tales of his future happiness. Zohak, learning of Feridun's approach, clad himself in armour. He attacked Feridun with his sword, whereupon Feridun smashed it with a club. However, an angel told Feridun not to kill the king but to chain him in a cave under a mountain. Feridun did as he was told and then succeeded to

FATIMA, daughter of the prophet Muhammad, on her way to a Jewish wedding party with Muhammad, A'isha, Umm Salma and Umm al-Ayman, receives a gift of a green cloak brought by Gabriel from paradise.

the throne. His reign lasted for several hundred years. (See also *SERPENTS AND DRAGONS*)

THE FRAVASHIS, according to the mythology of ancient Iran, were benevolent spirits or guardian angels. They helped *AHURA MAZDA* to create the world, and defended heaven from its enemies with their sharp spears while riding their fleet-

GEB, the Egyptian god of the earth, was the brother and consort of the sky goddess, Nut. (PAPYRUS.)

footed steeds. They were believed to be the ancestral spirits of believers, a part of the human soul that Ahura Mazda had created before each individual's birth, and thus might be regarded as prototypes for living beings. Fravashi is usually translated as "She who is Chosen".

GABRIEL, or Jibril, is known as the spirit of truth or "Angel of Revelations" in Islamic tradition. He stands at the apex of the angelic host and is said to have dictated the Qur'an to Muhammad. Gabriel is also believed to stand at the north-east corner of the *KA'ABA*, Islam's most sacred shrine.

In the Bible, Gabriel appears as the messenger of *YAHWEH*. He visited the Old Testament patriarch *DANIEL* twice, to announce the return of the Hebrews from captivity in Babylon and to explain the diversity of nations. In the New Testament, it is the archangel Gabriel who brings Mary the tidings that she is to conceive Jesus. Gabriel is also the trumpeter who will sound the Last Judgment. According to Hebrew apocalyptic literature, Gabriel is an angel of retribution and death. (See also *ANGELS AND DJINN*)

GADD was the name given to a variety of beneficent deities in pre-Islamic northern Arabia. It is sometimes believed to refer merely to a personification of good luck.

GAYOMART was the primeval being of ancient Iranian mythology. His corpse, together with that of the primeval bull *GEUSH URVAN*, was said to have given rise to all life. According to tradition, Gayomart existed for 3,000 years as a spirit until, in the second great epoch, he was made into a physical being by *AHURA MAZDA*, the principle of

GABRIEL, *angel of the Annunciation, tells Mary that she is to conceive Jesus. He is also believed to stand at the Ka'aba, Islam's most sacred shrine, containing the Black Stone.* (ICON, 12TH CENTURY.)

goodness. He was killed by *ANGRA MAINYU*, the principle of darkness. According to one myth, all the parts of the universe were created from his body; another tale tells how the seed of Gayomart was buried in the ground for 40 years, until it gave rise to the first human couple, *MASHYA AND MASHYOI*, as well as the seven metals. Gayomart's name is translated as "Mortal Life", or "Dying Life".

GEB, the Egyptian god of the earth, was the brother and consort of *NUT*, and the eldest son of *SHU* and Tefnut, the deities of air and moisture. Shu, or in some stories *RA*, was said to have separated Geb and Nut from a passionate embrace by violently pushing them apart so that Nut formed the sky and Geb the earth. Until then, there had not been sufficient space between the two bodies for Nut to give birth. Geb was said to grieve continuously for having been parted from his beloved Nut, and his distress was said to cause earthquakes.

He was usually regarded as a beneficent deity who provided humanity with crops for their fields, and who healed the sick. However, it was also feared that he might trap the dead within his body and thereby prevent them from entering the underworld. The god was usually depicted as a bearded man, often lying under the feet of Shu. He was sometimes coloured green, to indicate that vegetation was believed to grow from his body. Occasionally he was accompanied by a goose or portrayed as a bull.

Geb, the "Father of the Gods", and Nut were said to have begat *OSIRIS, ISIS, NEPHTHYS* and *SETH*. The kings of Egypt called themselves the "Heirs of Geb".

281

GEUSH URVAN, the primeval bull of ancient Iranian mythology, was created, along with the primeval man *GAYOMART*, by *AHURA MAZDA*, the essence of good. According to one tradition, Geush Urvan died, like Gayomart, at the hands of *ANGRA MAINYU*, the essence of darkness. Another tradition teaches that Geush Urvan was slain by *MITHRA*. All kinds of plants and animals were said to emerge from his corpse.

Widely believed to be the guardian of cattle, Geush Urvan's name means "Soul of the Cow". The sacrifice of a bull was an important part of Mithraic rituals.

GILGAMESH, the famous Mesopotamian hero, is believed to be based on a real person, who was most probably a Sumerian king. *The Epic of Gilgamesh*, a poem recording the hero's exploits, was transcribed on to tablets in the second millennium BC.

Gilgamesh was two-thirds god, one-third man. He was so active and such a womanizer that the inhabitants of Uruk, or Erech, the city where he lived, appealed to the gods for help. The deities responded by creating another man called Enkidu, or Eabani, who turned out to be a wild and savage being, even more troublesome than Gilgamesh. Eventually, it was Gilgamesh who helped the people of Uruk to hatch a plot whereby they succeeded in taming the wild being. Enkidu subsequently became Gilgamesh's friend and constant companion, and the two men lived a life of luxury together.

In time, however, Gilgamesh was instructed by the gods to leave his home in order to fight Khumbaba, or Huwawa, the horrible monster who lived some 20,000 marching hours away from Uruk at Cedar Mountain. Enkidu and Gilgamesh set off on their quest and, after entering the cedar forest, eventually found Khumbaba's home. Gilgamesh

challenged the monster to battle and, after a fearsome struggle, the two men overcame him, although it was Enkidu's spear that struck the fatal blow.

Soon afterwards, the goddess *INANA* tried to seduce Gilgamesh. When the hero turned her down, she complained to the god An (see *ANU*) who was eventually persuaded to give Inana the bull of heaven to send against Gilgamesh. However, Enkidu caught the bull and Gilgamesh stabbed it to death. The gods, outraged that the bull had been killed, took their revenge by striking Enkidu down with illness. After a few days, he died.

Gilgamesh was devastated at the death of his friend, and became terrified at the thought of death. He decided to try and discover the secret of immortality and set out on a quest to find *UTNAPISHTIM*, the hero who, after surviving the flood, had been granted immortality by the gods. When he reached Mount Mashu, Gilgamesh was confronted by the scorpion men who guarded its gates. However, they recognized that he was in part divine and let him pass by them to proceed into the mountain.

At length, Gilgamesh came to a beautiful garden beside a sea and saw before him the tree of the gods,

GILGAMESH with a lion. Gilgamesh is the Mesopotamian hero of an epic poem, which describes his legendary adventures, taking him to death and back. (RELIEF FROM PALACE OF SARGON, KHORSABAD, 8TH CENTURY BC.)

laden with amazing fruits, the ground covered with jewels. There, he met the goddess Siduri Sabitu, who tried to deter the hero from his quest. At Gilgamesh's insistence, the goddess eventually advised him to seek the help of Ushanabi, Utnapishtim's boatman. Ushanabi took Gilgamesh through the waters of death into the underworld, and at last, the hero reached Utnapishtim. Gilgamesh told him: "Because of my brother I am afraid of death; because of my brother I stray through the wilderness. His fate lies heavy upon me. How can I be silent, how can I rest? He is dust, and I shall die also and be laid in the earth for ever." The hero of the flood told Gilgamesh that death, like sleep, was necessary for humankind. To prove his point, he told Gilgamesh to try staying awake for six days and seven nights. Gilgamesh agreed, but fell fast asleep almost as soon as he had sat down.

Before Gilgamesh returned home, Utnapishtim showed him the plant of youth, which lay at the bottom of the ocean. Gilgamesh found the plant, but as he bent to pick it, it was stolen by a snake. The tale ends on a sad note, with the ghost of Enkidu telling Gilgamesh of the misery of life in the underworld. (See also *UNDERWORLDS; HEROES AND QUESTS*)

GUBABA see *KUBABA*.

GULA see *NINURTA*.

GULASES see *GULSES*.

THE GULSES, or Gulases, were Hittite goddesses whose name means either "Scribes", or "Female Determiners of Fate". The Gulses allotted the destinies of individual

H

men and women, dispensing good and evil as well as life and death. The Hurrians called them Hutena.

HADAD see *BAAL*.

THE HAFAZA, according to Islamic mythology, are a type of guardian spirit. They look after people, protecting them from *DJINN*, or demons. Everybody is said to be protected by four hafaza: two to watch over them during the day and two during the night. The hafaza record each individual's good and bad deeds. People are said to be most at risk from the djinn at sunset and at dawn since, at those times, the hafaza are changing guard.

HAHHIMAS, the disappearing god, according to one version of the Hittite myth of *TELEPINU*, was responsible for having caused the great devastation that afflicted the earth. The myth tells how "Hahhimas has paralysed the whole earth, he has dried up the waters, Hahhimas is mighty!" In response to this desperate state of affairs, the weather god *TARU* called on his brother, the wind, to breathe on the earth, thereby reinvigorating it. However, on his return, the wind simply reported that the whole earth was paralysed and that people were doing nothing but eating and drinking. Hahhimas then began to seize and paralyse the gods, including Telepinu. Hahhimas's name is sometimes translated as "Torpor".

HAN-UZZAI see *AL-UZZA*.

HANNAHANNA was the Hittite mother goddess and goddess of birth. Her name is usually translated as "Grandmother". She was served by the bee who eventually found the fertility god *TELEPINU* after he had disappeared from the world, leaving decay and death behind him. *TESHUB* protested at the bee being sent on the mission, saying, "The gods great and small have sought him but have not found him. Shall this bee now search and find him?" However, Hannahanna ignored Teshub's objections and told the bee to bring Telepinu home.

The bee searched the earth, and eventually found Telepinu asleep in a field. As directed by Hannahanna, the insect stung the god. Enraged, Telepinu embarked on a bout of destruction, killing humans and animals. The story may be influenced by the belief that honey has the power to expel evil spirits.

HAOMA, according to ancient Iranian mythology, was the lord of all medicinal plants. He was able to confer immortality on his followers and was sometimes said to be the son of *AHURA MAZDA*, the supreme god and principle of good. Equivalent to the Indian Soma, haoma was also a real herb from which an intoxicating drink could be made. The drink was believed to heighten spiritual awareness and also to confer immortality. It was used in sacrificial rituals, which

GILGAMESH and his friend Enkidu fought bulls during their quest together, which culminated in the death of the monster Khumbaba. (AKKADIAN CYLINDER SEAL IMPRESSION, 3RD MILLENNIUM BC.)

were said to drive away evil spirits. The spirit of the great religious reformer *ZOROASTER* was said to be strengthened by drinking haoma.

HAOSHYANGHA, or Hoshang or Husheng, the son of Siyamek, was the first king, according to ancient Iranian mythology. Siyamek, the son of *MASHYA AND MASHYOI*, the first human couple, was killed by a demon. After killing the demon, Haoshyangha spread peace throughout his kingdom and then proceeded to spread justice throughout the world. He introduced all the arts of civilization to human beings. After extracting iron from a stone, he taught humankind how to make axes, saws and hoes. He then organized a system of irrigation, leading water from the rivers to the fields, and tamed wild animals so that they could be used to cultivate the land. He also taught people to make clothing from the skins of wild animals.

HAPI see *APIS*.

HARSIESIS see *HORUS*.

HAOMA was both a god of medicine and the name of a magical herb. Zoroaster was said to have drunk a fortifying potion made from haoma. (LIEBIG "CHROMO" CARD, 19TH CENTURY.)

HATHOR (above), was depicted as a cow, or as a woman wearing a horned headdress with a solar disc. (TEMPLE OF HUREMHEB, EGYPT.)

HATHOR (left), daughter of the god Ra, in her usual form of a cow. She nourished the living with her milk and carried the dead to the underworld. (TEMPLE OF HATSHEPSUT, EGYPT.)

HATHOR, the Egyptian sky goddess and daughter of the sun god, *RA*, was usually represented as a cow. The goddess of joy and love, dance and song, she looked after mothers and children. She nurtured the living and carried the dead to the underworld. There, she refreshed them with food and drink from the sycamore tree, in which it was believed she was incarnated. Royal coffins were made from sycamore trees, in the belief or hope that death was no more than a return to the womb.

HATHOR, as the goddess Sekhmet, is depicted in human form, with the head of a lioness surmounted by a sun disc, identifying her as the daughter of Ra.

The Eye of Ra was identified with Hathor. When Ra grew old, humankind began to plot against him. Hearing of this, the enraged god decided to send the divine Eye, the terrifying, burning power of the sun, to slaughter them. The Eye took the form of Hathor who, as the lioness Sekhmet, or the "Powerful One", threw herself at all the wicked men and women and killed them in a massive bloodbath. Eventually, Ra decided that enough carnage had been inflicted, and he called an end to the slaughter. Only by Ra's intervention was Sekhmet prevented from destroying humanity.

In order to put an end to Sekhmet's relentless slaughter, Ra drenched the battleground in thousands of jugs of beer mixed with pomegranate juice. The bloodthirsty Sekhmet drank the bright red potion, believing it was blood, and became so inebriated that she ceased her attack and was transformed back into the beautiful Hathor. In remembrance of the event, great jugs of beer and pomegranate juice were drunk annually on Hathor's feast day. (See also *SACRED ANIMALS*)

HAZZI was a mountain god worshipped by both the Hurrians and the Hittites. He formed part of the retinue of the weather god, *TARU*, and was invoked at Hittite state occasions as a god of oaths. Hazzi was also the home of the gods; it is thought to have been situated on Mount Sapon, near Ugarit.

HEBAT see *HEPAT*.

HEPAT, or Hebat or Hepit, the chief goddess of the Hurrians, was sometimes referred to as the "Queen of Heaven". The wife of the tempest god *TESHUB*, she was often granted almost equal status with her husband, and occasionally took precedence over him. She and Teshub produced a son, Sharruma, who was represented as a pair of human legs. When Hepat heard that *ULLIKUMMI* had forced Teshub to abdicate, she nearly fell off the roof of a tower in horror: "If she had made a single step she would have fallen from the roof, but her women held her and did not let her fall." Hepat was assimilated into the Hittite pantheon, where she was often equated with *ARINNA*, the sun goddess. She was depicted either sitting on a throne or standing on a lion, her sacred animal.

HEPIT see *HEPAT*.

HERARHTY see *HORUS*.

HORUS, in the story of *ISIS* and *OSIRIS*, is sometimes known as Harsiesis to distinguish him from the twenty or so other Horuses in the Egyptian pantheon. He was depicted as a falcon or with a falcon's head. He was born, after Osiris had retired to the underworld, on the island of Chemmis near Bhutto and was raised there in secret by Isis. Harsiesis eventually avenged Osiris's death at the hands of *SETH*, and reclaimed the throne. He ruled peacefully, and was worshipped throughout Egypt.

Horus was worshipped as the god of the sky. His eyes were said to be the sun and moon.

Herakhty, or "Horus of the Horizon", was a sun god who rose each morning on the eastern horizon. He was often identified with the sun god, *RA*, and was eventually absorbed by him, forming Ra-Herakhty.

HOSHANG see *HAOSHYANGHA*.

monstrous dragon or snake *ILLUYANKAS* with a rope after Inaras had trapped the creature at a feast. The weather god *TARU* then killed Illuyankas. Inaras rewarded Hupasiyas for his help by building him a house. She warned him that he must never look out of the windows of his new home in case he saw his mortal wife and children. When Hupasiyas disobeyed the goddess, she killed him.

HUSHEDAR, according to ancient Iranian mythology, is a saviour and a son of the prophet *ZOROASTER*. Hushedar would be succeeded every thousand years by other saviours, culminating in *SAOSHYANT*, who is expected to introduce the universal judgment of humankind.

Eventually, after a final conflict between good and evil, the universe will be made pure again, and humanity will dwell in perfection with *AHURA MAZDA*.

HUSHENG see *HAOSHYANGHA*.

HUTENA see *GULSES*.

IBLIS is the name for the devil in Islamic belief. He is a rebel against God and tempts humankind to evil. Originally, he was the angel Arazil. When *ALLAH* created the first man, *ADAM*, out of clay, Arazil refused to worship him. When Allah summoned the angels to praise his creation, Arazil refused to attend. As a result, Arazil was thrown out of paradise, and from then onwards he encouraged the *DJINN* to make war against Allah. Eventually, he brought about Adam and Eve's fall from grace by tempting them into sin.

On the Day of Judgment, Iblis and his hosts of evil spirits will be consigned to the fires of hell. It is disputed whether Iblis was an angel or a djinn since, though he behaved like a fallen angel, he was said to have been made from smokeless fire like a djinn.

HORUS (above) was the son of Osiris and Isis, and a cosmic deity. He was depicted as a falcon or with a falcon's head. As the first ruler of all Egypt, he wore the double crown of the united kingdom. (RELIEF OF THE TEMPLE OF SETI I IN HYPOSTYLE, 1303–1290BC.)

HORUS (left) in battle. Raised in secret by his mother, Isis, he eventually avenged his father Osiris's death at the hands of Seth and reclaimed the throne.

HOURIS, in Islamic mythology, were black-eyed women who provided dead men in paradise with sexual pleasure. Each man was said to be given 72 houris, whose virginity was eternally renewed.

HUBAL was a god worshipped in Arabia in pre-Islamic times. His image, made from red carnelian, still stands in the sacred *KA'ABA* in Mecca, Islam's holiest city. It is believed that the Black Stone of the Ka'aba might be connected with the god in some way. Hubal was particularly famed for his oracle.

HUPASIYAS was the lover of *INARAS*, the Hittite goddess whose duties seem to have been those of protecting gods and tradesmen. A mortal being, Hupasiyas bound the

SERPENTS AND DRAGONS

HUMAN FEARS OF POWERFUL, ungovernable forces were crystallized in visions of huge and terrifying monsters. Serpents and dragons were composite images of everything that was inhuman: scales, claws and wings, of fantastic, fearful strength and size. They might also exhibit the characteristics of other animals, such as the head of a lion and the talons of an eagle. Their hybrid appearance added to their monstrous nature. Many were sea creatures, embodying the malign power of unpredictable nature and the threat of chaos. The most dramatic myths concern human or immortal heroes who killed dragons that threatened the world. By destroying the monsters, heroes were able to restore order and preserve the safety of civilization. As emblems of chaos, serpents featured in creation stories such as the myth of the snake Apep, coiled in the primeval water, who fertilized the cosmic egg of the Egyptians. In time, snakes came to represent not just disorder, but evil.

THE SERPENT (above) in the Garden of Eden is frequently portrayed with the face of Lilith, who in Hebrew legend was Adam's first wife. She considered herself his equal and left him – and Eden – rather than submit to him. She was often depicted as winged, with the body of a snake, and was said to be the temptress of Eve. She acquired the character of a wicked demon who killed new-born babies and was the enemy of men. (ANONYMOUS ENGRAVING.)

EVE (left), with her partner Adam, was free to eat the fruit of every tree in the Garden of Eden except one, the tree of the knowledge of good and evil. The serpent, more subtle than any other beast, persuaded Eve that this was the one fruit she desired and, having tasted it, Eve gave it to Adam to eat. According to the Old Testament of the Bible, their disobedience condemned humans to lives of toil, hardship and death. The serpent's punishment was to crawl on its belly and eat dust, and to be the enemy of humankind thereafter. (ILLUSTRATION BY RICHARD RIEMERSCHMID.)

LEVIATHAN (left), the great sea monster, was said to have existed from the fifth day of creation, and to represent the forces of chaos subordinated by Yahweh. According to later Hebrew traditions, Leviathan will be vanquished in a great final battle with the archangel Gabriel, and the banquet celebrating the eventual arrival of the Messiah will take place in a tent made from the monster's skin. (LEVIATHAN BY ARTHUR RACKHAM, 1908.)

AARON'S ROD (above), was turned into a serpent by Yahweh to help Moses and Aaron persuade the pharoah to allow the Israelites to leave Egypt. The pharaoh sent for all the sorcerers and magicians of Egypt, who responded by miraculously turning their own staffs into serpents as well, but they were all eaten by Aaron's. (AND HE THREW DOWN HIS ROD. . ., BY QAJAR, MINIATURE, C. 1860–70.)

APEP (left) the great serpent, lay in wait in the Egyptian underworld to ambush the sun god, who had to voyage through it each night ready to rise again. Night was a time of uncertainty and danger for the god, as it was for humans on earth. The return of the sun in the morning represented the triumph of life over death, symbolized by Ra-Herakhty, the falcon, vanquishing the serpent. (SMALL LIMESTONE PYRAMID.)

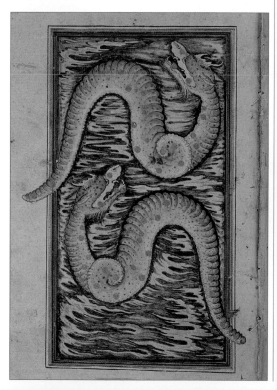

MARDUK'S (above) battle with Tiamat is part of the Babylonian creation myth. Tiamat was the primeval salt-water ocean, which had to be tamed to allow the universe to come into existence. Marduk subdued her and eventually split her in two to create the earth and sky. Her eyes became the sources of the rivers Tigris and Euphrates. Marduk went on to kill her son, Kingu, and mixed his blood with earth to create humankind. (ILLUSTRATION FROM GILGAMESH BY ZABELLE C BOYAJIAN, 1924.)

DRAGONS (right) were appropriate emblems for the stars mapped by Arabic astronomers. These cosmic creatures engaged in battles far beyond human realms, such as the encounter between the Persian hero Feridun and the mighty dragon Azhi Dahaka. When Feridun stabbed the monster, snakes, toads and scorpions began to pour out, so instead of cutting him up, the hero imprisoned him in Mount Demavend. (ILLUSTRATION FROM A DESCRIPTION OF THE FIXED STARS, 1629.)

IBRAHIM see *ABRAHAM*.

ILLUYANKAS was the monstrous snake or dragon of Hittite mythology. He waged war against the gods, particularly against the weather god, *TARU*. However, the monster was eventually slain by Taru, who was assisted in his assault by the goddess *INARAS* and her mortal lover, *HUPASIYAS*. In another version of the tale, Illuyankas seized the heart and eyes of the weather god. Taru responded by fathering a son whom he married to the daughter of Illuyankas, demanding the missing organs as a dowry payment. Taru then succeeded in slaying the monster.

The story of Illuyankas and Taru was assimilated into Canaanite mythology as the struggle of the gods against the *LEVIATHAN*. The Hittite monster was also the prototype for Typhon, the hundred-headed beast of Greek mythology. The tale of Taru's battle against Illuyankas was recited at an annual feast either of the New Year or of spring. The destruction of the monster was believed to signal the beginning of a new era.

IMHOTEP was a sage and scholar attached to the court of the ancient King Zoser, who ruled Egypt in the third millennium BC. A great architect, as well as an astronomer and scientist, Imhotep designed and oversaw the construction of the first pyramids. Until then, rulers had been buried in underground chambers. Imhotep's Step Pyramid at Saqqara was the first monumental stone building ever constructed. The sage was also credited with ending a seven-year famine by advising the king to make offerings to *KHNUM*, the god who controlled the flood waters of the Nile.

Admired during his lifetime, Imhotep gradually came to be celebrated as a god. According to some tales, he was the son of the great god *PTAH* and provided the high priest of Ptah with a son. The patron of scribes, he is usually depicted as a priest with a shaven head. He was also the patron of doctors. His name means "He Who Comes in Peace." (See also *GATEWAYS TO THE GODS*)

INANA, the goddess of love, fertility and war, queen of heaven and earth, was the most important goddess in the Sumerian pantheon. Her symbol was the reed bundle, and she was often portrayed with bright sunbeams radiating from her image. Inana's Babylonian equivalent was the goddess *ISHTAR*.

Like Ishtar, Inana descended to the underworld kingdom of *ERESHKIGAL*. At the gate, Inana explained why she had come: "Because of my sister Ereshkigal". Then, however, she claimed that she wanted to see the funeral of Gugalanna, the "Bull of Heaven".

IMHOTEP, *studying a papyrus. Probable architect of the famous Step Pyramid at Saqqara, and greatly admired during his lifetime, Imhotep gradually came to be celebrated as one of the gods.*

INANA *with Ea and Gilgamesh. She was the most important goddess in the Sumerian pantheon. (AKKADIAN CYLINDER SEAL, 3RD MILLENNIUM BC.)*

At each of the gates of the underworld, Inana divested herself of one of her items of clothing, or earthly attributes, including her priestly office, her sexual powers and her royal powers. Finally, she was condemned to death and killed, becoming part of the underworld kingdom.

The goddess Ninshubur, Inana's handmaiden, mourned grievously for her queen and eventually appealed to the gods for help. Neither *ENLIL* nor Nanna (see *SIN*) would become involved. However, the god *EA* came to Inana's aid. From the dirt of his fingernails, he created two beings who, because they were sexless, were able to enter the land of infertility. These beings were mourners who eased the ceaseless pain of Ereshkigal, whose existence had been one of continuous rejection. In reward for thus soothing the ruler of the underworld, the beings asked that they be allowed to revive Inana. Ereshkigal agreed and the goddess was reborn.

Before leaving, Inana had to agree to find someone to take her place in the underworld. The goddess was escorted on her homeward journey by a group of horrific demons.

When she reached the world of the living, Inana found her handmaiden, Ninshubur, waiting for her by the gates of the underworld and her two sons waiting for her in their temples. All three were in mourning. However, she was aghast to discover that her husband *DUMUZI*, far from mourning her death, was thoroughly enjoying himself. Not only was he seated on his throne but he was also dressed in the splendid garments which she herself had given him. Furious with rage, Inana immediately appointed Dumuzi as her substitute in the underworld.

Although Dumuzi attempted to hide, he was eventually dragged off by the demons who had accompanied Inana on her homeward journey. Geshtinanna, Dumuzi's sister, was so distraught that she offered to share Dumuzi's sentence with him. On the way to the underworld, Inana granted eternal life and death to both Dumuzi and Geshtinanna. For half of each year Inana and Dumuzi were together, while Geshtinanna took Dumuzi's place. When Dumuzi joined Inana, the milk flowed, the crops ripened and the fruit trees blossomed. During the barren months, however, Dumuzi had to return to the realm of Ereshkigal.

In ancient Sumer, a ceremony took place each year in which the king of each city would impersonate Dumuzi and the chief priestess would assume the role of Inana. The couple would take part in a marriage ritual, which was believed to ensure fertility and prosperity.

INANA (left), often identified with Ishtar, the goddess of love and war, is shown here with Anubanini, king of the Lullubians.

ISHTAR (right), the Babylonian goddess of love and war, had countless lovers, both men and gods, but was fickle and cruel. (*ILLUSTRATION FROM LEWIS SPENCE'S MYTHS OF BABYLONIA AND ASSYRIA.*)

INARAS features in Hittite mythology as the goddess who helped bring about the death of the monstrous dragon or serpent *ILLUYANKAS*. She is sometimes said to be the daughter of the weather god *TARU*. When Taru failed to overcome Illuyankas, Inaras devised a plot to bring about the monster's downfall. She prepared a marvellous feast, then asked a mortal, *HUPASIYAS*, to help her in her task. Hupasiyas agreed, on condition that she sleep with him.

Once she had carried out his request, Inaras invited the dragon, together with his offspring, to attend the banquet. When the monsters had eaten and drunk their fill, they found they were unable to squeeze back into their underground home. Hupasiyas then bound Illuyankas with a rope, and Taru killed him. Inaras built Hupasiyas a house in gratitude for his help. Then she said, "Farewell! I am now going out. Do not look out of the window; for if you look out, you will see your wife and children." When 20 days had passed, Hupasiyas threw open the window and saw his family. As soon as Inaras returned from her journey, Hupasiyas begged her to let him go home, whereupon the goddess killed him.

ISHTAR, the goddess of love and fertility, was a fearsome, often violent, deity, sometimes known as the "Lady of Battles". The Babylonian form of the Sumerian goddess *INANA*, she was the guardian spirit of life and the creator of wisdom. Her symbol was the eight-pointed star. Although she had countless lovers, she usually treated them cruelly.

On one momentous occasion, Ishtar descended to the underworld realm of her sister *ERESHKIGAL*. However, Ereshkigal cursed her sister, who subsequently died. As a result of Ishtar's death, the earth became infertile and neither birds nor beasts nor human beings mated. *EA*, the water god, eventually managed to save Ishtar by using his magic incantations, but Ereshkigal demanded she be given someone in her sister's stead. It was finally decided that *TAMMUZ*, her husband, should replace her for six months of each year.

Uruk or Erech, Ishtar's holy city, was called the town of the sacred courtesans, for prostitution formed part of her cult and she protected harlots, as well as alehouses. The personification of the planet Venus, Ishtar was sometimes believed to be the daughter of the moon god, *SIN*, sometimes of the sky god *ANU*. (See also *DYING AND RISING GODS; SACRED ANIMALS*)

ISHTAR (left) became the principal goddess of the Babylonians and Assyrians. Like Inana, she was identified with Venus, the evening star. (*ALABASTER, 2800–2300BC, SYRIA.*)

ISHTAR (right), in her violent form as "Lady of Battles", is shown heavily armed and mounted on a lion.

ISIS, the Egyptian mother goddess, was the daughter of *GEB* and *NUT*, and the sister and consort of *OSIRIS*. She is usually depicted with huge, sheltering wings, and she is sometimes regarded as a personification of the throne. The hieroglyph for her name is the image of a throne, and her lap came to be seen as the throne of Egypt.

Isis helped Osiris to civilize Egypt by teaching women to grind corn as well as how to spin and weave. She also taught people how to cure illness and instituted the rite of marriage. When Osiris left Egypt on his world travels, Isis ruled the country wisely and well in his stead. Aspects of the myth of Isis occur in various Egyptian texts, and were assembled into a single narrative by Plutarch in the first century AD.

On hearing of Osiris's death at the hands of the evil god *SETH*, Isis was distraught. She cut off her hair, put on mourning clothes and set off in search of his body. A group of children told Isis they had seen the chest that enclosed Osiris's body floating down the Nile and out into the sea. It was eventually washed up underneath a beautiful tree on the shores of Byblos in the Lebanon. The tree immediately began to grow, so quickly that it had soon enclosed the coffin in its trunk. Hearing of the astonishing tree, the king of Byblos ordered it to be cut down and brought to his palace, where it was used to support the roof.

News of the remarkable tree rapidly spread. Isis immediately guessed what had happened and rushed to Byblos where, after disguising herself, she sat by a well in the city centre. When some of the queen's servants came to fetch water from the well, Isis braided their hair for them, breathing on it such beautiful perfume that a short

ISIS (above) is usually depicted as a woman seated on a throne. She wears a headdress and huge wings which are outspread, protecting Egypt and its people. (SARCOPHAGUS OF RAMESES III, GRANITE.)

ISIS (left) was the sister and consort of Osiris, the murdered god. She sought his body throughout the land of Egypt when he was slain by the evil god Seth.

while later the queen sent for the stranger and made her the nurse of her child.

Each night, Isis placed the queen's child in the fire of immortality while she transformed herself into a swallow and flew around the pillar that enclosed Osiris's corpse. One evening, the queen came into the room and saw her son lying in the flames. She was so horrified that she let out a piercing scream, thereby causing her child to lose his chance of immortality. Isis then revealed her true identity and asked to be given the pillar.

Her wish was granted, and so at last she recovered Osiris's corpse. The goddess carried the body of Osiris back to Egypt where she hid it in a swamp. However, Seth discovered the body and cut it into 14 pieces, which he then scattered up and down the country. With the help of several other gods, Isis located all the pieces, except for the penis, which had been swallowed by a fish. According to one version of the story, Isis then reassembled the body and, using her healing and magical powers, restored Osiris to life. Before departing to the underworld, Osiris and Isis conceived a child, *HORUS*.

Isis became so famous throughout Egypt, and beyond, that in time she absorbed the qualities of almost all the other goddesses. She was a great mother goddess, a bird goddess, a goddess of the underworld who brought life to the dead and a goddess of the primeval waters. Her following spread beyond Egypt to Greece and throughout the Roman Empire. She was worshipped for more than 3,000 years, from before 3000BC until well into Christian times. Her cult, and many of her images, passed directly on to the figure of the Virgin Mary.

ISKUR was a Hittite weather god who controlled the rain and thunderstorms. The "King of Heaven", he assisted the earthly king in battles and was represented sitting on two mountain gods or riding on a chariot drawn by bulls, his sacred animals. His attributes were a club and shafts of lightning, and his sacred number was ten.

JAHWEH see YAHWEH.

JAM see YIMA.

JAMM see YAM.

JEHOVAH see YAHWEH.

JEMSHID see YIMA.

JIBRIL see GABRIEL.

THE KA'ABA, or "Square House" is an oblong stone building, draped with black silk, which contains the sacred Black Stone of Islam. Situated within the mosque at Mecca, Islam's holiest city, the Ka'aba symbolizes the meeting of heaven and earth, and was an important shrine long before the time of the Prophet Muhammad (*c.* AD570–632). It contained many images of gods and goddesses from the Arabian pantheon.

According to the Qur'an, the Ka'aba was rebuilt by ABRAHAM for the worship of the one true god – ALLAH – but the Meccans had enshrined a number of idols, the "Daughters of Allah", within it. Muhammad cleansed the Ka'aba of its idols and ordered that all prayers be directed to the structure. In pre-Islamic times, a four-month truce was called each year between the warring tribes of Arabia, and people from different tribes and towns would visit the shrine and circle round the structure.

Today, it is the sacred duty of all Muslim followers to try to make at least one pilgrimage to Mecca, specifically to the Ka'aba, in their lives. This pilgrimage is known as the hajj, and is one of the "Five Pillars of Islam". Its rites include seven circumambulations of the Ka'aba and, if possible, kissing the Black Stone.

Within Islam, the Black Stone is traditionally the place where Hagar conceived Ishmael, the ancestor of the Arabian people. Apocryphal stories abound as to its origins. One tale tells how it was once the most trustworthy of God's angels. God therefore placed the angel in the Garden of Eden, so that it might remind ADAM of his promise to God. However, with the Fall, Adam forgot his promise, and God

THE KA'ABA or "Square House" is an oblong stone building draped with black silk which contains the sacred Black Stone of Islam. (HAJJ CERTIFICATE, 1432.)

turned the angel into a white pearl. The pearl rolled towards Adam and then miraculously turned back into the angel once more. The angel reminded Adam of his promise, whereupon Adam kissed it. God then turned the angel into the Black Stone, to symbolize a world into which evil has entered. Adam carried the Black Stone across the world until he reached Mecca. There, the angel Gabriel told Adam to build the Ka'aba and to place the Black Stone within the structure.

Another story tells how the Abyssinian general Abraha determined to destroy the Ka'aba but was unable to enter the city of Mecca because the elephant upon which he was riding refused to move. Eventually, the general's army was forced to retreat.

KAMRUSEPAS see TELEPINU.

KERESASPA, according to some traditions within Iranian mythology, was the hero who would finally kill the monstrous dragon AZHI DAHAKA. Keresaspa was renowned for numerous brave deeds, and it is also told how he once went into battle against the vast bird Kamak, whose huge wings had covered the sky and thus prevented the fertilizing rain from reaching earth. Another monster to die at the hands of Keresaspa was Gandarewa, a demon who lived in the water and constantly threatened to swallow all that was good in creation.

KERET, the king of Sidon, was said to be a son of EL, the supreme god of the Ugaritic pantheon. A legend describing Keret's exploits was contained in texts dating from the 14th century BC, which were discovered in 1929 at Ras Shamra in Syria, on the site of the ancient city of Ugarit.

Keret had been married to seven wives, but all of them had died, and the king was despairing of ever fathering an heir to the throne. At this point, El appeared and ordered Keret to lead his army into battle against Sidon's enemies. Keret was terrified. He locked himself away and burst into tears. However, in a dream he discovered that he was to father a son, and this encouraged him to undertake the campaign. Afterwards, Keret took a wife and promised that he would give the goddess Asherat (see ASTARTE) presents of silver and gold in thanks. El blessed the king and said that he would father eight sons.

The children were born in due course, but Keret failed to keep his vow to Asherat. He became seriously ill and vegetation withered throughout his kingdom. A ceremony was held in the palace of the rain and fertility god, BAAL. The rains appeared, and Keret recovered from his illness.

KHNUM, an Egyptian creator god, was said to have fashioned the world on his potter's wheel. His name means "Moulder". The god is frequently depicted as a ram-headed man sitting in front of a potter's wheel on which stands the being he has created. Khnum made the gods as well as people. He was also said to control the annual inundation of the river Nile.

In one story, the historical sage *IMHOTEP*, a minister and architect to King Zoser in the third millennium BC, was consulted by the ruler about the cause of a seven-year famine. The Nile was failing to rise high enough to irrigate the fields, and the people were starving. Imhotep told Zoser that he should make offerings to Khnum. The king did as he was advised, whereupon Khnum appeared to him in a dream and promised him that he would release the waters. That year, the kingdom enjoyed a splendid harvest. (See also *SACRED ANIMALS*)

KINGU was a demon of ancient Mesopotamia. He was either the son or husband of *TIAMAT*, the mother goddess and monster of chaos. Kingu sided with his mother in her tremendous battle against *MARDUK*, leading an army of ferocious monsters into battle. However, like Tiamat, Kingu was

eventually slain by Marduk. According to one traditional story, Marduk mixed Kingu's blood with earth and used the clay to mould the first human beings. Kingu then went to live in the underworld kingdom of *ERESHKIGAL*, along with the other deities who had sided with Tiamat.

KHNUM (far left), the creator god, was portrayed with a ram's head as a symbol of potency and virility.

KHNUM (left) was said to have made men and women on his potter's wheel, and was also responsible for the flooding of the Nile.

KISHAR see *ANSHAR*.

THE KORYBANTES, or Corybantes, were the companions of *CYBELE*, the great mother of Phrygian mythology. They performed frenzied dances, took part in orgiastic revelries and were believed to have the power both to induce and to heal madness.

According to one tradition, they were the offspring of the Greek god Zeus, who impregnated the earth by falling on it as rain. According to another story, they were the offspring of the Greek deities Thalia and Apollo.

L

KUBABA (left), at first a local goddess of Carchemish, later became the neo-Hittite mother goddess. (BASALT RELIEF, CARCHEMISH, SYRIA, 9TH CENTURY BC.)

KOTAR see KOTHAR.

KOTHAR, or Kotar, was the divine craftsman or blacksmith of Phoenician mythology. Lord of magic spells and incantations, he appears in myths dating from the 14th century BC discovered at Ras Shamra in Syria, the site of the ancient city of Ugarit. Kothar created a marvellous bow for the hero *AHAT*. It was made from twisted horns and shaped like a serpent. The servant of the supreme god *EL*, Kothar helped to build a palace for *BAAL*, the god of rain and fertility.

KUBABA was an ancient goddess of Carchemish in Asia Minor. As a local goddess, she had only a minor role to play in the mythology of the region. In due course, however, she became the chief goddess of the neo-Hittite kingdoms and took on the characteristics of a mother goddess, whose attributes included a

KUBABA holds a mirror, one of the attributes inherited from her by the Phrygian goddess Cybele. (BASALT RELIEF, CARCHEMISH, SYRIA, 9TH CENTURY BC.)

mirror and a pomegranate. Her name, as well as some of her attributes, were taken over by the Phrygians for their mother goddess *CYBELE*, whose attributes also included a mirror and pomegranate. In Upper Mesopotamia she was known as Gubaba.

KUMARBI was the father of the gods in the mythology of the Hurrians, a people who lived in the mountainous regions south of the Caspian Sea and whose beliefs had a huge influence on those of the Hittites. Before acceding to the throne, Kumarbi had to depose *ANU*, to whom he had bowed down and ministered for nine years. At the end of the nine-year period, Kumarbi attacked Anu, who immediately flew up into the sky like a bird soaring to heaven. However, Kumarbi pulled Anu down by his feet and and bit off his penis. Anu told Kumarbi not to rejoice, for he had been impregnated by his sperm and would bear three terrible gods. These deities are believed to have been different aspects of the weather god *TESHUB*.

Kumarbi was eventually deposed by his son, Teshub. Kumarbi determined on revenge and, after seeking the help of the sea, proceeded to father another son. Known as *ULLIKUMMI*, he was made of diorite stone and was placed on the shoulders of the giant Upelluri, who lived in the middle of the sea. Teshub attacked Ullikummi, but he was unsuccessful in his onslaught and was forced to abdicate. Although the end of the myth is missing, it is widely agreed that Teshub eventually succeeded in defeating Kumarbi and regaining the throne.

KURUNTA was a Hittite god, generally believed to have been associated with the countryside. He appeared in a version of the myth of the disappearing god, *HAHHIMAS*, which describes the decline and death of all living

things. The weather god *TARU* sought to prevent Kurunta from being beguiled by Hahhimas, who paralysed people into inaction, but even Kurunta, a "child of the open country", fell prey to him. Kurunta was depicted standing on a stag, his sacred animal, and holding a hare and a falcon. Models of stags have been found in tombs dating from the third millennium BC.

LELWANI was originally a Hittite god of the underworld, referred to as "King". Over time, he seems to have developed into a female deity. She lived in the dark earth, and her shrines were connected with charnel houses and mausoleums.

LEVIATHAN was a ferocious monster of Phoenician mythology. His name means "Coiled". The figure of Leviathan drew on the Canaanite Lotan, a seven-headed monster killed by *ANAT*, as well as on the chaos monster *TIAMAT* of Mesopotamian mythology.

LEVIATHAN, the fearsome sea monster, was an expression of the chaos from which Yahweh protected humankind. (ILLUSTRATION BY GUSTAVE DORÉ FROM PARADISE LOST, 1866.)

In the Old Testament, Leviathan is the chaos dragon who is overcome by *YAHWEH*. He is referred to in Isaiah as the "crooked serpent", and in the Book of Job, God says, "His heart is as firm as a stone; yea as hard as a piece of the nether millstone." The lashings of his tail "maketh the deep to boil like a pot . . . Upon earth there is not his like, who is made without fear. He beholdeth all high things: he is a king over all the children of pride."

In apocalyptic writings, as well as in Christianity, the devil is said to manifest himself as the serpent Leviathan. In the apocryphal Book of Enoch, he appears as a vast creature, which inhabits "the abyss over the fountains of the waters." Leviathan's jaws were sometimes regarded as the very gates of hell. (See also *SERPENTS AND DRAGONS*)

GATEWAYS TO THE GODS

T HE EGYPTIANS BELIEVED THAT, on the death of the pharaoh, the sun god Ra would strengthen the rays of the sun to enable the king to ascend, as if he were climbing a heavenly staircase. The pyramid shape symbolized such a ramp, and the earliest pyramids were indeed designed in steps. Seen as a stylized mound, or hill, the pyramid also echoed the primeval hill which had risen out of the waters of Nun at the beginning of creation. The Mesopotamian equivalent of the pyramid was the ziggurat, a stepped structure that also rose skywards on a huge scale, with ramps and stairways connecting the levels and leading up to an altar at the top. The ancient builders of these colossal monuments saw the sun as an all-powerful creator and their ruler as a personification of the god. Their buildings, soaring skywards, connected them with the deity while glorifying his mortal embodiment on earth.

THE ZIGGURAT (above) of Ur was a temple dedicated to the Sumerian moon god Nanna, who measured time and brought fertility to the land. Built from rough, unbaked brick, it originally shone with a facing of glazed tiles. Long flights of steps connected the different levels and ultimately led to an altar at the very top: the ziggurat's function was to raise the worshippers closer to the sky deities.

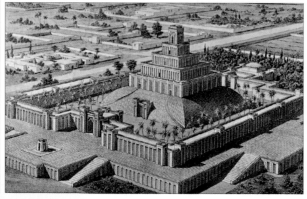

ZIGGURATS (left) were built in most major Mesopotamian cities. They were huge, stepped pyramids, surmounted by a temple where offerings were made, to which it was thought that the deity would descend to communicate with his or her devotees. The temple of Marduk in Babylon, seven storeys high, was possibly the inspiration for the biblical story of the Tower of Babel. (OTTO GIRARD, A ZIGGURAT RECONSTRUCTED, 19TH CENTURY.)

ANUBIS (above) presided over mummification and funeral rites. Since the Egyptians regarded the afterlife as a continuation of their earthly existence, the correct preservation of the corpse was vital. Detailed incantations, designed as a guide to the underworld, accompanied the body, at first carved inside tombs, and later written on an illustrated papyrus scroll known as the Book of the Dead. (THE BOOK OF THE DEAD OF KHENSUMOSE, 11TH–10TH CENTURY BC.)

THE PYRAMIDS' (below) vast size attested to the Egyptians' overriding concern with the continuation of life after death. Tens of thousands of men laboured for decades to construct them, under the direction of a single architect, who was given the title of "Overseer of All the King's Works". Most of the stone was quarried locally, and the huge blocks were hauled on sleds up ramps that rose higher and more steeply as the pyramid grew.

THE TOWER OF BABEL (above) was said to have been built on the plain of Shinar in Babylonia, according to the Bible, by the descendants of Noah, with the intention of reaching up to heaven. Yahweh, the god of the Israelites, disapproved of this product of human pride. He thwarted their plan by confusing their speech so that they no longer understood one another's instructions. The tower, and the planned city, were abandoned, and the people scattered. (MEDIEVAL MANUSCRIPT REPRODUCED IN STRUTT'S ANTIQUITIES, 1773.)

THE PYRAMIDS (above) of Giza were regarded by the Greeks as one of the Seven Wonders of the World, and are the only one of the seven to have survived virtually intact. Their awesome size and mysterious nature made it difficult to believe that they were the work of human hands. Imhotep, the architect of the first pyramid – and the first stone building in Egypt – achieved great renown by his feat: by the Late Period, 2,000 years after his death, he had become a god. (ENGRAVING BY JACQUES PICART FROM THE SEVEN WONDERS OF THE WORLD, 17TH CENTURY.)

295

LILITH is flanked by owls, her sacred animals. Created with Adam, she rejected his authority and consorted with demons. She wears a crown of lunar horns and a rainbow necklace. (TERRACOTTA.)

LILITH, according to Hebrew legend, was the first woman to be created. She was portrayed as part snake, part woman and wearing wings. *YAHWEH* blamed her for having tempted *EVE* to reveal the mysteries of the Garden of Eden to *ADAM*. In the Old Testament, she is the demon who disturbs the night. Her name means "Storm Goddess", or "She of the Night". The owl was her sacred creature.

According to Talmudic legend, Lilith was created at the same time as Adam. She refused to lie down beneath him, believing herself to be his equal, and flew away to the desert. There, she consorted with demons and became the mother of numerous other demons, at the rate of more than a hundred each day. God sent three angels to bring Lilith back from the desert, but she refused. The angels threatened to drown her, but she warned them that she had the power to kill children. Eventually she agreed not to harm children: "Whenever I shall see you or your names or your images on an amulet . . ." Lilith then wandered the world, looking for unprotected children who deserved to be punished because of the sins of their fathers. She killed them by smiling at them.

According to another tradition, Lilith desired to join the ranks of the cherubim, but God forced her to descend to the earth. When Lilith saw that Adam already had a partner, Eve, she attempted to return to the cherubim but instead found herself cast out into the desert. One Hebrew myth tells how Yahweh made Lilith, like Adam, from earth. However, instead of using clean earth, Yahweh made her from filth and sediments.

Lilith originated in Sumerian mythology as a goddess of desolation. She is also associated with the Babylonian demon Lilitu, who preyed upon men. (See also *SERPENTS AND DRAGONS*)

LILITU see *LILITH*.

LUCIFER see *SATAN*.

MAAT was the Egyptian goddess of truth, justice and harmony. A daughter of the sun god, *RA*, she ruled over the judgment of the dead in the throne room of *OSIRIS*. Each person, when they died, had to appear before the 42 judges of the dead and declare whether they were innocent or guilty of numerous crimes. The soul of the dead person would be weighed on a pair of scales against the goddess, represented by a single ostrich feather. The scales were held by the jackal-headed god, *ANUBIS*, and their verdict was recorded by Maat's consort, the moon god, *THOTH*. If the heart was weighed down by crimes, the terrifying female monster Ammut, part crocodile, part hippopotamus, part lion, would devour the dead person. If, however, the deceased had lived "with Maat in his heart", and was thus pure and virtuous, he became a spirit, and could live with the gods to fight against the serpent *APEP*.

Maat was depicted wearing on her head the feather that said to be put in the scales of judgment. As the "Breath of Life", she was often pictured ministering to the *PHARAOHS* by holding the ankh, a symbol of life, to their noses. All human beings were intended to live "by Maat, in Maat and for Maat."

MAAT, goddess of truth and justice, is depicted wearing a single ostrich feather, which is an ideogram of her name. (TOMB OF HUREMHEB, EGYPT.)

THE MALA'IKA, according to Islamic belief, are angels. They are sometimes said to be made from light and are believed to be superior to ordinary humankind but inferior to the prophets. The four chief angels are Jibril or *GABRIEL*, the holy spirit; Mikha'il, the guardian of the Jews; Israfil, the angel who will sound the trumpet at the resurrection; and Arazil, the "Angel of Death". *IBLIS* is either regarded as the fallen arazil or as one of the *DJINN*.

MANAT, or Menat, was a goddess of pre-Islamic Arabia who was worshipped in the region between the holy cities Mecca and Medina. She was believed to be one of the three daughters of *ALLAH*, the supreme god, the others being *AL-UZZA* and *AL-LAT*. As a goddess of fate, Manat had control over human destiny.

MANDAH was the name given to a pre-Islamic group of Arabian gods who were concerned with irrigation as well as being protective deities.

MARDUK, the chief god of Babylon, was the oldest son of *EA*, the water god. Born in the waters of *APSU*, the primordial, fresh-water ocean, Marduk was originally regarded as a fertility or agricultural deity whose attribute was an agricultural implement with a triangular blade, called a "mar". However, he gained a reputation as a fearless warrior and was usually depicted armed for battle. His name means "Calf of the Sun God", and he was associated with the planet Jupiter. This most splendid of gods apparently had four eyes and four ears, and fire blazed forth when his lips moved.

In time, Marduk's reputation for bravery grew to such an extent that he was chosen by the gods to attack the terrifying monster *TIAMAT*. He was given a thunderbolt as a weapon and also equipped himself with his bow, spear and mace. After a ferocious battle, Marduk slaughtered Tiamat: "When Tiamat opened her mouth to consume him, he drove in the evil wind that she close not her lips. As the fierce winds charged her belly, Her body was distended and her mouth was wide open. He released the arrow, it tore her belly, It cut through her insides, splitting the heart. Having thus subdued her, he extinguished her life."

The great god cast down Tiamat's carcass, stood upon it and, after slicing her body in two, thrust one half upwards to form the vault of the heavens and pushed the other half down to form the floor of the deep. Thus, the earth and sky were created. Marduk then divided the year up into 12 months, made the constellations and appointed the sun and moon to their places in the sky. He then addressed his father saying "Blood I will mass and cause bones to be. I will establish a savage, 'man' shall be his name."

The gods tied up *KINGU*, who had sided with his mother, Tiamat, in the battle, and severed his blood

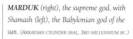

MARDUK (right), the supreme god, with Shamash (left), the Babylonian god of the sun. (AKKADIAN CYLINDER SEAL, 3RD MILLENNIUM BC.)

vessels. Out of his blood, which they mixed with clay, they fashioned human beings.

Before agreeing to attack Tiamat, Marduk had successfully persuaded the gods that, if he rose to the challenge, he should be granted additional powers, including the ability to determine fates and the right to pardon or kill captives taken in battle. After killing the monster, he was awarded 50 titles, each of which corresponded to a powerful divine attribute. In this manner, Marduk came to absorb all the other gods and to symbolize total divinity. He even threatened *ANU*'s status as supreme god, taking from him the power of his dignity.

According to one tale, the evil genies were annoyed by the moon god, *SIN*, whose light revealed their wrongdoings for all to see. The genies, together with *SHAMASH*, *ISHTAR* and *ADAD*, devised a plot whereby they eventually succeeded in eclipsing Sin's light. However, Marduk, displaying no fear whatsoever, simply overcame the conspirators and put them to flight. (See also *SACRED ANIMALS; SERPENTS AND DRAGONS*)

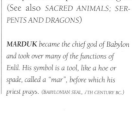

MARDUK became the chief god of Babylon and took over many of the functions of Enlil. His symbol is a tool, like a hoe or spade, called a "mar", before which his priest prays. (BABYLONIAN SEAL, 7TH CENTURY BC.)

MASHYA AND MASHYOI

were the first human couple of ancient Iranian mythology. In some traditions, they were said to have been born from the seed of *GAYOMART*, the primeval man, after it had lain in the soil for 40 years. Their first act was to walk, their second to eat. Then, however, they were sent a thought by a demon and, as a result, they became victims of *ANGRA MAINYU*, the principle of darkness. However, the good spirits continued to protect them. In time, Mashya and Mashyoi begat seven couples. One of these couples, Siyamek and Siyameki, became the parents of *HAOSHYANGHA* and of Fravak and Fravakain, who were said to be the ancestors of the 15 different peoples into which humankind was divided.

MEHUERET see NEITH.

MEN, a Phrygian moon god, was

said to rule over both the underworld and the heavens. He was attributed with the good health of plants and animals and was referred to as Tyrannos or "Master".

MENAT see MANAT.

MIN, an ancient and popular

Egyptian god, was always depicted with an erect phallus and with a flail raised in his right hand. On his

MIN (left), the god of roads and travellers, wore upon his head a crown decorated with two upright plumes. (RELIEF, KARNAK.)

head he wore a crown decorated with two tall, straight plumes. It is thought that Min may originally have been worshipped as a creator deity, but in classical times he was venerated as the god of roads and protector of those who travelled through the desert. His main cult centre was at Koptos, a centre for commercial travellers, and prayers were offered to the god before the travellers embarked on their expeditions. Min was also a god of fertility and growth, and a protector of crops. His main feast was known as the Feast of the Steps. Seated on his step, the god received the first sheaf of the harvest, which had been cut by the king.

MINUCHER, according to

ancient Iranian mythology, was a descendant of *FERIDUN*, the great hero. When Feridun grew old he gave each of his three sons, Selm, Tur and Irej, a share of his kingdom. However, Selm and Tur plotted to take Irej's share from him. Irej was willing simply to give his brothers his part of the kingdom, and so he came before them unarmed. Without hearing what he had to say, Tur struck him over the head with a golden chair and then slashed him with his sword from head to foot until Irej's body

was streaming with blood. Tur tore Irej's head from his body, filled his skull with musk and amber, and sent it to Feridun. The king, who was waiting for his youngest son to return home, was stricken with grief when he heard what had happened and sought revenge.

Eventually Irej's grandson *MINUCHER* attacked and killed Selm and Tur in a bloody and ferocious battle. Feridun then died, leaving the throne to Minucher.

MITHRA, known in Indian

mythology as Mitra, was originally a god of contracts and friendship. In Iran he developed into the protector of truth. Before the time of *ZOROASTER*, the religious reformer, Mithra was often

associated with *AHURA MAZDA*, the principle of good. Mithra was the light: he was believed to ride his golden chariot, the sun, across the sky, drawn by four white horses. He had 10,000 ears and eyes, possessed both strength and knowledge, and was renowned for his bravery in battle. The god was able to bless those who worshipped him with victory over their enemies as well as wisdom, but he showed no mercy to his foes. As a god of fertility, he caused the rain to fall and the plants to grow.

According to one tradition, Mithra, as the sun, formed a link between Ahura Mazda and *ANGRA MAINYU*, the principle of darkness. This supposition was built on the understanding that the sun marked the continual revolutions of light and dark. Under Zoroaster's reforms to Iranian religion, Mithra was ousted from power, and Ahura

MITHRA was a forerunner of the Graeco-Roman god Mithras, shown here. Mithra was worshipped in underground shrines, many of them decorated with a relief showing him slaying the bull Geush Urvan. (MITHRAEUM OF SIDON, 4TH CENTURY AD.)

MOSE

MOSES (left) was given the Ten Commandments on Mount Sinai. Here he presents them to the Hebrew people. (ILLUSTRATION BY H. PISAN.)

MOSES (right) loosens his sandal on Mount Horeb, or Sinai, obeying God's command from the burning bush. (MOSAIC, SAN VITALE, RAVENNA, ITALY.)

Mazda was given the position of supreme deity. Although, in the fourth century BC, Mithra returned as the focus of an extremely popular cult, Zoroastrians continued to give him no credence.

At his birth, Mithra was said to have emerged from a rock armed with a knife and a torch. He was worshipped in underground shrines, almost all of which were decorated with a relief showing him slaying the bull GEUSH URVAN, from whose corpse all plants and animals arose.

Regular sacrifices, particularly of bulls, were made to Mithra, in the belief that the fertility of nature would thereby be ensured. In the first century BC, when the Roman Empire expanded into western Asia, Mithra was assimilated into Graeco-Roman belief as the god Mithras.

MOLECH see *MOLOCH*.

MOLOCH, or Molech, was the name of an Ammonite god to whom human sacrifices were made. The Ammonites occupied the southern part of modern Jordan and were descended from Lot, who appears in the Old Testament as the nephew of the patriarch *ABRAHAM*. In the Second Book of Kings, Moloch is described as the "abomination of the children of Ammon."

Many Israelites are believed to have consecrated their children to Moloch by throwing them into the flames. It is sometimes argued that, rather than being the name of a god, Moloch refers simply to the sacrificial ritual. The children were burnt in a place called Tophet, in the valley of Hinnom, which had been built for the explicit purpose of sacrificial rituals.

The king was sometimes regarded as the son of Moloch, and the phrase "to the molech" may have meant "for the sake or life of the king" and referred to the sacrifice of a child conceived at a sacred marriage rite. Other research suggests that Moloch may have been the god Baal-Hammon who was worshipped at Tyre and Carthage.

MOSES was a great Hebrew prophet who is generally believed to have lived in the 13th century BC and who fulfilled many of the traditional functions of the mythic hero. He was the agent of God in delivering the tribes of Israel from their bondage in Egypt, and he presented them with the law establishing God's covenant with them. He is traditionally regarded as having written a portion of the Pentateuch, the first five books of the Bible.

During the period of the Israelites' exile in Egypt, Moses survived a decree to kill all male children by being hidden in the bulrushes. He was discovered there by an Egyptian princess and was brought up in the royal palace. Later, during a period in exile, Moses was grazing his flock when an angel of God appeared to him in a flame of fire, which issued from a bush. Speaking from the centre of the fire, the voice of God told Moses that he was called "I am that I am", which the Hebrews expressed by the four letters YHWH or JHWH, later pronounced as "YAHWEH".

In a later episode, recounted in the Book of Exodus, Moses led his people out of Egypt, and God drew back the Red Sea for them, so that they could walk across to freedom. On Mount Sinai, Moses received the Ten Commandments, written on tablets of stone, and the people of Israel made a pact, or covenant, with their new deity, Yahweh.

N

MOT, according to Phoenician mythology, was the god of death, drought and infertility. He ruled over the underworld and over the countryside when the ground lay dry. On one important occasion, *BAAL*, the god of rain, thunderstorms and fertility, challenged Mot to a contest, and banished death to the barren wastelands. In response, Mot challenged Baal to come to his underground home and eat mud, the food of the dead. Baal accepted the challenge but died as a result. The goddess *ANAT*, furious with grief, visited Mot to seek the release of her brother and consort. She carried off Baal's corpse and, when Mot refused to restore him to life, she killed Mot in a ritual slaughter: "With her sickle she cleaves him. With her flail she beats him. With fire she grills him. With her mill she

grinds him. In the fields she scatters him, to consume his leaven, so that he no longer withholds his share [of the crop]." The supreme god *EL* learned in a dream that Baal was to come back to life: he saw the skies dripping with oil and streams running with honey.

The story of Mot and Baal provides a dramatic account of the agricultural cycle, its periods of dryness and death under the rule of Mot, alternating with the revival of the land's fertility when Baal was brought back to life. According to the Jewish historian Philo (*c.* 30BC–AD45), Mot was created at the beginning of time when the dark forces of chaos mingled with air. However, Mot was usually regarded as the son of *EL*.

NAMTAR see *RESHEF*.

NANNA see *SIN*.

NASR, an Arabian deity of pre-Islamic times, is mentioned in the Qur'an. He was one of the five idols who were erected by the descendants of Cain, the others being *WADD*, Sowa, Yaghut and Ya'uk. His name is translated as either "Vulture" or "Eagle".

NEBTHET see *NEPHTHYS*.

NEITH, the great mother of the Egyptians, was originally the local goddess of Sais, situated in the Nile delta of Lower Egypt. She was also a warrior goddess and a goddess of the home. As a goddess of war, who was believed to march into battle ahead of the soldiers, her symbol was a shield with crossed arrows. She was often said to be the mother of *SEBEK*, the crocodile god, and was also said to have created the terrible cosmic serpent *APEP* by spitting into *NUN*, the watery abyss.

Neith came to be regarded as the mother of all the gods, and in particular of *RA*, and was sometimes seen as the celestial cow, Mehueret, who gave birth to the sky before life began. Neith also became the protectress of the dead. She is sometimes depicted offering them food and drink on their arrival in the underworld.

NEITH, the Egyptian great mother, was envisaged as the great weaver who wove the world with her shuttle. (TOMB OF RAMESES I.)

NEKHBET, the vulture goddess of Upper Egypt, protected the ruling pharaoh and suckled him and the royal children. (TEMPLE OF HATSHEPSUT, EGYPT.)

NEKHBET was the vulture goddess of Upper Egypt. She was often depicted with her wings outspread, holding the symbols of eternity in her claws. Nekhbet was widely regarded as a mother goddess who looked after the ruling *PHARAOH*, along with *WADJET*, the cobra goddess of Lower Egypt.

NEPHTHYS, or Nebthet, the consort of the evil Egyptian god *SETH*, was a daughter of the earth god *GEB* and sky goddess, *NUT*. Her name means "Mistress of the House or Castle". The goddess was sometimes regarded as a symbol of the desert edge; often barren but occasionally, after a flood, fruitful.

Nephthys and Seth had no children of their own. However, according to one tradition Nephthys plied her brother *OSIRIS* with drink, seduced him and conceived a child. In some stories, the baby she gave birth to was *ANUBIS*, the jackal-headed god. When Seth murdered Osiris, Nephthys immediately abandoned her husband and helped her sister *ISIS* to embalm Osiris's corpse. The two goddesses then took the form of kites and hovered over the body, protecting it while it awaited burial. Nephthys thus came to be associated with the dead.

NEPHTHYS with her sister Isis. After the death of Osiris, Nephthys helped Isis prepare him for burial. The sisters are often portrayed protecting the bodies of the dead. (PAPYRUS, EGYPT. C. 1300BC.)

NERGAL see *ERESHKIGAL*.

NINGAL see *SIN*.

NINGIRSU see *NINURTA*.

NINHURSAGA, the Sumerian goddess known as "Lady of the Great Mountain" or "Lady of the Stony Ground", was sometimes referred to as the mother of the gods, the great creative principle. As *NINLIL*, she was the wife of *ENLIL*, lord of the wind; and as Ninki, she was the wife of Enki (or *EA*), the god of water. Ninhursaga was said to nourish earthly kings with her milk, thereby making them divine. Many Mesopotamian rulers, including Nebuchadnezzar, called themselves her children.

The goddess was associated with birth; she was the power that gave shape to life in the womb and was the divine midwife of gods and mortals. However, she was also the stony ground that lies at the edges of the Arabian desert.

Enki and Ninki were believed to live together on the island of Dilmun, a paradise land sometimes thought to be present-day Bahrein. The divine couple had several children, and indeed, all the vegetation in the land was said to originate from their union. However, in time, Enki began to take a sexual interest in his daughters, whereupon Ninki fell into a terrifying rage. Retrieving Enki's semen from the body of Uttu, the spider goddess, she planted it in the ground. The seeds grew into eight plants. When Enki ate the plants, he was attacked by illness in eight parts of his body. Nobody but Ninki was able to cure him, which at length she did by placing him in her womb, from which he was reborn.

301

NINKI see *NINHURSAGA*.

NINLIL, the Sumerian grain goddess, was sometimes associated with the goddess *NINHURSAGA*. One day *ENLIL*, the god of the air, found Ninlil bathing in a canal near the city of Nippur and, unable to resist her beauty, raped her. In punishment, the gods banished Enlil from Nippur and sentenced him to death. Enlil departed for the land of the dead, but Ninlil followed him so that he should see her give birth to the son they had conceived. The child, when born, became the moon god, Nanna, or *SIN*. Enlil was overwhelmed with grief that his son would have to live with him in the land of the dead and tried to persuade Ninlil to have another child by him, who would act as Nanna's replacement while Nanna returned to the land of the living. Ninlil eventually agreed and in due course gave birth to three more children, thereby appeasing the underworld goddess *ERESHKIGAL* for the loss of Nanna.

NINURTA, or Ningirsu, was a Mesopotamian god of war. He was also associated with the irrigation of the land. Ninurta's warlike temperament prompted a vast army to rise up against him. All of nature joined in the battle, including the rocks and stones. Ninurta soon conquered his enemies. He rewarded those stones that had taken his side by giving them the power to shine and glitter, while those that had sided against him he left to be trodden underfoot.

In another story, Ninurta retrieved the tablets of destiny from the tempest bird, *ZU*. In some accounts, Ninurta is the son of *ENLIL* and *NINHURSAGA* and the husband of Gula, the goddess of healing. In early Sumerian tales, Ninurta took the form of Imdugud, the storm bird, but he gradually came to have human form. However, he was usually represented with wings, and when on the battlefield would still appear as a lion-headed storm bird.

NOAH is the hero of the Old Testament story of the flood. According to the Book of Genesis, God saw that humankind had become wicked and declared, "I will destroy man whom I have created from the face of the earth; *NOAH cursed Ham's son Canaan because Ham had seen "the nakedness of his father", Noah. This may be a later attempt to explain Canaan's subjugation to the tribes of Israel. (19TH CENTURY ENGRAVING.)*

both man, and beast, and the creeping things, and the fowls of the air; for it repenteth me that I have made them." However, because Noah was a good and faithful man, God decided to save him, together with his family.

God instructed Noah to make an ark and to take into it two of every living thing. When the day of the flood arrived, water gushed from the ground, and the rain began to fall. For 40 days and 40 nights the torrent continued until

NINURTA, the Mesopotamian god of war, taking part in a New Year or creation ritual with the winged goddess, Ishtar, the water god, Ea, and the sun god, Shamash.
(AKKADIAN CYLINDER SEAL, c. 2400–2200BC.)

the entire earth was submerged. After some time had passed, Noah sent out a dove to see if the flood had abated but it returned to the ark. Eventually, another dove returned with an olive leaf in its mouth. God promised never again to flood the earth and offered the rainbow as a sign of good faith: "This is the token of the covenant which I make between me and you and every living creature that is with you, for perpetual generations: I do set my bow in the cloud."

Flood myths are found throughout the ancient world, from Greece to India. The story of a flood destroying earth appears in the epic of *GILGAMESH* as well as in the myth of the Sumerian water god Enki (see *EA*) and the hero

NOAH was instructed by God to build an ark and take into it two of every living thing, to preserve them from the destruction of the flood. (FRENCH BOOK ILLUSTRATION, C. 1260.)

Atrahasis, or Ziusadra.(See also *MYTHS OF THE FLOOD*)

303

UNDERWORLDS

THE MYTHOLOGY OF EVERY CULTURE included the idea that life in some way continued after death. The spirit might inhabit another physical body and live on earth again, or lead a perpetual existence in a murky netherworld. The concept of judgment invariably accompanied death and determined the future of the soul. A tribunal of gods or angels awaited the deceased to weigh up their conduct. The religion of the Egyptians was dominated by their funerary cult, but far from being obsessed with death itself, they saw it simply as a brief interruption. They aspired to an afterlife that was a continuation of their existence on earth in every respect, preserving their social status, family connections and even their physical possessions. Only for those who had failed to please the gods during their mortal lives, or who had not prepared themselves for their journey through the underworld with the proper rituals and incantations, was death really a termination.

OSIRIS (right) was originally a deity of vegetation and agriculture, but the myth of his death became central to his cult and raised his status to that of a great god. The pharaoh, who was considered to be an incarnation of Ra the sun god while he was alive, became identified with Osiris on his death. Osiris was depicted wearing the crown of Egypt, and carrying the royal insignia of the crook and flail, but was tightly wrapped in mummy cloths. As lord of the underworld, he presided over the judgment of the dead on their arrival in his realm. (WALL PAINTING FROM THE GRAVE OF SENNUTEM, 14TH CENTURY BC.)

MASHU (right) was a magic mountain which formed the boundary of the Mesopotamian underworld, into which the sun set each night. When the hero Gilgamesh visited the underworld in search of the immortal Utnapishtim, he had to pass through the gates of Mashu, guarded by fearsome scorpion gods. After a journey in total darkness, he emerged into an enchanted garden of precious stones. (ILLUSTRATION FROM GILGAMESH BY ZABELLE C. BOYAJIAN, 1924.)

THE WEIGHING OF THE SOUL (above) was a decisive moment in the Egyptian journey to the underworld. The deceased was brought by Anubis before a panel of judges and his heart, where thought and memory resided, was weighed on the scales. It had to balance exactly with the goddess of truth, Maat. If it failed, the spirit was destroyed: the terrible Ammut, with the head of a crocodile and the mane of a lion, crouched by the scales waiting to eat the condemned. The ibis-headed god Thoth declared the result. (FROM THE BOOK OF THE DEAD OF HUNEFER, 13TH CENTURY BC.)

MUMMIFICATION (left) was practised to preserve a corpse so that life could continue after death, and this was the domain of the mortuary god, Anubis. He took the form of a black dog or jackal – the very animal who might scavenge a body that was incorrectly buried. The heart was the only internal organ left in the body, and it was protected by a scarab beetle bearing a spell that would keep it from confessing any sins during interrogation before Anubis. (WALL PAINTING FROM THE GRAVE OF SENNUTEM, 14TH CENTURY BC.)

NUN, according to Egyptian mythology, was the personification of the watery abyss that existed at the beginning of time and which contained the potential for all life.

According to one Egyptian creation myth, these formless, chaotic waters contained four pairs: Nun and Naunet, Kuk and Kauket, Huh and Hauhet, *AMON* and Amaunet. These pairs, known as the Ogdoad, symbolized the primeval waters. Eventually the four pairs formed an egg in the waters of Nun, and out of the egg burst a fabulous bird, or, according to some versions of the story, air. This bird was a manifestation of the creator god. According to one tradition, the sun god Atum rose from Nun in the form of a hill, a primeval mound, and gave birth to *SHU*, the god of air, and Tefnut, the goddess of moisture. Nun was depicted as a man standing in water, his arms raised to support the boat of the sun god. (See also *MYTHS OF THE FLOOD*)

NUSKU see *SIN*.

NUT, the Egyptian goddess of the sky, was the twin sister of the earth god, *GEB*. When, against *RA*'s wishes, she married her brother, Ra was so enraged that he commanded *SHU* to separate the couple. Shu pushed Nut upwards to form the sky and Geb down to form the earth. Ra was so angry with Nut that he decreed that she would be unable to bear children in any month of the year. However, the god *THOTH* took pity on her. He challenged the moon to a game of draughts, and, when he won, took as his prize enough of the moon's light to create five new days. On each of these days, Nut bore a child: *OSIRIS, SETH, ISIS, NEPHTHYS* and, according to some versions of the tale, *HORUS*.

Another myth tells how Nut helped Ra to distance himself from human beings when he became disillusioned with their ways.

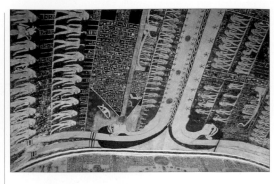

Taking the form of a cow, she raised the great god upwards on her back. However, the higher Nut rose, the dizzier she became, until she had to summon four gods to steady her legs. These gods became the pillars of the sky.

OG, according to Hebrew mythology, was one of the many giants who roamed the earth before the great flood that destroyed creation.

NUT, the Egyptian sky goddess, arches over the earth, formed by her consort, Geb. She balances on her outstretched fingers and toes, which touch the four cardinal points. (TOMB OF RAMESES VI.)

Of these giants, Og alone survived the flood. According to one story, the flood waters reached no higher than Og's ankles, and so he remained unharmed by the deluge. Other stories tell how *NOAH* allowed Og to sit on the roof of his ark while Noah fed him oxen.

After the flood had subsided, Og fell in love with Sarah, the wife of *ABRAHAM*, and jealously plotted against the patriarch. The enmity between Og and Abraham continued down the years, and it culminated in a battle with *MOSES*. After the great prophet had led the Israelites out of Egypt into the land of Canaan, he was forced to engage in numerous battles against the local people. One of these battles was against Edrei, a city ruled by Og. When the giant spotted the approaching forces, he lifted a mountain high above his head and was about to drop it on Moses and his followers when *YAHWEH* caused the monstrous missile to drop on to Og's own shoulders. The giant

NUT was depicted on funerary amulets which were attached to a mummy for protection. At death, the pharoah was said to pass into the body of Nut. A scarab was placed over the heart to keep it silent during the judgment of the dead. (MUMMY ACCESSORIES, PTOLEMAIC PERIOD, C. 100BC.)

struggled to throw off the mountain, but his teeth sank into it, and he was unable to see properly. Moses took an axe in his hands, leapt into the air and cut through the giant's ankles. Og crumpled, struck the ground and died. In the Old Testament Book of Deuteronomy, Og was said to be king of Bashan: "Behold, his bedstead was a bedstead of iron . . . nine cubits was the length thereof, and four cubits the breadth of it."

OGDOAD see NUN.

OHRMAZD see AHURA MAZDA.

OSIRIS, son of the Egyptian deities GEB and NUT, was originally a god of nature who symbolized the cycle of vegetation. In time, however, he became god of the dead. At his birth, he was pro-

claimed the "Universal Lord", and he grew into a tall and handsome deity. When his father retired, Osiris became king of Egypt and took his sister, ISIS, as his queen. He taught humankind how to make bread and wine, and oversaw the building of the first temples and statues to the gods. He also built towns, and laid down just and fair laws. Once Egypt was civilized, Osiris embarked on a great journey, civilizing each country to which he came. His success was largely due to the fact that everyone he encountered was immediately transfixed by his charisma.

When Osiris returned to Egypt many festivals were held in his honour. However, his younger brother, SETH, grew jealous of his popularity. He hatched a plan and invited Osiris to a feast, during which a superb coffin was carried in to

them. Feigning innocence, Seth announced that the coffin belonged to whomsoever fitted it. Osiris entered into the joke and lay down in the coffin. Immediately, the lid was nailed down and the coffin thrown into the Nile. The coffin was eventually washed up on the shores of Byblos.

According to another version of the story, Seth killed Osiris after first transforming himself into a crocodile; yet another tale tells how Seth turned himself into a bull and trampled Osiris to death.

When Isis heard what had happened to her husband and brother, she was overcome with grief and began to search for his body. She eventually found it and brought it back to Egypt, where she hid it in a swamp. Seth found the body and cut it into 14 pieces. Undeterred, Isis remade Osiris's body and then

OSIRIS, murdered by Seth and dying, gives his divine sperm, the source of life, to his consort, Isis. (BASALT RELIEF FROM THE SARCOPHAGUS OF NES-SHUTFENE, SAQQARA, 4TH CENTURY BC.)

performed a magic ritual whereby she restored Osiris to life. This was the first rite of embalment. Osiris was by now so disillusioned with his brother that he decided to retire from life and to reign over the dead in the underworld. There, in the court of the underworld, he supervised the judgment of the dead.

Osiris was usually depicted as a bearded man wrapped in mummy bandages and holding a crook and a flail to symbolize his kingship. He symbolizes the regenerative powers of the natural world, as well as the threat posed by severe weather conditions to the well-being of humanity. (See also UNDERWORLDS; DYING AND RISING GODS)

P

THE PHARAOHS' (top) treasure chambers were fabled for their unrivalled wealth of gold and magnificent artefacts, and many were rifled in antiquity. This is the treasure chamber of Rhampsinitus.

PAPAS see ATTIS.

PHARAOHS ruled over Egypt from around 3100BC, when the country became unified. In early times, the word pharaoh, meaning "Great House" or "Palace," was never used to refer to the king himself, but under the New Kingdom (c. 1570–1085BC) the term could be applied directly to the king. Regarded as a divine monarch, the pharaoh was sometimes depicted worshipping his own image, thereby drawing attention to his divine status. He was given the titles of "Horus"; "The Two Ladies" (referring to NEKHBET and WADJET,

the goddesses of Upper and Lower Egypt); "Horus of Gold"; "King of Upper and Lower Egypt and Lord of the Double Land"; and "Son of Ra and Lord of Diadems". Whenever there was a change of ruler, the queen was said to marry RA and to bear a son who became the new king. Pharaohs were often depicted suckling from a goddess to symbolize both their divinity and their relationship to the deity.

According to one papyrus, the wife of a high priest of Ra was made pregnant by the sun god. The ruling pharaoh, Khufu of the fourth dynasty, attempted to prevent the birth, but Ra sent several deities,

led by ISIS and NEPHTHYS, to look after the woman. The deities delivered and named the children and, before leaving the house, hid three crowns. When the priest found the crowns he realized that his children would become kings.

The pharaoh was responsible for the economic and spiritual welfare of his people, and for the construction and upkeep of the temples. Priests were regarded merely as his representatives. After his death, the pharaoh was believed both to join Ra in his boat which sailed across the sky and to take up kingship in the underworld, as OSIRIS. (See also GATEWAYS TO THE GODS)

THE PHARAOH RAMESES II (above) defeated the Khetans in battle. The god-kings were often called to mediate in battle as well as between the gods and the people.

THE PHARAOH RAMESES II (above left) as a young man. Regarded as a divine monarch, the pharaoh was sometimes depicted worshipping his own image. (BAS-RELIEF, 13TH CENTURY BC.)

THE PHARAOH TUTANKHAMEN (right) had a fairly undistinguished reign. However, his tomb at Thebes survived intact throughout the centuries until it was opened in 1922. This golden mask from the inner tomb was amongst the most splendid of the many treasures discovered. (14TH CENTURY BC.)

PTAH was the god of Memphis, the old capital in the north of Egypt where the *PHAROAHS* were crowned. His priests believed he created the world, although he probably originated as a fertility god. In the third millennium BC, he came to rank third in the divine hierarchy after *AMON* and *RA*.

Believed to be the inventor of the arts, Ptah designed and built secular buildings as well as overseeing the construction of temples, and he was said to have moulded the gods and kings out of metal. In one tradition, he created the world through the power of the word.

Ptah is usually depicted wearing a close-fitting linen wrap and skull cap, and holding the sceptre of dominion. Sometimes, however, he is shown as a twisted, frightening figure, in which guise he was believed to protect humanity from all kinds of evil.

When the power of Memphis declined, Ptah was often associated with other deities, including *OSIRIS*. His consort was the lioness goddess, Sekhmet (see *HATHOR*) and he was the father of Nefertum. The bull *APIS* was worshipped in a temple opposite his and was believed to be an incarnation of the god. (See also *SACRED ANIMALS*)

RA, the supreme manifestation of the sun god of Heliopolis, was a hugely important member of the Egyptian pantheon. He was said to have come into being on the primeval mound that rose out of *NUN* and to have proceeded to plan creation. Sometimes, however, he was depicted as a child rising out of a lotus flower. The Egyptians believed that each day the sun god was born. In the morning, after his bath and breakfast, he began his journey across the sky in his boat

PTAH, the creator god and patron of craftsmen, holds his sceptre of dominion, surmounted by the ankh, or symbol of life.
(STATUETTE FROM THE TREASURE OF TUTANKHAMEN, 14TH CENTURY BC.)

RA (above), the supreme Egyptian sun god, with Aten, another sun god, to the left. (WALL PAINTING FROM THE TOMB OF SENNEDJEM, THEBES, 13TH CENTURY BC.)

RA (left), the supreme Egyptian manifestation of the sun god, is usually portrayed as a falcon-headed man wearing the disc of the sun on his head. (GREAT TEMPLE, ABU SIMBEL.)

and would spend one of the hours of the day inspecting each of his 12 provinces. When the sun went down, Ra was believed to enter the underworld until the morning, when he was born again. All night long, the supreme god had to fight his enemy APEP, the terrible cosmic serpent of the underworld.

Ra gave birth to SHU, the god of air, and Tefnut, the goddess of moisture. According to one myth, the pair disappeared to explore the universe; when Ra finally found them, he was so relieved that he burst into tears. From his tears the

first human beings were formed. Another tale tells how, when Ra was an old and dribbling man, the goddess ISIS determined to discover his secret name. She made a snake from earth moistened with the great god's spit and positioned the snake beside a path where the god liked to walk. In due course, the snake bit Ra, poisoning him and causing him such agony that he cried out in pain. Isis agreed to cure him only if he would reveal his name. Ra's suffering was such that he eventually agreed to disclose his secret. Isis promised not to pass on her knowledge to anyone but HORUS and, by speaking the god's true name, healed him.

The PHARAOHS called themselves "Sons of Ra", not only because he was held in great awe but also because he was said to have created order out of chaos. Ra was usually depicted as a falcon wearing a sun disc on his head. (See also MYTHS OF THE FLOOD)

DYING AND RISING GODS

STORIES OF BEAUTIFUL AND WELL-LOVED semi-divine youths who died tragically, or were seized by the grim ruler of the underworld but were then miraculously restored to life, echoed through many ancient cultures. Like the promise of a serene afterlife, they raised the possibility that death itself could be conquered. They underlined the regenerative powers of nature, suggesting the continuance of humanity in future generations and, above all, the annual rebirth of the natural world. Dying and rising gods were associated with vegetation, fertility and the harvest: their devotees worshipped them because they needed reassurance that when the summer drought came and food crops died away, they could rely on the resurgence of the next season's growth. Faith in the annual return of a force that could defy death and the powers of darkness gave them confidence that the following year would be fruitful. Fresh green shoots pushing up through the soil can be clearly identified with the eternal youth of these deities rising from the underworld.

ADONIS (above), the beautiful youth, was the lover of Venus, the Roman version of Astarte, goddess of the Phoenicians and Canaanites. He was gored to death by a boar while out hunting and descended to the underworld, but at Venus's entreaty was permitted to return to her for half of each year. On his annual departure from earth, an ecstatic mourning festival was held in the Phoenician city of Byblos, the centre of his cult. (VENUS AND ADONIS BY PYOTR SOLOKOV, CANVAS, 1782.)

WILD ANEMONES (left) forming a red carpet at the foot of Mount Lebanon after the winter rains were said to represent the blood of Tammuz, before his descent to the underworld signalled the beginning of a season of parched earth and withered vegetation. Tammuz, the Mesopotamian god of vegetation, was the consort of the fertility goddess Ishtar. He was consigned by her to spend half the year in the underworld, in recompense for her own release from death.

OSIRIS's (right) death and the story of his grieving widow, Isis, contains elements common to other dying and rising myths. In some versions, Osiris was killed by Seth in the form of a bull or boar; in another he was encased in a coffin which became entwined in a living tree at Byblos, like the myrrh tree from which Adonis was born. Isis breathed new life into Osiris and conceived their son, Horus, but Seth dismembered his body and scattered the pieces, like grain being scattered in a field. Osiris crouches here on a pedestal, flanked by Isis and Horus. (EGYPTIAN GOLD AND LAPIS LAZULI, 9TH CENTURY BC.)

BAAL (left) was the son of the fertility god Dagan. He was armed with thunder (a mace) and lightning (a lance) for his epic battle with the sea god, Yam, who represented the forces of chaos and thus threatened nature. His victory spurred him to challenge the god of death, Mot, but he was killed. He was avenged by his sister and consort Anat, and Mot's defeat restored Baal to life so that fertility could return to the earth.
(SYRIAN LIMESTONE RELIEF, 17TH–13TH CENTURY BC.)

ATTIS (right) was the consort of the Phrygian mother goddess, Cybele. In one version of his myth, he was gored by a wild boar, but according to the most famous story he is said to have castrated himself in a fit of madness brought on by the jealous Cybele. This theme was taken up by adherents of his cult, who mourned his death and celebrated his rebirth in frenzied and bloody rituals each spring.

(MARBLE BUST, IMPERIAL ROME.)

RA-HERARHTY see *HORUS*.

RASHNU was the personification of righteousness and a judge of the dead in ancient Iranian mythology. When people died, their good and bad deeds were weighed in golden scales in order to determine their fate. It took the judges three days and three nights to come to their decision, during which time the soul of the dead person would hover by its body, meditating on its life and anxiously awaiting the verdict. When the judgment had been made, the soul would be sent across the Chinvat, or Cinvat, Bridge, which led to *AHURA MAZDA*'s paradise. A beautiful lady would help the good souls across the bridge. Bad souls would find that the bridge was as narrow and sharp as the edge of a razor and would plunge downwards into the depths where demons waited to inflict every imaginable type of cruelty on them. But the stay in heaven or hell was only temporary, for not until the day of the resurrection will the whole person, body and soul, be judged.

RESEF see *RESHEF*.

RESHEF, or Resef, was the Phoenician god of lightning and plagues. He was referred to as "Lord of the Arrow", probably due to the manner in which he spread disease and sickness all about him. The god could also be invoked for healing. Reshef was sometimes regarded as the consort of the ferocious goddess *ANAT* and was the equivalent of the Mesopotamian plague god, Namtar. The Egyptians assimilated Reshef into their pantheon, where he was regarded as a god of war and depicted brandishing an axe.

RESHEF, the Phoenician god of plagues. From earliest times he was depicted as wielding an axe, or mace and shield, and wearing a tall, pointed headdress. (BRONZE, CANAANITE, LATE BRONZE AGE OR EARLY IRON AGE.)

RUSTEM, the ancient Iranian hero, possessed a magnificent horse, Rakhsh, who was faithful and brave, and assisted him in his battles against dragons and demons. (ILLUSTRATION FROM SHAH-NAMEH MANUSCRIPT, 1486.)

RUDA, or "Gracious", was a pre-Islamic deity worshipped in northern Arabia. The deity sometimes appears in male form, sometimes female. Usually associated with the evening star, Ruda was sometimes known as Arsu.

RUSTEM, the hero of the 10th-century Iranian epic *Shah-Nameh*, was the son of ZAL, and a nobleman and adviser to the king. Whatever danger threatened the king's realm, Rustem always rode fearlessly into battle: he subdued countless earthly enemies, and fought and conquered demons. On one occasion, a demon surprised Rustem while he was asleep and threw him into the sea; none the less, the hero managed to escape.

Eventually the king, whom Rustem had looked after for countless years, became jealous of him. He ordered his men to dig deep ditches and to line their bases with sharp, upended spears and swords. The king then invited Rustem to go hunting on his land. Although Rustem's horse, Rakhsh, refused to enter the hunting ground, the hero spurred him onwards. Both horse and rider fell into a ditch and were pierced through and through. Rustem died, but before doing so, he shot the king dead with his bow and arrow. Rustem's bravery symbolized the battles between the Persians and the Turanians, Indians and Semites. (See also HEROES AND QUESTS)

SAHAR AND SALEM see SHACHAR AND SHALIM.

SANDA see SANTAS.

SANTAS was an ancient god of western Asia Minor. He was often associated with the mother goddess KUBABA and was sometimes referred to as "King". Santas sometimes appeared as the Babylonian god MARDUK, and he was assimilated into the Greek pantheon as the god Sandon.

SAOSHYANT is the name of the final saviour in Iranian mythology. His appearance will signal the arrival of the last days and the coming of Frashkart, the "final renewal". It is sometimes said that Saoshyant will be born of a virgin, who will become impregnated by the preserved seed of ZOROASTER while bathing in a lake. According to one tradition, the cycle of the world is made up of four ages, each lasting 3,000 years. The first 3,000 years were those of spiritual creation during which AHURA MAZDA brought the benign spirits and the FRAVASHIS, the guardian angels, into being. In the second 3,000 years, Ahura Mazda created the material world, GAYOMART, the primeval man, and GEUSH URVAN the primeval bull, although his work was hindered by ANGRA MAINYU, who introduced evil and destruction. In the third age, good and evil were locked in an intense struggle with one another and Angra Mainyu filled the world with evil spirits. At the beginning of the fourth and final period – the present age – the religious reformer Zoroaster appeared. This last age is that of Saoshyant, the saviour who will finally appear in order to renew the world and resurrect the dead.

A flood of molten metal will submerge and purify the whole planet, and Angra Mainyu will finally be destroyed. During the final renewal itself, the whole of humanity will be subjected to a burning torrent, which will cleanse them of all their evil ways and thus allow them to live with Ahura Mazda. Those who have lived blameless lives will experience the scalding torrent as no more than "warm milk". According to one tradition, Saoshyant will sacrifice a bull and mix its fat with the magical elixir, HAOMA, thereby creating a drink of immortality, which he will give to all humanity.

RUSTEM was surprised while sleeping by the demon Akwan, who tried to hurl him into the sea. Needless to say, the hero managed to escape. (ILLUSTRATION FROM SHAH-NAMEH, LITHOGRAPH.)

SATAN *or Lucifer, the fallen angel, came to be seen as the ruler of hell. Here, with a triple face, he devours the traitor Judas Iscariot and two other sinners.* (HAND-COLOURED WOODCUT, 1512.)

SATAN, whose name means the "Adversary", plays a minor role in the Old Testament as the opponent of humankind, ordered by *YAHWEH* to test humanity's faith. He is an angel in the kingdom of heaven and deals directly with Yahweh.

In the Book of Job, Yahweh instructs Satan to destroy Job's family and possessions and cover him with boils, with the intention of tempting him into cursing God. However, the patient Job declares: "'What? Shall we receive good at the hand of God, and shall we not receive evil?' In all this did not Job sin with his lips."

Satan came to be viewed by the Hebrews as the supreme evil being, under whom was ranged a hierarchy of demons. In opposition to the demons were the angels. Thus, the Hebrews came to see creation as a battle between the forces of good and evil, suggesting the influence of Persian thinking.

One tale relates how Satan, the devil and "prince of this world", rebelled against Yahweh and was hurled by an angel into the abyss. He is imagined in the form of a snake or a dragon. In Christianity, Satan became the embodiment of evil. He was pictured as a handsome man with horns, a pointed tail and cloven hoofs.

In the apocryphal Book of John the Evangelist, Jesus describes Satan's transformation: "My Father changed his appearance because of his pride, and the light was taken from him, and his face became unto a heated iron, and his face became wholly like that of a man: and he drew with his tail the third part of the angels of God and was cast out from the seat of God and the stewardship of the heavens." (See also *ANGELS AND DJINN*)

SEBEK, or Sobek, the Egyptian crocodile god, was represented either as the reptile itself or as a man with a crocodile's head. Sebek's following was greatest at Crocodilopolis, capital of the province of Fayum. A live crocodile called Petsuchos, said to be an incarnation of the god, was kept in a lake attached to Sebek's main sanctuary. Sebek's devotees sought the god's protection by drinking water from the pool and feeding the crocodile on delicacies. In the 13th dynasty, during the second millennium BC, many of the kings were called Sebekhotep, or "Sebek is Satisfied", and it is thought that many people regarded the god as the chief deity. According to some stories, the evil god *SETH* hid himself in Sebek's body to escape being punished for murdering *OSIRIS*.

Sebek was sometimes regarded as the son of *NEITH*, the great mother and warrior goddess, who was also credited with having given birth to the terrifying snake *APEP*. (See also *SACRED ANIMALS*)

SEKHMET see *HATHOR*.

SETH, an Egyptian god of storms and chaos, came to signify evil, although he was widely held in high esteem. The son of the earth god *GEB* and sky goddess *NUT*, he was rough and wild, with red hair and white skin.

Seth became so jealous of his gracious elder brother, *OSIRIS*, that he murdered him and appointed himself king of Egypt. However, unknown to Seth, Osiris and *ISIS* had conceived a child, *HORUS*. Isis nursed Horus in secret until he was old enough to avenge his father, and Osiris himself occasionally returned from the underworld to

SEBEK *embodied the deadly power of the crocodile against its prey, and epitomized the military might of the pharaoh.* (RELIEF FROM TEMPLE OF SEBEK AND HORUS, KOM OMBO.)

SETH (above), the slayer of Osiris, was not always considered evil. He was worshipped in prehistoric times, and again by the Ramessid pharaohs.

SETH (left), god of evil and the desert, with his wife Nephthys, the sister of Isis. He is depicted as a brutish animal, part pig, part ass. (BASALT SCULPTURE.)

tells how the god came upon HATHOR, the cow goddess, when she was bathing in a river and raped her. Seth was immediately struck down with a terrible illness and his wife, Anat, appealed to Ra for help. Eventually Isis helped Anat cure Seth. The god symbolizes the harsh aspects of the natural world and was said to live in the arid desert.

SHACHAR AND SHALIM, or Shar and Shalim, "Dawn" and "Dusk", were the offspring of EL, the supreme god of the Phoenician pantheon. They were also known as Sahar and Salem. In ancient texts discovered at Ras Shamra in Syria, on the site of the city of Ugarit, the deities are described as having been conceived when El stretched out his hands like waves to the sea, making his two wives fruitful. The two wives are generally believed to be Ashera (see ASTARTE) and ANAT.

instruct his son in the art of war. When the right moment arrived, Horus went into battle against Seth and overcame him.

Before a divine tribunal, Seth declared that he was entitled to the throne of Egypt because he was the only deity strong and brave enough to protect RA. Although some of the gods sided with Seth, Isis per-

suaded them to change their minds. When Osiris was consulted in the underworld, he demanded to know why his son had not been allowed to take his rightful place on the throne and threatened to send demons to attack the gods. Ra finally agreed to Horus's claim.

According to one story, Seth went to live with Ra in the sky.

Another version of the myth tells how Seth was condemned to carry Osiris on his shoulders for all eternity. Yet another tale relates how the goddess NEITH suggested that Seth should be given two foreign goddesses, ANAT and ASTARTE, as his wives, in order to console him for having lost the throne to Horus. A tale concerning Seth and Anat

SHAMASH was the Babylonian sun god, able to expose injustice and falsehood with his searching rays. He was also the god of divination, and could be consulted through a soothsayer. He is shown here in his emanation as Mrn, chief deity of the city of Hatra. (PARTHIAN SCULPTURE, C. AD150–200.)

SHU, the Egyptian god of air, was the male half of the first divine couple. His name is sometimes translated as "Emptiness", sometimes as "He Who Holds Up". Shu was created when the supreme god *RA*, as Ra-Atum, spat or sneezed him out of his mouth. His consort was Tefnut, goddess of moisture, who was created in the same fashion. Shu and Tefnut left Ra-Atum to explore *NUN*, the dark abyss that existed at the very beginning of time. Ra-Atum was distraught, thinking he had lost his children. When they returned, he wept tears of joy, from which the first human beings were formed.

Shu and Tefnut begat *GEB*, the earth, and *NUT*, the sky. Eventually, Shu separated his two children by pushing Nut upwards with his arms. He is often depicted as supporting the sky.

Shu succeeded Ra to the throne, but the followers of the terrifying snake *APEP* continually attacked him and, growing tired of the ceaseless conflict, Shu abdicated, leaving his son Geb to become king. After a terrible storm lasting more than a week, Shu took up residence in the sky. Sometimes, as son of the sun god, Ra, Shu is represented with the head of a lion.

SHAMASH was the Babylonian god of the sun, who saw all things and thus also came to be regarded as a god of justice and divination. Known to the Sumerians as Utu, his light uncovered every misdeed and enabled him to see into the future. Each morning, the scorpion men opened a gate in the vast mountain of Mashu and Shamash made his way out into the sky. Slowly, he climbed the mountain until he reached the high point of the sky; as evening approached, he rode his chariot towards another great mountain and disappeared through its gates. During the night, Shamash journeyed through the depths of the earth until he reached the first gate once more. The sun god's consort was Aya, who gave birth to Kittu, justice, and Misharu, law and righteousness. Shamash was depicted seated on a throne.

SHAR AND SHALIM see *SHACHAR AND SHALIM.*

SHAUSHKA was an important Hurrian deity who was identified with *ISHTAR*, the Babylonian goddess of love, fertility and war. Like Ishtar, she was depicted as a winged figure standing on a lion, and was attended by two women. The goddess seems to have had a dual nature.

SIN, the Sumerian-Babylonian moon god, was the father of *SHAMASH*, the sun god, *INANA* (or *ISHTAR*), the planet Venus, and Nusku, the god of fire. Sometimes known as Suen, or Nanna, he was conceived when the air god *ENLIL* raped the grain goddess *NINLIL* and was born in the underworld. Sin's consort was Ningal, or the "Great Lady". Sin was usually depicted as an old man with a blue beard, and he was called the "Shining Boat of Heaven". Every evening, he would climb into his crescent-shaped boat and sail across the skies. Sometimes, the crescent moon was regarded as the god's weapon and the full moon as his crown.

Sin was the enemy of the wicked, for his light revealed their evil ways. On one occasion, the utukku, or evil genies, hatched a plot against Sin and, with the help of Shamash, Ishtar, the goddess of love and fertility, and *ADAD*, the god of thunder, they eclipsed his light. However, the great god *MARDUK* waged war against the conspirators and gave Sin back his radiance.

Sin was also held to be wise and was believed to measure time with his waxing and waning. Moreover, by raising the marsh waters around the city of Ur, where his temple stood, he ensured the well-being of cattle by enabling them to enjoy an abundant supply of food. (See also *GATEWAYS TO THE GODS*)

SIYAMEK see *HAOSHYANGHA*.

SOBEK see *SEBEK*.

SIN (right) was the Babylonian moon god, whose symbol, the crescent moon, is depicted on this carved stone. The god was held in supreme regard in Mesopotamia. His chief cult centres were at Ur and Harran. (KUDURRU, C. 1120BC.)

SHU (below), supports a head-rest found in the tomb of Tutankhamen. The god of air, Shu was the father of the sky goddess, Nut, and was often depicted in this position, supporting the sky above his head. (CARVED IVORY, 14TH CENTURY BC.)

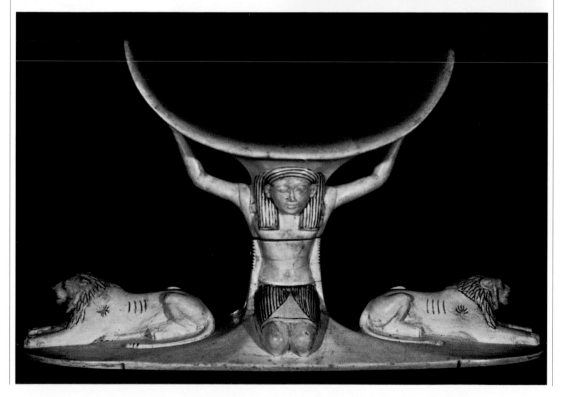

T

SOLOMON's (left) wisdom and proverbs, led to this Old Testament king, the second son of David, becoming a legendary figure. It was said that he commanded djinn.

SOLOMON (right) reigned over Israel for 40 years. His great achievement was the building of the temple at Jerusalem. (BYZANTINE BOOK ILLUSTRATION, 11TH CENTURY.)

SOLOMON was the Old Testament king who ruled over Israel in the tenth century BC. He was noted for his great wisdom and for building YAHWEH's marvellous temple at Jerusalem. Under the influence of his many foreign wives, Solomon also built shrines for other gods, thereby incurring Yahweh's wrath. Solomon's seal, a six-sided star, became an important symbol used as an amulet or talisman. According to Arabic mythology, the star and the real name of God were etched on King Solomon's magic ring, thereby enabling him to command armies of demons. (See also ANGELS AND DJINN)

SPENTA ARMAITI is one of the AMESA SPENTAS, or the "Holy Immortals", of ancient Iranian mythology. Like the other Amesa Spentas, she is believed to have originated before the religious reforms of ZOROASTER and to have been assimilated into the purified religion as an aspect of AHURA MAZDA, the supreme being. Spenta Armaiti was patroness of the earth, and symbolized submission and devotion. She was widely believed to be the spiritual mother of all human beings, and people were taught to say, "My mother is Spendarmat, Archangel of the Earth, and my father is Ohrmazd, the Lord Wisdom."

According to one tradition, she was the mother of GAYOMART, the primordial being. As Gayomart lay dying, his body separated into seven metals. Spenta Armaiti gathered together the gold and grew a plant from it. From this plant came the first human couple.

The name Spenta Armaiti is sometimes translated as "Wisdom" or "Devotion".

SRAOSHA was known as the "Ear" of AHURA MAZDA, the principle of good in ancient Iranian mythology. He was one of the YAZATAS, Zoroastrianism's "Beings Worthy of Worship". As the "Ear" of Ahura Mazda, he was the means by which those who worshipped the supreme being could gain access to him. During the night, Sraosha guarded the whole of creation from evil demons.

SUEN see SIN.

TAHMURAS, according to ancient Iranian mythology, was the son of HAOSHYANGHA, the first king. He taught people how to spin and weave, and how to train birds of prey. On one occasion, he succeeded in capturing ANGRA MAINYU and, after leaping on to his back, forced the evil being to carry him on a tour of the world. However, while Tahmuras was away on his travels, the DAEVAS began to create havoc, so Tahmuras had to return and take up arms against them.

The daevas gathered together a noisy army, which hid itself in thick black smoke. Undeterred by this, Tahmuras captured two-thirds of the aggressors with the help of his magic arts and struck down the remainder with his massive club. The daevas pleaded for mercy and promised Tahmuras that if he spared their lives, they would teach him a marvellous secret. Tahmuras relented and, in return, the daevas taught him how to write and made him extremely wise and learned.

TAMMUZ, the Babylonian god of vegetation and the harvest, was a dying and rising god. Relatively low in standing among the gods, he was nevertheless extremely popular with the people and had a widespread following. His marriage to ISHTAR, the lustful goddess of love and fertility, led to his death: just as corn is cut down suddenly at the height of its splendour, so Tammuz was forced to retire to the underworld. Ishtar was devastated at his loss and underwent a period of wailing and lamentation. Each year after the harvest, those who worshipped Ishtar and Tammuz took part in a mourning ritual.

Ishtar eventually sought out Tammuz in the underworld and managed to secure his release, on condition that he return to the underworld for half of each year. Tammuz returned to the land of the living and took up his position at the gate of the sky god, ANU. It was there that the wise man ADAPA encountered him, when Adapa was summoned before Anu for demonstrating too much power. Adapa flattered Tammuz, who rewarded him by interceding on his behalf.

Tammuz's sister was Belili. In Sumerian myth, he was known as DUMUZI, the consort of INANA. (See also DYING AND RISING GODS)

TAMMUZ (below) was sought after his death by the goddess Ishtar, who followed him to the underworld. (ILLUSTRATION FROM GILGAMESH BY ZABELLE C. BOYAJIAN, 1924.)

ϹΟΛΟΜΩΝ

HEROES AND QUESTS

MYTHS ABOUT MORTAL HEROES HAVE AN immediacy that comes from their recognizable human characteristics. Though the great heroes performed astonishing acts of bravery and achieved feats that were far beyond the capability of any real man, their adventures took place on earth and, in some ways, they behaved as other men did – falling in love, falling asleep, making friends, making mistakes – so that those who listened to their stories could identify with them as they could not with remote gods and goddesses. These men feared death and could not avoid it, hard as they tried. A perilous journey was usually central to the hero's story. There were many thrilling adventures on the way, with twists and turns that diverted

him from his path, and selfless deeds such as killing monsters that frustrated him in his quest but saved the day for ordinary folk.

GILGAMESH (above), king of Uruk, or Erech, was the hero of a number of Sumerian stories that were combined and written down by Babylonian scribes in about 2000BC. Gilgamesh was said to be two-thirds god and one-third man because his mother was the goddess Ninsun. From her he derived his great strength. Despite his heroic stature, he began his reign as a tyrannical king, whose people were eventually driven to call on the gods for help in subduing him. (ASSYRIAN CYLINDER SEAL IMPRESSION, 1350–1000BC.)

ENKIDU (above left) was a wild man sent by the gods to deal with Gilgamesh, in answer to his people's prayers. He was, however, even more unruly than the king. Gilgamesh conceived a plan to civilize Enkidu. As a test of strength, they fought in a great wrestling match, but neither could outdo the other, and the two became friends. Their adventures together included the killing of fierce bulls and the fire-breathing demon Humbaba. (AKKADIAN CYLINDER SEAL IMPRESSION, C. 2300BC.)

GILGAMESH (left) resisted the seductive advances of the goddess Ishtar. Incensed, she sent the bull of heaven to avenge her honour, but with Enkidu's help, Gilgamesh managed to stab the bull. The gods were outraged and decided that Enkidu must pay for his part in the exploit. Within a few days, he had fallen ill and died. The loss of his friend instilled the fear of death in Gilgamesh and he embarked on a quest to find eternal life. (ILLUSTRATION BY E. WALLCOUSINS FROM MYTHS OF BABYLONIA AND ASSYRIA BY DONALD MACKENZIE.)

USHANABI (above), the ferryman, was the only man who knew how to cross the treacherous waters of death safely. He guided Gilgamesh over them on his way to reach the old man Utnapishtim, the sole survivor of the great flood, who had been granted immortality by the gods. Gilgamesh hoped that Utnapishtim would be able to tell him the secret of eternal life. (ILLUSTRATION FROM GILGAMESH BY ZABELLE C. BOYAJIAN, 1924.)

UTNAPISHTIM (above) reluctantly told Gilgamesh of a plant growing at the bottom of the sea which had the power to give him eternal youth. Gilgamesh found the plant, but as he bent to pick it, a serpent smelt it and stole it. In this way, snakes acquired the ability to stay young forever by simply shedding their ageing skin. Gilgamesh was forced to understand that his death was inevitable and returned to his kingdom. (ILLUSTRATION FROM GILGAMESH BY ZABELLE C. BOYAJIAN, 1924.)

RUSTEM (left), alone of all men, dared to fight the great White Demon in order to free the king, who had been inspired by the evil Angra Mainyu to try to usurp the throne of the ruler of Mazinderan. Rustem found the demon sleeping in his mountain lair, woke him and wrestled with him until "blood and sweat ran down in rivers from their bodies." Rustem was victorious and cut off the demon's head. (ILLUSTRATION FROM SHAH-NAMEH, LITHOGRAPH.)

RUSTEM (above), the Iranian hero, was born in a mysterious fashion, as a result of the incantations of a wizard and with the help of the magical feathers of the Simurgh bird. He was as tall as eight normal men and was famed for his strength and prowess in battle. One of his exploits in his youth was the killing of a rogue white elephant with a blow from an ox-headed mace.
(ILLUSTRATION FROM SHAH-NAMEH BY SHIRAZ, C. 1545.)

RUSTEM (left) searched the country for a horse and eventually caught one that had in fact been set aside for him from birth. Rakhsh was as magnificent and brave as the hero himself, with the strength of an elephant and the speed of a racing camel. On one occasion, when Rustem was sleeping and unarmed, his horse saved his life by killing a lion before it could attack him.
(ILLUSTRATION FROM SHAH-NAMEH BY INJU SHIRAZ, 1341.)

TARU, the Hittite weather god, was the father of *TELEPINU*. Like many other myths originating in West Asia, those featuring Taru are concerned with the annual cycle of vegetation. The tales relate his battles against a terrible monster, the giant serpent or dragon *ILLUYANKAS*. When Taru overcame the monster, vegetation flourished, but when he was vanquished all plant life withered and died.

According to one tale, Illuyankas managed to defeat the weather god. However, the goddess *INARAS* then hatched a plot whereby she managed to trap the terrible monster. The goddess prepared an enormous banquet and invited Illuyankas and his numerous offspring to come and join her in feasting.

When they had eaten their fill, the monsters discovered that they were too fat to fit through the tunnel that led to their underground home. The hero *HUPASIYAS*, Inaras's human consort, then tied the monsters up with a rope, whereupon Taru, assisted by the other gods, overcame them.

According to another version of the myth, the serpent overcame Taru, and seized his heart and eyes. Taru then fathered a son whom he married to the daughter of Illuyankas. The son asked for his father's missing organs as a dowry

payment and returned them to Taru. The weather god then slew Illuyankas in a terrifying sea battle. He also killed his son, probably in revenge for his having sided with the monster during the battle.

TEFNUT see *SHU*.

TELEPINU was a Hittite god of agriculture who controlled the fertility of plants and animals. His father, *TARU*, the weather god, said of him: "This son of mine is mighty; he harrows and ploughs, he irrigates the fields and makes the crops grow."

On one famous occasion, which has become known as the "myth of the disappearing god", Telepinu suddenly vanished; his haste was such that he put his boots on the wrong feet. Immediately, all life on earth began to wither and die. Even the gods began to starve. Fire was extinguished, animals perished, the trees lost their leaves, and the fields became dry and parched. "Barley and emmer wheat throve no more, oxen, sheep and humans ceased to conceive, and those who were pregnant could not bear." The sun threw an enormous feast for the gods, but his guests were unable to eat their fill or quench their thirst. Finally Taru explained that his son was angry and had disappeared, taking all good things with him.

TESHUB (above) god of the tempest and head of the Hittite pantheon, bears an axe and a three-pronged lightning fork. He was also a god of battle and overcame Kumarbi, the father of the gods. Kumarbi's son Ullikummi fought to take control of Teshub's city, but without success.

THOTH (below), the Egyptian moon god and vizier of Osiris, records the result of the weighing of a heart. As Osiris' sacred scribe, he was associated with secret knowledge and helped at the burial of Osiris. (FROM THE BOOK OF THE DEAD OF HUNEFER, c. 1310BC.)

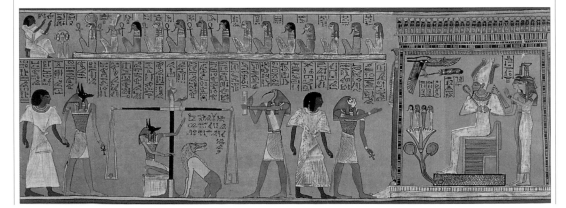

All the gods, both great and small, proceeded to search for Telepinu. The sun sent out the eagle saying, "Go, search the high mountains, search the hollow valleys, search the dark-blue waters." However, although the eagle explored the entire country, he failed to find the missing god. Then, the weather god asked the mother goddess, HANNAHANNA, for advice. Hannahanna told the weather god to go himself and look for Telepinu, but Taru soon gave up and sat down to rest. Then Hannahanna suggested sending a bee to look for the god. Although the weather god objected, the goddess ignored him and told the bee to find the Telepinu, sting him on his hands and feet to wake him up, and then bring him back home.

At length, the bee found Telepinu asleep in a field. When the bee stung him, the god fell into such a frenzy that he proceeded to cause yet more devastation, killing human beings, oxen and sheep in his wake.

Eventually, the goddess Kamrusepas managed to calm him down using her magic spells: "She stilled his anger, she stilled his wrath, she stilled his rage, she stilled his fury." Telepinu flew home on the back of an eagle, and life returned to normal: "He released the embers of the hearth, he released the sheep in the fold, he released the oxen in the stall. The mother attended to her child, the ewe attended to her lamb, the cow attended to her calf."

TESHUB was a god of the tempest who was worshipped throughout western Asia. He is believed to have originated among the Hurrians, although the chief myth concerning his activities has been passed down by the Hittites. In the Hittite mythological texts, it is recorded how the fearsome god Teshub overcame KUMARBI, the father of the gods. Kumarbi

fathered a son, ULLIKUMMI, who was made of diorite stone and grew to a huge size on the back of the giant, Upelluri. In order to view the vast creature, Teshub climbed to the summit of a high mountain. On seeing the monster, the terrified weather god persuaded the other deities to join him in launching an attack. However, their assault proved unsuccessful. Ullikummi succeeded in advancing as far as the gates of Teshub's city, whereupon he forced the god to abdicate his throne.

Teshub sought advice from the wise god EA who, after pondering a while, unearthed the ancient saw with which heaven and earth had been divided, and used the tool to sever the diorite stone at its feet. As a result, Ullikummi's power quickly faded, whereupon the gods decided to renew their attack on him. Although the end of the myth is missing, it is generally believed that Teshub eventually regained his kingdom and throne.

Teshub was the husband of HEPAT, who was often given almost equal standing with her husband, and sometimes took precedence over him. Teshub's attributes were an axe and lightning flashes, and he was sometimes depicted as a bearded figure, holding a club, with his feet resting on mountain deities. His chariot was drawn by two bulls.

THOTH, the Egyptian moon god, presided over scribes and knowledge, and was "Lord of the Sacred Words". He was sometimes said to be the sun god RA's eldest son, although, according to one tradition, he sprang from the head of the evil god, SETH.

Thoth is usually regarded as the vizier of OSIRIS, god of vegetation and the dead, as well as his sacred scribe. Because he was associated with secret knowledge, Thoth was able to help at the burial of Osiris. He also helped to look after HORUS when ISIS was bringing him up.

Eventually, Thoth succeeded Horus to the throne of Egypt and reigned peacefully over the land for more than 3,000 years. Afterwards, he took his place in the sky as the moon.

According to one story, he was ordered by Ra to light up the sky at night. There, he was slowly devoured by monsters who were, however, repeatedly forced to disgorge him bit by bit. Thoth was usually depicted as an ibis or as a baboon. It was said that Thoth

wrote a book of magic, known as the *Book of Thoth*, which lies buried in a tomb near Memphis. The spells within the book were said to give the user power over the gods. Thoth was also said to record the verdict of the judgment of the dead in the underworld. (See also *SACRED ANIMALS*)

THOTH, god of the moon, writing and knowledge, with a scribe. Thoth was often depicted as a baboon, one of his sacred animals. (BRONZE, ARMARNA, C. 1340BC.)

TIAMAT embodied the raw energy of the ocean. In the Babylonian creation story, she was split in two by Marduk to form the sky and the ocean floor. Her eyes became the sources of the great rivers Tigris (left) and Euphrates, on which the lives of the Mesopotamians depended.

useful plants. It was said that he helped AHURA MAZDA, the principle of goodness, in his struggle against every evil.

TISTRIYN see TISHTRYA.

ULLIKUMMI was the son of KUMARBI, originally an ancient Anatolian deity who was later introduced into Hittite mythology. The myth of Ullikummi concerns Kumarbi's attempt to wreak vengeance on his first son, TESHUB, who had overthrown him.

Kumarbi nursed the thought of creating an evil being and eventually slept with a vast stone, which subsequently gave birth to a son, Ullikummi. The boy was made of diorite stone, and in order that he might grow up in safety the deities placed him on the shoulders of the giant Upelluri in the middle of the sea. The child rapidly grew bigger and bigger until the water reached no higher than his middle, at which point the sun god noticed him and immediately told Teshub of the impending threat. Teshub wept

TIAMAT was the personification of the primeval ocean who, with Apsu, initiated the creation of the gods. Depicted as a mighty dragon, she eventually marched against Ea and the other gods. Only Marduk, Ea's son, stood against her and overcame her. (ILLUSTRATION BY EVELYN PAUL.)

TIAMAT, according to Mesopotamian mythology, was the turbulent, salt-water ocean that existed at the beginning of time. The universal primeval mother, she was depicted as a monstrous female dragon and was believed to embody the forces of chaos. The waters of Tiamat mingled with the fresh-water primordial ocean, APSU, and, in doing so, initiated the creation of the gods.

In time, Apsu grew tired of the clamour of the gods and began to plot their destruction. Tiamat at first refused to take part in Apsu's plan, but when the water god EA captured both Apsu and Mummu, the waves, Tiamat was spurred into action. After giving birth to an army of monsters, "sharp of tooth and merciless of fang", she marched against Ea and the other gods.

For some time, all attempts to subdue Tiamat failed until finally MARDUK, Ea's son, was chosen to confront her. Tiamat opened her jaws to swallow Marduk, but the god threw a raging storm into her mouth so that she was unable to close it. Marduk then caught Tiamat in a net and, after piercing her with an arrow, tore her innards apart. After slaughtering Tiamat's army of monsters, Marduk split Tiamat's skull and slashed her body in two. From one half of her body, he made the vault of the heavens, from the other half, the floor of the ocean. Then Marduk pierced Tiamat's eyes to form the sources of the rivers Tigris and Euphrates and bent her tail up into the sky to make the Milky Way. (See also SERPENTS AND DRAGONS)

TISHTRYA, or Tistriyn, was the name given by the ancient Iranians to the dog star. He was regarded as the god of water, whether that of the clouds, lakes, rivers or seas. Tishtrya also provided the seeds of

with fear but, after being comforted by his sister, resolved to attack the monstrous being. However, though Teshub summoned the thunder and rain to help him, he was unable to defeat the creature.

Before long, Ullikummi had reached the gates of Teshub's city and forced the weather god to abdicate. Distraught, Teshub sought help from the wise god EA, who retrieved a saw that had originally been used to separate heaven from earth. Ea sliced through Ullikummi's ankles, and the monster's power

UTNAPISHTIM was told by Ea to build a boat and take every kind of living thing aboard. The gods were about to punish the wicked city of Shurripak with a deluge, but Ea wished Utnapishtim to survive.
(ILLUSTRATION FROM GILGAMESH BY ZABELLE C. BOYAJIAN, 1924.)

faded. The gods then renewed their attack on Ullikummi, and Teshub regained the throne.

UTNAPISHTIM, according to one version of the Mesopotamian flood myth, was the wise man who alone survived the flood. The gods ANU, ENLIL, NINURTA and Ennugi decided to destroy humankind, having grown tired of their ways. However, EA, the water god, warned Utnapishtim of the conspiracy, and told him to build a boat and in it store the seeds of all life. Utnapishtim built a huge vessel 120 cubits high and loaded it with his family, his cattle and numerous other animals and birds.

On the evening that he finished his work, a filthy rain began to fall, and everyone on earth was stricken with terror. For six days and six

nights, the deluge continued until, at daybreak on the seventh day, it suddenly ceased and all that was left of humanity was a vast heap of thick mud.

Utnapishtim, whose marvellous boat had come to rest on the summit of Mount Nisir, cried out in grief. He let loose one bird after another from his boat, but they all returned, having found nowhere they could alight. However, when at last Utnapishtim released a raven, it failed to return, signifying that it must have found dry land.

In gratitude to the gods, Utnapishtim placed offerings to them on the summit of the mountain. Enlil, however, was furious to see that a human being had escaped the wrath of the gods. Ea eventually managed to calm Enlil down, whereupon Enlil took

Utnapishtim and his wife by the hand and said that from now on they would be immortal, like the gods themselves.

Some time after these events, the hero GILGAMESH, a descendent of Utnapishtim, sought out the immortal in the hope of learning the secret of eternal life from him. Utnapishtim refused to disclose the secret, but nonetheless directed Gilgamesh to the bottom of the sea to find the plant of rejuvenation. Unfortunately, on Gilgamesh's journey home, it was stolen from him by a serpent when the hero stopped to bathe and rest. (See also *MYTHS OF THE FLOOD; HEROES AND QUESTS*)

UTTUKU see SIN.

UTU see SHAMASH.

W

VOHU MANO was one of the *AMESA SPENTAS*, or "Holy Immortals", of ancient Iranian mythology. These divine beings were believed to people the universe and to look after humanity. They are thought to have been worshipped before the time of the religious reformer *ZOROASTER*. Although Zoroaster denounced the old gods, he continued to venerate the Amesa Spentas as aspects of *AHURA MAZDA*, the one true spirit set in opposition to *ANGRA MAINYU*, the spirit of darkness. It was said that when Zoroaster was about 30 years old, Vohu Mano transported his spirit to Ahura Mazda, thereby bringing about his spiritual enlightenment. Vohu Mano ("Good Thought" or "Spirit of Good") reigned over useful animals and was often represented by the cow.

WADD was a moon god worshipped in certain parts of southern Arabia from the fifth to second centuries BC. His name means "Love" or "Friendship", and his sacred animal was the snake. Wadd is referred

VOHU MANU, the "Good Thought", was one of the Amesa Spentas of Iranian mythology. He personified the wisdom of Ahura Mazda, portrayed here presenting the crown of the kingdom of Persia to Ardechir I. (ROCK CARVING, EARLY 3RD CENTURY BC.)

to in the Qur'an as a pagan divinity, one of five idols erected by the descendants of Cain.

WADJET was the cobra goddess of Lower Egypt. She was usually represented as a cobra about to strike, although she sometimes appeared as a lioness. In the myth that relates how *ISIS* brought up her child *HORUS* in secret, Wadjet appears as the young god's nurse. Both Wadjet and *NEKHBET* were believed to protect the *PHARAOH*. (See also *SACRED ANIMALS*)

YAHWEH, or Jahweh, was regarded by the tribes of Israel as the creator of all things and the judge of all nations. He probably originated as a mountain god and was identified with *EL*, the supreme deity of the Canaanite pantheon. Yahweh intervened in earthly affairs, often through his prophets. He demanded that his followers should worship no other deity and was a jealous god. Though he dealt severely with anyone who strayed from his teachings, he was a god of

YAHWEH's followers avoided pronouncing the four Hebrew letters that made up his name, considering it too sacred to be pronounced aloud.

righteousness and ultimately merciful. No physical likeness was ever attributed to him.

The Third Commandment decrees, "Thou shalt not take the name of the Lord thy God in vain", so his followers avoided pronouncing the four Hebrew letters, YHWH or JHWH, which made up his name. The letters are supposed to represent the identity of God and are usually interpreted as meaning "I am that I am". From the 13th century, Yahweh was sometimes known in English as Jehovah. (See also *SERPENTS AND DRAGONS; ANGELS AND DJINN*)

YAM, or Yamm, or Jamm, was the Phoenician god of the sea and water in general. One of his titles was "Ruler River". According to one myth, Yam asked the supreme god, *EL*, to grant him power over the other gods. El agreed but warned him that he must first conquer *BAAL*.

The fertility god equipped himself with magical weapons made by the smith gods and went into battle. He succeeded in killing Yam, proceeded to scatter his remains and then crowned himself king. The myth symbolizes the chaotic forces of nature being overcome by its civilizing aspect, which ensures the fertility of the crops.

Another tale tells how Yam was compensated for his defeat by being given the goddess *ASTARTE* as his bride. Yam was sometimes referred to as a dragon or serpent, or as the sea monster, *LEVIATHAN*.

YAMM see *YAM*.

THE YAZATAS, or "Beings Worthy of Worship", were the protective spirits of Zoroastrianism. Most of them were ancient Iranian gods who were incorporated into *ZOROASTER's* reformed religion as helpers of the supreme being, *AHURA MAZDA*. Some of the Yazatas corresponded to the stars and planets, others to the elements, while many embodied abstract concepts. Sometimes, the celestial Yazatas were said to be led by Ahura Mazda and the terrestrial Yazatas by Zoroaster. They included in their number *RASHNU* and *SRAOSHA*.

YAM, the Phoenician sea god, represented the turbulence of nature. He was defeated by the fertility god, Baal. In some versions of his myth he married the goddess Astarte, though she is more often described as the consort of Baal himself. (GILDED BRONZE, 19TH–18TH CENTURY BC.)

ANGELS AND DJINN

NGELS ARE INTERMEDIARIES BETWEEN heaven and earth, sent to bring messages to humankind – their name comes from the Greek word for "messenger". The Hebrew patriarch Jacob had a vision of angels on foot, ascending and descending a ladder which stood on the earth and reached up to heaven. Later concepts of heaven were of a more remote realm, from which winged angels flew down to earth. Angels are mentioned frequently in the Bible, praising Yahweh or appearing to humans bearing announcements or instructions from him. Islamic angels are also winged messengers; another of their tasks is to record the good and bad deeds of men, and they examine the faith of the dead on their first night in the grave. Djinn are less predictable. Originally nature spirits, they are a disruptive influence on humankind, capable of causing madness. A sinful man risks being turned into a djinnee (a lesser djinn) after his death.

THE PROTECTIVE SPIRITS (above) of ancient Iranian mythology were portrayed as winged creatures, and it was perhaps this imagery that influenced the development of the idea of angels' wings. Protective, sheltering wings were an important symbol of the beneficence of Ahura Mazda, the supreme god of the Iranians, and are used to represent him. (PERSIAN MINIATURE, C. 1370–80.)

THE DJINN (above) were ugly and evil supernatural beings in pre-Islamic times, the fiery spirits of wild, desolate places who exercised their malign powers under a cloak of invisibility or by changing their shape at will. Their name means "furious" or "possessed". Though they were capable of redemption under Islam, those who refused to acknowledge Allah became demons. (SYRIAN RELIEF SCULPTURE, 9TH CENTURY BC.)

THE ANGELS (left), who were created before human beings, objected to Allah's plan to populate the earth, on the grounds that humanity would rebel against him. However, when Allah created Adam as the first prophet and taught him the names of all things, all the angels agreed to bow down before him. The single exception was Iblis, the devil, who considered that as he was born of fire he was superior to a being made of earth. (OTTOMAN MINIATURE, 1558.)

LUCIFER (above left), arriving in hell with Beelzebub, entered a new and dreadful domain, where he plotted his revenge as the adversary of humankind. Early Christian tradition, based on a passage of Isaiah and the words of Jesus – "I beheld Satan falling as lightning from heaven" – held that Satan had originated as an angel who had been thrown out of heaven because he was too proud to acknowledge the supremacy of Yahweh. (ILLUSTRATION TO MILTON'S PARADISE LOST BY JOHN MARTIN, 1827.)

THE ARCHANGEL GABRIEL (below) sits on the left hand of Yahweh and, in Hebrew literature, guards the left side of humans while they sleep. As a warrior, he will fight the last great battle with Leviathan, the symbol of chaos, at the end of time. According to Christian tradition it was Gabriel who was sent to announce the births of John the Baptist and Jesus. In Islam, he is Jibril, the angel of revelations. (ARCHANGEL GABRIEL, BYZANTINE SERBIAN ICON, 14TH CENTURY.)

SOLOMON (left), the son of David, was king of Israel for 40 years in the tenth century BC. His wisdom was legendary, and his reign prodigiously successful: his wealth and knowledge, together with his interest in the various religious practices of his many wives, led to his being credited with supernatural powers. He was said to converse with spirits such as peri and djinn, and the six-pointed star called Solomon's Seal was a powerful talisman. (KING SOLOMON AND A PERI BY QAZWIN, C. 1570.)

THE TEMPLE (above) in Jerusalem was the outstanding achievement of Solomon's long reign. It was built using a labour force of 180,000 men, but its scale and splendour prompted the legend that Solomon's magic powers gave him command over an army of djinn who had carried out the work. When the temple was completed, it was dedicated in a ceremony lasting 14 days, during which 22,000 oxen and 120,000 sheep were sacrificed. (ILLUSTRATION FROM CALMET'S DICTIONARY OF THE HOLY BIBLE, 1732.)

MUHAMMAD (above) travelled as a young man to Syria, where he met Christians, Jews and others who believed in a single god. He became convinced that they were right. When he was about 40 he retreated to a cave on Mount Hira to wrestle with his beliefs alone. There, he was visited by the angel Jibril, who insisted that Muhammad should "recite" his beliefs, in other words, that he should preach the truth about Allah. (ILLUSTRATION FROM AN UNDATED MINIATURE.)

Z

YIMA, or Jam, or Jemshid, according to ancient Iranian mythology, was a great king. He was usually regarded as the son of *TAHMURAS*, one of the civilizing heroes, although according to some traditions the boy was born in a pillar of fire when a bolt of lightning struck the earth.

Yima governed the land wisely and justly, earning the title of the "Good Shepherd". As a priest, he was pious; as a warrior, he was strong; and as a herdsman, he was rich in cattle. He lived in a time known as the Golden Age, when death did not exist.

Because nobody died, Yima had to enlarge the earth three times, with the aid of his magic instruments. However, it came to pass that Mahrkusha, an evil demon, sent terrible floods followed by scorching summers down to earth, with the intention of annihilating all living creatures, both human beings and animals. Seeing what was about to happen, *AHURA MAZDA*, the principle of good, decided that the noble and upright Yima should be saved. He told him to build an underground dwelling place and to take into it every variety of man and beast. The fabulous chamber should also contain running water and trees, flowers and fruits. No diseased, wicked, ill-natured or deformed creature should be allowed entrance. Yima asked how he was to make this chamber, and Ahura Mazda replied that he should mould the earth with his hands and feet, as potters do. After the disaster, Yima emerged unscathed.

A later tradition claims that Yima eventually fell victim to the evil monster *AZHI DAHAKA*, who sawed him in two. It seems that he deserved this fate because he had committed the sin of pride.

ZAL, a hero of ancient Iranian mythology, was the son of Sam, a descendant of *FERIDUN*. Zal was born with white hair. Horrified by his strange appearance, his father ordered him to be left to die on the slope of a mountain. However, Simurgh, a noble vulture, rescued the baby and carried him to her nest on the peak of Mount Elburz. Simurgh was a mythical bird, said to be so old that she had seen the world destroyed three times, and had thus acquired great wisdom.

Zal grew up to become an extraordinarily beautiful young man. Sam, by now consumed with guilt for having abandoned his son, went in search of the child. He reached the home of Simurgh and entreated the vulture to return the young man to him. The bird agreed, and Sam blessed his son and called him Zal.

Zal had many adventures. On one occasion, he visited Kabul, which lay in his father's land of Hindustan. While staying with Mihrab, one of his father's servants, he learnt that his host had a beautiful daughter, Rudabeh. Without even having seen the young woman, Zal fell in love with her and she, hearing of Zal, fell in love with him. They arranged to meet in secret in a palace, which Rudabeh had filled with beautiful flowers and strewn with jewels. Rudabeh stood on a high terrace and looked down on Zal. Then, let-

ZAL was rejected as a baby by his father Sam, and exposed on a mountain. He was rescued by a fabulous bird called Simurgh, who raised him in her nest. (MINIATURE, MID 15TH CENTURY.)

ting down her beautiful hair, she told Zal to climb up it to her. Zal refused to do anything that might harm Rudabeh and instead climbed up a rope, which he managed to throw on to the terrace.

Although the young couple were deeply in love, they had to overcome the fact that Rudabeh's family were old enemies of Sam's employer, King MINUCHER. At length, Sam agreed to let Zal marry Rudabeh, particularly since astrologers had said that the couple would give birth to a great hero. That hero proved to be RUSTEM.

ZARATHUSTRA see ZOROASTER.

ZOHAK, according to ancient Iranian mythology, was the son of a desert king. He was persuaded by ANGRA MAINYU, the principle of darkness, to kill his father and seize the throne. Angra Mainyu then took up residence in Zohak's castle as his cook and persuaded the new king to introduce meat to his diet. Zohak was so pleased with his new cuisine that he promised Angra Mainyu a gift of his choosing. Angra Mainyu asked that he might kiss Zohak's shoulders, and rest his

face and eyes there. After kissing the king, Angra Mainyu disappeared. Suddenly, a snake appeared from each of Zohak's shoulders. His courtiers tried to destroy them, but each time the snakes were sliced off, they grew again.

Disguised as a doctor, Angra Mainyu returned and told Zohak that he should feed the snakes each day with human brains. In this way, Zohak himself became a demon and ruled over the world for a thousand years, during which time evil reigned supreme. Finally, one night Zohak had a terrifying dream; when

ZAL was carried by Simurgh to the highest peaks of Mount Elburz, where he grew up without his father's knowledge. Eventually, Sam was prompted by a dream to seek his son in the mountains, and the two were reconciled.

his advisers interpreted it for him, they said that it signified that he would be overthrown by a man called FERIDUN. Zohak ordered all children to be put to death, but the baby Feridun survived. When Feridun grew up he succeeded in killing Zohak and taking over the reins of power.

ZOROASTER, or Zarathustra, was a great religious reformer of ancient Iran. He was thought to have lived in the north-east of the country, some time in the sixth or fifth centuries BC, but scholars now believe that he lived much earlier, around 1200BC. The compelling figure of Zoroaster gave rise to many myths. It was said that his birth was foretold from the beginning of time. The moment he was born, he burst out laughing and the whole universe rejoiced with him.

Although the evil demons, the *DRUJS*, tried to destroy the child, he was protected by *AHURA MAZDA*, the principle of good. When he reached the age of 30, Zoroaster was given numerous revelations from the *AMESA SPENTAS*, or "Holy Immortals". Once armed with these spiritual insights, Zoroaster was able to resist the temptations of *ANGRA MAINYU*, or Ahriman, the principle of darkness.

Zoroaster denounced the worship of numerous gods, which until then had been prevalent in Iran, and instead preached a purified faith, focused on the struggle between good and evil, or Ahura Mazda and Angra Mainyu. His faith was a type of monotheism, although it inclined to dualism.

It was said that on one occasion, Zoroaster visited the court of a king and performed numerous miracles, including curing the king's favourite horse, before finally winning him over to his religion. The king then waged war against numerous neighbouring kings in an attempt to convert them. According to tradition, Zoroaster was murdered at the age of 77 while at his prayers.

ZOROASTER was traditionally said to have had a miraculous birth. According to legend, his mother, Dughdova, who was a virgin, conceived after she had been visited by a shaft of light. Though evil forces repeatedly tried to destroy the baby, he was protected by Ahura Mazda. (LIEBIG "CHROMO" CARD, 19TH CENTURY.)

ZOROASTER's teaching was embraced by the Achamenian rulers of Iran, who built this square tower facing the royal rock tombs at Naqsh-i-Rustam near their capital, Persepolis. Known as the Ka'bah-i-Zardusht, it may have been used as a fire temple; fire was a Zoroastrian symbol of purity and wisdom.

It is probable that Zurvan Akarana originated as an important god of early Iranian mythology. However, in the centuries following *ZOROASTER*, devotees of the religious movement known as Zurvanism came to regard him as the primal and eternal being, beyond good and evil, who formed Ahura Mazda and Angra Mainyu in order that they should both struggle to dominate creation.

According to one tradition, Zurvan Akarana promised authority to the firstborn, leading Angra Mainyu to tear his way out of the womb. As a result, evil reigned for several thousand years. It was also said that Zurvan Akarana conceived his two offspring at the very moment when he began to doubt that he would ever give birth. In consequence, Ahura Mazda embodied his wisdom and Angra Mainyu his doubt.

ZU was the demonic tempest bird of Mesopotamian mythology who lived in the underworld and stole the tablets of fate from *ENLIL*, "Lord of the Wind". The tablets gave whoever possessed them control of the universe. The supreme god *ANU* promised sovereignty over the gods to whoever recovered the tablets. Although the fragmentary nature of the surviving text makes the outcome difficult to establish for certain, it seems that the god *MARDUK* succeeded in regaining the tablets, although in some versions of the tale Zu is overcome by *NINURTA*, Enlil's son.

ZURVAN AKARANA came to prominence in Iranian mythology as the transcendent being who gave rise to *AHURA MAZDA*, the principle of good or light, and *ANGRA MAINYU*, or Ahriman, the principle of evil or darkness.

The religious reformer *ZOROASTER* had taught that Ahura Mazda was the one true god, who was set in eternal opposition to Angra Mainyu. This dualism, which became sharper as time passed, presented a problem: if Ahura Mazda was all-powerful, then he must have created evil. The concept of Zurvan Akarana, or "Infinite Time", managed to circumvent this intellectual dilemma.

ZOROASTER was a priest, prophet and thinker who made huge innovations in religious thought. He preached a purified faith that focused on the struggle between light and darkness, or Ahura Mazda and Angra Mainyu. (SYRIAN MURAL.)

THE MYTHS OF
SOUTH AND
CENTRAL ASIA

INTRODUCTION

THE IMMENSE INDIAN subcontinent encompasses an astonishing diversity of geographical regions. In the north lie the rugged Himalayan mountains, further south the vast agricultural plains of the river Ganges; there are high plateaux and low-lying coastal regions, vast rainforests and deserts. The climate is extreme, with scorching heat followed by drenching monsoons. This tremendously varied and unpredictable land has given rise to a rich mythology, many of whose deities have spread elsewhere, for example to Tibet and Sri Lanka, the other countries that are under consideration here.

A significant feature of Indian belief is the desire to transcend the chaos and unpredictability of the world in order to find the truth, nirvana (spiritual ecstasy) or enlightenment. From the earliest times, evidence suggests that people believed that they might achieve this goal through the practice of meditation. For example, modern excavations have uncovered evidence that the people of the Indus Valley civilization, which flourished around the middle of the third millennium BC in the region of modern Pakistan, worshipped a deity associated with meditation.

In the second millennium BC, the remarkable Indus Valley civilization collapsed under the constant incursions of the Aryan invaders, a group of Bronze Age tribes. The Aryans, or

GAUTAMA BUDDHA, the founder of Buddhism, attained enlightenment after many incarnations as a bodhisattva, or "buddha-to-be", setting an example for all Buddhists to follow. (GANDHARA-STYLE RELIEF, 3RD CENTURY BC.)

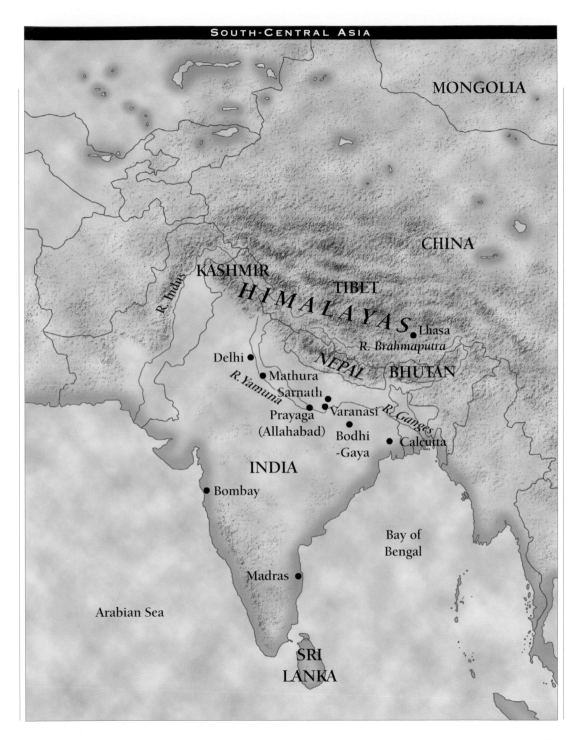

SOUTH-CENTRAL ASIA

MONGOLIA

CHINA

KASHMIR

R. Indus

HIMALAYAS

TIBET

Lhasa

R. Brahmaputra

NEPAL

BHUTAN

Delhi

R. Yamuna

Mathura

Sarnath

Prayaga
(Allahabad)

Varanasi

R. Ganges

Bodhi
-Gaya

Calcutta

INDIA

Bombay

Bay of
Bengal

Madras

Arabian Sea

SRI
LANKA

"Noble Folk", believed in many gods, spirits and demons. Among their most important deities were Indra, a weather and warrior god; Varuna, a maintainer of order and morality; Agni, a fire god; Surya, a sun god; and Yama, king of the dead.

Many of the gods of the Aryan invaders are venerated in India to this day. None the less, some of the beliefs attributed to the people of the Indus Valley civilization were to resurface. For example, the great Hindu god Shiva is believed to have taken on some of the characteristics of the Indus Valley civilization's fertility god. Indeed, this ancient figure is sometimes known as "proto-Shiva". The god also demonstrates something of the continuity of Indian belief, the willingness of the people to adopt and assimilate deities into their own world-view. In the *Rig Veda*, a

collection of sacred hymns composed between the 14th and tenth centuries BC, Shiva is only a minor deity known as Rudra. However, he later rose to become one of the three major gods of Hinduism, the belief system that developed from India's earlier religious traditions and prevails. Shiva also embodies the implicit contradictions of Hindu belief: that genesis cannot take place without previous destruction and that the ordered cosmos can only evolve from an initial state of chaos. Thus, though Shiva is known as the "Destroyer", his name means "Auspicious"; he is an ascetic (denying physical pleasures), but he is also extremely wild and has a huge sexual appetite.

Whereas the Aryans believed that after death they would either ascend to the heavens or descend to the underworld, by the

MANDALAS symbolize the universe as a circle. Though often found in paintings, for ritual purposes they are drawn in rice or coloured powder on consecrated ground. The dance called mandala-nrtya, performed in a circle, is based on Krishna's dance with the gopis and symbolizes the constant presence of the god. (DETAIL OF MANDALA OF BODHISATTVA AMOGHAPASA, GOUACHE, NEPAL, 1860.)

time of the *Upanishads*, sacred teachings composed between the eighth and fifth centuries BC, the human condition had come to be seen as one in which people were trapped within a relentless cycle of birth and death. The goal was to transcend the cycle and achieve liberation. It may be that such ideas, totally absent from the teachings of the Aryan invaders, had their roots in the beliefs of the Indus Valley civilization.

Followers of Buddhism and Jainism, two religions which arose in India in the sixth century BC, were also dedicated to the use of

SHIVA *as Nataraja, "Lord of the Dance", represents creation and destruction in balance. He is supported by the bull, Nandi. (STONE CARVING, 12–13TH CENTURY.)*

meditative techniques as a means of release from the cycle of death and rebirth. For Jains, the path to liberation demanded that stringent austerities, including self-mortifications, be practised, while Buddhists emphasized the inward struggle. Although both Buddhism and Jainism deny the existence of a creator god, they have a rich mythology. Jainism focuses on the tirthankaras, the great teachers who show the way to achieve liberation. Buddhism, on the other hand, gave rise to the cult of buddhas and bodhisattvas ("buddhas-to-be"), who helped people along the path to enlightenment.

Veneration of the numerous buddhas and bodhisattvas smoothed the way for the assimilation of Buddhism by people used to deity worship. Moreover, the adoption of many deities from Hinduism, as well as other religions, helped Buddhism to spread and flourish. At the same time, such a policy produced a vast and often bewildering pantheon.

In the third century BC, Mahinda, a close relative of the great Indian emperor Ashoka, introduced Buddhism to Sri Lanka. The king of Sri Lanka was converted, and Buddhism became the country's dominant religion, remaining so to this day. In the seventh century AD, Buddhist missionaries travelled from

India to Tibet. Although the new beliefs faced resistance from followers of the indigenous Bon religion, by the 12th century, Buddhism was firmly entrenched.

The Bon religion was characterized by a belief in the existence of two creator deities, the principles of good and evil, as well as a host of lesser gods and goddesses, and shared some similarities with shamanism. Buddhist teachers adopted many of the old shamanistic rites, attempting to contact the spirit world, and would often take the role of oracles or divine soothsayers for those Bon deities that had been brought into the new religion. This assimilation produced a very individual form of Buddhism, sometimes known as Lamaism,

VISHNU *was seen as the protector of the world. His first incarnation, or avatar, was as the fish, Matsya. (WOODCUT BY BERNARD PICART, 18TH CENTURY.)*

from the title, "Lama", given to Tibetan Buddhist religious masters or gurus. In time, Lamaism spread to Nepal, Mongolia and Bhutan.

Within India, Buddhism was largely reabsorbed into Hinduism; the Buddha himself was said to have come into being as the ninth incarnation of the great Hindu god Vishnu. This continual absorption and assimilation of different beliefs is perhaps the dominant characteristic of Indian religion. Certainly, it is what has helped give rise to such a rich and varied mythology.

THE ADIBUDDHA, or "Primordial Buddha", rose to prominence in the 11th century as a result of an attempt to transform Mahayana, or "Great Vehicle" Buddhism, into a monotheistic religion, inspired by a sentence within a Buddhist text, which claimed that there was a self-emanating buddha who existed long before anything else. In Nepal, the Adibuddha came to be seen as infinite, omniscient and the supreme creator. It was said that he emanated from the mystic syllable "Om" and gave rise to the five DHYANIBUDDHAS, or "Great Buddhas of Wisdom".

In Tantric Buddhism, Vajradhara is identified with the Adibuddha, and is portrayed holding a bell and a thunderbolt. In Nepal and Tibet, the Adibuddha is usually shown wearing robes and the ornaments of a BODHISATTVA. His SHAKTI, or female energy, is Adidharma.

THE ADIBUDDHA or "Primordial Buddha", in the posture of Yab-Yum ("Father-Mother") with his shakti. (BRASS AND COPPER, TIBET, 16TH CENTURY.)

ADITI, a Hindu mother goddess, is regarded as the personification of the earth, and her bosom as its navel. Her name means "Infinity" or "Free from Bounds". She is symbolized by the immortal cow and is said to embody unlimited light, consciousness and unity.

Aditi is usually said to be the mother of the great god VISHNU, and she appears in the Veda, the "sacred knowledge" of the Hindus, as the consort of BRAHMA or KASYAPA. DAKSHA, the son of Brahma, is said to have been born of Aditi, and Aditi to have been born of him. The goddess is also the mother of the ADITYAS, the deities who protect the world from chaos and ignorance. She rules over the divine ordering of the world and is said to be able to free all those who believe in her from sickness and sin. Whereas Aditi corresponds to the universal and divine in humankind, her sister, Diti, corresponds to all that is individual, human and divided.

THE ADITYAS are the offspring of ADITI, the Hindu mother goddess. They are usually said to number seven or eight deities, including MITRA and VARUNA. However, in later times, there were sometimes said to be 12 Adityas, each of whom was associated with the sun as the source of life, and each connected with a month of the year.

The Adityas are believed to offer salvation from all ills. Martanda, the eighth son of Aditi, is sometimes regarded as the divine ancestor of human beings.

THE ADIBUDDHA, in Tibetan Buddhism, is the personification of pure sunyata, or emptiness, combined with wisdom. All buddhas are aspects of his nature. (TIBETAN PAINTING.)

AGASTYA was a great Hindu sage who was said to have been conceived when the beautiful Urvasi, one of the APSARAS, slept with both MITRA (or sometimes SURYA) and VARUNA. Agastya caused any obstacle that stood in the way of the well-being of the universe to disappear. When a range of mountains threatened to grow so high that it hid the light of the sun, Agastya begged it to shrink back down in order to let him pass, and to stay that size until he returned. The sage then tricked the mountain range by returning home along another route. On another occasion, Agastya helped the hero RAMA, an AVATAR of the great god VISHNU. When Rama went into battle against RAVANA, the king of LANKA, he shot off each of the demon's ten heads with his arrows. However, the hero found that as soon as one head was removed, another sprang up in its place. Rama finally produced a miraculous weapon which had been given to him by Agastya. The weapon's point was made of sunlight and fire, and it weighed as much as the mountains MERU and

AGNI (left) spouts flames and carries a torch or flaming spear. (FRENCH, 19TH CENTURY.)

AGNI (right), as the god of sacrificial fire, is a mediator between gods and humankind. (BRONZE, ORISSA, 11–12TH CENTURY.)

Mandara put together. The arrow struck Ravana, killed him, and then magically returned to Rama.

AGNI, or "Fire", is one of the chief deities of the *Rig Veda*, the sacred hymns of Hinduism. He is both the protective god of the hearth and the god of the sacrificial fire. In the latter role, he mediates between deities and human beings by taking sacrifices to the gods. Agni appears in the sky as lightning and is regarded as both cruel and kind: although he dispels darkness, he devoured his parents as soon as he was born and consumes the bodies on the cremation pyre. He is referred to as the son of heaven and earth, and is usually said to have emerged either from the sun or from lightning. Other sources regard him as the son of *ADITI* and *KASYAPA*, and he is sometimes said to have been born from stone or from the rubbing together of two pieces of wood.

One of the guardian deities of the world, Agni can grant immortality and purify people of their sins after death. He looked after the monkey god *HANUMAN* when the demon king of *LANKA*, *RAVANA*, set light to his tail. The god is portrayed as red in colour, with two or three heads, several arms, a long beard and clothes of flames. He is sometimes shown riding in a chariot drawn by horses but is also said to ride a ram or a goat.

AIRAVATA, according to Hindu mythology, was the great white elephant ridden by *INDRA*, the king of the gods. One myth tells how the goddess *PARVATI* invited all the gods to a great party held to celebrate the birth of her son, *GANESHA*. Sani, the planet Saturn, at first refused the invitation, but Parvati insisted that he accept. When Sani looked at Ganesha, the child's head was reduced to ashes. *VISHNU*, the preserver of the universe, went in search of another head for Ganesha, and returned with that of the elephant Airavata.

AIRAVATA, the great white elephant, carries Indra into combat with Krishna, who is mounted on Garuda. Krishna was to overcome Indra. (WATERCOLOUR, C. 1590.)

AKSOBHYA, one of the five *DHYANIBUDDHAS*, or "Great Buddhas of Wisdom", rules over the eastern paradise Abhirati. His name means "Immovable", and he is said to subjugate the passions and enjoy mirror-like wisdom. Long ago, when Aksobhya was a monk, he vowed before the buddha who then ruled over Abhirati that he would never experience anger or repulsion. After endlessly striving to achieve this goal, he finally became a buddha and took up rulership over Abhirati. Anyone who is reborn in Abhirati will never fall into lower levels of consciousness, so all believers seek, like Aksobhya, to conquer passion.

In Tibet, Aksobhya is represented as *GAUTAMA BUDDHA*. He is usually depicted as blue in colour, and he is sometimes shown supported by a blue elephant. His main attribute is the thunderbolt and he is associated with the element. His *SHAKTI*, or corresponding female energy, is Locana. Aksobhya

AKSOBHYA (above), whose name means "Immovable", rules over the eastern paradise Abrihati, a land without evil, ugliness or suffering. (BRASS AND SILVER, TIBET, 13TH CENTURY.)

emanates the *BODHISATTVA MANJUSHRI*, the patron of the kings of Tibet. (See also *DHYANIBUDDHAS*)

AMITABHA is one of the five *DHYANIBUDDHAS*, and one of the most important buddhas of Mahayana or "Great Vehicle" Buddhism. His name means "Boundless Light" or "He Whose Splendour is Immeasurable".

Amitabha rules over the western paradise, a state of consciousness known as Sukhavati. Everyone who believes in the buddha is promised entry to Sukhavati, where they are reborn. Amitabha is thus a type of saviour who assures people of a life after death: individuals are able to achieve liberation through calling on his name, rather than having to endure countless rebirths.

AMITABHA (above) seated on a lotus flower, emits rays of golden light.

AMITABHA (left), who gave up his throne to become the monk Dharmakara, is shown here with a begging bowl. He achieved enlightenment and rules over the western paradise, Sukhavati. (GILT BRONZE, TIBET.)

In a previous existence, Amitabha was a king who, after encountering the Buddhist teaching, gave up his throne to become the monk Dharmakara. The buddha is thus sometimes depicted with a shaven head. Dharmakara took 48 vows in which he promised to help all those who attempted to tread the path towards enlightenment. Through meditation, the monk eventually fulfilled his vows and became the buddha Amitabha.

His element is water, and he is associated with the twilight and life in the beyond. He is usually shown as red in colour, sitting on a lotus blossom; sometimes, however, he is depicted riding a pair of peacocks.

Although he originated in India, Amitabha achieved his greatest popularity in China and Japan, where he is known as Amida, the buddha who inspired the "Pure Land" school of Buddhism. In the eighth century, the Indian monk *PADMASAMBHAVA* introduced Amitabha's cult to Tibet, where it also gained a wide following. In both Tibet and Nepal, Amitabha is often depicted in Yab-Yum, the posture of embrace, with his *SHAKTI*, or corresponding female energy, Pandara. (See also *DHYANIBUDDHAS*)

AMOGHASIDDHI is one of the five *DHYANIBUDDHAS*. He presides over the paradise of the north, and his name means "He Whose Accomplishment is Not in Vain".

Amoghasiddhi is sometimes identified with *GAUTAMA BUDDHA* and is normally coloured green. In Tibet, he is sometimes shown in Yab-Yum, the posture of embrace, with his *SHAKTI*, or corresponding female energy, Aryatara. The buddha sometimes sits on a throne decorated with garudas, eagle-like mythological birds. He may hold a sword in one hand and make the

AMOGHASIDDHI (above) one of the five Dhyanibuddhas, makes his characteristic mudra, or gesture, of fearlessness with his right hand. (BRONZE ENGRAVED WITH SILVER, 14TH CENTURY, TIBET.)

gesture of "Fear not" with the other. Amoghasiddhi's element is the earth and he is associated with the future buddha *MAITREYA*. (See also *DHYANIBUDDHAS*)

AMRITA is the elixir of immortality that features in the popular Indian myth of the churning of the ocean. The tale tells how, when the authority of the old gods was weakened, the ASURAS, or demons, began to threaten to usurp their power. The great god VISHNU, the preserver of the universe, suggested that the gods revitalize themselves by drinking the miraculous elixir Amrita, which they would have to produce by churning the celestial ocean. However, Vishnu said that they would need the assistance of the demons to accomplish the task.

In accordance with his instructions, the gods uprooted Mount Mandara and placed it in the middle of the ocean. Using the snake Vasuki as a churning rope, they whirled the mountain around and around until eventually it bored downwards into the earth, forcing the gods to turn to Vishnu once again for help. In his incarnation as the turtle KURMA, Vishnu took the mountain on to his back and the churning began again, this time more smoothly. However, the snake Vasuki began to suffer terribly and eventually poured forth venom, which threatened to engulf the whole of creation. SHIVA then came to the rescue. He succeeded in swallowing the poison, although it burned his throat, leaving a blue mark on his neck.

In due course, the ocean turned to milk and then to butter. By now the gods were growing tired, but they persisted in their efforts until at long last the water gave rise to the sacred cow Surabhi. After Surabhi came Varuni, goddess of wine; Parijati, the tree of paradise; the sun, the moon and LAKSHMI, goddess of wealth and good fortune. Finally, the divine doctor DHANVANTARI appeared holding the precious drink Amrita.

According to one version of the tale, the evil demon Rahu snatched the Amrita and began to drink it. Quickly, Vishnu chopped off Rahu's head in order to prevent the

elixir from spreading throughout the demon's body. None the less, Rahu's ghastly head remained immortal. According to another version of the myth, the drink penetrated throughout Rahu's body, whereupon Vishnu cut the demon into little pieces and set them among the stars. Yet another tale tells how the demons ran off with the sacred drink, whereupon Vishnu transformed himself into a beautiful woman, beguiled the demons and then succeeded in snatching the elixir back from them. The gods at last drank the Amrita and, having regained their power, drove the demons away.

ANANGA see KAMA.

ANANTA see NAGAS.

ANIRUDDHA, in Hindu mythology, is an epithet of Vahara, the third AVATAR of VISHNU. A DAITYA princess, Usha, fell in love with him and, assisted by her magical powers, brought him to her chambers. Hearing what had happened, Bana, the princess's father, sent his men to capture Aniruddha. The hero killed his assailants, whereupon Bana used his powers to kidnap the young man. When KRISHNA, his brother BALARAMA and his son, PRADYUMNA discovered what had happened, they determined to rescue Aniruddha. A tremendous battle ensued. SHIVA, the destroyer, and the god of

AMRITA (left), nectar of the gods and the elixir of immortality, is held by the buddha Amitayus, sitting in meditation with the vase in his lap. (BRONZE, TIBET, 10TH CENTURY.)

AMRITA (right) came into being when the gods stirred up the oceans using the snake Vasuki as a churning rope.

war, KARTTIKEYA, both sided with Bana but, despite their help, Bana lost the battle. After acknowledging that Krishna was the supreme god, Shiva persuaded him to spare Bana's life. Aniruddha then returned home with the princess.

THE APSARAS, according to Hindu mythology, are heavenly nymphs who were originally associated with water and later with the countryside. According to the great epic, the *Ramayana*, their origin can be traced to the churning of the ocean (see AMRITA). When the Apsaras emerged from the water, neither the gods nor the ASURAS wanted to marry them, so they belonged to everyone and were known as the "Daughters of Joy".

The Apsaras are charming and beautiful dancers, and are said to be fond of games of chance. However, according to one tradition, they can also cause madness. They are sometimes said to live in fig trees and banana plants.

One myth tells how when King Pururavas was out hunting one day, he heard cries for help and discovered that two Apsaras were being carried off by demons. The king rescued the Apsaras and, struck by their beauty, begged one of them, Urvasi, to become his lover. Urvasi agreed on condition that she was never forced to see the king's naked body.

After living together for a while, Urvasi discovered she was pregnant. By this time, however, the GANDHARVAS, the friends of the Apsaras, missed Urvasi and hatched a plot, which would enable her to return to them. Urvasi possessed two pet lambs,

which she kept by her bed at night. One evening, the Gandharvas approached Urvasi and Pururavas as they lay sleeping, and stole one of the lambs. Urvasi loudly protested that she was shocked that anyone had managed to steal her lamb when "a man and a hero" lay next to her. The Gandharvas then took Urvasi's second lamb, whereupon she made the same comment. This time, Pururavas leapt out of bed, unable to bear the suggestion that he was not a man, and went to catch the thieves. The Gandharvas then lit up the sky with flashes of lightning so that Urvasi saw the naked body of her husband. At once, as she had sworn, she disappeared.

Pururavas set off in pursuit of Urvasi and eventually found her as one of a flock of swans, swimming on a lake with other Apsaras. He begged Urvasi to return to him, but she refused. Eventually she promised him that he could spend the last night of the year with her, in order that he might see his son.

On the last night of the year, the Gandharvas took Pururavas to a golden palace and brought Urvasi to him. Urvasi told him that, the following morning, the Gandharvas would grant him a wish. When Pururavas asked Urvasi what she thought he should ask for, she told him that he should seek to become a Gandharva.

The next morning, Pururavas did as Urvasi had advised. The Gandharvas gave him some sacred fire in a dish and said he must return home and offer up sacrifices. Back at home, Pururavas neglected the fire for a moment and it disappeared. One tree grew where he had left the fire, and another where he had left the dish. The Gandharvas told him that he should make another fire by rubbing together two pieces of wood, one from each tree. Having made the fire, Pururavas cast his offerings into it and achieved his wish to become a Gandharva. He lived with Urvasi ever after.

Another Apsara, Shakuntala, the mother of King Bharata, was said to live in the hermitage of a *RISHI*, or seer. King Dushyanta fell in love with her and asked her to marry him, then gave her a ring and returned home. Shakuntala, dreaming of her love, forgot to look after one of the hermitage's guests. In punishment, the guest told her that unless she journeyed to find Dushyanta and showed him her ring, the king would fall out of love with her. On her way to find the king, Shakuntala lost the ring in a lake, where it was swallowed by a fish. The fish was later caught and sold to the king who then remembered the Apsara and sent for her to come and live with him.

THE APSARAS, or "Daughters of Joy",
are invoked at weddings to bring good
fortune. They are dancers in Indra's
heaven. (ANGKOR WAT, CAMBODIA, 12TH CENTURY.)

ARJUNA, the Hindu hero, was the son of the great god INDRA and Kunti, the wife of Pandu. Although Kunti was married to Pandu, he was under a curse and could not father children. Kunti conceived Arjuna and the other PANDAVA heroes after worshipping a variety of different gods.

ARJUNA is best known for his role in the *Bhagavad Gita* or "Song of the Lord", part of the Hindu epic, the *Mahabharata*. While waiting for the start of the great battle of Kurukshetra, Arjuna was troubled by the thought of the bloodshed and suffering that would ensue, especially since his opponents, the Kauravas, were his relatives. KRISHNA, the eighth AVATAR of the great god VISHNU, disguised himself as Arjuna's charioteer, and offered the hero comfort and spiritual teaching. He then urged Arjuna to do his duty as a kshatriya, or member of the warrior caste. Arjuna, overwhelmed with awe and devotion, was filled with renewed resolution. On another occasion, Arjuna and Krishna helped the fire god AGNI recover his power by burning down a huge forest.

ARUNA see GARUDA.

ASANGA see MAITREYA.

THE ASURAS, according to early Indian mythology, were beings who possessed supernatural or divine power. They were power-seeking and dangerous, and were opposed to the gods, or DEVAS. They are sometimes misleadingly described as demons, though they were not necessarily evil.

According to later Hindu texts, the creator being PRAJAPATI was the ancestor of both the devas and the asuras. The devas chose to follow truth, and the asuras chose to follow falsehood. At first, the asuras became rich through telling lies,

ARJUNA (above) and Krishna, the eighth avatar of the great god Vishnu, sound their transcendental conch shells. Krishna is disguised as Arjuna's charioteer.

ARJUNA (left) the archer, a Pandava prince, rides into the battle of Kurukshetra against the Kauravas, which ended with the total destruction of both armies.

but eventually they were destroyed. Occasionally, the devas were obliged to join forces with the asuras – as, for instance, during the churning of the ocean, when the gods sought to obtain AMRITA, the elixir of immortality.

One famous asura, Jalamdhara, was the product of the union of GANGA, the goddess of the river Ganges, with the ocean. There came a time when the power of the war god INDRA rose to equal that of SHIVA. Feeling threatened, Shiva manifested a towering form of anger and ordered it to wed the goddess Ganga to the ocean. The asura Jalamdhara was produced from their union, and BRAHMA bestowed upon him the ability to conquer the gods. Jalamdhara performed countless miracles in his youth before marrying Vrinda, the daughter of a nymph. He then gathered together an army of asuras and declared war on the gods.

A tremendous battle ensued and the great asura even succeeded in overcoming VISHNU, although the goddess LAKSHMI persuaded Jalamdhara to spare his life. Eventually, Jalamdhara succeeded in driving the devas from heaven.

The devas sought help from Brahma, who directed them to Shiva. He advised the devas to combine their powers and to make a fabulous weapon, whereupon the

ARJUNA, having broken a vow he had made to his brothers, had to endure 14 years' exile. During this time, he journeyed to the river Ganges, where he became the lover of the river goddess Ganga. She gave him the power to become invisible in water.
(PAINTING BY WARWICK GOBLE.)

devas forged a huge and dazzling disc, so bright that no-one could look at it.

Meanwhile, Jalamdhara tried to seduce Shiva's wife, PARVATI, although the goddess managed to escape him. Vishnu then disguised himself as Jalamdhara and succeeded in seducing Vrinda. When Vrinda realized what had happened, she died of grief.

Jalamdhara was furious. He resurrected his dead asuras and summoned them to battle once more. Shiva threw the marvellous disc at Jalamdhara, cutting off his head. However, the asura simply grew a new head in the old one's place each time Shiva beheaded him. Eventually, Shiva summoned the wives of the gods. Taking the form of monstrous ogres, the goddesses drank all the asuras' blood, whereupon the gods won the battle and regained their kingdom.

The Hindu epic the *Mahabharata* tells how Brahma granted three DAITYAS – asuras descended from Diti – permission to establish three cities: one of gold in heaven, one of silver in the air and one of iron on earth. The three brothers ruled over them for many years. Countless asuras flocked to the cities where they were provided with their every desire. Eventually, Shiva burned the three cities to the ground, together with all the asuras, and threw them into the depths of the ocean.

THE ASVINS, or "Horse Drivers", according to Hindu mythology, are golden-coloured twins who drive a three-wheeled golden chariot drawn by horses or birds. Known individually as Nasatya and Dasra, they bring divine bliss to humankind, and symbolize strength and energy. The offspring of the sun and the cloud goddess Saranyu, the Asvins are both married to daughters of the light. Each morning, they make a path through the clouds for the dawn goddess USHAS and scatter the dew with their whips.

In the *Rig Veda*, the ancient Hindu hymns, the Asvins often intervene with the gods on behalf of humankind. They also guard the RISHIS, or seers, from drowning in the sea of ignorance. The doctors of the gods, they are friends of the sick and unfortunate. They heal the blind and the lame, and rejuvenate the aged. They are chiefly associated with the war god INDRA and prepare the equipment of the warrior gods.

THE ASURAS, outwitted by Vishnu, chose to hold the head end of the serpent Vasuki during the churning of the ocean, and were nearly suffocated by the creature's hot breath. (KANGRA MINIATURE, 18TH CENTURY.)

Although they are kind and beautiful, the gods originally forbade the Asvins entry to heaven. However, the rishi Syavana eventually came to their aid. Despite being well advanced in years, Syavana had a beautiful young wife, Sukanya. One day, the twins saw her bathing in a river and, after flattering her, tried to persuade her to leave her husband for one of them. Sukanya refused, whereupon the twins said that they would make Syavana young and beautiful again and that Sukanya should then choose from among the three of them. Syavana agreed and, after bathing in the river, the three men emerged, all looking young and handsome. Sukanya took a long time to come to a decision, but finally chose to stay with her husband. Syavana was delighted: not only had he kept his wife, but he had regained his youth and beauty. In gratitude, he persuaded Indra to allow the Asvins into heaven.

349

MYTHICAL MOUNTAINS

THE VAST MOUNTAIN RANGE OF THE Himalayas inspired awe in all those who beheld it. Its peaks appeared to reach up out of the human world to touch the realms of the gods, and the range was regarded as sacred by both Tibetans and Hindus as a transitional domain between the human and the heavenly worlds. Mount Meru, the mythical axis of the cosmos, lay at its centre. One legend credited the mighty god Indra with the formation of the mountains: it was said that they had been a herd of flying elephants who had displeased him. He punished them by cutting off their wings. All the gods were thought to make sacrifices on the mountains, but Shiva was particularly associated with them. Mount Kailasa was his mythological paradise and, as an ascetic, his deep meditation on this mountain ensured the continued existence of the world.

PARVATI (above right) was the daughter of the god Himavat, king of the Himalayas, who was a deified personification of the mountains. Parvati's name means "Daughter of the Mountain" and she was an aspect of the mother goddess, Devi. She became the consort of the great god Shiva, who had his home on Mount Kailasa. Another daughter of Himavat was Ganga, the deity of the sacred river whose source is in the Himalayas and was said to flow through Shiva's hair. (SHIVA AND PARVATI WITH SKANDA, BRONZE, 10–11TH CENTURY.)

MERU was supported on the hood of the coiled primeval cobra, Vasuki, who created earthquakes when he yawned and will consume the whole world with his fiery breath at the end of the present age. Both Hindus and Buddhists acknowledge the mountain's sacred status, and its shape is symbolized in conical objects of worship and meditation called yantras, on which the material world is depicted at the outer edge, and the absolute and eternal at the centre. (NEPALESE YANTRA.)

MERU (left) *was the mythical mountain at the centre of the cosmos, the navel of the world, and was sacred to both Hindus and Buddhists. All the spheres of existence, from Brahma's heavenly city of gold at its summit, to the seven nether worlds at its foot, centred on the mountain, and the sacred river Ganges sprang from it. Its slopes glittered with precious stones and were clothed with trees laden with delectable fruits. It was surrounded by a vast lake and ringed with golden peaks.* (MURAL PAINTING, WAT KO KEO SUTTHARAM, THAILAND.)

THE GODS (below) *assembled on Mount Meru in search of the elixir of immortality, Amrita, which had been lost with other precious treasures in a catastrophic flood. Vishnu's solution was to churn the cosmic ocean until the treasures emerged. The gods uprooted Mount Mandara and set it on the back of the tortoise Kurma. The gods, with the help of the asuras, coiled the world serpent Vasuki around the mountain like a rope and each took an end.* (THE CHURNING OF THE MILKY OCEAN, BASOHLI, C. 1700.)

MOUNT MANDARA (right), *as it was spun, churned the cosmic ocean until it turned to milk, and then to butter. Eventually, the precious things it contained began to emerge: the sacred cow, Surabhi; the sun; the moon; Lakshmi, the goddess of good fortune; and, finally, the physician of the gods, Dhanvantari, holding the precious Amrita. The demon Rahu got hold of the elixir, but Vishnu rescued it by chopping off Rahu's head. The gods drank the Amrita to regain their power, and restored Mount Mandara to its proper place.* (KANGRA MINIATURE, 18TH CENTURY.)

AVALOKITESHVARA is the most popular *BODHISATTVA* or "buddha-to-be" of Mahayana or "Great Vehicle" Buddhism. His name is translated as "Lord of Compassionate Sight" or "Lord Who Looks From On High". The Bodhisattva of the present age, Avalokiteshvara is said to have emanated from the great buddha *AMITABHA*. Although his residence is in Amitabha's paradise, he remains in this world in order to attend to the salvation of humans and animals. He is usually represented as a handsome man, with several heads and arms.

According to one myth, when Avalokiteshvara was looking down on the suffering in the world, his head burst open in pain. Amitabha put the pieces back together as nine new heads. Then, because Avalokiteshvara wanted to help all creatures, he grew 1,000 arms, and in the palm of each hand was an eye: "From his eyes were derived the sun and the moon, from his forehead, Mahesvara, from his shoulders, *BRAHMA* and other gods, from his heart, Narayana, from his thighs, *SARASVATI*, from his mouth, the winds, from his feet, the earth, from his belly, *VARUNA*."

Avalokiteshvara helps everyone who asks for his assistance. He visits hell to take cooling drinks to those suffering the heat of the damned, and he preaches the Buddhist law to beings incarnated as insects or worms. He is also said to protect people from natural disasters and to bless children. Moreover, the bodhisattva is said to have converted the female ogres of Sri Lanka and to have been given the task of converting Tibet to Buddhism.

In Tibet, his name is sPyan-ras-gzigs or *CHENREZIG*. In China, Avalokiteshvara developed into the goddess Kuan Yin, or Guanyin, and in Japan into the god, or sometimes goddess, Kwannon. (See also *BODHISATTVAS*)

AVALOKITESHVARA (left) is also known as Padmapani, or "Lotus-bearer", and holds a pink lotus blossom in his hand. In eastern religions, the lotus signifies non-attachment, freedom from ignorance, and the path to enlightenment.

AVALOKITESHVARA (above) the bodhisattva of universal compassion, is an emanation of the meditation of the Dhyanibuddha Anitabha, and therefore wears an effigy of the great buddha in his headdress. (BRONZE, 14TH CENTURY.)

THE AVATARS of *VISHNU* are his incarnations on earth in order to help humankind in moments of great crisis. It is generally accepted that Vishnu has ten avatars, although their number varies, and their identities are also flexible. Usually, the incarnations are said to consist of Matsya, *KURMA*, Varaha, *NARASIMHA*, Vamana, Parashurama, *RAMA*, *KRISHNA*, *GAUTAMA BUDDHA* and Kalkin.

Matsya, the first avatar, appeared as a fish who protected *MANU*, the first man, during the great deluge. The second avatar, Kurma the tortoise, supported Mount Mandara on his back during the churning of the ocean. Varaha, the boar, rescued the earth. The story tells how the earth, lost beneath floods, had been captured by a demon, whereupon Vishnu, as the boar Varaha, plunged into the waters and traced the earth by its smell. He killed the demon who had captured the earth and raised it out of the ocean on his tusks. Vishnu as Varaha is depicted as a giant with a boar's head, carrying the goddess of the earth.

The fourth avatar was Narasimha, who killed the powerful demon Hiranyakashipu, an incarnation of *RAVANA*. The demon had persuaded *BRAHMA* to give him the power to dethrone the storm god, *INDRA*, and to send the sky gods into exile. The demon then proclaimed himself king of the universe. Hiranyakashipu's son, Prahlada, was, however, a devotee of Vishnu. This so enraged Hiranyakashipu that he tortured the young man in an effort to dissuade him from his worship. Prahlada remained unswayed. Hiranyakashipu then ordered Prahlada to be put to death, but nothing could harm the young man. Eventually, Hiranyakashipu flew into such a rage that he struck a pillar, saying that if Vishnu was so important and omnipresent, why was he not right there, within the pillar? Immediately, the pillar collapsed, and Vishnu emerged

in the form of Narasimha, a man with a lion's head. Narasimha immediately seized Hiranyakashipu and tore him to pieces, whereupon Prahlada succeeded his father to the throne.

Vamana, a dwarf, was the fifth avatar who came to save the world from the demon Bali. The sixth avatar was Parashurama. When his mother had impure thoughts, Parashurama decapitated her at his father's command. However, when his father granted him a wish, Parashurama asked that his mother be brought back to life. Later, when

King Kartavirya insulted his father, Parashurama destroyed the whole kshatriya, or warrior, caste to which the king belonged. He then ordered the brahmans to sleep with the widows of the kshatriya men, in order to produce a new and purer warrior caste.

Rama, the warrior, is the seventh avatar of Vishnu, and the god, Krishna, is the eighth. Vishnu was said to assume his ninth avatar, the Buddha, in order to mislead the sinful so that they would receive their just deserts. Kalkin, the final avatar, has yet to come. He will

THE AVATARS surround this picture of the god Vishnu. Taking the form of various animals, the avatars appeared on earth to help humankind during times of crisis.

(JAIPUR, RAJASTHAN, 18TH CENTURY.)

appear at the end of the present age, or Kali *YUGA*, to establish a new era. It is thought that he will take the form of a warrior on a white horse, or a man with a horse's head. Kalkin will put an end to the wicked, and everything will be reabsorbed into the "Absolute" until creation begins again. (See also *THE AVATARS OF VISHNU*)

B

BALARAMA was the elder brother of *KRISHNA*, the eighth *AVATAR* of *VISHNU*, and was himself regarded as a partial avatar of the great Hindu "Preserver of the Universe". When the evil King Kamsa heard of Krishna's amazing exploits, he determined to kill him. He announced a wrestling match, challenging all the local young men to try their strength against the champions of his court. Krishna and Balarama, eager to take up the challenge, immediately made their way to the city where the contest was to take place. However, when it was their turn to fight, King Kamsa released a wild elephant into the ring. The elephant charged towards the two young men, but Krishna simply leapt on to its back, put his arms round its neck and squeezed it to death. King Kamsa then sent his two strongest champions into the ring, but Krishna broke the neck of the first and Balarama crushed the other so hard that his heart burst.

Krishna later killed King Kamsa, but Balarama was killed in a drunken brawl involving Krishna's kinsmen, the Yadavas.

BALARAMA holding a horn, with his younger brother Krishna, playing the flute. The brothers overcame the champions of the court of the evil King Kamsa. (PAINTING BY BECHERAM DAS PANDEC, 1865.)

BALI see *VISHNU*.

BANA see *ANIRUDDHA*.

BANDARA was the title that was originally given to important officials within the Singhalese kingdom of Sri Lanka. In time, however, the term came to be used for a group of gods who were considered superior to the lesser deities, or *YAKSHAS*. For example, the god *DADIMUNDA*, treasurer to the supreme god *UPULVAN* and protector of Buddhism, is held to be a Bandara. Very often, a principal local god will be known simply as Bandara.

BCAN see *BTSAN*.

BODHISATTVAS are living symbols of compassion. They choose to delay the moment of entering nirvana in order to help others along the path to enlightenment. (STONE, 2ND–4TH CENTURY AD.)

THE BDUD were the heavenly spirits of the indigenous Bon religion of Tibet. However, within Tibetan Buddhism, the bDud came to be seen as devils. They were said to be black and to live in a castle.

BEG-TSE, a *DHARMAPALA*, or "Protector of the Teaching", is a mythical warrior who is regarded as a symbol of the conversion of the Mongols to Tibetan Buddhism. He

on to his head. For several years, the river meandered around the god's tangled locks, until at last Shiva divided it into seven streams and allowed it to flow safely out over the world.

BODHISATTVAS are "enlightenment beings" who are destined to become buddhas. They put off the moment when they will enter nirvana and escape the cycle of death and rebirth, in order that they may help others along the long path to enlightenment. Bodhisattvas are thus living symbols of compassion.

According to Mahayana, or "Great Vehicle" Buddhism, human beings are sometimes able to enter paradise by means of a bodhisattva's merits and spiritual power rather than through their own, provided that they call on the bodhisattva in faith.

Bodhisattvas are usually shown robed as princes, wearing five-leaved crowns. *AVALOKITESHVARA* and *MANJUSHRI* are two of the best known bodhisattvas. (See also *BODHISATTVAS*)

BHAGIRATHA (below) endured rigorous austerities to induce the gods to allow the sacred river Ganges to flow down to earth, to carry away the ashes of his ancestors so that their spirits might be freed. (ROCK CARVING AT MAMALLAPURAM, INDIA, 7TH CENTURY.)

BEG-TSE (above), flanked by dakini, supernatural beings who are said to devour humans. He stands in his characteristic warlike pose, with one foot on a horse and the other on a man.

wears armour and carries a garland of human heads. In Lamaism, he is a god of war. According to tradition, in the 17th century, Beg-tse sided with the Mongolian warriors and led an army of animals against the Dalai Lama. However, the Dalai Lama assumed the form of the *BODHISATTVA AVALOKITESHVARA* and converted Beg-tse to Buddhism.

BHAGIRATHA, according to Hindu mythology, was the sage who persuaded *BRAHMA* and *SHIVA* to send the sacred river Ganges down to earth from heaven. The earth had become littered with the ashes of the dead, and Bhagiratha realized that the waters of the Ganges would wash them away and liberate the spirits of those who had been cremated. In order to prevent a disastrous flood, the great god Shiva allowed the river to fall

BRAHMA, according to Hindu mythology, was the creator and director of the universe. He was the father of gods and humans alike, and in classical Indian thought, he forms a trinity with VISHNU and SHIVA. The three gods are collectively known as the Trimurti. Vishnu and Shiva represent opposing forces and Brahma, the all-inclusive deity, represents their balancing force.

Brahma was also the personalized form of Brahman. Originally, this term referred to the sacred power inherent within a sacrifice, but it came to refer to the power, known as the "Absolute", which lay behind all creation.

While the god Brahma meditated, he produced all the material elements of the universe and the concepts that enabled human beings to understand them. In each day of Brahma's existence, the universe is created, and in each night, it is reabsorbed. Within each of these cycles, there are four successive ages, or YUGAS, beginning with the Krita Yuga, or golden age, and ending with the Kali Yuga, the present age of conflict and despair.

According to one myth, Brahma produced the beautiful goddess Satarupa from his own body. She was so lovely that he was unable to stop staring at her, and whenever she moved aside to avoid his gaze, he sprouted a new head in order that he might continue looking at her. Eventually, Brahma overcame her shyness and persuaded Satarupa to marry him, and they retired to a secret place for 100 divine years, at the end of which MANU, the first man, was born.

Another creation myth describes how, in the beginning, the universe was shrouded in darkness. Eventually, a seed floating in the cosmic ocean gave rise to a beautiful, shining egg. According to the sacred texts known as the *Laws of Manu,* "In this egg the blessed one remained a whole year, then of himself, by the effort of his thought

only, he divided the egg into two." From the two halves, he made heaven, the celestial sphere, and earth, the material sphere. Between the two halves of the egg he placed the air, the eight cardinal points and the eternal abodes of the waters. "From himself he drew the

Spirit, including in itself being and not-being, and from the Spirit, he drew the feeling of self which is conscious of personality and is master." The egg finally revealed Brahma the god, who divided himself into two people, a male and a female. In due course, these two

BRAHMA, the creator of the universe. His attributes include a vessel containing water from the sacred Ganges river. He is attended by Hamsa, a goose or swan.

beings gave rise to the whole of the rest of creation. Another version of the myth describes how Brahma

Brahma is often shown with four heads and four hands in which he holds the four Vedas, the holy scriptures of ancient India. His other attributes include a vessel containing water from the Ganges and a garland of roses. He rides on Hamsa, a goose or swan. Brahma's wife is the beautiful *SARASVATI*, the goddess of learning and patroness of arts, sciences and speech.

THE bTSAN, or bCan, are Tibetan demons who live in the air and appear before human beings as fierce hunters who ride their red steeds over the mountains. Anyone who finds themselves alone in wild and deserted places may be killed by the arrows of the bTsan.

CANDI see *DURGA*.

CANDRA see *CUNDA*.

CHAKRA SAMVARA see *SAMVARA*.

BRAHMA (above) produced a beautiful young woman from his own body. Each time she moved to avoid his gaze, he sprouted a new head so that he might continue looking at her. (STONE, CHOLA PERIOD, 11TH CENTURY.)

BRAHMA (right) receives an offering in the presence of a sacred fire. In one of his left hands he holds the Vedas, the collections of sacred writings that form the basis of Hindu belief and religious practice.

came forth from the egg as the primeval being known as *PURUSHA*. This creature had 1,000 thighs, 1,000 feet, 1,000 arms, 1,000 eyes, 1,000 faces and 1,000 heads. In order that the universe might come into being, he offered himself as a sacrifice. The gods and the brahman caste came from his mouth, the seasons came from his armpits, earth came from his feet and the sun emerged from his eyes.

Brahma was also sometimes known as Narayana, or "He Who Comes From the Waters". In this guise, he was regarded as lying on a leaf, floating on the primeval waters sucking his toe – a symbol of eternity.

Brahma's following was probably at its height in the early centuries of the first millennium

AD, when he seems to have been the focus of a cult. Usually, however, he was regarded as less important than Vishnu and Shiva, the other two great gods. Today, there is only one temple dedicated to him in the whole of India.

Brahma's fall from supremacy is accounted for in a myth concerning the origins of Shiva. According to the tale, Brahma and Vishnu were arguing over which of them was the most powerful. At the height of their quarrel a huge lingam, the phallic-shaped symbol of Shiva, arose from the cosmic ocean, crowned with a flame. When Brahma and Vishnu examined the lingam, it burst open. Deep within it the gods found the ultimate creator deity, Shiva, and they had to admit his supremacy.

CHENREZIG, or sPyan-rasgzigs, means "Looking with Clear Eyes" and he is the Tibetan form of *AVALOKITESHVARA*, the *BODHISATTVA* of compassion. He is believed to be the protector of Tibet and, according to tradition, is the founding father of the Tibetan people.

One tale tells how the Buddha *AMITABHA* saw the suffering of human beings and created Chenrezig out of his compassion for them. The bodhisattva is said to have appeared on a small island in the middle of Lhasa and, on seeing the immense suffering of all the creatures who surrounded him, to have vowed that he would never leave the world until every one attained peace.

The innumerable creatures all begged to be given bodies. Chenrezig did as they requested and, in order that they might achieve spiritual liberation, he preached the Buddhist teachings to them. However, more and more creatures kept appearing. Eventually, Chenrezig despaired of ever being able to help everybody. He begged Amitabha to allow him to break his vow and, in despair, his body broke into countless pieces.

Amitabha felt sorry for Chenrezig and re-created him, giving him even greater power. The bodhisattva now had numerous heads, 1,000 arms and an eye in the palm of each hand. Chenrezig still felt daunted by the task that lay ahead of him and began to weep at the thought. From one of his tears, the goddess *TARA* was born, and together, they proceeded to help everyone attain liberation.

Tibetans traditionally regard their original ancestors as Avalokiteshvara in the form of a monkey and the goddess Tara (sGrol-ma) in the form of a rock ogress. One story tells how the monkey journeyed to the Himalayas in order to engage in a prolonged and undisturbed period of meditation. When he arrived at his destination, he was soon spot-

ted by a rock ogress. Although the ogress attempted to seduce the monkey, none of her charms succeeded in persuading him to break his vow of chastity. The ogress became so frustrated and angry that it seemed that she might be about to destroy the world, whereupon the monkey finally gave in to her entreaties. The couple eventually produced six children. From these children, the entire population of Tibet arose.

King Songtsen Gampo (AD620–49), who was responsible for the introduction of Buddhism to Tibet, is traditionally said to have been an incarnation of Chenrezig. The Dalai Lama is also regarded as an incarnation of the bodhisattva.

CUNDA, or Candra, or Cundi, is a *BODHISATTVA*, regarded either as a female form of *AVALOKITESHVARA* or as an emanation of Vajrasattva or *VAIROCANA*, whose image she

CHENREZIG, the bodhisattva, is the protector of Tibet and is believed to be incarnated in its spiritual leaders.

sometimes bears on her crown. She is said to have given birth to 700,000 buddhas and is therefore sometimes referred to as "Mother of the Buddhas".

Cunda may have developed from the Hindu goddess of the dawn, *USHAS*. She has one face, numerous arms and is coloured

D

white, like the autumn moon, or green. She rides upon the back of a prostrate man. The bodhisattva is kindly but threatening and possesses numerous weapons, including a thunderbolt, sword, bow, arrow, axe and trident. However, two of her hands are held in the gestures of teaching and charity. Although she helps the good, she is terrifying to the wicked. According to one Tibetan tale, she helped a warrior to destroy a wicked queen, who took a different king to her bed each night and killed him. (See also *BODHISATTVAS*)

CUNDI see *CUNDA*.

DADIMUNDA, or Devata Bandara, is one of the most popular gods of the Singhalese people of Sri Lanka. Originally, he looked after temples, but later he became treasurer to the supreme god *UPULVAN*.

Dadimunda finally emerged as the protector of Buddhism in Sri Lanka. He is said to ride on an elephant, attended by numerous *YAKSHAS*, or lesser deities.

THE DAITYAS, according to Hindu mythology, are giant *ASURAS* who oppose the gods. They are the

offspring of Diti, the sister of *ADITI* and one of the wives of the sage *KASYAPA* who fathered *GARUDA*.

HAYAGRIVA is a famous daitya who appears in both Hindu and Buddhist mythology. On one occasion, he attacked *BRAHMA* and stole from him the four books that make up the Veda, the "sacred knowledge" of the Hindus. *VISHNU*, reincarnated as the *AVATAR* Matsya the fish, managed to kill Hayagriva and retrieve the sacred texts. In

Tibetan Buddhism, Hayagriva was a lord of wrath, the leader of the terrifying gods known as Drag-shed (see *DHARMAPALAS*.)

Another daitya, Prahlada, was renowned for his devotion to Vishnu. According to one tradition, Prahlada was raised by Vishnu in order that one day he might become king of the daityas. Prahlada's father, the demon king Hiranyakashipu and avatar of *RAVANA*, was furious that his son

THE DAITYAS, with the other asuras, were persuaded by the gods to help them obtain Amrita. The daityas wanted to drink the elixir, but the gods offered them wine instead. When the daityas were all drunk, the gods made off with the Amrita. (ILLUSTRATION TO THE MAHABHARATA.)

worshipped Vishnu, but eventually Vishnu, as the avatar *NARASIMHA*, killed Hiranyakashipu.

The Hindu epic, the *Mahabharata*, tells how three daitya brothers asked Brahma to grant them invulnerability. Brahma said it was impossible to do so, whereupon the brothers asked that they might establish three cities and return to them after 1,000 years. Brahma agreed. He told the great asura Maya to build the cities: one of gold in heaven, one of silver in the air and one of iron on earth. The three brothers then ruled over their realms, populated by countless asuras, for many years, until, eventually, *SHIVA* burned the three cities, together with all the asuras, and threw them into the ocean.

THE DAITYAS fought the gods for possession of Amrita, which the gods needed to restore their superior power. Here, it is carried by Brahma, in the midst of the battle. (ILLUSTRATION TO THE MAHABHARATA.)

BODHISATTVAS

BODHISATTVAS ARE FUTURE BUDDHAS. They have such compassion for humanity that they take a vow to attain enlightenment, not just for their personal liberation but to show others the path they have found. In Mahayana Buddhism, this means that, even though they have reached the threshold of nirvana, they delay their own freedom and resolve to stay in the world to help others. For them, their own achievement of nirvana is not their only goal. They perceive further stages of enlightenment to be attained on the route to becoming a buddha. Celestial bodhisattvas, such as Manjushri and Avalokiteshvara, are very near to becoming buddhas themselves, and they act as mediators between the buddhas and mortals. They are not monks, but lay figures who are often portrayed as princes, wearing elaborate jewellery and a five-leaved crown. The bodhisattva Maitreya is the buddha of the future, a benevolent character who will arrive on earth in about 30,000 years, when the Buddhism of the present age has expired.

PADMAPANI (left), the "Lotus Bearer", is an aspect of Avalokiteshvara, depicted holding a lotus blossom. The lotus is a religious symbol in both Hinduism and Buddhism; in the latter it represents those who have conquered ignorance and achieved enlightenment. Padmapani is associated with the colours red and white, and wears an image of the buddha Amitabha on his crown, since Avalokiteshvara is Amitabha's attendant. (BODHISATTVA PADMAPANI, KHARA KHOTO, 13TH CENTURY.)

AVALOKITESHVARA (above), "The Lord Who Looks Down", is greatly revered in Mahayana Buddhism as the embodiment of compassion. He is sometimes depicted with as many as a thousand arms, all of which he uses to help humanity. The bodhisattva's compassion is so great that he even enters the realms of hell to alleviate the sufferings he finds there. In Tibet, where he is known as Chenrezig, the successive Dalai Lamas are regarded as incarnations of the bodhisattva. (TIBETAN STATUE, 14TH CENTURY.)

A MANDALA (left) has Avalokiteshvara at its centre. He is shown with many heads because he was so distraught by his vision of the sufferings on earth that his head split open with pain. In the mandala, a symbolic representation of the universe, the four walls and four open gateways are taken to include within them the whole external world, at the centre of which sits the bodhisattva in the position of lord of the world. (TIBETAN PAINTING.)

MANJUSHRI (above), the great bodhisattva, personifies wisdom and learning. The sword he wields in his right hand is used to cut through the veil of ignorance. In his left hand he carries a lotus blossom, holding a scroll which contains the "Perfection of Wisdom": these writings describe the ideal of the bodhisattva as the highest aspiration of religious life, and the emptiness of phenomena which characterizes Mahayana Buddhism. (CHINESE, 15TH CENTURY.)

CUNDA (left) is a female bodhisattva, sometimes called the "Mother of the Buddhas". She is said to be kindly to the good but terrifying to the wicked: she is portrayed with as many as 16 arms, each of which holds a threatening weapon, but for a worshipper who knows how to regard her, her hands are in the positions of teaching and charity. (RELIEF FROM CENTRAL INDIA, 10TH CENTURY.)

VAJRAPANI (left), the indigo bodhisattva, is one of the most important wrathful deities. Vajrapani is the destroyer of evil. His fierce demeanour represents the attitude needed to turn hatred against itself and transcend it. He is armed with a Vajra, or thunderbolt, which is the weapon of the Hindu gods Indra and Karttikeya. Vajrapani is also said to be the embodiment of skilful actions. (TIBETAN PAINTING.)

THE DAKINI, according to traditional Buddhist belief, are supernatural beings, or low-ranking goddesses. They fly through the air and are said to eat human beings. The dakini have magical powers and are able to initiate novices into the secret wisdom of the Tantra, a series of ritual texts dealing with the attainment of enlightenment. They can also help Yogis who wish to further their spiritual progress since they are able to concentrate the powers that the Yogi releases.

The dakini are usually shown dancing and appear as young naked women, as horrible monsters, or with the heads of lions or birds or the faces of horses or dogs. They also feature in Hindu mythology, as witch attendants on the goddess KALI.

In Tibetan Buddhism, dakinis are known as khadromas, female beings who move in celestial space. Their nakedness symbolizes their knowledge of perfect truth. The khadromas are said to live in Urgyen, a mythical realm that is also regarded as the birthplace of PADMASAMBHAVA, one of the founders of Tibetan Buddhism. In Tibet, eight goddesses, represented as beautiful young women, are sometimes included within the group of dakinis. They are known as the "Eight Mothers" and are thought to have developed from Tibetan shamanism.

DAKSHA, according to Hindu mythology, is the lord of cattle and the son of the mother goddess ADITI. He chose Sati, one of his 60 beautiful daughters, to be the wife of the great god, SHIVA. One tale tells how Daksha prepared an important sacrifice to which he invited all the gods, including INDRA. However, he failed to invite Shiva. Sati was outraged at this slight to her husband but decided that, even if her husband were not invited, she herself would attend the ceremony. Shiva was highly impressed by his wife's loyalty. However, he told her that Daksha was sure to insult him and that she must be strong and not respond to his insults.

When Sati arrived at her father's house, Daksha immediately began to insult Shiva, scorning his wild dancing and his appearance. Sati, finally overwhelmed with fury, denounced her father in front of all the gods. Then, since she had broken her promise to Shiva, she threw herself on to the sacrificial fire and was burnt to death.

Shiva was so angry and distraught at this turn of events that he sent one of his emanations, a terrifying demon, to kill everyone who had attended the ceremony. At length, the great god VISHNU, the preserver of the universe, persuaded Shiva to bring the guests back to life. Daksha finally acknowledged that Shiva was indeed a great god, and as a sign that he recognized his own stupidity he adopted the head of a goat. Shiva entered into a deep and prolonged meditation and awaited the time when Sati would be reincarnated as PARVATI.

In another version of the myth, Daksha's head was torn off, and Sati was brought back to life after the massacre. The goddess begged Shiva to restore her father to life. The great god agreed but, because nobody could find Daksha's head, he was given that of a ram.

THE DANAVAS are half-divine, half-demonic beings of Hindu mythology who were banished by the war god, INDRA, to live in the ocean. The monster Bali, whom it is said that VISHNU overcame in his incarnation as Vamana the dwarf, was a danava. The danavas were ASURAS, and although they are often described as "demons", they were not totally evil.

Vishnu, for example, recognized that Bali had shown himself to be capable of honourable behaviour and so rewarded him by making him king of the underworld.

DASRA see ASVINS.

DEVADATTA was a cousin of GAUTAMA BUDDHA. He became a member of the Buddhist community but grew jealous of Gautama and planned to murder him. First of all, he sent a group of assassins to murder the great teacher. However, the men were so impressed by the Buddha that they repented their evil intentions and became his followers. Then, Devadatta tried to crush Gautama by rolling an enormous boulder on

DHANVANTARI features in the ancient Indian myth of the churning of the ocean. It was he who appeared bearing *AMRITA*, the elixir of immortality, from the milk ocean. Dhanvantari was also known as Sudapani, or "One Who Bears Nectar in His Hands". The master of universal knowledge, he came to be regarded as the physician of the gods. He is the guardian deity of hospitals which are usually in the vicinity of a sanctuary of *VISHNU*.

top of him. However, the boulder stopped before it reached its target. Finally, he sent a wild elephant to gore the Buddha to death. The elephant was, however, tamed by the Buddha's kindness. When he died, Devadatta was condemned to lengthy sufferings in hell.

DEVAKI see *KRISHNA*.

DEVI (above), the great Hindu goddess, is the subject of an attempted seduction by her husband Shiva. On the right, he praises her for having resisted temptation. (SANDSTONE, CAMBODIA, 13TH CENTURY.)

DEVI (left) is honoured by the Hindu gods, Shiva, Vishnu, Brahma, Ganesha and Indra. (ILLUSTRATION BY J. HIGGINBOTHAM, 1864.)

THE DEVAS are the divine beings of the Veda, the ancient sacred teachings of India. The devas were regarded as immortal, and their chief attribute was their power, which enabled them to help human beings.

They later came to be regarded as those gods who are less important than great gods such as *ISHNU* and *SHIVA*. Although they inhabit a realm higher than that of human beings, they are still mortal. Among these Hindu devas are groups such as the *ADITYAS*, the rudras and the vasus.

In Buddhism, the devas are divine beings who live in the celestial heavens but are none the less subject to the ongoing cycle of death and rebirth. Most of the Buddhist devas originated in the Indian pantheon. They have long, pleasurable lives, and promote and protect Buddhism.

DEVATA BANDARA see *DADIMUNDA*.

DEVI is an aspect of the "Great Goddess" in Hindu mythology. It is the name by which the god *SHIVA*'s wife is sometimes known and is also the name given to female Hindu deities in general. Devi, as Shiva's *SHAKTI*, or consort, is both a benevolent and a fearsome deity, and is regarded as a major goddess within Hinduism.

She is a complex figure, taking many different forms, including those of *DURGA*, *KALI*, *PARVATI* and Sati. Sometimes, she also takes the form of goddesses who are independent of Shiva. Her main attributes are the conch, hook, prayer wheel and trident. (See also *THE MOTHER GODDESS*)

DEVADATTA, the Buddha's cousin and his rival from childhood, hatched a plot to murder him, but his hired assassins were all stricken with remorse as soon as the Buddha touched the wall behind which they were hidden.

THE DAKINI include eight Tibetan goddesses, of which images such as this one were used in rites of exorcism which drew on shamanistic practices. (CARVED HUMAN BONE, TIBET, 18TH CENTURY.)

DHARMAPALAS are "Protectors of the Dharma", or teaching. In Buddhism, particularly in Tibetan belief, they are regarded as ferocious divine beings who protect the faithful from the evil demons and bad influences which might thwart their spiritual progress. As such, the Dharmapalas are similar to the GUARDIAN KINGS. In Tibet, the Dharmapalas are worshipped either individually or in groups of eight, when they are known as the "Eight Terrible Ones" or Drag-shed. The eight are usually said to be KALADEVI (Lha-mo), BRAHMA (Tsangs-pa), BEG-TSE, YAMA, Kuvera (Vaishravana), HAYAGRIVA, MAHAKALA or Mahalka ("Great Black One") and YAMANTAKA. Vaishravana is also one of the Guardian or Celestial Kings.

In Tibet, the Dharmapalas are usually shown frowning, with tangled hair surmounted by a crown of five skulls. Most of them are in Yab-Yum, the posture of embrace, with their SHAKTI.

Some of the Dharmapalas were also Lokapalas (Guardian Kings) who existed in pre-Buddhist times as members of the Bon pantheon. PADMASAMBHAVA, one of the founders of Tibetan Buddhism, assimilated some of these ancient deities and transformed them into deities who protected the Buddhist law. However, some of the Lokapalas were adopted from the Hindu religion.

THE DHYANIBUDDHAS, or five "Great Buddhas of Wisdom", are the five meditating buddhas who, according to some traditions, are said to have arisen from the primeval buddha, ADIBUDDHA. They are sometimes referred to as Tathagatas ("Perfected Ones"), Transcendent Buddhas, or Jinas.

DHARMAPALAS with ferocious frowns decorate these ritual implements. They wear jewellery of writhing snakes and each have a third eye in its forehead. (NEPALESE RITUAL FLAYING KNIVES, 18–19TH CENTURY.)

DURGA, mounted on a lion, in combat with Mahisha, the terrible buffalo demon who threatened the power of the gods. (PAINTING BY BIKANER, RAJPUT SCHOOL, 1750.)

to the occasion. The demon changed first into a buffalo, then into a lion, whereupon Durga sliced off his head. Mahisha then turned into an elephant, but the goddess cut off his trunk. Although he hurled mountains at her, Durga overcame the monster, crushing him and killing him with her spear (See also THE MOTHER GODDESS).

DUSHYANTA see APSARAS.

THE GANDHARVAS are a class of Hindu demigods who are said to inhabit the heaven of the war god INDRA along with the APSARAS. They are part human, part horse and, as nature spirits, are associated with the fertility of the earth. The gandharvas guard the SOMA, the sacred drink that conveys divine powers. Some of them appear at Indra's court as divine musicians and singers. According to the Rig Veda, the ancient hymns composed by Vedic Aryans who came to India from central Asia, at the beginning of existence a gandharva united with an apsara to produce the first pair of human beings, YAMA and Yami.

DURGA is a slayer of demons who threaten the order of creation. She killed Mahisha, who was invulnerable to man and beast. (ILLUSTRATION BY J. HIGGINBOTHAM, 1864.)

The term Jina means "Conqueror", and refers to someone who has succeeded in overcoming the cycle of rebirth and suffering.

The Dhyanibuddhas are VAIROCANA or Mahavairocana, AKSOBHYA, RATNASAMBHAVA, AMITABHA and AMOGHASIDDHI. They are sometimes regarded as symbols of the various aspects of enlightened consciousness. On the other hand, they are sometimes believed to represent the body of the Dharma or teaching. Whereas followers of the non-Mahayana schools of Buddhism tend to venerate GAUTAMA BUDDHA, Mahayana Buddhists make any one of the five Dhyanibuddhas their chief object of worship. Occasionally, Gautama Buddha replaces Amoghasiddhi as one of the Dhyanibuddhas and sometimes KSHITIGARBHA is considered one of their number. (See also DHYANIBUDDHAS)

DIPANKARA, or the "Lighter of Lamps", was a Buddha of a past age whom Shakyamuni, or GAUTAMA BUDDHA, met in a previ-

ous life when he was the sage Sumedha. After having honoured Dipankara, Sumedha determined that he would become a Buddha himself. He became a BODHISATTVA, or "buddha-to-be", and passed through countless lives before entering the TUSHITA heaven prior to his final birth, to Queen MAYA. Dipankara recognized that Sumedha would become Gautama Buddha, and proclaimed his glorious future.

DITI see ADITI.

THE DMU were supernatural beings of the indigenous Bon religion of Tibet. They are said to have lived in heaven.

DRAG-SHED see DHARMAPALAS.

DURGA is the great Hindu mother goddess whose name means "She Who is Difficult to Approach", or "Inaccessible". She is an aspect of the SHAKTI of SHIVA, and can be terrifying and ferociously protective. She is usually depicted with a beautiful face and

with eight or ten arms, in which she carries various weapons given to her by the gods.

Other goddesses are often identified with her, including Candi, who protects against wild animals, and Shitala, who protects against smallpox. She also manifests herself as the bloodthirsty KALI.

Durga is said to have been born fully formed, ready to do battle against demons. When the terrible buffalo demon Mahisha threatened the power of the gods, not even VISHNU nor Shiva dared stand against him. However, Durga rose

GANESHA is the Hindu god of wisdom and literature, and the son of *PARVATI*, the wife of the great god *SHIVA*. He is portrayed with the head of an elephant and a pot belly, a symbol both of his greed and his ability to dispense success. He has four arms but only one tusk. An extremely popular deity, he is invoked at the outset of new undertakings. He is regarded as the patron of business, and businesspeople hold ceremonies in his honour. He was traditionally the first scribe of the great Hindu epic, the *Mahabharata*. He was said to have been so keen to write it down that he tore off one of his tusks to use as a pen.

One myth tells how, when Shiva was away from home, Parvati grew bored and lonely. She decided to make herself a baby and created Ganesha, either from the rubbings of her own body, from dew and dust, or from clay. She later ordered the child to stand guard outside the entrance to her rooms. When Shiva returned home and tried to see his wife, Ganesha, not realizing who he was, barred his entrance, whereupon Shiva knocked his head off. Parvati was distraught and demanded that her son be brought back to life. The first head Shiva

GANESHA (below), patron of literature, with Sarasvati, goddess of learning and the arts, mounted on a peacock and holding a lute. (ILLUSTRATION BY J. HIGGINBOTHAM, 1864.)

GANESHA's (above) mount, the rat, was originally a demon, who was vanquished and transformed by the elephant-headed god. (STONE, 11TH CENTURY.)

could find was that of an elephant. Parvati was delighted. Ganesha subsequently looked after the ganas, Shiva's attendants.

According to another myth, Parvati invited the god Sani, the planet Saturn, to visit her son. However, she had forgotten how dangerous the god could be and when he looked at Ganesha, the child's head burst into flames. *BRAHMA* told Parvati to repair her child with whatever she could find, which turned out to be the head of the elephant, *AIRAVATA*.

GANGA (right) the personification of the sacred river Ganges, is usually depicted holding a waterpot and a lotus in her hands. (STONE, BENGAL, 12TH CENTURY.)

GANGA, according to Hindu mythology, is the goddess of the sacred river Ganges. Ganga is the holiest of the three great river goddesses, the others being Yamuna and *SARASVATI*. The confluence of the three rivers, known as the Tirtha, is regarded as particularly sacred and is situated at the town of Allahabad, where a great mass pilgrimage takes place each year.

Ganga is said to have emerged from one of *VISHNU's* toes. Until her descent, she was believed to live in the sky, but when the earth became filled with the ashes of the dead, the sage *BHAGIRATHA* prayed that the gods might allow her purifying waters to come down to earth. The gods agreed. However, the descent of the great river threatened to engulf and destroy the entire earth, so *SHIVA* allowed it to land on his head as he sat meditating on Mount Kailasa. After spending several years in Shiva's hair, the river separated into seven different streams and flowed down over the earth.

According to one myth, Ganga nourished the semen of Shiva in her waters, eventually producing the warrior god Skanda, also known as *KARTTIKEYA*. The tale tells how Shiva offered up six of his seeds to the fire god *AGNI*, who gave them to Ganga for safekeeping. Swaha, the daughter of a sage, visited the river on six successive nights and was impregnated by the seeds, eventually giving birth to Karttikeya. The child had six heads, and six or 12 arms and legs.

Another myth tells how *INDRA's* power was beginning to threaten that of Shiva, whereupon a form of anger manifested itself before Shiva and asked that it might serve him. Shiva told the form to submerge itself in the Ganges and to marry the goddess to the ocean. A son called Jalamdhara, an *ASURA*, resulted from the union, and *BRAHMA* gave the asura the power to conquer the gods. (See also *SACRED RIVERS*)

GARUDA, according to Hindu mythology, was the prince of birds and the son of the sage *KASYAPA*. According to one account of Garuda's birth, Kasyapa had two beautiful wives, Kadru and Vinata. The sage promised to provide both wives with heirs. Kadru chose to give birth to 1,000 splendid serpents, whereas Vinata asked for only two sons. However, Vinata requested that her sons' strength and prowess should surpass that of Kadru's offspring.

Eventually, Kadru laid 1,000 eggs and Vinata laid two. After 500 years, 1,000 serpents emerged from Kadru's eggs. However, Vinata's two sons failed to appear. Impatient, Vinata broke open one of her eggs to find an embryo with only the upper half developed. The embryo became Aruna, the red glow of dawn. Aruna cursed his mother and ascended into the sky, where he remains to this day. Another 500 years passed and Vinata's remaining egg finally broke open to reveal Garuda.

Another tale tells how, in order to free herself from a curse, Vinata was forced to acquire *AMRITA*, the elixir of immortality and to give it to her nephews, the 1,000 serpents. Vinata asked Garuda to seize the drink from the gods and, after a mighty struggle, he succeeded in doing so. He put the drink down in front of the serpents, but said that they must purify themselves before drinking it. While they were busy performing their ablutions, *INDRA* retrieved the Amrita, as had been previously arranged with Garuda.

Garuda was a devotee of *VISHNU*, the preserver of the universe, and he was chosen by the god to be his mount. He appeared whenever summoned by Vishnu's thought, and fought with him against demons and demonic ser-

GARUDA, half human, half eagle, was the chosen mount of Vishnu, who rides him with his consort, Lakshmi, seated on a lotus flower. (PAINTING, BUNDI, C. 1770.)

pents. Garuda is depicted with the head, wings and claws of an eagle. In Buddhism, garudas are divine bird-like creatures.

GAURI see *PARVATI*.

GAUTAMA BUDDHA was the founding master of Buddhism and is regarded as the most perfect of holy men, rather than as a deity. By most accounts, he was born in the sixth century BC into the kshatriya, or warrior, caste at Kapilavastu, just inside the border of what is now Nepal. Gautama was the Buddha's family name; his given name was Siddhartha. In later legend he was known as Shakyamuni, or the sage of the Shakya clan. Gautama is venerated by all Buddhists, although for the "Pure Land" sect of Japanese and Chinese Buddhism, the Buddha AMITABHA, or Amida, has supreme importance.

The story of Gautama's life has become a legend. According to tradition, while in one of the Buddhist heavens, Gautama realized that the time had come for him to descend to earth. The spirit of the Buddha appeared in a dream to Queen MAYA: a small, snow-white elephant floating on a raincloud, a symbol of fertility, seemed to circle around the queen three times and then enter her womb. At that moment, all around the world, musical instruments played, trees and flowers bloomed and lakes were suddenly covered with lotus blossoms. Astrologers forecast that Queen Maya and the Buddha's father, the local ruler King Suddhodana, would have a son who would become either a universal emperor or a buddha.

When the boy was born, he immediately began to walk, and a lotus sprang from the place where his foot first touched the ground. The child took seven steps in the directions of the seven cardinal points, and thus symbolically took possession of the world. Soon after his birth, his mother died of joy.

When Gautama was 12 years old, a wise man predicted that, if he were to witness old age, sickness or death, or to see a recluse, he would leave the palace in order to become an ascetic, one who shuns physical pleasures. In fear of the prophesy, the king surrounded his son with luxury and had high walls built around his palaces.

When Gautama reached the age of 16, he was married to Princess Yasodhara and 12 years later, their son RAHULA was born. At about this time, Gautama's curiosity about the outside world was aroused and he decided to set out to explore the land outside the palace grounds. The king immediately ordered that every sign of suffering and sadness should be removed from his son's path. However, on the first day of his excursion, Gautama saw a wrinkled old man; on the second day, he saw someone suffering from an incurable disease, as well as a funeral procession; and on another day, he came across a wandering ascetic. Gautama finally decided to leave home and become an ascetic. His father was devastated and provided even more amusements for the prince. However, nothing would deter the young man.

After six years of asceticism, Gautama realized that he was no nearer enlightenment than he had

GAUTAMA BUDDHA (left), seated in the witness attitude, is assailed by the powers of evil, led by the demon Mara. Demons in threatening human and animal shapes seek to terrify him, and Mara's daughters try to seduce him. (MURAL, AJANTA, BERAR.)

GAUTAMA BUDDHA (left) has an urna, or symbolic circle of hair, between his eyebrows, derived from Indian images of Shiva's third eye: it indicates spiritual vision. (GILT-COPPER, NEPAL.)

GAUTAMA BUDDHA (right), having decided to renounce the world, cuts off his hair. (TIBET, 18TH CENTURY.)

been while living his former life of luxury. Deciding that he must free himself from desire, he set off for the town of Bodh Gaya; as he journeyed, light radiated from his body, attracting peacocks and kingfishers. When Gautama reached Bodh Gaya, he sat down beneath the branches of a sacred tree, whereupon the earth shook six times.

While Gautama was meditating, he was tested by the demon MARA, the Buddhist equivalent of Satan. First, he was subjected to fear, then enticed with pleasure. However, Gautama remained unmoved. Eventually he became aware of the "Four Noble Truths" that became the basis of his teaching: that life is full of suffering, that suffering depends on certain conditions such as craving, that these conditions can be removed, and that the way to make suffering cease is to practise the eightfold path: right view, right thought, right speech, right action, right livelihood, right effort, right mindfulness and right concentration or contemplation.

Gautama had reached a state of perfection and at that moment attained complete spiritual insight. The earth swayed, breezes blew, flowers rained down from heaven, the gods rejoiced and all living things were happy. Seven weeks later, he preached his first sermon at Sarnath, on the outskirts of the holy city of Benares.

Gautama preached for more than 40 years, during which time he performed many miracles and converted all who heard him, including his father, his son, his first cousin Ananda, his wife and his adoptive mother,

MAHAPRAJ-APATI GAUTAMI. He even ascended into heaven, where he converted his mother, Queen Maya, before climbing back down to earth on a ladder, accompanied by the gods. At the age of 80, Gautama entered nirvana, the ultimate state of spiritual bliss, near his birthplace. (See also *THE AVATARS OF VISHNU; THE LIFE OF THE BUDDHA*)

GESAR was a mythical king who inspired the greatest epic of Tibetan Buddhism. Tales of his exploits began to arise in the 11th century, at the time when Buddhism was beginning to infiltrate Tibet and threaten the indigenous Bon religion. The legends describe King Gesar's battle against the ancient beliefs and are said to be several times the length of the Bible.

Gesar, whose name means "Lotus Temple", was said to have been born in the kingdom of Ling in eastern Tibet. He is regarded as the embodiment of the *BOD-HISATTVA AVALOKITESHVARA,* as well as of *PADMASAMBHAVA,* one of the founders of Tibetan Buddhism. His warriors are said to be incarnations of the Mahasiddhas, great ascetics.

Although the stories about Gesar are influenced above all by Buddhism, traces of the Bon religion can also be found in the tales that tell of mountain deities and spirits of places. Travelling singers transmitted the early versions of the epic, whereas the later tales were said to arise from Tibetan monks.

The story of Gesar tells how an old woman died cursing all religions. Her final wish was that in a future life she and her three sons might rule over all Buddhist lands and wreak their revenge on the Buddhist teaching. The gods, hearing that the woman and her sons were threatening to return to the world as horrifying monsters, decided to send one of their number, Gesar, down to earth in order to do battle against them.

Gesar was reluctant to assume human form and so, before agreeing to descend to earth, he drew up several conditions that he set before the gods, believing that they would be impossible to fulfil. He demanded that his father should be a god and his mother a snake; that he should be given an immortal horse, which could fly through the sky and speak all languages; that he should be supplied with a magical bow and arrow and strong companions; that he should be given a beautiful wife, for whom everybody would be willing to fight; and a clever uncle, who would be able to assist him with battle plans. He also insisted that the gods should protect and help him at all times. To Gesar's distress, the gods agreed to all his demands, so he was forced to descend to earth.

The earthly Gesar was conceived when a god descended in the form of a rainbow and gave Gongmo – a *NAGA* who had transformed herself into a beautiful young girl – a drink of water from a holy vase. Gongmo became pregnant, and in due course, Gesar emerged from his mother as a globe of golden light, which eventually broke open to reveal a baby. According to some versions of the tale, the baby had three eyes, whereupon his horrified mother immediately plucked one out.

Having been warned that he would be overthrown by Gesar, the ruling king tried to kill the child almost as soon as he was born, but, despite his every effort, the boy remained unharmed. However, Gesar and his mother were forced into exile. At the age of 15, Gesar entered a horse race, and on winning it, was made King of Ling and given the former king's daughter as his wife. King Gesar then fought and conquered several demons and converted several countries to Buddhism.

He finally returned to heaven, although in the knowledge that he would have to return to earth one day. Gesar came to be regarded as a warrior god and god of wealth; his consort was a *DAKINI.*

TIRTHANKARAS

JAINISM IS AN INDIAN RELIGION and philosophy which offers an austere path to enlightenment. Much of its mythology was inherited from Hinduism, including huge numbers of gods, and ideas on the structure of the universe, but Jains differ from Hindus in that they do not believe in the idea of creation, considering that time is cyclic. Jain ascetics attempt to conduct their lives following five vows: to injure no living thing (because everything has a soul); to speak the truth; to take only what is given; to be chaste; and to achieve detachment from places, people and things. Their examples in following this discipline are 24 tirthankaras, or "spiritual teachers", who have appeared in the present cycle of time. A *tirtha* is a ford or crossing-place, or a sacred place, person or path which enables believers to cross over into liberation from an endless round of rebirth: for Jains, the tirthankaras were the builders of the ford.

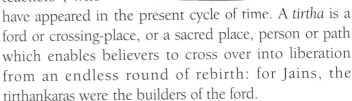

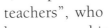

RISHABHA (left) also called Adinatha, was the first tirthankara of the present cycle. He lived for an extremely long time, and was credited by Jains with the establishment of the caste system, the monarchy and the rule of law. He also organized the cultivation of the land, the pursuit of the arts, and taught humankind the 72 sciences, including arithmetic and writing. In Hindu mythology, he was a minor avatar of Vishnu. He is represented by the bull motif and is usually shown naked in a standing yoga posture. (TIRTHANKARA, SRI ADINATH TEMPLE, KHAJURAHO, INDIA.)

MAHAVIRA (above), the twenty-fourth tirthankara, was a contemporary of Gautama Buddha. At the age of 30, he renounced family life and embarked on life as a wandering ascetic. He endured 12 years of fasting, silence and meditation to achieve enlightenment, then spent the next 30 years preaching throughout northern India. He and his followers went about naked to indicate their conquest of passion, and he and other tirthankaras are traditionally portrayed with downcast eyes, dead to the world. (HEAD OF A TIRTHANKARA, STONE, 10TH CENTURY.)

THE TIRTHANKARAS (above) were all considered to have come from the kshatriya, or warrior caste, and were not deities but human teachers who had achieved enlightenment. Worship of their images focuses on their teaching and achievements rather than on themselves. They are all depicted as identical, except for an animal or other symbol which identifies each one, such as the boar that is associated with Vimala (top) and the goat that distinguishes Kunthu (bottom). (DETAIL FROM THE TWENTY-FOUR JAIN TIRTHANKARAS, BUNDI, c. 1720.)

PARSHVA (left) was the twenty-third tirthankara, born to Vama, queen of Benares, in the ninth century BC. He spent 70 years as a wandering ascetic before attaining nirvana when he died at the age of 100 on Mount Sammeda. His symbol was the snake, and he was often depicted under a canopy of cobras. He systematized the Jain religion, dividing its adherents into monks, nuns, and male and female laity, and giving his chief disciples responsibility for the Jain community. (TIRTHANKARA PARSHVANATHA, ORISSA, 11TH CENTURY.)

GNOD-SBYIN see *YAKSHAS*.

THE GNYAN are Tibetan spirits who live in trees and stones. They send plagues, diseases and death down on humankind.

GREAT BUDDHAS OF WISDOM see *DHYANIBUDDHAS*.

GRI-GUM, according to Tibetan belief, was a king who, unlike the rulers who preceded him, cut the magic rope that connected him to heaven. The first human ruler was said to have come down from the sky, landing on top of a mountain. At the end of his reign, he returned to heaven by means of a magic rope. The six kings who followed him did the same. However, Gri-gum, the eighth king, failed to return to heaven. During a duel, the air became so filled with soot that, unable to see while waving his sword around, he severed the magic rope. He was then killed by his opponent.

GSHEN-LHA-OD-DKAR, in the Tibetan Bon religion, was the "God of White Light" from whom all other gods emanated. When nothing else existed, two lights emerged; one was black and the other was white. A rainbow then appeared and gave rise to hardness, fluidity, heat, motion and space.

THE GUARDIAN KINGS (below) who guard the four quarters of the world. Acolytes of the bodhisattva Avalokiteshvara, they are said to have assisted at the birth of Gautama Buddha.

These phenomena merged with one another and formed a gigantic egg. From that egg, the black light produced sickness, disease, pain and countless demons, whereas the white light produced joy, prosperity and numerous gods. The gods and demons together gave rise to all kinds of creatures. These beings inhabit the mountains, trees and lakes of the land.

GSHEN-RAB, or Shenrab Miwo, is traditionally said to have been the founder of the later or purified form of the Bon religion of Tibet, which came into being after the introduction of Buddhism to the country. He is said to have come from a mystic land known as Zhang Zhung, and he came to be regarded as identical to *GAUTAMA BUDDHA*. Some scholars have also identified him with Laozi, the founder of Daoism. He is represented seated on a lotus.

THE GUARDIAN KINGS, according to Buddhist belief, guard the four quarters of the world and protect the Buddhist law. They are said to live on the mythical Mount *MERU*, at the gates of the paradise of *INDRA*, the protector of Buddhism. The Guardian Kings are acolytes of the *BODHISATTVA AVALOKITESHVARA*.

Originally, they were regarded as benevolent, but they developed into menacing warriors. They are usually shown wearing armour and helmets or crowns. The kings are said to have assisted at the birth of *GAUTAMA BUDDHA* and to have held

up the hooves of his horse when he left the palace of his father for the outside world. In Indian art, they are usually shown riding elephants, whereas in Tantrism they are often shown trampling demons.

The chief Guardian King is Vaishravana, the guardian of the north and of winter. His name means "He Who is Knowing", and he is lord of the *YAKSHAS*, divine beings who protect and serve their ruler.

The guardian of the south, Virudhaka or the "Powerful One", fights ignorance and protects the root of goodness in human beings. He rules over the summer, and, in

Tibet, he is often shown with a helmet made from an elephant's head. The guardian of the east, Dhritarashtra, or "He Who Maintains the Kingdom of the Law", presides over the spring and maintains the state. The guardian of the west, Virupaksha, or "He Who Sees All" presides over the autumn. Virupaksha is usually represented standing on a rock or on demons, and wearing armour.

In Hinduism, the guardians are known as Lokapalas. Vaishravana is worshipped as Kuvera, a god of wealth who guards his buried treasure. Kuvera became the king of

HANUMAN (above) wrestles with the demons of Ravana as he strives to find Rama's wife, Sita. (TERRACOTTA, 5TH CENTURY.)

HANUMAN (left), the Hindu monkey god, was well known for his extraordinary agility, which enabled him to escape from the demon Ravana. (JAIPUR, 17TH CENTURY.)

LANKA and drove a magnificent chariot, which the demon king RAVANA used in battle in the Hindu epic, the *Ramayana*.

HANUMAN is the monkey god

of Hindu mythology. He is regarded as the patron of learning and is the son of VAYU, god of the winds. According to one myth, Hanuman once tried to snatch the sun from the sky, thinking it was something to eat. To prevent the catastrophe, the war god INDRA threw his thunderbolt at the monkey, smashing his jaw.

In the great Hindu epic the *Ramayana*, Hanuman is the minister of the monkey king Sugriva and the loyal companion of RAMA, the famous AVATAR or incarnation of VISHNU, the preserver of the universe. Hanuman assisted Rama when the hero was locked in battle with the demon king RAVANA, who had run off with Rama's wife, SITA. It was Hanuman who discovered Sita's whereabouts, on the island of LANKA, Ravana's kingdom.

Hanuman's extraordinary agility enabled him to leap across the waters to the island like an arrow.

However, in mid-flight, a sister of the demon king caught Hanuman's shadow and managed to pull the monkey beneath the waters, where another demon tried to swallow him. Hanuman succeeded in escaping by stretching out so that the demon had to open her jaws, then contracting, so that he was able to leap from her mouth.

Hanuman finally found Sita in a grove of trees. Each day, Ravana threatened the goddess with torture and death if she refused to marry him, but Sita insisted on remaining faithful to Rama. Although Hanuman offered to carry her away, Sita refused to touch any man but her husband. As Hanuman left to tell Rama that he had found Sita, Ravana and his demons set his tail on fire. However, the fire failed to hurt the monkey god, who instead caused vast destruction on the island by swishing his tail from side to side, setting light to countless buildings.

Back in India, Hanuman encouraged an army of monkeys to build a bridge across the sea from India to Lanka, thereby enabling Rama and his troops to approach and attack the demon king. Rama rewarded Hanuman for his help by giving him the gift of eternal life.

Hanuman was said to be as large as a mountain, with yellow skin, a red face and a tremendously long tail. His roar was like thunder, and he flew through the clouds with a great rushing sound.

HAYAGRIVA is one of Tibetan Buddhism's DHARMAPALAS, or "Protectors of the Teaching". He is the lord of wrath, the leader of the terrifying gods known as Drag-shed. His name means "Horse's Neck", and he is small, with a pot belly and a horse's head. In Buddhism, Hayagriva is regarded as an emanation of either the buddha AMITABHA or the buddha AKSOBHYA and as the terrifying aspect of the BODHISATTVA AVALOKITESHVARA.

In a Hindu myth, Hayagriva was one of the DAITYAS, giant ASURAS who opposed the gods. He stole the Veda, the sacred knowledge of Hinduism, when it fell from BRAHMA's mouth. VISHNU, reincarnated as the AVATAR Matsya the fish, managed to kill Hayagriva and retrieve the sacred texts.

Hayagriva is also regarded as an avatar of the god Vishnu, who is said to have taken on this form in order to retrieve the Veda, after it had been stolen from the gods by two daityas.

HERUKA is a Buddhist deity, an emanation of the buddha AKSOBHYA. In Tibet he is regarded as one of the protective deities, or ISHTADEVATAS. Heruka is usually depicted with three eyes, wild hair and bared teeth. His body is smeared with ashes, and he holds a severed human head in his hand. The deity sits or dances on a corpse and is sometimes shown with his female partner, Prajna, with whom he creates nirvana (spiritual bliss). Heruka confers buddhahood and protects the world from evil.

The herukas as a group are terrifying energies who are usually portrayed with haloes of flame. They dance with their huge and terrifying consorts. The herukas exist in the head region, and meditators who achieve their level are believed to be capable of reaching a realm of the ultimate reality.

HAYAGRIVA, the leader of the terrifying gods known as Drag-shed, wreathed with his enemies' heads. (BRONZE, TIBET.)

I

HEVAJRA is a *YIDAM*, or tutelary god, worshipped in Mongolia, Cambodia, Thailand and Tibet. He is usually represented with four legs and eight heads; his body is blue, and his heads are different colours. He is sometimes shown alone, but often in Yab-Yum, the posture of embrace, with his *SHAKTI* or corresponding female energy.

HIMAVAT see *PARVATI*.

HIRANYAKASHIPU see *AVATARS* and *RAVANA*.

INDRA, one of the chief deities of Indian mythology, is a god of storms and war. He appears in the *Rig Veda* – the ancient hymns forming part of the Veda, the sacred knowledge of Hinduism – as the king of the gods. Indra is red or gold in colour, and is large, fierce and warlike. In his right hand he carries a thunderbolt, which he uses either to slay his enemies or to revive those killed in battle. He is said to ride through the heavens in a chariot, often said to be the sun. In later times, he was frequently depicted on the elephant, *AIRAVATA*.

Indra was born from heaven and earth, which he separated for ever. He challenged the old order and became the leading deity, a less remote figure than the Vedic god, *VARUNA*. Indra was best known as a destroyer of demons, who led the gods against the *ASURAS*. He fought and destroyed the serpent *VRITRA* with a pillar of foam and, in doing so, gave form to chaos, liberating the waters, generating life and causing the sun to rise.

On another occasion, Indra set free some cows which had been stolen from the gods. This myth is interpreted as symbolizing how Indra released the sacred force, or light of the world. Indra was also worshipped as the god who provided rain. As the bringer of light and water, he absorbed many of Varuna's functions, becoming a fertility god and a god of creation.

A vast drinker with a huge belly, Indra was also associated with *SOMA*, an intoxicating drink used in religious rituals. It was from Soma that the god was said to derive his special powers. After drinking it, he became so large that he filled both heaven and earth.

Indra's importance gradually declined. Although he remained a terrifying god of thunder, he came to be regarded as a divine earthly monarch who reigned in Swarga, a luxurious heaven situated on the sacred Mount *MERU*.

According to one myth, it was Indra, rather than *VISHNU*'s *AVATAR* Vamana, who fought the demon Bali. While Indra was attacking a host of demons led by Jalamdhara, Bali fell, and a stream of jewels poured from his mouth. Indra was

HEVAJRA is the Buddhist equivalent of the Hindu god Shiva Nataraja. He is shown in Yab-Yum with his shakti, Nairamata, who stands on two corpses. (TANTRIC BRONZE.)

so amazed that he struck open the demon's body with one of his thunderbolts. The different parts of Bali's body then gave rise to the seeds of precious stones. Diamonds were produced from his

K

INDRA (above) is a weather and fertility god, and a leading Hindu deity. He is shown wielding a vajra, or thunderbolt, and is seated on his mount, the elephant Airavata. (11TH CENTURY.)

bones, sapphires from his eyes, rubies from his blood, emeralds from his marrow, crystal from his flesh, coral from his tongue and pearls from his teeth.

In a story from the Hindu epic, the *Ramayana*, Indra seduced Ahalya, the wife of the great sage Gautama. One day, when he knew that the sage was away from his home, Indra disguised himself, visited Gautama's wife and pressed her to become his lover. Despite his disguise, Ahalya immediately recognized Indra and, because she was curious about the chief god, she

agreed. Afterwards, as Indra was leaving, he met Gautama returning. Realizing what had happened, the sage caused the god's testicles to fall off. Gautama then cursed Ahalya, condemning her to lie on ashes and eat only air until *RAMA* visited her. The gods later replaced Indra's testicles with those of a ram. (See also *MYTHICAL MOUNTAINS*)

ISHTADEVATAS are protective Buddhist deities or sacred beings who are especially common in Tibet. Ishtadevata means "Beloved (or Desired) Divinity".

Each individual who decides to enter the path of Bhakti yoga – that of loving submission to a deity – chooses their own ishtadevata. Alternatively, the individual's guru may choose the ishtadevata, since

the guru will be able to discern which aspect of the divine will be most useful to the disciple.

JALAMDHARA see *THE ASURAS* and *GANGA*.

JINAS see *DHYANIBUDDHAS*.

KADAVUL see *KATAVUL*.

KADRU see *GARUDA*.

KALADEVI, known in Tibet as Lha-mo, is the only female *DHARMAPALA*, or protector of the Buddhist law. She is said to have been created by the other deities and provided with weapons, in order that she might defend Tantrism, a tradition of gaining enlightenment through ritual practices. Kaladevi rides a mule whose

reins are made from poisonous snakes and whose back is covered with the skin of a *YAKSHA*. According to one myth, the skin is that of Kaladevi's son, whom she is said to have devoured. Kaladevi has three protruding eyes, ten arms and, like all Dharmapalas, wears a crown and garland of skulls. She is sometimes said to be the wife of a yaksha king of Sri Lanka and is occasionally depicted walking on a lake of blood along with two other female beings. A terrifying and bloodthirsty goddess, she is often regarded as a consort of *YAMA*, god of the dead. She helps those who earnestly seek her protection.

KALADEVI, a bloodthirsty goddess who is the only female Dharmapala, or protector of the Buddhist teaching. (BRONZE AND ENAMEL, TIBET, 18TH CENTURY.)

KALI, the "Black One", is the terrifying aspect of the great mother goddess and *SHAKTI* of *SHIVA*. The personification of death and destruction, she is said to spring from the forehead of *DURGA*, another aspect of the goddess, when she becomes angry. Kali is usually depicted with blood-red eyes, four arms and with her tongue lolling out of her mouth in search of blood. She is naked, but for a girdle of severed heads or hands, a necklace of skulls and a tiger skin.

Like Shiva, Kali has a third eye in her forehead. In one hand she holds a weapon, in another the severed head of a giant, while her remaining two hands, in contrast, are raised in blessing. Her devotees regard her as a loving mother goddess who can destroy death as well as demons.

One myth tells how a monster, Raktabija, was destroying the world. Each time he was wounded, 1,000 demons sprang from each drop of his blood. The gods asked Kali to destroy the monster and, as she set about killing the demons, she drank their blood before it reached the ground, so that they were unable to multiply. When only the original monster remained, Kali gulped him down in one mouthful.

In celebration of her victory, she began to dance. As her movements became more and more frenzied, all creation began to shake, and the whole of existence was threatened with destruction. The gods begged Shiva to stop the goddess from dancing, but even the great god was unable to calm her. Eventually, Shiva threw himself on the ground in front of the goddess, whereupon she began to dance on his body. Finally, Kali realized what she was doing and stopped dancing.

The city of Calcutta is called after the goddess: its name means "Kali Ghat" or "Kali's Steps". Each day, animals are sacrificed to her, and it is believed that human sacrifices were made to her in the past. (See also THE MOTHER GODDESS)

KAMA, in the form of Kamadeva, is the god of love. Often depicted as a young man riding on a parrot, he bears a bow and arrows made of sugar cane and decorated with flowers. (ILLUSTRATION BY J. HIGGINBOTHAM.)

KALKIN see *AVATARS*.

KAMA, according to the ancient sacred teachings of India, is either sexual desire or the impulse towards good. However, Kama is sometimes regarded as a deity. Described as the first being to be born, he is superior to gods and humanity and, as a symbol of original desire, he is said to have brought about the created world.

In the form of Kamadeva, he is the god of love. He is sometimes regarded as the son of Dharma, god of justice and Shraddha, goddess of faith. Elsewhere he is described as the son of *LAKSHMI*, or as having arisen from the heart of *BRAHMA*. His consort is Rati, or "Voluptuousness", the goddess of sexual passion. Kama is said to rule over the *APSARAS*, the heavenly nymphs.

According to one myth, the goddess *PARVATI* grew bored because her consort, the great god *SHIVA*, was deep in meditation on Mount Kailasa. Parvati persuaded Kama to come to her aid. Kama was loathe to intervene, but Parvati insisted, whereupon Kama prepared to fire his arrow at Shiva's heart in order to remind him of his duties to his wife. The god Mahesvara saw what was about to happen; since it was

KARTTIKEYA, the Hindu warrior god, is named after the Kirttikah, or Pleiades.
(SANDSTONE, PUNJAB, 6TH CENTURY.)

self-born, emerged from Time". One of his wives, Kadru, gave birth to 1,000 serpents, while the other, Vinata, gave birth to *GARUDA*, the bird chosen by the great god Vishnu to be his mount. Kasyapa is sometimes said to have fathered the *ADITYAS* by *ADITI* and the demonic *DAITYAS* by her sister, Diti. He is described in the Hindu epics, the *Mahabharata* and the *Ramayana*, as the son of *BRAHMA* and the father of Vivasvat, or the sun, who in turn was the father of *MANU*, the first man, from whom all human beings are descended.

In Buddhism, Kasyapa is one of the six Manushi, or "human", buddhas. He is the immediate predecessor to *GAUTAMA BUDDHA*. He is often shown seated on a lion, and is coloured yellow or gold because he represents the light of the sun and the moon.

KATARAGAMA DEVIYO is one of the four great gods of Sri Lanka. He is the equivalent of the Indian god *KARTTIKEYA* and the southern Indian Tamil god, *MURUKAN*. Originally, Kataragama Deviyo was called Ceyon, or "God with the Red-coloured Body".

KATAVUL, or Kadavul, is the name for the supreme personal being of the Tamils of southern India and Sri Lanka. The source of all existence, his name means "He Who Is". He is the judge of humankind, rewarding or punishing people according to their deeds during life.

KATUKILAL see *KORRAWI*.

KHADROMAS see *DAKINI*.

KHYUNG-GAI mGO-CAN was an ancient Tibetan god who may have been connected with the sun. He was said to have had the head of a bird.

KORRAWI is the Tamil goddess of battle and victory. She also takes the form of Katukilal, a goddess of the woods. The mother of *MURUKAN*, her temples are guarded by demons and spirits.

necessary for Shiva to finish his meditation in order for the cycles of creation to run their course, he struck Kama with a thunderbolt. Later, however, he brought Kama back to life. In another version of the myth, Shiva struck Kama with a flash of his third eye and burned him to ashes. As a result, Kama was sometimes called Ananga, or "Bodiless".

KAMSA see *KRISHNA*.

KARTTIKEYA, also known as Skanda, is a warrior god who campaigns against demons. The deity is sometimes said to have been raised by the stars of the Pleiades, or Kirttikah. He is sometimes also regarded as a god of fertility.

In the great Hindu epics the *Mahabharata* and the *Ramayana*, Karttikeya is described as the son of *SHIVA*. He is said to have been conceived when Shiva offered his seeds to the fire god *AGNI*, who gave them for safekeeping to the river goddess *GANGA*. Eventually, a child with six heads, and six or 12 arms, was born.

Alternatively, Shiva is said to have directed the fire of his third eye at a lake. Six children emerged and were brought up by the wives of the *RISHIS*, or seers. One day, *PARVATI* hugged the children so tightly that they were squeezed together into one child, although the six heads remained.

KASYAPA was an ancient Indian sage whose name means "Tortoise". According to the sacred Hindu *Atharva Veda*, "Kasyapa, the

KARTTIKEYA is sometimes shown riding a peacock, holding a bow in one hand and an arrow in the other.

THE AVATARS OF VISHNU

THE GREAT GOD VISHNU WAS SEEN as the protector of the world, having measured out the universe in three giant strides and established it as the home of both gods and humanity. He was a benevolent deity, and his consort Shri, or Lakshmi, was the beautiful goddess of good fortune. In token of his willing involvement with the human race, he descended to earth and became incarnate at times when the world of mortals was threatened by evil. His incarnations, or avatars, follow an evolutionary pattern, from fish and reptile, through animals and the dwarf Vamana, to men and finally to the future creator, Kalkin. The number was traditionally fixed at ten, although the individual avatars varied slightly in different texts. The Buddha was assimilated into the series much later than the others, while the seventh and eighth avatars, Rama and Krishna, are important heroes of Hindu mythology.

MATSYA (above), the fish, was Vishnu's first incarnation. It was rescued by Manu from being eaten by a larger fish. Manu looked after it while it grew, then released it to the ocean. In return, the fish warned Manu of a catastrophic flood. It helped him build a boat on which he could save seeds and animals to repopulate the world, and towed the boat to safety. (ILLUSTRATION FROM DEVOTIONAL TEXT, 17TH CENTURY.)

KURMA (left), the tortoise, supported Mount Mandara on his back during the churning of the cosmic ocean. As the gods had uprooted the mountain and turned it upside down for this task, the peak drilled into the earth when the churning began. Vishnu, in his second incarnation as Kurma, dived underneath it and twisted with the mountain, acting as a paddle to speed up the operation. The milk ocean turned to butter and tossed up Amrita, the elixir of immortality. (ILLUSTRATION BY J. HIGGINBOTHAM, 1864.)

VARAHA (right) was the rescuer of the earth. The demon Hiranyaksha tossed the earth into the cosmic ocean, but in his third avatar, as Varaha the boar, Vishnu plunged into the ocean and killed the demon. He then found the earth in the form of a beautiful woman, whom he carried back up to the surface on his tusks. (BRONZE, GURJARA PRATIHARA, 10TH CENTURY.)

NARASIMHA (above) was the fourth avatar. Hiranyakashipu the demon, the twin brother of Hiranyaksha, dethroned the god Indra and proclaimed himself king of the universe. He was enraged by his son's veneration of Vishnu and condemned him to death, but failed to kill him. In his anger, the demon struck a pillar demanding to know why Vishnu did not show himself. The pillar split open, and Vishnu was incarnated as the man-lion Narasimha, who disembowelled Hiranyakashipu. (ILLUSTRATION BY J. HIGGINBOTHAM, 1864.)

VAMANA (above), the dwarf, rescued the universe from the demon Bali, who had assumed power over it. To release it from his grasp, Vishnu assumed the form of a dwarf for his fifth incarnation. He requested from Bali as much territory as he could cover in three strides. Bali easily granted this apparently trivial request, and Vishnu, transformed into the giant, Trivikrama, covered the underworld, the earth and the heavens in three vast strides. (ILLUSTRATION BY J. HIGGINBOTHAM, 1864.)

PARASHURAMA (above), although he was born a brahman, was destined to lead the life of a warrior. He was armed with a celebrated axe that had been given to him by Shiva. In revenge for insulting his father, he wiped out all the male members of the warrior caste and ordered their widows to sleep with brahmans to produce a new and purer caste of warriors. He was Vishnu's sixth avatar. (PARASHURAMA KILLING ARJUNA KARTAVIRYA BY CHAMBA OR BILASPUR, C. 1750–60.)

RAMA (left) was Vishnu's seventh avatar, assumed at the gods' request to destroy Ravana, the evil ruler of Lanka (the island of Sri Lanka). Rama, son of the king of Ayodhya, won his wife, Sita, by bending and breaking Shiva's unbendable bow. He was banished by his stepmother for 14 years to the forest, where Sita was abducted by Ravana. After many adventures, Rama killed Ravana, won Sita back, returned to his kingdom and reigned for 1,000 years. (ILLUSTRATION TO THE RAMAYANA BY MIR KALAN, C. 1750–60.)

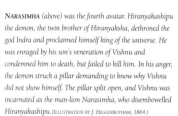

GAUTAMA BUDDHA (left), Vishnu's ninth incarnation, was not identified until the third or fourth century AD. In the earliest accounts of it, Vishnu was said to have assumed this avatar in order to convert demons to Buddhist beliefs, with the intention of weakening them in their war against the gods, or to mislead sinful mortals so that they would receive their just punishment. Later, a more positive reason was suggested: Vishnu was said to want to abolish animal sacrifices.

KRISHNA (above), the god and the eighth avatar, was hidden at birth because of a prophecy that his mother's eighth child would kill the evil King Kamsa. Krishna was brought up in obscurity among a community of cowherds. After killing a succession of demons, including Vatsasura, who came in the guise of a calf, Krishna killed Kamsa. He assisted the hero Arjuna in the great battle of Kurukshetra, disguised as his charioteer. (ILLUSTRATION TO THE BHAGAVATA PURANA BY MANKOT, C. 1730–40.)

KALKIN (above right) is Vishnu's tenth and final avatar, and is still to come: he will appear at the end of the present age, the Kali Yuga, which began in 3102BC and will last 432,000 years. In its final years, humanity will face a breakdown of civilization and a loss of spiritual and moral values. The divine incarnation of Kalkin, riding a white horse, will be needed to wipe out the wickedness of the world and establish a new era. (STONE CARVING ON PRASANNA CHENNAKESHAVA TEMPLE, SOMNATHPUR.)

KRISHNA, according to Hindu mythology, is an AVATAR of VISHNU, the preserver of the universe. He is traditionally referred to as the only complete avatar. A divine hero, Krishna is said to have been miraculously born in the town of Mathura in northern India. The gods wanted to destroy the evil oppressor King Kamsa, and so Vishnu decided to be born as the eighth son of the king's sister Devaki. According to one story, Vishnu plucked out two of his hairs, one black, one white. The black hair became Krishna and the white hair BALARAMA, Krishna's older brother. Krishna's name means the "Dark One".

King Kamsa learned that he was to be assassinated by one of his nephews, so he imprisoned Devaki and her husband Vasudev and killed each of their sons as they were born. When Devaki gave birth to Krishna, Vishnu told the couple to exchange their baby for the daughter of some cowherds who lived on the other side of the river Yamuna. The doors of the prison miraculously opened, and Vasudev carried the baby to the river. As soon as the child's toe touched the waters, they parted, allowing the father and son to pass through safely. Vasudev left the baby with the cowherds Yashoda and Nanda. However, King Kamsa discovered what had happened and sent a demon disguised as a nurse to look after the infant. Krishna sucked at the demon's breast until he drained her life away.

Krishna was a playful child, teasing

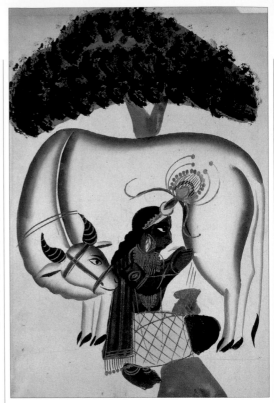

KRISHNA (above), an avatar of Vishnu, spent his childhood as the adopted son of cowherds. (KALIGHAT PAINTING, C. 1860.)

KRISHNA (left) is said to have taught the science of Bhakti yoga to the sun god, Surga, who instructed Manu, father of humankind.

the cows, laughing at his elders and stealing butter and sweets. He also displayed signs of his divine origins by, among other pranks, uprooting two trees at once; on another occasion, his adopted mother, Yashoda, was amazed to see the whole universe when she looked down his throat. Once, when the cowherds were about to worship the great god INDRA, Krishna told them that instead they should worship Mount Govardhana and their herds. The mountain, he explained, provided their herds with food and the cows themselves gave them milk to drink. Krishna then declared that he himself was the mountain. Indra was furious and sent down torrents of rain. However, Krishna lifted Mount Govardhana and held it above the storms for seven days and seven nights. Indra was so amazed that he came down from the heavens and asked Krishna to befriend his son, the hero ARJUNA.

One of the most popular myths concerning Krishna is that of his youthful dalliances with the gopis, the female cowgirls, and in particular with a girl called RADHA with whom the young hero fell passionately in love. Once, when the cowgirls were bathing in the river Yamuna, Krishna stole their clothes, then hid in a tree. He refused to return their garments to them until they came out, one by one, their hands clasped in prayer. Because all the cowgirls wanted to hold Krishna's hands when they danced, he multiplied his hands countless times. The sound of

Krishna's flute, calling the cowgirls out to dance in the moonlight, is believed to symbolize the voice of the supreme lord calling all who hear him to divine pleasures.

As Krishna grew older, he began to rid the neighbourhood of monsters and demons. Eventually, King Kamsa heard of his exploits and determined to kill him. However, Krishna not only succeeded in killing Kamsa but also went on to destroy numerous other oppressive kings as well as demons.

The most important battle he participated in was that of Kurukshetra. On the eve of the

KRISHNA visiting Radha, a young gopi, or cowgirl, with whom he fell passionately in love. His name means "Dark One" and he is often depicted as dark-skinned.
(ILLUSTRATION TO RASAMANJARI BY BHANUDETTA, BASOHLI, C. 1865.)

battle, Krishna, disguised as a charioteer, is said to have preached to the hero Arjuna the *Bhagavad Gita*, or "Song of the Lord", which forms part of the great Hindu epic, the *Mahabharata*. The war ended in the destruction of both armies, with only the merest handful of survivors on each side. Krishna died shortly afterwards. He was sitting in the forest, meditating, when a huntsman mistook him for a deer and shot an arrow, which struck him on his left heel, his only vulnerable spot. Krishna told the huntsman not to grieve or be afraid, and then ascended into the sky in a beacon of light.

Krishna is believed to embody divine beauty, joy and love, using his charm, playfulness and compassion to draw his devotees into the embrace of the supreme lord. (See also *THE AVATARS OF VISHNU*)

KSHITIGARBHA, who is a BOD-HISATTVA, or "buddha-to-be", is said to look after the six paths taken by souls after they have been judged. These paths are the destinies of humankind, ASURAS, demons, gods, animals and the damned. Patient and persevering, he consoles those who live in hell, seeking to lighten the burdens that they have brought upon themselves by evil actions when alive.

Kshitigarbha came to be regarded as the protector of all travellers. In India, he had only a small following, but he attracted many devotees both in China and Japan. According to one Chinese myth, he was a young Indian boy of the brahman caste who was so upset by how his late mother was suffering in hell that he determined to save all the other inhabitants of hell from such a terrible fate.

Kshitigarbha's name means "He Who Encompasses the Earth". In China, he is known as Dizang Wang, and in Japan as Jizo-Bosatsu.

KUNTI see ARJUNA.

KUN-TU-BZAN-PO, according to the Bon religion of Tibet, created the world from a lump of mud, and living beings from an egg.

KURMA, the tortoise, was the second incarnation, or AVATAR, of the Hindu god VISHNU, the preserver of the universe. During the churning of the ocean, Kurma supported Mount Mandara on his back in order to prevent the mountain from boring a hole in the earth. The gods were thus able to obtain AMRITA, the elixir of immortality, to restore their power. (See also *THE AVATARS OF VISHNU*)

L

KURUKULLA is a Buddhist goddess who emanates from *AMITABHA*. She is said to be able to cast spells on men and women in order to ensure that they serve her. In Tibet, she became a goddess of riches. Her main attributes are a red lotus, a bow and an arrow. She is often represented as reddish in colour, seated in a cave and with four arms. Her two upper arms are held in a threatening posture, while the two lower arms offer comfort.

KUVERA see *GUARDIAN KINGS*.

LAKSHMANA, according to Hindu myth, was the son of King Dasaratha and Sumitra and the half-brother of *RAMA*, an incarnation of the great god *VISHNU*. When Rama was exiled from his late father's kingdom, Lakshmana accompanied him on his travels. While the two brothers were living in the wilderness, Surpanaka, one of the demon king *RAVANA*'s sisters fell in love with Rama. He sent the woman to Lakshmana who in turn sent her back to Rama. The demoness, seeking revenge for being thus insulted, attacked Rama's wife *SITA*, but to no avail. Rama then asked Lakshmana to disfigure the seductress, which he did by cutting off her nose and ears. The demoness demanded that Ravana avenge her, and it was during this great battle that the demon king succeeded in abducting Sita.

LAKSHMI, or Shri, according to the Veda, the sacred knowledge of the Hindus, was alleged to have been many deities, including the consort of *VARUNA* or *SURYA*. However, she is best known as the beautiful consort or *SHAKTI* (female power) of the great Hindu god *VISHNU*. The goddess of wealth and good fortune, Lakshmi is usually depicted as a beautiful golden woman sitting on a lotus flower, the symbol of the womb, immortality and spiritual purity. During the Hindu celebration of Diwali, the

LAKSHMANA and Rama wandering in search of Rama's abducted wife, Sita.
(ILLUSTRATION TO THE RAMAYANA, KANGRA, 1780.)

festival of lights, thousands of lanterns are lit and fireworks exploded in order to please the goddess. People gamble and feast, while the goddess is said to wander from house to house looking for somewhere to rest, and blessing with prosperity all houses that are well lit.

Lakshmi was said to have been born several times. For example, when Vishnu was incarnated as *RAMA*, Lakshmi was born as *SITA*.

Everyone wants to possess Lakshmi, but she insists that no one can keep her for long. She immediately leaves anyone who puts her on their head, which is what the demons do whenever they manage to catch hold of her. In early myths, Lakshmi was sometimes associated with *INDRA*, the war god. However, even Indra had to divide her into four parts in order to keep hold of her for any length of time. Lakshmi's presence is believed to bring fertility. According to one tale, when the goddess sat down next to Indra, he

began to pour down rain so that the crops flourished. Another myth tells how Lakshmi was born by her own will in a beautiful field, which had been cut open by a plough.

Lakshmi appears in the famous myth of the churning of the ocean. Using the snake Vasuki as a rope to turn Mount Mandara, the gods churned the cosmic ocean for 100 years. Eventually the ocean turned to milk and gave rise not only to *AMRITA*, the elixir of immortality, but also to the "Fourteen Precious Things", including the beautiful goddess Lakshmi, who rose seated on a lotus flower. The heavenly musicians and great sages began to sing Lakshmi's praises; the sacred rivers asked her to bathe in their

LAKSHMI (far left), laden with flowers, is a beautiful golden woman. Her presence is believed to bring fertility, and ancient Indian rulers would perform a marriage ritual in which they took Lakshmi as their bride to secure wealth and fertility.

LAKSHMI (left) sat on Vishnu's lap and refused to look at the demons who wanted to own her as goddess of prosperity when she emerged from the cosmic ocean.
(ILLUSTRATION BY J. HIGGINBOTHAM, 1864.)

LANKA was the site of the battle between Rama and Ravana, the demon king. Ravana's horde of demons was eventually defeated by Rama's army of monkeys, assembled by Hanuman. (ILLUSTRATION TO THE RAMAYANA, RAJASTHAN, EARLY 19TH CENTURY.)

MAHALKA see *MAHAKALA*.

MAHAMAYA see *MAYA*.

MAHAPRAJAPATI GAUTAMI was the stepmother and aunt of *GAUTAMA BUDDHA*. She raised him after his mother, Queen *MAYA*, died of joy a few days after his miraculous birth. The devotion of Mahaprajapati became legendary. After the death of her husband, Mahaprajapati persuaded the Buddha to allow her to found a Buddhist order of nuns.

MAHAKALA is a destructive aspect of the god Shiva. Threatening and armed with a sword, he is known as the "Great Black One". (TIBETAN, 19TH CENTURY.)

waters; the sea of milk offered her a crown of immortal flowers; and the sacred elephants who hold up the world poured the holy water of the Ganges over her.

LANKA was the old name given to Ceylon, now Sri Lanka. It was also the name of its capital. The walls of Lanka are said to have been made from gold by Vishvakarma, a creator deity and the architect of the gods. Originally, Lanka was intended as a home for Kuvera, god of riches, but the demon king *RAVANA* later captured it and took it as his own.

According to one tale, *VAYU*, a god of the winds, was responsible for creating the island. Narada, a sage, or *RISHI*, challenged Vayu to break off the summit of Mount *MERU*, the world mountain. *GARUDA*, the mythical bird, normally protected the mountain,

but one day, in the bird's absence, Vayu succeeded in breaking off the summit. He immediately threw the summit into the depths of the ocean, where it remained as the island of Lanka.

THE LHA-DRE are gods, or supernatural beings, of the indigenous Bon religion of Tibet. When Buddhism entered Tibet, the Buddhist teachers assigned to the Lha-Dre the role of protectors of the new faith, thereby assimilating them into the Buddhist pantheon, where they are regarded as "Deities of the World" rather than the symbolic deities of Buddhism.

LHA-MO see *KALADEVI*.

LOKAPALAS see *DHARMAPALAS* and *GUARDIAN KINGS*.

THE LU are supernatural beings of the indigenous Bon religion of Tibet, who were assimilated into Buddhism as protectors of the faith. They live in lakes and rivers, and require regular placation.

MAHAKALA, or Mahalka, is known in Tibet as Mgon-po. The destructive form of the god *SHIVA*, he is one of the *DHARMAPALAS* of Tibetan Buddhism, and a *YIDAM*, a tutelary god of Tibet. He is known

as the "Great Black One", and has three eyes. He is covered with a tiger or elephant skin and holds a noose made from snakes.

His function, like that of all Dharmapalas, is to destroy all known enemies of the Buddhist teaching. Mahakala's most important duties are to pacify, enrich, magnetize and destroy. In the 17th century, he was accepted as the tutelary god of Mongolia, then under Tibetan influence.

LANKA (left) burns as Hanuman, the monkey god of Hindu mythology, leaps across the water to safety.

MAITREYA is the buddha of the future and the last earthly buddha. Regarded as the embodiment of love, his name means the "Benevolent" or "Friendly One". Maitreya is currently a *BODHISATTVA* dwelling in the *TUSHITA* or "Joyful" Heaven. In due course, *GAUTAMA BUDDHA* will enthrone him as his successor. Maitreya is expected to appear at the end of the present Buddhist age, in around 30,000 years' time.

Maitreya is often depicted as one of a triad with Gautama and the bodhisattva *AVALOKITESHVARA*. In non-Mahayana, or "Great Vehicle" Buddhism, the term *bodhisattva* usually refers either to Maitreya or to the historical Gautama Buddha, prior to his spiritual enlightenment.

The cult of Maitreya is very widespread in Tibetan Buddhism. According to one Tibetan tale, Asanga, a learned sage who founded the Yogachara school of Mahayana Buddhism, received his teaching directly from Maitreya. The Yogachara school teaches that everything consists of "mind only" and puts particular emphasis on the practice of yoga.

Asanga spent many years meditating on the future buddha. He eventually began to feel that his efforts to attain wisdom were fruitless and started to feel frustrated. One day, Asanga noticed that the wings of birds had worn a groove in a rock against which they always brushed when landing. The sage then heard the drip of water on a stone and saw that the drip had cut a deep passage through the rock. These two observations caused him to renew his determination to attain wisdom. However, though he continued to meditate, and though he continued to invoke Maitreya, he still got nowhere.

Some time later, while he was searching for food, Asanga met a man who was rubbing an iron bar with a piece of cotton. When Asanga asked the man what he was doing, the man replied that he was making a needle. Once again, Asanga determined to continue his pursuit of wisdom.

Many years passed, and still Asanga had failed to achieve his goal. Finally, he decided to leave his cave for good. As he was making his return to the outside world, Asanga met a dog who was suffering excruciating pain from a wound infested with worms. Although Asanga felt great compassion for the animal, he knew that if he removed the worms, they would die for want of food. Eventually, he decided that he would pick off the worms and allow them to eat his own flesh. However, he then worried that he might crush the worms, and so he decided to lick them off the dog instead.

Just as his tongue brushed against the worms, the dog disappeared and in its place stood Maitreya. Asanga asked Maitreya why he had failed to appear to him during his many years of meditation, whereupon the future buddha replied that only in this act of pure

MAITREYA (above) will appear far in the future, when India becomes an earthly paradise. (TIBETAN BRONZE, 11TH CENTURY.)

MAITREYA (right), the buddha of the future, and the last earthly buddha.

compassion had Asanga's vision been cleansed, although he had been with the sage throughout his many years of meditation.

Maitreya then told Asanga to carry him on his back into the city so that everyone might see him. Asanga did as instructed, but

nobody saw Maitreya because their vision was so clouded. Maitreya then took Asanga to the Tushita heaven, where he was able to gain the spiritual insight which he had sought for so many years.

MANJUSHRI is the *BOD-HISATTVA* of wisdom and one of the most important members of the Buddhist pantheon. His name means "He Who is Noble and Gentle", and his *SHAKTI*, or female energy, is *SARASVATI*. Manjushri is usually depicted with two lotus blossoms, on which rest his attributes, a sword of wisdom and a sacred text. He dispels ignorance, bestows eloquence and is a symbol of the enlightenment that can be reached through learning. He is said to be the father and mother of the bodhisattvas, as well as their spiritual friend.

In Tibetan Buddhism, certain great saints and scholars are regarded as incarnations of Manjushri. The Tibetans often depict Manjushri with several heads and arms. In Nepal, he is believed to have introduced civilized life, and his festival is celebrated on the first day of the year. According to legend, Manjushri originally came from China. In Japan he is known as Monju-Bosatzu. (See also *BOD-HISATTVAS*)

MANU, according to Hindu mythology, was the first man and the precursor of humankind. One myth tells how Manu was the son of *BRAHMA* and a young woman whom the god had produced from his own body. According to

MANJUSHRI, enthroned and surrounded by deities, is flanked by two lotus blossoms, on which rest a sword of wisdom and the Prajnaparamita-sutra, a holy text that advocates the ideal of the bodhisattva. (TIBETAN PAINTING.)

another tradition, Manu was the son of the sun god *SURYA*. Manu was saved from a cataclysmic flood by Matsya, an *AVATAR* or incarnation of the great god *VISHNU*, the preserver of the universe.

One day, Manu was washing in the river when he found a tiny fish, Matsya, which begged the sage to protect it. Manu took the fish home, where it grew bigger and bigger until eventually it asked to be taken to the sea. Before the fish swam away, it warned Manu that there would be a huge flood, which would engulf the earth, and it advised the sage to save himself by building a huge boat. Manu did as the fish advised, taking on board the boat all kinds of creatures and seeds of plants.

Almost before he had finished his task, the rains began to fall heavily and soon the whole world was flooded. The waters grew rough and threatened to capsize Manu's craft. However, Matsya appeared again, this time as a gigantic fish, and towed the boat safely through the waters. The fish then told Manu to fasten the boat to the summit of a mountain, which still remained above the water, and to wait for the floods to subside. Before leaving, the fish confessed to Manu that he was in fact Vishnu.

In gratitude to the god, Manu made a sacrifice of milk and melted butter. After a year, the offering turned into a beautiful woman who revealed that she was his daughter, Ida. The couple proceeded to engender the human race.

MANJUSHRI, seated on a lotus-moon throne, wields his sword of wisdom, poised to strike down ignorance.

MARA is the evil demon of Buddhist belief who tempted *GAUTAMA BUDDHA* as he sat meditating under the sacred tree at Bodh Gaya. Mara's name means "Death". He realized that if Gautama achieved enlightenment, his own power would be destroyed, and he therefore sent his three beautiful daughters to tempt the sage. Although Mara's daughters sang and danced and tried every trick they knew to beguile him, Gautama remained unmoved. Eventually, they admitted defeat.

Mara then sent an army of terrifying devils to threaten Gautama. Some of the creatures had 1,000 eyes, others were horrifically deformed; they drank blood and ate snakes. However, as soon as they came near to the sacred tree, they found that their arms were bound to their sides. Finally, Mara himself attacked Gautama with his fearsome weapon, a disc which could slice mountains in two. None the less, when the disc

MAYA (above) gave birth to Gautama Buddha while holding on to the branch of a tree. He is also shown taking seven symbolic steps. (TIBETAN PAINTING, 18TH CENTURY.)

MARA (below) sent his three beautiful daughters to tempt Gautama and tried in every way to threaten the sage as he sat meditating under the sacred tree at Bodh Gaya. (TIBETAN PAINTING, 18TH CENTURY.)

reached Gautama, it was transformed into a garland of flowers. At last, the demon realized that he was beaten.

THE MARUTS are a group of either 27 or 60 storm gods, usually said to be the sons of the goddess Prisni and *RUDRA*, an ancient Vedic deity who later came to be identified with *SHIVA*. The Maruts accompanied the war god *INDRA* and were armed with lightning arrows and thunderbolts. According to the *Rig Veda,* the ancient collection of sacred hymns, they wore golden helmets and breastplates, and used their axes to split the clouds so that rain could fall. They were widely regarded as clouds, capable of shaking mountains and destroying forests.

According to a later tradition, the Maruts were born from the broken womb of the goddess Diti, after Indra hurled a thunderbolt at her to prevent her from giving birth to too powerful a son. The goddess

had intended to remain pregnant for a century before giving birth to a son who would threaten Indra.

MATSYA see *MANU.*

MAYA, or Queen Mahamaya, was the mother of *GAUTAMA BUDDHA*. According to Buddhist tradition, she possessed all the qualities required of a woman destined to bear a buddha. She was not passionate, she drank no alcohol and she observed the precepts of a lay Buddhist. On the day she conceived Gautama, she is said to have had a dream in which a small white elephant, carrying a white lotus in its trunk, entered her right side. In due course, Maya gave birth to Gautama from her side as she stood holding on to a tree. She suffered no pain. Seven days later, she died of joy and joined the gods.

Maya, or "Miraculous Power", was a term used in Hinduism to describe the power of the Vedic gods. Later, Maya was regarded as the illusion of reality which we perceive, which will be dispelled when the universal reality of Brahman or the "Absolute" is understood. (See also *THE LIFE OF THE BUDDHA*)

MAYA (above) dreams of a small white elephant and conceives Gautama Buddha, who is seen arriving for reincarnation, riding on the elephant.

MERU is a mythical world mountain, also known as Sumeru. According to ancient Indian beliefs, both Buddhist and Hindu, it is situated at the centre of the universe and is the dwelling place of the gods. In Hindu tradition, the sacred Ganges flows from the summit of Mount Meru, and BRAHMA's magnificent golden city is situated at its peak. Beneath the mountain lie seven lower worlds, in the lowest of which lives the snake Vasuki, who bears Mount Meru and all the worlds on his coils and destroys them at the end of each YUGA.

In Buddhist belief, Meru is surrounded by seas and worlds, beneath which lie the hells. The realms of the gods and the Buddhafields are situated above the mountain. According to one Tibetan myth, in the very beginning, there was nothing but emptiness. Eventually, a wind began to stir, caused by the karma of the inhabitants of a previous universe. After many ages, the winds grew stronger, and rain began to fall. Many years later, the primeval or cosmic ocean arose, and the winds began to move the waters of the ocean, churning them until they gave rise to the cosmic mountain Meru, or Rirap Lhunpo. In due course, Meru became the abode of the gods and semi-divine beings.

Meru is made of precious stones; its slopes are covered with trees and fruits. Around the mountain lies a vast lake, and around the lake lies a ring of golden mountains. Altogether, there are seven rings of mountains and seven lakes. The final lake is Chi Gyatso, within which lie the four worlds. Each world is like an island and has its own unique inhabitants. Our own world is called Czambu Ling. At first, Czambu Ling was inhabited by gods from Mount Meru. Everyone was happy, there was no illness or pain.

However, it so happened that one day, one of the gods noticed a creamy substance lying on the surface of the earth. The cream tasted delicious, and soon all the other gods began to eat it. The more the gods ate, the less powerful they became. Eventually, the light the gods had radiated was extinguished, the world became dark and the gods became human beings. When the creamy food ran out, the people began to eat fruit. Each individual had his own plant, and each day the plant would produce just one piece of fruit, which was just enough to satisfy one person's hunger.

One day, a man noticed that his plant had produced two pieces of fruit. He ate both pieces and, when the next day his plant produced no fruit, he stole some from his neighbour's plant. In this way, theft and greed were introduced to the world. (See also MYTHICAL MOUNTAINS)

MGON-PO see MAHAKALA.

MITRA, according to Vedic mythology, was a god of light. He was one of the ADITYAS, and was closely associated with VARUNA, the supreme Vedic deity. Sometimes regarded as twins, Mitra and Varuna maintained universal order and justice and were said to embody the power that formed the essence of the kshatriya, or warrior caste. A good-natured deity, Mitra has particular responsibility for friendships and contracts. He is believed to direct human beings towards the light and to enable them to live happily with one another. In Iran, his parallel is the god Mithra.

MURUKAN, or the "Youthful One", was a deity of the Dravidians of southern India. He is sometimes known as Ceyon, or the "Red One". He is an important figure in present-day Tamil religion. Murukan is usually represented riding an elephant or a peacock, and he carries a spear and a garland of flowers. He is sometimes identified with KARTTIKEYA, the Hindu warrior god. His equivalent in Sri Lanka is KATARAGAMA DEVIYO.

MERU (right), the golden mountain, is the centre of the world in both Hindu and Buddhist mythology. (MURAL PAINTING, WAT KO KEO SUTTHARAM, THAILAND.)

SACRED RIVERS

THE GREAT RIVER GANGES, which rises in the Himalayas and flows across north-east India, is sacred to Hindus, who believe that bathing in her water will enable them to reach Indra's heaven, Svarga, on Mount Meru. They also revere the holy city of Prayaga (now Allahabad), where the Ganges is joined by her two tributaries, the Yamuna and the subterranean Sarasvati. This is a place of pilgrimage so sacred that a tiny piece of its soil is believed to be capable of wiping away sin. Each of these great rivers was deified as a goddess, of which the most holy was Ganga, daughter of the mountain god Himavat and an aspect of the great mother goddess, Devi. She was said to have emerged from the toe of Vishnu, and to have descended from heaven to cleanse the earth of the accumulated ashes of the dead. The ashes of the faithful are still committed to her care.

SARASVATI (above), the goddess, was originally identified with the sacred river which flows into the Ganges at Prayaga. As the deity of a natural force, she had the power to smash mountains and spoke with the roar of the waterfall. Later, she was said to be the creation and consort of Brahma. She became the goddess of music and wisdom, was credited with the invention of Sanskrit, and was known as the "Mother of the Veda". (MARBLE STATUE, 12TH CENTURY.)

VARANASI (left), the city on the west bank of the Ganges, is a holy place for Hindus. They believe that to die here, or to have their ashes committed to the river, will release their souls from the cycle of rebirth and death. The dead are cremated on the "burning" ghats (the stone steps that run down to the water), and their ashes are given to the Ganges to be carried down to the sea.

YAMUNA (left), the river goddess, was the daughter of the sun god Surya and his wife Sanjna, and was also sometimes said to be the sister of Yama, the Vedic god of death. As a river goddess, she was thought to bring fertility and good harvests, and was therefore identified with prosperity. The river Yamuna, a tributary of the Ganges, parted miraculously to allow Krishna's father, Vasudev, to carry him to safety as a baby. (STONE CARVING, 9TH CENTURY.)

GANGA'S (above) fall from heaven was cushioned by the matted hair of Shiva, sitting on Mount Kailasa. It separated the river into seven different streams so that it would not engulf the earth. Ganga was believed to flow through the underworld too, linking all three worlds. She was seen as a symbol of purity and was portrayed as a beautiful woman, the consort of Vishnu and Shiva, and also of a mortal king, Shantanu. (ILLUSTRATION BY WARWICK GOBLE.)

THE YAMUNA (left) is one of the seven great rivers of India – the others are the Ganges, Sarasvati, Godavari, Narmada, Sindhu and Kaveri – that are particularly revered, though Hindus hold all water to be sacred. On the bank of the Yamuna lies the ancient city of Mathura, the mythical birthplace of Krishna, which is also a place of pilgrimage for Buddhists and Jains.

P

NAGAS, according to Hindu belief, are semi-divine but powerful serpents who guard the treasures of the earth. They are often associated with fertility but can occasionally prove dangerous. Whereas some nagas are depicted with several heads, others are represented as human beings. The naga Vasuki was used as a rope in the myth of the churning of the ocean and was afterwards worn by *SHIVA* as a girdle that had the power to dispel demons. When the great god *VISHNU* is resting, he sleeps on the naga known as Sesha, or Ananta. Seshas's hoods shade the god, but his yawns cause earthquakes.

In Buddhist belief, the nagas are often regarded as water deities who guard Buddhist texts. One story tells how the nagas took the Buddhist philosopher Nagarjuna to their realm, where he rediscovered the *Prajnaparamita-sutra* of Mahayana Buddhism. The *GAUTAMA BUDDHA* is said to have given the text to the nagas for safekeeping until a time when humans were ready to receive it. Another story tells how the naga king Elapatra disguised himself as a man to listen to the Buddha preach.

Naga kings are depicted in representations of Gautama Buddha's birth. One such king, Mucilinda, is said to have sheltered the meditating Buddha during a great storm by surrounding him with the coils of his body and forming an awning

NAGAS are semi-divine but powerful serpents who guard the treasures of the earth. (ALAMPUR, 7TH–8TH CENTURY.)

with his hood. The naga kings are said to control rainfall and to look after rivers, lakes and seas. They protect against fires caused by lightning. In spring, the nagas climb to the heavens, whereas in winter they live deep in the earth.

NANDA see *KRISHNA*.

NANDI, or Nandin, is the milk-white bull who is an animal form of *SHIVA*, the great Hindu god. As well

NANDI's statue stands at the entrance of many temples dedicated to Shiva, and devotees customarily touch the bull's testicles as they enter the shrine. Nandi is Shiva's principal attendant.

as being Shiva's chosen mount, Nandi is a member of his retinue and represents the great god's virility and fertility.

When Shiva took the form of Nataraja, Nandi provided the music for his wild dancing. In the *Puranas*, Hindu scriptures dating from the fifth century AD, Nandi is invoked as a divinity. He is the son of Surabhi, the divine cow who arose from the churning of the ocean, and *KASYAPA*, the sage.

Nandi looks after all four-legged creatures and stands guard at the four corners of the world. A sculpture of the bull is usually situated at the entrance of temples dedicated to Shiva.

NANDIN see *NANDI*.

NANG-LHA is one of the supernatural beings of the indigenous Bon religion of Tibet. He was assimilated into the Buddhist pantheon as a protector of the religion.

Nang-Lha looks after the house and is usually shown with the head of a pig and the body of a human being.

NARASIMHA was the fourth incarnation, or *AVATAR*, of the great Hindu god *VISHNU*, preserver of the universe. A man-lion, he overcame the king Hiranyakashipu, an incarnation of *RAVANA*. See also *THE AVATARS OF VISHNU*)

NARAYANA see *BRAHMA*.

NASATYA see *ASVINS*.

NATARAJA see *SHIVA*.

NATHA is one of the four principal gods of Sri Lanka. His name means "Master". He was identified with the *BODHISATTVA*, or "buddha-to-be", *AVALOKITESHVARA*, and was also sometimes regarded as *MAITREYA*, the future Buddha. The Buddhist goddess *TARA* is said to be his consort.

NILARANTHA see *SHIVA*.

PADMASAMBHAVA was one of the founders of Tibetan Buddhism. His followers worship him as the

NARASIMHA *was a man-lion, the fourth avatar of the Hindu god Vishnu. He overcame the demon king Hiranyakashipu.* (CARVING, HALEBIDU, KARNATAKA.)

"second Buddha". A contemporary of the Tibetan king Trisong Detsen (AD755–97), Padmasambhava was allegedly born in the mythical land of Urgyen, believed to be situated in north-west Kashmir. He is said to have been created by the buddha AMITABHA and to have appeared, aged eight years old, in a lotus blossom, thereby earning his name, which means "He Who is Born from the Lotus".

After murdering a king's minister, Padmasambhava was condemned to live in the charnel grounds. However, while there, he mastered all the learned disciplines of his time, in particular the teachings of the Tantras, and achieved great spiritual power through conversing with the DAKINI, the female "Sky-goers". At that time, the ancient Bon religion still flourished in Tibet. King Trisong Detsen decided that he wanted to intro-

duce Buddhism to the country, and so sent messengers to India, instructing them to find the most learned men in order that they might teach his people. The messengers advised the king to send for Padmasambhava.

Padmasambhava arrived in Tibet and imparted the Buddhist teachings to 25 main students, as well as to the king. Some accounts say that he stayed for a few months, others that he was in Tibet for 50 years. He transformed many demons into DHARMAPALAS, or "Protectors of the Teaching", founded the "Inconceivable" temple with the help of local spirits, and composed the "Hidden Treasures". The treasures, known as Gter-ma, are religious instructions, which are said to have been hidden away in order to be revealed sometime in the future when the world needs a fresh revelation.

PADMASAMBHAVA *was worshipped as the "second Buddha" and instrumental in introducing Buddhism to Tibet.* (PAINTING, TANKA LAMA SCHOOL, 19TH CENTURY.)

One story tells how the king eventually grew worried that his people showed greater reverence for Padmasambhava than for himself. In order to demonstrate his supreme authority, he summoned all his courtiers to watch Padmasambhava bow down before him. However, as Padmasambhava raised his arms as if to prostrate himself before the king, flames sprang from his fingertips, setting the ruler's clothes on fire. Immediately, the king tore off his ceremonial scarf, already smouldering, and threw himself at Padmasambhava's feet in submission. He later gave Padmasambhava the scarf as a token of his humility, establishing the tradition of giving scarves as a sign of respect.

Before leaving Tibet, the sage promised to return every month on the tenth day of the waxing moon in order to bless anyone who called out his name. According to legend, he travelled to Bhutan, where he

PADMASAMBHAVA *in his eight forms. He built the first Tibetan Buddhist monastery, at Samyé, where previous attempts had been foiled by demons, who tore down the buildings as soon as they were erected.*

continued his religious teaching. Padmasambhava is said to have lived for more than 1,000 years.

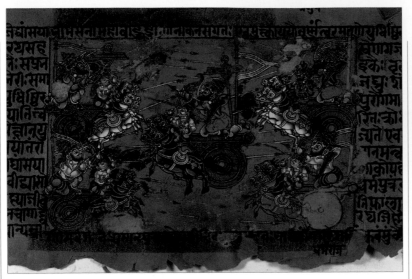

THE PANDAVAS were descended from King Pandu. Two of their number, Bhima and Arjuna, fought against Drona, the leader of the Kauravas. (ILLUSTRATION TO THE MAHABHARATA, INDIA, C. 1542.)

PATTINI is the most important Singhalese goddess. She is said to look after marriages and to keep epidemics at bay. According to one myth, she was born from a mango, which had been struck by a divine arrow. Another myth tells how she introduced the cultivation of rice into Sri Lanka.

THE PEY, according to the Tamils of southern India and Sri Lanka, are demons who drink the blood of the dead and of wounded warriors, and bring misery and bad luck to the living. They are wild creatures with tangled hair.

PRADYUMNA, according to Hindu mythology, was the son of KRISHNA, the eighth AVATAR of VISHNU, and his wife Rukmuni. He is sometimes said to have been a reincarnation of KAMA, god of desire. When he was six days old, Pradyumna was kidnapped by a demon, Shambhara, who threw him into the sea. The infant was swallowed by a fish, which was later caught and brought to Shambhara's home. Pradyumna

THE PANDAVAS were the descendants of King Pandu. The five Pandava princes fought the Kauravas in the famous battle of Kurukshetra, which is described in the Hindu epic, the *Mahabharata*.

On the eve of the battle, ARJUNA, one of the five brothers, received spiritual instruction from KRISHNA, an AVATAR of the great god VISHNU, who disguised himself as Arjuna's charioteer. Krishna's teaching forms the *Bhagavad Gita* or "Song of the Lord".

PARASHURAMA see AVATARS.

PARVATI is an aspect of the divine mother of Hindu mythology, the consort of the great god SHIVA. She is the graceful aspect of the SHAKTI of Shiva. Parvati's name means "Daughter of the Mountains"; her father was Himavat, king of the mountains, and she was the mother of the elephant god GANESHA, whom she is sometimes said to have created from the rubbings of her own body. According to one myth, Shiva produced six

children without Parvati's assistance. The goddess became extremely fond of her husband's offspring and one day hugged them so tightly that they merged into one child, although the six heads remained. The boy grew up to become the warrior god KARTTIKEYA, or Skanda. According to another story, when Parvati first saw Karttikeya, she felt such maternal love for him that milk flowed from her breasts.

Another tale tells how Shiva criticized Parvati's dark skin, whereupon the goddess retired to the forest in shame and became an

ascetic. However, BRAHMA was so impressed by Parvati's austerities that he transformed her into Gauri, the golden-skinned goddess. In some versions of the story, Parvati's dark skin became the goddess KALI.

Shiva once turned Parvati into a fisherwoman to punish her disobedience. On another occasion, Parvati crept up behind Shiva and put her fingers over his eyes. Darkness enveloped the world, and so Shiva made a third eye appear in the middle of his forehead. (See also MYTHICAL MOUNTAINS; THE MOTHER GODDESS)

PARVATI (right), mother of the elephant-headed god Ganesha, with Shiva, who is shown with the goddess Ganga in his hair. (ILLUSTRATION BY J. HIGGINBOTHAM, 1864.)

PARVATI with her husband, Shiva, and children Karttikeya and Ganesha, in their home on Mount Kailasa, attended by Nandi, the bull. (MINIATURE, 18TH CENTURY.)

Prajapati then created night and day, the seasons, death, and people to relieve his loneliness.

The name Prajapati sometimes refers to a variety of gods, including INDRA, SOMA, SHIVA, GARUDA, KRISHNA and MANU. It is also the name given to ten sages from whom humanity is said to be descended, and to seven RISHIS, or seers. BRAHMA is sometimes attributed with myths that later became associated with Prajapati.

PRAJNA see HERUKA.

PRAJNAPARAMITA, according to Buddhist belief, is the deification of the *Prajnaparamita-sutra*, a sacred text in which GAUTAMA BUDDHA is said to have set out his teachings. According to tradition, the Buddha gave the text to the NAGAS until the time was ripe for it to be revealed to the faithful. The sutra is said to have been "restored" by the Buddhist philosopher Nagarjuna.

Prajnaparamita is thus regarded as an incarnation of the divine word. Her name means "Perfection of Insight" or "Wisdom that Reaches the Other Shore". In Tibet, the goddess is usually depicted coloured white or yellow, holding a lotus flower in one hand and the sacred text in the other.

emerged from the fish, and Mayadevi, the mistress of the house, looked after him. The sage Narada, lord of the GANDHARVAS, told her who the child was. When Pradyumna became a young man, Mayadevi fell in love with him and told him the truth about his origins. Pradyumna then killed Shambhara and fled with Mayadevi to Krishna's palace.

PRAHLADA see AVATARS.

PRAJAPATI, according to Hindu mythology, is the lord or master of created beings. In the Hindu epic, the *Mahabharata*, he is the protector of the sexual organ. By his own powers, he produced numerous children including a daughter, USHAS, or "Dawn".

On one occasion, Prajapati attempted to commit incest with Ushas, whereupon she transformed herself into a gazelle or deer. Prajapati then took the form of a stag, whose seed gave rise to the first humans. In other versions of the myth, Prajapati succeeded in mating with Ushas when she appeared in numerous different animal forms. The couple thereby gave rise to all living creatures. Another myth tells how Prajapati rose weeping from the primordial waters. The tears that fell into the water became the earth, whereas those that the god wiped away became the sky and the air.

PRITHIVI, a Vedic earth goddess, is sometimes said to be the mother of USHAS, the dawn, AGNI, the god of fire, and INDRA, the great war god. She is also the consort of Dyaus, the sky father of the Vedic religion. When giving birth to Indra, numerous portents warned the goddess that this particular son was destined to supplant the old order. As a result, she hid the child away. Prithivi is usually depicted in the form of a cow.

393

R

PURURAVAS see *APSARAS*.

PURUSHA was the primordial man or cosmic giant of Indian mythology. According to the ancient sacred hymns known as the *Rig Veda*, Purusha was three-quarters immortal and one-quarter mortal. From his mortal quarter, he released his wife, Viraj, and he was then born from her as a universal spirit. Purusha assumed the form of a giant with 1,000 thighs, 1,000 feet, 1,000 arms, 1,000 eyes, 1,000 faces and 1,000 heads.

In order that the world might be created, he offered himself up to be sacrificed. His head became the heavens, his navel, the atmosphere and his feet, the earth. The seasons came from his armpits, the earth from his feet, the sun from his eyes, and the moon from his mind. The gods and people of the brahman caste came from his mouth, and the wind was born from his breath. His arms became the kshatriyas, or warrior caste; his thighs became the vaishyas, or the traders and farmers; and his feet became the shudras, or servant class.

In the *Brahmanas* and the *Upanishads*, religious texts composed after the *Rig Veda*, Purusha was regarded as *PRAJAPATI*, the lord of created beings. His name is also used to denote the spiritual core of a person; in Buddhist texts, it is sometimes applied to the Buddha.

RADHA (above) and Krishna walking by the Yamuna river in the moonlight, having exchanged clothes. (ILLUSTRATION TO THE BHAGAVATA PURANA, KANGRA, C. 1820.)

PURUSHA (left) was the primal being of Indian mythology. He was sacrificed to create all living things.

RADHA, according to Hindu mythology, was the favourite gopi, or cowgirl, of *KRISHNA*, the eighth *AVATAR* of the great god *VISHNU*. She lived in Vrindavan, the village in northern India where Krishna was brought up. Radha is sometimes regarded as Krishna's wife, sometimes as his lover. According to one tale, she was married to Ayanagosha, a cowherd. When Ayanagosha heard of Radha's adultery, he went in search of the couple. However, Krishna assumed the form of a goddess, and they thereby escaped Ayanagosha's

RADHA (left) has her toenails painted by her lover, Krishna. (KANGRA. C. 1820.)

asleep with Rahula in her arms, feared he might wake them and so left them sleeping.

Rahula entered a Buddhist community at the age of seven and is regarded as the guardian of novices. He is one of the ten great disciples of the Buddha and was said to be "first in esoteric practices and in desire for instruction in the Law". He died before the Buddha. He is sometimes represented holding a fly whisk (swatter) and a scroll of scriptures, and is often accompanied by a deer or a disciple.

RAKSHASAS, according to Hindu belief, are semi-divine, usually evil-natured, spirits. They are able to assume any shape they choose. Whereas they tend to be good-natured and faithful towards one another, with outsiders they can be gluttonous, lustful and violent. They live in a magnificent city, designed by Vishvakarma, the architect of the gods. Harmless beings, such as the YAKSHAS, are rakshasas, as are numerous enemies of the gods, including demons who live in cemeteries and harass human beings.

According to one tradition, the rakshasas emerged from BRAHMA's foot, whereas another tradition tells how they are descendants of KASYAPA, the great RISHI, or sage. In some texts, the rakshasas are described as the original inhabitants of India who were subjugated by the Aryans.

wrath. According to another tradition, Radha is an incarnation of LAKSHMI, the goddess of good fortune and wife of Vishnu. The goddess took the form of Radha in order that she might not be separated from her husband.

Radha's love for Krishna is seen as a symbol of the interplay between the individual soul and the divine. When Radha is apart from Krishna, she longs for his return, and Krishna likewise pines for Radha. Devotees of Krishna regard the human feeling of love and surrender as a means of achieving knowledge of and union with the divine.

RAHU see AMRITA.

RAHULA, whose name means "Fetter", was the son of GAUTAMA BUDDHA and the princess Yasodhara. He is usually said to have been born shortly before Gautama left his family to seek enlightenment, although he is sometimes said to have been born on the day of his father's enlightenment. According to the former version of the myth, Gautama crept into his wife's rooms to kiss her goodbye but, seeing her

RADHA (right) listens to her lover, Krishna, (left), entertaining her with his flute as she attends to her toilette. (MINIATURE, 18TH CENTURY.)

THE MOTHER GODDESS

EVI, OR MAHADEVI ("THE GREAT GODDESS"), is a composite figure who includes various aspects of the female deity in a series of contrasting incarnations. In the earliest Indian cultures, the mother goddess was Shakti, the source of all energy in the universe, the creative force who brought fertility to the earth. Some of her manifestations were associated with natural forces, such as Ushas, the dawn, and Ganga, the river. Later she was subsumed in the patriarchal Hindu creation myth as the consort of Shiva. In this role she continued to appear in a variety of incarnations. Some were benign, such as Sati and Parvati, both of whom were loving and caring, but others were terrifying, such as the warrior goddesses Durga and Kali. Although she lost her autonomy in her new role as consort, she was still the creative force. While Shiva embodied potency, Shakti was the energy needed to release his power.

KALI (above), the "Black One", was the most terrifying aspect of the goddess Devi. She was portrayed as a black-skinned hag with pendulous breasts and a necklace of skulls or severed heads. Like Shiva, she had an all-seeing third eye in her forehead. Her male victims, made impotent without the goddess's activating energy, had no way of resisting her attack. (THE GODDESS BEHEADING A MAN, BUNDI, C. 1650.)

UMA (right) was an early form of the goddess Parvati, the shakti of Shiva. Uma was the consort of Chandrashekhara, an aspect of Shiva who was also called Umapati ("Uma's spouse"). She was the daughter of Himavat, the king of the Himalayas. In her fierce aspect as Uma Maheshvara, she fought with demons. (KHMER STATUE, 11TH CENTURY.)

PARVATI (above right), the wife of Shiva (above left), was a reincarnation of his first wife, Sati, who had immolated herself in shame when Shiva was not invited to her father Daksha's sacrifice. Shiva showed no interest in Parvati at first, objecting to her dark skin, but she won his love by enduring austerities. She became the personification of the loving wife and mother, domesticating Shiva, and they led an idyllic family life with their children Karttikeya (above centre) and Ganesha. (BRONZE SOMASKANDA GROUP, 16TH CENTURY.)

DURGA (left) the invincible warrior goddess, fought demons that threatened the world. She was the embodiment of the anger of the gods, whether of Shiva and Vishnu, or of Parvati. When Durga herself was angry, Kali emerged from her forehead. Durga fought the demon Mahisha in an epic battle, in which he transformed himself into a buffalo, a lion, an armed man and an elephant. Finally, Durga cut off Mahisha's head. (DURGA SLAYS MAHISHASURA, MANDI, C. 1750–60.)

KALI (right) set out to kill demons but could become so intoxicated with blood that she threatened the world as well. She vanquished the demon Raktabija, who was reproduced with every drop of his blood that touched the ground, by catching the drops in her huge mouth before they fell, and then sucking the demon dry. Inflamed by her feast, she began to dance wildly, and when Shiva tried to stop her, she danced on his body, nearly destroying the cosmos. (ILLUSTRATION BY J. HIGGINBOTHAM, 1864.)

RAMA (above) and his brothers getting married. Rama was married to Sita, regarded by devotees of Vishnu as the ideal woman. (KULU-MANDI, PAHARI SCHOOL, 1760–5.)

RAMA (left) and his half-brother, Lakshmana left Sita alone to hunt a golden deer planted in the forest by Ravana. Meanwhile, the demon captured Sita. (MUGHAL PAINTING, EARLY 17TH CENTURY.)

RAMA was an *AVATAR*, or incarnation, of *VISHNU*, the great Hindu deity known as the preserver of the universe. He is said to have been sent down to earth in order to overcome the powers of darkness as embodied by the evil demon *RAVANA*, king of *LANKA*. His life and exploits are immortalized in the Hindu epic, the *Ramayana*.

Rama probably originated as a folk hero and only gradually came to be regarded as an avatar of Vishnu. He was courageous and peace-loving, dutiful and virtuous. Devotees of Vishnu regard him as the ideal man and they regard his wife, *SITA*, as the ideal woman: chaste, faithful and devout.

Rama was said to be the son of King Dasaratha of Ayodhya. On his father's death, his stepmother Sumitra cheated him out of his inheritance and banished him into exile in the forest for 14 years. Although Rama advised his wife to stay in the palace, away from the hardships of forest life, Sita insisted on accompanying her husband: "With you it is heaven, away from you hell," she said. Once in the forest, Rama protected the sages who had their hermitages there. When Rama failed to respond to the advances of a horrible female demon, Surpanaka, she persuaded her brother, Ravana, to kidnap Sita. Ravana succeeded in abducting Sita and carried her off to the island of Lanka. Rama, mad with grief, went in search of his wife and succeeded in overcoming numerous demons, often with the help of the monkey god *HANUMAN*.

In order to reach Sita, Rama had to take his army across the sea. He asked the ocean for help and, when none was forthcoming, became so enraged that he shot his arrows at the waters in an attempt to dry them up. Nothing happened. Rama then fired an arrow tipped with a charm given to him by *BRAHMA*. Immediately, the sky grew dark, and all living creatures trembled with fear. Finally, the ocean spoke and explained that, though he was unable to halt the movements of his waters, he would support a bridge over which Rama's soldiers could cross. Soon, Hanuman's army of monkeys had built a bridge and the troops began to cross over to Lanka. Immediately, Rama and Ravana entered into a fearsome battle. Rama's army appeared to be winning when Ravana approached to attack Rama in person. Rama destroyed the demon's ten heads one after another, but new ones kept growing in their place. Finally, Rama fired an arrow which the sage *AGASTYA* had given to him. The arrow killed Ravana, then returned to Rama. The battle was won.

Despite Sita's innocence, she repulsed Rama, since her reputation had been stained by her long stay with Ravana. Sita despaired and threw herself on to a funeral pyre. *AGNI*, the fire god, rescued her from the flames. In another version of the story, Sita remained unharmed by the flames, thus publicly proving her innocence.

Rama regained his kingdom and ruled over it with wisdom, fairness and tenderness for 1,000 years. He finally returned to heaven where he was reunited with Vishnu. The

RAMA (far left) spurned the advances of the sister of the demon Ravana. In revenge, she persuaded Ravana to kidnap Rama's wife Sita. (ILLUSTRATION BY WARWICK GOBLE.)

RAMA (left) gives his ring to Hanuman for the monkey god to send to Sita. Hanuman is the courageous and ever-loyal supporter of Rama. (ILLUSTRATION BY WARWICK GOBLE.)

victory of Rama over Ravana continues to be celebrated annually in India at the festival of Dussehra. In northern India, his name refers to the supreme god. His attributes are a bow and arrows. (See also *THE AVATARS OF VISHNU*)

RATI see *KAMA*.

RATNASAMBHAVA is one of the *DHYANIBUDDHAS*, "Great Buddhas of Wisdom". He is the "Source of Secret Things" and "He Who is Born of the Jewel". In Tibet he is often shown embracing Mamaki, his *SHAKTI*. His element is fire, his heavenly quarter the south, and he is yellow in colour. His carriage is drawn by a pair of lions or a horse.

RAVANA was the demon king of *LANKA* whom *RAMA*, an *AVATAR* of the great god *VISHNU*, was sent down to earth to vanquish. He had ten heads and was said to be indestructible. In the Hindu epic, the *Ramayana*, he is portrayed as the embodiment of evil. According to one tradition, a high-ranking member of Vishnu's heaven committed a sin and was given the choice of two means to clear his name: he could either descend to earth and live out seven incarnations as a friend of Vishnu or three incarnations as the enemy of the god. The offender chose the latter option, believing that he would thereby return to heaven more quickly.

Ravana's first incarnation was as the demon king Hiranyakashipu. Such was his power that he

dethroned the mighty god *INDRA* and shut the gods out of heaven. He proclaimed himself king of the universe and ordered everyone to worship him. However, his son Prahlada persisted in worshipping Vishnu; try as he might, the demon king was unable to sway him from his vocation. Hiranyakashipu determined to kill Prahlada, but Vishnu protected him. Eventually, Vishnu destroyed the demon and Prahlada became king.

Ravana's second incarnation was as the enemy of Rama, another avatar of Vishnu. Ravana abducted Vishnu's wife, *SITA*, and took her away to the island of Lanka. Helped by the monkey god *HANUMAN*, Rama found her there and made war against the demon, eventually killing him. On the eve of the great battle in which he was slain, the demon admitted that he had only kidnapped Sita in order that he might be killed and so go on to live out his third incarnation as a demon, after which he would be able to return to heaven.

In his third incarnation, Ravana appeared as the demon Sisupala. The son of a king, he had three eyes

RATNASAMBHAVA's element is fire, and he represents the branch of the cosmos conerned with sensation. (TIBETAN BRONZE, WITH SILVER AND COPPER, 15TH CENTURY.)

and four arms. Although his parents were horrified at the sight of him, they were reassured by a voice which told them that, until the time of his death, Sisupala would be both famous and fortunate. The voice also announced that his mother would be able to recognize whoever it was that would eventually kill the boy: when the child sat on his knee, his third eye and extra arms would disappear.

The king and queen travelled from kingdom to kingdom, placing their son on the knee of each ruler, but nothing happened. When they returned home the young prince *KRISHNA*, the eighth avatar of Vishnu, visited the palace. As soon as Sisupala sat on Krishna's knee, his third eye vanished, and his extra two arms fell off. The queen then begged Krishna to forgive her child should he ever offend him. Krishna agreed that he would.

Years later, Sisupala attended a great sacrifice along with numerous important kings. Krishna was also present. The celebration was hosted by King Yudhishthira, who decided that the first homage should be paid to Krishna. Sisupala was outraged, saying that many of the guests present were more important than Krishna. Sisupala appealed to *BRAHMA* for advice, who simply said that Krishna himself should settle the dispute. Sisupala was furious and insulted Brahma, who proceeded to tell the guests the story of Sisupala and the predictions made about him at his birth. Sisupala became increasingly angry and, drawing his sword, continued to insult Brahma. Krishna's flaming disc then rose into the air, shot towards Sisupala and cut him in two. Sisupala's soul appeared as leaping fire and, moving towards Krishna, was absorbed into the hero's feet.

RAVANA (above left), the demon king of Lanka, is conquered by Rama, who rides away in triumph with his wife Sita.

RAVANA (above right) with Hanuman, the monkey god. When Ravana abducted Rama's wife Sita, Hanuman leapt across

the waters to the island of Lanka to discover where Ravana had hidden her. (ILLUSTRATIONS BY J. HIGGINBOTHAM, 1864.)

S

RIRAP LHUNPO see *MERU*.

RISHIS are usually regarded as the seers and great sages of Hinduism, but the term is also applied to saints and inspired poets. The Veda, the sacred knowledge of the Hindus, was said to have been revealed to the seven great rishis who preserved and transmitted it. The identity of these seven great rishis varies. According to the *Shatapatha Brahmana*, a commentary on the Veda, they were *GAUTAMA*, Bharadvaja, Vishvamitra, Janmadagni, Vasishtha, *KASYAPA* and Atri. The seven great rishis were sometimes regarded as holy beings who were identified with the seven stars of the Great Bear.

RUDRA appears in the *Rig Veda*, the great collection of ancient Indian hymns. His name means "Howler" or the "Red One". A god of storms and the dead, he was sometimes associated with the destructive aspect of the fire god *AGNI*. According to one myth, he emerged from the forehead of *BRAHMA* when the god became angry. Rudra fired his arrows of disease at gods, men and animals, but he also brought health and performed good deeds.

When *PRAJAPATI* committed incest with *USHAS*, the dawn, Rudra was about to shoot him when Prajapati promised to make

him lord of animals. In this role, Rudra was represented in the form of a bull. He gradually came to be seen as an increasingly dark god who developed into the destructive aspect of *SHIVA*. He is often regarded as the father of the *MARUTS*, companions of *INDRA*.

THE SA-DAG are the supernatural "Lords of the Soil" of the indigenous Bon religion of Tibet. They were assimilated into the Buddhist pantheon as protectors of the religion and are propitiated before any building work or farming is carried out.

SAMANTABHADRA is an emanation of the *DHYANIBUDDHA VAIROCANA*, and represents the Buddhist law and compassion. He is one of the most important *BODHISATTVAS* of Mahayana, or "Great Vehicle" Buddhism, and is worshipped as the protector of all those

SAMANTABHADRA, enthroned on a lotus, is mounted on his six-tusked white elephant, which also stands on lotus flowers. (EMEI, SICHUAN, CHINA.)

who teach the dharma, or law. Samantabhadra is often depicted together with *GAUTAMA BUDDHA* and *MANJUSHRI*, bodhisattva of wisdom. He is shown riding on a white elephant with six tusks, a symbol of the ability of wisdom to overcome all obstructions to enlightenment, including the six senses.

SAMVARA, or Chakra Samvara, is a god of initiation in Tantrism, a tradition that uses ritual practices as a path to enlightenment. One of the *YIDAMS* or tutelary gods of Tibet, he is depicted with 12 arms and four or five heads. He is associated with the buddha *AKSOBHYA*. In China, he is believed to be incarnated in the chief Tibetan Buddhist priest in Beijing. His *SHAKTI*, or corresponding female energy, is *VAJRAVARAHI*.

SANI see *AIRAVATA*.

SANJNA see *SURYA*.

SARASVATI is one of the three sacred rivers mentioned in the *Rig Veda*, a collection of ancient Hindu hymns. The Sarasvati is believed to

SAMVARA (above) in the posture of Yab-Yum with his shakti, wears a garland of heads and a crown of skulls. (BRASS AND COPPER, KASHMIR, 9TH CENTURY.)

flow underground to join the other two sacred rivers, the Ganges and the Yamuna, at Allahabad, a town in northern India where mass pilgrimages occur each year.

Sarasvati means "Watery"; as the river, she gives fertility and wisdom to the earth. In later times, Sarasvati became the wife and the creation of *BRAHMA*, the creator of the universe.

Sometimes identified with Vak, the goddess of eloquence, Sarasvati was herself the goddess of language, art and learning. She was sometimes called the "Mother of the Veda", the sacred texts of Hinduism, and was also credited with having invented the Sanskrit alphabet. Offerings are made to her by schoolchildren before classes.

Beautiful but temperamental, she was sometimes depicted with four arms and was represented riding on a swan or peacock, or sitting on a lotus. In some branches of

SARASVATI (right) with Brahma. Sarasvati was the creation and the wife of Brahma, the creator of the universe. (CHAPRA ILLUSTRATION, BIHAR, 1802.)

Buddhism, Sarasvati is the goddess of instruction and a companion of the *BODHISATTVA MANJUSHRI*. (See also *SACRED RIVERS*)

SATI see *DAKSHA*.

SESHA see *NAGAS*.

SHAKTI means "Force", "Power" or "Energy". In Buddhism, shaktis, who are female, embody the active energy of the male deities with whom they are often shown in a sexual embrace known as Yab-Yum. The five main shaktis correspond to the five male *DHYANIBUDDHAS*, or the "Great Buddhas of Wisdom": Vajradharisvari corresponds to *VAIROCANA*, Locana corresponds to *AKSOBHYA*, Mamaki corresponds to *RATNASAMBHAVA*, Pandara corresponds to *AMITABHA* and Tara to *AMOGHASIDDHI*. When in Yab-Yum, these shaktis may hold a cup made from a skull.

In Hinduism, Shakti is regarded as the creative force of *SHIVA* and is worshipped under many names, including *PARVATI*, Uma, *DURGA* and *KALI*. Shaktism is an aspect of Tantrism. Shaktas worship Shakti

and revere her as the life-force and the energy that maintains the universe. As a means towards experiencing the supreme reality, Shaktas use sexual practices, including those shown in the *Kamasutra*, the manual of erotic art. However, in some sects, these practices are meditated upon rather than actually performed.

SARASVATI, one of the three sacred rivers mentioned in the Rig Veda, was also a beautiful but temperamental goddess, sometimes depicted with four arms and sitting on a lotus.

SHAKUNTALA see *APSARAS*.

SHAMBHALA, according to Tibetan Buddhist mythology, is a mythical kingdom generally said to lie to the north-east of India, although it is also believed to be located in China and at the North Pole. It is claimed that the saviour of the world will appear from Shambhala when war and destruction threaten civilization. The Kalachakra teachings, a complex system of meditation, are also said to have arisen in Shambhala. According to tradition, a mythical king Suchandra ruled over Shambhala and received the Kalachakra teachings from the Buddha in his 80th year. The king wrote the teachings down and passed them on through six further kings and 25 "Proclaimers". At the time of the 25th teacher, Rigden Pema Karpo, a golden age will dawn and Shambhala will become a universal kingdom.

SHENRAB MIWO see *GSHEN-RAB*.

SHITALA see *DURGA*.

SHIVA, sitting on a lotus throne and ringed by a circle of flames, sustains the world with his meditation. (PAINTING, C. 1890.)

visited the rishis in order to persuade them to become his devotees. The rishis responded by cursing Shiva and, when this had no effect, they sent a fearsome tiger to devour him. The great god simply removed the skin of the tiger with his fingernail and draped it around his neck like a shawl. The rishis then sent a snake to attack Shiva, who merely hung it around his neck as a garland. Finally, the rishis sent an evil dwarf armed with a club to attack the god, but Shiva responded by placing his foot on the dwarf's back and beginning to dance. The rishis watched the performance in wonder. Even the heavens opened so that the gods were able to look down at the astounding dance. Eventually, the rishis were no longer able to resist the dancing Shiva and threw themselves at his feet.

Shiva's principal symbolic representation is the lingam, a phallic shaped stone. One myth tells how the god visited a pine forest where some sages were meditating. The sages, not recognizing Shiva, suspected him of trying to seduce their wives and caused him to lose his phallus. Immediately, the world grew dark, and the sages lost their virility. Eventually, they made offerings to Shiva, and the world returned to normal.

Shiva is often shown with four arms and with a third eye, the eye of inner vision, in the middle of his forehead. He frequently has a serpent as a necklace, one around his waist and others wrapped around his arms. He may also be depicted smeared with ashes as a symbol of his asceticism. His throat is often coloured blue, and he is sometimes

SHIVA, as Nataraja, the "Lord of the Dance", orders the universe with his dance, with one foot on the back of the dwarf who personifies ignorance. (BRONZE, C. AD846.)

SHIVA is one of the principal Hindu deities who, together with *VISHNU* and *BRAHMA*, forms the Trimurti, or triad of great gods. He is believed to have developed from *RUDRA*, a minor deity who appears in the *Rig Veda*, the collection of ancient Hindu hymns dating from between 1500 and 900BC. It seems that the god grew in stature after absorbing some of the characteristics of an ancient fertility god sometimes referred to as "proto-Shiva". Representations of this god, sitting in the position of a yogi and associated with animals and plants, have been ascribed to the Indus Valley culture, which dates from before 1500BC.

Shiva can be kind and protective, but he is also terrifying and is found in such places as battlefields and cremation grounds. He is often shown decorated with a string of skulls. Although he is a god of creation, he is also the god of time and thus the great destroyer. He is a fertility god, but he is also an ascetic who has conquered his desires and lives on Mount Kailasa in the high Himalayas, deep in the meditation which keeps the world in existence.

Although Shiva brings death, he also conquers death as well as disease and is invoked to cure sickness. He is sometimes depicted as half-male, half-female. The conflicting qualities and attributes found within the god are intended to symbolize a deity within whom all opposites are reconciled. Even Shiva's name, which means "Auspicious", is intended to reconcile and propitiate the dark aspect of his character, which caused him to be known as the "Destroyer".

As Nataraja, Shiva is the "Lord of the Dance", and is often depicted as such. He dances out the creation of the world, but when he grows tired he relapses into inactivity and the universe becomes chaotic. Destruction thus follows the period of creation. One myth about Shiva as Nataraja concerns the 10,000 *RISHIS*, or sages. Shiva

known as Nilakantha, or "Blue Throat", due to the important part he played in the myth of the churning of the ocean.

According to this popular tale, the great snake Vasuki was used as a rope with which to turn Mount Mandara and so churn the seas in order to produce AMRITA, the elixir of immortality. However, the snake became so exhausted that he eventually spewed out venom, which threatened to destroy all existence. Shiva came to the rescue by swallowing the poison, which stained his throat.

Shiva is the father of the elephant god GANESHA and the warrior god KARTTIKEYA. His mount is the bull NANDI. His consort or SHAKTI (female power) is called PARVATI in her gentle aspect.

SHIVA with the wives of the rishis, whose husbands feared he was trying to seduce them: an episode from the Puranas. *(PAHARI SCHOOL, 1710–25.)*

Her other aspects are called Uma, the gracious; Bhairavi, the terrible; Ambika, the generatrix; Sati, the good wife; Gauri, the brilliant; KALI, the black; and DURGA, the inaccessible.

One myth tells how Shiva gained his third eye as a result of a prank played by Parvati. While Shiva was meditating on Mount Kailasa, Parvati crept up behind him and covered his eyes with her hands. Immediately, the sun grew pale, and every living being trembled with fear. Suddenly, a burning eye appeared on Shiva's forehead, banishing the darkness. Flames shot out from the eye and set light to the whole of the Himalayas. Parvati was devastated and, in due course, Shiva was moved by her distress to restore the mountains to their former glory.

According to another myth, when Shiva was deep in meditation on Mount Kailasa, Parvati grew bored. She persuaded KAMA, god of

SHIVA, as Nataraja, dances holding a drum, symbolizing the rhythm of creation, and a flame, symbolizing destruction.

desire, to come to her aid. Kama was loathe to intervene, but Parvati insisted, whereupon Kama prepared to fire his arrow at Shiva's heart in order to remind him of his duties to his wife. The god Mahesvara saw what was about to happen; since it was necessary for Shiva to finish his meditation in order for the cycles of creation to

run their course, he struck Kama down with a thunderbolt. Later, however, Mahesvara brought Kama back to life.

In another version of the myth, Shiva destroyed Kama with a flash of his third eye. Parvati retired from life, having become tired of Shiva's lack of interest in her. One day she was visited by a young man who, while praising her for her asceticism, tried to persuade her to give it up. Parvati grew angry, and eventually the man revealed himself to be none other than Shiva.

The god promised his wife that he would demonstrate his love to her, but Parvati demanded that he should first return Kama to his wife. Shiva did as she requested, and the couple then retired into the mountains. The intensity of their love-making shook the whole world.

DHYANIBUDDHAS

FIVE GREAT MYSTIC BUDDHAS appear together in the "Mandala of the Five Jinas", and are therefore known collectively as Dhyanibuddhas, or "Meditation Buddhas". They are said to have arisen from the Adibuddha, or "Primeval Buddha". Jinas, or spiritual conquerors, are those who have overcome the perpetual cycle of rebirth and human suffering. As subjects for meditation, they each represent a different aspect of the enlightened consciousness.

Mandala is the Sanskrit word for a circle: a mandala is both a symbolic picture of the universe and an aid to meditation, helping the onlooker to achieve different states of mind. For ritual purposes, the mandala is traced on the ground using coloured powders which are brushed away afterwards. It may also be a picture or a three-dimensional object, such as a sculpture or even a building. Mandalas can also be visualized during meditation – they do not have to exist physically.

AMITABHA reigns in the western paradise of Sukhavati, or "Pure Land". Once a king, the buddha renounced his throne and vowed to create a realm which combined all the perfections of existing lands. As its ruler, he devoted himself to good deeds and eventually became a buddha. Sitting on his lotus, his aura is bigger than a billion worlds and he has 84,000 marks of his virtues. Rebirth in Pure Land leads to the attainment of nirvana without difficulty. (TIBETAN PAINTING.)

AMOGHASIDDHI (right) rules the paradise of the north, seated on a throne flanked by a pair of garudas, or mythical birds with human heads, on which he travels. He is coloured green, and his hand is traditionally raised in a posture meaning "Fear not". His emblem is the Vajra, the thunderbolt, an indestructible weapon, as hard as a diamond. (TIBETAN PAINTING, 15TH CENTURY.)

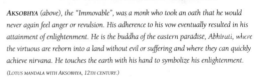

AKSOBHYA (above), the "Immovable", was a monk who took an oath that he would never again feel anger or revulsion. His adherence to his vow eventually resulted in his attainment of enlightenment. He is the buddha of the eastern paradise, Abhirati, where the virtuous are reborn into a land without evil or suffering and where they can quickly achieve nirvana. He touches the earth with his hand to symbolize his enlightenment. (LOTUS MANDALA WITH AKSOBHYA, 12TH CENTURY.)

VAIROCANA (left) is the oldest of the Dhyanibuddhas. His name means "Coming from the Sun", and he was at one time identified with the Adibuddha. He is often depicted clasping his hands in the gesture of supreme wisdom. The great monument of Borobodur, in Java, is itself a mandala, designed in concentric circles and squares with four open entrances. A long series of stone reliefs depicting the Buddha's life story is designed to aid meditation. (RELIEF OF BUDDHA MAHAVAIROCANA AT BOROBODUR, JAVA, 9TH CENTURY.)

THE MANDALA (left) has a fixed, symbolic format. It has an outer ring of flames, protecting the area within, and burning away the impurities of the onlooker. A ring of Vajras indicates the indestructability of enlightenment, and lotus petals show the nature of the Pure Land. Within the circles is a palace, with four walls and four open gates, symbolizing the whole world. At the centre sits a presiding deity, with whom the meditator attempts to identify. (SAMVARA MANDALA, TIBET.)

405

SITA (left) and Lakshmana, Rama's half-brother, watch the monkey god Hanuman worshipping Rama.

SITA (right) finds Rama among the lotus blooms. (PAINTING BY WARWICK GOBLE.)

SHRI see *LAKSHMI*.

SISUPALA see *RAVANA*.

SITA appears in the Veda, the sacred knowledge of the Hindus, as a goddess who rules over agriculture and vegetation and is the wife of the war god *INDRA*. However, according to the Hindu epic, the *Ramayana*, she is the wife of *RAMA*, an *AVATAR* of the great god *VISHNU*, and the daughter of King Janaka.

Rama won Sita as his wife after proving his worth by stringing a miraculous bow, which the god *SHIVA* had given to the king. *RAVANA*, the demon king of *LANKA*, later abducted Sita and took her to his kingdom.

According to one version of the myth, when Rama finally reclaimed his wife, he suspected her of having committed adultery with the demon. Sita proved her innocence and was immediately swallowed by the earth, her mother. Shortly afterwards, Rama drowned. In another version of the traditional tale, Sita demonstrated her innocence by throwing herself on to a funeral pyre, which left her unscathed. The goddess is believed to embody all the virtues of an ideal wife: chaste and devout.

SKANDA see *KARTTIKEYA*.

SOMA, according to Hindu mythology, is the vital life force in all living beings. A plant, as well as the state of ecstasy induced by the sacred drink extracted from the plant, it played a central role in Vedic sacrificial rituals.

Soma was regarded as a deity, and one entire book of the ten that comprise the *Rig Veda*, the sacred Hindu hymns, is devoted to his glory. After swallowing the juice, the war god *INDRA* grew so vast that he filled heaven and earth. It was said to be the power of Soma that enabled Indra to overcome the monstrous snake *VRITRA* and to make the sun rise. In due course, Soma developed into the moon god. The source of water, he was associated with fertility and the powers of creation.

Sometimes regarded as the father of the gods, Soma was married to the daughters of *DAKSHA*, a lord of creation. One myth tells how Daksha believed that Soma was showing one of his daughters preference over the others, and so sentenced the moon to death by consumption. However, Daksha's other daughters intervened, causing Soma's punishment to be only periodic rather than eternal. According to another traditional myth, the waxing and waning of the moon is due to the gods'

SITA before Rama – her husband and an incarnation of Vishnu. Lakshmana waves a fan. (ILLUSTRATION BY J. HIGGINBOTHAM, 1864.)

gradual consumption of the Soma it contains. Soma is the equivalent of the ancient Iranian Haoma. Soma can appear as either a bull or a bird.

SUDAPANI see *DHANVANTARI*.

SUMERU see *MERU*.

SURABHI see *AMRITA*.

SURYA, the sun god, was one of the most important deities in the Veda, the sacred knowledge of the Hindus. His father was either the sky god Dyaus or the warrior god *INDRA*.

Sometimes, however, Surya is said to form a trinity with Indra and the fire god *AGNI*, who are regarded as his brothers. His mother is *ADITI*, the mother goddess. According to the *Rig Veda*, the sacred Hindu hymns, Aditi had eight sons known as the *ADITYAS*. She threw one of her offspring, the sun, away from her, possibly because she did not want to be associated with its burning heat. Another myth tells how Surya arose from the eye of a great giant, *PURUSHA*.

Surya has golden hair and golden arms, although sometimes he is represented as dark red in colour. His chariot is drawn by a team of horses and he holds a lotus flower in his hands. His symbol is

the swastika, which was widely used throughout the ancient world as a symbol of the sun.

Surya's scorching heat was so intense that his wife Sanjna became exhausted and left him. Before abandoning the god, she persuaded her handmaid to take her place. Surya went in search of Sanjna and found her in the forest in the form of a mare. The god transformed himself into a horse, and the couple produced the warrior Revanta and the two ASVINS. The Asvins are golden youths who act as messengers of the dawn.

Eventually, Sanjna's father cut off some of Surya's brightness so that Sanjna was able to bear his heat. Surya's shavings fell to earth, where they were made into weapons for the gods.

In the *Brahmapuranas*, sacred writings dating from the fourth century AD, Surya is attributed with 12 "splendours" and given 12 names of distinct deities including INDRA, VISHNU, VARUNA and MITRA. Surya himself is said to be "the supreme spirit who, by means of these splendours, permeates the universe and radiates as far as the secret soul of men."

SURYA (left), the sun god in Hindu mythology. (LIMESTONE VOTIVE IMAGE FROM THE SUN TEMPLE AT KONARAK, ORISSA, 11TH CENTURY.)

SURYA (below), the Hindu sun god, drives his chariot across the sky. (ILLUSTRATION BY J. HIGGINBOTHAM, 1864.)

T

TAKSHAKA, according to Hindu mythology, was king of the *NAGAS*, the semi-divine serpents. He ruled over a glorious city in the underworld. One myth tells how King Parikchit, when out hunting, mistakenly insulted a hermit who had taken a vow of silence. The hermit's son cursed the king, saying that within a week the snake Takshaka would burn and kill him with his poison. The king decided to protect himself by building a palace on top of a column in the middle of a lake. Takshaka transformed an army of serpents into monks and sent them to the king with gifts. Among the gifts, the king found a strange insect. He was so relieved that Takshaka had spared him that he boasted to his courtiers that, having no fear of death, he dared to put the insect on his neck. Immediately, the insect turned into Takshaka. The serpent bound the king in his massive coils and uttered a tremendous roar, whereupon the king's courtiers burst into tears and fled. Meanwhile,

Takshaka rose high into the air, king Parikchit fell down dead, and his palace burst into flames.

According to another tale, Takshaka coveted some beautiful jewels, which belonged to the queen, wife of King Parikchit's son. The queen decided to give the jewels to the wife of a tutor and asked Utanka, one of the tutor's students, to take them to her. On the journey, Utanka stopped to wash. Immediately, a beggar stole the jewels and ran off with them. Utanka pursued the beggar, but when he finally caught hold of him, the man turned into the serpent Takshaka, slid into a hole in the ground, and hid in his palace.

The god *INDRA* saw Utanka's distress and sent a thunderbolt down to earth. The bolt split the ground open, allowing Utanka to continue pursuing the thief. Beneath the earth, Utanka discovered a glorious kingdom filled with beautiful palaces and temples. He chanted a hymn of praise to the nagas, but the snakes remained

TARA (above) as the Green Tara, is regarded as the saviour of Tibet, and holds the blue lotus of compassion in each hand. (MONGOLIA, 19TH CENTURY.)

unmoved. Utanka then began to praise Indra. Flattered, Indra again offered to help the student, whose horse burst into flames and engulfed the nagas' kingdom in smoke. Terrified, Takshaka returned the jewels to Utanka. At long last, riding Indra's horse, Utanka arrived at the appointed place to deliver the jewels to his tutor's wife.

TARA is one of Tibetan Buddhism's most popular deities. Her name means both "She Who Delivers" and "Star". She is regarded as an emanation of the *BODHISATTVA AVALOKITESHVARA* and is said to have been born from a lotus floating in one of his tears in order to help him in his work. According to another account, Tara was born in a beam of blue light

TARA (left), in her white form, is the symbol of transcendent knowledge.

TARA (right), the patron goddess of Tibet, has 21 forms, including that of the Green Tara, who embodies the feminine aspect of compassion.

which shone from one of Avalokiteshvara's eyes. She embodies the feminine aspect of compassion and incorporates the essence of the goddess. As a result, her name is sometimes applied to other female deities.

The earliest representations of the goddess date from the sixth century AD, when Tara came to be regarded as the *SHAKTI*, or sometimes the wife, of Avalokiteshvara. In Tibet, where her cult spread widely in the 11th century, it was said that the goddess was reincarnated in every virtuous woman. Since then she has been worshipped widely as a personal deity. There are 21 different forms of Tara, each of which has its own colour, posture and attributes, and they all can appear to be either peaceful or wrathful.

The most common forms are Green Tara and White Tara. In Tibet, the White Tara is often said to be a form of the Green Tara. She is believed to be a form of *SARASVATI*, the wife of *BRAHMA*. The Green Tara, said to be the original Tara, holds a blue lotus in each hand to signify her compassion. The consorts of the seventh-century Tibetan king Songtsen Gampo are said to have been embodiments of these two Taras. When red, yellow or blue, Tara is said to be in a menacing mood, whereas when green or white she is said to be gentle and loving. Tibetan Buddhists believe that their ancestors are

Avalokiteshvara in the form of a monkey and Tara (sGrol-ma) in the form of a rock ogress.

TATHAGATAS see *THE DHYANI-BUDDHAS*.

THE TIRTHANKARAS are the ancient "Ford-makers" of Jainism, who taught the Jain doctrine. These leaders, through their own ascetic observances, succeeded in finding a way of escaping the continual round of death and rebirth, and were thus able to show others the path to enlightenment.

According to Jain belief, there are ten regions of the universe, in each of which 24 tirthankaras appear in each of the three ages – past, present and future. Since Jains do not believe in a creator god, their mythology concentrates on the figures of these tirthankaras, who have become objects of worship. Tirthankaras are usually depicted naked, each with his own characteristic colour and posture, but otherwise identical.

In the current age, the first tirthankara was Rishabha, who is usually said to be the founder of Jainism. At his birth, the great warrior god *INDRA* appeared in order to welcome the child into the world. Rishabha taught human beings how to cultivate the land, how to ply different trades and how to execute the arts. He also organized people into three castes. He then left worldly affairs and became a monk. After meditating for six months, Rishabha achieved enlightenment and finally entered nirvana. 21 tirthankaras followed Rishabha, ending with Neminatha, a cousin of *KRISHNA*.

The twenty-third tirthankara, Parshva, appeared 84,000 years after Neminatha's death. Before being born, Parshva lived in heaven as the god Indra. In order to descend to earth, he entered the womb of Queen Vama. As a child, Parshva disdained worldly life and finally withdrew to live in the forest

as a recluse. Eventually, he learned how to achieve liberation from the world and from then onwards he passed on his knowledge to his followers. When he died, at the age of 100, his soul entered nirvana. His death occurred 246 years before the birth of Mahavira, the twenty-fourth Tirthankara.

Mahavira, or the "Great Hero" was also known as Vardhamana. One night, he entered the womb of Devananda, the wife of a brahman. That same night, Devananda saw 14 apparitions, all of favourable omen – an elephant, a bull, a lion, the goddess Shri, or *LAKSHMI*, a garland, the moon, the sun, a standard, a vase, a lake of lotuses, the ocean, a heavenly dwelling, a heap of jewels and a flame.

Devananda's husband was delighted by this omen, as he felt sure it meant that he would father a wise and learned son. However, the

THE TIRTHANKARA Malli, the nineteenth, was a woman according to one Jain tradition. Tirthankaras are portrayed with downcast eyes, to indicate their detachment. (CHAUHAN SCULPTURE, 11TH CENTURY.)

king of the gods decided that he would prefer Trisala, the wife of Siddhartha, a kshatriya (member of the warrior caste) to bear the child, and so the embryo was transferred. Trisala also witnessed 14 splendid apparitions before the birth.

When Mahavira was born, the gods rejoiced and the demons threw gifts. As a youth, Mahavira married Yasoda, but at the age of 30, he gave away his wealth and withdrew from the world. After 12 years of austerity, he achieved enlightenment. When Mahavira died, his soul ascended to nirvana. Jainism still requires its followers to practise austerity for at least 12 years.

TRANSCENDENT BUDDHAS
see *DHYANIBUDDHAS*.

TUSHITA is the Buddhist heaven inhabited by contented or joyful gods. It is home to all the buddhas who need to be born on earth only once more, and is thus the abode of *MAITREYA*, the future buddha. Before his final incarnation, *GAUTAMA BUDDHA* lived in the Tushita heaven as a *BODHISATTVA*. From there, he descended to earth to enter the right side of Queen *MAYA*, his mother. In the Tushita heaven, one day corresponds to 400 years of human life.

UPULVAN is the highest of the four great gods in the Singhalese pantheon. His name means the "Water-lily Coloured One". He is said to have been the only god who remained faithful to *GAUTAMA BUDDHA* during his battle with the demon *MARA*.

URVASI see *APSARAS*.

USHA see *ANIRUDDHA*.

USHAS, the dawn, is the daughter of *PRITHIVI*, the earth goddess of Hindu mythology. Her father is usually said to be the sky god Dyaus and her lover *SURYA*, the sun god. Sometimes, however, the fire god *AGNI* is regarded as her lover, and she herself is said to be the mother of the sun. According to another tradition, Ushas was the daughter of *PRAJAPATI*, the lord or master of created beings. When the god attempted to commit incest with her, Ushas turned into a deer in order to escape his advances.

Ushas is the bringer of life in all its richness. She drives away the dark but is the source of aging. She herself is born each morning, yet because she exists for ever, she is regarded as old. It is said that through the light provided by Ushas, human beings can find their way towards the truth. Each morning, like a good housewife, she

wakes all living beings and directs them towards their work. The gods implore her to leave the wicked asleep and wake only the good. In the *Rig Veda*, the ancient sacred hymns, Ushas is depicted as a bride dressed in rose-coloured garments and a golden veil. She is sometimes described as a dancing girl, covered with jewels, or as a beautiful young woman who is stepping out of her bath. The goddess drives a carriage pulled by rosy-hued cows or horses, who represent the morning clouds.

VAIROCANA, according to Hindu mythology, was an *ASURA*, the son of Prahlada, who became king of the *DAITYAS*. He was the father of Bali, who was overcome by *VISHNU* in his incarnation as a dwarf.

One account tells how, together with *INDRA*, Vairocana attempted to discover Atman, or the "Self". The gods sent Indra and Vairocana to ask *PRAJAPATI* to help them in their quest, whereupon Prajapati told them, "That which is reflected in the eye, that is the Self." Vairocana

VAIROCANA is the principal of the five Dhyanibuddhas, or "Great Buddhas of Wisdom". (TIBET, 15TH CENTURY.)

and Indra then asked whether that which was reflected in the water was the Self. Prajapati confirmed their suspicion and told them to look at themselves in the water. He added that they should let him know if there was anything they failed to understand. Vairocana decided that he now knew the Self, and returned to the asuras. Indra looked at himself in the water but was troubled by numerous questions which he put to Prajapati. Eventually, Indra achieved absolute certainty about the Self and became fully enlightened.

Vairocana appears in Buddhist teaching as the principal of the five DHYANIBUDDHAS, or the "Great Buddhas of Wisdom". He is said to be the personification of the "Absolute" and is sometimes regarded as a type of ADIBUDDHA, or primordial Buddha. In Tibet, the snow lion is regarded as Vairocana's mount. His colour is white, and he is often shown holding a disc. Vairocana is sometimes said to have introduced humankind to the Yogacara school of Mahayana, or "Great Vehicle" Buddhism, which teaches that everything is "mind only" and that the disciple's aim is to achieve mystical union with the divine. (See also DHYANIBUDDHAS)

VAISHRAVANA see GUARDIAN KINGS.

THE VAJRA, or Vajrakila, is a deified spike, sometimes known as a "Thunderbolt Sceptre", which is believed to embody a powerful god and is said to be capable of dispelling evil forces. It is mainly employed by Tantric Buddhists in Tibet. The Vajra originated in India, where the thunderbolt sceptre is the favourite weapon of INDRA.

VAJRAVARAHI is regarded as an important Buddhist deity in both Tibet and Nepal. Her name means "Diamond Sow", and she is represented with the head of a pig. Her attributes are a thunderbolt, a skull and a club.

VAMANA see AVATARS.

VARAHA see AVATARS.

VARUNA appears in the *Rig Veda*, an ancient collection of sacred Hindu hymns, as a sky god. He symbolized the heavens and lived in his palace high above the realm in which INDRA operated. In one sense, then, he was more important than Indra, but because he was more remote, the part he played was of less consequence. He could see everything going on in the world and surveyed the affairs of human beings, reading their secret thoughts and sending his messengers out to oversee their activities. Varuna was omnipresent and knew both the past and the future. Above all, he was concerned with the moral order. He presided over oaths and he initiated and sustained the *rta* or order, which was believed to govern both nature and society, and which human beings had to obey. Those who failed to follow the *rta* would be bound with Varuna's noose. However, the god had a reputation for gentleness and could undo sin easily. Varuna was sometimes said to have created the sun; at other times, the sun was said to be his eye. Later, he came to be seen as lord of the night and as the god of water, ruler of the rivers and seas. The wind was his breath,

VARUNA (left) was represented riding a sea monster and holding the noose he used to bind the disobedient. (STONE, 8TH CENTURY.)

THE VAJRA, or "Thunderbolt Sceptre", is carried by the god Indra, the Hindu god of weather, mounted on Airavata.

and the stars his eyes. He was linked with the moon, and presided over the care of SOMA, the sacred drink. He also shared with YAMA, the first person who died, the title of "King of the Dead". Sometimes regarded as one of the ADITYAS and the twin brother of MITRA, Varuna is also known as "King of the Snakes".

VASUDEV see KRISHNA.

VASUKI see NAGAS.

VAYU appears in the *Veda*. He is god of the winds and sometimes shares a chariot with INDRA. He is said to have been born from the breath of PURUSHA, the original being or world giant.

According to one myth, Vayu was responsible for creating the island of LANKA, now known as Sri Lanka. Narada, a sage or RISHI, challenged Vayu, who was known for his unstable temper, to break off the summit of Mount MERU. GARUDA, the mythical bird, protected the mountain, but one day, in the bird's absence, Vayu succeeded in his efforts. He immediately threw the mountain peak into the sea where it became the island of Lanka.

THE LIFE OF THE BUDDHA

BEFORE HE ACHIEVED enlightenment, the Buddha had lived through a long series of existences as a bodhisattva, striving to be generous and moral, to shun possessions and to gain insight. He was eventually reborn in the Tushita heaven, the domain of those who need be born only once more, where he prepared for his final miraculous birth as Siddharta Gautama. King Snddhodana, his father, had been told in a prophecy that if his son were to be king, he must be prevented from seeing the miseries of life. So, Siddharta enjoyed a splendid and carefree life in three

palaces, surrounded by guards to stop him from looking out. He married Yasodhara and had a son, Rahula. But at about the age of 30, he ventured out of his palaces and encountered the "Four Sights": old age, disease, death and an ascetic looking for a way to transcend suffering. Siddharta resolved to do the same and left his royal existence behind.

QUEEN MAYA (above), the Buddha's mother, dreamed on the night of his conception that an elephant laid a lotus blossom in her womb while the whole of nature shook with joy. At his birth, the Buddha emerged from his mother's side while she rested by a tree in a garden. He began to walk immediately, and lotus flowers sprang up each time his feet touched the ground. With seven symbolic steps, one in each of the cardinal directions, he took possession of the world and declared that there would be no more rebirth for him. (SCENES FROM BUDDHA'S LIFE BY MULGANDHA VIGARA.)

GAUTAMA BUDDHA (left), having left behind his early life of absolute luxury, endured six years of strict austerities which reduced him to little more than a skeleton. Eventually, however, he realized that this way of life would do nothing to end human suffering and that he needed to achieve a middle way. On the bank of the river Nairanjana, a woman called Sujata mistook him for a god and made him an offering of rice milk, which he accepted. Knowing now that his enlightenment was near, he divided the milk into 49 mouthfuls, one for each day he would spend in contemplation, striving to see things as they really are. (FROM A PAINTING BY ABANINDRO NATH TAGORE.)

GAUTAMA BUDDHA (left) spent the 45 years following his enlightenment wandering and preaching the truths he had learnt. He taught everywhere he went, talking to everyone from kings to beggars, and lived by begging himself. He converted all those he met and performed many miracles, and his following increased in number. A community of Buddhist monks, the Sangha, grew up. (THE BUDDHA BEING OFFERED HERBS, TIBETAN, 18TH CENTURY.)

ANANDA (below), the Buddha's first cousin and devoted attendant, was one of his disciples who attained enlightenment in his presence. Ananda recited the Buddha's teachings at the first Buddhist council. He could explain all 60,000 words and was known as the "Treasurer of the Teachings". He was also responsible for encouraging women to join the Sangha, and established an order of nuns. (BURMESE SHRINE.)

GAUTAMA BUDDHA (above) sat under the Bodhi tree in Bodh Gaya for 49 days, and achieved enlightenment when his knowledge was crystallized into the "Four Noble Truths": that life is full of suffering, that suffering depends on craving, that suffering can be ended, that the way to end it is to follow the eightfold path: right view, right thought, right speech, right action, right livelihood, right effort, right mindfulness and right concentration. His initial response was to remain where he was, but he was persuaded by the god Brahma to preach the truth he had discovered to his growing band of disciples.

THE VIDYARAJAS are Buddhism's semi-divine kings of mystical knowledge. They symbolize the power which the five DHYANIBUDDHAS, "Great Buddhas of Wisdom", exert over the passions and forces of evil. They are sometimes regarded as wrathful emanations of the Dhyanibuddhas, or as the energy which the adept assumes on meeting obstacles.

In India and the Hindu pantheon, the Vidyarajas are represented by the Bhairavas, the "Terrifying Ones", and the Krodharajas, or "Kings of Wrath", who eat flesh. The five great Vidyarajas correspond to the five Dhyanibuddhas, while other Vidyarajas correspond to the BODHISATTVAS. Acalanatha corresponds to the Dhyanibuddha VAIROCANA, Trailokyavijaya corresponds to AKSOBHYA, Kundali corresponds to RATNASAMBHAVA, YAMANTAKA corresponds to AMITABHA, and Vajrayaksa or Vajrapani corresponds to AMOGHASIDDHI.

VINATA see GARUDA.

VISHNU is one of the most important gods of Hinduism and the most widely worshipped. Together with SHIVA and BRAHMA, he belongs to the triad of great gods known as the Trimurti. The preserver of the world, Vishnu is majestic and at times terrifying. On the whole, however, he is a benevolent deity and far less frightening than Shiva. Vishnu's devotees, the Vaishnavas, regard him as the supreme god: one of his many epithets is the "Highest God". Brahman, the Hindu concept of the "Absolute" or supreme reality, is sometimes depicted as Vishnu.

According to one myth, a lotus flower emerged from Vishnu's navel on the end of a long stalk held by VAYU, the vital force and god of the winds. Seated in the centre of the flower was Brahma, who subsequently proceeded with the act of creation.

VISHNU sits enthroned on the coils of the world snake Ananta or Sesha, on which he sleeps during the intervals between Brahma's successive creations. He holds a shell, mace, disc and lotus.
(IVORY STATUETTE.)

Vishnu's main function is to ensure the triumph of good over evil. In the *Rig Veda*, the ancient sacred hymns of Hinduism, Vishnu appears as only a minor deity. He seems to have originated as a solar god, and in his manifestation as the sun, he was said to be able to traverse the cosmos in only three steps, an act probably intended to symbolize the god measuring out the universe, making it habitable for gods and humans. Later, Vishnu began to be associated with other figures, including a fish and a dwarf. This association developed into the concept of Vishnu's incarnations, known as AVATARS, or "descents". Vishnu appears in these different guises in order to combat demons and to restore divine order when the cosmos is threatened. The most important of Vishnu's avatars are the hero, RAMA, and the god, KRISHNA. Within Hinduism, GAUTAMA BUDDHA also came to be regarded as one of the great god's incarnations.

In his incarnation as the fish Matsya, Vishnu saved MANU, the first man, from a great flood. The tale tells how Manu found a tiny fish, which begged him to rescue it from the other fish, which were trying to eat it. Manu took the fish home and kept it in a pot. Soon the fish grew too big for the pot, so Manu put it into a pond. Matsya then grew too big for the pond, so Manu took it to the ocean.

As Manu released the fish into the waters, Matsya turned and warned him that there was to be a great flood, which would drown the whole world. He advised Manu to save himself by building a boat. The floods arrived and Manu took shelter in his boat. Fierce waves and winds attacked the boat, and Matsya again appeared, this time as a gigantic fish. Matsya towed the boat behind him for several years until he reached Mount Hemavat, the summit of which remained above the waters. Manu moored the boat to the mountain and awaited the end of the flood. Matsya then announced that he was in fact Vishnu and that he had saved Manu so that he could repopulate the world.

In his incarnation as the dwarf Vamana, Vishnu saved the world from the demon Bali. He persuaded Bali to give him as much land as he could cover in three strides. As soon as Bali granted his request, Vishnu was transformed into a giant. In two strides, he crossed the universe, which he returned to the gods. He then turned to the demon and insisted that he be allowed to take a third step, as promised. Bali offered Vishnu his head to stand upon and, in recognition of this honourable behaviour, Vishnu gave the demon the underworld to rule as his kingdom.

In the intervals between Brahma's successive creations, Vishnu is believed to lie asleep on the cosmic waters, on top of the many-headed world snake Ananta or Sesha. During his sleep, he slowly develops into another avatar, who will appear in the impending cycle of creation.

Vishnu is usually depicted as a beautiful young man, blue in colour and with four arms. His attributes include the club, associated with the power of knowledge; a conch shell, associated with the origins of existence; a wheel, associated with the powers of creation and destruction; and the lotus, which is associated with the sun and with the tree of life that springs from Vishnu's navel. His mount is the mythical bird GARUDA.

The god is also identified with the cosmic pillar, the centre of the universe which was believed to support the heavens. His consort is LAKSHMI, the goddess of wealth and good fortune. (See also THE AVATARS OF VISHNU)

VISHVAKARMA see LANKA.

VIVASVAT see YAMA.

VRINDA see ASURAS.

VRITRA was the fearsome serpent of Hindu mythology whom the great god INDRA destroyed. He embodied the dark and unproductive forces of nature, and deprived humanity of the light of knowledge. A powerful Brahman called Tvashtri was determined to overthrow Indra. He fathered a son, Trisiras, whom he strengthened with his own powers. The son had three heads; he read the Veda with

his first head, he fed himself with the second head and he used his third head for surveying the world. He was exceedingly pious, and Indra became worried as his power seemed to increase day after day. Indra sent beautiful young women to seduce Trisiras, but nothing tempted him from his path of asceticism. Eventually, Indra decided to kill him and struck him down with his thunderbolt. However, even then the boy continued to radiate such a splendid light over the entire world that Indra's fears were unallayed.

Tvashtri, the boy's father, determined to avenge the death of his son and created a huge and terrifying demon called Vritra. The demon challenged Indra to a battle, and a bloody and terrifying onslaught ensued. Eventually,

VISHNU, attended by his consort, Lakshmi, sleeps on the world snake, Sesha, while Brahma, the creator, emerges from the lotus growing from Vishnu's navel. (MINIATURE, RAJASTHAN, 18TH CENTURY.)

VISHNU, the supreme cosmic principle, forms a triad of great gods with Brahma and Shiva. (STONE, 10TH CENTURY.)

Vritra swallowed the god. The assembly of deities was horrified and decided to make the demon open his mouth. As soon as Vritra did so, Indra jumped out, and the battle began again.

Eventually, a great RISHI, or sage, was consulted and, with the help of VISHNU, a truce was agreed upon. Vritra promised to make peace, provided that Indra never attacked him with a weapon of wood, stone or iron, nor with anything wet or dry, nor during the night or day. Indra agreed, but he continued to plot his revenge on the demon.

At sunset one evening he saw a pillar of foam, neither wet nor dry nor wood, stone, nor iron, arising from the sea. He took the pillar and threw it at Vritra, who immediately fell dead. After slaying the demon, Indra liberated the waters, the sun, the sky and the dawn.

Y

THE YAKSHAS, according to Hindu mythology, are followers of the god of riches, Kuvera. They live in the Himalayas and guard hidden treasure. The yakshas are usually depicted with short limbs and pot bellies. They are often benign, and are worshipped as protective spirits and bringers of fertility. Female yakshas are known as yakshis. In Buddhism, the yakshas are sometimes wild creatures who haunt lonely places and show hostility towards people by disturbing their meditations.

In Tibet, the yakshas are known as gnod-sbyin. Regarded as semi-divine beings, they resemble nature

YAKSHAS (left) are Hindu nature spirits. The female spirits, yakshis, though graceful, can be spiteful and sometimes eat children. (SANDSTONE BRACKET, 2ND CENTURY AD.)

spirits and protect Buddha and the Buddhist law. According to one tradition, Tibet was originally ruled over by a succession of beings, the first of whom were the black and warlike gnod-sbyin.

YAMA appears in the *Rig Veda*, the ancient sacred hymns of Hinduism. He is the guardian of hell and is regarded as "King of the Dead". A fierce deity, he is usually said to be the son of Vivasvat, the sun, and the brother of MANU, the only survivor of the great flood. Yama's companion and sister was Yamuna, or Yami.

The brother and sister are sometimes said to have been the first human couple, and Yama to have been the first man who died. According to one story, Yama set out to explore the world and discovered a path to heaven. As a result, mortality was introduced to the world. As the guardian of the dead, Yama was originally regarded as a friendly deity. However, by the time of the *Brahmanas*, the Hindu texts, which were commentaries on the Veda, or "Sacred Knowledge", Yama had become a sinister and destructive force. He developed into the terrifying punisher of human beings, and was depicted armed with a noose and a mace, green in colour, and with two four-eyed dogs as companions. These dogs would sometimes wander the world, gathering together the souls of the dying.

When the soul leaves the body, it is said to cross the river Vaitarani to the land of the dead, where it proceeds towards the judgment room. There, an account of the

YAMA (right) with Naciketas, a man to whom Yama taught the secret of immortality. Yama is regarded as the guardian of hell and "King of the Dead".

soul's deeds is read out, whereupon Yama makes his judgment. The soul will be sent either to a paradise, to one of many hells, or back to the world of the living, where it will be reborn.

One myth tells how the devoted Savitri persuaded Yama to give her back her husband Satyavan. Yama, impressed by her love, offered to grant her a wish as long as she did not ask him to restore Satyavan to life. She agreed, but wished for more sons fathered by her husband, so Yama had to send him back to keep his promise.

In Buddhist mythology, Yama is the ruler of the hells. Originally he was a king of Vaishali, a city in north-eastern India. During a ferocious battle, the king wished that he was the ruler of hell and was reborn as Yama. He was accompanied to hell by his eight generals and 80,000 soldiers. There, he has molten copper poured into his mouth three times a day. The punishment will last until all Yama's deeds have been atoned for. In the meantime, he inflicts disease and old age on humans, to prevent them from living immoral lives.

Yama's sister, Yami, is said to rule over the females in hell. In Tibetan Buddhism, Yama is often shown accompanied by Yami and is sometimes regarded as one of the DHARMAPALAS, or "Protectors of the Teaching".

YAMA with his shakti, Yami, goddess of death. They stand in the posture of Yab-Yum on Yama's attendant animal, a black buffalo. Yama is a guardian of the south, the direction associated with the dead.

YAMANTAKA, or "He Who Puts an End to Yama", is one of Buddhism's VIDYARAJAS, or kings of mystical knowledge. He conquers YAMA, god of the dead, and is sometimes shown trampling him. A wrathful manifestation of the buddha AKSOBHYA, he is one of the BODHISATTVAS who welcome the faithful into Aksobhya's paradise. He is also regarded as a DHARMAPALA, or "Protector of the Teaching", and is said to fight pain.

Yamantaka is often shown with six arms and legs as well as six horribly contorted faces, each with three eyes. He is usually represented seated on a white cow, although he sometimes rests on a rock. His body is coloured black, dark blue or green, and he is surrounded by flames. In Tibet, he is sometimes shown holding an axe and a skull, and he may wear a tiara of skulls, a belt of skulls and carry a human corpse.

YAMI; YAMUNA see YAMA.

YASHODA see KRISHNA.

THE YIDAMS are the tutelary deities of Tibet. There are numerous yidams since each deity in the Tibetan pantheon can be adopted

YAMANTAKA is a wrathful guardian deity of Tibetan Buddhism, depicted in the posture of embrace, or Yab-Yum, with his shakti, Vidyadhara.

as a tutelary god. Their name means "Firm Mind". The yidams are invoked by people for protection, but they are more usually regarded as deities who can help in an individual's transformation. They are nearly always depicted with their SHAKTI, their corresponding female energies, and are usually coloured blue. The male yidams are divided into bhagavats, dakas and herukas, whereas the female yidams are divided into bhagavatis and DAKINIS.

THE YUGAS are Hinduism's cycles, or ages of the world. Each yuga lasts for thousands, even millions, of years.

The yugas decline in length through the cycle, reflecting the decline in righteousness. The Krita Yuga, lasting 1,728,000 human years, was the golden age, when there were no gods, demons or diseases and when human beings were saints. The Treta Yuga lasted 1,296,000 years and was the age when sacrifices began and people became less virtuous. The Dwapara Yuga was a decadent age, lasting 864,000 years, when virtue lessened even more and desire, disease and disasters entered the world. The Kali Yuga, 432,000 years long, is the degenerate age, when only a quarter of virtue remains and people have sunk into wickedness. The Kali Yuga is the age in which we are currently living.

More than four million human years make up a Maha Yuga, or great age, and one Maha Yuga equals a day and a night in the life of Brahma. Each Maha Yuga is preceded and followed by periods of twilight, which last a tenth of the length of a Maha Yuga. During this time, BRAHMA sleeps.

ZHANG ZHUNG see GSHEN-RAB.

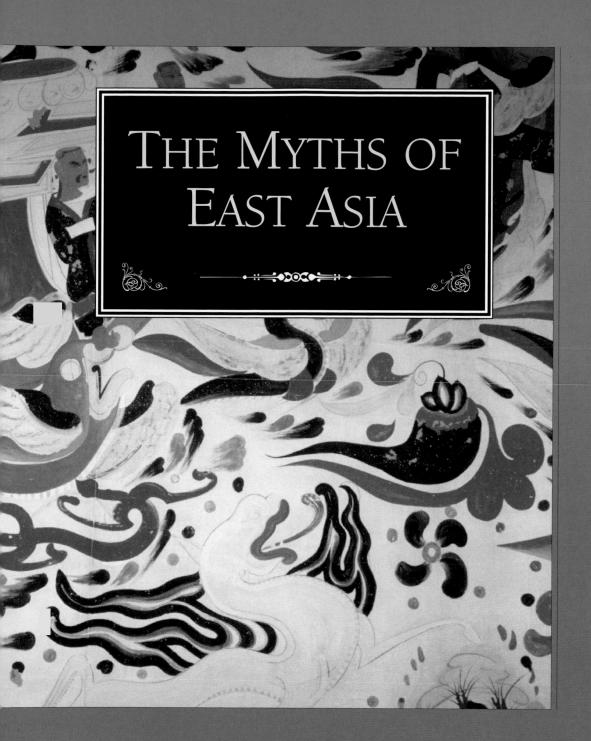

THE MYTHS OF
EAST ASIA

INTRODUCTION

THE GREAT WORLD religions founded in West and Central Asia gradually spread eastwards until they encountered the gods and goddesses of the Far East. To a greater or lesser extent, Hinduism, Buddhism and Islam all influenced the indigenous beliefs of East and South-east Asia. However, the host countries tended to make the encroaching deities their own, embracing them within their own mythologies by a process of adaptation and assimilation.

China, the so-called "Mother Civilization of East Asia", did not view the incoming gods and goddesses as a threat. The immensely stable structure of Chinese society meant that, rather than feeling threatened by outside beliefs, the Chinese were able to modify and absorb outside influences while maintaining their own culture.

China has its origins in the second millennium BC, when the Shang kings founded a state which formed the basis for all subsequent development. During the ancient Shang dynasty, ancestor worship was already in evidence, and numerous gods were also venerated, including the great Shang Di. Worshipped as the ancestor of the dynasty, Shang Di came to have an important role in Chinese religious thought. The Zhou invaders, who overthrew the Shang dynasty in about 1050BC, worshipped a deity known as Tian, or "Heaven".

In the sixth century BC, Confucianism emerged, although it was not until the Han dynasty (206BC–AD220) that it became the philosophy of the state. Founded by Master Kong (551–479BC), Confucianism propounded a belief in a highly structured society and stressed the importance of the bonds of family life. Master Kong remained, however, noncommittal about the existence of supernatural beings.

Whereas Confucianism drew its adherents from all social classes, Daoism, which emerged at about the same time, tended to appeal to the underprivileged. Daoists seek out the Dao, or "Way", a type of divine

BUDDHA was widely venerated in China, especially during the Tang dynasty between the seventh and ninth centuries AD. Buddhism offered a consoling message about the transience of suffering and the possibility of eventual salvation. (BUDDHA PREACHING, BANNER FROM DUNUANG CAVES, CHINA, 8TH CENTURY AD.)

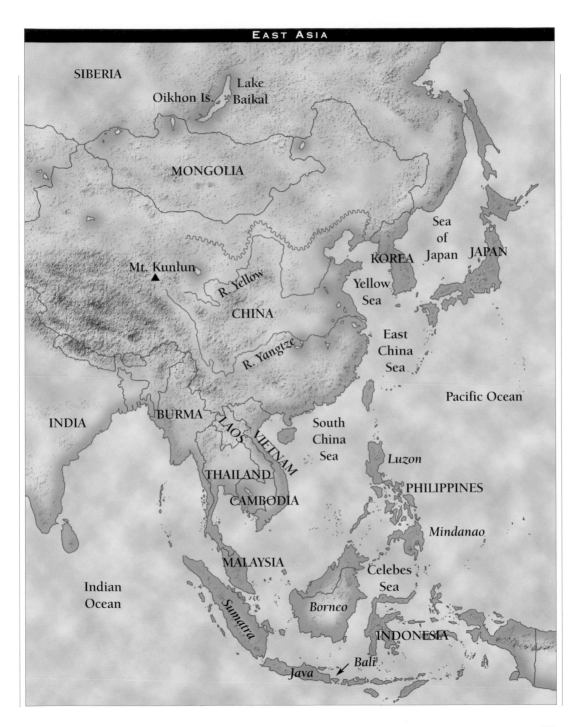

EAST ASIA

SIBERIA

Oikhon Is.

Lake
Baikal

MONGOLIA

Sea
of
Japan   JAPAN

KOREA

Mt. Kunlun

R. Yellow

Yellow
Sea

CHINA

East
China
Sea

R. Yangtze

Pacific Ocean

INDIA

BURMA

LAOS

VIETNAM

South
China
Sea

Luzon

THAILAND

PHILIPPINES

CAMBODIA

Mindanao

MALAYSIA

Celebes
Sea

Indian
Ocean

Sumatra

Borneo

INDONESIA

Java

Bali

JAPAN

Hokkaido

Sea of
Japan

Sado Is.

Honshu

Oki Is.

Izumo

JAPAN

Kyoto

Inland
Sea

Yamato

Edo (Tokyo)

Ise

Kyushu

Shikoku

Pacific
Ocean

principle underlying nature. Its followers aim to achieve harmony with the principle by stilling and emptying the mind. During the first millennium AD, Daoism developed an elaborate pantheon of gods and goddesses. Its principal deity was the "Jade Emperor", whose heaven, modelled on that of the earthly emperor, contained numerous ministries and officials.

Around the beginning of the Christian era, Buddhism entered China, introduced by Buddhist monks travelling along the ancient trade route, known as the Silk Road, from India and Central Asia. It was a peaceful invasion, since Buddhism did not feel it necessary to reject the gods and spirits of popular religion, provided that people realized that only the Buddha could offer true salvation. What made the incursion of Buddhism even smoother was the fact that the incoming religion had similarities with Daoism: both Buddhism and Daoism aimed to control mental processes. As a result, there came to be an interplay between the two faiths after Buddhism's arrival in China.

China had a widespread cultural influence on its neighbouring countries, including Japan. Shinto, the early religion of Japan, took

YU HUANG (below), the "Jade Emperor", was the chief deity of the Daoist pantheon. His supremacy in heaven mirrored that of the emperor on earth, with whom he was said to correspond directly. (CHINESE WALL PAINTING, C. 1325.)

CONFUCIUS is known in the West by the Latin rendering of his name, Kong Fuzi. Benevolence was central to his doctrine, which was adopted by the state during the Han dynasty. (CHINESE DRAWING.)

much of its cosmology, including that of an egg-shaped cosmos, from Chinese sources. However, whereas the Chinese regarded their "Jade Emperor" as a reflection of the earthly emperor, the Japanese claimed that the members of the imperial family were descended from their chief deity, the sun goddess Amaterasu, giving them a divine right to govern. In the sixth century AD, Buddhism entered Japan, spreading from China and Korea. Japan adopted Buddhism and used it to complement Shintoism, so that it still remains unclear whether some deities are Shinto or Buddhist. The overlap of Shinto and Buddhist ideas gave Japanese Buddhism its own distinctive flavour.

Chinese civilization also influenced South-east Asia, in particular Vietnam. However, Burma, Thailand, Cambodia, Laos, peninsular Malaysia and the Indonesian islands of Sumatra, Java and Bali were all affected by the advance of Indian culture, and especially by the cults of the great Hindu gods Vishnu and Shiva. On the island of Bali, Shiva and Buddha were sometimes worshipped as a joint deity.

From the beginning of the 17th century, Islam became the dominant religion of insular South-east Asia, carried there by Muslim traders. However, despite the impact of these major religions, indigenous beliefs persisted. For example, on Bali, where Hinduism is the official religion, mediums still communicate with deities and spirits; among the peoples of Borneo, the indigenous animistic beliefs continue to produce a mythology peopled by ghosts and spirits connected with natural phenomena.

In other areas of East Asia, traditional beliefs have been lost under the force of incoming religions. Many of the shamanic myths of Mongolia were lost after the introduction of Buddhism to the country in the 13th century. In Siberia, shamanism came under threat from Muslim missionaries from the tenth century onwards. However, while Islam won many converts, a reverse process also took place, with certain Central Asian Sufi orders being influenced by shamanism. Later, shamanism declined in the face of missionary activity of the Russian orthodox church in the 19th century and, after the Russian revolution of 1917, Siberian shamans were persecuted by the Communists. Today, however, there are movements to revive shamanism to the level of influence it held in times gone by.

In general, the countries of East Asia have contributed to the already rich mythologies of the religions to which they have become hosts. In China, the goddess of mercy,

SHAMANS of Mongolia perform ritual dances with the use of drums to induce a trance state. These charismatic figures have the power to control spirits and to make journeys out of their bodies to the upper and lower spirit worlds. They are central figures in many communities, combining the functions of priest and doctor. (ILLUSTRATION FROM LE TOUR DU MONDE. C. 1850.)

Guanyin, evolved out of the Indian bodhisattva Avalokiteshvara and became a powerful mother goddess. Amitabha, the buddha of boundless light, became an important deity in both China and Japan. As Omito Fu in China and as Amida in Japan, he came to have an immense impact, in particular on the Japanese mind.

Initially identified with the great Shinto goddess Amaterasu, Amida became the focus of a school of Buddhism that teaches that all of those who call on the Buddha in faith will gain entry to his wondrous paradise. By confidently looking forward to a glorious hereafter, Chinese and Japanese devotees came to view earthly life as simply transitory. The figure of Omito Fu/Amida thus demonstrates the manner in which an incoming deity can both be transformed by and, in turn, come to transform the society in which it makes its home.

A

THE ABAASY, according to the Yakut people of Siberia, are evil supernatural beings who live in the lower world and are ruled over by the malevolent spirit *ULU TOYO'N*. The son of the chief Abaasy is said to have only one eye and iron teeth.

AIZEN-MYOO is regarded as the god of love in popular Japanese belief. He is a deity of both physical and intellectual desire and represents love transformed through the desire for enlightenment. His body is red and he has six arms holding various weapons, three eyes and the head of a lion in his hair. Despite his frightening appearance, he shows great compassion for humankind.

AJYSYT see *ITCHITA*.

AMATERASU is the sun goddess of Japanese mythology and one of the most important deities within the Shinto pantheon. Her full name, Amaterasu-O-Mi-Kami, means "August Person who Makes the Heavens Shine". Amaterasu was brought into being when *IZANAGI*, the male half of the primal couple, washed his face after returning from *YOMI*, the land of the dead. The sun goddess emerged from Izanagi's left eye and the moon god *TSUKIYOMI* from his right. Izanagi told Amaterasu that she should rule the high plains of heaven and gave her his sacred bead necklace.

The storm god *SUSANO-WO*, who had been born from Izanagi's nose, angered his father by saying that, rather than rule over the waters as Izanagi had decreed, he wanted to join his mother *IZANAMI* in Yomi. As a result, Izanagi banished Susano-Wo. Before leaving, Susano-Wo said that he wanted to say goodbye to Amaterasu, his sister. However, Amaterasu suspected that her brother wanted to take her kingdom from her, so she prepared for battle. Arming herself with a bow and two quivers of arrows, she

shook her bow in challenge and stamped the earth beneath her feet. Susano-Wo claimed that he had no wish to usurp Amaterasu's power. Instead, he said that they could prove which of them was the most powerful by seeing who could produce male deities.

Amaterasu began the contest by breaking her brother's sword into three, chewing the pieces, then spitting them out. A mist appeared from her mouth, soon taking the form of three goddesses. Susano-Wo then took the fertility beads with which Amaterasu bound her hair and arms. He cracked the beads with his teeth, and from them produced five male gods. He then announced that he had won the contest. However, Amaterasu said that because the gods had

AIZEN-MYOO *sits on a blossoming lotus, a symbol of enlightenment. He is popularly seen as the god of romantic and erotic love.* (JAPANESE SCULPTURE, C. 12TH CENTURY.)

come from her own jewels, she had won the contest. Susano-Wo ignored her protest and celebrated his victory by wreaking havoc on earth. He destroyed the rice fields, filled in the irrigation ditches and

the priestesses who officiate at ceremonies associated with the sun goddess's cult. Another theory argues that the women were weaving the fabric of the universe, which remained incomplete.

Until 1945, Amaterasu was worshipped as a sacred ancestor of the Japanese imperial family, and a mirror forms part of the imperial regalia. A major shrine to the goddess at Ise is visited by millions of pilgrims each year. (See also *CREATION MYTHS*)

AME-NO-UZUME, or simply Uzume, is the dawn goddess and the goddess of laughter, according to the Shinto mythology of Japan. She helped to tempt *AMATERASU* out of a cave after the sun deity, enraged by the behaviour of the storm god *SUSANO-WO*, had taken

shelter there. Ame-No-Uzume danced at the entrance to the cave, eventually becoming so carried away by her antics that she flung off all her clothes. The assembled gods burst out laughing, and the disturbance caused Amaterasu to look out of her hiding-place to see what was happening. As a result, her light returned to the world.

Another myth tells how Ame-No-Uzume distracted a local solar deity, the "Monkey Prince", who had attempted to block the descent from heaven of *NINIGI* or Honinigi, Amaterasu's grandson. In due course, Ame-No-Uzume and the Monkey Prince were married.

AME-NO-UZUME (below) helped to lure Amaterasu out of a cave by arousing her curiosity with an erotic dance. (ILLUSTRATION FROM MYTHS AND LEGENDS OF JAPAN.)

AMATERASU (above), hearing the commotion outside her cave, looked out in curiosity and light returned to the world. (WOODBLOCK PRINT BY TAISO YOSHITOSHI, 1882.)

finished his rampage by skinning a young pony and hurling it through the roof of the sacred weaving hall, where Amaterasu and her attendants sat weaving. One of the maidens died of fright, and Amaterasu fled in terror and fury.

The goddess hid in a cave, thereby casting the world into darkness. The evil gods were delighted, as the darkness enabled them to perform their wicked deeds undetected. However, the good deities beseeched Amaterasu to return to the world. The goddess refused, and so the deities hatched a plot. They found the cock whose crow

precedes the dawn and made a mirror strung with jewels. Then, after setting the cock and the mirror outside Amaterasu's hiding place, they asked the goddess *AME-NO-UZUME* to dance on an upturned tub. The cock began to crow and the goddess began to dance, her feet creating a frenzied drumming noise. Eventually, the goddess was carried away by the ecstasy of her dance and removed her clothes, whereupon all the gods began to laugh. Unable to contain her curiosity, Amaterasu emerged from the cave and caught sight of her reflection in the mirror. As she was lured out to gaze at her own beauty, the world was again lit by the sun.

Amaterasu and her attendants are said to have been weaving the garments of the gods, or those of

B

AMIDA is a Japanese deity who derives from the buddha Amitabha, or "Boundless Light", who postponed his own entry into nirvana in order that he might save humankind. In China, Amida is known as Omito Fu. He is the central figure in the "Pure Land" sects of Buddhism. The devotees believe that, by invoking the buddha at the hour of their death, they may be reborn in the Pure Land, Amida's western paradise. Once in the Pure Land, the faithful remain free from pain and desire until the time for their final enlightenment arrives.

Amida was originally identified with *AMATERASU*, the sun goddess and the most important Shinto deity. He is often represented welcoming the faithful to his Pure Land, surrounded by numerous bodhisattvas and celestial beings.

ANTABOGA is the world serpent of Balinese mythology. At the beginning of time, only Antaboga existed. By means of meditation, the great serpent created the world turtle, *BEDAWANG*. Two snakes lie on top of the world turtle, as well as the Black Stone, which forms the lid of the underworld.

The underworld is ruled by the goddess *SETESUYARA* and the god *BATARA KALA*, who created the light and the earth. Above the earth lies a layer of water and, above the water, a series of skies. *SEMARA*, the god of love, lives in the floating sky, and above that lies the dark blue sky, home to the sun and moon. Next is the perfumed sky, which is full of beautiful flowers and is inhabited by Tjak, a bird with a human face; the serpent Taksaka; and a group of snakes known as the Awan, who appear as falling stars. The ancestors live in a flame-filled heaven above the perfumed heaven, and beyond that is the abode of the gods.

ARA is a spirit who features in a creation myth of the Iban, one of the Dayak peoples of Borneo. The

AMIDA sits on a lotus, emitting rays of golden light, with an aura larger than a billion worlds. (WOOD SCULPTURE, 18TH CENTURY.)

story tells how, at the beginning of time, Ara floated in the form of a bird above a boundless ocean together with another spirit, *IRIK*. The birds eventually plucked two enormous eggs from the water. From one of the eggs, Ara formed the sky, and from the other, Irik formed the earth. However, because the earth was too large for the sky, the two spirits had to squash it until it became the right size. During the process, mountains and valleys, rivers and streams were created. Plants began to appear, and then the two spirits decided to create human beings. At first they tried to make them from the sap of trees but, when this proved unsuccessful, they used the soil. After fashioning the first humans, they gave them life with their bird-song.

AS-IGA, according to the Ostyak people of Siberia, is a benevolent spirit. His name means "Old Man of the Ob", the great river that runs through Siberia.

THE BA XIAN, or Pa Hsien, or "Eight Immortals", are symbols of good luck and important figures within the Daoist mythology of China. They are not, however, gods, although they are often viewed as such. The Ba Xian are said to have achieved immortality through the practice of the Dao, or "Way". Although accounts of how

they became immortal did not appear until the 15th century, some of the Ba Xian featured in earlier myths.

The first figure to achieve immortality was Li Tieguai ("Li with the Iron Crutch"). An ascetic, Li Tieguai was taught by Laozi, said to be the founding father of Daoism, who descended from heaven in order to help him. One day, soon after gaining immortality, Li decided to visit a sacred mountain. He left his body behind, asking his disciple to look after it for seven days and telling him that, if by then he had not returned, the disciple was to burn it.

On the sixth day, the disciple's mother fell ill. Anxious to visit her, the disciple burned Li's body. When Li's soul returned, it found only a heap of ashes, and so entered the body of an ugly beggar with a crippled leg who had died of hunger. Although Li did not want to live in such a horrible body, Laozi persuaded him to do so and gave him a crutch to help him to walk. According to another tale, Li was given the crutch by *XI WANG MU*, the "Queen Mother of the West", who healed a wound on Li's leg and taught him how to become immortal. Li is usually depicted as a beggar leaning on an iron crutch.

Li Tieguai is said to have instructed Zhong-li Quan in the Daoist doctrine. According to one tradition, Zhong-li Quan found instructions for gaining immortality behind the wall of his dwelling when it collapsed one day. Zhong-li Quan followed the guidelines, whereupon he disappeared to the heavens on a cloud. Another tale tells how, during a famine, Zhong-li Quan miraculously produced silver coins and gave them to the poor, thereby saving them from starvation. Zhong-li Quan was fat, bald and sported a long beard. He was

THE BA XIAN *included Zhang Guolao, who is represented here, riding his mule back-to-front, in a paper model outside a temple during a festival in Taiwan.*

often represented with a fan made from feathers or palm leaves. After gaining immortality, he became a messenger of heaven.

Lu Dongbin was born in the tenth century AD. While still a student, he met a fire dragon who gave him a magic sword with which he could conceal himself in heaven. Later, Lu Dongbin visited an inn where he met a man called Han Zhongli. While Han Zhongli warmed up a pot of wine, Lu fell asleep and saw the whole of his future life in a dream. He dreamt that he would enjoy good fortune for 50 years but then his luck would run out, his family ruined and he himself killed by bandits.

When Lu Dongbin woke up, he became convinced of the worthlessness of earthly ambition and decided to renounce the world. He followed Han Zhongli into the mountains in order to seek the Dao and achieve immortality. Lu Dongbin is said to mingle with ordinary mortals, rewarding the good and punishing the wicked. He uses his sword to conquer ignorance, passion and aggression. He is the patriarch of many Chinese sects and the most popular immortal in Chinese culture.

Han Xiang is usually said to be a nephew of a Tang dynasty philosopher. He became a disciple of Lu Dongbin, who took Han to heaven and showed him the tree that bears the peaches of eternal life. Han began to climb the tree but slipped and crashed to earth. Just before landing, he achieved immortality. Han Xiang is said to have a wild temper and supernatural powers. On one occasion, he caused peonies to blossom in the middle of winter. A prophecy was written on their petals and, though at the time the words appeared to mean nothing, they later came true. Han is traditionally portrayed carrying a peach, a flute or a bouquet of flowers.

Cao Guojiu was a brother of Empress Cao of the Song dynasty. He lived in the 11th century AD and is said either to have become disillusioned by the corrupt life of the court or to have been overwhelmed with shame when his brother was found to be a murderer. Whatever the reason, he disappeared into the mountains in pursuit of the Dao.

On coming to a river, Cao tried to persuade the boatman to carry him across by showing him the golden tablet that had allowed him entrance to court. The boatman was unimpressed and Cao, ashamed, threw the tablet into the river. The boatman turned out to be Lu Dongbin in disguise. Lu Dongbin adopted Cao as his disciple and instructed him in the Dao.

Another version of the story tells how the emperor gave Cao a golden medal, which had the ability to allow its owner to overcome all obstacles. When Cao showed the medal to the boatman, a priest asked him why he found it necessary to use such methods of persuasion. Ashamed, Cao threw the medal into the river, whereupon the priest revealed himself as Lu Dongbin and promised to help Cao gain immortality.

Zhang Guolao was an old man who lived at the time of the Empress Wu of the Tang dynasty, in the eighth century AD. He is often shown riding back-to-front on a white mule. The mule was said to be capable of travelling thousands of miles each day and, when not being ridden, could be folded up and put in a bag. To bring the mule back to life, Zhang just sprinkled it with water.

The emperor grew intrigued by Zhang and asked a Daoist master to tell him his true identity. The master replied that he was afraid to answer the emperor's question because he had been told that if he did so, he would immediately die. He finally agreed to reveal who Zhang was, on condition that the emperor promised afterwards to go barefoot and bareheaded to Zhang and ask him to forgive the master for his betrayal. The emperor agreed, whereupon the master said that Zhang was an incarnation of the chaos that existed at the beginning of time. The master died, but when the emperor went to ask Zhang for forgiveness, he was brought back to life.

Zhang could endow the childless and the newly married with children. He is sometimes shown holding the peaches of eternal life or the bag that contains his mule.

Lan Caihe was either a girl or a man who looked like a woman. In summer she wore a thick overcoat and in winter only light clothing. She wore a belt made of black wood and a boot on only one foot. Her family dealt in medicinal herbs. One day, when she was collecting herbs, Lan Caihe met a beggar dressed in filthy rags, his body covered in boils. The girl looked after the beggar, who turned out to be Li Tieguai in disguise. For her kindness, Li Tieguai rewarded the girl with immortality. Lan Caihe then toured the country singing songs and urging people to seek the Dao. One day, she took off her coat, boot and belt, and rose into the sky riding on a crane. She is sometimes represented carrying a basket of fruit or flowers.

He Xiangu became immortal after grinding and eating a mother-of-pearl stone. After swallowing the stone, He Xiangu became as light as a feather and found that she was able to fly over the mountains gathering fruits and berries. One day the emperor summoned her to his court, but she became immortal and disappeared. She is usually depicted holding either a peach or a lotus blossom. (See also THE EIGHT IMMORTALS)

THE BAJANG is an evil spirit who, in the folk-tales of the Malay-speaking people of South-east Asia, appears when a disaster or illness is about to occur. He usually takes the form of a giant polecat (ferret) and is particularly harmful to children.

The master of the household is said to be able to catch the Bajang and keep him in a container. If the master feeds the Bajang milk and eggs, the spirit becomes friendly and will cause the master's enemies to fall ill. However, if the master fails to feed the spirit, he will attack him.

BARONG, according to Balinese mythology, is the leader of the forces of good and the enemy of *RANGDA*, the demon queen. He is regarded as the king of the spirits and traditionally takes the form of a lion. Ritual battles, usually ending in Rangda's defeat or a compromise, are staged between the two beings. (See also *DEMONS*)

BASUKI is a giant serpent of Balinese mythology. He lives in the underworld cave that is ruled over by the god *BATARA KALA* and the goddess *SETESUYARA*.

BATARA GURU is the name by which the Hindu god Shiva was known in South-east Asia before the arrival of Islam. He was the omnipotent sky god and was also viewed as a god of the ocean. Shiva was introduced to Java, Sumatra, Bali and the Malay peninsula sometime before the fifth century AD.

The Malay people added their own stories to the Indian tales of the great god's exploits. In Sumatra, for example, Batara Guru was said to have created the earth by sending a handful of soil to his daughter, *BORU DEAK PARUDJAR*, who had jumped from heaven into a vast ocean in order to avoid the unwelcome advances of the god Mangalabulan. A swallow told Batara Guru what had happened, and the god sent the bird down to earth with the soil. When the girl

BENKEI was the companion of the hero Yoshitsune. They were once attacked by a ghostly company of the Taira clan. (ILLUSTRATION FROM MYTHS AND LEGENDS OF JAPAN.)

threw the soil into the water, it immediately formed an island. This

so annoyed the sea serpent NAGA PADOHA that he arched his back, causing the island to float away. Batara Guru then sent down more soil, as well as an incarnation of himself in the form of a hero. The hero managed to keep the serpent

still by placing an iron weight on his back so that he sank to the lower depths. Try as he might, Naga Padoha was unable to move the huge weight, but his writhings caused the formation of mountains and valleys.

After he had created the islands of the South-east Asian archipelago, Batara Guru sprinkled them with seeds, from which arose all animals and plants. Boru Deak Parudjar and the hero then produced the first human beings.

BATARA KALA, according to the creation myth of the Balinese, is the god who rules over the underworld cave together with the goddess *SETESUYARA*. Batara Kala created the light and the earth.

BEDAWANG is the Balinese world turtle whom the world serpent *ANTABOGA* created through meditation. Two snakes lie on top of the world turtle as well as the Black Stone, which forms the lid of the underworld. The god *BATARA KALA* and the goddess *SETESUYARA* rule over the underworld.

BENKEI, according to Japanese mythology, is the companion of the hero *YOSHITSUNE*. He is said to have been conceived by a *TENGU*, or demon. He soon grew to a great height and became very strong. None the less, Yoshitsune succeeded in overpowering Benkei in a duel, whereupon the giant became the hero's servant.

BENTEN, or Benzai, was one of the *SHICHI FUKUJIN*, or seven deities of good fortune or happiness, an assembly of immortals grouped together in the 17th century by a monk who intended them to symbolize the virtues of a man of his time. Benten was said to be the sister of the king of the Buddhist hells. Later, due to a mistake, she was attributed with the virtues of good luck and was included in the group of seven deities of happiness.

Benten helps human beings acquire material gains. She is said to have married a dragon in order to render him harmless, and is sometimes represented riding a dragon or sea serpent. She is associated with the sea. The goddess is

BENTEN holding a zither and riding on a dragon, is visited in her cave at Enoshima by a nobleman asking her to grant prosperity to his house. The goddess is associated with material wealth. (GOLD LACQUER SCREEN, 19TH CENTURY.)

also believed to be an exemplar of the feminine accomplishments, and she is often shown playing a musical instrument. Venerated by gamblers and jealous women, as well as by speculators and tradesmen, Benten is believed to bring good luck in marriage and is the patron saint of the geishas. (See also *THE SHICHI FUKUJIN*)

BENZAI see *BENTEN*.

BISHAMON is a Japanese god who was derived from Vaishravana, one of the Guardian Kings of Buddhism. Bishamon, like Vaishravana, was originally the heavenly guardian of the north, but he later became the protector of the law who guarded people from illness and demons. He was also a god of war. Bishamon is believed to possess enormous wealth and to dispense ten sorts of treasure or good luck. As a result, he was included in the list of SHICHI FUKUJIN, the seven deities of happiness or good luck, an assembly of immortals grouped together in the 17th century by a monk who intended them to symbolize the virtues of a man of his time.

Bishamon is normally represented as a blue-faced warrior clad in full armour, and his attributes include a spear and a pagoda, a symbol of religious devotion. He is sometimes known by the name Bishamon-tenno or Bishamonten, and is often shown trampling two demons. In the sixth century, Prince Shotoku called upon the god to help him in his crusade against anti-Buddhist factions. (See also THE SHICHI FUKUJIN)

BORU DEAK PARUDJAR, according to the mythology of Sumatra, is the daughter of the god BATARA GURU, the name by which the Hindu god Shiva was known in South-east Asia before the arrival of Islam. Batara Guru is said to have created the earth by sending a handful of soil to his daughter, Boru Deak Parudjar, who had jumped from heaven into a vast ocean in order to avoid the unwelcome advances of the god Mangalabulan. A swallow told Batara Guru what had happened, and the god sent the bird down to earth with the soil. When Boru Deak Parudjar threw the soil into the water, it immediately formed an island. This so annoyed the sea serpent NAGA PADOHA that he arched his back, making it float away.

Batara Guru then sent down more soil, as well as an incarnation of himself in the form of a hero. The hero managed to keep the serpent still by placing an iron weight on his back so that he sank to the depths. Try as he might, Naga Padoha was unable to move the weight, but his writhings caused the formation of mountains and valleys.

After he had created the islands of the South-east Asian archipelago, Batara Guru sprinkled them with seeds from which arose all the animals and plants. Boru Deak Parudjar and the hero then produced the first human beings.

BOTA ILI, according to the Kedang people of eastern Indonesia, was a wild woman who lived at the top of a mountain. Her

BISHAMON is a Japanese god of war whose attributes include a spear and a pagoda, a symbol of religious devotion. He is shown here with a ministering demon.
(WOODBLOCK PRINT BY ISAI, 19TH CENTURY.)

body was covered with hair, and she had long, pointed fingernails and toenails. She ate lizards and snakes and would cook them over a fire, which she lit by striking her bottom against a stone.

One day, a man called WATA RIAN noticed the smoke of Bota Ili's fire and set off to find its source. He took with him a fish to eat and some wine. When he reached the top of the mountain, Wata Rian climbed a tree and waited for Bota Ili to return with her catch of reptiles. The wild woman struck her bottom against a rock to start a fire, but to no effect. Looking up, she saw Wata Rian and shrieked at him to come down from the tree so that she could bite him to death. Wata

C

THE CITY GOD stands resplendent on his altar in the City God Temple in Xi Gang in Taiwan.

the god of wind. With their help he smothered Huang Di's soldiers in a thick, black fog, whereupon the latter invented the compass in order to find his whereabouts. Chiyou then called down the wind and rain, whereupon Huang Di summoned the goddess of drought, Ba, to clear the skies. Eventually, Chiyou was defeated and decapitated, although his headless body continued to run across the battlefield before finally falling down dead.

Chiyou was said to have invented warfare and weapons and was also a renowned dancer. Although his body was that of a human being, he had the feet of an ox. He was said to have four eyes and six arms, pointed horns, a head made from iron and hair as sharp as spears. He lived on a diet of sand and stones.

CH'IYU see *CHIYOU.*

CHORMUSTA see *QORMUSTA.*

CHU JONG see *ZHU RONG.*

THE CITY GOD was the impersonal tutelary deity of walled cities and towns, responsible to YU HUANG, the "Jade Emperor", in heaven. In each town, his temple was regarded as the "yamen", or celestial court, the counterpart to the terrestrial state yamen with its human mandarin responsible to the emperor in Beijing. The City God performed the same duties "on the other side", controlling harmful ghosts and spirits with his retinue of tamed demons within the city bounds. Prayers were addressed to him on behalf of a deceased, asking him to intercede with the ten judges of the purgatorial courts in the underworld, reflecting the widespread Buddhist concept of reincarnation.

Rian, unafraid, told her to calm herself or he would set his dog on her. The two of them lit a fire and cooked their food together.

Bota Ili drank so much wine that she fell asleep, whereupon Wata Rian shaved the hair from her body and discovered that she was really a woman. The two were eventually married.

BUJAEGN YED is a culture hero of the Chewong, a Malayan people. One day, Bujaegn Yed, a hunter, was eating the food he had caught when YINLUGEN BUD, an ancient spirit, appeared to him. The spirit warned the hero that he was committing a terrible sin in failing to share his food. Bujaegn Yed took heed of the warning and took some of the food home to give to his wife, who was pregnant.

When Bujaegn Yed's wife was about to give birth, the hero was on the point of cutting open her stomach to allow the baby out, as was customary at that time, when Yinlugen Bud again appeared. The spirit showed Bujaegn Yed how to deliver a baby in the correct manner, and also taught him the rules and rituals of childbirth. Then, after teaching Bujaegn Yed's wife how to breastfeed a baby, the spirit disappeared. From that time on, women did not have to die when their children were born.

CAO GUOJIU see *BA XIAN.*

CHANG E see *ZHANG E.*

CHIYOU or Ch'iyu, is variously described as a son, descendant or minister of SHEN NONG, the ancient Chinese god, or culture hero, associated with medicine and agriculture. Chiyou rebelled against HUANG DI, the "Yellow Emperor", in a struggle for the succession. After Chiyou had driven Huang Di's forces on to an immense plain, the enemies engaged in a tremendous battle.

Huang Di's army was composed of bears, tigers and other ferocious animals, whereas Chiyou's army was composed of demons. Chiyou was also supported by Chi Song Zi, the "Master of Rain", and Fei Lian,

D

DAIKOKU, *one of the gods of good fortune, performs a New Year dance carrying his bulging sack of rice. Tucked into his belt is his rice mallet, which grants wishes and from which money spills when it is shaken.* (FUNDAME INRO, C. 1850.)

been led from a country near Mecca to their present home. Demong married the daughter of a local ruler in order to ensure good relations with the existing inhabitants of Borneo. The woman, Rinda, had several children. When Demong was about to die, he ordered that a boundary stone be erected in order to mark the Ibans' territory. The stone stands to this day, and it is said that whoever attempts to move it risks incurring the wrath of Demong.

DIDIS MAHENDERA was a fabulous creature who, according to the Dayak people of Borneo, appeared together with *ROWANG RIWO* during the first epoch of creation, when a part of the universe was brought into being with each successive clash of the two cosmic mountains. The creature had eyes made from jewels.

DIMU see *DIYA*.

DIYA and Tian-Long were attendants of *WEN CHANG*, the Chinese god of literature. Diya, whose name means "Earthly Dumb", and Tian-Long, meaning "Heavenly Deaf", helped Wen Chang with the setting and marking of his examination papers, since, being deaf and dumb, they could be relied on not to leak the questions in advance. Another myth mentions these two as the primal couple, who gave rise to human beings and all other creatures. Diya was sometimes known as Dimu, meaning "Earth Mother".

DIZANG WANG, or *TI-TS'ANG WANG*, is one of the four great bodhisattvas ("buddhas-to-be") of Chinese buddhism. Long ago, Dizang Wang vowed that he would

become a buddha, but only when he had liberated all creatures on earth from the relentless cycle of death and rebirth.

In one of his existences, he was a girl whose mother killed animals for food. Through meditating, the girl succeeded in saving her mother from hell. Dizang Wang is believed to succour all those who are detained in the courts of hell. He is depicted as a monk holding a metal staff which opens the gates of hell, and is often surrounded by the ten judges. He is the equivalent of the Indian bodhisattva Kshitigarbha and the Japanese *JIZO-BOSATSU*.

DONGYUE DADI, or Tung-yüeh Ta-ti, is the "Great Emperor of the Eastern Peak" according to Chinese mythology. He assists the "Jade Emperor" *YU HUANG* and supervises all areas of earthly life.

There are 75 departments within Dongyue Dadi's offices. One lays down the time for the births and deaths of all creatures, another determines people's social

DAIKOKU *stands on two bulging bales of rice to symbolize his prosperity, and holds his magic mallet. As the patron of agriculture he was the protector of the soil and he was also seen as a friend of children.* (JAPANESE SCULPTURE.)

DAIKOKU was one of the *SHICHI FUKUJIN*, or seven gods of good fortune, a group of deities assembled in the 17th century by a monk who intended them to symbolize the virtues of a man of his time.

Daikoku was regarded as the god of wealth and a patron of farmers. He is often depicted standing or sitting on bales of rice, which are sometimes being eaten away by rats. Daikoku remains untroubled by the rats' greed because he is so wealthy. He usually carries a mallet, with which he is able to grant wishes. His picture was sometimes placed in kitchens, and he is sometimes said to have provided for the nourishment of priests. (See also *THE SHICHI FUKUJIN*)

DAINICHI-NYORAI is the Japanese form of the buddha Mahavairocana, or the "Great Illuminator". He was introduced to Japan at the beginning of the ninth century, together with numerous other Buddhist figures. He became the supreme deity of some esoteric sects and is sometimes regarded as the "Primordial Buddha". *YAKUSHI-NYORAI*, the divine healer, is sometimes seen as an aspect of Dainichi-Nyorai.

DAISHO-KANGITEN see *SHOTEN*.

DEMONG, according to the Iban of Borneo, governed the ancestors of the Iban people after they had

standing, another their wealth and another the number of children they will have. Dongyue Dadi's offices are staffed by the souls of the dead. His daughter, Sheng Mu, looks after women and children. Dongyue Dadi is usually represented sitting down and wearing the garments of an emperor.

THE EARTH GOD, the ubiq-
uitous local territorial deity, is the closest to the lives of villagers and is amongst those most frequently seen on the altars of the common people. The Earth God is not looked upon as powerful or fearsome. He is a celestial deity, the lowest ranking official in the bureaucracy of the celestial pantheon, and is the tutelary god of each sector of a large village or suburb; the protector of the well-being of both town and country dwellers. He has control over the wealth and fortune of the people.

The Earth God is almost universally thought to be an impersonal spirit. People appeal to him for anything that affects their lives and

livelihoods. In times of peril, images of the Earth God have sometimes been taken from their shrines to be shown the cause of a problem, such as drought, flood, frost, caterpillars, locusts or mildew, to enable the deity to understand fully what his devotees are suffering.

EBISU, in Japanese mythology, was one of the SHICHI FUKUJIN, or seven gods of good fortune or happiness, an assembly of deities grouped together in the 17th century by a monk who intended them to symbolize the virtues of a man of his time. Ebisu himself is credited with the virtue of candour.

THE EARTH GOD (right) sits on the altar of a local temple, clutching his staff and tael of gold, symbolizing wealth.

DAINICHI-NYORAI (below), the "Great Sun Buddha", was the supreme deity of the Shingon sect. Its members held that the esoteric teachings of the Buddha were too obscure to be expressed in writing, but could be presented in painting (PAINTING ON SILK, 13TH CENTURY.)

He is said to be the patron of labourers, wealth and prosperity, and to promote hard work. Ebisu is believed to have originated in Shinto belief as the son of OKUNINUSHI, the mythical hero. He is also sometimes identified with the third son of IZANAGI AND IZANAMI, the primal couple, and as such is regarded as one of the ancestors of the first people of Japan.

In some areas of Japan, the god of farms is called Ebisu; fishermen also invoke the god before going to sea. Ebisu is symbolized by a large stone, which a boy must retrieve from the bottom of the water. He is

usually represented dressed as a peasant and smiling. He holds a fishing rod in one hand and a sea bream (sunfish), a symbol of good luck, in the other hand. (See also THE SHICHI FUKUJIN)

EC, according to the Yenisei people of Siberia, is the supreme god. He regularly descends to earth in order to ensure the well-being of creation. Ec drove his wife, KHOSADAM, out of the sky in punishment for being unfaithful to him with the moon.

THE EIGHT IMMORTALS see BA XIAN.

YIN AND YANG

DAOIST PHILOSOPHY CENTRED ON the principle of unity in the cosmos and the belief that a natural order, based on balance and harmony, determined the behaviour of everything in existence. Two interacting forces held the Chinese universe in delicate balance: yin, the female element, was associated with coldness, darkness, softness and the earth. It originally referred to the shady side of the mountain. Yang, the sunny side, was the male principle, associated with light, warmth, hardness and the heavens. The two forces were opposites but mutually dependent, and needed to be in equilibrium for harmony to exist. They were present in every aspect of the world, in contrasting pairs such as life and death, or good and evil, as well as in everyday activities, objects, animals and human characters. In the ancient Chinese creation myth, yin and yang were held inside the cosmic egg until the struggle of the opposing forces cracked the shell.

THE YIN/YANG SYMBOL (above) expresses the interaction between opposites that gives rise to the universe and everything in it. The dark section (yin) and the light section (yang) are directly opposed, yet interlocking and mutually dependent. Together they form a perfect circle. The two small spots show that each opposing force contains a small seed of the other within it. (CARVED CHINESE JOSS BOARD.)

THE BAGUA (left) were discovered by Fu Xi, the legendary emperor, who saw them inscribed on the back of a tortoise he found on the banks of the Yellow River in about 3000BC. The constantly changing interactions of yin and yang gave rise to the infinite variety of patterns of life, symbolized in the three-line symbols of the eight trigrams. The top line of each trigram represents heaven, the bottom is earth and the middle line is humankind. (ILLUSTRATION FROM SUPERSTITIONS EN CHINE, 1915.)

THE YIN/YANG SYMBOL (below), surrounded by the trigrams of
the bagua, was hung on the house door as a protective amulet to
prevent the entry of devils. With it might hang a picture of the
immortal Liu Hai with his three-legged bowl, who brought good
luck to those involved in commercial ventures. He carried a string
of gold pieces to remind him of a visiting philosopher who
suggested he tried to pile eggs to demonstrate the precariousness
of high office. (ILLUSTRATION FROM SUPERSTITIONS EN CHINE, 1915.)

THE PEI TOU IMMORTALS (above) were star spirits of which the most
important were the "Three Stars of Happiness": Shou Lao, the god of
longevity; Fu Shen, the god of luck; and Cai Shen, the god of wealth. They
are shown here contemplating the yin/yang symbol on a scroll, and
surrounded by symbolic figures of long life and immortality: the pine tree
with Shou Lao's white crane, the stag and a child presenting a peach.
(CHINESE SILK EMBROIDERY, 17TH CENTURY.)

THE DRAGON (right) and the phoenix were often used together decoratively.
For the Chinese, dragons represented the male, yang element and were a
beneficent force of nature, even though they had fiery tempers. The mythical
phoenix represented the female, yin element. The dragon was the emblem of
the Chinese emperor, and the phoenix of the empress, and together the two
creatures were used to symbolize marital harmony. (JADE RITUAL DISC WITH DRAGON
AND PHOENIX, C. 481–221BC.)

EMMA-O (left), the king of hell, was no match for the strong man Asahina Saburo, and was humiliated by having to crawl between his legs. (KINJI INRO, 19TH CENTURY.)

EMMA-O (right) wears a magistrate's hat to indicate his office as judge of the dead. (NASHIJI INRO, 18TH CENTURY.)

EMMA-O, according to Japanese Buddhism, is the ruler of hell and the judge of the dead. He is identified with the Chinese deity YANLUO WANG and derives from the Hindu god of death, Yama.

Emma-O rules over the underground hell Jigoku, where he is surrounded by 18 generals and thousands of soldiers as well as demons and guards with horses' heads. The underworld is divided into eight hells of fire and eight of ice. According to one tradition, death begins as a journey across a vast, empty plain. In other versions of the tale, infernal beings guard the dead during their journey. At the entrance to hell lies a steep mountain, which the deceased have to climb before encountering, on the other side of the mountain, a river with three crossings. One of the crossings is a shallow ford, which those who have committed only minor sins may cross. Another is a bridge over which good people may pass. The third is a horrific torrent filled with monsters, through which evil sinners must struggle. At the other side of this third crossing waits a horrible old woman who strips her victims naked. They are then taken before Emma-O by the guards of hell. Emma-O judges only men; his sister decides the fate of women. The god sits between two severed heads, and a magic mirror reflects all the sinner's past wrongdoings. Emma-O then judges the individual's sins and allocates them to the appropriate hell. The souls of the dead can, however, be saved with the help of a bosatsu, the Japanese form of the bodhisattva.

ERLIK, according to the Altaic people of southern Siberia, is the king of the dead, an adversary of the supreme god, ULGAN. He incurred Ulgan's wrath by leading the first men to commit sin. The great sky god sent the saviour MAIDERE down to earth in order to teach men to respect and fear him, but Erlik succeeded in killing him. Flames shot forth from the saviour's blood, eventually reaching up to heaven and destroying Erlik and his followers. Erlik was then banished to the underworld. Erlik is regarded both as the first man and as the elder brother of the creator. He is depicted as a terrifying being, having taken on some of the characteristics of Yama, the Buddhist god of the underworld. He sometimes appears as a bear.

ES is the sky god of the Ket people of Siberia. Although he is invisible, he is depicted as an old man with a long black beard.

Es created the world and made the first human beings from clay. When he threw clay with his left hand towards the right, it became a woman; when he threw clay with his right hand towards the left, it became a man.

ESEGE MALAN TENGRI, or "Father Bald-head Tengri", is the sky god of the Buriat people of Siberia.

FANGCHANG see *PENGLAI*.

FU HSI see *FU XI*

FU XI, or Fu Hsi, according to Chinese mythology, is the brother and husband of *NU GUA*. Whereas Nu Gua rules over the earth, Fu Xi rules over the sky. They are both represented with the tails of dragons.

One popular myth tells how, long ago, a man was labouring in his fields when he heard a rumble of thunder. He ordered his son and daughter into his house, hung an iron cage under its eaves and stood in wait, holding a large iron fork. All at once, there was an enormous clap of thunder and a flash of lightning, and the monstrous thunder god, *LEI GONG*, appeared wielding a huge axe. The man attacked Lei Gong with his fork, pushed him into the iron cage and slammed the door shut. Immediately, the rain and wind ceased.

FU XI's (above) legacy to Chinese civilization included the invention of the calendar, the fishing net and the bagua, or eight trigrams. (19TH CENTURY ILLUSTRATION.)

The following morning, the man prepared to journey to the local market in order to buy spices with which to pickle the thunder god. Before leaving home, he warned his children not to give Lei Gong anything to eat or drink. As soon as the man had left, Lei Gong began to beg the children for just the merest drop of water. At first the children heeded their father's instructions, but eventually they relented. As soon as the water touched his lips, Lei Gong became strong again and burst out of his cage. Before leaving, he thanked the children for helping him and gave them one of his teeth, which he told them to plant in the ground. The children planted the tooth and, within a few hours, it grew into a plant bearing a gourd.

It began to rain, and by the time the man returned from market, the rain had covered the whole earth. The man told his children to climb inside the gourd for safety, then he built a boat and rose up to heaven on the swelling water. There, he knocked on the door and begged the lord of heaven to end the flood. The lord of heaven commanded the water god to put an end to the flood, but the god was so diligent that the water immediately subsided, and the man's boat crashed down to earth, killing him. However, the children were unharmed because the gourd cushioned their fall.

The children proved to be the only survivors of the flood. They became known as Fu Xi. When they grew up, the young man suggested that they have children. The young woman was reluctant, since they were brother and sister, but agreed on condition that her brother was able to catch her in a chase. Fu Xi caught his sister, and so began the custom of marriage. The woman then changed her name to Nu Gua.

According to another version of the tale, although the two beings wanted to marry and have children, they knew that they would first have to be granted permission from the gods because, being brother and sister, the marriage would be incestuous. The couple climbed a sacred mountain, and each built a bonfire on its summit. The smoke from the two fires mingled, and Nu Gua and Fu Xi took this to mean that they had been granted permission to marry. Time passed and eventually Nu Gua gave birth to a ball of flesh. Fu Xi chopped the ball into numerous pieces with an axe and carried the fragments up a ladder to heaven. A gust of wind scattered the pieces of flesh all over the earth; when they landed, they became human beings. In this way, the earth was repopulated. (See also *CREATION MYTHS; YIN AND YANG*)

FU XI (below centre) became the first of the legendary emperors of China, followed by Shen Nong and Huang Di.

FUDO-MYOO (left), a terrifying deity who protects Buddhism and its adherents, holds a sword in one hand and a rope in the other. (SCULPTURE, 12TH–14TH CENTURY.)

Fugen is often depicted sitting on a white elephant with six tusks, or sometimes riding four elephants. He may be shown with 20 arms.

FUKUROKUJU is one of the *SHICHI FUKUJIN*, the seven gods of good fortune or happiness, a group of deities assembled in the 17th century by a monk who intended them to symbolize the virtues of a man of his time.

Fukurokuju himself symbolizes the virtue of popularity as well as wisdom, longevity, virility and fertility. He is usually depicted with a very long, thin head to indicate his intelligence and a short, fat body. He is sometimes accompanied by a crane, a stag or tortoise, all creatures which symbolize longevity. Fukurokuju is of Chinese origin

FUDO-MYOO (above) is surrounded by a halo of flames, the symbol of his virtues. (PAINTING, C. 13TH CENTURY)

FUGEN-BOSATSU (below) sits on a lotus blossom carried by a white elephant. (JAPANESE SILK PAINTING, 14TH CENTURY)

FUDO-MYOO is the most important of the five great Japanese myoos, the equivalent of Indian Buddhism's vidyarajas, terrifying emanations of the five "Great Buddhas of Wisdom". Fudo-Myoo corresponds to the Buddha *DAINICHI-NYORAI*. He is usually portrayed with a terrifying face half-concealed by long hair and surrounded by a halo of flames. The flames are believed to consume the passions. In one hand, he holds a sword, which is used to conquer greed, anger and ignorance, and in the other hand he holds a rope with which he catches those who oppose the Buddha.

FUGEN-BOSATSU is the Japanese form of the bodhisattva or "buddha-to-be", Samantabhadra. He represents innate reason and is believed to be able to prolong people's lives. One tale tells how Fugen-Bosatsu appeared before a monk disguised as a courtesan with the intention of demonstrating that the nature of Buddha was latent in even the most sinful of women.

and may have been a Daoist sage. He is the godfather of *JUROJIN*, the god of longevity and happy old age. (See also *THE SHICHI FUKUJIN*)

FUXING see *SAN XING*

GAO YAO, or Ting-jian, was an ancient Chinese god of judgement. His accompanying animal, a mythical one-horned goat, helped him to detect injustice.

GIMOKODAN is the name that the Bagobo people of the Philippines give to the underworld. The Bagobo are a hill tribe living on the island of Mindanao. According to tradition, Gimokodan, the land of the dead, lies below the earth and is divided into two parts. One part is reserved for brave warriors who die in battle, the other part houses everyone else. A giantess lives in the second section and feeds the spirits of dead children with milk from her breasts. Most of the spirits, however, turn to dew as soon as it is daylight and only become spirits again at night. A river lies at the entrance of Gimokodan, and all those who bathe in it forget their former lives.

GONG-GONG appears in Chinese mythology as a terrible monster who brings about a disastrous flood. He takes the form of a black dragon and is attended by a nine-headed snake. As the sworn enemy of the legendary benevolent emperor *YAO*, Gong-Gong decided to impale Mount Buzhou with his horn, thereby disturbing the balance of the earth and causing the rivers to overflow. He then tore a hole in the sky, disturbing the course of the sun. The monster is thus held responsible for all irregularities of weather and light.

According to another version of the tale, Gong-Gong and *ZHU RONG*, the divine lord of fire, decided to fight each other in order to determine which of them was the most powerful. The battle

GAO YAO'S (above) assistant in his pursuit of justice was a mythical one-horned animal, sometimes described as a qilin, or unicorn, who butted the guilty but spared the innocent. (SINO-TIBETAN ENAMEL QILIN.)

continued for several days. Eventually, the two creatures fell out of heaven, and Gong-Gong was defeated. Gong-Gong was so humiliated by having lost the battle that he determined to kill himself by running head first at Mount Buzhou, one of the mountains which supported the sky. When Gong-Gong struck the mountain, a great chunk fell off, a huge hole was torn in the sky and enormous cracks appeared in the earth. Fire and water gushed out, and a massive flood covered almost the entire surface of the world. The few areas that escaped the flood were destroyed by fire.

The goddess *NU GUA* selected some coloured stones from the bed of a river and melted them down. She then patched the sky with the melted stones and propped up the four points of the compass with the legs of a tortoise. However, when Gong-Gong collided with the mountain, he caused the heavens to tilt towards the northwest, which is why all the great rivers of China flow eastwards.

FUKUROKUJU (left), the god of long life and wisdom, is portrayed as a benevolent old man with an enormous brain. (JAPANESE LACQUERED VASE, 19TH CENTURY)

GUAN DI was worshipped as the protector of state officials in thousands of temples throughout China, in which the swords of public executioners were housed.
(CHINESE PORCELAIN, 16–17TH CENTURY.)

Guanyin is believed to live on a mountain or an island in the Eastern Sea. She is said to have introduced humankind to the cultivation of rice, which she makes wholesome by filling each kernel with her own milk. The goddess comes to the aid of all those who need her help, especially when they are threatened by water, demons, fire or the sword. She is sometimes said to stand on a cliff in the middle of flaming waves and rescue shipwrecked people from the sea, the symbol of samsara, the ceaseless round of earthly existence.

The 14th-century novel *Journey to the West*, which is said to provide a popular record of Chinese mythology, tells how the "Monkey King" went up to heaven where he stole the peaches of immortality from the garden of XI WANG MU, the "Queen Mother of the West". The monkey incurred the wrath of all the gods and was finally taken captive by Buddha. However, Guanyin interceded on the monkey's behalf and he was allowed to accompany a Buddhist pilgrim during his journey to India.

Another myth tells how Guanyin was the third daughter of King Miao Zhong. She entered a religious order against the wishes of her father, who did all he could to persuade her to remain in the outside world. Eventually, the king decided that he would have to kill her. However, YANLUO WANG, lord of death, appeared and led Guanyin away to his underworld kingdom. There, Guanyin soothed the damned and transformed hell

GUAN DI is sometimes portrayed as a mandarin, sitting unarmed, stroking his beard. (SOAPSTONE FIGURE, 17–18TH CENTURY.)

GUAN DI, or Kuan-ti, is the Daoist patron deity of soldiers and policemen. He protects the realm and looks after state officials. During the Chinese Qing dynasty (1644–1912), Guan Di was venerated for his warlike functions. In other periods he was regarded as the guardian of righteousness who protects men from strife and evil. In popular belief, Guan Di was famed for casting out demons. He was also called upon to provide information about people who had died and to predict the future.

Guan Di was originally a general called Guan Gong, who lived in the third century AD, during a time of turmoil at the close of the Han dynasty. He was renowned for his military skill, but he also came to be admired for his great courage and loyalty, since he was eventually executed by his enemy as a prisoner of war because he refused to change his allegiance. Because of his many virtues he was later deified, being officially recognized as a god at the end of the 16th century. Guan Di is represented as a giant dressed in green with a long beard and a red face. He is often depicted standing next to his horse and clad in full armour.

GUANYIN, or Kuan Yin, is Chinese Buddhism's goddess of mercy or compassion. She developed from the male bodhisattva, or "buddha-to-be", Avalokiteshvara, known in Japan as KWANNON, and helps all beings on earth to attain enlightenment. Guanyin was herself originally regarded as male but increasingly gained female characteristics. Believed to bless women with children, she is sometimes depicted holding a child in her arms. However, she may also be represented as a bodhisattva with a thousand arms and a thousand eyes. She sometimes appears in the guise of a young woman holding a fish basket, standing on clouds or riding on the back of a dragon in front of a waterfall.

GUANYIN (above), Chinese Buddhism's goddess of mercy and compassion, is often depicted holding a willow branch and a vase filled with the dew of compassion.

GUANYIN (right) helps all beings attain enlightenment. Originally a male deity, she increasingly gained female characteristics. (CHINESE PORCELAIN, 13–14TH CENTURY.)

into a paradise. Yanluo Wang then released Guanyin, and she was reborn on an island where she protected seafarers from storms. Her father then fell ill, and Guanyin healed him by cooking a piece of her own flesh for him to eat. In gratitude, the king ordered a statue of his daughter to be made. However, the sculptor misunderstood the king's instructions and made a statue with a thousand arms and a thousand eyes.

Guanyin is also credited with the ability to release prisoners from their chains, remove poison from snakes and deprive lightning of its power. She is believed to be capable of curing almost every sickness. A very popular goddess, her image is often found in people's homes and the festivals of her birth and enlightenment are endowed with great significance by Buddhists.

GUEI, or Kuei, according to Chinese mythology, are spirits formed from the *YIN*, or negative essence, of people's souls. These spirits or emanations are always feared because they are said to take their revenge on those people who ill-treated them when they were alive. They can be identified because they wear clothes which have no hems and their bodies cast no shadows.

HACHIMAN is the Japanese god of war. However, he is also a god of peace, and sometimes serves as a god of agriculture and protector of children. A historical figure, he is the deified form of the Emperor Ojin, who died at the end of the fourth century AD and was famed for his military deeds and bravery. Within the Shinto religion, Hachiman became a very popular deity, although his name does not appear in the sacred texts of Shintoism. He came to be regarded as a protector of Buddhism and is viewed by Buddhists as a bosatsu, the Japanese form of a bodhisattva, or "buddha-to-be". His sacred creature is the dove.

HAN XIANG see BA XIAN.

HE XIANGU see BA XIAN.

HIKOHOHODEMI is the great-grandson of the Japanese sun goddess AMATERASU and the son of NINIGI, or Honinigi, and his wife, Kono-Hana-Sakuyu-Hime.

Hikohohodemi's name means "Fireshade". His brother is called HONOSUSERI, or "Fireshine". Hikohohodemi hunted land animals, whereas his brother was a fisherman. One day the brothers tried to swap their means of livelihood but discovered that neither was able to perform the other's tasks. Honosuseri returned the bow, but Hikohohodemi had lost Honosuseri's fish hook and so offered him another in its stead. Honosuseri, however, refused to accept the replacement.

Upset, Hikohohodemi visited the sea god Watatsumi-No-Kami at the bottom of the ocean. Having previously found the fish hook in the mouth of a fish, the sea god returned it to Hikohohodemi. Meanwhile, Watatsumi-No-Kami's daughter had fallen in love with the young god. The couple were married and lived together for many years. Eventually, Hikohohodemi decided to return home. Before leaving, Hikohohodemi's father-in-law gave him two jewels, which made the tide rise and fall; he also gave him a friendly crocodile to transport him on his journey.

Back on land, the god returned the fish hook to Honosuseri, who, despite this gesture, continued to pester his brother. Eventually, Hikohohodemi lost all patience and made the tide rise. When Honosuseri was almost covered by the sea, he begged forgiveness and promised to serve Hikohohodemi, whereupon the latter caused the tide to go out.

The daughter of the sea god joined Hikohohodemi on land and announced that she was about to have her child. She made Hikohohodemi promise not to look at her while she gave birth,

HACHIMAN is the Japanese god of war, the deified form of the Emperor Ojin. Centuries after his death, a vision of a child appeared at his birthplace, identifying itself with an ideogram representing the name Hachiman. (STATUE BY KAIKEI, 13TH CENTURY.)

but the god was unable to resist the temptation and peeped through a crack in the wall of his wife's hut. There, he saw his wife transformed

HIKOHOHODEMI was the grandfather of Jimmu-Tenno, the first emperor of Japan.

HONOSUSERI, according to the Shinto mythology of Japan, was the elder brother of *HIKOHOHODEMI*. Honosuseri was a great fisherman, while his brother hunted animals on land. Honosuseri's name means "Fireshine", and his brother's name means "Fireshade". The brothers are the great-grandsons of the sun goddess *AMATERASU* and the sons of *NINIGI*, or Honinigi, and his wife Kono-Hana-Sakuyu-Hime.

HOTEI is one of the *SHICHI FUKUJIN*, or seven Japanese gods of good fortune or happiness. He is represented as a Buddhist monk and is recognizable by his bald head and vast belly, a symbol both of his wealth and friendly nature and of a soul that has achieved serenity through Buddhism. Hotei is often shown leaning on a large sack, which is said to contain endless gifts for his followers. He is regarded as a friend of the weak and of children. He may have originated as a Chinese hermit called Budaishi who lived in the 10th century AD and was believed to be an incarnation of Maitreya. (See also *THE SHICHI FUKUJIN*)

HSI HO see *XI-HE.*

HSI WANG MU see *XI WANG MU.*

HSIEN see *XIAN.*

HSÜAN TSANG see *XUAN ZONG.*

HOTEI is depicted as a smiling monk with a large belly, which signifies contentment, not greed. He carries a fan and a sack.
(IVORY NETSUKE, LATE 19TH CENTURY.)

into an enormous dragon. Afterwards, Hikohohodemi's wife returned to the sea and sent her sister to look after the child.

When the boy grew up, he married his aunt, the sea-god's daughter Tamayori-Hime, who had brought him up. They produced a son with two names, Toyo-Mike-Nu and Kamu-Yamato-Iware-Hiko. After his death, the boy was known as *JIMMU-TENNO*. He was the first emperor of Japan.

HINKON, according to the Tungu people of Siberia, is the god of hunting and lord of animals.

HKUN AI is a hero of Burmese mythology. He married a dragon who had taken the form of a beautiful woman. During each water festival, the woman became a dragon again, and Hkun Ai eventually became upset by his wife's metamorphoses. He decided to leave her, but before he did so, she gave him an egg. In due course the egg cracked open to reveal a son whom Hkun Ai called Tung Hkam.

When the boy grew up, he fell in love with a princess who lived on an island. Tung Hkam could not find a way to cross over the water to reach his beloved, until one day his mother appeared and formed a bridge with her back. Tung Hkam eventually became a great king.

HOMOSUBI see *KAGUTSUCHI.*

HONINIGI see *NINIGI.*

CREATION MYTHS

MYTHS OF THE CREATION OF THE WORLD begin with emptiness, darkness, a floating, drifting lack of form or a fathomless expanse of water. Out of this dim swirl comes a more tangible object which holds the promise of both solid land and human life. The egg is a potent symbol of creation, and features in mythologies all over the world, including those of China and Southeast Asia. According to the folklore of the Iban in Borneo, the world began with two spirits floating like birds on the ocean, who created the earth and sky from two eggs. In Sumatra, a primordial blue chicken, Manuk Manuk, laid three eggs, from which hatched the gods who created the world. A Chinese creation myth, which may have originated in Thailand, begins with the duality governing the universe – yin and yang – struggling within the cosmic egg until it splits, and the deity Pangu emerges.

IZANAGI AND IZANAMI were the primal couple in the Japanese creation myth. The gods arose in a remote heaven far above the floating world, and generations of gods and goddesses were born before these two were instructed to complete and solidify the world below. As a result of their union Izanami gave birth to all the islands of Japan and numerous gods and goddesses, including the fire god Kagutsuchi who burnt her so badly that she died. These rocks off the Japanese coast, near Ise, are known as the Myoto-Iwa, or wedded rocks, and symbolize Izanagi and Izanami. They are bound together by a rice-straw rope.

PANGU (above) grew 3 metres (10 feet) every day, pushing the earth and sky apart. He lived for 18,000 years and when he died his body formed the world, each part becoming one of its elements. His flesh became the soil, his hair the vegetation, his perspiration the dew, and so on. Finally, the fleas and other parasites inhabiting his body became the first humans. He was said to be responsible for the weather: when he smiled the sun shone, but if he was sad or angry, storms would ensue. (LITHOGRAPH, 19TH CENTURY.)

AMATERASU (above) the sun goddess, was born from the left eye of Izanagi as he washed his face. The unruly behaviour of her brother, the storm god Susano-Wo, frightened and angered her so much that she hid in a cave, plunging the whole world into darkness. All the other gods assembled in front of the cave and lured her back out by showing her her own glorious reflection in a divine mirror. As she emerged, the sun reappeared. (UTAGAWA KUNISADA, THE GODDESS AMATERASU EMERGING FROM EARTH, WOODBLOCK PRINT, 1860.)

FU XI (top centre) was the creator god who figured in the oldest Chinese myths, but when legendary dynasties were devised in accounts of ancient history, he became the first emperor, and was said to have reigned from 2852–2737BC. He taught his subjects how to make fishing nets and rear domestic animals, and discovered the bagua inscribed on the shell of a tortoise. These were the eight trigrams, based on combinations of the symbols for yin and yang, which formed the basis of Chinese calligraphy. (MA LIN, FU XI, 13TH CENTURY.)

SUSANO-WO (top right) was the storm god, the brother of Amaterasu. Sometimes known as the "Raging Male", he caused chaos in the world with his unpredictable behaviour, and the gods punished him by throwing him out of heaven. Once living on earth, his conduct improved, and he killed a terrible eight-headed serpent to win the hand of his beautiful wife, Kushi-Inada-Hime. While chopping through the serpent's tail, he discovered the legendary sword called Kusanagi, or "Grass Mower", which he sent to heaven as a gift for his sister.

I

HUANG DI, or Huang Ti, is the legendary "Yellow Emperor" of Chinese mythology who is said to have lived in the 3rd millennium BC. According to one story, Huang Di came into being when the energies that instigated the beginning of the world merged with one another, and created human beings by placing earthen statues at the cardinal points of the world and leaving them exposed for 300 years. During that time, the statues became filled with the breath of creation and eventually began to move. Huang Di allegedly received his magical powers when he was 100 years old. He achieved immortality and, riding a dragon, rose to heaven where he became one of the five mythological emperors who rule over the cardinal points. Huang Di himself rules over the fifth cardinal point, the centre. (See also *CHINA'S SACRED PEAKS*)

HUANG TI see *HUANG DI.*

IDA-TEN, according to Japanese mythology, is a god who protects monks and is the guardian of their

HUANG-DI is worshipped as one of the founders of Chinese culture and is said to have invented writing, the compass and the pottery wheel, and instituted the breeding of silkworms.

good conduct. He is depicted as a young man wearing armour and holding a sword. Ida-Ten is the Japanese equivalent of the Hindu warrior god Skanda, or Karttikeya, and was adopted by Buddhism in the seventh century.

ILA-ILAI LANGIT is a mythical fish who features in the creation story of the Dayak people of Borneo. The tale tells how, at the beginning of time, all creation was enclosed in the mouth of a gigantic snake. Eventually, a gold mountain arose and became home to the supreme god of the upper region, while a jewel mountain arose and became home to the supreme god of the lower region. The two mountains collided together on numerous occasions, each time creating part of the universe. This period has become known as the first epoch of cre-

ation, when the clouds, the sky, the mountains, the cliffs, the sun and moon were made. Afterwards, the "Hawk of Heaven" and the great fish Ila-Ilai Langit were brought into being, followed by two fabu-

lous creatures: *DIDIS MAHENDERA,* who had eyes made of jewels, and *ROWANG RIWO,* who had golden saliva. Finally, the golden headdress of the god *MAHATALA* appeared.

In the second epoch of creation, *JATA,* the divine maiden, created the land. Soon afterwards, hills and rivers were formed. In the third epoch of creation, the tree of life appeared and united the upper and lower worlds.

INARI is the god of rice, according to the Shinto mythology of Japan. His cult is extremely widespread since he is believed to ensure an abundant rice harvest and therefore brings prosperity.

In popular belief, Inari is represented as an old, bearded man sitting on a sack of rice, but the deity also appears in female form, with flowing hair. He, or she, is accompanied by two foxes. It is sometimes said that the god lives

HUANG DI (far left) was the third of the legendary emperors described in the Han dynasty to explain early Chinese history. Fu Xi and Shen Nong preceded him.

INARI's shrine at Kobe. Inari was the god of rice and is sometimes referred to as the god of food. He came to be regarded as a god of prosperity and is invoked by tradespeople. (THE SHRINE OF INARI AT KOBE BY WALTER TYNDALE, CANVAS, C. 1910.)

in the distant mountains and that the foxes act as his messengers. Alternatively, the god himself is occasionally regarded as a fox. Images of foxes are found in front of all of his shrines. Inari's wife was the food goddess UKE-MOCHI. When SUSANO-WO or, according to some versions of the myth, TSUKIYOMI, killed Uke-Mochi for producing food from her orifices, Inari took over her role as the deity of agriculture.

IRIK is a spirit who features in a creation myth of the Iban, one of the Dayak peoples of Borneo. Together with another spirit, ARA, Irik floated in the form of a bird above a boundless ocean. The birds eventually plucked two enormous

eggs from the water. From one of the eggs, Irik formed the earth and from the other, Ara formed the sky. However, because the earth was too large for the sky, the two spirits had to squash it until it was the right size. During the process, mountains and valleys, rivers and streams were created. Immediately, plants began to appear. The two spirits then decided to create human beings. At first they tried to make them from the sap of trees but, when this proved unsuccessful, they used the soil. After fashioning the first humans, they gave them life with their bird-song.

ISSUN BOSHI is a diminutive hero of Japanese mythology whose name means "Little One-Inch". His parents, despite being married for many years, had failed to conceive a child. In desperation, they prayed that they might be given a son even if he were only as tall as a fingertip. The gods took the couple literally and gave them a tiny child.

When Issun Boshi was 15 years old, he set off for Kyoto, taking with him a rice bowl, a pair of chopsticks and a needle stuck in a bamboo sheath. He paddled down the river, using the rice bowl as a boat and the chopsticks as oars. After arriving at Kyoto, Issun Boshi secured a job in the service of a noble family. For many years, he worked hard and his employers were pleased with him.

One day, the young hero accompanied the daughter of the house to the temple. On the way there, two giant ONI, horned devils, jumped out at them. Issun Boshi immediately attracted their attention so that the daughter could escape. One of the oni succeeded in swallowing Issun Boshi. Undeterred, the tiny man drew his needle out of its sheath and stabbed the devil in the stomach. As he crawled up the devil's throat, he continued to stab him until, with huge relief, the oni spat him out. Immediately, the other oni pre-

pared to attack Issun Boshi, whereupon the hero leapt up and began attacking its eyes with his needle. Both oni soon fled, leaving behind them a mallet, an object of good luck. Issun Boshi and the girl struck the mallet on the ground and made a wish. Immediately, Issun Boshi grew into a full-size samurai. The couple returned home, and the girl's father agreed to allow them to be married.

ITCHITA, according to the Yakut people of Siberia, is an earth goddess and an aspect of the great mother goddess. She keeps sickness away from human beings, and is attended by the spirits of the grass and trees. She herself lives in the white beech tree. Other aspects of the great mother are the goddess Ynakhsyt, who protects cattle, and Ajysyt, who looks after children and helps women in childbirth. Ajysyt constantly sways backwards and forwards, thereby encouraging the growth of the life force.

J

IZANAGI AND IZANAMI, according to Shinto belief, were the eighth pair of deities to appear after heaven and earth had been created out of chaos. Their full names, Izanagi-No-Mikoto and Izanami-No-Mikoto, mean "The August Male" and "The August Female".

Izanagi and Izanami were ordered to create the islands of Japan. They stood side by side on the "Floating Bridge of Heaven", lowered the heavenly jewelled spear into the sea and began to stir. When they lifted the spear out of the water, droplets fell from its tip and became an island, the first solid land. The two gods then descended on to the island and built a heavenly pillar and a splendid palace.

One day, the deities realized that each of their bodies differed from that of the other. Izanami said that her body was not fully formed in one place and Izanagi said that his body had been formed in excess in one place. Izanagi then suggested that they bring these two parts together. The two deities circled around the heavenly pillar until they met one another and

joined their bodies together. Izanami bore a child, but he was a deformed creature called Hiruko, or "Leech Child", whom the couple immediately abandoned at sea. The gods decided that the child had been born imperfect as a result of Izanami having spoken first during the couple's courting ritual. Once again, the couple circled the pillar and this time, Izanagi spoke first.

Izanami subsequently gave birth to the islands of Japan as well as to the gods and goddesses of waterfalls, mountains, trees, plants and the wind. While giving birth to the god of fire, *KAGUTSUCHI*, Izanami was so badly burned that she died. However, even while dying she continued to bear more and more gods. Eventually, she disappeared to *YOMI*, the land of the dead.

Izanagi was desperately upset. Many deities were formed from his tears, and when he sliced off the fire god's head, even more deities came into being. Izanagi determined to follow his wife to Yomi, but by the time he arrived there she had already eaten the food of the dead. Although Izanami tried to

persuade the gods to allow her to return to the land of the living, they refused her request. Izanagi then stormed into the hall of the dead and, after lighting a tooth of his comb and using it as a torch, he saw Izanami. She was horribly transformed: her corpse was squirming with maggots and eight thunder deities had taken up residence in her body.

Horrified at the sight of his wife, Izanagi fled back home. His behaviour infuriated Izanami, who sent the hags of Yomi, together with numerous thunder deities and warriors, to hunt him down. However, by employing various magic tricks, Izanagi succeeded in escaping them. When the god finally reached the outer edge of the land of the dead, he found three peaches. Picking them up, he threw them at the hags, who immediately ran away. Izanagi told the peaches that from that time onwards they would save mortals, just as they had saved him.

At length, Izanami, who by now had herself become a demon, set off in pursuit of Izanagi. In order to block her way, her husband pushed

IZANAMI AND IZANAGI, standing on the "Floating Bridge of Heaven", stir the sea with the heavenly jewelled spear to create the world. (WOODBLOCK PRINT, 19TH CENTURY.)

a huge boulder into the passage that separated Yomi from the land of the living. The husband and wife stood on either side of the boulder, and Izanami told Izanagi that in punishment for his behaviour she would strangle a thousand people each day. Izanagi replied that, each day, he would ensure that 1,500 people were born.

The god then purified himself by washing in a river. When he removed his clothes, a new deity came into being as each garment fell to the ground. Finally, Izanagi washed his face and, in so doing, brought into existence the sun goddess *AMATERASU*, the moon god *TSUKIYOMI* and the storm god *SUSANO-WO*. Izanagi decided to divide his kingdom equally among these three deities. (See also *CREATION MYTHS*)

JAR-SUB, according to the ancient Turkic and modern Altaic peoples of Siberia, personifies the

which to rule his kingdom, he was bewitched by a god who took the form of a bear and caused the invaders to fall asleep. One of Jimmu-Tenno's followers dreamt of a magic sword sent by Amaterasu to help Jimmu-Tenno pacify the land now known as Yamato. When he awoke, the soldier found the sword and gave it to his leader. The forces continued on their journey, led by a crow. When they reached Yamato, Jimmu-Tenno built a magnificent palace and married a local princess.

JIZO-BOSATSU is the Japanese form of Kshitigarbha, the bodhisattva or "buddha-to-be" who protects children. He is also said to help pregnant women and travellers. His cult is extremely popular in Japan, where he tends to be regarded as a venerable person rather than as a deity. Each year, his devotees confess their faults to him in the ceremony known as the "Confession of Jizo".

According to one tale, dead children whose parents simply lament their deaths, rather than offering up prayers to help them to be reborn, are sent to a sandy beach or river bank in hell. There, they spend their time building shrines, which are destroyed each night by demons. However, Jizo eventually appears to console the children. He wraps them in the folds of his robe and tells them that he is their father and mother.

JIMMU-TENNO (below) was the legendary first emperor of Japan, from whom the Japanese Imperial family claims direct descent. (DRAWING, ANON. 20TH CENTURY.)

combination of earth and water. Jar-Sub can refer either to the universe as a whole, or to the native land.

JATA, according to a creation myth of the Dayak people of Borneo, was a divine maiden who made the land and the hills during the second epoch of creation. In the first epoch of creation, the clouds, the sky, the mountains, the cliffs, the sun and moon all came into being. Afterwards, the "Hawk of Heaven" and the great fish *ILA-ILAI LANGIT* were created, followed by two fabulous creatures, *DIDIS MAHENDERA* with the jewel eyes and *ROWANG RIWO* with the golden saliva. Finally, the golden headdress of the god *MAHATALA* appeared. In the third epoch of creation, the tree of life arose, thereby uniting the upper and lower worlds.

JIZO-BOSATSU (above) is sometimes represented as a monk. He carries a staff with rings whose jingling warns small creatures of his approach so he will not step on them. (CARVED WOOD, 11TH CENTURY.)

JIMMU-TENNO, according to Japanese mythology, was the first Emperor of Japan and thus the founder of the Imperial line. He was said to be the descendant of the sun goddess *AMATERASU* and the grandson of *HIKOHOHODEMI*. During his life, Jimmu-Tenno was known by two names, Toyo-Mike-Nu and Kamu-Yamato-Iware-Hiko; it was only after his death that he became known as Jimmu-Tenno. Jimmu-Tenno was said to have acceded to the throne in 660BC.

One story tells how, while moving east with his troops in search of new territories and a place from

K

JUROJIN *(left) is shown as a small old man with a long white beard. One of the Shichi Fukujin, or seven gods of good fortune or happiness, he holds the promise of happiness in old age.* (IVORY NETSUKE.)

JUROJIN is one of the *SHICHI FUKUJIN* or seven gods of fortune or happiness, an assembly of deities gathered together in the 17th century by a monk who intended them to symbolize the virtues of a man of his time.

Jurojin was the god of longevity and happy old age. He is depicted as a small old man with a long white beard and is shown in the company of a crane, tortoise or deer, all symbols of longevity. The god also carries a staff to which is attached a scroll or book, which is said to contain the wisdom of the world. He is said to be extremely fond of rice wine. (See also *THE SHICHI FUKUJIN*)

KADAKLAN, according to the mythology of the Tinguian people of Luzon in the Philippines, is the god of thunder. He lives in the sky and beats his drum to create thunder. His dog Kimat is the lightning; he bites whatever Kadaklan chooses.

KAGUTSUCHI, or Homosubi, is the fire god of Japanese Shinto mythology. He is the son of *IZANAMI*, the female half of the primal couple. When she gave birth to him, the goddess was so badly burned that she died. In revenge, *IZANAGI*, Kagutsuchi's father,

attacked the fire god, slicing off his head. In doing so, Izanagi created several more deities. Kagutsuchi was greatly feared by the Japanese.

KAMI was the word used in ancient Japan to refer to anything mysterious or sacred. Its range of application covered everything from objects of folk cults to important deities. The kami came to be regarded as supernatural beings with human qualities. Sometimes, they are nature deities such as mountains, trees and rivers; sometimes they embody values or ideals. They may be protective deities or important men. The Buddha was thought of as the kami of China, and, later on, local kami came to be regarded as protectors of Buddhism. Some became identified with Buddhist deities.

KAMI-MUSUBI see *OKUNINUSHI*.

KANNON see *KWANNON*.

THE KAPPA, according to Japanese mythology, are a race of monkey-like demons. They live in ponds and rivers, and lure human beings, as well as other creatures, down into the depths of the water where they then feed on them. As well as being particularly fond of blood, the kappa like cucumbers.

They are malicious creatures who can, however, sometimes be appeased or bargained with. For example, if a cucumber is inscribed with the names and ages of a particular family and thrown into the water where a kappa lives, the creature will not harm that family. The kappa also display a certain vulnerability. They always return a low bow, and in doing so they spill the water, which empowers them,

from the saucer-shaped depressions in the tops of their heads.

Because they are very knowing, they can sometimes prove helpful to human beings. According to one tale, a kappa persuaded a man on a horse to play tug-of-war with him. As soon as they had grasped hold of one another, the man spurred on his horse, and the water began to spill from the top of the kappa's head. The kappa begged the man to stop, promising that if he did so, he would teach him how to mend bones. The rider agreed, and his family became renowned for their knowledge of bone-setting.

The kappa have monkey-like faces, webbed hands and feet and yellow-green skin. They wear shells like tortoises.

KARITEI-MO see *KISHIMO-JIN*.

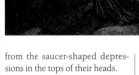

THE KAPPA *(above) are demons who drag animals or people into rivers to feed on. They resemble monkeys but stink of fish.* (ILLUSTRATION FROM MYTHS AND LEGENDS OF JAPAN.)

KHADAU see *MAMALDI*.

KHORI TUMED is a hero of Mongolian shamanism. One day, he saw nine swans fly on to the island of Oikhon on Lake Baikal. The swans removed their feathered garments and revealed themselves to be beautiful women. Believing that they were alone, they bathed naked in the lake. However, while the women were bathing, Khori Tumed stole one of their dresses and so, when they left the water, one of them was unable to fly away.

Khori Tumed married the swan woman and they lived happily together, eventually producing 11

sons. However, the time came when the swan woman asked Khori Tumed to give her back her feathers. The hero refused, but his wife continued to ask him for her dress, assuring him that she would not fly away. Eventually, Khori Tumed relented and allowed her to try the dress on. Immediately, she flew up and out of a window in their tent. Before she finally escaped, Khori Tumed persuaded her to name their sons. The swan woman did so and then flew around the tent, bestowing blessings on the tribes.

KHOSADAM, according to the Yenisei people of Siberia, is the wife of *EC*, the supreme god. Ec drove her out of the sky after discovering that she had been unfaithful to him with the moon. Khosadam is an evil, destructive deity and appears as a devourer of souls.

KHUN K'AN see THENS.

KHUN K'ET see THENS.

KIMAT see KADAKLAN.

KISHIMO-JIN, or Karitei-Mo, is Japanese mythology's "Goddess Mother of Demons". She is said to eat children and to have destroyed a town in India while Gautama Buddha was living there. When the townspeople begged the Buddha to save them, he hid Kishimo-Jin's son beneath his begging bowl. The demoness was distraught and finally asked the Buddha for help. The Buddha converted her by explaining that the pain she felt at the loss of her son was similar to that she wilfully inflicted on other

KUNLUN, where Gautama Buddha sits enthroned, is regarded as a kind of earthly paradise by both Buddhists and Daoists.
(BUDDHIST SCROLL.)

people. Kishimo-Jin was thus converted to Buddhism and became a protector of children. She is often represented seated on a chair and holding a child in her arms.

KUAN-TI see GUAN DI.

KUAN YIN see GUAN YIN.

KUEI see GUEI.

K'UN LUN see KUNLUN.

KUNLUN, or K'un Lun, is a mountain range in western China that is regarded as a Daoist paradise. It is said to be the home of *XI WANG MU* and the immortals. As well as rising above the ground, it is said to descend underground, thereby connecting the realm of the dead with that of the gods. Xi Wang Mu, the "Queen Mother of the West" is said to grow the peaches of immortality in the garden of her splendid palace on Kunlun.

KUNLUN, beyond the western limits of the ancient Chinese empire, was home to the "Queen Mother of the West".

THE EIGHT IMMORTALS

DAOISM EMERGED AS A philosophical system at about the same time as Confucianism, around the sixth century BC. Later, in response to the growing popularity of Buddhism, it acquired all the trappings of a religion, including a mythology. The "Eight Immortals" were central figures in Daoist myth and Chinese folk religion. They had all gained eternal life through seeking the Daoist "Way", and each set an example of ideal behaviour that could be followed by ordinary people to gain enlightenment. Though they were not gods, their immortality gave them superhuman powers: they practised magic and could fly through the air at great speed. They had many adventures while pursuing their mission to banish evil from the world, and were all cheerfully addicted to wine, so that they were sometimes described as the Jiu-zhong Ba Xian – the "Eight Drunken Immortals".

LI TIEGUAI (far left, above) was the first immortal. His body was prematurely cremated while his soul was visiting a sacred mountain. As his own body was no longer available to him, his soul had to inhabit that of a lame beggar, and he used an iron crutch to support himself. Li later revived his disciple's dead mother with a phial of magic medicine, and came to be regarded as the patron of pharmacists. (RELIEF TILE, QING DYNASTY.)

HE XIANGU (second from right), the patron of unmarried girls, was a young woman herself who acquired immortality when a spirit appeared to her on the mountain where she lived and instructed her to grind and eat a mother-of-pearl stone. The stone made her weightless and able to fly over the mountains. She is usually shown carrying a peach or a lotus blossom. (RELIEF TILE, QING DYNASTY.)

CAO GUOJIU (far left) carried a golden tablet which allowed him admission to the imperial court, because he was the brother of the empress. He left the court to seek the Daoist "Way" but, when he found he had no money to pay a ferryman, he tried to impress him with his court credentials. The ferryman, who was Lu Donghin in disguise, pointed out his folly, and Cao threw the tablet into the river. As an immortal, Cao Guojiu was the patron of the nobility. (RELIEF TILE, QING DYNASTY.)

SHOU LAO (left) the Daoist god of longevity, was visited by the "Eight Immortals" on one of their journeys together. Originally a stellar deity, the "Old Man of the South Pole", he had evolved into an old man who carried a gourd containing the water of life. He rode on a stag, a symbol of happiness. (CHINESE DISH, C. 1680.)

HAN XIANG (left), Lu Donghin's disciple, was said to be the great-nephew of a Daoist philosopher. He was a wandering minstrel who played the flute. During the sea voyage of the "Eight Immortals", Ao Bing, son of the "Dragon King of the Eastern Sea", tried to steal the flute and take Han Xiang prisoner. There was a great battle to rescue Han Xiang, in which the immortals were, naturally, victorious. (IVORY FIGURE, MING DYNASTY.)

LU DONGBIN's (below) blessing on parents was believed to bestow intelligent children, so Chinese scholars regarded him especially highly, and he was the guardian of ink makers. When the "Eight Immortals" decided to cross the sea, they each threw down an object on which to ride, which each turned into a sea monster. Lu Dongbin used his magic sword. (LU DONGBIN RIDING ON A KRAKEN, FROM SUPERSTITIONS EN CHINE, 1915.)

LAN CAIHE (above) was either a girl or an effeminate man. She was the patron of the poor, because she gained her immortality by her kindness in attending to the needs of a filthy beggar, whose wounds she washed and dressed. The beggar turned out to be Li Tieguai, the first of the "Eight Immortals". Lan Caihe was sometimes shown with a basket of flowers, because of her skill in growing marvellous blooms from a small pot of earth. (FRESCO, QING DYNASTY.)

ZHANG GUOLAO (above) rode on a white mule, sometimes sitting facing the animal's tail. He was a great necromancer, and his mule had extraordinary powers. It could travel over vast distances but, when no longer required, it could be folded up like a sheet of paper and kept in a bag. Zhang Guolao is often depicted with the bag containing his mule, or hitting a bamboo drum. He granted both happy marriage and the gift of children. (IVORY AND BRONZE FIGURE, MING DYNASTY.)

ZHONG-LI QUAN (left) learnt the "Way" of Daoism from Li Tieguai, then disappeared into the clouds on achieving immortality and became the messenger of heaven. Bald, with a long beard, he carried a feather fan and was the patron of soldiers. Zhong-li Quan was sometimes also shown holding a peach. The peaches of Xi Wang Mu, the "Queen Mother of the West" ripened every 3,000 years, when the immortals ate them to renew their immortality. (IVORY FIGURE, MING DYNASTY.)

L

KWANNON, or Kannon, according to Japanese Buddhist belief, is the god or goddess of mercy. She is the Japanese form of the Chinese goddess *GUANYIN*, or Kuan Yin, who herself derives from the Indian male bodhisattva Avalokiteshvara. The feminization of Kwannon is relatively modern. Kwannon, as a bosatsu, or bodhisattva, is a "buddha-to-be" who has decided to remain on earth in order to help other people to achieve enlightenment. She is known as the "Lady Giver of Children" and is a very popular deity, the protector of women and children. Kwannon is said to have been born from a ray of light, which emerged from the right of the Buddha Amitabha. There is also a Kwannon with a horse's head and one with numerous arms. According to one

KWANNON (above) lived in a cave in the Iwai Valley. (WOODBLOCK PRINT BY HIROSHIGE, ANDO OR UTAGAWA, 1853.)

KWANNON (right), the Japanese god or goddess of mercy, could assume 33 different forms, including this one with 11 heads. (WOOD SCULPTURE, 12TH CENTURY.)

tradition, Kwannon could assume 33 different forms, which gave rise to a great ritual pilgrimage to 33 sanctuaries dedicated to her.

LAN CAIHE see *BA XIAN*.

LAO CHÜN see *LAO JUN*.

LAO JUN, or Lao Chün, is the name given to the deified form of Laozi, who, by tradition, wrote the Dao-de Jing, the text which forms the basis of Daoism. He is believed to have lived in the sixth century BC; his deification began in the second century BC. Lao Jun became one of the most important Daoist gods and was sometimes said to have arisen from the primordial chaos. According to another legend, he emerged from his mother's side after a gestation of 80 years.

LEI GONG, or Lei Kung, is the god of thunder in China's Daoist pantheon. Known as "My Lord Thunder", or "Thunder Duke", he is depicted as a horribly ugly man with wings, claws, and a blue body. He carries a drum, and in his hands he holds a mallet and a chisel. Lei Gong attacks any human being

guilty of an undetected crime or who remains beyond the reach of the earthly law.

One story tells how a fierce storm arose in the middle of a thick forest. A hunter looked up into the trees and saw a child holding a flag. Lei Gong, the thunder god, approached the child but as soon as the child waved the flag, he retreated. Immediately, the hunter realized that the child must be an evil spirit and that the flag must be made of some unclean material, since all deities dislike impure objects. The hunter shot down the flag, and Lei Gong instantly struck the tree in which the child was perched. Unfortunately, being so

LAO JUN (above) is said to have been a contemporary of Confucius and a teacher of the Buddha. (PAINTED SCROLL, 18TH CENTURY.)

LAO JUN (above right), who was reputed to have been born with white hair and the power of speech, lived to a very great age. (PAINTING BY QIAN GU, 16TH CENTURY.)

close to the tree, the hunter was also struck by the thunder. However, when he came round, the hunter found a message on his body saying that his life had been prolonged for 12 years in thanks for having assisted with the work of heaven. At the foot of the tree, the hunter found the body of a vast lizard, the real form of the child.

LEI GONG (above), the winged thunder god, harasses sheep and swine in a storm of   *thunder clouds and explosive lightning flashes. (WOODBLOCK PRINT, 19TH CENTURY.)*

455

M

LEI KUNG see *LEI GONG.*

LI NAZHA see *NAZHA.*

LI TIEGUAI see *BA XIAN.*

THE LIGHTNING GODDESS is one of the nature deities referred to in early Chinese legends. She is the wife of the god of thunder, *LEI GONG,* and carries a pair of mirrors which she uses to create flashes of lightning and, occasionally, fires. The gods of thunder, lightning, wind and rain were invoked by the people during times of drought.

LING CHIH see *LING ZHI.*

LING ZHI, or Ling Chih, according to Daoist belief, is a plant of immortality. Its name means "magic herb". Ling zhi is believed to be either a type of grass or a mushroom. It grows on the three islands of the immortals, and anyone who eats it is said to gain immortality for at least 500 years.

LONG WANG, or Lung Wang, are "Dragon Kings" according to Chinese mythology. They are the servants either of Yuanshi Tian-Zong, the "Celestial Venerable of the Primordial Beginning", or *YU HUANG,* the "Jade Emperor", who was Yuanshi Tian-Zong's assistant and later came to surpass him in power. According to Daoist belief, there are different varieties of Long Wang: the celestial dragon kings, the dragon kings of the five cardinal points and the dragon kings of the oceans. Each of the dragon kings of the oceans has responsibility for one of the four oceans, helped by an army of sea creatures. The Long Wang bring rain.

LU DONGBIN see *BA XIAN.*

THE LIGHTNING GODDESS
holding her two mirrors, which she flashes to cause lightning.

LUNG WANG see *LONG WANG.*

LUXING see *SAN XING.*

MAHATALA is the supreme god of the Dayak people of Borneo. He rules over the upper regions and lives on Jewel Mountain.

MAIDERE, according to the Altaic people of Siberia, was the saviour whom the great sky god *ULGAN* sent to earth in order to protect human beings from the evil ways of the god and first man *ERLIK.* Erlik succeeded in killing Maidere, whereupon the saviour's blood gave rise to vast flames, which leapt up to the skies, destroying Erlik's heaven.

MAIN is a mythical hero of the Evenk people of Siberia. One story tells how a great elk ran to the top of a hill in the upper world and impaled the sun on its antlers. Immediately, human beings, who lived in the middle world, were subjected to continual darkness. The hero Main flew to the upper world on a pair of skis and proceeded to hunt down the elk. He eventually succeeded in shooting

LONG WANG (above), a dragon king, holds court in this modern mural in a mountain temple in Shanxi province in northern China. It is said that the dragon kings live in their own crystal palaces beneath the water.

the animal with an arrow, whereupon sunshine returned to the middle world of human beings. Main remained in the upper world, guarding the sun. According to Evenk tradition, each evening the elk catches the sun and each night, Main pursues the elk and reclaims the sun in order to rise the next morning.

MAMALDI, according to the Amur people of Siberia, created the continent of Asia. She and her husband, Khadau, are regarded either as the first human couple or as the parents of the first shaman. Whereas Khadau created the souls

LONG WANG (left), a celestial dragon king. Because they were the bringers of rain, dragon kings controlled life and death.

of shamans, Mamaldi breathed life into them. She was eventually killed by Khadau.

MANUK MANUK, according to Sumatran mythology, is a fabulous blue chicken, which belonged to the supreme god. One day, the chicken laid three gigantic eggs from which emerged three gods. The gods created the three levels of the universe: the upper world, or heaven; the middle world, or the earth; and the underworld.

MARISHI-TEN is Japanese Buddhism's goddess, or sometimes god, of war and victory. In the Middle Ages, Japanese warriors believed that Marishi-Ten made them invisible. She is depicted either sitting or standing on a boar or herd of boars. She sometimes has as many as eight arms in which she holds numerous weapons.

LING ZHI (right), the fabled mushrooms of immortality, being gathered by a boy.
(DRAWING BY ZHANG LING, 16TH CENTURY.)

MEN SHEN consist of a pair of Chinese gods who look after entrances and doorways. One of the gods is usually represented with a red or black face, the other with a white one. They are armed with weapons and magic symbols, and guard houses as well as palaces. During the New Year festivities, paper images of the gods are stuck on doors to protect those that live within from evil demons.

Although their origins are supposed to lie in the ancient past – when they were said to prevent spirits escaping from hell – one pair of Men Shen was later said to represent two historical generals who heroically guarded the palace of a Tang dynasty emperor against demons. According to one myth, the emperor had promised to look after a dragon king who had made a mistake while distributing the rain and had been condemned to death by the "Jade Emperor", YU HUANG. However, the emperor was unable to keep his promise and the spirit of the dragon king held him responsible for his death. Each night, the dragon king would come and cause a commotion outside the palace gates. Unable to sleep, the emperor fell ill, so his two generals guarded the doors. Eventually, the dragon king was driven away.

MIROKU-BOSATSU is the Japanese form of Maitreya, the future buddha. He currently lives in the Tushita heaven awaiting his future birth as a human being and finally as a buddha.

MOMOTARO is a Japanese hero who was born from a peach and was renowned for conquering demons. An elderly couple, who had been unable to have children, found a peach floating in a stream. When they cut the fruit open, they found a tiny baby boy inside. The baby sat up and ate the peach, whereupon the delighted couple called him Momotaro or "Peach Child". They raised Momotaro to be a brave and noble boy.

When he was 15, he decided to repay his parents and friends for looking after him, and determined to rid a neighbouring island of the ONI, or devils, which were persecuting them. Momotaro pocketed three dumplings, which the old woman had cooked, and set off for the island. He soon encountered a dog, a pheasant and a monkey, each of whom agreed to accompany him on his quest in return for a dumpling. The four adventurers then took a boat and crossed over to the island. There, they found

MEN SHEN (above left), one of a pair of entrance gods, guards a Chinese temple door in Yogjakarta, Java.

MEN SHEN (above), guarding a temple entrance, are sometimes represented as two generals, Heng and Ha, whose weapons include poisonous breath and fire.

numerous girls who had been taken prisoner by the oni. Momotaro attacked the castle of the oni and, together with his companions, succeeded in killing all the devils. He then piled his boat high with the treasure that the oni had stolen from the village people, helped the captive girls on board and returned home a hero.

MONJU-BOSATSU is the Japanese form of the bodhisattva, or "buddha-to-be", Manjushri. His name means "he whose beauty

MOMOTARO (left), before his battle with the oni, enlisted the help of a pheasant in exchange for a dumpling. (ILLUSTRATION FROM MYTHS AND LEGENDS OF JAPAN.)

MOYANG KAPIR is a civilizing hero spirit, according to the Ma'Betisek people of Malaysia. He stole the bag that contained the rules of civilized human behaviour from the ferocious spirit *MOYANG MELUR* and then distributed them among his people in order that they might no longer commit murder, cannibalism and incest.

MOYANG MELUR, according to the Ma'Betisek people of Malaysia, is a spirit being who guarded the rules of civilized behaviour. He is said to live on the moon and to be half-human, half-tiger. For a long time, Moyang

charms", and he personifies wisdom, compassion and contemplation. Monju-Bosatsu is often shown accompanied by a lion and is usually seated, holding the sword of intelligence, which cuts through ignorance.

Melur kept the rules of civilized behaviour to himself and, as a result, human beings constantly committed murder, incest and cannibalism.

One night, Moyang Melur was so enthralled by the chaos and destruction that was taking place below him that he leaned right out of the moon in order to take a closer look. However, he leaned too far and fell to earth. There, he met a hunter called *MOYANG KAPIR*. Moyang Melur told Moyang Kapir that unless he was able to return to

MIROKU (left), the future buddha, sits in contemplation, awaiting the time of his coming on earth. (JAPANESE SCULPTURE.)

MONJU-BOSATSU (above right), the Japanese form of Manjushri, with the Buddha (seated in the centre) and the bodhisattva Fugen-Bosatsu. (14TH CENTURY.)

the moon immediately, he would kill every single human being. Moyang Kapir promptly threw a rope to the moon, and they both climbed up it.

Moyang Melur was looking forward to killing and eating Moyang Kapir, but the latter quickly slid back down to earth, taking with him the rules of civilized behaviour, which he had found hidden in a bag under a mat. The hunter then distributed the rules among his people.

SHAMANS OF MONGOLIA

IN MANY TRADITIONAL COMMUNITIES, the shaman is a central figure combining the function of priest and doctor. He or she has the power to control spirits which, though neither good nor evil, may be destructive: to protect the community he or she incorporates them in him or herself. The shaman's ability to make out-of-body journeys to the upper and lower spirit worlds is also part of a protective role in the tribe. In shamanistic myths the world was once peopled by beings who could easily travel between heaven and earth, but after the bridge between the two was broken, most people lost their original wisdom. Eventually only a few – the shamans – were able to reach heaven, and they could do so only in spirit, by separating their souls from their bodies. Shamanistic myths, passed down through successive generations in an oral tradition, tell of a process of decline, from a golden age, when great spirits brought knowledge to the world, to the present, when not even all shamans can fly away from it.

DRUMMING (above) is used to induce a trance state in which the shaman's soul can leave his body. The drum beat excludes other stimuli while its insistent rhythm works on the consciousness. According to Mongolian legend, early shamans could use their drums to call back the souls of the dead. The lord of the dead, fearing that he would lose all his subjects, ordained that the shamans' drums, originally double-headed, should have only a single head to reduce their power.

ANIMALS (left) are used by Siberian Yakut shamans as receptacles for their souls. Each shaman keeps his chosen animal far away from other people, so that its life is protected and his spiritual well-being ensured. However, once a year, when the last snow melts, the animals are said to come down from the mountains and walk into the villages. The most powerful shamans keep their souls in horses, elks, bears, eagles or boars; the weakest keep them in dogs. Sometimes the animals fight, and if one is harmed, its shaman will fall ill or die.

YAKUT SHAMANS (above) claim descent from a primordial shaman who rebelled against the supreme god and was condemned to eternal fire. His body, which was composed of reptiles, was consumed, but a single frog escaped the flames and gave rise to a line of shamanic demons from whom Yakut shamans are still drawn. (LITHOGRAPH, C. 1835.)

A SHAMAN (left) enacts a healing ceremony over a sick man. Illness is thought to be due to the loss of the person's soul, which may have wandered to the land of the dead in error, looking for its home. The shaman's task is to retrieve the soul and for this he or she needs to be able to fly to the underworld and persuade it to return. The shaman may also massage, stroke or blow on the patient, and suck harmful material out through the skin. (A SHAMAN OF YAKUTIA, C. 1805.)

N

MUCILINDA (left) coiled his body under the Buddha beneath the sacred fig tree at Bodhi-gaya. (STONE CARVING, 3RD CENTURY AD.)

other great demiurge, and asked him for advice. Num instructed the shaman to descend below the earth and call upon Nga. The shaman did so and married Nga's daughter. He then supported the earth in his hand and became known as the "Old Man of the Earth".

NINIGI, or Honinigi, is the grandson of the great AMATERASU, the sun goddess of Japanese Shinto

NAGAS (below) are spirits in the form of serpents. They may be benevolent and protective, like Mucilinda sheltering the Buddha from the rain. (THAI BRONZE, 1291.)

MUCILINDA is the king of the serpent deities, or water spirits, known as *NAGAS*. According to a legend, Mucilinda sheltered the Buddha with the outspread hoods of his seven heads during a downpour that lasted for seven days. When the sun returned, the serpent was transformed into a young prince who proceeded to pay homage to the Buddha. In India, and especially in South-east Asia, Mucilinda is often depicted protecting the Buddha.

NAGA PADOHA is the great sea serpent of South-east Asian mythology. In the tale of creation, *BATARA GURU*, a form of the great Hindu god Shiva, created the first solid land whereupon Naga Padoha sought to destroy it by writhing and thrashing about in the ocean. However, Batara Guru, in his incarnation as a hero figure, managed to control the serpent, pressing him down with a vast iron weight so that he descended to the lower regions of the cosmos.

NAGAS, according to the mythology of South-east Asia, are supernatural beings who take the form of serpents. The great serpent

Sesha, on whose coils the god Vishnu rested in the intervals between creation, was served by nagas. In Buddhist belief, the serpent *MUCILINDA* was a naga king who sheltered Gautama Buddha from the weather. In Tibetan Buddhism, the nagas are said to guard the Buddhist scriptures. (See also *DEMONS*)

NAZHA, the "Third Prince" and *enfant terrible* of Chinese mythology, is an exorcising spirit and a deity of popular religion. Nazha is also said to have been a powerful deity in his own right, dispatched down to the human world by *YU HUANG*, the "Jade Emperor", to subdue or destroy the demons raging through the world. He was incarnated as the third son of Li Jing, a general who fought for the Zhou dynasty in the 12th century BC. Nazha grew up to be full of mischief and the numerous legends surrounding his life are probably better known to Chinese peasants than recent imperial history.

NGA, according to the mythology of the Samoyed Yuraks of Siberia, is the god of death and hell, and one of the two great demiurges, or

supreme deities. One tale relates how the earth threatened to collapse, so a shaman visited *NUM*, the

mythology. Amaterasu had been trying for some time to find someone to rule over earth. At first, she decided to send her son, Ame-No-Oshido-Mimi, down from the heavens. However, the god looked over the Floating Bridge of Heaven, saw the many disturbances happening below, and refused to go.

The gods all met together in order to decide what to do and eventually determined to send down Ame-No-Hohi. Three years passed but the gods heard nothing from Ame-No-Hohi. They then decided to send down his son, Ame-No-Wakahiko. Before he left, they gave him a bow and arrows.

Ame-No-Wakahiko descended to earth and soon married Shitateru-Hime, the daughter of OKUNINUSHI, the god of medicine and magic. This time, eight years passed without the gods hearing any news. At the end of that time, they sent down a pheasant to find out what Ame-No-Wakahiko had

NAZHA (above), the "Third Prince" and son of Li Jing, is the enfant terrible of Chinese Mythology. Numerous popular legends are told about his escapades.

been doing. The pheasant perched on a tree outside the god's house.

One of the women of the house noticed the bird and told Ame-No-Wakahiko that it was an evil omen. Immediately, the god shot it with his bow and arrow. The arrow passed straight through the bird, entered heaven and fell at the feet of Amaterasu and the god Takami-Masubi. The god recognized the arrow and, in fury, flung it back down to earth where it killed Ame-No-Wakahiko. Shitateru-Hime, his wife, was devastated.

The gods then sent two of their number down to visit Okuninushi. They told him that they had been sent by the sun goddess in order to bring the land under her command. Okuninushi spoke to his two sons. The older son agreed to

worship Amaterasu, but the younger son tried to resist. However, the two gods soon overpowered the younger son, who then promised not to put up any resistance against the sun goddess. Okuninushi also agreed to the sun goddess's rule, on condition that a place should be reserved for him among the major deities worshipped at the famous shrine at Izumo. Amaterasu agreed to this.

At last, Amaterasu sent her grandson, Ninigi, down to earth. Before leaving heaven, Ninigi was given various divine objects, including the mirror into which the sun goddess had gazed after emerging from hiding in the cave, the heavenly jewels that had produced Amaterasu's sons and the sword Kusanagi, which the storm god SUSANO-WO had found in the tail of the eight-headed snake, Yamato-No-Orochi. These three items became the emblems of Japanese imperial power.

NAZHA's (above) father, Li Jing, was a commander who fought during the mythological wars between dynasties in the 12th century BC.

Ninigi married Kono-Hana-Sakuyu-Hime, the daughter of a mountain god. When Kono-Hana-Sakuyu-Hime conceived on the first night that she slept with her husband, Ninigi suspected her of having been unfaithful to him. In response, Kono-Hana-Sakuyu-Hime built a house with no doors, and, when she was about to give birth, she entered the house and set it alight saying that if she had been unfaithful, her child would die. As it turned out, Kono-Hana-Sakuyu-Hime produced three sons. One of them, HIKOHOHODEMI, married the daughter of the sea god. Their child later fathered a boy who, after his death, became known as JIMMU-TENNO. Jimmu-Tenno was the founder of the imperial line of Japan.

THE NIO, according to Japanese Buddhism, are the two guardian kings, or kings of compassion. They are usually represented as giants who guard the entrances to temples and monasteries, and are dressed either in sarongs or in armour. They are believed to banish evil spirits and thieves, and to protect children.

NU GUA or Nü Kua, is an ancient Chinese creator deity who, after the great flood, became the consort of *FU XI*. Her name is derived from the words for gourd or melon, a symbol of fertility, and she is sometimes known as the "Gourd Girl". Nu Gua is said to have been half-human and half-serpent or dragon and to have had the ability to change her shape at will. She is sometimes shown holding a pair of compasses while Fu Xi holds a set square, symbolizing their part in the creation. Nu Gua is also said to have invented the flute.

According to one story, Nu Gua descended to earth after it had been separated from the sky, and after the mountains, rivers, animals and plants had been created. She tamed the wild animals and, together with other mythological figures, taught humankind how to irrigate the land. However, Nu Gua is most famous for having created human beings out of clay or mud.

One day, as Nu Gua wandered through the world, she began to feel that something was missing and longed to have some companionship. She sat down on the bank of a river and, gazing at her reflection in the water, she began to play with some mud from the riverbed. Almost without thinking, she began to model the clay into a little figure. However, rather than giving the figure a tail like herself, she gave it legs and feet. When Nu Gua had finished moulding the figure, she stood it on the ground and it immediately came to life, dancing and laughing with happiness.

Nu Gua was so happy with her creation that she decided to fill the whole world with people. She worked until it grew dark, and as soon as the sun rose the next morning, she set to work once more. Although the people wandered off, Nu Gua could still hear their voices and so she never again felt lonely. Before long, Nu Gua realized that she could not possibly create enough people to populate the whole earth. She decided to call on her magic power and, taking a length of vine, she trailed it in the mud and then whirled it about in the air. As soon as the drops of mud touched the ground, they were transformed into human beings.

It is sometimes said that those people whom Nu Gua fashioned with her hands became rich and fortunate, whereas those who were created when the drops of mud fell to the ground were the poor and humble people.

NU GUA'S (left) image on a Chinese temple altar in Singapore. She is known as the "Dark Lady of the Ninth Heaven".

THE NIO (left) are the two guardian kings or kings of compassion. They are usually represented as temple guardians, with fierce expressions which are designed to deter evil spirits from entering the sacred precinct.

Realizing that her little people might eventually die and become extinct, Nu Gua divided them into male and female so that they could bear children.

Nu Gua and Fu Xi are also renowned for having saved the world from a flood. One tale tells how the world had become wild and chaotic: human beings were eaten by wild animals, immense fires raged continuously and water flowed without ceasing. Nu Gua mended the skies with melted stones, supported the heavens with the legs of a turtle and piled ashes of reeds on a river bank to dam the waters until, at last, everything became calm again.

NÜ KUA see *NU GUA*.

NUM and *NGA*, according to the mythology of the Samoyed Yuraks of Siberia, are the two great demiurges, or supreme deities. At the beginning of time, Num sent several birds one after the other to explore the endless stretches of water. Eventually, one of the birds returned with a small piece of sand or mud, from which Num created a floating island.

Another tale relates how the earth threatened to collapse, whereupon a shaman visited Num and asked him for advice. Num instructed the shaman to descend to Nga, the god of death and hell, who lived beneath the earth. The shaman did as instructed and married the daughter of Nga. He then supported the earth in his hand and became known as the "Old Man of the Earth". Num lives in a place of light, but he regularly visits earth to ensure it is secure.

OGETSU-NO-HIME see *UKE-MOCHI*.

OKUNINUSHI, according to Japanese Shinto mythology, is the god of medicine and magic. His name means "Great Land Master", and he ruled the earth after its creation until *AMATERASU* sent her grandson *NINIGI* to take his place. As god of medicine, he is credited with having invented therapeutic methods of healing.

Okuninushi had 80 brothers, all of whom wanted to marry the beautiful princess *YAKAMI* or Ya-Gami-Hime. While the brothers were on their way to visit the princess, a flayed hare stopped them and asked them for help. The brothers told the hare to wash in the sea and then dry itself in the wind. The hare suffered excruciating pain and distress. The creature then met Okuninushi who, feeling sorry for it, told it to bathe in fresh water and then roll around in the pollen of kama grass. The hare did as Okuninushi advised and immediately felt better. In gratitude, the hare, who was really a god, told Okuninushi that the beautiful princess Yakami would be his.

Okuninushi's brothers were furious. They heated a vast rock until it was white-hot and rolled it down a mountain towards their brother. Okuninushi mistook the rock for a boar, caught hold of it and was burned to death. However, with the help of his mother, Kami-Musubi, he was brought back to life. The brothers then crushed Okuninushi to death. This time, Kami-Musubi advised her son to avoid further attacks by taking refuge in the underworld.

There, Okuninushi met the storm god *SUSANO-WO* and his daughter Suseri-Hime. The couple fell in love. When Susano-Wo discovered this, he sent Okuninushi to sleep in a room full of snakes. However, the god was protected by a scarf, which Suseri-Hime had given him. The following night, Susano-Wo sent him to sleep in a room full of centipedes and wasps, but again Okuninushi was protected. Susano-Wo then fired an arrow into the middle of an enormous field and told Okuninushi to look for it. When Okuninushi reached the middle of the field, Susano-Wo set fire to the grass. However, a mouse showed Okuninushi a hole in which he could take shelter from the fire and then brought the arrow to him.

By this time, Susano-Wo was beginning to approve of Okuninushi. He asked him to wash his hair and then went to sleep. While Susano-Wo was sleeping, Okuninushi tied the storm god's hair to the rafters of his palace and fled with Suseri-Hime. He took with him Susano-Wo's sword, bow and arrows and his harp, called Koto. As Okuninushi and Suseri-Hime made their escape, the harp brushed against a tree, and the noise of its strings awoke Susano-Wo. The god jumped up and in so doing pulled down his house with his hair.

Okuninushi hurried onwards. Eventually, at the borders of the underworld, Susano-Wo almost caught up with the elopers and called out to them, advising Okuninushi to fight his brothers with Susano-Wo's weapons in order that he might rule the world. It seems that Okuninushi's trickery had finally convinced the storm god that he would make a suitable husband for Suseri-Hime, because he then asked the god to make Suseri-Hime his wife and to build a palace at the foot of Mount Uka. Okuninushi became ruler of the province of Izumo.

OKUNINUSHI is seen here with the white hare of Inaoa, who foretold his success in his quest for the hand of Yakami.

P

OTSHIRVANI, according to Siberian mythology, is a god of light. He was sent by the supreme god to fight Losy, a monstrous serpent who killed all mortal beings by covering the world with poison. Otshirvani took the form of an enormous bird and, seizing Losy in his claws, threw him against the world mountain, killing him.

PA HSIEN see BA XIAN.

PAMALAK BAGOBO, according to the Bagobo people of Mindanao in the Philippines, is the god who created human beings. According to tradition, monkeys once behaved and looked like humans and only acquired their current appearance when Pamalak decided to create humankind as a separate race.

P'AN-KU see PANGU.

PANGU, or P'an-ku, is the cosmic giant of Chinese mythology. He is said to be the child of YIN and

THE ONI are giant horned demons. They are said to have come to Japan from China with the arrival of Buddhism, and Buddhist priests perform annual rites in order to expel them. The oni can be a variety of colours and have three fingers, three toes and sometimes three eyes. They are usually cruel and lecherous, and they are said to sweep down from the sky in order to steal the souls of people who are about to die. One story tells how the diminutive hero MOMOTARO freed numerous young girls whom the oni had captured and raped.

The oni of hell have the heads of oxen or horses; they hunt down sinners and take them away in their chariot of fire to EMMA-O, the ruler of the underworld. Some oni are held responsible for illness and disease, and others are said to have once been mortal women whose jealousy or grief transformed them into demons.

OT, the fire queen of the Mongols, is said to have been born at the beginning of the world, when the earth and sky separated. Her blessing is invoked at weddings and her radiance is said to penetrate throughout all the realms. Ot is believed originally to have been identical with UMAI, mother goddess of the Turkic people of Siberia.

PANGU *is the giant who emerged from the cosmic egg when it split to form the earth and sky. He held the two apart to create the world.*

PANGU, the cosmic creator and mythological deity, on an altar in a temple in Tainan, in southern Taiwan.

the myth tells how Pangu was born from the five basic elements and formed heaven and earth with a chisel and hammer. Pangu is still worshipped by some of the people of South China. (See also CREATION MYTHS; CHINA'S SACRED PEAKS)

PENG LAI, or P'eng-lai, according to Daoist belief, is an island in the East China Sea inhabited by the immortals or XIAN. The plant of immortality, LING ZHI, grows there. Many explorers have attempted to discover the mythical island, but all expeditions have failed – some-times, it is said, because the island sinks beneath the waves. Everything on the miraculous island is made of gold and jewels: the trees are made of pearl and coral, and the animals and birds are glittering white.

The two other islands of the immortals are Fangchang and Yingzhou. Originally, there were five islands, but a giant caused two of them to break away from their moorings and sink without trace. Fangchang, lying off the east coast of China, is said to be inhabited by dragons and to boast marvellous palaces made of gold, jade and crystal. Thousands of immortals live there, cultivating the plant of immortality. Yingzhou is also cred-ited with a marvellous appearance and inhabitants.

P'ENG-LAI see PENG LAI.

POLONG, according to Malayan and Indonesian tradition, is a flying demon created from the blood of a murdered man. Whoever owns the Polong can order it to attack his enemies. The victims tear their clothes, go blind and eventually lose consciousness. However, the Polong also feeds on the blood of its owner.

PU LANG SEUNG see TIIENS.

YANG, the vital forces of the universe. The myth of Pangu's birth tells how, at the very beginning of time, only chaos existed. Chaos took the form of a primordial egg, and eventually Pangu took shape inside its shell. The creature slept and grew inside the egg for 18,000 years until, eventually, he woke up and stretched. The light part of the egg, which was pervaded by yang, rose up to become the sky; the heavy part, pervaded by yin, sank down and became the earth.

Pangu, fearing that the earth and sky might merge together again, stood between them, his head keeping the sky aloft and his feet treading down the earth. For 18,000 years, the distance between heaven and earth increased at a rate of 3 metres (ten feet) a day. Pangu grew at the same rate to continue to hold heaven and earth apart.

Eventually, when Pangu considered that there was no risk of the earth and sky rejoining, he fell asleep and eventually died. The giant's enormous corpse gave rise to all the elements. His breath became the wind and clouds, his voice became the thunder and lightning, his left eye became the sun, and his right eye became the moon. His four limbs and his trunk were transformed into the cardinal directions and the mountains, his blood became the rivers and his veins the roads. His flesh became trees and soil, the hair on his head and his beard became the stars in the sky, and the hairs on his body were transformed into grass and flowers. His teeth and bones became metal and stones, and his sweat produced the dew. Finally, the fleas and parasites on his body became the ancestors of the different races of human beings.

Many later tales elaborate the story of Pangu. According to one, the alternation of night and day occurs when Pangu opens and closes his eyes. Another version of

467

CHINESE DRAGONS

THE CHINESE DRAGON CAME FIRST in the mythical hierarchy of 360 scaly creatures, and was one of the four animals who symbolized the cardinal points. Associated with the east, the dragon stood for sunrise, spring and fertility and was opposed by the white tiger of the west, who represented death. Daoist dragons were benevolent spirits associated with happiness and prosperity, and were kind to humans. However, when Buddhism became popular, their character was modified by the Indian concept of the naga, which was a more menacing creature. In folk religion, the Long Wang

were dragon kings who had authority over life and death because they were responsible for rain, without which life could not continue, and funerals. They were gods of rivers, lakes and oceans, and represented wisdom, strength and goodness. Because they had power over the rain, offerings were made to dragons during droughts, but angry Long Wang sent storms, fog and earthquakes. They protected ferrymen and water-carriers, and punished anyone who wasted water.

THE CHINESE DRAGON (above) was a mythical hybrid monster with the "horns of a deer, head of a camel, abdomen of a cockle, scales of a carp, claws of an eagle, feet of a tiger, and ears of an ox." Because dragons represented the yang principle, their images were traditionally accompanied by water or clouds, which were yin. (QIANLONG, FAMILLE ROSE BOTTLE VASE, 18TH CENTURY.)

DRAGON PROCESSIONS (left), which were held all over China in spring, welcomed the annual return of these generous creatures and ensured fertility. Dragons spent the winter underground, emerging on the second day of the second lunar month. Their arrival, announced by claps of thunder, coincided with the beginning of the spring rains, and this was the time to go out into the fields and begin the year's cultivation. As bringers of rain, dragons were coloured blue-green. (HSIE YANG, PROCESSION OF THE BLUE DRAGON.)

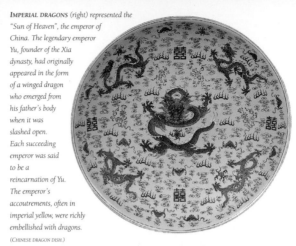

IMPERIAL DRAGONS (right) represented the "Sun of Heaven", the emperor of China. The legendary emperor Yu, founder of the Xia dynasty, had originally appeared in the form of a winged dragon who emerged from his father's body when it was slashed open. Each succeeding emperor was said to be a reincarnation of Yu. The emperor's accoutrements, often in imperial yellow, were richly embellished with dragons. (CHINESE DRAGON DISH.)

A DRAGON (above) was often depicted playing with a flaming pearl or ball, which symbolized thunder. It was this heavenly sport which was thought to cause the rain to fall. Only imperial dragons were represented with five claws on each foot. Those with four claws signified the status of a prince, while court officials were allowed only three claws for the dragons embroidered on their robes and other possessions. (CHINESE PILLAR RUG.)

HUI-NENG (right), the Chinese Buddhist patriarch, persuaded a fierce dragon to shrink so small that it would fit into a tiny rice bowl and was thus able to subdue it. The magic powers of dragons included the ability to make themselves invisible at will and change their shape and size. They could shrink to the size of a silkworm or swell to fill all the space between heaven and earth. (ILLUSTRATION FROM SUPERSTITIONS EN CHINE, 1914.)

R

PUDAI (left), in the "Cave of the Laughing
Buddha" in Zhejiang Province, China, is
portrayed with a fat belly and a wide grin.

PUDAI (right), also known as the
"Hempbag Monk", on a temple altar in
Tainan, in southern Taiwan.

the "Wind God" and the "Master
of Rain" to bring on a major storm,
with gales and torrential rains to
help him. Along with the LIGHT-
NING GODDESS and the God of
Thunder, these nature spirits were
invoked during times of drought.
The Goddess of Lightning flashes
the two mirrors she carries to cause
lightning, while thunder is made by
the thunder god with his hammer
and drums, and has the power to
kill. The Master of Rain is said to
own a mysterious one-legged bird,
which can drink the seas dry.

PU-TAI see PUDAI.

PUDAI, or Pu-tai, was a Chinese
monk who is said to have lived in
the tenth century AD and whose
original name was Qizi. He is said
to have earned his name, which
means "Hempen Sack", from his
habit of wandering through towns
with a beggar's sack on his back.
He was believed to be able to predict the weather, and his life was
filled with miraculous events. At his
death, he revealed himself to be an
incarnation of Maitreya, the future
Buddha. Pudai is often represented
as the "Laughing Buddha", the
Chinese style of depicting Maitreya.

PULANG GANA, according to
the Iban people of Borneo, is an
earth spirit who ensures the abundant growth of rice. According to
tradition, a long time ago the Iban
began to clear the jungle in order to
create the first rice farm. However,
when they arose the next morning,
they found that all the trees had
grown back. The same happened
after their next attempt to clear the
jungle, and the next. At last, the
Iban decided to keep watch during
the night in order to try and solve
the mystery.

That night, they saw Pulang
Gana coax the trees back to life and
ensure that they became rooted in

the soil once more. They tried to
catch the spirit, who explained that
he owned the earth and everything
that grew in it, and that he alone
could ensure that the plants flourished. When the people asked the
spirit what they should do before
cultivating rice, he told them that
they should offer up gifts to him.

QORMUSTA, or Chormusta,
according to Mongolian belief, is
king of the Tengri, the realms of

heaven. The supreme god, he lives
in the centre of the world and is
associated with the creation of fire.

RADIN is a mythical hero of the
Iban people of Borneo. One tale
tells how, after winning a battle,
Radin began to be troubled by a
hungry ghost. When the ghost
introduced smallpox to Radin's
tribe, the hero determined to kill it.
One night, Radin hid inside a roll
of matting, and when the ghost
approached, he jumped out and
cut it into pieces with his sword.
Before falling asleep again, Radin
heard something fall to the ground
and, when daylight came, he found
a carving of a hornbill, a sacred
bird, lying on the ground in pieces.
Radin realized that this signified
that the ghost was far too powerful
a being to overcome, so he and his
people moved to another area.

THE RAIN SPIRIT is one of the
early nature gods who were referred
to in Chinese legendary stories. In
his struggle with HUANG DI, the
"Yellow Emperor", CHIYOU begged

THE RAIN SPIRIT (left), with his vase of
water, sometimes also holds a dragon on a
plate, since the dragon is a symbol of rain.

RANGDA (right), the Balinese demon
queen, is represented by a terrifying mask.

RANGDA is the terrifying demon
queen of Bali. She leads an army of
evil witches against BARONG, the
leader of the forces of good. The
evil demon is usually represented
as scantily clad, with long hair and
with claws in place of fingernails
and toenails.

It is sometimes suggested that
Rangda derived from an 11th-cen-
tury Balinese queen who was exiled

S

by the king for practising witchcraft against his second wife. In revenge, Rangda attempted to destroy the kingdom. Half the population died of plague before she was overcome by the superior powers of a holy man. The name Rangda means "widow". (See also DEMONS)

ROWANG RIWO is a fabulous creature who, according to the Dayak people of Borneo, appeared during the first epoch of creation with *DIDIS MAHENDERA*. Rowang Riwo had golden saliva and Didis Mahendera had eyes of jewels.

THE SAN QING DAOZU's senior deity is Yuanshi Tian-zong, "Jade Pure", who is invisible and eternal.

THE SAN GUAN DADI, or San Kuan Ta-ti, are the "Three Great Primordial Rulers" and "Controllers of Heaven, Earth and the Waters". Also known as the San Yuan Dadi, they are of mythical origin and are revered as the source of all happiness and forgiveness of sins, able to avert calamities and sickness. Legend has it that *YU HUANG*, the "Jade Emperor", sent them down to earth to govern it, and observe men's good and evil thoughts and deeds.

SAN-HSING see *SAN XING*.

THE SAN QING DAOZU's second deity is Ling-bao Tian-zong, who regulates time and yin and yang.

SAN KUAN TA-TI see *SAN GUAN DADI*.

THE SAN QING DAOZU, or, as they are sometimes known, "The Three Pure Ones", are the supreme deities of the orthodox Daoist pantheon, ruling the entire cosmos from the highest heaven. In the "Doctrine of the Three Pure Ones", they are the symbolic personification of the three life principles: breath, vital essence and spirit. They are prayed to as a group for assistance in coping with the problems of life.

THE SAN QING DAOZU's third deity is Lao Jun. He is the deified form of the legendary founder of Daoism, Laozi.

SAN GUAN DADI, the three great primordial rulers, are transcendent powers who bestow happiness, forgive sins and protect from evil.

The first is the "Perfect One", or "Jade Pure", Yuanshi Tian-zong, the deity of the beginning representing primeval origins. He is in charge of the "Heaven of the Heavenly Ones" and is said to have formulated the heavens and earth and dominated the first phase of creation.

The "Highest Holy One", Ling-bao Tian-zong, the "High Pure", represents energy and activity. He is in charge of the "Heaven of the Perfect Ones", Zhenren, and is said to have devised the rules for calculating time and controlling the interaction of YIN and YANG, as well as the doctrine for the heavens and earth. He is the guardian of magical writings. Ling-bao dominated the second phase of creation.

The "Greatest Holy One", the "Supreme Pure", *LAO JUN*, representing humankind, is the deified philosopher Laozi who is in charge of the third and lowest heaven, that of the immortals. He is said to have dominated the third phase of the creation of the cosmos, and inspired the formation of religious Daoism at a later stage.

THE SAN XING, or San-hsing, or "Three Stars", are the three Chinese gods of good fortune. They were historical figures who were given divine status in recognition of their special merits. Fuxing or "Lucky Star" is usually depicted alongside a child or as a bat, a symbol of good luck. He is the god of happiness. Luxing or "Star of Honour" is the god of salaries and is often shown as a deer. Shouxing, "Star of Longevity", is shown with the face of an old man, a white beard and eyebrows, a high bald head and holding a knotty staff, a symbol of the immortals.

Fuxing is said to have been a government official called Yang Cheng who lived during the sixth century BC. He came from a village whose inhabitants were all very short in height. Each year, the emperor, who enjoyed surrounding himself with dwarfs, would call a number of the villagers to his court and insist that they remain there. As a result, as time went by, the population of the village began to dwindle. Eventually, Yang Cheng asked the emperor to take pity on the village folk. The emperor was impressed by Yang Cheng's petition and so ceased his demands.

Luxing is sometimes identified with Guo Ziyi, who had many sons, or is said to have been Shi Fei, a servant of the founder of the Han dynasty, who lived at the end of the third century BC.

Shouxing came to be known as *SHOU LAO*, the god of long life and "Old Man of the South Pole". He is said to fix the date of everyone's death, writing it down beforehand. However, although the digits of the appointed date cannot be changed, they can sometimes be juggled.

According to one tale, a child called Zao Yan was told that he had only 19 more years to live. One day, the boy was told to go to a field, taking with him some food and wine. There, he would find two men playing a game of draughts (checkers) under a mulberry tree. Zao Yan was advised to offer the men food and drink but to refuse to answer any of their questions. The boy did as he was told. He gave the two men the food and drink, then waited quietly

while they argued over how they should thank him. The men finally decided to reverse the order of the digits of the number of years Zao Yan was to live, thereby decreeing that he should live for a further 91 years. Zao Yan later discovered that one of the men had been Shou Lao.

SEMARA, according to the mythology of the Balinese, is the god of love who lives in the floating sky, one of a series of skies that lies above the layer of water hanging over the earth.

THE SAN XING *Luxing and Fuxing are dressed as mandarins, while Shouxing, the god of longevity, holds a sprig of Ling Zhi, the plant of immortality. (JADEITE FIGURES, LATE QING DYNASTY.)*

THE SAN XING *(above) are usually portrayed as three good-humoured old men, surrounded by symbols of good fortune, longevity and immortality. (PAINTED SILK SCROLL BY WANG CHAO, C. 1500.)*

SENGALONG BURONG see *SURONG GUNTING.*

SETESUYARA, according to Balinese mythology, is the goddess who rules over the underworld together with the god *BATARA KALA*.

SHAKA-NYORAI is the Japanese name for the Buddha Shakyamuni Gautama. Although Shaka is worshipped in Japan, the dominant form of Buddhism is the "Pure Land" school, whose followers chiefly venerate the buddha *AMIDA* or Amitabha.

*SHAKA-NYORAI, the Japanese buddha,
preaching at Ryoj-Usen Mountain. (WALL
PAINTING, 8TH CENTURY.)*

SHANG DI, or Shang Ti, was worshipped as the ancestor of China's Shang dynasty, established around 1500BC. The supreme god, he ruled over heaven and controlled natural phenomena such as the thunder, lightning, wind and rain. He was also regarded as the god of agriculture and was believed to determine people's fates. He was sometimes known simply as Di, which means "Lord" or "God".

SHANG TI see *SHANG DI*.

SHEN NONG, or Shen Nung, is an ancient Chinese god of medicine, health, agriculture and forestry. Together with *FU XI* and *HUANG DI*, he was one of the San Huang, or "Three Nobles", legendary emperors of China. He was sometimes referred to as the "Divine Husbandman", although, as god of the hot winds, he could also bring harm. Shen Nong is said to have invented the plough to improve the lives of the ancient Chinese. He taught them how to grow food and revealed the medicinal properties of plants.

Because he had a transparent stomach, he was able to observe the effect of food and drink on his body. However, while investigating the effect of an unusual piece of grass, he turned black and died.

SHENG MU see *DONGYUE DADI*.

THE SHICHI FUKUJIN are the seven Japanese gods of good fortune or happiness. Their names are *DAIKOKU, EBISU, BENTEN,* *BISHAMON, FUKUROKUJU, JUROJIN* and *HOTEI*. Among the group are deities from Buddhism, Japanese folklore and Chinese Daoism. The group was assembled in the 17th century by the monk Tenkai, who intended the gods to symbolize the virtues of fortune, magnanimity, candour, dignity, popularity, longevity and amiability. The deities are said to travel together on a treasure ship and are sometimes portrayed thus. (See also *THE SHICHI FUKUJIN*)

SHEN NONG (below left), with Huang Di, another legendary emperor of China.

SHEN NONG (below) is portrayed dressed in green leaves because he is a "primitive" deity and lived before cloth was ever invented.

SHOTEN, or Daisho-Kangiten, is a Japanese form of the Indian elephant-headed god Ganesha, who was adopted by certain Buddhist sects. His cult was introduced to Japan in the ninth century. Shoten both creates obstacles and overcomes them. He is worshipped by esoteric sects, and the god's tremendous power is believed to help people to gain enlightenment.

SHOU LAO is the Daoist god of long life. Originally known as Shouxing, he was one of the SAN XING or Chinese gods of good fortune. In due course, he came to rule over the department of the heavens that decrees the life-span of human beings. The god is usually shown with a large head and carrying a staff as well as a gourd, which holds the water of life. In his other hand, he holds the peach of eternal life. His creature is the white crane, a symbol of immortality. (See also THE EIGHT IMMORTALS)

SHOUXING see SHOU LAO.

SHUN is one of the five legendary emperors, or Wu Di, of Chinese mythology. The emperor YAO chose Shun, rather than his own son, as his successor. Shun was said to be a potter who travelled throughout the four directions and banished all the threatening creatures guarding their entrances. He is said to have lived in the third century BC and to have been succeeded by YU.

SUKU-NA-BIKONA, a dwarf deity, assisted OKUNINUSHI, one of Japan's great mythological heroes. He is regarded as a benevolent deity who is learned in both healing and cultivation.

After Okuninushi had settled in his palace with his wife, Suku-Na-Bikona arrived in a tiny boat on the crest of a wave. Okuninushi put the dwarf in the palm of his hand in order to examine him, whereupon the creature leapt up and bit the hero on his cheek. Okuninushi was

SHOU LAO (left) wears the robes and hat of a mandarin in his capacity as the heavenly official who determines human life-spans. (CHINESE PORCELAIN, 18TH CENTURY.)

SHOU LAO (right), the Daoist god of long life, has a large head and carries a staff. (JADE CARVING, 17TH CENTURY.)

annoyed and told the gods what had happened. One of the gods realized that the dwarf must be his son, a mischievous child who had fallen to earth. The god asked Okuninushi to look after his child, who proceeded to help the hero to establish his rule. Eventually, however, Suku-Na-Bikona disappeared.

SURONG GUNTING is a culture hero of the Iban people of Borneo. He went to visit his grandfather, a spirit called Sengalong Burong and, during his journey, the stars taught him about the agricultural cycle. When he reached his destination, his grandfather taught him about rituals and omens.

In due course Sengalong Burong threw the young man out of his house in punishment for having slept with his aunt, Dara Chempaka Tempurong. According to Sengalong Burong, if people of adjacent generations slept with one another there would be a terrible harvest. Surong Gunting returned to his home and taught his people all that he had learned.

SUSANO-WO is the storm god of Japanese Shinto mythology. He came into being when IZANAGI, the male half of the primal pair, washed his face after returning from the land of the dead. Susano-Wo emerged from Izanagi's nose.

Izanagi divided his kingdom between his three children, the others being the sun goddess AMATERASU and the moon god TSUKIYOMI. To Susano-Wo he allocated rulership of the ocean. Susano-Wo was dismayed with his lot and protested, saying that he wanted to join his mother IZANAMI in the underworld. Izanagi immediately banished Susano-Wo.

Before leaving, Susano-Wo visited his sister Amaterasu. He challenged her to a contest in order to determine which of them was the most powerful. The task was to see who of them could give rise to male deities. Susano-Wo took Amaterasu's fertility beads from her hair and arms and, breaking them with his teeth, blew them out as five male deities. He then pronounced himself victorious. Amaterasu disagreed, saying that the beads belonged to her, and therefore she had won the contest. Susano-Wo ignored his sister's protests and proceeded to celebrate

his victory by causing devastation on earth. He finished his riotous activities by throwing a flayed pony through the roof of the sacred weaving hall where Amaterasu sat with her attendants. Amaterasu was so angry that she hid in a cave, thereby bringing darkness to the world. Although Amaterasu was eventually lured out of the cave, the gods decided that Susano-Wo ought to be punished. They ordered him to give them numerous gifts and cut off his beard and the nails of his hands and feet. Finally, the gods threw Susano-Wo out of heaven.

According to another tale, Susano-Wo ordered the food goddess *UKE-MOCHI* to give him something to eat. The goddess responded by pulling food from her nose, mouth and rectum whereupon the disgusted Susano-Wo killed her. From her corpse sprouted all the basic food crops: rice seeds grew from her eyes, millet from her ears, wheat from her genitals, red beans from her nose

and soy beans from her rectum. In some versions of the legend, it is the moon god Tsukiyomi, rather than Susano-Wo, who kills the food goddess.

When Susano-Wo arrived on earth he set out to find some human beings. He soon came across an elderly couple and a beautiful young woman. The couple, weeping, told Susano-Wo that an eight-tailed, eight-headed monster called Yamato-no-Orochi had eaten seven of their eight daughters and was about to take their youngest daughter too. Susano-Wo promised to kill the monster and in return asked to be allowed to marry the daughter.

The couple agreed, whereupon Susano-Wo turned the daughter into a comb, which he fastened in his hair. The god then told the man and woman to place eight large

TAI SUI is surrounded by some of the 60 images which portray the annual Tai Sui. These are all subsidiary deities of the "Lord of Time".

tubs of rice wine on eight platforms and to surround the platforms with a fence containing eight openings. When the monster approached, it began to drink up the wine with its eight heads and soon fell down drunk. The god then chopped up the monster's body with his sword, discovering in the process the famous sword called Kusanagi or "Grass Mower" in its tail. (See also *CREATION MYTHS*)

SUSERI-HIME see *OKUNINUSHI*.

T'AI-I see *TAIYI*.

TAI SUI, the "President of the Celestial Ministry of Time" and "Ruler of the Year", is an arbiter of human destiny worshipped to avert calamities. He rules the cycle of 60 years, each of which is controlled by one of the subsidiary Tai Sui.

Astrology concerns human fortune, and the stellar deity Tai Sui presides over dates and times, auspicious or otherwise. Astrologers match a person's birth date and time with the cycle to provide a guide to auspicious and inauspicious years. Tai Sui was an early

deity honoured at the beginning of spring by the official religion and the official class in imperial China, as well as by Daoists. He is one of the fiercest gods in the pantheon and must be placated whenever ground is disturbed for any reason.

TAIYANG DIJUNG see *YI*.

TAIYI, or T'ai-i, has various meanings within Daoism. Sometimes it is said to be identical with the Dao, but over time it came to be personified as the highest deity within the Daoist pantheon. Taiyi is sometimes said to live in the polar star and to be served by the five mythical emperors.

TAIYI TIANZUN, or T'ai-i T'ien-tsun, is an early Daoist deity who is the saviour of sufferers and unfortunates. He is one of the more senior and significant of the Daoist gods, and is said to be equal to the "Jade Emperor" in rank.

Before the time of *HUANG DI*, the "Yellow Emperor", Taiyi Tianzun had been regarded as the supreme deity. He became the medical adviser to the "Yellow Emperor".

THE SHICHI FUKUJIN

SEVEN POPULAR JAPANESE DEITIES, the Shichi Fukujin, were considered to bring good luck and happiness. Each one personified a different aspect of good fortune. Although they were included in the Shinto pantheon, only two of them, Daikoku and Ebisu, were indigenous Japanese gods. Others were versions of popular Buddhist gods imported from China, while Benten and Bishamon originated as Hindu deities, and Hotei as a Daoist god. Buddhism was declared the official religion of the Japanese imperial court in AD593, but instead of trying to stamp out the existing faith, Buddhist missionaries in Japan drew parallels between the two faiths and proclaimed the identities of the deities to be the same. Because of this peaceable marriage of the two faiths, it was easy for attractive and popular Buddhist gods, such as those of good fortune, to be assimilated with the innumerable kami of the old religion.

BISHAMON (above) the god of war, came from the Hindu pantheon. He stood for benevolent authority. He was a warrior and always wore full armour, so that he was forever ready for battle. He is always shown carrying a lance and a miniature pagoda to symbolize his dual virtues as a soldier and a missionary. (HERIAN PERIOD FIGURE, 11TH CENTURY.)

THE SEVEN GODS (above left) were often depicted travelling together on their treasure ship Takara-Bune, representing a cargo of all the good luck anyone could ask for in life. The ship carried various magical articles on board, such as a hat which rendered the wearer invisible, and a purse that was always full of money. (HIROSHIGE, TREASURE SHIP WITH SEVEN GODS OF GOOD FORTUNE, WOODBLOCK PRINT, 19TH CENTURY.)

BENTEN (left), the only goddess in the group of seven, was a goddess of love, and was believed to bring good luck in marriage. She rode on a dragon or a sea serpent and was associated with the sea, so her shrines were often located by the sea or on islands. She was a patron of music and played a stringed instrument called a biwa. (GILDED KOMAI BOX, LATE 19TH CENTURY.)

FUKUROKUJU (left), perhaps originally a Daoist sage, was the god of long life, wisdom and popularity. He was a little old man with a short body and legs and a very long, narrow bald head, which indicated his intelligence. His traditional companions were animals associated with longevity: a crane, a stag or a tortoise. (JAPANESE IVORY NETSUKE, 18TH CENTURY.)

HOTEI (left) was a fat, bald monk who carried a large sack and a small screen. His enormous belly was meant to indicate his contentment and serene good nature, rather than greed. He is often depicted seated comfortably on his sack, laughing merrily. (ARITA MODEL, LATE 17TH CENTURY.)

JUROJIN was the godson of Fukurokuju, and also promised long life and a happy old age. He had a long white beard to indicate his great age and was portrayed carrying a staff to which was attached a scroll containing all the wisdom of the world, including the life-span of each individual. (JAPANESE INRO, 19TH CENTURY.)

DAIKOKU was the god of wealth and agriculture. He was portrayed wearing a cap and hunter's clothes, surrounded by the symbols of prosperity. Standing or sitting on a bag of rice, he carried another large sack of rice over his shoulder and a rice mallet in his hand, with which he granted wishes. He was sometimes said to be the father of Ebisu. (SATSUMA MODEL, LATE 19TH CENTURY.)

EBISU was the Shinto god of work. The most popular of the seven gods, he was a fisherman, and was fat and cheerful. He was usually shown holding a large fish. Later, he became associated with profit and could bring good luck to commercial ventures. Ebisu was deaf, so he did not join the other gods for the Shinto festival at Izumo which takes place in October. Instead, his festival was held in his own temple. (SATSUMA MODEL, LATE 19TH CENTURY.)

TARVAA was one of the first shamans of Mongolia. As a young man, he fell ill, and his relatives assumed he was dead. Tarvaa was so displeased at this presumption that his soul left his body and flew up to the spirit world. There, he met the judge of the dead who demanded to know why he had arrived so early. The judge, impressed that the youth possessed the courage to visit his kingdom, offered to give him a present before he returned to the land of the living. Tarvaa, rather than choosing wealth or glory, asked to be given knowledge of all the marvels that he had encountered in the spirit world, together with the gift of eloquence. He then returned to his body. However, he found that in his absence, birds had pecked out his eyes, and so he spent the rest of his days unable to see. He became famous for his wisdom and his tales of the spirit world.

TAWARA-TODA is a hero, possibly of historic origins, who features in the mythology of Japan. He defeated an enormous centipede which had been ravaging the territory of the king of the dragons. In gratitude, the king gave Tawara-Toda several supernatural gifts, including a bag of rice which constantly refilled itself.

THE TENGRI, according to the mythology of the Buriats of Siberia, are a type of spirit being. It is said that 54 good-natured Tengri live in the west, whereas 45 bad-natured Tengri live in the east. The Tengri are also regarded as realms, all of which are interconnected, and which together form a cosmic tree.

THE TENGU are creatures of Japanese mythology who are said to live in trees and mountainous areas. Part human, part bird, they have long noses and are sometimes depicted wearing cloaks of feathers or leaves. Although they play tricks, they are not outrightly evil.

TEVNE, according to traditional Mongolian belief, is a hero who managed to appropriate the yellow book of divination from the king. The king had a beautiful daughter whom he desperately tried to protect by keeping her hidden from the outside world. All the king's servants knew that if they revealed the princess's whereabouts, the yellow book of divination would reveal their guilt. As a result, for many years the princess remained in hiding.

One day, Tevne decided that he would attempt to confuse the book. He dug a deep hole in the ground and trapped one of the princess's servants in it. He then built a fire on top of the hole, placed a kettle over the fire and, taking a piece of iron piping, passed it through the kettle. Then, speaking through the pipe, he asked the woman how he could find the princess. The woman told Tevne how the beautiful girl could be identified, so he released her.

Later, Tevne succeeded in picking out the princess from girls of similar appearance. Although the king was furious, he was forced to allow Tevne to marry her. In order

TIAN (above), the sky or heaven, is symbolized by a ceremonial Bi disc. (CHINESE JADE, 3RD–2ND CENTURY BC.)

THE TENGU (left), though wicked, could also be helpful, and rescued the hero Tameto from a giant fish. (WOODBLOCK PRINT BY KUNIYOSHI, 19TH CENTURY.)

to discover who had revealed the secret of his daughter's identity, the king sought advice from his yellow book. The book told him that he had been tricked by a man with earthen buttocks, a body of fire, lungs of water and an iron pipe for vocal cords. The king decided that the book's abilities had deserted it, and so he burned it. Sheep licked up the ashes and thereby acquired divinatory powers.

THE THENS, according to the people of Laos and northern Thailand, are the three divine ancestors who, together with three great men, Pu Lang Seung, Khun K'an and Khun K'et, established human society.

The Thens lived in the upper world, whereas the three great men ruled over the lower world, living by means of fishing and growing rice. A vast bridge joined together the two worlds.

One day, the Thens suddenly announced that all human beings should give them a portion of their food before they sat down to eat a meal. When the people refused, the Thens caused a huge flood to cover the earth. The three great men built a raft on top of which

they constructed a house. Taking women and children with them, they travelled over the flood to the upper world in order to seek a reprieve from the chief Then.

The king of the Thens told the travellers to seek shelter in heaven with one of his relatives, Grandfather Then Lo. However, the three great men noticed that the flood was beginning to recede, and they told the king that they would rather return to the lower kingdom, since in heaven they were unable to walk or run because there was no solid ground. The king gave the divine ancestors a buffalo and sent them back down to earth.

Three years passed, after which time the buffalo died. A plant began to grow from its nostrils, and

before long gave rise to three gourds. A strange noise issued from the gourds, whereupon one of the great men bored a hole in each of the fruit. Immediately, human beings began to emerge from the plants. The first people to emerge were the aboriginal slaves, followed in due course by the Thai people.

The three great men taught the people how to cultivate fields and how to weave. Later, Then Teng and Then Pitsanukukan descended from the upper world in order to teach the Thais about time as well as how to make tools, weave cotton and silk and prepare food.

Finally, the king of heaven sent the lord of the divine musicians to teach the people how to make and play instruments, and how to sing and dance. When the divine musician had finished his work he returned to heaven, and the bridge that connected the two worlds was destroyed.

TI see SHANG DI.

TI TS'ANG WANG see DIZANG WANG.

TIAN, or T'ien, is the Chinese word that refers both to the sky, or heaven, and to its personification as a deity. According to Daoism, there are 36 heavens, which are arranged on six levels. Each level is inhabited by different deities. The highest heaven is that of the "Great Web", which is sometimes said to be the home of the "Celestial Venerable of the Primordial Beginning", Yuanshi Tianzun.

From ancient times, Tian, or Tian Di, was regarded as a supreme being who had the power to influence the destiny of human beings, bringing order and calm, or catastrophe and punishment. The Chinese emperor is regarded as the "Son of Heaven", or Tianzi, and is believed to mediate between Tian and humankind.

TIAN DI see TIAN.

U

TIAN LONG see *DIYA*.

T'IEN see *TIAN*.

TING-JIAN see *GAO YAO*.

TOKOYO, according to Japanese mythology, was the daughter of a samurai called Oribe Shima who had displeased the emperor and been banished from the kingdom. Oribe Shima set up home on a desolate group of islands known as the Oki Islands.

He was extremely unhappy as he missed his daughter. Tokoyo was also miserable at being separated from her father and determined to find him. She sold all her property and set out for a place called Akasaki on the coast, from where the Oki Islands could just be seen. Although Tokoyo tried to persuade the fishermen to row her out to the islands, they all refused, since it was forbidden to visit anyone who had been sent there.

One night, Tokoyo took a boat and sailed out to the islands alone. She fell asleep on the beach, and the next morning she began to search for her father. The young woman soon encountered a fisherman and asked him if he had seen her father. He replied that he had not, and warned her not to ask anyone where he was as it might cause immense trouble. As a result, Tokoyo wandered all over the islands, listening to what people were saying, but never asking the whereabouts of her father.

One evening, she came to a shrine of the Buddha and after praying to him, fell asleep. She was soon woken by the sound of a girl crying and looking up she saw a young girl and a priest. The priest led the girl to the edge of the cliffs and was about to push her into the sea when Tokoyo ran up and stopped him. The priest confessed that he was forced to carry out the ritual in order to appease the evil god *OKUNINUSHI*. If he were not sent a young girl each year, the god

would become very angry and cause great storms and many fishermen would drown.

Tokoyo offered to take the girl's place, saying that she was so unhappy without her father that the loss of her life meant nothing to her. Then, Tokoyo prayed to the Buddha again and, with a dagger between her teeth, dived into the ocean intending to hunt down the evil god and kill him.

At the bottom of the ocean, Tokoyo spied a marvellous cave. Inside, instead of the evil god, she found a statue of the emperor who had banished her father. She began to destroy the statue, but then thought better of it and, tying it to herself, she began to swim back. Just as she was leaving the cave, Tokoyo found herself confronted by

a serpentine creature. Unafraid, she swam up to it and stabbed it in the eye. Blinded, the creature was unable to gain entrance to the cave, and Tokoyo succeeded in attacking it until finally she killed it.

When Tokoyo arrived at the shore, the priest and the girl carried her to town, and word of her heroic deeds soon spread. The emperor himself, who had suddenly found himself cured of an unknown disease, heard what had happened and realized that Tokoyo must have released him from an evil spell. He ordered the release of Oribe Shima, and the father and daughter returned to their home town.

TOMAM, according to the Ket people of Siberia, is a goddess who looks after migratory birds.

TOKOYO succeeded in killing a monstrous sea serpent and thus freed the emperor from an evil curse. (ILLUSTRATION FROM MYTHS AND LEGENDS OF JAPAN.)

TSAO-CHÜN see *ZAO JUN*.

TS'AO KUO-CHIU see *BA XIAN*.

TSUKIYOMI, in Shinto mythology, is the god of the moon. His name means "Counter of the Months". Tsukiyomi is said to have come into being when *IZANAGI*, the male half of the primal couple, purified himself after visiting the underworld. When he washed his face, Tsukiyomi appeared from Izanagi's right eye, the sun goddess *AMATERASU* from his left eye and the storm god *SUSANO-WO* from his nose. Izanagi divided his kingdom between his three offspring, allocating to Tsukiyomi the realms of the night.

According to one version of the myth relating how the staple crops of Japan were created, Tsukiyomi asked the food goddess *UKE-MOCHI* for a meal, but when she produced the food from her orifices, he was so disgusted that he killed her. The basic foodstuffs then appeared from the corpse of the goddess. When Amaterasu learned what had happened, she was displeased and said that she would never set eyes on her brother again. It is for this reason that the sun and the moon inhabit the sky at different times.

TUNG-YÜEH TA-TI see *DONGYUE DADI*.

UKE-MOCHI, or Ogetsu-No-Hime, is the food goddess, according to the Shinto mythology of Japan. She is married to *INARI*, the god of rice. The storm god *SUSANO-WO* or, in some versions of the story, the moon god *TSUKIYOMI* ordered the food goddess to give him something to eat. The goddess responded by pulling food from her nose, mouth and rectum

歸
國
浦
島

whereupon the god, disgusted, killed her. From Uke-Mochi's corpse sprouted all the basic food crops: rice seeds grew from her eyes, millet from her ears, wheat from her genitals, red beans from her nose and soy beans from her rectum. She is also said to have produced a cow and a horse.

ULGAN is the great sky god of the Altaic people of Siberia. He sent the saviour MAIDERE to earth in order to teach men to respect the true god. Maidere was slain by the evil ERLIK, but flames arose from his blood and reached up to heaven, destroying Erlik and his followers. Ulgan is sometimes depicted surrounded by rays of light.

ULU TOYO'N is the malevolent creator spirit of the Yakut people of Siberia. He lives in the third sky

and rules over the ABAASY, evil beings who live in the lower world. Ulu Toyo'n is also the lord of thunder and is said to have given fire to human beings, as well as one of their three souls.

UMAI is the mother goddess of the Turkic people of Siberia. She is said to have 60 golden tresses, which resemble the rays of the sun, and to look after newborn babies and help couples to conceive. Sometimes known as Ymai, or Mai, she is believed to have originally been identical with OT, the fire queen of the Mongols.

URASHIMA was a young fisherman who features in the mythology of Japan. One day, when out fishing, he caught an old turtle. Rather than killing the creature, he took pity on it and threw it back into the

water, whereupon a beautiful girl emerged from the spray. The girl stepped into Urashima's boat, told him that she was the daughter of the sea god, a dragon king, and invited him to come and live with her in their palace under the ocean. The palace was made of seashells, pearls and coral, and Urashima found himself waited upon by seven golden-tailed dragons.

For four years, Urashima lived in perfect happiness with his wife, the dragon princess. However, one day he began to long to see his parents and the streets where he used to play. Before he left for his former home, Urashima's wife gave him a casket, telling him that, provided it remained closed, it would enable him to return to her. When Urashima reached his homeland, he found that everything looked strange to him. Eventually, he

URASHIMA returned from his stay under the ocean riding on the back of a turtle.
(WOODBLOCK PRINT BY TAISO YOSHITOSHI, 1882.)

asked an old man if he knew the whereabouts of Urashima's cottage. The old man replied that Urashima had drowned 400 years ago while out fishing. Urashima was so shocked that he failed to remember his wife's instructions and opened the casket. Immediately, a puff of white smoke escaped from the casket and drifted towards the sea. Urashima himself suddenly began to grow old. His hair grew white and his hands shook, until finally he became no more than a pile of dust and was blown away on the wind.

USHIWAKA see YOSHITSUNE.

UZUME see AME-NO-UZUME.

481

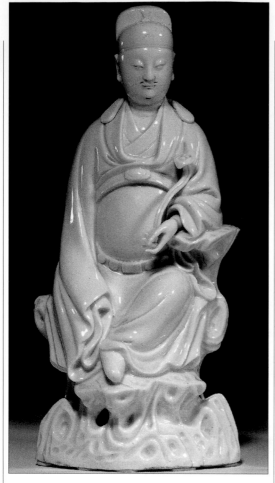

VIZI-ANYA see *VIZI-EMBER*.

VIZI-EMBER, according to the mythology of the Magyars of Siberia, is a water spirit who lives in lakes and rivers. He devours human beings and, if none are forthcoming, he will call out, demanding to be satisfied. Those who hear his voice know that someone is about to drown.

There are also two female water spirits, the water mother Vizi-anya and the water maiden Vizi-leany. Whenever one of these spirits appears to humankind, the vision signifies that something unfortunate is about to happen.

VIZI-LEANY see *VIZI-EMBER*.

WAKAHIRU-ME, according to Japanese Shinto belief, is the younger sister of the sun goddess *AMATERASU*. She is said to have been sitting with Amaterasu in the divine weaving hall when the storm god *SUSANO-WO* threw a flayed horse into the chamber.

The divine weaving hall was the place where Amaterasu and her attendants were said to weave garments, for the gods themselves or for the priestesses of the sun goddess. Alternatively, the deities were said to be weaving the unfinished parts of the universe.

WEN CHANG, the god of literature, is dressed as a mandarin and holds a sceptre as a symbol of his official position in the heavenly hierarchy. (CHINESE BLANC-DE-CHINE FIGURE, 17TH CENTURY.)

WATA RIAN, according to the Kedang people of eastern Indonesia, was the hero who civilized the wild woman *BOTA ILI*. Bota Ili lived on top of a mountain; her body was covered with hair and the nails of her fingers and toes were long and pointed. She ate lizards and snakes, and would cook them over a fire, which she lit by striking her bottom against a stone. One day, Wata Rian noticed the smoke of Bota Ili's fire and set off to find its source.

When he reached the top of the mountain, Wata Rian climbed a tree and waited for Bota Ili to return with her catch of reptiles. In due course, the wild woman returned. She struck her bottom against a rock to start a fire, but to no effect. Looking up, she saw Wata Rian and shrieked at him to come down from the tree in order that she might bite him to death. Wata Rian, unafraid, told her to calm herself or he would set his dog on her. The two of them lit a fire and cooked their food together. Bota Ili drank so much wine that she fell asleep, whereupon Wata Rian shaved the hair from her body and discovered that she was a woman. The couple were eventually married.

WEN CHANG is the Daoist god of literature. Originally a stellar deity, he descended from his home in the stars and lived through 17 lives, each of which was filled with remarkable events and achievements. At the end of this time, Wen Chang was finally rewarded by the "Jade Emperor" with the title "Grand Emperor of Literature".

THE WIND GOD is a nature spirit, like the gods of rain, thunder and lightning. He is portrayed as an old man carrying a sack of wind.

According to one story, a student was disappointed with his performance in an examination and, fearing he had failed, begged Wen Chang to help him. That night, while he was asleep, the student saw the god throwing several essays into a fire. Among them, the student recognized his own. After the essays had disintegrated into tiny pieces of ash, the god transformed them. Wen Chang gave the student his corrected essay, and the young man memorized it.

The following morning, the student discovered that a fire had destroyed the building where all the essays had been kept and that he would have to repeat the examination. This time, he wrote the essay as the god had instructed him and passed.

The deity is usually represented sitting down, wearing the robes of a mandarin and holding a sceptre. Wen Chang is in fact a constellation of six stars. When the stars are bright, literature is said to flourish. He is accompanied by several officials who set and mark exam papers and bear tidings to those who pass. They include *DIYA* and Tian Long.

THE WIND GOD, an impersonal nature deity, assumed human form as Feng Po during the Tang or Song dynasties. Images in mainland China portrayed him as an

elderly man carrying a sack of cold wind which he pointed in the direction he wished wind to blow. In northern and central China he was sometimes portrayed astride a tiger, and was also often depicted holding a pair of open fans with which he produced gentle breezes. He was accompanied by a shrimp spirit carrying a vase filled with rainwater which he sprinkled as he went.

THE WU DI, or Wu Ti, are the "Five Perfect Emperors" of Chinese mythology who are said to have lived during the third century BC. They are the "Yellow Emperor" (*HUANG DI*), Zhuan Xu, Du Gu, *YAO* and *SHUN*. One of the five elements is associated with each emperor.

XI-HE, or Hsi Ho, according to Chinese mythology, is the mother of the ten suns and the wife of Taiyang Dijun, the god of the eastern sky. Each morning, Xi-He would carry one of her sons to the edge of the sky in her chariot in order that he might spend the day lighting up the world. Eventually, the suns rebelled against their ordered existence and appeared in the sky together, thus causing devastation on earth. Nine of them were shot down by the divine archer *YI*.

XI WANG MU, or Hsi Wang-mu, is described in ancient Chinese texts as a monster with a human face, the teeth of a tiger and a leopard's tail. She ruled over the demons of the plague and was known as the goddess of epidemics. However, by the first century AD she had become a noble lady. Known as the "Queen Mother of the West", she was said to rule over the western paradise of the immortals in the Kunlun Mountains where she was attended by the "Jade Girls" and three-legged birds.

Xi Wang Mu is portrayed as a beautiful woman wearing a royal gown and sometimes riding on a crane. She is said to live in a palace of jade, nine storeys high and surrounded by a golden wall more than a thousand miles long. The male immortals live in the right wing of her palace and the female immortals in the left.

In her garden, Xi Wang Mu grows the peaches of immortality, which release all those who eat them from death. However, the tree bears fruit only once every 3,000 years. When the peaches are ripe, Xi Wang Mu invites all the immortals to a feast during which they eat the marvellous fruit.

Xi Wang Mu is said to have given a peach of immortality to several ancient Chinese rulers. In the myth of the divine archer *YI* and his wife *ZHANG E*, Yi is given the elixir of immortality by the "Queen Mother of the West", but Zhang E drinks it all up, thereby condemning her husband to life as a mortal. According to some versions of the tale of the immortal Li Tieguai, it was the Queen Mother of the West who taught him the secret of immortality.

In popular mythology, she is regarded as Wang Mu Niangniang, the wife of the "Jade Emperor", *YU HUANG*. Once a year, she is said to meet her consort, Dong Wang Gong, who lives in the east. The occasion is believed to symbolize the union of *YIN* and *YANG*.

XI WANG MU, with other deities, rides through the heavens in a celestial chariot drawn by cranes. (CAVE PAINTING AT DUNHUANG, CHINA, C. AD535–56.)

DEMONS

DEMONS APPEARED IN ALL KINDS OF mythologies as servants and ministers of deities, including the ruler of the underworld. They usually personified forces of evil, and appeared on earth to wreak havoc among mortals by bringing disease and famine, or inhabiting the living. In the afterlife, they existed to punish the wicked with cruelly appropriate tortures for the sins they had committed in life. For a Buddhist, this state of torment could not be everlasting because rebirth continued, but the time in Naraka (the underworld) represented the lowest point of the soul's journey. In Japan, demons were called oni. Most were invisible, though some appeared in the form of animals, and they were the source of sin and misfortune. Even so, they were not viewed as wholly evil. The fox oni, for instance, was considered especially dangerous, yet was the companion of Inari, the rice god, who was popular and benevolent.

HELL (above) for the Chinese was divided into ten levels, presided over by the "Kings of the Law Courts". Souls had first to appear before Yanluo Wang, the supreme master, who heard their case then sent them on to each court in turn for their punishments to be decided. The kings, dressed like emperors, presided over the ghastly tortures that were carried out by demons. Souls could avoid hell only by living blameless lives and by making regular offerings to Guanyin, goddess of mercy. (ILLUSTRATION FROM SUPERSTITIONS EN CHINE, 1914.)

JIGOKUDAYU (left), the "Lady from Hell", was a Japanese courtesan who experienced enlightenment when she looked in her mirror and, instead of her reflection, saw a vision of a skeleton gazing back at her. She became a disciple of the 15th-century Zen master Ikkyu Sojun, the "Holy Madman" who frequented inns and brothels and danced in the street with a skull on a pole. Here, two laughing demons hold up a mirror for her to see her vision. (JIGOKUDAYU SEES HERSELF IN A MIRROR, BY TAISO YOSHITISHI, WOODBLOCK PRINT, 1882.)

BARONG (above) the spirit king, is the opponent of Rangda, the demon queen, in the great battle between good and evil, which is presented as a dance in Bali and other parts of South-east Asia. He takes the form of a lion, representing day, light and the forces of goodness. During their battle, the humans who try to help Barong are put under a spell by Rangda, which makes them turn their weapons on themselves, but Barong keeps them from harm. (BALINESE STONE CARVING.)

RANGDA (left), the ferocious female demon of Bali, had a lolling, fiery tongue, pendulous breasts and rolling eyes. A creature of darkness, sickness and death, she was the leader of a band of witches. Her name means "widow", and she may derive from an 11th-century Balinese queen exiled for practising sorcery. In revenge she tried to destroy the kingdom, and half the population died of plague before a holy man put an end to her black magic. (BALINESE RITUAL MASK.)

NAGAS (right) are dragon-like demons, and were dangerous and destructive spirits. Of Indian origin, their mythology spread with Buddhism into China and beyond. Some are half-human, half-snake, while others are monstrous water creatures who guard the depths of lakes. Naga Padoha is the serpent ruler of the underworld who, according to the mythology of South-east Asia, was confined there by the creator god Batara Guru when he tried to destroy the earth. (NAGA SCULPTURE IN A BALINESE SHRINE FOUNTAIN.)

Y

THE XIAN were said to live in the Kunlun Mountains, the location of the sacred peach garden where Xi Wang Mu, the "Queen Mother of the West", grew the peaches of immortality which they ate to ensure eternal life. (PAINTING, C 14TH CENTURY.)

THE XIAN

THE XIAN, or Hsien, according to Chinese mythology, are beings who have gained immortality. They are not deities, but have been granted the gift of eternal life.

The immortals are either celestial or terrestrial. Celestial immortals live in Tian, the Daoist heaven, or on the isles of the immortals situated in the Eastern Sea, or in the Kunlun Mountains.

They can change their appearance at will and are often represented riding on the backs of cranes. The terrestrial immortals live in forests and mountains.

XUAN ZANG

XUAN ZANG, or Hsüan Tsang, was a celebrated Buddhist monk of the seventh century AD. Said to have been commissioned by the emperor of China, he journeyed to the source of Buddhism in India in quest of instruction, and returned with Buddhist scriptures. Some of his bones are still revered in temples in China and Japan.

Xuan Zang's great pilgrimage was immortalized in the 16th-century novel Xi You Ji (The Journey to the West) by Wu Zheng-en. According to this story, the monk was accompanied by four aides on his hazardous journey. Of the four, the most important and active was the "Monkey King". The other three were part players, the illiterate and slow-witted monk Sha; Piggy; and the White Horse on which Xuan Zang rode.

YA-GAMI-HIME see YAKAMI.

YAKAMI

YAKAMI, or Ya-Gami-Hime, was a beautiful princess of Japanese mythology who lived at Inaba, a province near Izumo. The 80 brothers of the great hero *OKUNINUSHI* all wished to marry the princess. On their way to woo her, they met a hare that had been flayed. The brothers cruelly advised the hare to cure itself by bathing in the sea and drying itself in the wind. Naturally, this caused the animal to suffer severe pain. Later, when Okuninushi came across the hare, he told it to bathe in fresh water and then roll in the pollen of kama grass. On doing so, the hare found itself cured. It revealed itself to be a deity and told Okuninushi that he would marry Yakami.

YAKUSHI-NYORAI

YAKUSHI-NYORAI was one of the first buddhas to be venerated in Japan and became one of the most important. While still a bodhisattva, he is said to have made 12 vows, including promising to find a cure for all illnesses.

His name means "Master with Remedies", and he is commonly known as the "King of Medicines", or the "Divine Healer". Yakushi also vowed to transform his body into beryl in order that he might light up the whole world with his radiance. His home, situated in the east, was known as the "Land of Pure Beryl".

Yakushi-Nyorai is usually shown carrying a medicine bowl, and miraculous powers are attributed to his effigies.

THE XIAN included figures such as Han Shan, one of "The Four Sleepers" who is usually depicted holding a scroll. He would explain its contents to his fellow sleeper, Shi De, in unintelligible gibberish. (PAINTED SILK SCROLL, 14TH CENTURY.)

YAMATO TAKERU

YAMATO TAKERU is a hero who features in the mythology of Japan. Originally called O-Usu-No-Ikoto, he was the son of Emperor Keiko. The emperor told his other son to bring two beautiful young women to him, but the son made the maidens his own wives and sent two other women in their place. The emperor, who was planning to punish his son, ordered Yamato Takeru to bring his brother to dine.

After five days, there was still no sign of the brother. Puzzled, the emperor asked Yamato Takeru what had happened to him. Yamato replied that he had crushed his brother to death and pulled off his limbs. The emperor, impressed at his son's strength, sent Yamato Takeru to destroy some rebels who threatened his kingdom.

For his first quest, the hero was sent to the west to slaughter two brothers. The palace of the brothers was surrounded by countless

warriors, so Yamato Takeru disguised himself as a girl and entered the palace during a feast. While everyone was busy eating and drinking, Yamato Takeru caught hold of one of the brothers and stabbed him. The other brother tried to escape, but Yamato Takeru seized and killed him, too. As the second brother lay dying, he named his killer Yamato Takeru or "Brave One of the Yamato".

On his journey home, Yamato Takeru brought all the mountain, river and sea deities under control. However, he had not been at home long when the emperor sent him off on another mission. Yamato Takeru complained to his aunt Yamato Pime that he needed time to rest, as well as more protection, and so his aunt gave him a sword and a bag, which she told him to open only in an emergency. The hero then did as his father, the emperor, had asked and killed many more enemies.

Eventually, a man lured Yamato Takeru into a trap. He begged the hero to go to a pond in the middle of a vast plain and kill a deity who lived in its waters. Once Yamato Takeru was in the middle of the plain, the man set fire to the area, trapping the hero. Undeterred,

Yamato Takeru cut down the grass with his magic sword. Then, opening the bag his aunt had given him, the hero found it contained a flint. Immediately, he lit another fire, which overcame the first, killing the man and all his followers.

Yamato Takeru performed many other brave and glorious deeds. On his long homeward journey, while crossing the sea in a boat with his wife Oto Tatiban Pime or Miyazu-Hime, the sea deity began to stir up the waves. Oto Tatiban Pime offered to sacrifice herself in order to save her husband and, stepping out of the boat, disappeared beneath the waves. Once on shore again, Yamato Takeru broke his journey by a mountain pass in order to eat some food. Seeing a deer, the hero threw the remains of his meal at the animal, not realizing that it was the deity of the pass. The deer fell down dead. Soon afterwards, Yamato Takeru encountered another deity in the form of a white boar and broke a taboo by saying that he would kill it. A fearsome hailstorm then descended, dazing the hero. None the less, Yamato Takeru struggled onwards until eventually he fell down dead. His soul was transformed into a huge white bird.

XUAN ZANG (above), the fabled travelling monk, is accompanied by his aides, the Monkey King, Piggy, the slow-witted Sha and the White Horse.

YAKUSHI-NYORAI (below) is the "Divine Healer" of Japanese Buddhism. Effigies of the buddha are credited with miraculous curative powers. (GILT BRONZE, 8TH CENTURY.)

YAN DI see *SHEN NONG*.

YAN WANG see *YANLUO WANG*.

YANG, according to Daoist belief, originally stood for the mountain slope facing the sun, and was associated with light and warmth. This ancient concept came to be viewed as one of the two cosmic forces, the other being *YIN*, which interacted to produce the universe. Yang represents masculinity, activity, heat, dryness and hardness. It is believed that yang may have originally been a sky deity. (See also *YIN AND YANG*)

YANLUO WANG is the senior king of the ten courts of the Chinese underworld. He investigates the past lives of the dead and sends them on to the other kings for punishment in the hells which are attached to each court. Eight of the "Kings of the Law Courts" punish particular souls while the remaining king allocates souls to bodies in preparation for their reincarnation. However, according to some versions of the tale, every soul has to appear before each of the courts in turn.

Horrific tortures await serious offenders: corrupt officials are forced to swallow molten gold, and the worst offenders are plunged into boiling oil, crushed by stones or cut in half.

YAO is one of the five legendary emperors of Chinese mythology. He is said to have ruled over China during the third century BC. Within Confucianism, Yao is regarded as the examplar of a good ruler. He is credited with having established the calendar, and with introducing official posts whose holders were responsible for making correct use of the four seasons of the year.

It was during his reign that the divine archer *YI* shot nine of the ten suns out of the sky and that a huge flood threatened to destroy the world. Yao made *SHUN* his succes-

YANLUO WANG is the terrifying king of hell who presides over the judgement and punishment of souls. (CHINESE CERAMIC, 1523.)

sor, subjecting him to a series of tests before allowing him to take over the reins of power.

YI is the divine archer of Chinese mythology. He performed many brave deeds, including shooting nine of the ten suns from the sky, obtaining the elixir of immortality from *XI WANG MU*, and bringing under control the winds which plagued the "Yellow Emperor".

The ten suns lived in a giant mulberry tree known as Fu Sang, which grew in a hot spring beyond the eastern ocean. They were the children of Taiyang Dijun, the god of the east and lord of heaven, and *XI-HE*, goddess of the sun. Xi-He ordained that only one sun should appear in the sky at a time so, each morning, she would drive a sun to the edge of the sky in her chariot,

and at the end of the day would return it to the Fu Sang tree. In this way, light and warmth were brought to the world.

After a thousand years, the ten suns grew tired of their ordered way of life and decided to rebel. One day, they all appeared in the sky together. They were delighted with themselves, but their continual presence in the sky caused devastation on earth: the soil dried up, the crops withered and died and even the rocks began to melt. Soon there was scarcely anything left to eat or drink. Monsters and wild animals came out of the forest in search of food and began to devour human beings.

Eventually, the people begged their ruler, *YAO*, to help them. Yao prayed to Taiyang Dijun to take pity on humankind. Taiyang Dijun and

Xi-He heard Yao's prayers and ordered nine of the suns to return to the Fu Sang tree. However, their entreaties fell on deaf ears.

Taiyang Dijun then called on the divine archer Yi for help. The great god gave Yi a red bow and a quiver of white arrows, and told him to bring his sons under control and to kill the wild animals. Yi, together with his wife *ZHANG E*, proceeded to do as Taiyang Dijun had instructed him. However, whereas Dijun had intended Yi merely to frighten the suns into submission, Yi decided that the only solution was to kill them. Taking an arrow from his quiver, he fired it high into the sky. Immediately, a huge ball of

fire appeared, and the air was filled with flames. On the ground lay a three-legged raven. Yi then shot another arrow at the sky, and another; each time, one of the suns was extinguished and fell to earth as a three-legged raven.

Yao realized that if Yi carried on, no light or warmth whatsoever would be left, so he told one of his courtiers to steal one of Yi's arrows so that he could destroy only nine of the ten suns. When there was only one sun left in the sky, Yi began to kill the wild animals and monsters that were devouring human beings.

Peace returned to the earth, and everyone praised Yi. The divine archer returned to heaven with Zhang E. However, to Yi's surprise, and Zhang E's anger, the god Taiyang Dijun spurned Yi for having killed his sons and ordered him and his wife to leave heaven and live on earth as mortals.

Yi was happy enough, hunting in the forests, but Zhang E grew bored and worried that now, one day, she would die. As a result, Zhang E persuaded Yi to visit the "Queen Mother of the West" and ask her for the elixir of immortality. The Queen Mother agreed to help Yi and Zhang E. She gave them a box containing enough elixir to enable them to live for ever, but said that there was only sufficient elixir for one of them to gain complete immortality.

Zhang E swallowed all of the elixir herself, and was punished by being stranded on the moon. When Yi discovered his wife's treachery, he was dismayed. However, he decided that, since he was to die, he should pass on his skills. He took a pupil, Peng Meng, who soon became an expert archer, although not so proficient as Yi. In time, Peng Meng grew jealous of Yi's superior ability and killed him. Another version tells how Yi was finally forgiven by the gods and returned to heaven.

YIN, according to Daoist belief, originally referred to the mountain slope facing away from the sun. Together with *YANG*, Yin was viewed as one of the two cosmic forces whose interaction produced the universe. Yin represents the female principle – the cold, the dark and softness – and may have originated as an earth deity. (See also *YIN AND YANG*).

YINGZHOU see *PENG LAI*.

YINLUGEN BUD, the ghost of the tree trunk, is an ancient spirit of the Chewong people of Malaysia. He taught the hero *BUJAEGN YED* how to deliver children and instructed him in many other rituals associated with childbirth. He also warned Bujaegn Yed that it was sinful not to share his food when he ate a meal.

YMAI see *UMAI*.

YNAKHSYT see *ITCHITA*.

YOMI is the land of the dead in Japanese Shinto mythology. It is a land of filth rather than of punishment, and it is known as the "Land of Darkness", or the "Land of Roots". *IZANAGI*, the male half of the primal couple, followed his wife *IZANAMI* to Yomi, but failed to secure her release.

YOSHITSUNE, also known as Ushiwaka, is a hero who features in Japanese mythology. He was trained in the art of warfare by the Tengu and then succeeded in

YOSHITSUNE was trained in swordplay by the Tengu, the bird-like imps of Japanese myth. (WOODBLOCK PRINT BY KUNISADA, C. 1815.)

avenging the defeat of his people, the Minamoto clan. He defeated the giant *BENKEI* in a duel whereupon the giant became his servant.

YAO, fourth of the legendary emperors of China, was the pattern of the good ruler. (PAINTING BY MA LIN.)

YU was the hero of the flood in Chinese mythology. He is revered for his dedication to hard work. Yu was sometimes shown as half-dragon, half-human, but eventually he came to be represented as entirely human.

Yu laboured for 13 years to put an end to the flood. He controlled and directed all the waters of the earth by cutting holes through the mountains, creating rivers, springs and estuaries. Eventually, his hands and feet grew callused, and he became so exhausted, he could scarcely walk. However, he struggled on, building an irrigation system in order to drain the flood waters into the sea.

In the course of his mammoth drainage work, he made the land fit for cultivation and connected the nine provinces of China to one another. The ruling emperor was so grateful that he abdicated and gave the throne to Yu, who became the first emperor of the Xia dynasty. Yu is said to have reigned from 2205 to 2197BC. Each succeeding emperor was seen as an incarnation of the dragon Yu.

Another myth tells how, in order to carry out his work, Yu would transform himself into a bear. Each day, when the time came for him to eat, he would beat his drum, and his wife would carry out food for him. One day, when Yu was breaking up rocks, his wife

YU HUANG (above), the "Jade Emperor" or "August Personage of Jade" is the supreme ruler of heaven and earth.

mistook the sound for the beating of his drum. She rushed out with his food, but as soon as she saw the bear she fled. Yu ran after her but, being pregnant, she fell to the ground exhausted and turned to stone. The stone continued to grow and, when the time of the expected birth arrived, Yu split it open, whereupon his son, Qi, was born.

YU DI was another name given to *YU HUANG*, the so-called "Jade Emperor" of Chinese mythology.

YU HUANG, or the "Jade Emperor", came to be regarded as the supreme ruler of heaven in Chinese mythology. He was responsible for determining events both in the heavens and on earth, and he had a vast number of underlings to carry out his commands. Yu Huang's chief assistant was *DONGYUE DADI*, or "Great Emperor of the Eastern Peak". Dongyue Dadi alone had 75 gods to help him in his work.

At the beginning of each year, Yu Huang would summon all the deities to his palace, which was in

YU (left) the Lord of the Flood, was given the task of controlling and draining the waters that covered the plains of China.

is usually depicted sitting on his throne wearing the ceremonial robes of an emperor, embroidered with dragons.

The "Queen Mother of the West", *XI WANG MU*, who is known by many titles, including Wang Mu Niangniang, was said to be the wife of Yu Huang. He has a large family of sisters, daughters and nephews, and a celestial dog, who helps to protect the heavenly household from evil spirits.

YUANSHI TIAN-ZONG see
SAN QING DAOZU.

YUQIANG, or Yü-ch'iang, in
Chinese mythology, is the god of the sea and of ocean winds. As a god of the sea, he is represented with the body of a fish and riding two dragons. As a god of the winds, he is represented with the body of a bird and a human face.

According to one tale, Yuqiang was ordered by the king of heaven to anchor the five floating islands of the immortals. Yuqiang succeeded in the task by enlisting the help of 15 giant tortoises. He allocated three of the tortoises to each island and ordered them to take it in turns to carry one of the islands on their backs. Each turn was to last 60,000 years. Unfortunately, a giant caught six of the tortoises, and so two islands were set adrift. They floated away and sank, leaving only three.

QING LONG PA JIANGJUN (left), the Green Dragon General, guards the entrance to the Jade Emperor Hall.

YUQIANG (below), the god of the ocean winds, listens to the Buddhist doctrine.
(*PAINTING BY ZHAO BOZHU, SONG DYNASTY.*)

the highest of the heavens, and was guarded by the "Transcendental Official". The deities would then be allocated new positions, according to how they had performed their duties during the previous year. The various ministries oversaw everything, from water and time, to war and wealth.

The heavenly administration was a replica of the earthly one. If, for example, there was a flood, the earthly official would warn the heavenly official – the deity – that his work was substandard and, if necessary, he would be fired. New deities would be confirmed by the Daoist priests. The "Jade Emperor" was said to deal directly with the emperor of China, whereas his attendants dealt with less important human beings. In the 11th century AD, when the emperor of China was losing his power, he attempted to regain support by claiming to be in direct communication with heaven and to have received a letter from Yu Huang.

One myth tells how before Yu Huang was born, his mother dreamt that *LAO JUN*, the deified form of Laozi, the putative founding father of Daoism, handed her a child. The young Yu Huang succeeded his father, the king, to the throne but abdicated after a few days in order to retire to the mountains and study the Dao. He attained perfection and, for the rest of his life, he instructed the sick and poor in the Dao. Eventually, he became an immortal and after millions more years was transformed into the "Jade Emperor". Yu Huang

CHINA'S SACRED PEAKS

THE GREAT CREATOR PANGU lived for 18,000 years, growing every day and filling the space between the earth and the sky. When he died, his body formed the world. In one version of the myth, his head became Tai Shan mountain in the east; his feet, Hua Shan in the west; his right arm, the northern Heng Shan; his left arm, the southern Heng Shan; and his stomach Song Shan, the mountain of the centre. These were the five sacred Daoist mountains of China. They were worshipped as deities in their own right: pilgrims climbed stairways to the summits and made sacrifices to them. In the heavenly bureaucracy of the Chinese pantheon, the "Ministry of the Five Sacred Mountains" was controlled by Tai Shan, the grandson of Yu Huang, the "Jade Emperor".

TAI SHAN's (above) summit is reached by climbing the "Stairway to Heaven", which consists of about 7,000 steps lined with shrines and temples. Sacrifices were offered at the top of the mountain by the emperor each spring, but he could not presume to do this unless his reign was a successful one. Successive emperors made ceremonial journeys to the holy mountains that marked the limits of the empire, to assert their claim to their territory.

TAI SHAN (left), the holiest peak, is the sacred mountain of the east. Its presiding deity ("Lord of the Yellow Springs") ruled the earth and regulated birth and death, while his daughter Bixia Shengmu ("Princess of Streaked Clouds") protected women and children. Souls left the mountain at birth and returned there at death. The mountain was granted various noble titles by the Jade Emperor.

A PAGODA (right) stands at the summit of Mount Song Shan, the mountain of the centre, in the heart of the ancient Chinese empire.

HUANG DI (below left) the "Yellow Emperor", was the third and most splendid of the legendary emperors of China, preceded by Fu Xi and Shen Nong. Huang Di ordered roads to be built and mountain passes to be cut throughout his empire. When he journeyed to Tai Shan to make sacrifices, his chariot was drawn by six dragons. Tigers and wolves preceded it, serpents slithered beside it, phoenixes flew overhead and spirits followed behind. The road ahead was cleaned and swept by the gods of wind and rain.

HUA SHAN (above) was the sacred mountain of the west. The hero Yu, who controlled the great flood of China, visited the four corners of the world, marked by the sacred peaks. At Hua Shan he found people who drank dew and ate the air, who had three faces each but only one arm. Daoists believed that mountain-tops brought them closest to the Dao and built many of their temples on or near the summits of the sacred mountains.

HENG SHAN (left) in Shanxi Province, has a monastery clinging precariously to the sheer rock face. This is the northern Heng Shan, said to have been formed from the right arm of the giant Pangu.

Z

爆竹生花
王承熙[題]

ZAO JUN, or Tsao-chun, is a Daoist kitchen god, worshipped since at least the second century BC. He is still widely worshipped, and his picture is placed above the kitchen stove. At New Year, his spirit is offered a meal of meat, fruit and wine, and his lips are smeared with honey. The portrait is then burned in order to help the god on his way to heaven. The honey is supposed to keep Zao Jun sweet for when he reports on each family's conduct to *YU HUANG*.

According to one story, Zao Jun was once a poor man who, because he was unable to support his wife,

or because of a trick she played on him, had to allow her to marry someone else. He wandered far and wide begging. One day, he realized he had come to the home of his former wife and was so ashamed that he tried to hide in the hearth, where he was burned to death.

Another version of the tale tells how, before he became a deity, Zao Jun was a man called Zhang Lang. He was married to a good and faithful woman but left her for a young girl. Things went badly for him. In due course, the young girl became bored with Zhang Lang; he lost his sight and had to beg for food.

One day, Zhang Lang appeared at the door of his former wife. However, being blind, he did not know her. The woman invited Zhang Lang in and gave him his favourite meal. He was reminded of his wife and told the apparent stranger his story. His wife told Zhang Lang to open his eyes, and when he did so, he found he was able to see again. However, Zhang Lang was so ashamed at his former behaviour that he jumped into the hearth and was burned to death. His wife managed to seize one of his legs, which is why the fire poker is described as "Zhang Lang's leg".

ZAO JUN, the kitchen god, is honoured with fire crackers during the New Year celebrations. (CHINESE PAINTING, 19TH CENTURY.)

ZHANG E, or Chang O, according to Chinese mythology, is the wife of the divine archer *YI*. The lord of heaven, Taiyang Dijun, condemned Yi and Zhang E to live on earth as mortals in punishment for killing nine of his ten sons. Zhang E was furious and persuaded Yi to obtain the elixir of immortality from *XI WANG MU*, who lived on Mount Kunlun. The myth varies slightly, but, according to one version, the Queen Mother took pity

月宮 晴嬨 秦月

ZHANG E (left) stole the elixir of eternal life from her husband Yi, and fled to live on the moon. (CHANG E FLEES TO THE MOON, BY TAISO YOSHITOSHI, WOODBLOCK PRINT, 1885.)

down a tree. According to one version of the myth, Zhang E did finally regain her human appearance and lived the rest of her life in the palace of the moon. She is often shown wearing regal garments and carrying the disc of the moon in her right hand. She is regarded as a symbol of YIN, the female principle.

ZHANG GUOLAO see BA XIAN.

ZHONG-LI QUAN see BA XIAN.

ZHU RONG, or Chu Jong, according to Chinese mythology, is regent of the southern quarter of heaven and the divine lord of fire. He helped to divide heaven and earth from each other. One myth tells how Zhu Rong and the ferocious monster GONG-GONG decided to fight each other in order to determine which of them was the most powerful. Zhu Rong managed to defeat Gong-gong, who was so ashamed that he tried to kill himself and in the process caused a massive flood.

ZHU RONG (below), the God of Fire, on a temple altar in Taipei, Taiwan.

on Yi and gave him enough elixir to enable two people to live for ever, but only sufficient for one person to gain complete immortality. Yi returned home with the elixir, and Zhang E immediately began to toy with the idea of swallowing all the elixir herself. However, she was worried that the gods might be angry with her if she abandoned her husband, so she consulted an

astrologer. The astrologer suggested that Zhang E should travel to the moon where she would be free both from the accusations of the gods and the hardships of life as a mortal. He also promised that Zhang E would be miraculously transformed.

Zhang E was immediately persuaded by the astrologer's suggestion. She stole the elixir of

immortality from where it was hidden in the rafters of her house and swallowed it. Immediately, she began to float up to the moon. However, when she tried to call out, she discovered that she could only croak: she had been transformed into a toad.

Zhang E's companions on the moon were a hare and an old man who constantly attempted to chop

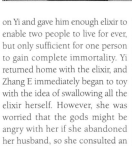

FAMILY TREES

Greek and Roman Family Trees
THE CHILDREN OF ZEUS

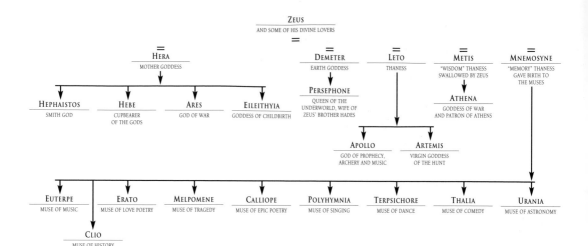

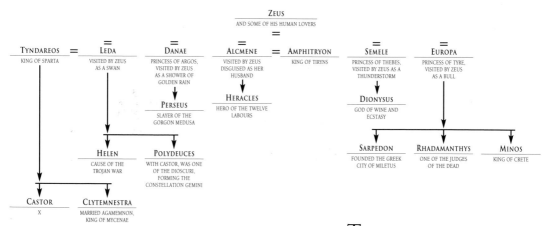

EXPLANATORY NOTE

The following family trees have been laid out to illustrate the various unions and children between important gods and goddesses described in this book. The = sign denotes sexual relationships and lines descending from the sign shows the child or children of that union.

The most powerful of the Greek gods, Zeus was married to Hera, a mother goddess, with whom he had several children. He was also, however, a great lover both of other goddesses and of mortal women, to whom he often appeared in disguise, thereby incurring the anger of Hera. In some cases these unions can be seen as mythological accounts of the union between two cultures, as when Zeus takes the Asiatic Europa to Crete. In others, it appears that particular cities or provinces of Greece have sought to give themselves divine antecedents by tracing the line of their rulers back to the greatest of the gods.

THE HOUSE OF ATREUS

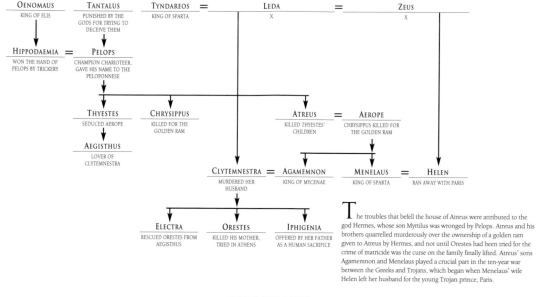

OENOMAUS
KING OF ELIS

TANTALUS
PUNISHED BY THE
GODS FOR TRYING TO
DECEIVE THEM

TYNDAREOS =
KING OF SPARTA

LEDA
X

= **ZEUS**
X

HIPPODAEMIA =
WON THE HAND OF
PELOPS BY TRICKERY

PELOPS
CHAMPION CHARIOTEER,
GAVE HIS NAME TO THE
PELOPONNESE

THYESTES
SEDUCED AEROPE

CHRYSIPPUS
KILLED FOR THE
GOLDEN RAM

ATREUS =
KILLED THYESTES'
CHILDREN

AEROPE
CHRYSIPPUS KILLED FOR
THE GOLDEN RAM

AEGISTHUS
LOVER OF
CLYTEMNESTRA

CLYTEMNESTRA =
MURDERED HER
HUSBAND

AGAMEMNON
KING OF MYCENAE

MENELAUS
KING OF SPARTA

= **HELEN**
RAN AWAY WITH PARIS

ELECTRA
RESCUED ORESTES FROM
AEGISTHUS

ORESTES
KILLED HIS MOTHER,
TRIED IN ATHENS

IPHIGENIA
OFFERED BY HER FATHER
AS A HUMAN SACRIFICE

The troubles that befell the house of Atreus were attributed to the god Hermes, whose son Myrtilus was wronged by Pelops. Atreus and his brothers quarrelled murderously over the ownership of a golden ram given to Atreus by Hermes, and not until Orestes had been tried for the crime of matricide was the curse on the family finally lifted. Atreus' sons Agamemnon and Menelaus played a crucial part in the ten-year war between the Greeks and Trojans, which began when Menelaus' wife Helen left her husband for the young Trojan prince, Paris.

THE MINOANS

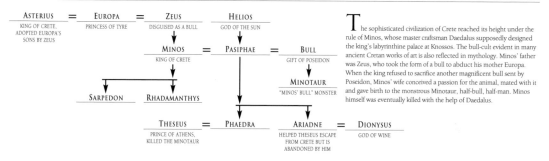

ASTERIUS =
KING OF CRETE,
ADOPTED EUROPA'S
SONS BY ZEUS

EUROPA =
PRINCESS OF TYRE

ZEUS
DISGUISED AS A BULL

HELIOS
GOD OF THE SUN

MINOS =
KING OF CRETE

PASIPHAE =
BULL
GIFT OF POSEIDON

MINOTAUR
"MINOS' BULL" MONSTER

SARPEDON

RHADAMANTHYS

THESEUS =
PRINCE OF ATHENS,
KILLED THE MINOTAUR

PHAEDRA

ARIADNE =
HELPED THESEUS ESCAPE
FROM CRETE BUT IS
ABANDONED BY HIM

DIONYSUS
GOD OF WINE

The sophisticated civilization of Crete reached its height under the rule of Minos, whose master craftsman Daedalus supposedly designed the king's labyrinthine palace at Knossos. The bull-cult evident in many ancient Cretan works of art is also reflected in mythology. Minos' father was Zeus, who took the form of a bull to abduct his mother Europa. When the king refused to sacrifice another magnificent bull sent by Poseidon, Minos' wife conceived a passion for the animal, mated with it and gave birth to the monstrous Minotaur, half-bull, half-man. Minos himself was eventually killed with the help of Daedalus.

THE FAMILY OF THESEUS

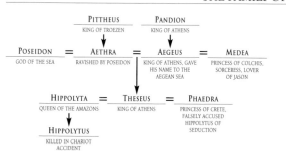

PITTHEUS
KING OF TROEZEN

PANDION
KING OF ATHENS

POSEIDON =
GOD OF THE SEA

AETHRA =
RAVISHED BY POSEIDON

AEGEUS =
KING OF ATHENS, GAVE
HIS NAME TO THE
AEGEAN SEA

MEDEA
PRINCESS OF COLCHIS,
SORCERESS, LOVER
OF JASON

HIPPOLYTA =
QUEEN OF THE AMAZONS

THESEUS =
KING OF ATHENS

PHAEDRA
PRINCESS OF CRETE,
FALSELY ACCUSED
HIPPOLYTUS OF
SEDUCTION

HIPPOLYTUS
KILLED IN CHARIOT
ACCIDENT

Although a mortal hero, Theseus was said by some to be the son of the god Poseidon. A brave fighter, he was a powerful monarch, uniting the twelve states of Attica into one kingdom with its capital at Athens. It was through Theseus that the two civilizations of island Crete and mainland Greece became closely connected, since he married the Cretan princess Phaedra, having abandoned her sister. Theseus himself died in exile, but his bones were eventually returned to Athens, where the people saw him as a saviour of the city.

Celtic Family Trees

THE DAGDA

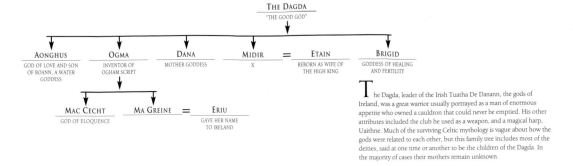

THE DAGDA
"THE GOOD GOD"

AONGHUS
GOD OF LOVE AND SON
OF BOANN, A WATER
GODDESS

OGMA
INVENTOR OF
OGHAM SCRIPT

DANA
MOTHER GODDESS

MIDIR = **ETAIN**
X   REBORN AS WIFE OF
THE HIGH KING

BRIGID
GODDESS OF HEALING
AND FERTILITY

MAC CECHT
GOD OF ELOQUENCE

MA GREINE = **ERIU**
GAVE HER NAME
TO IRELAND

The Dagda, leader of the Irish Tuatha De Danann, the gods of Ireland, was a great warrior usually portrayed as a man of enormous appetite who owned a cauldron that could never be emptied. His other attributes included the club he used as a weapon, and a magical harp, Uaithne. Much of the surviving Celtic mythology is vague about how the gods were related to each other, but this family tree includes most of the deities, said at one time or another to be the children of the Dagda. In the majority of cases their mothers remain unknown.

THE ROYAL HOUSE OF ULSTER

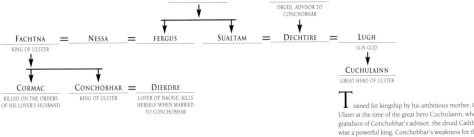

ROTH

CATHBAD
DRUID, ADVISOR TO
CONCHOBHAR

FACHTNA = **NESSA** = **FERGUS**
KING OF ULSTER

SUALTAM = **DECHTIRE** = **LUGH**
SUN GOD

CUCHULAINN
GREAT HERO OF ULSTER

CORMAC
KILLED ON THE ORDERS
OF HIS LOVER'S HUSBAND

CONCHOBHAR = **DIERDRE**
KING OF ULSTER   LOVER OF NAOISE, KILLS
HERSELF WHEN MARRIED
TO CONCHOBHAR

Trained for kingship by his ambitious mother, Conchobhar ruled Ulster at the time of the great hero Cuchulainn, who was said to be the grandson of Conchobhar's advisor, the druid Cathbad. Although otherwise a powerful king, Conchobhar's weakness for the beautiful Deirdre led him into a prolonged war. For, having killed Deirdre's lover so that he might marry her, he found his disgusted step-father Fergus siding against him with the enemies of Ulster. Conchobhar finally perished as the result of a magical sling-shot made by Cuchulainn's foster-brother Conall, which became embedded in the king's skull.

THE FAMILY OF FINN MACCOOL

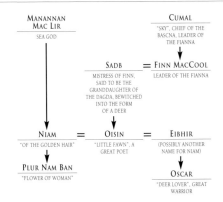

**MANANNAN
MAC LIR**
SEA GOD

CUMAL
"SKY", CHIEF OF THE
BASCNA, LEADER OF
THE FIANNA

SADB = **FINN MACCOOL**
MISTRESS OF FINN,   LEADER OF THE FIANNA
SAID TO BE THE
GRANDDAUGHTER OF
THE DAGDA, BEWITCHED
INTO THE FORM
OF A DEER

NIAM = **OISIN** = **EIBHIR**
"OF THE GOLDEN HAIR"   "LITTLE FAWN", A   (POSSIBLY ANOTHER
GREAT POET   NAME FOR NIAM)

PLUR NAM BAN
"FLOWER OF WOMAN"

OSCAR
"DEER LOVER", GREAT
WARRIOR

As leader of the Fianna, the warrior bodyguards of the High King of Ireland, Finn can be compared with the British King Arthur. Like Arthur, he was believed to lie asleep for ever in a hillside, waiting until his country needed him. His men, who came mostly from the clan Bascna or the clan Morna, were carefully selected for their physical strength and their skill in battle, and they became involved in various adventures throughout the island. Through Finn's relationship with Sadb, his story also enters the realm of enchantment, a mythical element reinforced in the tales of his son and grandson.

ARTHUR AND THE KNIGHTS OF THE ROUND TABLE

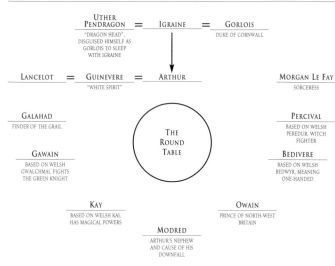

The original Arthur of Welsh and Irish tradition was a warrior king whose band of heroes followed him into a variety of adventures. Medieval legend transformed them into courtly knights and altered many of the Celtic ingredients of the old tales for a Christian audience. The magic cauldrons of inspiration and plenty, for example, became the Holy Grail used at the Last Supper. The concept of rebirth survives in Arthur's title of "Once and Future King". The Round Table, too, was a later addition, but many of those who sat at it were based on characters found in much earlier stories.

THE CHILDREN OF DON

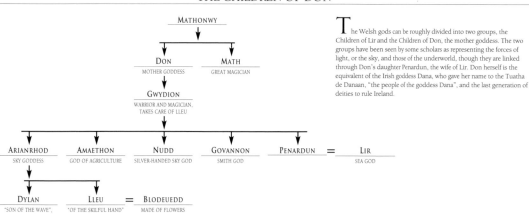

The Welsh gods can be roughly divided into two groups, the Children of Lir and the Children of Don, the mother goddess. The two groups have been seen by some scholars as representing the forces of light, or the sky, and those of the underworld, though they are linked through Don's daughter Penardun, the wife of Lir. Don herself is the equivalent of the Irish goddess Dana, who gave her name to the Tuatha de Danaan, "the people of the goddess Dana", and the last generation of deities to rule Ireland.

THE FAMILY OF PWYLL AND THE CHILDREN OF LIR

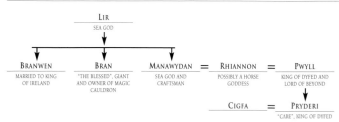

Common to both Welsh and Irish mythical tradition are heroes who are part mortal and part divine. A king of Dyfed, Pwyll is also connected with the otherworld, both through his own adventures there and through his wife Rhiannon, whose magical birds could wake the dead with their song. Indeed, Rhiannon's second husband Manawydan was the son of the Welsh sea god Lir, whose other children Bran and Branwen were similarly seen as humans with supernatural powers. Later Celtic writing absorbed these earlier influences into Arthurian legend, where Pwyll became Pelles, keeper of the Holy Grail.

Norse Family Trees

THE AESIR

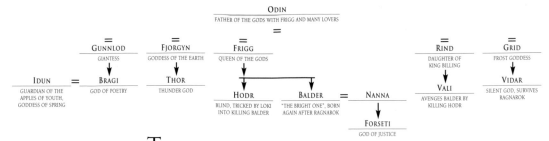

The Aesir were the gods and goddesses led by Odin. Predominantly connected with warfare, they lived in Asgard, a mighty stronghold where the souls of the bravest men killed in battle were taken after death by the Valkyries. After settling an early conflict with Vanir, another race of gods, the Aesir turned their attention to fighting the frost giants. Despite their divinity, the Aesir were not immortal. Many of them were fated to die during Ragnarok, the doom of the gods, when Loki and his children united with the giants to attack Asgard. Although Odin was widely rec-

ognized as the father of all gods, there were deities among the Aesir whose parentage was disputed. Tyr, for example, the war god who gave his name to Tuesday, was said by some to be the son of Odin, but by others to be the son of a giant named Humir. Heimdall, the watchman of the gods who stood guard on the rainbow bridge Bifrost, was the son of nine mothers, and himself fathered children in the human world of Midgard. Furthermore, Odin's brothers Vili and Ve, while far less important, were counted among the Aesir.

THE CHILDREN OF LOKI

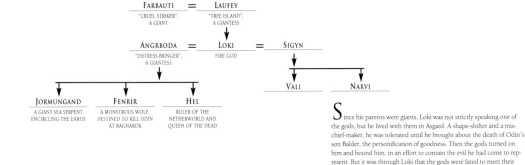

Since his parents were giants, Loki was not strictly speaking one of the gods, but he lived with them in Asgard. A shape-shifter and a mischief-maker, he was tolerated until he brought about the death of Odin's son Balder, the personification of goodness. Then the gods turned on him and bound him, in an effort to contain the evil he had come to represent. But it was through Loki that the gods were fated to meet their doom, for at the end of the world he would be freed from his prison and join his monstrous children to fight the last battle of Ragnarok.

THE VANIR

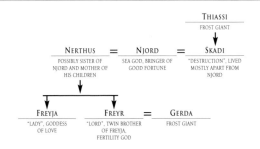

Unlike the warrior Aesir, the Vanir were a race of gods associated with fertility, with wealth and with good weather. They were believed by some to have existed before the Aesir and lived in their own world of Vannaheim. At first the two divine races were hostile to each other and conflict broke out between them. They eventually agreed to live in peace with each other, but the Vanir faded in significance. The best-known of their number were Freyr and Freyja, twins endowed with magical powers, who went to live in the Aesir's home of Asgard.

YGGDRASIL

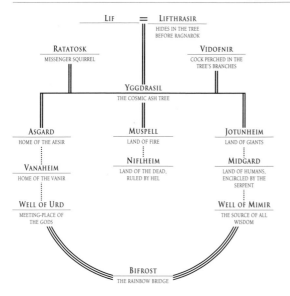

The world picture of Norse myth centred round the sacred tree, Yggdrasil. The branches of this vast ash were believed to hang over the Nine Worlds and its three roots to lead to them. Odin hanged himself from one branch for nine days and then died, in order that he might acquire the wisdom of the dead and bring back from their lands the magic Runes. After Ragnarok, when the Nine Worlds are destroyed, Yggdrasil will survive and the human couple, Lif and Lifthrasir, who took shelter in its branches, will descend to begin a new race of humans.

EXPLANATORY NOTE
The double lines denote the roots of the tree, Yggdrasil. The triple lines denote the link made by Bifrost between Asgard and Midgard, heaven and earth respectively.

THE FAMILY OF SIGURD

The story of the young hero Sigurd (known by the Germans as Siegfried) belongs as much to heroic legend as to myth, though it is connected with the Norse gods through the part played in the tale by Loki and through Sigmund's magic sword, thrust into a tree by Odin. As in many folk traditions, the possession of fabulous treasure brings disaster to the man who acquires it. Even Sigurd, otherwise an innocent figure, is fated to lose Brynhild, the beautiful Valkyrie whom he loves, when he is bewitched into marrying Gudrun.

THOR

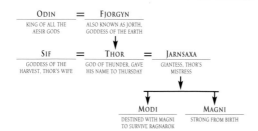

One of the most popular of the Aesir, Thor was renowned as a great warrior. He was enormous, even for a god, and his strength and courage made him a formidable enemy of the giants in many adventures. Although his simple-mindedness laid him open to mockery from the other gods, it endeared him to the ordinary farmers who worshipped him throughout Scandinavia. Thor's chief weapon was Mjollnir, his magic hammer, which created thunder when he flung it down on the earth. The vast hall in Asgard where he lived with Sif was called Bilskirnir, or Lightning.

Egypt / Mesopotamia / Iran

THE DESCENDANTS OF RA

The Egyptian creator god Ra and his descendants are known collectively as the Ennead, or "Nine Gods" of Heliopolis, the site of Ra's principal sanctuary. Ra needed no consort, but spat or sneezed out Shu and Tefnut and later, from his own tears, created humanity. The children of Nut were two pairs of twins.

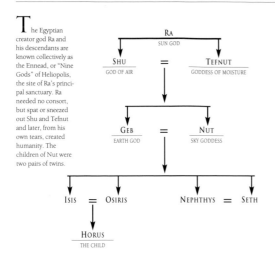

THE SUMERIAN PANTHEON

The Sumerians, living in Mesopotamia in the fourth and third millennia BC, developed a religious framework which was adapted by the Akkadians, Babylonians and other later civilizations in the region. Sumerian deities were organized into a settled pantheon by priests, who inscribed their myths on clay tablets.

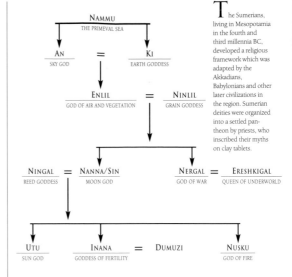

THE BABYLONIAN PANTHEON

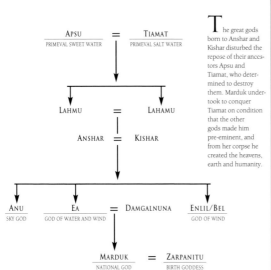

The great gods born to Anshar and Kishar disturbed the repose of their ancestors Apsu and Tiamat, who determined to destroy them. Marduk undertook to conquer Tiamat on condition that the other gods made him pre-eminent, and from her corpse he created the heavens, earth and humanity.

THE ZOROASTRIAN HEAVENLY HIERARCHY

AHURA MAZDA/SPENTA MAINYU
THE WISE LORD

HUMANITY

AMESA SPENTAS
SONS AND DAUGHTERS OF, OR ASPECTS OF, GOD

VOHU MANO	ASHA VAHISHTA	SPENTA ARMAITI	KHSHATHRA VAIRYA	HAURVATAT	AMERETAT
GOOD THOUGHT *animals/cattle*	RIGHTEOUSNESS *fire*	DEVOTION *earth*	DOMINION *sun and heavens*	WHOLENESS *waters*	IMMORTALITY *plants*

YAZATAS
PROTECTIVE SPIRITS

ANAHITA	ATAR	HAOMA	SRAOSHA	RASHNU	MITHRA	TISHTRYA
WATER, FERTILITY	FIRE	HEALING PLANTS	OBEDIENCE, THE HEARER OF PRAYERS	JUDGEMENT	TRUTH	THE DOG-STAR, SOURCE OF RAIN AND FERTILITY

In the Zoroastrian tradition, Ahura Mazda is alone worthy of worship. The Amesa Spentas are his creations and act as intermediaries between Ahura Mazda and his devotees. Many of the Yazatas were ancient Iranian deities who were included in the reformed religion as the servants of Ahura Mazda.

India / Japan

SHIVA'S FAMILY

Shiva is both the creator and the destroyer, and Parvati is the gentle aspect of his shakti, or creative energy. She is also an aspect of the great goddess, Devi, and a reincarnation of Shiva's wife Sati, who committed suicide. In her subservience to her husband, Parvati is a model for mortal devotees of Shiva.

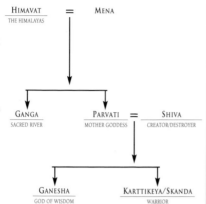

HIMAVAT — MENA
THE HIMALAYAS

GANGA
SACRED RIVER

PARVATI = SHIVA
MOTHER GODDESS — CREATOR/DESTROYER

GANESHA
GOD OF WISDOM

KARTTIKEYA/SKANDA
WARRIOR

VEDIC CREATION MYTH

The Vedic religion acknowledged that the origin of the universe is a mystery, and offered many differing accounts of the creation. The lineage of humanity, represented by Manu, the first man, is sometimes traced back through the sun god, the source of heat and life on earth, to the mother of the gods, Aditi.

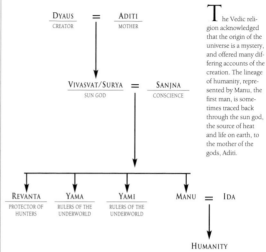

DYAUS = ADITI
CREATOR — MOTHER

VIVASVAT/SURYA = SANJNA
SUN GOD — CONSCIENCE

REVANTA
PROTECTOR OF HUNTERS

YAMA
RULERS OF THE UNDERWORLD

YAMI
RULERS OF THE UNDERWORLD

MANU = IDA

HUMANITY

HIERARCHY OF VEDIC DEITIES

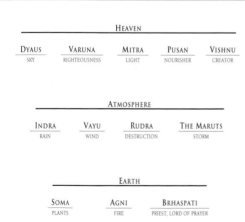

HEAVEN

DYAUS	VARUNA	MITRA	PUSAN	VISHNU
SKY	RIGHTEOUSNESS	LIGHT	NOURISHER	CREATOR

ATMOSPHERE

INDRA	VAYU	RUDRA	THE MARUTS
RAIN	WIND	DESTRUCTION	STORM

EARTH

SOMA	AGNI	BRHASPATI
PLANTS	FIRE	PRIEST, LORD OF PRAYER

The ancient heavenly deities were endowed with universal power, but were remote figures, whereas Indra and the other gods of the atmosphere exert a more direct influence over human life. Agni is the god of the sacrificial fire, and is therefore an intercessor between the gods and humankind.

SHINTO CREATION MYTH

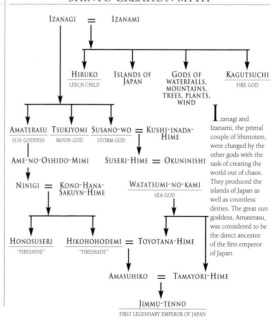

IZANAGI = IZANAMI

HIRUKO
LEECH CHILD

ISLANDS OF JAPAN

GODS OF WATERFALLS, MOUNTAINS, TREES, PLANTS, WIND

KAGUTSUCHI
FIRE GOD

AMATERASU
SUN GODDESS

TSUKIYOMI
MOON GOD

SUSANO-WO = KUSHI-INADA-HIME
STORM GOD

AME-NO-OSHIDO-MIMI

SUSERI-HIME = OKUNINISHI

NINIGI = KONO-HANA-SAKUYN-HIME

WATATSUMI-NO-KAMI
SEA GOD

HONOSUSERI
"FIRESHINE"

HIKOHOHODEMI = TOYOTANA-HIME
"FIRESHADE"

AMASUHIKO = TAMAYORI-HIME

JIMMU-TENNO
FIRST LEGENDARY EMPEROR OF JAPAN

Izanagi and Izanami, the primal couple of Shintoism, were charged by the other gods with the task of creating the world out of chaos. They produced the islands of Japan as well as countless deities. The great sun goddess, Amaterasu, was considered to be the direct ancestor of the first emperor of Japan.

PICTURE ACKNOWLEDGEMENTS

The Publishers are grateful to the agencies listed below for kind permission to reproduce the following images in this book.

Alan Lee: 44BR, 103, 108T, 109R, 110R, 113B, 127L, 127L, 134R, 139TR, 143TR, 143BR, 145T, 147TL, 148T, 149L, 151TL, 151BR, 152TM, 155R, 158, 159BL, 159BR, 160, 161BR, 163, 164, 166L, 167L, 171T, 172, 173BR, 183T, 185T, 186T, 196T, 197B, 207T, 224TR, 238BL, 239TR, 242, 247MR.

AKG: 14, 15BL, 16B, 17T, 18T, 20L, 21T, 22, 23L, 25, 26, 32, 36BR, 36TR, 37, 38L, 40TR, 41T, 42R, 43T, 43BR,45R, 46TR, 47, 49T, 50TL, 51TL, 52BL, 54TR, 55, 57 58T, 59T, 60BR, 61T, 61B, 62BR, 63TR, 64T, 65T, 66T, 67T, 68T, 68BR, 69T, 70B, 71BR, 72R, 74T, 76TL, 77, 78, 80B, 81B, 82T, 83TM, 84T, 85, 89T, 89B, 90B, 91T, 192B, 267TR, 267BL, 269TL, 271BR, 270BR, 273TR, 274TR, 276BL, 277TR, 278TL, 279R, 281, 285, 295TR, 297B, 301, 303, 304, 306B, 307, 308TL, 309, 310, 311T, 313TR, 313BL, 313BR, 314, 318, 321, 325, 331TL, 335B, 338, 341TR, 342T, 344L, 345R, 360T, 360B, 361TL, 361TR, 361BR, 363T, 366T, 372T, 373T, 373B, 375B, 381, 395BR, 399T, 405TL, 408T, 410, 415B, 441.

Ancient Art and Architecture: 260BL, 262B, 263TL, 264B, 273TL, 275BL, 278BR, 282, 284TL, 288TR, 288BL, 291, 292BL, 293B, 297TR, 298TL, 298B, 300B, 305BL, 316T, 316B, 319B, 324T, 328, 341TL, 350T, 352T, 355T, 357TL, 367, 371TL, 375T, 383BR, 385T, 389TL, 405BR, 405TR, 411B, 415T, 417B, 430, 432B, 438BR, 440TL, 442, 450TL, 453TR, 454R, 459TR, 462TL, 462TR, 464T, 473TL, 473BL, 475T, 476TR, 476M, 478, 487B.

Ancient Egypt Picture Library: 267MR, 269BR, 272BL, 280B, 284TR, 284BL, 287MR, 292BL, 297TL, 300TR, 306T, 311B.

Arnamagnean Institute: 178L, 204BL, 205BR.

Ateneum, Helsinki: 199BL, 205T, 222R, 223TL, 223TR, 243B.

Bildarchiv Foto, Marburg: 451B.

Bildarchiv Preussisher: 226T.

Birmingham Museum and Art Gallery: 103T, 122BR, 137, 143L, 153B, 159T, 169T.

The Bodleian Library: 141TL.

The Bridgeman Art Library: 79B, 86B, 87BL, 87BR, 92, 96BR, 96L, 130R, 140TR, 143L, 157T, 181L, 200BR, 203, 261TL, 268, 272TL, 279, 280T, 289BL, 307, 343B, 346, 353, 356, 363BR, 365T, 366BR, 368T, 377T, 378T, 378BR, 379TR, 379BR, 382T, 383T, 392T 393, 398TL, 398TR, 401T, 402T, 402B, 403B, 406TL, 407BL, 414, 447, 449TL, 454L, 466T, 470BR.

Dundee Art Gallery: 105T, 106B, 109L, 133T, 135T, 138B

E Davison: 121L

The British Museum: 445TL, 455B.

Christie's Art Gallery: 272BR, 287TR, 287BR, 323BL, 23BR, 330TL, 330BR, 331TR, 332, 336, 379MT, 351TR, 364, 370T, 371TR, 379BL, 396BL, 397T, 397BL, 400T, 426, 429, 432T, 436TL, 436TR, 439L, 439TR, 443B, 452B, 453BM, 453BR, 457B, 468T, 469TL, 469TR, 472BL, 476B, 477, 482T, 486TR

Corbis: 261BR, 263BR, 277TL, 294T, 312T, 326, 328, 329R, 330TR, 331BL 333, 335, 343TL, 347B, 351TL, 355B, 387B, 388T, 396BR, 405BL, 409T, 411T, 413BR, 418, 422, 424, 425TL, 435BR, 438TL, 438TR, 444, 451T, 456B, 459B, 461T, 462B, 465, 470T, 472TR, 479, 481, 483, 484B, 485T, 485BR, 485BT, 486TL 488, 491T, 492T 492B, 493TR, 493MR, 493B, 495T

CM Dixon: 264T, 267ML, 283, 302B, 343TR, 350B, 363BL, 416T, 423TL, 440BR, 452T, 453TL, 472TL, 474, 494.

Edimedia: 263LT, 354T, 374.

E.T. Archive: 33TR, 52TR, 53BR, 70T, 87TL, 188T, 215B, 258BL, 265BR, 266T, 266B, 267TL 283, 287MR, 290TR, 292TR, 296 317L, 334, 340, 342B, 344R, 349TR, 351B, 354B, 369, 376T, 380T, 384, 386T, 386B, 391B, 395T 413T, 420, 435TL, 445B, 455TL, 455TR, 468B, 489T, 494.

Fine Art Photographic Library: 76BR, 94, 106T, 104T, 105B, 126BL, 128B, 142R, 144Bl, 168BL, 188T, 245B.

Duncan Baird Publishing: 448.

Glasgow Museums: 117T.

Hutchison Library: 388B, 389B.

Icorec: 466B.

Image Solutions: 390T, 390B, 391TL, 412T.

Images of India: 400B.

Jean Loup Charmet: 199TR, 226B.

King Arthurs Great Hall, Tintagel: 102T, 136TL, 136TR, 139TL, 153TR.

Manchester City Art Galleries: 19B, 54BL, 103B, 194B.

Mary Evans: 277BR, 286T, 286B, 287TL, 287BL, 293T, 294B, 295BL, 295BM, 305T, 320B, 322B, 323TR, 323TL, 327B, 330BL, 331MR, 370B, 423TR, 434B, 435TR, 449BR, 453BL, 461B, 469B, 484R.

Michael Holford: 265TR, 315T, 319T, 322TR, 322ML, 361BL, 404, 434T.

Miranda Gray: 104BL, 130Bl, 146T, 148BL, 170B.

Nasjonalgalleriet, Oslo: 188B, 216B.

National Galleries of Scotland: 101L, 112, 120B, 124T.

National Museum Stockholm: 184T, 192T, 198R, 217T, 232BL.

National Palace Museum, Tapei: 489B, 491B.

Panos Pictures: 312B

Royal Asiatic Society: 359B&T.

Scala Florence: 31TL.

Statens Museum fur Kunst, Copenhagen: 183B, 201T, 247TR, 250B.

K Stevens: 427, 431, 433t, 456t, 457t, 458tr, 458tl, 463r, 463l, 464b, 467, 470bl, 471tr, 471tl, 471br, 471bm, 471bl, 475b, 482b, 487t, 490b, 490t, 495b.

Stuart Littlejohn: 116T, 117BL, 132BR, 170T.

The Tate Gallery: 44T, 136B.

Werner Forman Archive: 176, 177, 212BL, 252TR, 238BR, 191TL, 199TL, 207, 211BL, 215TR, 235, 247TL.

Yvonne Gilbert: 150ML.

INDEX

Index